Introducing

"Hubie" RE Internet Mouse™

He proudly stands next to Internet addresses.

(2 nd printing and re-edited version)

California Real Estate Principles

8th Edition

Walt Huber

Glendale Community College

TM

Introducing

"Hubie" RE Internet Mouse™

He stands next to Internet Addresses

Educational Textbook Company
P.O. BOX 3597
Covina, California 91722
ISBN:0-916772-04-7

COPYRIGHT   1976, 1977, 1978, 1979, 1985, 1989, 1994, 1995, 1998   8th EDITION

EDUCATIONAL TEXTBOOK COMPANY
(etcbooks.com)
P.O. Box 3597
Covina, California 91722
1(626) 339-7733

Library of Congress Cataloging in Publication Data

Huber, Walter Roy, 1941 -
California Real Estate Principles

Summary: Covers all material in Real Estate Principles classes with special stress on California real estate laws. Very clear and simple language, easy-to-read format with photographs, charts, and graphs. Includes glossary and index; suitable for the consumer, students and teachers wishing information about personal real estate transactions.

HD 266   C2H824   333.3   98-81926

ISBN 0-916-772-04-7

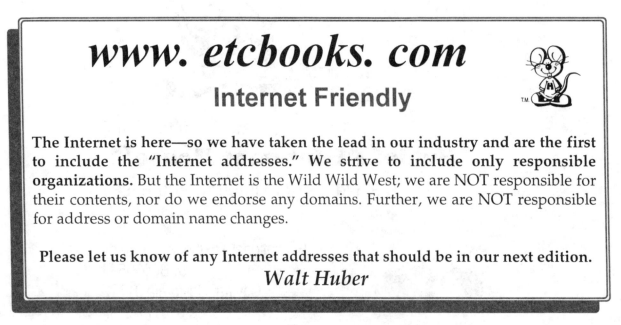

www. etcbooks. com
Internet Friendly

The Internet is here—so we have taken the lead in our industry and are the first to include the "Internet addresses." We strive to include only responsible **organizations.** But the Internet is the Wild Wild West; we are NOT responsible for their contents, nor do we endorse any domains. Further, we are NOT responsible for address or domain name changes.

Please let us know of any Internet addresses that should be in our next edition.
Walt Huber

Preface

The 8th edition of **CALIFORNIA REAL ESTATE PRINCIPLES** has moved into a new generation, with essential real estate concepts highlighted in green ink for special emphasis. We've selected key topics and reinforced them in this way so they jump off the page and stand out in the student's mind. This unique approach makes **CALIFORNIA REAL ESTATE PRINCIPLES** not only an excellent beginning real estate text, but also an essential review and reference book for those students planning to take the California Real Estate License Examination.

This new edition covers all matters related to the ownership and transfer of real property, from deposit receipt to completed escrow, and beyond. All the commonly used forms are shown and explained in detail, including the CAR five-page deposit receipt. Each chapter includes a multiple-choice quiz to test the reader's comprehension of material contained in the preceding pages. We also have a vocabulary test at the end of every chapter so students can match important real estate terms with concise definitions. Correct answers are given in the back of the book, enabling students to test themselves and work at their own pace.

I want to express my appreciation to the many people who helped to make this text possible. I received advice and helpful suggestions from the California Department of Real Estate (www.dre.ca.gov.), the California Association of Realtors® (www.car.org).

Special thanks, too, for the valuable assistance I received from the people who helped to design and produce this book: Rick Lee, executive editor; Philip Dockter, art director; and Melinda Winters, cover design.

The additions and revisions for this printing were made with the help of: Appraiser Edward S. Stahl; Donna Grogan, CPM from El Camino College; William Nunally and Robert Topping, from Sacramento City College; Evelyn Winkel, real estate law specialist from Rancho Santiago College; Kim Tyler, real estate law specialist from Shasta College; Jim Michaelsen, Santa Rosa Junior College; Nick Zoumbos, accounting specialist, from Crafton Hills College and Joe Newton, fellow author from Bakersfield College; all to whom I am very grateful. Thanks William Pivar—on some lake, somewhere.

A special thanks to Mary Ann Zamel and Arlette Lyons the two inspiring brokers from Covina who teach at Mount San Antonio College.

I must also offer special recognition to Drs. Joan and Jim Harrison from Quick Prep Real Estate Schools, for showing us their exceptional word association approach to Real Estate Exam preparation. I thank Ernie Hubert from Real Estate School 2000 for his improvement tips. And a heartfelt thanks to our friend Joe Ribertelli for lending us the benefit of his long expertise and intimate knowledge of concepts usually found on the state license exam.

WALT HUBER

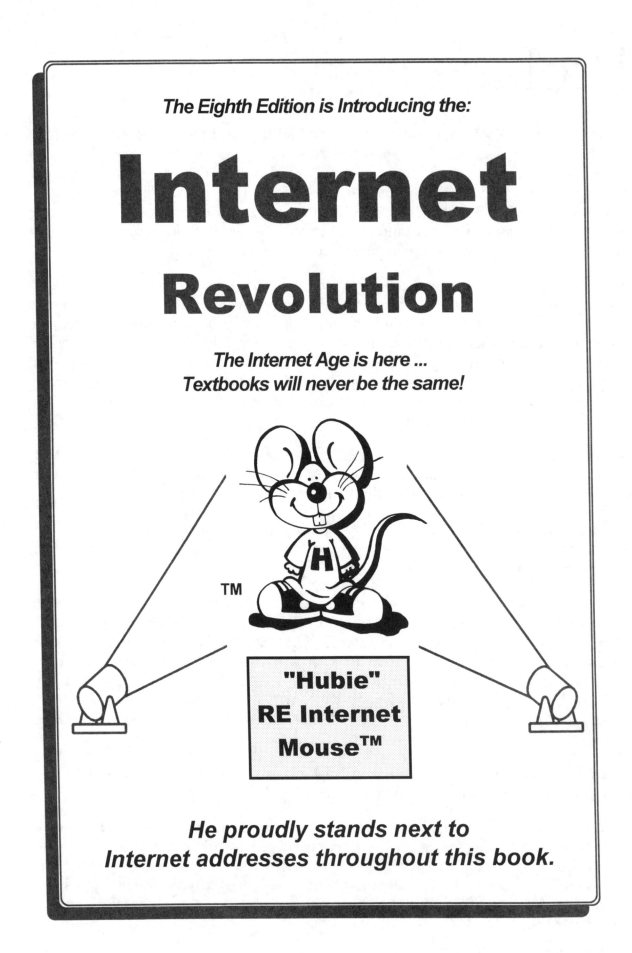

The Eighth Edition is Introducing the:

Internet
Revolution

The Internet Age is here ...
Textbooks will never be the same!

™

"Hubie"
RE Internet
Mouse™

He proudly stands next to
Internet addresses throughout this book.

Books change about every three years.

We include <u>Internet sites</u>, so you can get the latest information "<u>instantly!</u>"

Our Internet ICON is "Hubie," a mouse
who is placed in front of each of our Internet sites.

Just look for "Hubie" and you will find an Internet domain
where you will get the latest information.

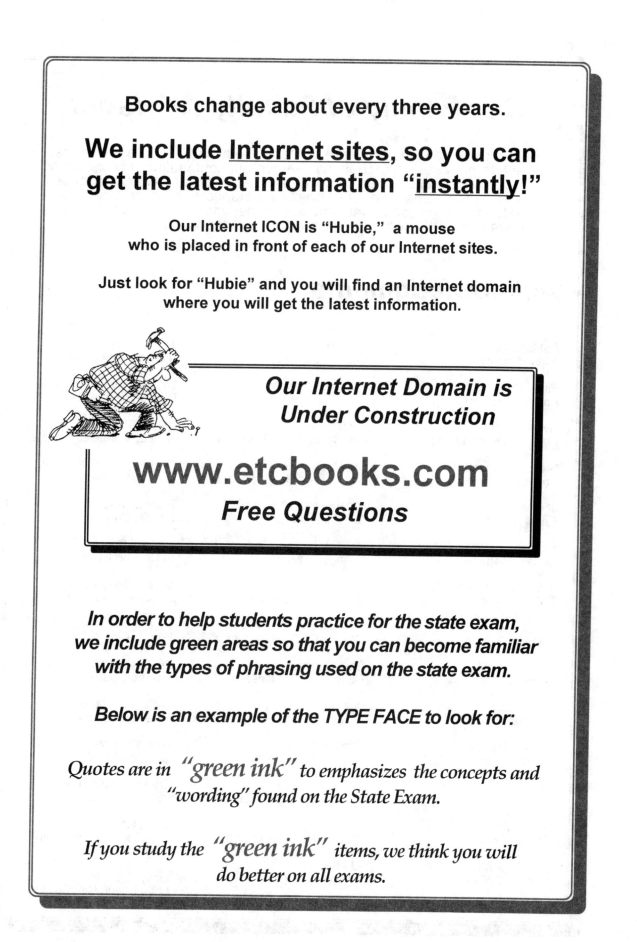

*Our Internet Domain is
Under Construction*

www.etcbooks.com
Free Questions

*In order to help students practice for the state exam,
we include green areas so that you can become familiar
with the types of phrasing used on the state exam.*

Below is an example of the TYPE FACE to look for:

Quotes are in *"green ink"* to emphasizes the concepts and
"wording" found on the State Exam.

If you study the *"green ink"* items, we think you will
do better on all exams.

Our Family of Faculty Advisors

This book contains the input of many prominent educators and real estate professionals. Their involvement as contributing advisors has made it possible for us to cover a wide range of material in detail and, at the same time, offer practical perspectives based upon their extensive classroom and industry experience. Their contributions were invaluable and merit my most sincere thanks.

Acknowledgments

Hal Madson
Allan Hancock College

Alfred J. Guetling
American River College

Ryan M. Polstra
American River College

Steve Sodergren
Antelope Valley College

Joe Newton
Bakersfield College

Donald T. Brown
Butte College

Jos. F. Belohlavek
Cabrillo College

Robin Sherman
Cabrillo College

Martin Carrick
Canada College

Melvin Brady
Cerritos College

John T. Martinez
Chabot College

Richard McCartney
Chabot College

Robert Andersen
Chabot College

Earl H. Bond
Chaffey College

J. O. Wright
Chaffey College

Frederick A. Henning
Citrus College

Keith H. Kerr
City College San Francisco

Fred Martinez
City College San Francisco

Hal Bouley
Coastline College

Ray Bennigson
College Of Marin

Bart J. Kearney
College Of San Mateo

Allen C. Shute
College Of The Canyons

Stan Reyburn
College Of The Desert

Jeff Eddy
College Of The Sequoias

John A. Miller
Contra Costa College

Ronald G. Rueb
Contra Costa College

Mike Hoey
Cosumnes River College

D. Blazej
Cuesta College

John R. Morrissey
Diablo Valley College

Leo Saunders, GRI, CRB
Diablo Valley College

Dr. Elliott J. Dixon
East Los Angeles College

Olivia Vasquez Anderson
East Los Angeles College

Frances K. Jackson
E.C.C., San Diego

Michael Botello
El Camino College

Donna Grogan, CPM
El Camino College

Dr. Eugene C. Azamber
Fresno City College

Peter Kirianoff
Fullerton College

William B. Harwood
Fullerton College

Dino Vlachos
Golden West College

Frank Pangborn
Irvine Valley College

Doug Rosner
Lake Tahoe Community College

Larry R. Hoffman
Long Beach City College

Sherry F. Tunison
Long Beach City College

Bill Monroe
Los Angeles City College

John J. Meichtry
Los Angeles Mission College

Harold Lerner
Los Angeles Pierce College

Robert R. Enger
Los Angeles Pierce College

Bernard Grabois
Los Angeles Valley College

Joseph H. Albaum
Los Angeles Valley College

Patricia Moore
Los Medanos College

Frank Coon
Los Medanos College

R. Joseph Banuat, CRS, CRB
Los Medanos College

Ignacio Gonzalez
Mendocino College

Edward L. Culbertson
Mira Costa College

Frank Diaz
Mission College

Gerald A. W. Haight
Modesto Junior College

Joseph G. Ansel
Monterey Peninsula College

Thomas A. Hester
Moorpark College

Mary Ann Zamel
Mt. San Antonio College

Arlette A. Lyons
Mt. San Antonio College

R. Glenn Vice
Mt. San Antonio College

Heli Sairanen
Napa Valley College

Bruce Gold
Orange Coast College

William R. Parks
Orange Coast College

Jim Crow
Oxnard College

Edwin Estes, Jr.
Palomar College

David Kemp
Palomar College

Dr. Evelyn D. Winkel
Rancho Santiago College

June Ann Reese
Rio Hondo College

Gilbert Mosqueda
Rio Hondo College

Devonne W. Armstrong
Riverside Community College

Michael Bernston
Riverside Community College

Robert J. Topping
Sacramento City College

Willie L. Nunally
Sacramento City College

S. Martin Welc
Saddleback College

Paul Grutsis
San Bernardino Valley
College

Nick Zoumbos
San Bernardino Valley
College

Dr. Shad Jefferies
San Diego Mesa College

Norma F. Hurley
San Joaquin Delta College

Victoria Armstrong
San Joaquin Delta College

Raymond O' Connor
Santa Barbara City College

Steve Herndon
Santa Rosa Junior College

William Rawlings
Santiago Canyon College

Kim Tyler
Shasta College

M. Wurschmidt
Shasta College

Joseph A. Mcneill, Jr.
Solano Community College

Robert C. Cass
Southwestern College

Ron Jackson
Southwestern College

Anne Havey
Southwestern College

Francis Robinson
Ventura College

Chris Grover
Victor Valley College

Carl W. Hefke
West Hills College

Abraham H. Farkas
West Los Angeles College

Faz Elahi
West Los Angeles College

Don Holman
West Los Angeles College

George H. Miller
West Valley College

James R. Overton
Yuba College

Real Estate Specialists

Charles Ellis
UCLA Extension

James Short
San Diego State Univ.

Lorraine Abrams
West Valley Occupational
Center

Stan Hechinger
CAL-LAND International

Hugh C. Damon
TMH Home Mortgage Co.

To the people closest to me, my family,
I dedicate this book:

To my mother and father
Walter and Tillie Huber, my sister
Carol Hamilton and my loving wife
Debbie.

Walt Huber

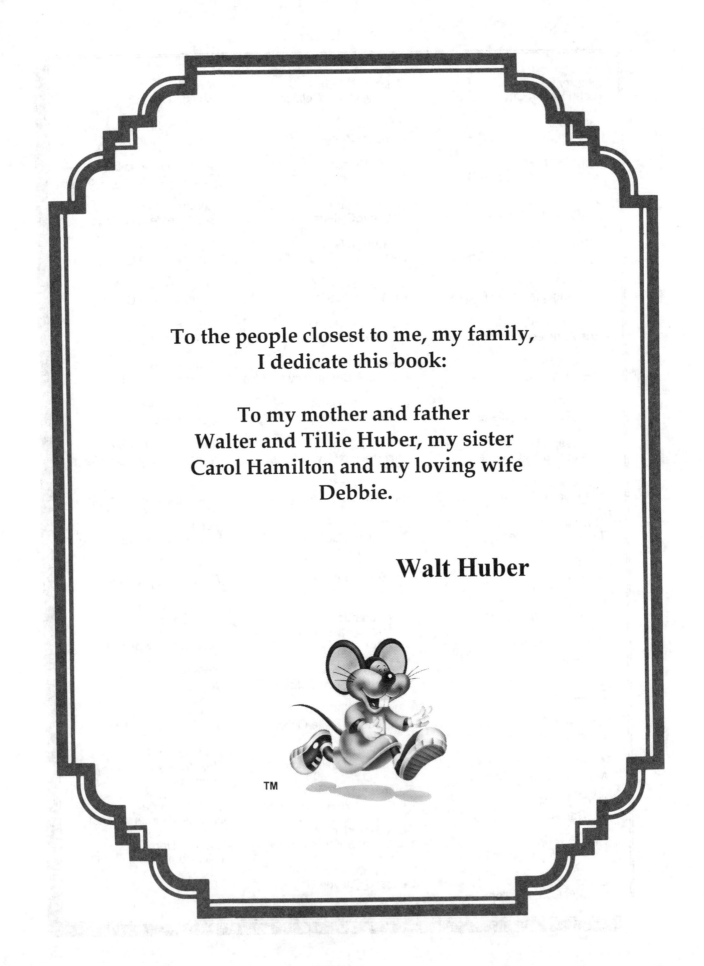

TM

Table of Contents

Chapter 4 - Agency & Its Responsibilities .. 73

Chapter 5 - Contracts 109

Chapter 6 - Landlord and Tenant 145
(Lessor and Lessee)

Chapter 8 - Real Estate Finance 203

Chapter 9 - Financial Institutions *249*

Chapter 12 - Subdivision & Government Control 351

Chapter 13 - Taxation of Real Estate 395

CHAPTER 1
Introduction to Real Estate

IMPORTANCE - COST - COMMISSIONS

No other investment, such as your car, boat or television, is as important as your home. Your home is a created environment that expresses **YOU**, just as the neighborhood you choose reflects your lifestyle.

Your home will probably be the most important and largest investment you make in your lifetime.

DRE is on the Internet

http://www.dre.ca..gov (Department of Real Estate - Homepage)
http://www.dre.cahwnet.gov (Department of Real Estate - Homepage)

(California Department of Real Estate)

The California Department of Real Estate (DRE) is on the Internet. They supply all the procedural information (See Chapter 14 of this book) you need to know about a license. We advise you to first look at the section called **"About Obtaining a Broker or Salespersons License."**

HIGH HOUSING COST

With a few exceptions, California has, more or less, continually experienced a huge increase in the value of land. It was (and is) due to our ever-increasing population, drawn to the state by plentiful jobs and the climate.

From 1990 to 1997 California was caught in the depreciation statewide real estate depression (the worst since the Great Depression in 1929), caused by a combination of federal defense and aerospace down-sizing, base closures, collapse of the construction industry and the loss of retail sales because California's confidence dropped. Remember is that real estate goes in cycles. Real estate is the first to feel any economic downturn and the last to recover.

Now California's economy is in a decade of expansion. This is due to the state's leadership in the following areas: 1) high technology and biotech; 2) foreign trade; 3) tourism & entertainment; and 4) professional services. The projections for the next decade imply that California will "almost double" the national average in: 1) job creation; 2) income increases; 3) household formation; and 4) population increases. California is the creative hub of the world because we have so many college educated people starting new creative businesses each day.

The scarcity of buildable land close to urban areas keeps driving the price of land higher. A home is an expensive venture that includes a monthly home loan payment. This payment usually equals one-fourth of the wages earned monthly by the homeowner. The monthly payment is only part of owning a home. Property taxes, fire insurance, repairs and furnishings are expenses that will further increase the monthly cost of maintaining a home.

BROKER'S COMMISSION (FULLY NEGOTIABLE)

A *COMMISSION is an amount paid, usually as a percentage, to a broker for services.* The broker is responsible for paying his or her salespeople their part of any commissions. Commissions paid to licensees are fully negotiable, but real estate brokers in California normally receive around five or six percent of the sales price of a home as their commission. For example, if a home sells for $300,000 and the broker involved in the sale receives a 6% commission, she would collect a total of $18,000 ($300,000 x .06) which is split between the salespeople.

As you can see, the real estate business is a profitable one. It requires a person who is ambitious, willing to work and enjoys helping a qualified buyer find the home. There is always a need for knowledgeable, well-trained salespeople.

HISTORICAL INFLUENCE

www.lib.berkeley.edu (California History)
www.calhist.org (California History)

NATIVE AMERICAN INDIANS WERE FIRST

California's colorful history gives a unique flavor to its customs and lifestyles. The first Europeans to actively settle California were Spaniards. In 1768 they began the famous mission system along El Camino Real, now known as U.S.Highway 101 and California 1. *They established fortified trading posts (called* ***PRESIDIOS****)* at San Francisco and Monterey.

*The first cities (called **PUEBLOS**)* were Los Angeles and San Jose. Spain's king granted vast ranchos to favored civil and military officers. Many streets, towns and landmarks in California still bear their names. The state's distinct architectural style, the rambling, cool, thick-walled adobe structure with red tile roof, dates from the Spanish period.

In the early 1800's California became a self-governing province of newly independent Mexico. The ruling government attempted land reform, breaking up the huge Spanish ranchos and giving ownership to Mexican citizens. This disturbed the American population in California and led to war with Mexico.

The United States war with Mexico ended on February 2, 1848, with the Treaty of Guadalupe Hidalgo. As part of the settlement, Mexico gave more than 500,000 square miles of land to the United States, including the present states of Nevada, Utah and California. In an extraordinary example of political-economic timing, Mexico deeded over all rights to this province within a few weeks of John Sutter's explosive discovery of gold near Sacramento.

The Gold Rush brought thousands of new citizens swarming to the west coast. Many settled permanently, founding towns and businesses, and expanding the already well-established orchards, vineyards and cattle ranches. Foreign trade crowded the coastal cities with goods and increased immigration. California achieved full statehood on September 9, 1850, and from that time on the state's population increased until it could boast of having the largest population in the nation. The newly established legislature adopted a land ownership recording system that recognized and protected the early land grants and provides a complete ownership history of California lands and their subdivision.

California statehood: September 9, 1850. California had the first licensing law in 1917—each state sets own licensing laws.

In 1917 California passed the first real estate licensing law in the nation. Although this first law was declared unconstitutional the **Real Estate Act of 1919** was upheld by the State Supreme Court. Licensing laws are a reasonable exercise by the state to regulate professions in the interest of the public good.

REAL & PERSONAL PROPERTY

OWNERSHIP IS A BUNDLE OF RIGHTS

In the historical legal sense, property refers to "all the rights" or interests one has in the "thing" owned, rather the thing itself. These rights, commonly referred to as a "bundle of rights," include the rights of possession, enjoyment, control and disposition. See Figure 1-1 for more details.

FIGURE 1-1

OWNERSHIP IS A "BUNDLE OF RIGHTS"

BUNDLE OF RIGHTS THEORY

The bundle of rights theory views property ownership rights as a large bundle of sticks, where each "stick" is a property right. Individually, these rights represent various, specific forms of ownership; the more of these you hold the more completely you own the property. So if you lease the property to someone, you give up one of your "sticks" (the right of possession). The basic rights of ownership include the following:

1. **Possession** — is the right to occupy, rent or keep others out.

2. **Enjoyment** — is the right to "peace and quiet" without interference from past owners and others.

3. **Control** — is the right to physically change or keep the property the way you like it.

4. **Disposition** — is the right to transfer all or part of your property to others as you see fit.

All of your ownership rights are, subject to governmental limitations and restrictions.

There are two types of property: **REAL PROPERTY** (*immovable*) and **PERSONAL PROPERTY** (*movable*), formerly called "chattel property."

Real property is "immovable"; title to real property is passed with a deed.

REAL PROPERTY

REAL PROPERTY *is the rights or interests that a person has in the land or anything attached to the land.* **LICENSE** *is permission to use a property.* A license may be revoked at any time. Real property is legally defined as:

1. Land
2. Anything permanently attached or affixed to the land
3. Anything incidental or appurtenant to the land
4. That which is immovable by law.

1. *LAND* ownership is commonly thought of as owning the surface of the earth; in other words, the ground we walk and build upon. But ownership also gives us rights to the space that is above our land and extends below our feet to the center of the earth, as Figure 1-2 illustrates.

FIGURE 1-2

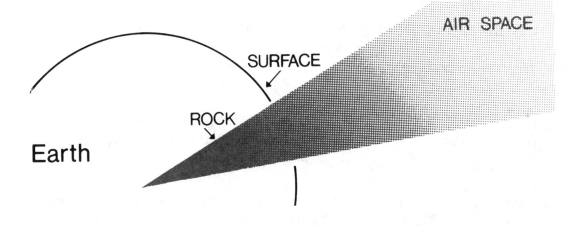

An *AIR SPACE RIGHT* is the right to the use of the air space above the surface of the earth. It is real property. In reality, the courts have restricted, to a reasonable height, the right of the property owner to use this space. An example for allowing only **reasonable use** of land is the need for airlines to have public "air highways" to provide us with transportation.

This airspace above the ground can be leased or sold in the same manner that mineral rights can be leased or sold. Airspace is an effective way to fully utilize the prime construction sites in many of our larger cites. Every day we are seeing an increased use of airspace for restaurants, office buildings, freeways, apartments and condominiums. An example of effective airspace use is space leased under our freeway overpasses (for storage or other business purposes) by Caltrans, our state highway maintenance division.

Condominiums are another good example of airspace use. Technically, a condominium (condo) buyer purchases:

A) the **air space** within the walls of the condominium and

B) a proportional share in the structural part of the **building, improvements and land** called the "common area."

Each owner may use the airspace within his or her unit in any manner he or she wishes, unless it violates the by-laws of the homeowner's group.

Generally, all that is beneath the surface of the earth belongs to the owner as real property. Substances such as gold, silver and borax are solids that are part of the real property. However, there are some exceptions: oil and other minerals can be claimed by the owner as personal property when removed from the ground. This is because they are considered by law to be "moving substances." As an owner, you may sell your mineral rights below 500 feet; or you may exercise your "right of surface entry" above the 500 foot level.

A ***RIPARIAN RIGHT*** *is the right of a landowner to use the water on, under and adjacent to his or her land, providing that its use does not infringe on the rights of any neighboring landowners.*

> *A "riparian right" is the right to reasonable use of water from a river, stream or water course, if the land borders it. "Potable water" refers to water suitable for drinking.*

2. Anything attached to the land, such as buildings, fences, walls, walks and shrubs, become ***REAL PROPERTY*** *when they are permanently incorporated or integrated in, or affixed or attached to, the land.* Buildings that rest on the land or anything attached by cement, nails, screws and plaster would be examples of real property.

> *Real property is the land and anything affixed to the land (called "improvements"). A bearing wall, which supports the upper part of a structure, is another example of real property.*

3. *Anything that is incidental or appurtenant to the land is* ***REAL PROPERTY.*** ***APPURTENANT*** *means ownership runs with the land.* Certain things that are a part of the land must be sold with the land or else the usefulness of the land is reduced. For example, some small communities own shares of stock in their own mutual water companies that supply them with water. When the land is sold, the shares in the water company go with the land. Easements that allow the use of someone else's land, such as a driveway to enter your land, also go with the land being sold if it is the only way to access the land.

> *Appurtenant means ownership "runs with the land"; it transfers automatically without the need of a separate conveyance. Stock in a mutual water company is appurtenant to real property: it transfers with the deed.*

Title to real property is passed with a "deed," whereas title to personal property is passed with a "bill of sale."

4. *That which by law is considered immovable is* **REAL PROPERTY**. Under California law, established crops and trees are a part of the land. Growing vegetables or fruits are considered personal property. Trees are sold with the land. The only exception is when a contract of sale for these items is made before the land is sold. If you have such a contract, it is a good idea to record it at the appropriate county recorder's office to assure that everyone has notice of the sale.

PERSONAL PROPERTY

PERSONAL PROPERTY *is any property that is movable and cannot be properly classified under the definition of Real Property.* Items such as clothes, furniture and automobiles are tangible, but easily movable. Personal property can also be documents that represent value, such as stocks, bonds or leases.

Personal property could be funiture, a refrigerator or a washer and dryer, etc.. It is personal property because it is "movable." Sellers take personal property with them unless negotiated otherwise. Personal property, not specifically included in a real estate sale's contract, may be subject to negotiation.

Planted growing crops are called **EMBLEMENTS** *if they are cultivated annually by a tenant farmer on leased land. These crops belong to the tenant even after the expiration of the lease. Such crops are considered personal property because they are harvested yearly (removed from the ground).*

A lease is personal property, as are stocks and bonds. Trust deeds are personal property.

When buying personal property, your receipt is called a "Bill of Sale." The Bill of Sale states that the goods have been paid for and that no outstanding loans exist on the personal property. It is always considered good practice to obtain a Bill of Sale. Figure 1-3 is an example of a Bill of Sale.

FIGURE 1-3

TRANSFERS TITLE OF PERSONAL PROPERTY

BILL OF SALE

In consideration for the sum of _Three hundred fifty and . . . no/100_

_$350.00_ as payment in full is hereby acknowledged from

(Mr. John Q. Smart) for the purchase of _(A Maytag washer_

and dryer, serial numbers #H02257 and #D376240).

Executed on _April 19, 19XX,_

in the county of _Sacramento,_ California.

Robert Seller
Signature of Seller

Personal property can be sold, can be used as security for a debt or can be changed into real property by becoming "affixed" to the land.

FIXTURES

FIXTURES are items of personal property that are attached to, or incorporated into, the land in such a manner as to become real property. The courts use these five tests to determine if an item is a fixture:

M	1) **Method of attachment**
A	2) **Adaptability**
R	3) **Relationship of the parties**
I	4) **Intention**
A	5) **Agreement**

> We sometimes place an acronym in front of a word to help you remember! **MARIA** stands for the first letter of each test.

1. The method of attachment to the land or buildings. If an item can be removed by simply being unplugged, it is probably personal property. On the other hand, if it is attached by cement, plaster, screws, nails or plumbing, it is probably real property. If removal of an item would leave permanent damage or an unusable area, it is surely real property. A rug lying in a living room would be considered personal property; carpet affixed to the floor would be considered real property.

Cost, size and time installed are not tests in determining what is real property.

2. The adaptability of the personal property. If property is well adapted for the land or building, it is probably a fixture or real property. An example would be an item attached by plumbing or plaster. On the other hand, a fan attached only by a wall plug would be considered personal property.

3. The relationship of the parties. If a fixture is not mentioned in a contract, and is affixed to the property, most courts will give the seller the benefit of the doubt. A refrigerator that is just plugged in would be considered personal property and would remain with the seller. To protect yourself, any questionable fixtures should be mentioned in the purchase agreement (deposit receipt). **Real estate salespeople remember: your client should secure a bill of sale for personal items.** In the case of a tenant and landlord, the court usually rules in favor of the tenant. There are, however, no set rules. A court decision is dependent upon the facts of each individual case.

4. The intention of the person attaching the personal property to the land is the most important test in a court of law. If you plan to remove an item of personal property, you may not permanently attach it to the land.

5. The agreement between the parties. Any item can be deemed real or personal property if it is so stated in a contract.

> *It is advisable to secure, in writing, any personal property that you want to remain as personal property. If you are buying a house, list all items you want to accompany the house, such as light fixtures, drapes or a fireplace screen. If you are selling, list only the items that will remain with the house. Remember: if in doubt, put it in writing!*

The five tests stated above are used to determine facts, and the facts are what the courts use to settle disputes.

TRADE FIXTURES
(REMOVABLE - EXCEPTION TO THE RULE)

TRADE FIXTURES are personal property used in the normal course of business, such as shelving or refrigeration units. A tenant may remove any trade fixture he or she installed provided the real property is left in the same condition as he or she found it. In this sense, trade fixtures are an exception to the rules of personal property.

Tenants own trade fixtures (built-in business furniture), so trade fixtures are removed by tenants when they leave.

METHODS OF LAND DESCRIPTION

A *COMMON ADDRESS is the address that is used for mail delivery, or the address posted on the property.* For example, let us assume that you live at 732 MAIN STREET, SAN DIEGO, CALIFORNIA. There may be several Main Streets in San Diego. Does the street run north and south or east and west? What are the boundaries of the property? As you can see, in a real estate transaction it is important to identify a property more precisely. A common address does not give all the information needed to properly describe or locate a property.

In California, every parcel of land must be properly described or identified. If the property is to be sold, financed or leased, a recognized legal description is required. The following three methods are accepted as means of property identification:

> **I. METES AND BOUNDS (SURVEYOR'S MAPS--IRREGULAR PARCELS)**
> **II. SECTIONS AND TOWNSHIPS (U.S. GOVERNMENT SURVEY--RURAL)**
> **III. LOTS, BLOCKS AND TRACTS (RECORDED SUBDIVISIONS--CITIES)**

I. METES AND BOUNDS (SURVEYOR'S MAPS)

METES AND BOUNDS is the method of identifying (describing) property in relationship to its boundaries, distances and angles from a given starting point. In the past, surveyors often used natural objects as a starting point in their descriptions. An outdated surveyor's report might read:

> *"Starting at the old oak tree at the stream, go 300 feet north along the river bed, then make a 90 degree right turn and proceed 100 feet..."*

The weakness in this type of description is that when natural objects are used as starting points, there is a chance that time, or man, many move or destroy these objects. Modern day surveying is a complicated method of property description better left to the professionals. It is also unnecessary for the average real estate salesperson to study this method in depth, but a basic working knowledge can be helpful. The following (Figure 1-4) is an example of how a simple surveyor's report might look.

FIGURE 1-4

II. SECTIONS AND TOWNSHIPS (U.S. GOVERNMENT SURVEY)

The United States Government Survey system was established to identify all public lands by the use of "base lines" and "meridians" starting from a precise surveying point. There are many such starting points throughout the country. There are three main starting points in California (see Figure 1-5).

The three starting points are:

1) **Humboldt Base Line and Meridian** in Northern California;
2) **Mt. Diablo Base Line and Meridian** in Central California;
3) **San Bernardino Base Line and Meridian** in Southern California.

From these three starting points, all of California may be described using sections, townships and ranges to define any given parcel.

BASE LINES AND MERIDIAN LINES

A BASE LINE is a horizontal line that runs east and west from any given starting point. Each base line is marked in six-mile increments. Every six-mile increment is called a **range** and each range is six miles in width. It is possible to move east or west a designated number of ranges from any starting point.

FIGURE 1-5

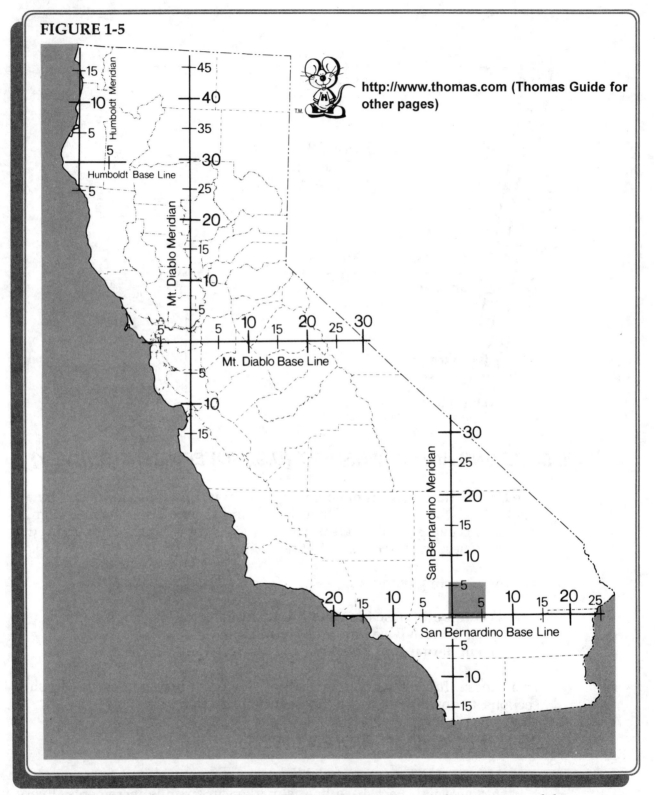

http://www.thomas.com (Thomas Guide for other pages)

MERIDIANS are vertical lines that run north and south from any one of the three starting points in California. Meridians are also marked off in increments of six miles each, but each six mile increment on a meridian is called a *township*.

TOWNSHIPS (EACH IS SIX MILES SQUARE)

A *TOWNSHIP is a square of land that measures six miles by six miles and thus contains 36 square miles.* Townships run north and south from the base line in rows.

The location of any township is determined by its distance from the nearest base line and meridian line. For example, to determine the location of a township northeast of the San Bernardino Base Line and Meridian (T. 4N, R. 3E), see Figure 1-6.

FIGURE 1-6

The following steps are used:

First, move east along the San Bernardino Base Line three ranges. This is the range located between the 2nd and 3rd range lines east of the San Bernardino Meridian. Second, move north from the San Bernardino Base Line four townships. This is the township located between the 3rd. and 4th. township lines north of the base line.

READING TOWNSHIP AND SECTION DESCRIPTIONS

The above description would be written:

T. 4N, R. 3E San Bernardino Base Line and Meridian.

In this form "R" represents the word range and "3E" tells you to move three ranges east of the meridian. Likewise, "T" means township, and "4N" tells you to go four townships north of the San Bernardino Base Line.

To locate a property, work backwards on the description. When reading a description, read it from right to left. A verbal interpretation of our above description would read: "Starting from the San Bernardino Base Line and Meridian, go three ranges east and four townships north." You have located the township in which the property is located.

SECTIONS (A SECTION IS ONE MILE SQUARE)

Each township is divided into 36 sections. A *SECTION is one mile square of land consisting of 640 acres. There are 36 sections in a township.*

A section contains 640 acres; 1/2 section 320 acres; 1/4 section 160 acres.

These sections are numbered in sequential order starting at the upper right-hand corner, as illustrated in Figure 1-7. Since each township is 6 miles square and consists of 36 sections, each section measures 1 mile square. If we wanted to located section 29 (See Figure 1-7), the description would read:

Section 29, T. 4N, R. 3E San Bernardino Base Line and Meridian.

FIGURE 1-7

36	31	32	33	34	35	36	31
1	6	5	4	3	2	1	6
12	7	8	9	10	11	12	7
13	18	17	16	15	14	13	18
24	19	20	21	22	23	24	19
25	30	29	28	27	26	25	30
36	31	32	33	34	35	36	31
1	6	5	4	3	2	1	6

Each section measures one mile square and consists of 640 acres. A section can be broken down into halves or quarters. For example, the description for the Northeast quarter of section 29 (See Figure 1-8) would read:

NE 1/4 of Section 29, T. 4N, R. 3E San Bernardino Base Line and Meridian.

That quarter can then be broken down further into halves or quarters. The description of the southwest quarter of the northeast quarter of section 29 (See Figure 1-8) would read:

SW 1/4 of the NE 1/4 of section 29, T. 4N, R. 3E San Bernardino Base Line and Meridian.

This procedure can continue until the property is completely described.

FIGURE 1-8

SECTION 29

See Figure 1-9 for a handy reference table and Figure 1-10 for math problems.

FIGURE 1-9   REFERENCE TABLE

One **ACRE** is 43,560 square feet.

One **SQUARE ACRE** is 208.71 feet, but this number is generally rounded off to 209 feet square.

One **MILE** is 5,280 feet long.

One **SQUARE MILE** contains 640 acres.

One **SECTION** is one square mile

One **TOWNSHIP** is six miles square (36 square miles).

One **COMMERCIAL ACRE** is an acre minus any required public dedications.

One **ROD** is 16.5 feet long (5.5 yards).

FIGURE 1-10

How do you find the area of an acre?

An *ACRE is an area of land that contains 43,560 square feet*. So if the area of a lot has more than 43,560 square feet, there is more than an acre of land. On the other hand, if there is less than 43,560 square feet in a lot it is smaller than an acre.

AREA is a definite amount of space within a shape. In America area is usually measured in square feet, but can possibly be measured in square yards or square meters in other parts of the world. Most test questions about area refer to a rectangular or square shape. The area of a rectangular or square shape is obtained by multiplying length **x** (times) width. The answer is in square feet. The area of a square lot 100 feet x 100 feet is 10,000 square feet.

Example (1): How many acres is a parcel of land that measures 330 feet by 660 feet?
Answer:
Area   = Length x Width
217,800   = 330 feet x 660 feet
Note: 1 acre = 43,560 square feet

$\dfrac{\textbf{217,800}}{\textbf{43,560}}$ = **5 ACRES** (Round if necessary)

Example (2): If an acre is divided into four equal lots, with each lot placed parallel to the other and having a depth of 240 feet, what is the width of each lot?

Answer:
Area   = Length x Width
43,560   = 240 feet (x 4 lots) x   ? feet
43,560   = 960 feet   x   ? feet

$\dfrac{\textbf{43,560}}{\textbf{960}}$ = **45.375 feet wide (Round to 45.4 feet wide)**

See Chapter 15 (Math) for more problems.

III. LOTS, BLOCKS, AND TRACTS (RECORDED SUBDIVISIONS)

In California, subdivisions are granted by the Department of Real Estate. The subdivision map, however, is approved by the county or city in which the property is located. The approved subdivision map is recorded at the County Recorder's Office. Once it is recorded, all future transactions can be referenced to that map. The following is a description of a home located in Venice, California (see Figure 1-11).

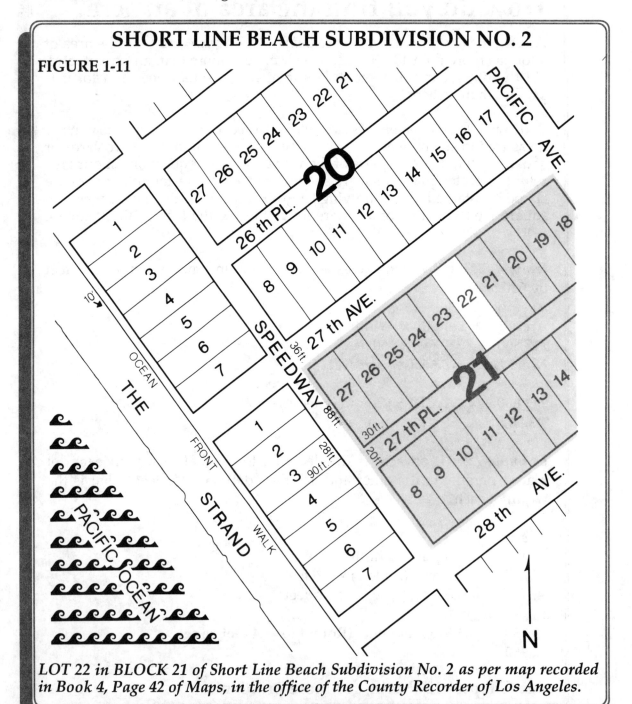

SHORT LINE BEACH SUBDIVISION NO. 2

FIGURE 1-11

LOT 22 in BLOCK 21 of Short Line Beach Subdivision No. 2 as per map recorded in Book 4, Page 42 of Maps, in the office of the County Recorder of Los Angeles.

CALIFORNIA FACTS

CALIFORNIA LAND

California, which is the largest state in population, is also one of the largest states in size with 101,803,000 acres. The Pacific Ocean touches over 840 miles of the California coastline, and the inland waterways account for 2,332 square miles of water. Over 45% of all the land (mostly National Forest and park land) in the state is owned by the Federal Government.

LAND OWNERSHIP

OWNERSHIP	ACRES	PERCENTAGE OF TOTAL
Federal	46,183,000	45%
State	3,125,000	3%
Local	2,059,000	2%
Private	50,436,000	50%
	101,803,000	100%

California, in recent decades, has become the most popular state. The Mediterranean climate has enticed millions to settle down in California. Because winters are mild for work or play, and because there is a great variety of lifestyles available, California will continue to be a magnet for the people of the United States and the World.

CALIFORNIA'S FAVORABLE FUTURE

California has a favorable future. We have the largest population in the United States and we're still growing! Because of our variable climate, California enjoys agricultural superiority, a thriving tourist trade and unchallenged status as the center of the entertainment industry. We also dominate in high technology, such as the computer industry. Our strategic trade position on the Pacific Rim gives us excellent access to such booming economic centers as Japan, Korea, Taiwan, Singapore and Australia.

In 1998, the number of people living in California was 32 million. Population estimates forecast the following population trends:

2000 - 34 million people

2010 - 40 million people

TERMINOLOGY - CHAPTER 1

A. Commission	**I.** Riparian Right	**Q.** Meridian Lines
B. Admission Date	**J.** Chattel Or Chattel Real	**R.** Range
C. Real Property	**K.** Emblements	**S.** Township
D. Potable Water	**L.** Bill Of Sale	**T.** Rod
E. Personal Property	**M.** Fixtures	**U.** Section
F. Air Space	**N.** Trade Fixtures	**V.** Acre
G. Bundle Of Rights	**O.** Metes And Bounds	
H. Condominium	**P.** Base Lines	

1.____ A column of land six miles wide, determined by a government survey, running in a north-south direction, lying east or west of a principal meridian.

2.____ Personal property that has become permanently attached to the land or improvements that are legally treated as real property; examples: plumbing fixtures, or built in range, etc..

3.____ Personal property used in a business, attached to the property, but removable by the tenant.

4.____ A structure of two or more units where the interior air space of each unit is individually owned; the balance of land and improvements is owned in common by all the owners.

5.____ Imaginary north-south lines used in surveying.

6.____ Property that is movable and not real property.

7.____ A written instrument that passes title of personal property from vendor (seller) to the vendee (buyer).

8.____ An amount, usually a percentage, paid to an agent as compensation for his or her services.

9.____ A legal description of land, setting forth all the boundary lines with their terminal points and angles. The distances between points are the metes and the directions are the bounds.

10.____ All of the legal rights relevant to ownership of property including rights of use, possession, encumbering and disposition.

11.____ In the survey of public lands, a territorial subdivision six miles long, six miles wide and containing 36 sections, each one mile square.

12.____ Land, improvements, items permanently attached to the land, appurtenances and that which is immovable by law.

13.____ A personal property and personal property interest in real property. An old term meaning personal property. Chattel real refers to a lease.

14.____ An area of land equaling 43,560 square feet, or a tract about 208.71 feet square.

15.____ The right of a landowner, whose land borders a stream or waterway, to use and enjoy the water, provided such use does not injure the rights of other owners.

16.____ A square of land (government survey) that contains 640 acres and is one mile square.

17.____ This old unit of measurement is 16 1/2 feet long (5.5 yards).

18.____ The space above a parcel or in a condominium; the cubic area of a space within the walls.

19.____ Imaginary east-west lines that intersect meridian lines to form a starting point for the measurement of land.

20.____ Water that is suitable for human consumption.

21.____ Crops (produced on leased land by a tenant farmer) from an annual cultivation considered personal property.

22.____ September 9, 1850.

Answers to the matching terminology are found on page 546.

MULTIPLE CHOICE

1. How many square miles are there in a section?

    A. 6   B. 9
    C. 4   D. 1

2. Metes and bounds is best described as:

    A. horizontal lines that run east and west   B. vertical lines that run north and south
    C. a method to measure land   D. a method to describe land

3. What percentage of California land is owned by the federal government?

    A. 2%   B. 3%
    C. 45%   D. 50%

4. The number of the section just below section one is:

    A. 7   B. 8
    C. 12   D. 36

5. A township is:

    A. 1 square mile   B. 6 square miles
    C. 36 square miles   D. 640 acres

6. California became a state on September 9,:

    A. 1825   B. 1849
    C. 1850   D. 1878

7. As long as it does NOT infringe on the rights of neighboring properties, landowners may claim a "riparian right" to what substance on, under or adjacent to his or her land?

    A. Water   B. Silver
    C. Gold   D. None of the above

8. Emblements are considered:

    A. annually cultivated crops   B. designs on houses
    C. transfer of ownership documents   D. none of the above

9. The commission paid for the sale of a condominum is:

    A. 6%   B. 10%
    C. set by law   D. fully negotiable

10. The address posted on the property is the :

    A. legal address   B. common address
    C. assessor's address   D. lot, block and tract

Answers to the multiple choice questions are found on page 545.

CHAPTER 2
Estates, Transfers and Titles

The previous chapter explained the differences between real and personal property. This chapter illustrates the types of estates (ownership) that you may have, the ways in which you can hold title and the methods of transferring real property.

ESTATE OWNERSHIP

ESTATES
Freehold & Less-Than-Freehold

Freehold	Less-Than-Freehold
(Real Property)	**(Personal Property)**

ESTATES (OWNERSHIP)

An **ESTATE** *is an interest, share, right or equity in real estate that varies from the minimal right of a renter to the maximum right of a full owner.*

Estates are either **(1) freehold** or **(2) less-than-freehold**, depending upon the degree of ownership and the duration of interest. Freehold estates are real property and less-than-freehold estates are personal property. Less-than-freehold estates come with certain rights for the use of real property. See Figure 2-1.

FREEHOLD ESTATES (REAL PROPERTY)

Freehold estates are 1) fee estates or 2) life estates.

The two types of freehold estates are: 1) a fee simple estate or 2) a life estate. These freehold estates are the greatest degree of ownership you can have under the law.

ESTATES IN FEE (FEE OR SIMPLE)

Fee or simple is the most interest (greatest) one can hold; it is of "indefinite duration," freely transferable and "inheritable" (referred to as an estate of inheritance).

It is okay for fee or simple property to have a loan against it.

An estate in fee is the most complete form of ownership and the most common in California. This can be referred to as fee, fee ownership, or simple. *FEE or SIMPLE means an owner has transferred all rights of a property to a new owner for an indefinite duration of time (perpetual).* All transfers are assumed to be fee or simple unless the grant part of the deed limits, by the use of conditions, the property's use.

CONDITIONS THAT RESTRICT A FEE ESTATE
(FEE SIMPLE DEFEASIBLE ESTATE)

If there are conditions to the property's use, it is a **FEE SIMPLE DEFEASIBLE ESTATE**. Breaking any condition of the transfer may be grounds for terminating or revoking the property transfer. The transfer can be undone ("defeased") and would revert to the grantor or the grantor's heirs. There are two categories of conditions:

> 1) condition precedent and
> 2) condition subsequent.

A **CONDITION PRECEDENT** *is an event that must happen* **before** *the property can be transferred.* For example, a property owner will give the state a parcel if the state agrees to build a college on the site. In such a case, if the state did not agree, the owner would not transfer the property. A **CONDITION SUBSEQUENT** *is an event that happens* **after (in the future)** *the property is transferred that causes the property to revert (go back) to the grantor.* The above example could become a condition subsequent by stating that "if actual construction of the college has not started within five years, the property will revert to the grantor."

A "fee simple defeasible estate" is an estate that can be defeated if a condition placed upon the estate is violated in the future (condition subsequent). For example, if a person takes title subject to a condition that liquor not be served on the premises, and then turns around and breaks this promise, the previous title holder has grounds to reclaim title through a court action. A fee simple defeasible estate, with a condition (precedent or subsequent) hanging over it, has less value than a fee simple estate.

In this chapter we have briefly discussed conditions, as in C,C&Rs (Covenants, Conditions & Restrictions). For a more complete discussion of other types of private restrictions, please see Chapter 3.

LIFE ESTATE (INDEFINITE PERIOD)

"Life" and "fee" are the two types of freehold estates.

A **LIFE ESTATE** *is an ownership interest in real property that only exists for the life of any designated person or persons (grantee).* The usual intent of this type of estate is to provide a lifetime residence for an individual. A life estate can be created by either a will or a deed.

A "life estate" is a freehold estate with a limited duration based upon someone's lifetime. This can be the lifetime of the person granting the estate or any other person so designated. When that designated person dies, the estate reverts back to the original owner (reversion). A person holding a life estate is free to lease the property to someone else, but this lease is also subject to the lifetime limitation. If the designated person dies, the estate ends and all rights, including any tenant rights, revert back to the original owner.

A person holding a life estate cannot grant more rights than he or she holds.

The life tenant usually has certain interests and obligations as long as the life estate is in effect. The life tenant:

1. has the right of physical possession of the property.
2. has the right to all rents and profits, but this terminates when the life estate holder dies.
3. can usually lease, sell or finance the property, but not beyond the time frame of the life estate.
4. is obligated to keep the property in good repair, although he or she is not required to make improvements.
5. may not damage or destroy any permanent part of the property to the detriment of succeeding interests.
6. is usually responsible for all annual costs and expenses.

If I give you a life estate, you hold "possession" for as long as you live. You can lease it out. However if you lease it out, the property is subject to how long you live. When you die, possession reverts back to me: you cannot give away more rights than you received from me. My estate is a (fee, simple) freehold estate and your estate is a (life) freehold estate.

The party (grantor) granting a life estate is said to hold an **ESTATE IN REVERSION**. The property returns (reverts back) to the grantor when the life estate holder dies.

If an owner granting a life estate names another person to receive title upon the death of the current life estate holder, that other person claims an **ESTATE IN REMAINDER**. The holder of an estate in remainder or estate in reversion has no right to the use and enjoyment of the property until the current life tenant dies.

LESS-THAN-FREEHOLD ESTATES (A LEASEHOLD IS PERSONAL PROPERTY)

LESS-THAN-FREEHOLD ESTATES *are personal rights to the use of real property for a period of time.* They are more commonly referred to as leases or rental agreements, which give a tenant various rights to use real property for a specified period. The lease or rental agreement is personal property because there is no true ownership in the property. The tenant only has possession of the property. See Figure 2-2.

A lease is a less-than-freehold estate because it is for a definite period of time. The lease is the personal property of the lessee (renter).

1) ESTATE FOR YEARS — *a lease for a fixed period of time, agreed to in advance.* This period can be from a few days up to 99 years. No notice to terminate is necessary.

A "definite period of time," fixed in advance, from three hours at a wedding chapel to a 99-year lease, is called an estate for years.

FIGURE 2-2

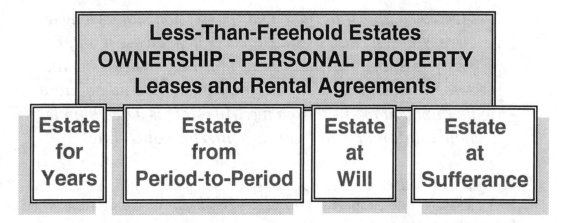

Less-Than-Freehold Estates OWNERSHIP - PERSONAL PROPERTY Leases and Rental Agreements			
Estate for Years	Estate from Period-to-Period	Estate at Will	Estate at Sufferance

ESTATE FROM PERIOD-TO-PERIOD — *a renewable agreement to rent or lease a property for a period of time,* where the rental or lease amount is fixed at an agreed to sum per week, month or year. A notice to terminate must be given.

ESTATE AT WILL — *a rental agreement that can be terminated by either party at any time.* By California law, there must be at least 30 day's notice.

ESTATE AT SUFFERANCE — *occurs when the person renting or leasing a particular property remains after the expiration of the stated term.*

The four main types of less-than-freehold estates are explained in detail in Chapter 6 - "Landlord and Tenant."

ACQUISITIONS AND TRANSFERS

TRANSFERS

A sale is the means by which real estate is usually transferred. A sale is the most familiar way of transferring property, but it is not the only way. The six basic ways to transfer real property are:

1. Deed
2. Will
3. Intestate succession (no will)
4. Accession
5. Occupancy
6. Dedication

Figure 2-3 illustrates the six methods of transferring real property.

FIGURE 2-3

Acquisition and Transfer

BY DEED	BY A WILL	BY INTESTATE SUCCESSION	BY ACCESSION	BY OCCUPANCY	BY DEDICATION
Grant Deed	Witnessed	Disposal by Law	Natural Causes	Abandonment	Voluntary
Quitclaim Deed	Holographic	No Will	Permanent Fixtures	Adverse Possession	Mandatory
			Encroachment	Prescription	

TRANSFER BY DEED

The deed is not the title, but is "evidence" of the title.

The most common method of acquiring title to a property is by deed transfer. In California, the transfer of ownership of real property is usually accomplished by a simple written document known as a deed. A **DEED** *is a written instrument that conveys and evidences title.*

The **GRANTOR** *is the person who grants property or property rights (seller).* The **GRANTEE** *is the person to whom the grant is made (buyer).* A grantee cannot be a fictitious person (example: Batman or Catwoman). It can be a person with a fictitious name (example: Microsoft, Inc.).

All deeds must have a "granting" type clause (action clause). The grantor is the person transferring real property. Both grant deeds and quitclaim deeds are signed only by the grantor. The deed is said to be executed when signed by the grantor.

There are two basic types of deeds: (1) grant deed and (2) quitclaim deed.

All other deeds are versions of these two deeds.

A **GRANT DEED** *is a document that transfers title with the key word being "grant."* (See Figure 2-4)

FIGURE 2-4

827367

320

BK D5061 PG 621

WHEN RECORDED MAIL TO

RECORDED IN OFFICIAL RECORDS
OF LOS ANGELES COUNTY. CALIF.
FOR TITLE INSURANCE & TRUST CO

MAY 19 1971 AT 8 A.M.

Registrar-Recorder

FEE
$2
C

NAME Philip S. Dockter
Street Address 1212 Lincoln Avenue
City & State Pomona, California 91767

#61638

MAIL TAX STATEMENTS TO

— SPACE ABOVE THIS LINE FOR RECORDER'S USE —

NAME SAME AS SHOWN ABOVE:
Street Address
City & State

DOCUMENTARY TRANSFER TAX $33.00
...Computed on full value of property conveyed
.....Or computed on full value less liens and encumbrances remaining at time of sale.
WILSHIRE ESCROW COMPANY
Signature of Declarant or Agent determining tax. Firm name

Grant Deed

FOR A VALUABLE CONSIDERATION, receipt of which is hereby acknowledged,

HENRY W. SPLITTER, a widower, who acquired title as HENRY SPLITTER, , does hereby

GRANT to   Philip S. Dockter   , a single man,

the real property in the   City of Los Angeles   County of   Los Angeles
State of California, described as:

Lot 22 in Block 21 of Short Line Beach Subdivision No. 2, as per map recorded in
Book 4 Page 42 of Maps, in the office of the County Recorder of said County.

RESERVING UNTO THE GRANTOR 50% of all oil, minerals, coals, petroleum, gas and
kindred substances in and under said land, from a depth below 500 feet from the
surface of said land, but without the right of entry of the surface thereof.

SUBJECT TO:
1. General and Special Taxes for the fiscal year 1971-72.
2. Covenants, conditions, restrictions, reservations, easements, rights and rights
   of way of record, if any.
3. Trust Deed to file concurrently herewith.

Dated   April 15, 1971

Henry W. Splitter
Henry W. Splitter

STATE OF CALIFORNIA
COUNTY OF   Los Angeles   } SS.
On   May 4, 1971   before me, the undersigned, a Notary Public in and for said State, personally appeared
Henry W. Splitter

320

_____, known to me
to be the person   whose name   is   subscribed to the within
instrument and acknowledged that   he   executed the same.
WITNESS my hand and official seal.

Signature _____
Donald R. Shewfelt

OFFICIAL SEAL
DONALD R. SHEWFELT
NOTARY PUBLIC — CALIFORNIA
PRINCIPAL OFFICE IN
LOS ANGELES COUNTY
My Commission Expires Aug. 17, 1971

Name (Typed or Printed)

(This area for official notarial seal)

MAIL TAX STATEMENTS AS DIRECTED ABOVE

The granting (or warranty) aspect of the deed is a promise that:

1. The owner (grantor) has not conveyed title to the property to any other person (grantee).

2. The property is free of any encumbrances (liens or other restrictions) other than those already disclosed to the grantee. A grant deed also transfers any after-acquired title, meaning that rights obtained after the sale has been completed are also conveyed.

These warranties are part of the grant deed although they are not written into the deed. They are called *IMPLIED WARRANTIES because they are not expressed in writing but are present.*

Grant deeds contain "implied warranties" even if they are not expressed in writing.

It should be noted that the grant deed does not necessarily give one all the rights to a property. Easements, rights of way, mineral rights, building restrictions and other types of restrictions may still restrict the use of the property.

A person who transfers title to real property is the grantor; therefore anyone who signs a grant deed is a "grantor" and anyone who signs a quitclaim deed is a "grantor." The person receiving property is the "grantee."

A *QUITCLAIM DEED is a deed that conveys only the present rights or interest that a person may have in a property.*

A quitclaim deed can give absolute ownership or only such title as one may hold. If there is no ownership interest, then nothing can be acquired. Read the quitclaim deed in Figure 2-5. Note that there are no warranties; just the clause, I quitclaim. This deed is used primarily to clear a cloud on title from the records. A *CLOUD ON TITLE is a claim, encumbrance or condition that impairs the title to real property until disproved or eliminated as, for example, through a quitclaim deed or a quiet title legal action.* It is usually a minor defect that requires a quitclaim deed before a title insurance company will clear the transfer. A quitclaim deed is often used in divorce actions, so that one party may have clear title.

Quitclaim deeds make no "covenants" (promises); they guarantee nothing, only convey all rights the grantor may have.

FIGURE 2-5

RECORDING REQUESTED BY

AND WHEN RECORDED MAIL THIS DEED AND, UNLESS OTHER-
WISE SHOWN BELOW, MAIL TAX STATEMENTS TO:

NAME

ADDRESS

CITY &
STATE
ZIP

Title Order No.   Escrow No.

——— SPACE ABOVE THIS LINE FOR RECORDER'S USE ———

Quitclaim Deed

The undersigned declares that the documentary transfer tax is $ .... and is
☐ computed on the full value of the interest or property conveyed, or is
☐ computed on the full value less the value of liens or encumbrances remaining thereon at the time of sale. The land, tenements or realty
is located in
☐ unincorporated area   ☐ city of ....

FOR A VALUABLE CONSIDERATION, receipt of which is hereby acknowledged,

do   . hereby remise, release and forever quitclaim to

the following described real property in the   county of
state of California:

Dated _____

STATE OF CALIFORNIA

COUNTY OF _____ } SS

On this the _____ day of _____ 19 ___, before me,
the undersigned, a Notary Public in and for said County and State,
personally appeared _____
_____
_____
_____, personally known to me
or proved to me on the basis of satisfactory evidence to be the
person____ whose name____ subscribed to the within instrument
and acknowledged that _____ executed the same.

_____
Signature of Notary

FOR NOTARY SEAL OR STAMP

MAIL TAX STATEMENTS TO PARTY SHOWN ON FOLLOWING LINE; IF NO PARTY SO SHOWN, MAIL AS DIRECTED ABOVE

_____
Name   Street Address   City & State

SAFECO Stock No. **CAL-0011A**

32

A **VALID DEED** has all the following essentials:

1. It must be in writing.
2. The parties must be properly described.
3. The grantor must have legal capacity.
4. The property must be adequately described.
5. There must be a granting clause (action clause).
6. It must be signed by the granting party.
7. It must be intentionally delivered, and accepted by the grantee.

Some subtypes of grant or quitclaim deeds used in California are:

GIFT DEED . . . *granted as a gift of love and affection.* No other consideration is necessary, but is void if given to defraud creditors.

TAX DEED . . . *given if property is sold as payment of past-due property taxes.*

ADMINISTRATOR'S DEED OR EXECUTOR'S DEED . . . *given to the purchaser of the deceased person's real property.*

SHERIFF'S DEED . . . *granted to the purchaser at a court-ordered sale.*

TRUSTEE'S DEED . . . *given to the purchaser of property at a trust deed foreclosure sale.*

GUARDIAN'S DEED . . . *used by a guardian to transfer the real property of minors or incompetents.*

LAND PATENT . . . *used by the government to grant public land to an individual.*

A trust deed is NOT a deed!

A **TRUST DEED** *is a security device; it pledges real property as security for the payment of a loan.*

A trust deed is a security device; it gives legal title to a trustee with the power to sell.

A **RECONVEYANCE** *is a document granted by a trustee to clear a trustor's debt from the title after a trust deed has been paid in full.*

A reconveyance is NOT a deed; it is proof of payment (satisfaction). Not used in a trustee's sale. (See Chapter 8.)

A deed does not take effect until it is delivered and accepted. In order for title to be transferred, the grantor must sign the deed and deliver it **with the intention of passing title immediately**.

Delivery and acceptance of the deed conveys title if it is "intentional." It becomes effective immediately.

The following are the three basic methods of delivery.

1. MANUAL DELIVERY is a direct transfer of the deed from the grantor to the grantee.

2. DELIVERY THROUGH RECORDING is the act of putting the title of record in the grantee's name at the county recorder's office. The grantee must have agreed to the recording.

3. CONDITIONAL DELIVERY requires that a specific event take place before title can be passed. The deed is then delivered manually.

TRANSFER BY WILL (TESTATE)

A **WILL** *is a document, created by a person, stating how that person's property is to be conveyed or distributed upon his or her death. It also leaves instructions as to the disposition of the body upon death.* This is known as dying **TESTATE,** *which means having made and left a valid will.*

There are two types of wills that can legally dispose of real and personal property:

1. Witnessed will (typed)
2. Holographic will (handwritten)

A **WITNESSED WILL** *is a typed document usually prepared by an attorney, dated, signed by the property owners and declared to be a will by at least two witnesses.*

A **HOLOGRAPHIC WILL** *is entirely handwritten by the owner, dated and signed.* Since it is in the owner's own handwriting, no other formalities and no witnesses are required, unless the will is signed with an "X", in which case it must be witnessed.

A holographic will signed "X" must be witnessed.

Note: A *REVOCABLE LIVING TRUST* *is a trust that is effective during the life of the owner, rather than upon his or her death.* It can eliminate probate (to prove a will) and serve the same function as a will. The property is placed in a trust created for the heirs and may consist of both real and personal property. It is revocable at the discretion of the benefactor (owner), but becomes fully enforceable upon that person's death. There can be a considerable estate tax savings under this arrangement, depending on the size of the estate. At the very least, a revocable living trust protects the interests of everyone involved while avoiding the time and expense of probate. This type of trust is, however, rather complicated to set up, so an attorney specializing in this field should be consulted.

TRANSFER BY PROBATE (SUPERIOR COURT APPROVAL)

PROBATE is a Superior Court procedure to determine the will's validity, any creditors' claims and establish the identity of the beneficiaries. There are charges for the court probate action and fees for any related attorney costs.

After a person dies, an **administrator (male)** or **administratrix (female)** is appointed by the court to temporarily take possession of the property until probate is finalized. If the will has appointed a particular custodian, then that person is known as an **executor (male)** or an **executrix (female).**

A probate court must approve the sale of real property for a commission.

A will is the best way of transferring property at death. If you do not take advantage of this legal device, the state will decide how your property will be divided among your heirs. This may be inconsistent with your wishes. To protect yourself, have an attorney draw up a will that reflects your desires, or leave your own handwritten (holographic) will.

TRANSFER BY INTESTATE SUCCESSION (NO WILL)

If there is no will, the procedure used for transferring the deceased's property to his or her heirs is called INTESTATE SUCCESSION. With intestate succession, the law provides for the disposition of the property. The rules for dividing the property are complex and dependent upon the relationship of the kin.

Separate property: If the decedent leaves a spouse and one child, property is divided equally, 50-50. If there is a surviving spouse and two or more children, 1/3 to spouse and 2/3 to children. If no surviving spouse, property is divided equally among the children.

ESCHEAT is the term used if there is no will and there are no heirs; the property reverts to the state of California. This is not automatic; it must be initiated through legal proceedings.

Individuals do not acquire property by escheat; if there are no heirs, it goes only to the state.

TRANSFER BY ACCESSION (NATURAL CAUSES)

ACCESSION occurs when an owner acquires title to additional land by natural causes, that is, additions to the property by improvements or natural growth. *The addition to land from natural causes, such as earthquakes, volcanoes or the action of moving water is known as ACCRETION.* For example, a river over time may slowly deposit soil on one of its banks. These *deposits of earth made through the natural action of water, called ALLUVIUM,* become the real property of the landowner who holds title to the river bank. *AVULSION is the sudden, violent tearing away of land by, for example, a river.* Title to that land is lost by the property owner.

Permanent fixtures attached to the land or buildings by residential tenants must be left with the building. Any improvements that are mistakenly placed on the property must also remain. *Placement of improvements and permanent fixtures on property that does not legally belong to the person who placed them is called ENCROACHMENT.*

TRANSFER BY OCCUPANCY

Ownership of real property, or the use of real property, can be gained through three types of occupancy:

1. Abandonment
2. Adverse Possession
3. Prescription (by use)

ABANDONMENT is the process of acquiring property that someone has left. One cannot acquire title to abandoned real property without court action, but a landlord can acquire possession of a property that is left (abandoned) by a tenant simply by gaining full control of the property. In the case of a lease, a financially troubled tenant might negotiate a release or abandon the property, thereby forfeiting part of the deposit.

Estates, Transfers and Titles

ADVERSE POSSESSION is acquiring title to another's property through continuous and notorious occupancy under a claim of title. It is the legal way to acquire title **without** a deed. Title may be obtained through adverse possession only as long as certain conditions are met:

1. **Property taxes** — The adverse possessor must have paid all taxes levied and assessed on the property for five consecutive years.

2. **Open and notorious occupancy** — The adverse possessor must live on, or openly use, the property in such a way that the titled owners might easily detect his or her presence.

3. **Uninterrupted use for five years** — The adverse possessor must use the property continuously for at least five consecutive years.

4. **Claim of title** — The adverse possessor must have some reasonable claim of right or color of title (perhaps a defective written instrument) as a basis for his or her assertion. For example, a person could claim that his uncle gave the property to him before he died, but the deed is missing.

5. **Hostile** — The adverse possessor must possess the property hostile to the legal owner, without his or her permission or any rental payment (consideration).

No fighting please, just confrontation in the legal sense.

The courts will require substantial proof before consenting to adverse possession. To obtain marketable title, or before a title insurance company can insure a property, clear title must be obtained by a court decree. This essentially means that a "quiet title" action is brought into court to prove that you have fulfilled all the five requirements. In the peoples' interest, adverse possession is not possible against public or government lands, but only against privately owned lands.

PRESCRIPTION is an easement, or the right to use another's land, which can be obtained through five years continuous use. Its requirements are similar to those of adverse possession, the differences being: **(1)** By prescription, only the use of the property has been obtained. **(2)** By prescription, taxes are still paid by the property owner. There is no confrontation and no property taxes.

TRANSFER BY DEDICATION

DEDICATION is the gift (appropriation) of land, by its owner, for some public use. To be fully dedicated, the land must be accepted for such use by authorized public officials. Dedication may be either (1) voluntary or (2) mandated by statute.

A developer will "dedicate land" for a street to the city.

TITLE (FORMS OF OWNERSHIP)

TITLE

TITLE is the evidence that one has the right to possess a parcel of real property. There are five distinct methods of holding title. Figure 2-6 displays the five ways a person, or persons, may hold title to real property and whether a single title holder has the right to will or sell his or her share independent of the other owners. *VESTING is the placing of a person's (or persons') name on the deed and the description of the method by which that person will hold title.*

"Vesting" is the method by which you hold "title" from among alternatives; it is the tenancy (method).

FIGURE 2-6

Methods of Holding Title
(Vesting) Concurrently or in Severalty

A SINGLE TITLE HOLDER	WILL	SELL
SEVERALTY	YES	YES
TENANTS IN COMMON	YES	YES
JOINT TENANTS	NO	YES
TENANCY IN PARTNERSHIP	NO	NO
COMMUNITY PROPERTY	YES	NO

SEVERALTY (SEPARATE OWNERSHIP)

SEVERALTY is the sole and separate ownership of property by one individual or by a corporation. The word "severed" means to sever, to cut off or separate. The name severalty is misleading; it does mean one.

Title can be held by a corporation (legal person) or individual (natural person). Severalty means ownership by "only one."

Property held by corporations is owned in severalty, as if by a single individual. A *CORPORATION is a body of persons treated by law as a single "legal person," having a personality and existence distinct from that of its shareholders.* A corporation can go on forever; it does not die.

Examples to show ownership by severalty are:

as a natural person, a real person

"Mary Smith, a single woman"

or

"Mary Smith, an unmarried woman"

or as a legal person; charter granted by the state

"Urban Analysis Inc., a corporation"

Sometimes married people wish to keep ownership to certain properties as separate property (in severalty). They could then use the phrase:

"Mary Smith, a married women, as her sole and separate property"

or

"Jim Smith, a married man, as his sole and separate property"

TENANCY IN COMMON

Ownership concurrently. The right to individually possess, will or sell.

When two or more people concurrently own property (without survivorship rights or community property rights) it is called TENANCY IN COMMON. If there is no other agreement, they will each share an equal interest in the property. All tenants in common have "unity of possession," which means they each have the right to occupy the property. Often, the property is rented to one of the owners or to a tenant. Tenancy in common gives all owners a share of the income and expenses of the property. An example of the wording illustrating this would be:

"Jim Smith and Mary Smith, husband and wife, as tenants in common"

Each owner may sell or transfer his or her interest separately from the others. For example, if one of the four owners of a building was to sell his or her 1/4 interest, there would be no restrictions. More commonly, if one of the owners dies, his or her heirs will inherit a 1/4 interest in the property.

If the owners do not agree on the ownership or management, and persistent disagreements exist, it would probably be best to sell the property and divide the profits accordingly. If an agreement cannot be reached by the owners, a court of law will sell the property and decide what is best for all concerned. *When the courts have the responsibility of selling the property, it is referred to as a **PARTITION ACTION**.* It is obviously better for the owners to sell the property themselves, as attorney's fees and court costs would be involved. Furthermore, the court would probably sell the land at a lower price to expedite the sale.

JOINT TENANCY

JOINT TENANCY occurs when two or more people own a property together with the rights of survivorship. If one of the joint tenancy owners should die, his or her interest is then split evenly with the surviving owners. Joint tenancy can never be willed.

> ### Joint tenants have the right of "survivorship." A joint tenancy cannot be willed.

When a joint tenancy is established, there are **four unites** (T-TIP) involved:

T   **1. Title** — All owners are granted title by the same instrument.

T   **2. Time** — All owners obtain title at the same time.

I   **3. Interest** — All owners share an equal interest.

P   **4. Possession** — All owners have an equal right to possess the property.

To create joint tenancy, there must be intention by the owners. The deed must be in writing and contain the phrase:

    "as joint tenants" or "in joint tenancy"

If it does not "state" that it is a joint tenancy, joint tenancy does not exist. Since this form of ownership is most common between married people, the usual phrase would read:

40

"Jim Smith and Mary Smith, husband and wife, as joint tenants"

If one of the parties should die, the property is automatically transferred to the remaining parties without having to go through the superior court procedure known as **"PROBATE"** (to prove a will). The transferred portion conveys the ownership and all debts on the property at the moment of death. Although probate costs may be avoided in joint tenancy, the surviving owners may end up paying higher income taxes later.

A joint tenant can sell or transfer his or her ownership interest. Any portion of joint tenancy transferred or sold to a nonowner will bring the nonowner into tenancy in common with the other owners, who remain as joint tenants. If A, B and C own a property together and C sells his interest to D, then D gets only the tenancy in common interest with A and B.

Because a corporation could, conceivably, go on forever, it is not permitted to enter into joint tenancies. Such a situation would give corporations an unfair survivorship advantage.

TENANCY IN PARTNERSHIP

*TENANCY IN PARTNERSHIP refers to two or more people who are co-owners in a business. A **GENERAL PARTNERSHIP** is where the partners share all profits and losses and share management responsibilities.* All partners must agree to a sale or transfer of real property. Each has a right to possess the partnership property. If a partner should die, his or her interest passes to any heirs who then have a right in the partnership, but not in any particular property. If an agreement cannot be reached with the heirs, the partnership may have to be dissolved.

In a partnership, the amount invested need not be equal but must be agreed upon mutually. The partnership agreement states the amount of money to be contributed by each, the duties of each and sets the proportional distribution of profits or losses.

*A **LIMITED PARTNERSHIP** is one consisting of one or more general partners and limited partners. A limited partner's losses are limited to the amount of his or her investment. A limited partner does not share management responsibilities.*

COMMUNITY PROPERTY

COMMUNITY PROPERTY refers to all the property acquired by a husband and wife during their marriage. California is a community property state, which means that any property acquired during a marriage is shared equally. This practice is derived from Spanish law and became incorporated into our legal system when California was a part of Mexico. Both husband and wife must sign all transfer documents to convey community real property. If only one spouse signs a transfer document, the "injured" spouse could void the sale within a one-year period. **Salespeople must make certain that both husband wife sign all real estate documents such as listings, deposit receipts and escrow instructions if the property being transferred is community property.**

The right to manage the community property is shared by both the husband and wife. Each can will his or her respective half to whomever they wish. If there is no will, the half belonging to the deceased would go to the surviving spouse. If willed to an heir, the heir and the remaining spouse would then be tenants in common.

> *Community property (husband and wife) vesting has equal interest.*

Debts can become a liability if they are incurred after marriage. Debts incurred by either spouse before marriage cannot be converted to the debts of the community property. The law also allows some community property to be transferred without going through probate. Questions about debts or probate should be directed to an attorney, as this issue is quite complex.

Any property obtained by either the husband or wife before marriage may remain as separate property. Both may inherit or receive gifts of property, which can remain as separate property. **However, any proceeds from the property held separately, such as rents or profit, cannot be commingled with community property, as this would cause them to become community property.**

> *Do NOT advise a buyer on how to hold title - that is giving legal advice. However, you can explain the different ways to take title. How a person holds title has a big impact upon income tax planning and estate planning.*

RECORDING & ACKNOWLEDGMENT

A deed does not have to be "acknowledged" or "recorded" to be valid, although it is wise to do both.

RECORDING

 http://www.co.sacramento.ca.us/ccr/index.html (County Clerk - Recorder for Sacramento County)

RECORDING is the legal process of making an instrument an official part of the records of a county, after it has been acknowledged. Instruments that affect real property are legal documents, such as deeds, mortgages, trust deeds, leases and contracts of sale. Recording gives constructive notice of the existence and content of these instruments.

> *CONSTRUCTIVE NOTICE is any recorded notice that can be obtained from the county recorder's office.* Any document recorded with the county recorder is assumed to be "public knowledge."

First to possess or record gets the property.

> *ACTUAL NOTICE is knowing, or one's responsibility for knowing, that a transaction has taken place.* If you have found, for example, that someone other than the owner is living in a house you are buying, you should have been aware of the existence of a signed lease. This is actual notice, whereas public records are representative of constructive notice. The act of taking possession (holding an unrecorded deed) gives constructive notice.

The recording process is a privilege rather than a legal requirement. Some documents have to be recorded to be valid. These include **mechanic's liens** and **declarations of homestead**. You may record an acknowledged instrument at any time. However, failure to utilize the privilege of recording at the earliest possible date can result in a question of legal or rightful title. **If the same property is sold to more than one party, the individual who has recorded first will usually be recognized as the rightful owner.** Therefore, time of recording is very important to a bonafide purchaser who is protected only if he or she records first.

If there are no prior arrangements (such as a subordination clause) the deed having priority is the one recorded first.

In order to establish priority, the documents affecting real property must be recorded by the county recorder in the county where the property is located. If the property is located in two counties, it should be recorded in both counties.

PRIORITY OF RECORDING

Under the recording system in California, "The first in time is the first in right." If an owner sells his or her house twice, the first deed recorded would be considered the valid deed. This person must not have knowledge of the rights of the other party. This is the reward granted in California for recording any real estate transaction. However, there are four exceptions to the rule that protects a person from later recordings.

They are:

1. Government liens, property taxes and special assessments
2. Actual or constructive notice of another person's prior rights
3. Mechanic's liens
4. Agreements to the contrary

ACKNOWLEDGMENT (OR NOTARY)

All documents must be acknowledged before they are recorded by the county recorder. *ACKNOWLEDGMENT refers to a signed statement by the named person that he or she has* **signed** *that document of his or her own free will*, in other words, that person "acknowledges" his or her signature. This acknowledgment must be performed in the presence or a witness, usually a notary public, authorized by law to witness acknowledgments.

> *A deed does NOT have to be acknowledged to be valid, but must be acknowledged to be recorded.*

A *NOTARY PUBLIC is a person who is authorized by the Secretary of State to witness the acknowledgment of documents.* All notarized documents must be stamped with a notary seal. The seal must contain the following information:

1. The word "Notary Public"
2. The name of the county
3. The name of the notary
4. The state seal
5. The expiration date

State, county, city or district officers and their deputies may also acknowledge a document. They include: court clerks, county clerks, court commissioners, municipal judges and county recorders.

VERIFICATION is an oath or affirmation made before a notary public that the content of an instrument is **true.** Notices of completion, non-responsibility and the statements used in filing a mechanic's lien are among instruments that must be verified rather than simply acknowledged.

An *AFFIRMATION is a solemn and legally binding* **declaration** *made by a person whose religious or other beliefs prohibit the taking of an oath.*

An *AFFIDAVIT is a written* **statement** *of circumstances, submitted under verification.*

Any the person signing a grant deed, quitclaim deed or trust deed is required to place a right thumb print on the notary's sequential journal. This is because of a high rate of fraud by the use of false deeds. Additionally, a notary must immediately notify the Secretary of State if the notary's sequential journal is stolen, lost, misplaced, destroyed, damaged or otherwise rendered unusable.

DO NOT GIVE LEGAL ADVICE

A real estate salesperson or broker may not give legal advice, as the law is a highly complex and specialize profession that requires years of preparation and training. In the state of California, only a licensed attorney who is a member of the State Bar is allowed to practice law. A broker cannot give legal advice, unless he or she is also an attorney, and must realize the truth in the saying:

"A man who is his own lawyer
has a fool for a client."

What appears to be a minor difficulty can often be the tip of the iceberg of concealed hazards. Any legal advice, counsel or preparation of legal instruments must, therefore, be handled by an attorney. An enterprising broker should establish a relationship with a local attorney specializing in real estate. If any problems arise, they can be cleared up in the shortest time possible to facilitate the sale.

It is illegal for **an agent**, except an attorney, to draw up legal documents. For this reason, real estate brokers use preprinted fill-in forms. These forms are drawn up by licensed attorneys who are familiar with the legalities involved in contracts.

TERMINOLOGY - CHAPTER 2

A. Freehold Estate
B. Condition Subsequent
C. Adverse Possession
D. Constructive Notice
E. Condition Precedent
F. Actual Notice
G. Life Estate
H. Affirmation, Affidavit, Verification
I. Grant Deed
J. Quitclaim Deed
K. Reversion

L. Remainder
M. Delivery
N. Witnessed Will
O. Holographic Will
P. Probate
Q. Intestate Succession
R. Escheat
S. Accession
T. Encroachment
U. Abandonment
V. Dedication

W. Prescription
X. Severalty
Y. Corporation
Z. Tenancy In Common
AA. Joint Tenancy
BB. Notary Public
CC. General & Limited
Partnerships
DD. Community Property
EE. Recording

1.____ The giving of private land by its owner for a public use; most commonly, the developer who gives it to a city.

2.____ The reverting of private property to the state when there are no valid heirs.

3.____ A voluntary association between two or more people to carry on a business with general and limited partners

4.____ A deed using the word "grant," or like words, containing warranties against prior conveyances and encumbrances. This is the most commonly used deed in California.

5.____ An estate of indeterminable duration, e.g., fee simple or life estate.

6.____ Undivided ownership of a property interest by two or more persons, each of whom has a right to an equal share in the interest and a right of survivorship.

7.____ It is notice that is actually and expressly given or implied.

8.____ A person authorized by the state to witness the signatures of persons executing documents, sign the certificate and affix the official seal.

9.____ An event that must happen before title is passed.

10.____ Documents filed with the County Recorder in such a way as are considered open notice to the world.

11.____ Co-ownership of property by two or more persons who hold undivided interest, without right of survivorship. The interests need not be equal.

12.____ An unlawful intrusion onto another's property by making improvements to real property, e.g., a swimming pool built across a property line.

13.____ A legal entity, sanctioned by the state, with rights and liabilities, distinct and apart from those of the persons composing it.

14.____ The intentional and voluntary relinquishment of any ownership interest (such as an easement) or possession of real property.

15.____ The means of acquiring interests in land, usually an easement, by continued use.

16.____ A condition attached to an estate whereby the estate is defeated or changed through the failure or non-performance of the condition.

17.____ A process of law by which the state lays out the correct succession of inheritance when a person dies without leaving a valid will.

18.____ Many different types of statements made before a professional witness.

19.____ An estate that reverts back to the grantor after the life of the tenant expires.

20.____ The court procedure of proving that a will is valid.

21.____ A method of acquiring title to real property, through possession of the property for a statutory period under certain conditions, by a person other than the owner.

22.____ A deed to relinquish any interest in property, which the grantor may have, without any warranty of title or interest.

23.____ An estate that is transferred to a third party (anyone other than the grantor) upon the death of the life estate holder.

24.____ A formal expression of a person's desires, witnessed by others, as to the disposition of his or her property after death.

25.____ Property acquired by husband and/or wife during marriage that is not acquired as separate property. Each spouse has equal rights of management, alienation and disposition.

26.____ An estate of a single entity held by a single person alone.

27.____ An estate or interest in real property that is held for the duration of the life of some certain person. It may be the person holding title to the estate or some other person.

28.____ A handwritten expression of a person's desires as to the disposition of their property after death.

29.____ Placing a document in the official records of the county.

30.____ The act of receiving a deed.

31.____ The acquiring of additional property.

MULTIPLE CHOICE

1. The most complete form of land ownership is:

   A. fee, simple, absolute estate
   C. estate at will

   B. estate for years
   D. none of the above

2. The two types of freehold estates are:

   A. life estate and estate at will
   C. fee simple and estate for years

   B. fee simple and life estate
   D. fee qualified and estate at will

3. A lease for a fixed period of time, agreed to in advance and requiring NO notice of termination is called a (an):

   A. estate for years
   C. estate at sufferance

   B. estate from period-to-period
   D. perpetual estate

4. A lease for a period of time that is renewable and requires a notice of termination is called a (an):

   A. life estate
   C. estate from period-to-period

   B. estate for years
   D. estate in reversion

5. A grant deed must be signed by:

   A. the grantee
   C. neither if the grantee takes possession of the property

   B. both the grantor and grantee
   D. the grantor

6. A holographic will that is signed with an "X":

   A. is not legal
   C. requires no other formalities to be legal

   B. must be reviewed by an attorney
   D. must be witnessed

7. A legal way to acquire title without a deed is through:

   A. adverse possession
   C. encroachment

   B. prescription
   D. dedication

8. Smart, Black and Curtis have a joint tenancy. Curtis sells his interest to Jones. A short time later, Smart dies. What method of holding title do Black and Jones have?

   A. Joint tenancy
   C. Tenancy in partnership

   B. Tenancy in common
   D. Severalty

9. Frank and Margaret Sharp purchased an income producing property through broker Finch. The Sharps asked Finch how they should hold title. Finch suggested they hold title as tenants in common. Finch's advice is:

   A. legal as long as the buyers asked him
   C. legal if Finch is a member of NAR

   B. legal as long as community property is not involved
   D. against the law; Finch is not an attorney

10. Frank is a life estate holder. He leases the property to Mary for a five-year period. After two years of the lease, Frank dies. The original grantor orders Mary to move out. Mary's lease was:

    A. not legal to begin with
    C. legal and valid for the full five years

    B. legal and valid until Frank's death
    D. valid only if confirmed by the administrator of the deceased's will

CHAPTER 3
Encumbrances

An encumbrance burdens (affects or limits title) the property by either:

1) money owed (liens) or 2) items that affect the physical use of the property (non-money).

The term encumbrance is usually new to the beginner in real estate. An **ENCUMBRANCE** *is a right or interest in real property other than an owner or tenancy interest.* It is a burden to the property that limits its use. The two main types of encumbrances, shown in Figure 3-1 and Figure 3-3, are: (1) liens and (2) items that affect the physical condition or use of the property. All liens are encumbrances but not all encumbrances are liens.

An encumbrance affects the fee simple title ... all liens are "encumbrances" but not all encumbrances are liens.

FIGURE 3-1

When an owner encumbers more than one lot, that owner has created a blanket encumbrance. A ***BLANKET ENCUMBRANCE*** *is a voluntary lien (money owed) placed over more than one parcel.* A release clause releases portions of the property.

A blanket encumbrance (one lien on several properties) usually has a "release clause" so that one or more of the parcels can be released under certain conditions.

Liens (money owed)

LIENS

Liens ("money owed") are money encumbrances.

A ***LIEN*** *is a document that uses a property to secure the payment of a debt or the discharge of an obligation.* It is money owed for one reason or another on a property. Liens include trust deeds or mortgages, tax liens, special assessments, mechanic's liens, judgments, attachments and bankruptcies. Liens are either:

       1) voluntary or
       2) involuntary;
       3) specific or
       4) general

VOLUNTARY AND INVOLUNTARY LIENS

VOLUNTARY LIENS are money debts that an owner agrees to pay. A lien is created when the buyer takes out a loan to finance the purchase of real estate. He or she voluntarily agrees to pay for the money borrowed. *INVOLUNTARY LIENS are money obligations that create a burden on a property by government taxes or legal action because of unpaid bills.* Both involuntary liens and voluntary liens must be paid, or assumed, in full before the owner can sell or refinance the property.

> *Liens are encumbrances against a property that can be either 1) voluntary or 2) involuntary.*

TRUST DEED (SECURITY DEVICE - VOLUNTARY & SPECIFIC)

A *TRUST DEED is a written instrument that makes real property collateral for a loan.* The evidence of debt is created by the promissory note that accompanies the trust deed. The trust deed pledges (hypothecates) the property as collateral, or security, for the note. In California, the trust deed is the usual security device for real property. In other states, the mortgage is the typical financing instrument. See Chapter 8 for details on trust deeds.

> *Trust deeds and mortgages are security devices that make property security for the debt. The accompanying promissory note is the evidence of the debt. Trust deeds and mortgages are personal property. Mortgages and trust deeds are examples of voluntary liens; therefore, a lien can be created by recording.*

MORTGAGE (SECURITY DEVICE - VOLUNTARY & SPECIFIC)

A *MORTGAGE is a lien that secures real property for the payment of a promissory note (debt).* Mortgages are rarely employed in financing California homes, but because of their wide use in other states, they are emphasized in the real estate licensing examination. In California many people use the term "mortgage" to mean a property loan, but they usually are talking about trust deeds. Therefore, it is essential to understand the difference between mortgages and trust deeds since almost every property transfer in California is financed through a trust deed. Details on mortgages are discussed further in Chapter 8.

> *Mortgages are covered on the state DRE exam, but are rare in California.*

MECHANIC'S LIENS (INVOLUNTARY & SPECIFIC)

MECHANIC'S LIENS are liens that may be filed against a **property** by a person who was not paid after furnishing labor or materials for construction work on that property. The form used to enforce a mechanic's lien action must be recorded to be effective. A mechanic's lien is a lien against the property itself. The property cannot be transferred until the obligation is paid and the title cleared. This gives a subcontractor, craftsman or general contractor, employed by an owner, the right to protect his or her interest. The same right applies to material suppliers who furnish such items as lumber, plumbing or roofing supplies. To determine the start time, the mechanic's lien dates back to the commencement of the project (see below).

A mechanic's lien is filed (recorded) against an individual's property; it is a specific (one property) and involuntary lien.

Preliminary Notice (To Protect Your Rights)

A *PRELIMINARY NOTICE* is a written notice that should be given before filing a mechanic's lien and within 20 days of supplying labor or services. This notice must be given, either by mail or in person, to the owner, general contractor and the lender. The notice must contain a general description of the labor or materials furnished, who supplied them and the person who contracted for these services. Failure to give the preliminary notice within 20 days does not restrict a supplier's right to file, but he or she may have allowed other claimants to file before him or her, which gives those claimants priority. As a matter of good practice, most suppliers include a preliminary notice as part of the original contract.

Lenders want to be first in priority.

Determining The Start Time For Mechanic's Liens

An important determination, when considering a mechanic's lien, is **the date that work started.** Mechanic's liens, once recorded, have priority over all other liens except taxes, assessments and trust deeds. To lenders, this is critical because lenders want their trust deeds recorded before any work starts. Before they will lend money, lenders will conduct a physical inspection of the property to make sure no construction has started.

A mechanic's lien must be recorded to become effective.

A mechanic's lien (labor or materials) dates back to the beginning (commencement) of work on the project. This is known as the "scheme of improvements."

Notice of Completion and Cessation (limits time to file)

A "Notice of Completion" (Shown in Figure 3-2) should be recorded by the owner within 10 days of completion. This gives everyone constructive notice. Completion technically occurs when the owner accepts the finished work of the contractor, but in some instances, the job is never completed. Guidelines have been set up by the state to allow suppliers of services and materials a filing period of up to 90 days. If one of these four alternatives occurs, the work is considered to be complete:

1. Occupation or use by owner after cessation of labor.
2. Acceptance of work improvements by owner.
3. A cessation of labor for 60 continuous days.
4. A cessation of labor for 30 continuous days if the owner files a "notice of cessation."

An unpaid pool contractor who supplied labor and materials could file a mechanic's lien in the county in which the work was done. The encumbrance created would be an unwelcome, involuntary and specific lien.

Filing Time

The filing period is very important because the rights of a person filing a mechanic's lien are valid for only a short time. A suit can be filed later, but it would not automatically become a lien against the real property. A mechanic's lien may be filed any time after the preliminary notice and until 30 days after completion, if you are a supplier or subcontractor, and 60 days after completion if you are the general contractor. If there is no notice of completion recorded for the project, all parties have 90 days after completion of the job to file.

30 days (sub), 60 days (general), 90 days (all parties).

FIGURE 3-2

RECORDING REQUESTED BY

AND WHEN RECORDED MAIL TO

Name

Street
Address

City &
State

——— SPACE ABOVE THIS LINE FOR RECORDER'S USE ———

INDIVIDUAL FORM

Notice of Completion

TO 1927 CA (3-75)   Before execution, refer to title company requirements stated on reverse side.   A. P. N.

Notice is hereby given that:

1. The undersigned is owner of the interest or estate stated below in the property hereinafter described.
2. The full name of the undersigned is _____
3. The full address of the undersigned is _____
4. The nature of the title of the undersigned is: In fee.
   (If other than fee, strike "In fee" and insert, for example, "purchaser under contract of purchase," or "lessee".)
5. The full names and full addresses of all persons, if any, who hold title with the undersigned as joint tenants or as tenants in common are:

   NAMES   ADDRESSES

6. The names of the predecessors in interest of the undersigned, if the property was transferred subsequent to the commencement of the work of improvement herein referred to:

   NAMES   ADDRESSES

   (If no transfer made, insert "none".)

7. A work of improvement on the property hereinafter described was completed on _____
8. The name of the contractor, if any, for such work of improvement was _____
   (If no contractor for work of improvement as a whole, insert "none".)
9. The property on which said work of improvement was completed is in the City of _____
   _____, County of _____, State of California, and is described as follows:

10. The street address of said property is _____
    (If no street address has been officially assigned, insert "none".)

Dated: _____

Signature of
owner named
in paragraph 2 _____
(Also sign verification below at X)

STATE OF CALIFORNIA,
COUNTY OF _____ } SS.   _____

The undersigned, being duly sworn, says: That ___he is the owner of the aforesaid interest or estate in the property described in the foregoing notice; that ___he has read the same, and knows the contents thereof, and that the facts stated therein are true.

SUBSCRIBED AND SWORN TO before me

Signature of
owner named
in paragraph 2 X _____

on _____

Signature _____

Notary Public in and for said State

Title Order No. _____
Escrow or Loan No. _____

SEE REVERSE SIDE FOR
TITLE COMPANY REQUIREMENTS AS TO NOTICE OF COMPLETION

(This area for official notarial seal)

Encumbrances

Notice Of Non-Responsibility
(Must Be Recorded And Posted)

An owner may file a notice of non-responsibility within 10 days of discovering that an unauthorized person is performing construction service on his or her property. A recorded and verified *NOTICE OF NON-RESPONSIBILITY is posted on the property stating that the owner is not responsible for the work being done.* This action releases an owner from any liability caused by the unauthorized activity. This notice of non-responsibility prevents suppliers from filing a valid mechanic's lien.

An apartment tenant may ask a painter, plumber or electrician to do work without the landlord's authorization and may try to charge the owner for the work done. This is the time for a landlord to file a notice of non-responsibility. If a tenant is installing carpet in your apartment without your authorization, a notice of non-responsibility would protect you against the claims of the carpet supplier.

TAX LIENS (SPECIFIC OR GENERAL LIENS)

If any government tax is not paid, it may become a lien, through law or a court action, on real property. If the lien is not settled, the property can be sold to pay back-taxes. Tax liens are either: (1) specific liens or (2) general liens. *SPECIFIC LIENS are liens against just one property.* Property taxes assessed against real property automatically become a specific lien on only that property on July 1st of each year. *GENERAL LIENS are liens on all the properties of the owner, not just one.* Federal or state income taxes and judgment liens can become a general lien on all your real property.

Example: Property taxes, mechanic's liens - specific liens
Income taxes, judgments - general liens

SPECIAL ASSESSMENTS

Local improvements are paid for by the property owners in a given district through SPECIAL ASSESSMENTS. Improvements such as streets, sewers, street lighting and irrigation projects are generally paid for by the property owners who have benefited from the work. If these assessments are not paid, they become a lien against the property. Most special assessments are 10 year bonds. This allows the property owner a reasonable amount of time to pay them off. Real property cannot be transferred until an outstanding bond is paid, unless there is an agreement between the parties involved in the transaction.

JUDGMENTS (INVOLUNTARY & GENERAL LIENS)

A *JUDGMENT* is a court decision determining the rights of the parties involved and the amount of compensation. A judgment can be appealed.

For a judgment to become a lien, an *ABSTRACT OF JUDGMENT, or formal filing of the judgment,* must be recorded. The judgment then becomes a lien upon all nonexempt property of the debtor. It also becomes a lien on all future property he or she later acquires until the lien is paid. A judgment lien is good for ten years. So, if any property is transferred within this ten year period, the lien must first be paid off. Under additional court action, the judgment holder may be able to force the debtor to sell the real property to pay off the lien.

Judgments are examples of general liens and involuntary liens against all real property only in the county in which the judgment is recorded. Once recorded, it is good for 10 years.

> At this point, it is important that you understand the use of the Small Claims Court. Anyone can take someone else to court regarding civil cases for a $6 filing fee plus the fee for serving the subpoena. Neither party is allowed to be represented in the courtroom by legal counsel. The current maximum amount of a judgment is $5,000. This limit will be adjusted periodically by the state legislature to meet inflationary trends. Night court is also available in some districts, making this process even more accessible. You should be aware, however, that for a plaintiff, the judge's decision in a small claims action is final. The defendant, though, has the right of appeal. This is an excellent way to settle a dispute with a minimal amount of time and expense.
>
> A judgment is not final until the appeal period has elapsed. In municipal court, the appeal period is up to 30 days. In a superior or federal court, the appeal period is up to 60 days.

TERMINATION OF JUDGMENT LIEN

Most judgment liens are terminated by the satisfaction of the judgment. *SATISFACTION OF JUDGMENT is compensation made by the payment of money or the return of property.* A notice that the judgment has been satisfied should be filed with the clerk of the court. It clears the lien from the record. Sometimes certain properties may be released from the judgment, but only with the judgment holder's consent. This partial release enables an owner to sell a property to satisfy a part of the judgment. A judgment may also be terminated if a bond is posted or if the judge grants a new trial.

Satisfaction of judgment clears the lien from the record.

ATTACHMENT (COURT-SEIZED PROPERTY)

ATTACHMENT (LIEN) is a process of the law that creates a lien. It gives custody of real or personal property to the courts to assure payment of a pending lawsuit in that county. This is to assure that there will be enough property to satisfy the judgment should the plaintiff prevail. The *PLAINTIFF is the person filing a court action to obtain an attachment lien.* The *DEFENDANT is the person who is being sued.* During an unlawful detainer action for collection of past due rents, for instance, it may be advantageous for a plaintiff to obtain an attachment against the defendant. This type of lien is good for three years, and is extended only if the plaintiff wins the court case. Use of the attachment lien is not very common because there are many rules and formalities involved in obtaining this type of lien. This is another area that requires the help of an attorney. The important thing to remember about an attachment lien is that it does exist, and can be a lien on real property.

An attachment creates a specific and involuntary lien on one property, which is good for 3 years.

LIS PENDENS "LAWSUIT PENDING"

LIS PENDENS is the recording of a notice that a lawsuit is pending concerning a particular property. Attorneys often file a lis pendens before a court date is set in order to stop the transfer of the property. A lis pendens places a cloud on the title, so this type of action should not be taken lightly. The property is not marketable until the lis pendens is removed.

A lis pendens is notice of a pending lawsuit that affects title (clouds title) and remains on the public record until judgment is rendered or suit is dismissed.

SHERIFF'S SALE (COURT ORDER TO SELL - EXECUTION)

A *SHERIFF'S SALE is the forced sale of a debtor's property to satisfy a judgment under a writ of execution.* In California, the sheriff's sale is the usual method of forcing someone to sell property to pay off a judgment. If a person refuses to pay off the judgment, the sheriff's sale is the next step. A *WRIT OF EXECUTION is a court order requiring the sale of certain property to satisfy a judgment.* The writ of execution extends the lien against the real property for one year. If the judgment has already been recorded as a lien on the property, the writ of execution will not create a new lien. The county sheriff, or other local officials, are then ordered to secure and sell the real or personal property to satisfy the lien.

A "writ of execution" is a court order to sell. The state controls lien and attachment laws, cities and counties do not.

Taxes and assessments have the priority to any proceeds from a sheriff's sale. Mechanic's liens and any previously recorded judgments have priority over paying the expenses of the sale. If these expenses are paid, a first trust deed is next to be satisfied. Any amount left over is applied toward a second trust deed and any subsequent liens, in the order of their recording, until the proceeds are exhausted.

INJUNCTION (ORDERED TO STOP)

An **INJUNCTION** *is a court order to stop doing something.* For example, the court may order a developer stop damming up a river.

Items That Affect Physical Use
(non-money encumbrances)

ITEMS THAT AFFECT PHYSICAL USE

***ITEMS THAT AFFECT PHYSICAL USE** are non-money encumbrances that affect the physical use of real property.* They include: easements, building restrictions, zoning and encroachments, which are conditions that limit the physical use of the property. See Figure 3-3.

Some encumbrances affect the physical use of the property.

They are:

1) *easements*
2) *restrictions*
3) *encroachments*
4) *leases (see Chapter 6).*

EASEMENTS (THE RIGHT TO USE ANOTHER'S LAND)

An easement is an interest in another's land; it is a right. Easements are non-money encumbrances; they are not liens. Land that is burdened with an easement is said to be "encumbered."

FIGURE 3-3

An *EASEMENT is the right to enter, use and exit another person's land for a certain purpose. The right to enter is called INGRESS and the right to exit is EGRESS.* Included in this definition is the right to profit from the easement, such as the right to take minerals, oil and gas. Easements are of two types: (1) easements appurtenant and (2) easements in gross.

> *An easement is the right to use another's land. It is a right, but NOT an estate.*

EASEMENT APPURTENANT (RUNS WITH THE LAND)

> *An easement is said to be appurtenant, which means the easement "runs with the land." The new buyer would have the "same rights" to the easement as did the seller.*

An *EASEMENT APPURTENANT is an easement "created for and beneficial to" the owner of adjoining or attached lands.* An easement is real property, not personal, but it is not an estate. In this case there are two parcels of land, with one owner giving another owner an easement. The *DOMINANT TENEMENT is the land that obtains the benefits of an easement.* Figure 3-4 is an illustration of a driveway easement. Owner A's land is the dominant tenement and Owner B's land is the servient tenement.

> *The dominant tenement is the land that benefits; the owner is the party who can terminate the easement.*

A **SERVIENT TENEMENT** *is the land that gives the easement for the benefit of another*. The appurtenant easement becomes part of the land and is transferred with the land. This easement cannot be transferred separately from the land.

The owner of the servient tenement cannot terminate the easement; it must "serve" the dominant tenement.

FIGURE 3-4

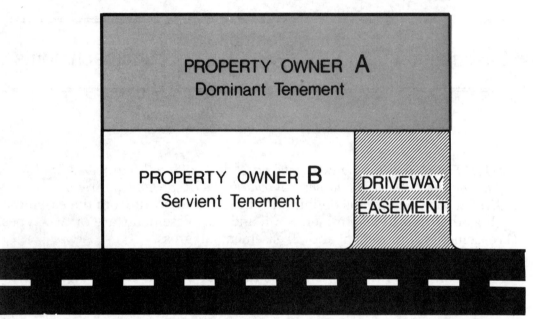

EASEMENT IN GROSS
(DOES NOT BENEFIT ADJOINING LANDOWNER)

An example of an easement in gross would be an easement for the telephone company (utility company) to enter the property to run telephone lines. Easements in gross do not benefit adjoining lands.

An **EASEMENT IN GROSS** *is an easement created for the benefit of others who do not own adjoining or attached lands*. It is a personal property right. Even though it is a personal right, there are still servient tenements. An example of an easement in gross would be a utility company obtaining the right to run natural gas lines across your land. In this instance you would become a servient tenement.

Other not-so-common easements are: rights to take water, wood or minerals; rights to transact business or conduct sports upon the land; rights to receive light, air or heat from the land; and the right to use a wall as a common party wall.

An easement that does not specify a special area for a right-of-way is also valid ... a property owner could give the right to cross his land and not limit how or where a person would have to cross ... This is known as an "unlocated easement."

CREATION OF AN EASEMENT

Easements are created in three basic ways:

1. Expressed in writing, as in a deed or contract
2. By implication of law (implied easement)
3. By virtue of long use (prescription)

1. EXPRESSED IN WRITING, AS IN A DEED OR CONTRACT. If a property is transferred as part of the deed, an easement appurtenant to the land would be included in the grant. The same thing is accomplished by transferring a property, but reserving an easement over the land. In any event, a written contract can create an easement between the parties. For legal protection, this contract should be acknowledged and recorded.

2. CREATION BY IMPLICATION OF LAW (IMPLIED EASEMENT). If an easement is implied in a transfer, or if it is necessary for use of the land, then the easement is said to be implied by law. The right to use the land for obtaining minerals implies that you have the right of surface entry in order to extract the minerals.

EASEMENT BY NECESSITY (LANDLOCKED) is an easement granted by a court if it is absolutely necessary for access. If a person is sold property that landlocks that person, he or she may acquire an easement by necessity. When the grantor transfers a portion of his or her land that leaves the grantee totally surrounded by the grantor (transferor), the grantor can be forced to give an easement of access to the grantee. An easement of access does not have to be the most convenient way of entering the property. If the grantee later acquires another access to his or her property, the easement by necessity is then terminated.

3. LONG USE (EASEMENT BY PRESCRIPTION). Prescription is an easement to continue using land by virtue of having used it for a long period of time.

A prescriptive easement can be obtained after 5 years of uninterrupted use of another's land; no confrontation or property tax payments required.

Possession for 5 continuous years can create a prescription, as long as there is:

1. Open and notorious use
2. Uninterrupted use for 5 years
3. Hostile (without permission of the owner)
4. Under a claim of right.

If a person acquired an easement by prescription, he or she would not have to confront the owner nor would that person have to pay taxes and assessments. An easement obtained by prescription can be terminated if not used.

TRANSFER OF EASEMENT

Easements are transferred automatically if they are easements appurtenant. Easements in gross can be transferred only by an expressed agreement, providing the easement is not made to a specific individual. An easement should be recorded. If it is not recorded, and the purchaser does not have knowledge of an easement, then the easement may not be considered to have been transferred with the property.

TERMINATION OF AN EASEMENT

Easements may be terminated in several ways:

1. **EXPRESSED RELEASE** Any written agreement can terminate an easement, but the usual form is a quitclaim deed. The servient tenement is the only one that could benefit from the termination of an easement.

2. **MERGER OF DOMINANT AND SERVIENT TENEMENTS** An easement is automatically terminated when the dominant and servient tenements merge into a common, or single, ownership. The easement can be created again if any part of the property is later transferred to a "separate owner."

3. EXCESSIVE USE The courts have held that excessive use of an easement that increases the burden on the servient tenement may be forfeited through a court injunction. If the dominant tenement refuses to correct the excessive use, and misuses of the easement can be established, the easement can be terminated. An example would be a dominant tenement owner allowing the entire neighborhood to use the easement as a through-street.

4. ABANDONMENT AND NON-USE If there is an obvious intent of an easement holder to abandon his or her easement, then that person may lose the easement through court action. In this way, an easement gained through prescription may be extinguished if non-use exists for a period of **five continuous years**.

Non-use of an easement acquired by prescription could terminate that easement. However, non-use of an easement appurtenant would not terminate the easement, unless it is abandoned.

5. DESTRUCTION OF SERVIENT TENEMENT When a governing body, by exercising the right of eminent domain, takes servient tenement property for its own use, the dominant tenement easement is considered automatically terminated.

Summary:

Easements are a right to use; not an estate
Easements are NOT liens
Easements are created by deed or prescription
Easements are appurtenant or in gross

ENCROACHMENTS (3 YEARS TO ACT)

As stated earlier, an **ENCROACHMENT** *is the wrongful, unauthorized placement of improvements or permanent fixtures on property by a nonowner of that property.* You must pursue the right to have an encroachment removed within 3 years or lose your right. If someone encroaches on your property, he or she is limiting the use of your property.

Encroachments are resolved or sue your neighbor.

Often fences, walls or buildings may extend over the recognized boundary line. The encroaching party may possibly gain legal title to the property through adverse possession, or legal use through an easement by prescription, if there is legal justification. In any event, encroachment may legally limit the use of your property.

RESTRICTIONS (C,C&Rs) AND ZONING

Restrictions are: 1) "private deed restrictions," such as those placed on a property by the grantor or developer, or 2) public restrictions, such as city zoning laws. The restrictions that are the most restrictive will always apply.

PRIVATE DEED RESTRICTIONS *limit the use or occupancy of the land. A typical restriction would be to limit the types of buildings on a given piece of land to single family residences.* Also, a restriction might require future construction to meet specific standards. For example, all houses erected on a property must be at least 5,000 square feet. Another example might be a setback requirement, which would require any structure to be set back so many feet from the street or adjoining property.

There are three types of private building restrictions: Covenants, Conditions and Restrictions. They are usually included in the deed at the time the property is subdivided, or may be created by a written contract. Their main purpose is to keep use of the land uniform throughout certain tracts of land. Subdivisions and condominiums usually include deed restrictions as a method to increase the aesthetics and economics of the project. These private deed restrictions (C,C&Rs) and bylaws are usually recorded separately, and are only referenced in the original grant deeds.

Covenants

A ***COVENANT*** *is a promise to do or not to do a certain thing.* For instance, a property could sell with a covenant stating that the property shall never be used to sell alcoholic beverages. If the covenant is broken, the usual court remedy would be an action for money damages. A court may also grant an injunction requiring compliance with the covenant.

Conditions

CONDITIONS *are promises to do or not to do something. The penalty for not following the set conditions is the reversion of the property to the grantor.* This penalty is so stiff that most courts will treat a condition as a covenant unless the terms are clearly stated in the deed or other contract. For a complete discussion of conditions, refer back to Chapter 2.

Deed restrictions are not liens.

Governmental Restrictions (Zoning)

PUBLIC RESTRICTIONS *are limits made by governmental agencies; usually cities and counties in the form of zoning.*

"Public restrictions" promote health, safety, morals and general welfare of the public. This is the use of police power.

Private restrictions are made by the present or previous landowners and are created only for their benefit. On the other hand, **zoning restrictions** are created by and for the benefit of the general public to insure its health, safety, comfort and morals.

Cities and counties can divide land into districts for control over local property through local laws that enforce zoning, rent control, building codes and other subdivision land use regulations.

Zoning is the restriction on the use of private property by the local government agency. Zoning dictates how the property can be used, the setbacks required and the height limit on any structures.

Private restrictions are placed on the property by the grantor or developer. If there are two restrictions, the most restrictive of the two will take precedence. For example, if a developer sets a deed restriction of 15,000 square feet to a lot but zoning only allows 10,000 square feet per lot, the zoning restriction is more restrictive and would prevail. This area is covered in depth in Chapter 12 under "Government Control."

RACE RESTRICTIONS (RULED ILLEGAL)

In 1961 the California State Legislature enacted a law that voided all restrictions as to race. Any race deed restriction before that law or after that law is now void. By law, we cannot erase recorded restrictions, but the 1961 law did make such restrictions illegal. It is illegal to restrict the right of an individual to sell, rent, lease, use or otherwise occupy a property because of race or membership in a certain ethnic group.

Race restrictions on a property by a grantor are unenforceable and illegal.

HOMESTEADING YOUR RESIDENCE

HOMESTEAD
(PROTECTS AGAINST JUDGMENT LIENS)

Although a homestead is not an encumbrance, it is appropriately discussed at this point. A *HOMESTEAD is a special provision of the California law that allows homeowners to protect their homes from forced sale to satisfy their debts, within certain limits.* There are two types of homesteads:

(1) Head of the household and (2) Federal Homestead Act of 1862, whereby the government encouraged settlements (gave land free to those who made certain improvements—this is not discussed here). It is basic to our society that a homeowner should have some protection against losing his or her home because of debts. A homestead consists of the house and adjoining dwellings in which the owner resides. This can include condominiums, farm and life estates. A homestead cannot include "unimproved" land such as vacant lots or a residence under construction.

DECLARATION OF HOMESTEAD

A *DECLARATION OF HOMESTEAD is the form that, after being acknowledged and recorded, protects a residence from judgments that become liens.* See Figure 3-5. This protects you for $75,000 if you are the head of a family. Persons who are mentally or physically disabled or over the age of 65 are entitled to protection for up to $100,000. Any resident who does not qualify under either of these conditions has a homestead valued at $50,000. It is a loose provision and almost everyone qualifies. When a person files a homestead, it does not protect that person against trust deeds, mechanic's liens or prior-to-filing liens.

> *You may only have one homestead at a time.*

In order for a declaration of homestead to be a valid, there are certain requirements that must be met. Omissions of any one of these will make the homestead void. The requirements are:

1. A statement showing the claimant is the head of a family and stating the name of the spouse.

2. A statement that the claimant is residing on the premises and claims it as his or her homestead.

3. A description for the premises and an estimate of cash value.

FIGURE 3-5

RECORDING REQUESTED BY

AND WHEN RECORDED MAIL TO

NAME
STREET
ADDRESS
CITY
STATE
ZIP

————————————(SPACE ABOVE THIS LINE FOR RECORDER'S USE)——————————

HOMESTEAD DECLARATION

——— ◄► ———

I, _____
(Full Name of Declarant)

do hereby certify and declare as follows:

(1) I hereby claim as a declared homestead the premises located in the City of _____,

County of _____, State of _____ commonly known as

_____
(Street Address)

and more particularly described as follows: [Give complete legal description]

(2) I am the declared homestead owner of the above declared homestead.

(3) I own the following interest in the above declared homestead:

(4) The above declared homestead is [strike inapplicable clause] my principal dwelling.
the principal dwelling of my spouse, and
[strike inapplicable clause] I am
my spouse is currently residing on that declared homestead.

(5) The facts stated in this Declaration are true as of my personal knowledge.

Dated: _____, 19____   _____
(Signature of Declarant)

STATE OF _____ ⎫
                                                              ⎬ ss
COUNTY OF _____ ⎭

On _____ before me, _____
(Name, title of officer—i.e. "Jane Doe, Notary Public")

_____

personally appeared _____

personally known to me (or proved to me on the basis of satisfactory evidence) to
be the person(s) whose name(s) is/are subscribed to the within instrument and
acknowledged to me that he/she/they executed the same in his/her/their authorized capacity(ies), and that by his/her/their signature(s) on the instrument the
person(s), or the entity upon behalf of which the person(s) acted, executed the
instrument.

WITNESS my hand and official seal.

_____
          Signature

(Seal)

WOLCOTTS FORM 756—HOMESTEAD DECLARATION —Rev 1-93
(price class 3)

© 1993 WOLCOTTS FORMS, INC

This standard form is intended for the typical situations encountered in the field indicated. However, before you sign, read it, fill in all blanks, and make
whatever changes are appropriate and necessary to your particular transaction. Consult a lawyer if you doubt the form's fitness for your purpose and use

4. It further provides that the declaration of homestead may need to contain a statement as to the character of the property; that no former declaration has been made and that it is within the limits prescribed by law.

The homeowner has time to file a declaration of homestead prior to court approval for a writ of execution. As part of the judicial process, the defendant must be informed of his or her right to file a declaration of homestead. This law change, in effect, has reduced the necessity of filing a homestead declaration until the homeowner is in financial trouble.

TERMINATION OF HOMESTEAD

A homestead may be terminated by a **DECLARATION OF ABANDONMENT.** The declaration of abandonment must be acknowledged and recorded by the involved parties. A sale or other conveyance of the property also terminates the homestead. The removal or destruction of the dwelling does not terminate the homestead. The reason for abandoning a homestead is to allow oneself the privilege of obtaining another homestead on a new residence.

A homestead is terminated by 1) Declaration of Abandonment or 2) the sale of the homesteaded property.

A. Encumbrance	**L.** Plaintiff	**W.** Conditions
B. Lien	**M.** Defendant	**X.** Restrictions
C. Blanket Encumbrance	**N.** Sheriff's Sale	**Y.** Homestead
D. Trust Deed	**O.** Writ of Execution	**Z.** Declaration of Homestead
E. Mortgage	**P.** Easement	**AA.** Declaration of Abandonment
F. Mechanic's Liens	**Q.** Easement Appurtenant	**BB.** Lis Pendens
G. Preliminary Notice	**R.** Dominant Tenement	**CC.** General Lien
H. Notice of Nonresponsibility	**S.** Servient Tenement	**DD.** Specific Lien
I. Abstract of Judgment	**T.** Easement In Gross	
J. Satisfaction	**U.** Encroachment	
K. Attachment	**V.** Covenant	

1.____ A right, limited to a specific use, that one party has in the land of another.

2.____ A statutory protection of a home from the claims of certain creditors and judgments up to a specified amount.

3.____ Anything that affects or limits the fee simple title to, or value of, property, e.g., mortgages or easements.

4.____ A notice, recorded and posted by the property owner to relieve them of responsibility for the cost of unauthorized work done on his or her property or materials furnished.

5.____ A limitation on the use of real property. These limitations fall into two general classifications -- public and private. Zoning ordinances are public, while a clause in the deed requiring the roof to be made of Spanish red title would be a private limitation.

6.____ The process by which real or personal property is seized by the court for the purpose of assuring payment.

7.____ A form of encumbrance that usually makes specific property security for the payment of a debt.

8.____ Discharge of a mortgage or trust deed from the records upon payment of the debt. Make sure you receive a Deed of Reconveyance to prove that you paid off the deed of trust.

9.____ A limiting restriction stating that upon the happening or not happening of some stated event, the estate shall be changed in some manner.

10.____ A promise to do or not to do a particular thing.

11.____ A person against whom a civil or criminal action is taken.

12.____ An instrument, recognized by law, by which property is hypothecated to secure the payment of a debt. This instrument is not commonly used in California, but is popular on the East coast.

13.____ In a court action, the one who sues; the complainant.

14.____ A recorded document of the essential provisions of a court judgment.

15.____ A lien, created by statute, which exists against real or personal property in favor of persons who have performed work or furnished materials for the improvement of real property.

16.____ A legal document by which a borrower pledges certain real property as collateral for the repayment of a loan. In addition to the buyer and seller, there is a third party to the transaction known as a trustee.

17.____ A formal statement that protects the head of the household from losing the property to the claims of creditors, usually up to a set maximum amount.

18.____ A lien, usually a trust deed in California, covering more than one property of the borrower.

19.____ A notice that informs or warns owners, lenders and general contractors that subcontractors have been hired, or materials have been supplied, to a particular job site.

20.____ A statement declaring the intent to give up a homestead, usually to declare a homestead on a new residence.

21.____ A court ordered sale of real or personal property by the sheriff pursuant to the execution of a judgment.

22.____ The construction of improvements on the property of another.

23.____ An easement for the benefit of the owner of an adjacent parcel of land.

24.____ Real property that benefits from an easement.

25.____ A writ to carry out a court order, usually arising from a judgment.

26.____ A property that is burdened by an easement.

27.____ An easement for the benefit of a person or utility company rather than for the benefit of adjacent landowners.

28.____ A notice filed or recorded for the purpose of warning all persons that the title to certain real property is in litigation.

29.____ A lien such as a tax lien or judgment lien that attaches to all property of the debtor rather than a specific property.

30.____ A lien that attaches to a specific property rather than all the property of the debtor.

MULTIPLE CHOICE

1. A mechanic's lien:

   A. is a general lien
   C. is a non-money encumbrance
   B. is a voluntary lien
   D. must be recorded to be effective

2. Income taxes would be an example of a (an):

   A. voluntary lien
   C. general lien
   B. attachment lien
   D. specific lien

3. An easement appurtenant:

   A. runs with the land
   C. has a separate conveyance
   B. cannot be transferred
   D. does not benefit the adjoining land

4. If you fail to pay a subcontractor and he or she files a mechanic's lien, the lien is:

   A. specific
   C. voluntary
   B. general
   D. both A and B

5. Homesteads allow homeowners to protect their homes from forced:

   A. robbery
   C. condemnation
   B. sale to pay bad debts
   D. eminent domain

6. A sheriff's sale CANNOT be the result of a (an):

   A. judgment
   C. writ of execution
   B. court action
   D. easement

7. Homesteading requires the claimant to:

   A. use the home as a residence
   C. describe the property in writing
   B. file a declaration of homestead
   D. all of the above

8. A document using property to secure the payment of a debt is called a:

   A. lien
   C. grant deed
   B. cloud on title
   D. reconveyance

9. Which of the following would be considered a voluntary lien?

   A. Special assessment
   C. Attachment
   B. Tax lien
   D. Mortgage

10. Local improvements that are paid for by the property owners who benefit from the work are called:

    A. special assessments
    C. property taxes
    B. tax liens
    D. district assessments

CHAPTER 4
Agency & Its Responsibilities

 http://www.sbaonline.sba.gov (Starting Your Business)

TECHNOLOGY AND THE BROKER

The evolution of the computer (both in the home and in the office) and the Internet has revolutionized the way brokers do business. The majority of the public will soon be able to transmit loan applications, check out credit histories and view color photos of properties, both in and out-of-state.

Customers must have the perception that the REALTOR® utilizes the latest technological trends. Customers will not feel confident in using an agent who is not up to speed.

AGENCY

AGENCY is the authority (or power) to act for a principal (person who hires) in a specified capacity for a stated period of time. An AGENT is one who acts for and with authority from another, called the principal. Agents (brokers) usually select and control their own professional approach to selling a property. Sellers are responsible for their representations to the buyer. While brokers share this responsibility, they also have a responsibility for their individual performance. This relationship is based on trust. The agent representing the seller must disclose all pertinent facts to the seller and must not take advantage of, or gain from, this relationship in an unethical manner.

Agent, Broker, Salesperson, Associate. Who Holds A Real Estate License?

Real Estate Agent

A **REAL ESTATE AGENT** *is a person, licensed by the Department of Real Estate (DRE), who holds either a broker or salesperson license and negotiates sales for other people.*

Real Estate Broker

A **REAL ESTATE BROKER** *is a license holder (boss/owner) and therefore permitted by law to employ those individuals holding a salesperson license.* A Salesperson is a individual who may negotiate sales for other people.

Real Estate Salesperson

A **REAL ESTATE SALESPERSON** *is an individual holding a salesperson license who must be employed by a real estate broker to perform any of the activities of a real estate broker.*

Real Estate Sales Associate

A **REAL ESTATE ASSOCIATE** *is another name for a real estate salesperson. An associate works for a broker as either an employee or an independent contractor.*

A licensee is either a Salesperson (employee) or Broker (boss/owner).

Department of Real Estate (DRE)

Check the status of a real estate salesperson or broker.

To check the status of a real estate salesperson or broker just connect with the following Department of Real Estate's Internet address.

http://www.dre.ca.gov/licstus.htm (Department of Real Estate)

Just click on LICENSEE RECORDS ON-LINE and enter the name or license number and the DRE will do the rest.

Agency & Its Responsibilities

A *PRINCIPAL (CLIENT)* is a person who hires or employs an agent to work for him or her. If the principal is a buyer, the agent represents the buyer. On the other hand, if the principal is a seller, the agent represents the seller.

The principal is the person who hires.

A *THIRD PARTY* is the other person in a contractual negotiation, besides the principal and his or her agent. If an agent works for the seller, the third party is the buyer, but if the agent works for the buyer, the third party is the seller. In effect it is the other party to the transaction.

In the agency relationship, the broker and other salespeople are required to make certain representations about the property they are selling. They are expected to do what is necessary, proper and usual to sell the real estate being offered. They must also make truthful representations to the buyer as to the condition of the property that may materially affect the value or desirability, and the terms of the sale. This is spelled out in the Agency Disclosure Form (discussed later).

An agency relationship may also come about by estoppel or ratification, although it is **not** advisable. The legal idea of *ESTOPPEL* is: *if you let a broker act as if he or she had your authorization to sell your house, you cannot later say he or she did it without your consent. When you authorize a broker to have acted for you after he or she has already done so, the action is called* **RATIFICATION.**

The best form for evidence of an agency relationship is a written agreement.

In California, most real estate transactions involve the use of a broker and his or her salespeople. To run a real estate office, a broker's license is required. A salesperson must also be licensed by the Department of Real Estate and can only work for a broker. In California, any person in real estate who is acting in return for compensation from others must have a real estate license to:

1. Sell or offer to sell
2. Buy or offer to buy
3. Solicit prospective buyers or sellers
4. Negotiate the purchase, sale, loan or exchange of business opportunities or real estate
5. Negotiate leases and collect rents.

Real estate license requirements are explained fully in Chapter 14.

You may buy, sell or lease your own property without a real estate license as often as you like in a given year because there is no agency involved.

The relationship between a seller, a broker (and his or her salespeople) and a buyer is called "agency."

TRADITIONAL AGENCY RELATIONSHIP

Traditionally, the broker was called the agent, the owner/seller was called the principal and the buyer was called the third party. Conventionally, the broker works for the seller. Figure 4-1 illustrates this agency relationship.

FIGURE 4-1

A. The principal = Owner/Seller
B. The agent = Broker/Salesperson
C. The third party = Buyer

The Principal is the person who hires.

However, the broker can act as an agent for the buyer, the seller or both. We will discuss these other agency relationships later in the chapter.

Real estate brokers are agents because they represent an interest other than their own and have a written agency contract called a listing, for which they may receive compensation. Whenever one person represents another in a business transaction, the "Law of Agency" applies.

> *The Law of Agency (defines agents' duties and responsibilities) is found in the California Civil Code; violations by agents are dealt with under the Business and Professions Code.*

Because the real estate broker is an agent, the California Civil Code, under the Law of Agency, defines his or her duties and responsibilities. Further, since the broker is a licensed real estate agent, he or she must comply with the rules and regulations of the California Administrative Code, which, in this case, is enforced by the Commissioner of Real Estate. Both codes govern, and can be enforced against, all brokers and their salespeople. Throughout this chapter, when we speak of a broker we are also referring to any salesperson that may be working for that broker.

The broker is technically the agent who supervises his or her salespeople and any brokers working for his or her agency.

A salesperson and broker may also be referred to as real estate agents. Since they are in an agency relationship, it is only logical to refer to them as agents.

RESPONSIBILITIES OF AGENCY

The California Civil Code boils the law of agency down to three basic rules applying to licensed brokers and licensed salespeople:

1. The agent **must** inform the principal of all facts pertaining to the handling of the principal's property. Agent must put client's interest above interest of self or others.

2. The agent **may not** gain any monetary interest in the property without the principal's prior consent.

3. An agent **may not** use the principal's property to his or her own advantage.

FIDUCIARY RELATIONSHIP

The broker (agent) works for the principal and forms with him or her a fiduciary relationship. On the other hand, the broker must maintain an honest and truthful relationship with the third party (plus give full disclosure of material facts affecting value or desirability).

The broker (agent) has certain duties, rights and responsibilities to both the principal and third party. To a principal the broker owes honesty, utmost care, integrity, accounting, disclosure and loyalty. This is called a "fiduciary" relationship. To a third party, an agent owes honesty and disclosure of material facts.

A *FIDUCIARY is a person acting in a position of trust and confidence in a business relationship. A FIDUCIARY RELATIONSHIP requires the highest good faith from the agent to his or her principal. In a legal context, an agent must act as though he or she is the principal and always seek to represent the principal's best interest. In this case, the agent takes on the responsibility of diligently finding a buyer or seller. See Figure 4-2.*

An agent must exercise honesty, reasonable skill and care, fair dealing and good faith in dealing with a third party. An agent of the principal must disclose to the third party any facts known to the agent that could materially affect the value or desirability of the property.

FIGURE 4-2

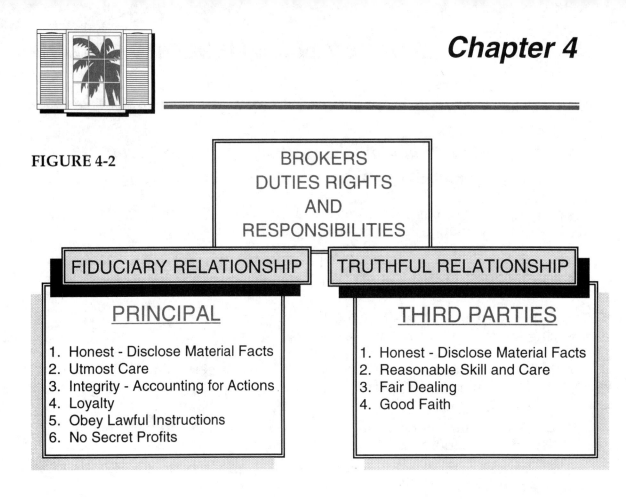

BROKERS
DUTIES RIGHTS
AND
RESPONSIBILITIES

FIDUCIARY RELATIONSHIP

PRINCIPAL

1. Honest - Disclose Material Facts
2. Utmost Care
3. Integrity - Accounting for Actions
4. Loyalty
5. Obey Lawful Instructions
6. No Secret Profits

TRUTHFUL RELATIONSHIP

THIRD PARTIES

1. Honest - Disclose Material Facts
2. Reasonable Skill and Care
3. Fair Dealing
4. Good Faith

THE GROWTH OF "BUYER BROKERAGES"

WE LOVE BUYERS

A large number of brokers are responding to a need in the industry by offering exclusive buyer's services. More than a fad, it is estimated that buyer's agents will represent 25% or more of the industry within the next ten years.

It is believed that good buyer representation will cut down on disputes and lawsuits. In the future, the trend will be toward joint buyer-seller agencies under one roof, so brokers don't exclude themselves from one entire side of the market.

LISTING AND SELLING AGENTS

When a salesperson obtains a listing agreement to sell a particular property, he or she is referred to as the "listing salesperson." That salesperson's broker is referred to as the "listing broker." If a different agency negotiates the sale, that agency is the "selling broker" and "selling salesperson." A broker or salesperson who both lists and sells the same property is referred to as the "listing and selling broker or salesperson."

> *In a real estate transaction, agents are identified as the "listing agent" or "selling agent."*

DISCLOSURE OF AGENCY RELATIONSHIP

According to the Agency Disclosure Law, the first thing the agent must do is establish if he or she is an agent for the seller, buyer or both.

The Agency Disclosure Law of January 1, 1988, states that an agent must disclose an agency relationship as soon as practical. An agent can represent a seller, a buyer or both.

The agency disclosure law states that both the listing broker and the selling broker must declare in writing, as soon as possible, who it is they represent:

1. The seller (owner)
2. The buyer, or
3. Both the seller and buyer (**dual agency**).

The only requirement is that the listing broker must at least represent the seller (owner). This law applies to all sales of residential property of from one to four units.

Be aware: This type of law, which differs from state to state, will profoundly affect the way brokers represent their clients and the way we as an industry are perceived by the public at large.

Figure 4-3 shows an Agency Disclosure Form used by the California Association of Realtors®. Civil law requires that both parties to a transaction be informed of the various options they have regarding agency representation. Both the buyer and the seller must sign the upper part of this form as an acknowledgment that they understand their rights and have received a copy of this disclosure. In addition, agency disclosure must again be confirmed on the Residential Purchase Agreement ("Deposit Receipt"—see Chapter 5). If it is not confirmed on the Deposit Receipt, then it must be confirmed on a separate form. This confirmation will protect the licensee against any future charges of misrepresentation in the agency relationship. It should be completed as soon as possible.

Because of the fiduciary relationship, the agent of the seller cannot tell the buyer that the seller is insolvent, unless the agent is given written notice to do so. But the seller's agent must inform the buyer about any material facts that affect the value of the property (for example, the property is in an earthquake zone or backs up to a freeway or school).

FIGURE 4-3

CALIFORNIA
ASSOCIATION
OF REALTORS®

DISCLOSURE REGARDING
REAL ESTATE AGENCY RELATIONSHIPS
(As required by the Civil Code)

When you enter into a discussion with a real estate agent regarding a real estate transaction, you should from the outset understand what type of agency relationship or representation you wish to have with the agent in the transaction.

SELLER'S AGENT

A Seller's agent under a listing agreement with the Seller acts as the agent for the Seller only. A Seller's agent or a subagent of that agent has the following affirmative obligations:
To the Seller:
    A Fiduciary duty of utmost care, integrity, honesty, and loyalty in dealings with the Seller.
To the Buyer and the Seller:
    (a) Diligent exercise of reasonable skill and care in performance of the agent's duties.
    (b) A duty of honest and fair dealing and good faith.
    (c) A duty to disclose all facts known to the agent materially affecting the value or desirability of the property that are not known to, or within the diligent attention and observation of, the parties.

An agent is not obligated to reveal to either party any confidential information obtained from the other party that does not involve the affirmative duties set forth above.

BUYER'S AGENT

A selling agent can, with a Buyer's consent, agree to act as agent for the Buyer only. In these situations, the agent is not the Seller's agent, even if by agreement the agent may receive compensation for services rendered, either in full or in part from the Seller. An agent acting only for a Buyer has the following affirmative obligations:
To the Buyer:
    A fiduciary duty of utmost care, integrity, honesty, and loyalty in dealings with the Buyer.
To the Buyer and the Seller:
    (a) Diligent exercise of reasonable skill and care in performance of the agent's duties.
    (b) A duty of honest and fair dealing and good faith.
    (c) A duty to disclose all facts known to the agent materially affecting the value or desirability of the property that are not known to, or within the diligent attention and observation of, the parties.

An agent is not obligated to reveal to either party any confidential information obtained from the other party that does not involve the affirmative duties set forth above.

AGENT REPRESENTING BOTH SELLER & BUYER

A real estate agent, either acting directly or through one or more associate licensees can legally be the agent of both the Seller and the Buyer in a transaction, but only with the knowledge and consent of both the Seller and the Buyer.

In a dual agency situation, the agent has the following affirmative obligations to both the Seller and the Buyer:
    (a) A fiduciary duty of utmost care, integrity, honest and loyalty in the dealings with either Seller or the Buyer.
    (b) Other duties to the Seller and the Buyer as stated above in their respective sections.

In representing both Seller and Buyer, the agent may not, without the express permission of the respective party, disclose to the other party that the Seller will accept a price less than the listing price or that the Buyer will pay a price greater than the price offered.

The above duties of the agent in a real estate transaction do not relieve a Seller or Buyer from the responsibility to protect his or her own interests. You should carefully read all agreements to assure that they adequately express your understanding of the transaction. A real estate agent is a person qualified to advise about real estate. If legal or tax advice is desired, consult a competent professional.

Throughout your real property transaction you may receive more than one disclosure form, depending upon the number of agents assisting in the transaction. The law requires each agent with whom you have more than a casual relationship to present you with this disclosure form. You should read its contents each time it is presented to you, considering the relationship between you and the real estate agent in your specific transaction.

This disclosure form includes the provisions of Sections 2079.13 to 2079.24, inclusive, of the Civil Code set forth on the reverse hereof. Read it carefully.

I/WE ACKNOWLEDGE RECEIPT OF A COPY OF THIS DISCLOSURE.

BUYER/SELLER _____ Date _____ Time _____ AM/PM

BUYER/SELLER _____ Date _____ Time _____ AM/PM

AGENT _____ By _____ Date _____
           (Please Print)   (Associate Licensee or Broker-Signature)

This Disclosure form must be provided in a listing, sale, exchange, installment land contract, or lease over one year, if the transaction involves one-to-four dwelling residential property, including a mobile home, as follows:
(a) From a Listing Agent to a Seller: Prior to entering into the listing.
(b) From an Agent selling a property he/she has listed to a Buyer: Prior to the Buyer's execution of the offer.
(c) From a Selling Agent to a Buyer: Prior to the Buyer's execution of the offer.
(d) From a Selling Agent (in a cooperating real estate firm) to a Seller: Prior to presentation of the offer to the Seller.

It is not necessary or required to confirm an agency relationship using a separate Confirmation form if the agency confirmation portion of the Real Estate Purchase Contract is properly completed in full. However, it is still necessary to use this Disclosure form.

┌ OFFICE USE ONLY ┐
Reviewed by Broker
or Designee _____
Date _____

EQUAL HOUSING
OPPORTUNITY

FORM AD-14 REVISED 10/95

FIGURE 4-4

BROKER REPRESENTS SELLER

| SELLER (PRINCIPAL) | FIDUCIARY RELATIONSHIP | BROKER (AGENT) | HONEST & TRUTHFUL RELATIONSHIP | BUYER (THIRD PARTY) |

BROKER REPRESENTS BUYER

| SELLER (THIRD PARTY) | HONEST & TRUTHFUL RELATIONSHIP | BROKER (AGENT) | FIDUCIARY RELATIONSHIP | BUYER (PRINCIPAL) |

BROKER REPRESENTS BOTH PARTIES

| SELLER (PRINCIPAL) | FIDUCIARY RELATIONSHIP | BROKER (AGENT) | FIDUCIARY RELATIONSHIP | BUYER (PRINCIPAL) |

Traditionally, the principal was usually a seller. Brokers are now free to represent the buyer, the seller, and sometimes both. Figure 4-4 illustrates the agency options.

> *It is legal for an agent to work for both the buyer and seller ("dual agency") if the agent has the acknowledgment and consent of all parties to the transaction.*

As you can see, there may be several brokers involved in a single transaction. In California, the seller (owner) and the buyer are usually represented by different brokers. The listing broker always represents the seller but may represent both. Traditionally the selling broker, who procures the buyer, seldom represents the buyer. In some other states, all the brokers and salespeople represent only the seller (owner).

SALESPEOPLE MAY BE INDEPENDENT CONTRACTORS OR EMPLOYEES

In California most salespeople working under a broker are not considered employees by the state, but rather act as independent contractors.

An **INDEPENDENT CONTRACTOR** *sells results rather than time, and his or her physical conduct is not subject to the control of another.* An **EMPLOYEE**, *on the other hand, works under the direct control and supervision of the employer.*

In most real estate offices the salespeople come and go at will, working no fixed hours and paying their own payroll taxes (Federal and State Income Taxes, Social Security, Unemployment Insurance and State Disability Insurance). More strictly supervised workers, such as secretaries, are generally considered employees. The broker is required, however, to carry workman's compensation and public liability insurance for salespeople in the same way that they do for employees.

> *The Department of Real Estate considers a salesperson an employee of the broker, even if he or she is usually an independent contractor. This makes the broker responsible for the real estate activities of the salesperson.*

TOP AGENTS HIRE TOP ASSISTANTS

It is estimated that 80 percent of the real estate business is handled by 10 percent of the agents. To handle the workload, more top agents are hiring personal assistants to take over the day-to-day brokerage chores, leaving the agents free to concentrate on sales. A **PERSONAL ASSISTANT** *handles such things as clerical tasks, paperwork, marketing, tickler files and conducts computer research.*

The growth in personal assistants is not without criticism. Among the complaints are that using assistants entrusts too many high-level tasks to unskilled employees and makes the agents inaccessible. It is important that the broker establish who is employing the assistants and who bears the responsibility for their actions.

WRITTEN BROKER - SALESPERSON AGREEMENTS

As required by the Real Estate Commissioner's Regulations, brokers must have a written contract with each licensed member of the sale's staff. A copy of this contract must be retained by all parties for three years from the date of termination. This is also required of salespeople who are themselves brokers but are working under another broker's license. The agreement shall be dated and signed by the parties and shall cover material aspects of the relationship between the parties, including supervision of licensed activities, duties and compensation.

> *Signed "broker-salesperson contracts" must be kept for "three years" from the date of termination of the contract.*

Figures 4-5 and 4-6 show the CAR® Broker-Associate Licensee Contract. It outlines the duties, responsibilities and compensation to be provided and must be signed and dated by both the broker and the salesperson.

FIGURE 4-5

CALIFORNIA
ASSOCIATION
OF REALTORS®

BROKER-ASSOCIATE LICENSEE CONTRACT
(Independent-Contractor)

THIS AGREEMENT, made this _____ day of _____, 19_____ by and between
_____
_____ (hereinafter "Broker") and
_____ (hereinafter "Associate Licensee").
IN CONSIDERATION of the respective representations and covenants herein, Broker and Associate Licensee agree and contract as follows:

1. **BROKER:** Broker represents that he/she/it is duly licensed as a real estate broker by the State of California, ☐ doing business as _____
_____ (Firm name), ☐ a sole proprietorship, ☐ a partnership, ☐ a corporation.
Broker is a member of the _____ Board(s)/Association(s) of REALTORS7, and a Participant in the
_____ multiple listing service(s).

2. **ASSOCIATE LICENSEE:** Associate Licensee represents that, (a) he/she is duly licensed by the State of California as a ☐ real estate broker, ☐ real estate salesperson, and (b) he/she has not used any other names within the past five years except _____
_____. Broker shall keep his/her/its license current during the term of this agreement. Associate Licensee shall keep his/her license current during the term of this agreement, including satisfying all applicable continuing education and provisional license requirements.

3. **LISTING AND SALES ACTIVITIES:** Broker shall make available to Associate Licensee, equally with other licensees associated with Broker, all current listings in Broker's office, except any listing which Broker may choose to place in the exclusive servicing of Associate Licensee or one or more other specific licensees associated with Broker. Associate Licensee shall not be required to accept or service any particular listing or prospective listing offered by Broker, or to see or service particular parties. Broker shall not restrict Associate Licensee's activities to particular geographical areas. Broker shall not, except to the extent required by law, direct or limit Associate Licensee's activities as to hours, leads, open houses, opportunity or floor time, production, prospects, sales meetings, schedule, inventory, time off, vacation, or similar activities. In compliance with Commissioner's Regulation 2780, et seq. (Title 10, California Code of Regulations, §2780, et seq.), Broker and Associate Licensee shall at all times be familiar with, all applicable federal, California and local anti-discrimination laws.

4. **BROKER SUPERVISION:**
   (a) Associate Licensee shall submit for Broker's review:
   i. All documents which may have a material effect upon the rights and duties of principals in a transaction, within 24 hours after preparing, signing, or receiving same. Broker may exercise this review responsibility through another licensee provided the Broker and the designated licensee have complied with Commissioner's Regulation 2725 (Title 10, California Code of Regulations, §2725).
   ii. Any documents or other items connected with a transaction pursuant to this agreement, in the possession of or available to Associate Licensee, (i) immediately upon request by Broker or Broker's designated licensee, and/or (ii) as provided in Broker's Office Policy Manual, if any.
   iii. All documents associated with any real estate transaction in which Associate Licensee is a principal.
   (b) In addition, without affecting Associate Licensee's status, Broker shall have the right to direct Associate Licensee's actions to the extent required by law, and Associate Licensee shall comply with such directions. All trust funds shall be handled in compliance with Business and Professions Code §10145, and other applicable laws.

5. **OFFICE FACILITIES:** Broker shall make available for Associate Licensee's use, along with other licensees associated with Broker, the facilities of the real estate office operated by Broker at _____
and the facilities of any other office locations made available by Broker pursuant to this agreement.

6. **ASSOCIATE LICENSEE'S REPORT:** Associate Licensee shall work diligently and with his/her best efforts, (a) To sell, exchange, lease, or rent properties listed with Broker or other cooperating Brokers, (b) To solicit additional listings, clients, and customers, and (c) To otherwise promote the business of serving the public in real estate transactions to the end that Broker and Associate Licensee may derive the greatest benefit possible, in accordance with law.

7. **UNLAWFUL ACTS:** Associate Licensee shall not commit any act for which the Real Estate Commissioner of the State of California is authorized to restrict, suspend, or revoke Associates Licensee's license or impose other discipline, under California Business and Professions Code Sections 10176 or 10177 or other provisions of law.

8. **LISTING COMMISSIONS:** Commissions shall be charged to parties who desire to enter into listing agreements and other contracts for services requiring a real estate license, with Broker.
   ☐ as shown in "Exhibit A" attached which is incorporated as a part of this agreement by reference, or
   ☐ as follows: _____
   _____
   _____
   Any proposed deviation from that schedule must be reviewed and approved in advance by Broker. Any permanent change in commission schedule shall be disseminated by Broker to Associate Licensee.

9. **COMPENSATION TO ASSOCIATE LICENSEE:** Associate Licensee shall receive a share of commissions which are actually collected by Broker, on listings and other contracts for services requiring a real estate license which are solicited and obtained by Associate Licensee, and on transactions of which Associate Licensee's activities are the procuring cause,
   ☐ as shown in "Exhibit B" attached which is incorporated as a part of this agreement by reference, or
   ☐ as follows: _____
   _____
   _____
   _____
   The above commissions may be varied by written agreement between Broker and Associate Licensee before completion of any particular transaction. Expenses which must be paid from commissions, or are incurred in the attempt to collect commissions, shall be paid by Broker and Associate Licensee in the same proportion as set forth for the division of commissions.

10. **DIVIDING COMPENSATION WITH OTHER LICENSEES IN OFFICE:** If Associate Licensee and one or more other licensees associated with Broker both participate on the same side (either listing or selling) of a transaction, the commission allocated to their combined activities shall be divided by Broker and paid to them according to the written agreement between them which shall be furnished in advance to Broker.

11. **COMMISSIONS PAID TO BROKER:** All commission will be received by Broker. Associate Licensee's share of commissions shall be paid to him/her, after deduction of offsets, immediately upon collection by Broker or as soon thereafter as practicable, except as otherwise provided in (a) Paragraph 9, above, (b) Broker's Office Policy Manual, or (c) A Separate written agreement between Broker and Associate Licensee. Broker may impound in Broker's account Associate Licensee's share of commissions on transactions in which there is a known or pending claim against Broker and/or Associate Licensee, until such claim is resolved.

12. **UNCOLLECTED COMMISSIONS:** Neither Broker nor Associate Licensee shall be liable to the other for any portion of commissions not collected. Associate Licensee shall not be entitled to any advance payment from Broker upon future commissions.

Published and Distributed by:
REAL ESTATE BUSINESS SERVICES, INC.
a subsidiary of the CALIFORNIA ASSOCIATION OF REALTORS®
525 South Virgil Avenue, Los Angeles, California 90020

OFFICE USE ONLY
Reviewed by Broker
or Designee _____
Date _____

EQUAL HOUSING
OPPORTUNITY

FORM I-14 REVISED 1990

FIGURE 4-6

13. **ASSOCIATE LICENSEE EXPENSES; OFFSETS:** Associate Licensee shall provide and pay for all professional licenses, supplies, services, and other items required in connection with Associate Licensee's activities under this agreement, or any listing or transaction, without reimbursement from Broker except as required by law. If Broker elects to advance funds to pay expenses or liabilities of Associate Licensee shall pay to Broker the full amount advanced on demand, or Broker may deduct the full amount advanced from commissions payable to Associate Licensee on any transaction without notice.

14. **INDEPENDENT CONTRACTOR RELATIONSHIP:** Broker and Associate Licensee intend that, to the maximum extent permissible by law, **(a)** This agreement does not constitute a hiring or employment agreement by either party, **(b)** Broker and Associate Licensee are independent contracting parties with respect to all services rendered under this agreement or in any resulting transactions, **(c)** Associate Licensee's only remuneration shall be his.her proportional share, if any, of commissions collected by Broker, **(d)** Associate Licensee retains sole and absolute discretion and judgment in the methods, techniques, and procedures to be used in soliciting and obtaining listings, sales, exchanges, leases, rentals, or other transactions, and in carrying out Associate Licensee's selling and soliciting activities, except as required by law or in Broker's Office Policy Manual, **(e)** Associate Licensee is under the control of Broker as to the results of Associate Licensee's work only, and not as to the means by which those results are accomplished except as required by law, or in Broker's Office Policy Manual, if any, **(f)** This Agreement shall not be construed as a partnership, **(g)** Associate Licensee has no authority to bind Broker by any promise or representation unless specifically authorized by Broker in writing, **(h)** Broker shall not be liable for any obligation or liability incurred by Associate Licensee, **(i)** Associate Licensee shall not be treated as an employee with respects to services performed as a real estate agent, for state and federal tax purposes, and **(j)** The fact the Broker may carry worker compensation insurance for his/her/its own benefit and for the mutual benefit of Broker and licensees associated with Broker, including Associate Licensee, shall not create or inference of employment.

15. **LISTING AND OTHER AGREEMENTS PROPERTY OF BROKER:** All listings of property, and all agreements for performance of licensed acts, and all acts or actions required a real estate license which are taken or performed in connection with this agreement, shall be taken and performed in the name of Broker. All listings shall be submitted to Broker within 24 hours after receipt by Associate Licensee. Associate Licensee agrees to and does hereby contribute all right and title to such listings to Broker for the benefit and use of Broker, Associate Licensee, and other licensees associated with Broker.

16. **TERMINATION OF RELATIONSHIP:** Broker or Associate Licensee may terminate their relationship under this agreement at any time, on 24 hours written notice, with or without cause. Even after termination, this agreement shall govern all disputes and claims between Broker and Associate Licensee connected with their relationship under this agreement, including obligations and liabilities arising from existing and completed listings, transactions, and services.

17. **COMMISSIONS AFTER TERMINATION AND OFFSET:** If this agreement is terminated while Associate Licensee has listings or pending transactions that require further work normally rendered by Associate Licensee, Broker shall make arrangements with another licensee associated with Broker to perform the required work, or shall perform the work him/herself. The licensee performing the work shall be reasonably compensated for completing work on those listings or transactions, and such reasonable compensation shall be deducted from Associate Licensee's share of commissions. Except for such offset, Associate Licensee shall receive his/her regular share of commissions on such sales or other transactions, if actually collected by Broker, after deduction of any other amounts or offsets provided in this agreement.

18. **ARBITRATION OF DISPUTES:** All disputes or claims between Associate Licensee and other licensee(s) associated with Broker, or between Associate Licensee and Broker, arising from or connected in any way with this agreement, which cannot be adjusted between the parties involved, shall be submitted to the Board of REALTORS® of which all such disputing parties are members for arbitration pursuant to the provisions of its Bylaws, as may be amended from time to time, which are incorporated as a part of this agreement by reference. If the Bylaws of the Board do not cover arbitration of the dispute, or if the Board declines jurisdiction over the dispute, then arbitration shall be pursuant to the rules of the American Arbitration Association, as may be amended from time to time, which are incorporated as a part of this agreement by reference. The Federal Arbitration Act, Title 9, U.S. Code, Section 1, et seq., shall govern this agreement.

19. **PROPRIETARY INFORMATION AND FILES:** Associate Licensee shall not use to his/her own advantage, or the advantage of any other person, business, or entity, except as specified provided in this agreement, either during Associate Licensee;s association with Broker or thereafter, any information gained for or from the business or files of Broker. All files and documents pertaining to listings and transactions are the property of Broker and shall be delivered to Broker by Associate Licensee immediately upon request or upon termination of their relationship under this agreement.

20. **INDEMNITY AND HOLD HARMLESS:** All claims, demands, liabilities, judgments, and arbitration awards, including costs and attorney's fees, to which Broker is subjected by reason of any action taken or omitted by Associate Licensee in connection with services rendered or to be rendered pursuant to this agreement, shall be:

    ☐ Paid in full by Associate Licensee, who hereby agrees to indemnify and hold harmless Broker for all such sums, or

    ☐ Other: _____
    _____
    _____

    Associate Licensee shall pay to Broker the full amount due by him/her demand, or Broker may deduct the full amount due by Associate Licensee from commissions due on any transaction without notice.

21. **ADDITIONAL PROVISIONS:** _____
    _____
    _____

22. **DEFINITIONS:** As used in this agreement, the following terms have the meanings indicated:

    (a) "Listing" means an agreement with a property owner or other party to locate a buyer, exchange party, lessee, or other party to a transaction involving real property, a mobile home, or other property or transaction which may be brokered by a real estate licensee, or an agreement with a party to locate or negotiate for any such property or transaction.

    (b) "Commission means compensation for acts requiring a real estate license, regardless of whether calculated as a percentage of transaction price, flat fee, hourly rate, or in any other manner.

    (c) "Transaction" means a sale, exchange, lease, or rental of real property, a business opportunity, or a mobile home which may lawfully be brokered by a real estate licensee, or a loan secured by any property of those types.

    (d) "Associate Licensee" means the real estate broker or real estate salesperson licensed by the State of California and rendering the services set forth herein for Associate Licensee.

23. **NOTICES:** All notices under this agreement shall be in writing. Notices may be delivered personally, or by certified U.S. mail, postage prepaid, or by facsimile, to the parties at the addresses noted below. Either party may designate a new address for purposes of this agreement by giving notice to the other party. Notices mailed shall be deemed received as of 5:00 P.M. on the second business day following the date of mailing.

24. **ATTORNEY FEES:** In any action, proceeding, or arbitration between Broker and Associate Licensee arising from or related to this agreement, the prevailing party shall, in the discretion of the court or arbitrator, be entitled to reasonable attorney fees in addition to other appropriate relief.

25. **ENTIRE AGREEMENT; MODIFICATION:** All prior agreements between the parties concerning their relationship as Broker and Associate Licensee are incorporated in this agreement, which constitutes the entire contract. Its terms are intended by the parties as a final and complete expression of their agreement with respect to its subject matter, and may not be contradicted by evidence of any prior agreement or contemporaneous oral agreement. This agreement may not be amended, modified, altered, or changed in any respect whatsoever except by a further agreement in writing duly executed by Broker and Associate Licensee.

BROKER:

_____
(Signature)

_____
(Name Printed)

_____
(Address)

_____
(City, State, Zip)

_____
(Telephone)   (Fax)

ASSOCIATE LICENSEE:

_____
(Signature)

_____
(Name Printed)

_____
(Address)

_____
(City, State, Zip)

_____
(Telephone)   (Fax)

NOTE: (1) Broker and Associate Licensee should each receive an executed copy of this agreement.

(2) Attach commission schedules Exhibits A and B if applicable.

Other specific rules and policies for handling procedures at a specific brokerage firm are usually set down in the company POLICY MANUAL. This manual must be read by all salespeople.

LISTINGS AND THE "MLS"

LISTING AGREEMENTS

> *Listings are employment contracts for personal service between an agent and a principal that create an agency relationship.*

The usual way to establish a broker's right to negotiate a sale of property is through a written contract, commonly called a listing. A **LISTING** *is a contract to employ a broker, legally referred to as an agent, to do certain things for the owner/seller. It is an employment contract for personal service.*

> *Listings are not assignable and death of the seller or broker cancels a listing, unless the seller is a corporation (which lives forever). A listing agreement signed by one spouse is enforceable but a Residential Purchase Agreement (deposit receipt-explained in Chapter 5) is not.*

There are three basic types of listings used in California. They are:

  1. Open Listing (non-exclusive)
  2. Exclusive Agency Listing
  3. Exclusive Right to Sell Listing

> *A listing may be for any period of time. If no beginning date is specified, the effective date is the date when the listing is signed. Real estate law requires that exclusive listings must have a definite, final termination date. If not, the agent may lose the commission and possibly his or her license.*

You should also know: all real estate listing agreements or contracts should be in writing, and must be in writing to assure collection of a commission.

> *All listings belong to the broker (not the salesperson). If you move, most brokers will allow you to take your listings.*

Open Listing (Unilateral, Non-Exclusive Contract)

An **OPEN LISTING** *is an authorization to sell a property. It may be given to several brokers or the property may be sold by the owner. If the owner sells the property, he or she is not required to pay a commission.* Usually, no time limit is placed on an open listing. A description of the property is included in the agreement along with the selling price and other terms.

Open listings are the simplest form of broker authorization. They can be given to several brokers concurrently and no notice of sale is required to terminate the listing. A broker should make sure an open listing is still valid before pursuing it. When an open listing is given to more than one broker, the first broker who finds a qualified buyer is entitled to the commission. On the other hand, if an owner finds his or her own buyer, that owner has no obligation to pay a commission to a broker.

> *NOT all listings are bilateral; NOT all listings are a promise for a promise because the open listing is unilateral (only seller promises). Exclusive listings are bilateral.*

Few brokers use this type of listing because of its uncertainty and the expense of advertising when working an open listing.

Exclusive Agency Listing (No Commission If Owner Sells)

The **EXCLUSIVE AGENCY LISTING** *is a listing where the listing broker is entitled to a commission. The owner, however, still has the right to independently sell the property without paying a commission to the listing broker.* The drawback with this type of listing is that the broker is, or could be, in competition with the owner for the sale.

> *An exclusive agency listing and exclusive right to sell listing both require a definite termination date.*

Exclusive Right To Sell Listing
(Commission If Sold Within The Listing Period)

The most common type of listing is the exclusive right to sell listing. Only the **EXCLUSIVE RIGHT TO SELL LISTING** *entitles the listing broker named in the agency contract to a commission even if the owner, himself, sells the property.* Figures 4-7 and 4-8; shows the "Exclusive Authorization and Right to Sell."

> *With an exclusive agency listing, the broker competes with the owner; with an exclusive right to sell listing, the broker is entitled to a commission even if the owner, himself, sells the property. An exclusive right to sell is the "strongest listing."*

FIGURE 4-7

CALIFORNIA
ASSOCIATION
OF REALTORS®

EXCLUSIVE AUTHORIZATION AND RIGHT TO SELL

1. **EXCLUSIVE RIGHT TO SELL:** _____ ("Seller") hereby employ and grants
_____ ("Broker") the exclusive and irrevocable right, commencing on
_____, 19 _____ and expiring at 11:59 P.M. on _____, 19 _____ ("Listing Period") to sell or exchange the
real property in the City of _____, County of _____, California,
described as follows: _____ ("Property").

2. **TERMS OF SALE:**
   A. **LIST PRICE:** The listing price shall be _____
   _____ ($_____).
   B. **PERSONAL PROPERTY:** The following items of personal property are included in the above price: _____
   _____
   _____
   C. **ADDITIONAL TERMS:** _____
   _____
   _____
   _____
   _____
   _____
   _____

3. **MULTIPLE LISTING SERVICE:** Information about this listing ☐ will, ☐ will not, be provided to a multiple listing service ("MLS") of Broker's selection and the Property sale, price, terms, and financing will be provided to the MLS for publication, dissemination and use by persons and entities on terms approved by the MLS. Seller authorizes Broker to comply with all applicable MLS rules.

4. **TITLE:** Seller warrants that Seller and no other persons have title to the Property, except as follows: _____
_____

5. **COMPENSATION TO BROKER:**
   Notice: The amount or rate of real estate commissions is not fixed by law. They are set by each Broker individually and may be negotiable between Seller and Broker.
   A. Seller agrees to pay to Broker as compensation for services, irrespective of agency relationships, _____ percent of the listing price (or if a sales contract is entered into, of the sales price), or $ _____,
   AND _____ as follows:
   1. If Broker, Seller, cooperating broker, or any other person, produces a buyer(s) who offers to purchase the Property on the above price and terms, or on any price and terms acceptable to Seller during the Listing Period, or any extension;
   2. If within _____ calendar days after expiration of the Listing Period or any extension, the Property is sold, conveyed, leased, or otherwise transferred to anyone with whom Broker or a cooperating broker has had negotiations, provided that Broker gives Seller, prior to or within 5(or ☐ _____) days after expiration of the Listing Period or any extension, a written notice including the name(s) of the prospective purchaser(s). This section shall not apply if Seller enters into a valid listing agreement with another licensed real estate broker after the final termination of this Agreement;
   3. If the Property is withdrawn from sale, conveyed, leased, rented, otherwise transferred, or made unmarketable by a voluntary act of Seller, without Broker's consent, prior to expiration of the Listing Period, or any extension;
   4. If completion of the sale is prevented by default of Seller;
   5. If completion of the sale is prevented by a party to the transaction other than Seller, then only if and when Seller collects damages by suit, settlement, or otherwise, and then in an amount equal to one-half of the damages recovered, not to exceed the above compensation, after first deducting title and escrow expenses and the expenses of collection, if any.
   B. In addition, Seller agrees to pay: _____
   _____
   C. Broker is authorized to cooperate with other brokers, and divide with other brokers the above compensation in any manner acceptable to Broker;
   D. Seller hereby irrevocably assigns to Broker the above compensation from Seller's funds and proceeds in escrow.

6. **AGENCY RELATIONSHIPS:** Broker shall act as the agent for Seller in any resulting transaction. Depending upon the circumstances, it may be necessary or appropriate for Broker to act as an agent for both Seller and buyer, exchange party, or one or more additional parties ("Buyer"). Broker shall, as soon as practicable, disclose to Seller any election to act as a dual agent representing both Seller and Buyer. If a Buyer is procured directly by Broker or an associate licensee in Broker's firm, Seller hereby consents to Broker acting as a dual agent for Seller and such Buyer. In the event of an exchange, Seller hereby consents to Broker collecting compensation from additional parties for services rendered, provided there is disclosure to all parties of such agency and compensation. Seller understands that Broker may have or obtain listings on other properties, and that potential buyers may consider, make offers on, or purchase through Broker property the same as or similar to Seller's Property. Seller consents to Broker's representation of sellers and buyers of other properties before, during, and after the expiration of this Agreement.

7. **BROKER'S AND SELLER'S DUTIES:** Broker agrees to exercise reasonable effort and due diligence to achieve the purposes of this Agreement, and is authorized to advertise and market the Property in any medium selected by Broker. Seller agrees to consider offers presented by Broker, and to act in good faith toward accomplishing the sale of the Property. Seller further agrees to indemnify and hold Broker harmless from all claims, disputes, litigation, and/or judgements arising from any incorrect information supplied by Seller, whether contained in any document, omitted therefrom, or otherwise, or from any material facts which Seller knows but fails to disclose.

Broker and Seller acknowledge receipt of copy of this page, which constitutes Page 1 of _____ Pages.
Seller's Initials (_____) (_____) Broker's Initials (_____) (_____)

Published and Distributed by:
REAL ESTATE BUSINESS SERVICES, INC.
a subsidiary of the CALIFORNIA ASSOCIATION OF REALTORS®
525 South Virgil Avenue, Los Angeles, California 90020
PRINT DATE

OFFICE USE ONLY
Reviewed by Broker
or Designee _____
Date _____

EQUAL HOUSING
OPPORTUNITY

EXCLUSIVE AUTHORIZATION AND RIGHT TO SELL (A-14 PAGE 1 OF 2) REVISED 1/96

FIGURE 4-8

Property Address: _____

8. **DEPOSIT:** Broker is authorized to accept and hold on Seller's behalf a deposit to be applied toward the sales price.

9. **LOCKBOX:** A LOCKBOX is designed to hold a key to the Property to permit access to the Property by Broker, cooperating brokers, MLS participants, their authorized licensees and representatives ("lockbox users"), and accompanied prospective buyers. Broker, cooperating brokers, MLS and Association/Board of REALTORS® are **not** insurers against theft, loss, vandalism, or damage attributed to the use of a LOCKBOX. Seller is advised to verify the existence of, or obtain, appropriate insurance through Seller's own insurance broker. If Seller does not occupy the Property, Seller shall be responsible for obtaining occupant(s)' written permission for use of a LOCKBOX. Seller authorizes Broker to install a LOCKBOX: (Initial) YES (___/___)   NO (___/___)

10. **SIGN:** Seller authorizes Broker to install a FOR SALE/SOLD sign on the property: (Initial) YES (___/___)   NO (___/___)

11. **MEDIATION OF DISPUTES:** Broker and Seller agree to mediate any dispute or claim arising between them out of this contract or any resulting transaction before resorting to arbitration or court action. Mediation fees, if any, shall be divided equally among the parties involved. IF ANY PARTY COMMENCES AN ARBITRATION OR COURT ACTION BASED ON A DISPUTE OR CLAIM TO WHICH THIS PARAGRAPH APPLIES WITHOUT FIRST ATTEMPTING TO RESOLVE THE MATTER THROUGH MEDIATION, THEN IN THE DISCRETION OF THE ARBITRATOR(S) OR JUDGE, THAT PARTY SHALL NOT BE ENTITLED TO RECOVER ATTORNEY'S FEES, EVEN IF THEY WOULD OTHERWISE BE AVAILABLE TO THAT PARTY IN ANY SUCH ARBITRATION OR COURT ACTION. This mediation provision applies whether or not the Arbitration of Disputes provision is initialed. Exclusions are listed in paragraph 13.

12. **ARBITRATION OF DISPUTES: (If initialed by Broker and Seller):** Any dispute or claim in law or equity arising between Broker and Seller out of this contract or any resulting transaction, which is not settled through mediation, shall be decided by neutral, binding arbitration. The arbitration shall be conducted in accordance with Part III, Title 9 of the California Code of Civil Procedure. Judgment upon the award of the arbitrator(s) may be entered in any court having jurisdiction. The parties shall have the right to discovery in accordance with Code of Civil Procedure §1283.05. Exclusions are listed in paragraph 13.

   "NOTICE: BY INITIALING IN THE SPACE BELOW YOU ARE AGREEING TO HAVE ANY DISPUTE ARISING OUT OF THE MATTERS INCLUDED IN THE 'ARBITRATION OF DISPUTES' PROVISION DECIDED BY NEUTRAL ARBITRATION AS PROVIDED BY CALIFORNIA LAW AND YOU ARE GIVING UP ANY RIGHTS YOU MIGHT POSSESS TO HAVE THE DISPUTE LITIGATED IN A COURT OR JURY TRIAL. BY INITIALING IN THE SPACE BELOW YOU ARE GIVING UP YOUR JUDICIAL RIGHTS TO DISCOVERY AND APPEAL, UNLESS THOSE RIGHTS ARE SPECIFICALLY INCLUDED IN THE 'ARBITRATION OF DISPUTES' PROVISION. IF YOU REFUSE TO SUBMIT TO ARBITRATION AFTER AGREEING TO THIS PROVISION, YOU MAY BE COMPELLED TO ARBITRATE UNDER THE AUTHORITY OF THE CALIFORNIA CODE OF CIVIL PROCEDURE. YOUR AGREEMENT TO THIS ARBITRATION PROVISION IS VOLUNTARY."

   "WE HAVE READ AND UNDERSTAND THE FOREGOING AND AGREE TO SUBMIT DISPUTES ARISING OUT OF THE MATTERS INCLUDED IN THE 'ARBITRATION OF DISPUTES' PROVISION TO NEUTRAL ARBITRATION."

   Broker's Initials ____/____   Seller's Initials ____/____

13. **EXCLUSIONS FROM MEDIATION AND ARBITRATION:** The following matters are excluded from mediation and arbitration hereunder: **(a)** Judicial or non-judicial foreclosure or other action or proceeding to enforce a deed of trust, mortgage, or installment land sale contract as defined in Civil Code §2985; **(b)** An unlawful detainer action; **(c)** The filing or enforcement of a mechanic's lien; **(d)** Any matter which is within the jurisdiction of a probate or small claims court; and **(e)** An action for bodily injury or wrongful death, or for latent or patent defects to which Code of Civil Procedure §337.1 or §337.15 applies. The filing of a court action to enable the recording of a notice of pending action, for order of attachment, receivership, injunction, or other provisional remedies, shall not constitute a violation of the Mediation of Disputes and Arbitration of Disputes provisions.

14. **EQUAL HOUSING OPPORTUNITY:** The Property is offered in compliance with federal, state, and local anti-discrimination laws.

15. **ATTORNEY'S FEES:** In any action, proceeding, or arbitration arising out of this Agreement, involving Seller and/or Broker(s), the prevailing party shall be entitled to reasonable attorney's fees and costs, except as provided in paragraph 11.

16. **ENTIRE CONTRACT:** All prior discussions, negotiations, and agreements between the parties concerning the subject matter of this Agreement are superseded by this Agreement, which constitutes the entire contract and a complete and exclusive expression of their agreement with respect to its general subject matter, and may not be contradicted by evidence of any prior agreement or contemporaneous oral agreement. This Agreement and any supplement, addendum, or modification, including any photocopy or facsimile, may be executed in counterparts.

Seller warrants that Seller is the owner of the Property or has the authority to execute this contract. Seller acknowledges that Seller has read and understands this Agreement, and has received a copy.

Date _____, 19 _____ at _____, California   Date _____, 19 _____ at _____, California

Seller _____   Address _____

Seller _____   City _____ State _____ Zip _____

Date _____, 19 _____ at _____, California   Date _____, 19 _____ at _____, California

Broker (Firm) _____   Address _____

By (Agent) _____   City _____ State _____ Zip _____

This form is available for use by the entire real estate industry. It is not intended to identify the user as a REALTOR®. REALTOR® is a registered collective membership mark which may be used only by members of the NATIONAL ASSOCIATION OF REALTORS® who subscribe to its Code of Ethics.
PRINT DATE

Page 2 of _____ Pages.

OFFICE USE ONLY
Reviewed by Broker
or Designee _____
Date _____

EQUAL HOUSING OPPORTUNITY

EXCLUSIVE AUTHORIZATION AND RIGHT TO SELL (A-14 PAGE 2 OF 2) REVISED 1/96

This type of listing often contains a section referred to as a safety clause. A **SAFETY CLAUSE** *is a negotiated period (any agreed to time period) after the termination of a listing in which the listing broker may still be entitled to a commission.* To protect themselves, brokers must furnish the owner/seller with a list of persons to whom they have shown the property during the listing period. If the owner sells the property himself to someone on the list within the negotiated period, the broker may be entitled to a commission. This would not apply if the homeowner secured a new broker and sold the property to someone on the original list.

Net Listing (Must Be Used With Other Listing; Seldom Used)

A **NET LISTING** *is an authorization to sell that must be used with one of the other three listings. The broker's commission is any amount above the selling price set by the owner.* This listing may take the form of an open listing, an exclusive agency listing or an exclusive right to sell listing.

With this type of listing it is imperative for the broker to explain, in writing, the exact meaning of a net listing so that there is no confusion about any earned compensation. Since this is a vague type of listing and the possibility of wide variations in commission, a net listing is seldom used in California.

The best way to create an agency relationship is in writing. In order to be entitled to a commission, it must be in writing.

MULTIPLE LISTING SERVICE (MLS) (SUBAGENTS AND COOPERATING BROKERS)

A **MULTIPLE LISTING SERVICE (MLS)** *is an association of real estate agents providing for a pooling of listings, recent sales and the sharing of commissions on a specified basis.* The advantage to the seller is that his or her home or property will receive wider market exposure because it will be shown by other cooperating brokers.

A **MULTIPLE LISTING** *is a listing, usually an exclusive right to sell, taken by a member of a multiple listing service, with the provision that all members of the multiple listing service have the opportunity to find an interested buyer.* Sometimes in exclusive areas, sellers will request that their listing not be put into the multiple listing service. This would limit the number of people (looky-loo's) who just look at their properties for curiosity's sake.

An agent can delegate some authority to his or her salespeople or other brokers and their salespeople. This is known as subagency. *A SUBAGENT is a licensed broker or salesperson upon whom the powers of an agent have been conferred, not by the principal, but by the agent with the principal's authorization.* The agent can delegate purely mechanical acts such as typing to anyone, but a subagency can only be created with the principal's consent. The subagent has the same duties and responsibilities as the agent.

Subagents only have the powers that are given to them by the listing agent.

MLS SERVICES ARE NOW ON THE INTERNET

Internet MLS services are here to stay. Some are independent but most are still controlled by the local Boards of Realtors®. The California Association of Realtors® has the most complete system linking the MLS services of the entire state into one Internet address.

California Association of Realtors® has developed the www.car.org Website. *WWW.CAR.ORG (WWW.CA.REALTOR.COM) is a source of California MLS databases that links and provides the largest directory of homes for sale in California.* This has become the main source of available California home listings on the Internet. It breaks down our state by regions, maps and counties in order to help locate the MLS that covers whatever geographical area the user wants. It is the gateway to real estate listing information.

www.car.org (Listings from CAR's local boards) or
www.realtor.com (The nation's largest directory of homes for sale—it is the main source of information from Realtors®)
www.themls.com (Example: Combined L.A./Westside MLS)

COOPERATING BROKERS

A listing agreement usually authorizes the principal's agent to use cooperating brokers (subagents). *A COOPERATING BROKER is a non-listing broker (subagent) who also works to sell the listed property.* The cooperating broker performs the same acts as the agent to find a buyer. Cooperating brokers and salespeople are therefore subagents of the broker but they can also represent the buyer if it is disclosed to all parties. The purpose of a multiple listing service is to authorize and encourage subagency so that their members can act as cooperating brokers, thus sharing listings and commissions.

Agreements between brokers need not be in writing, although it is obviously preferred. Agreements between brokers and salespeople, however, must be in writing.

Cooperating brokers can also solve the problem of selling in other states (each state has its own licensing laws). Since a broker can only sell in states where he or she has a license, how can one sell a property, for commission, in another state? The answer is simple. Find a licensed, cooperating broker in that state.

A "pocket listing" is the unethical practice of not giving a new listing to the MLS until the listing broker first tries to sell it within the company.

COMMISSIONS

In real estate, a *COMMISSION is a fee paid, usually as a percentage, to an agent as compensation for his or her services.* Traditionally, it is payment from the seller to the agent who finds a ready, willing and able buyer to purchase the seller's property, according to the listing terms or any other terms acceptable to the seller. A *COMMISSION SPLIT is a previously agreed to split between a broker and his or her salesperson of a commission earned on a sale.* Commission rates vary throughout California, but usually range from 3% to 10% of the selling price. The listing agreement states that a commission is to be paid only when all the terms of the listing or other acceptable terms of the sale are met.

Commission rates are negotiable; the listing must have this statement printed in TEN POINT BOLD. Note: No documents can imply commissions are not negotiable.

When a broker lists a property for sale and a cooperating broker sells it, the commission is shared. Although the ratio for dividing the commission varies, it is often 50% to the listing broker, and 50% to the selling broker. If a salesperson is involved, he or she shares in their broker's part of the commission.

Salespeople only receive compensation for real estate transactions from their employing broker. All persons performing real estate activities for compensation must hold a valid real estate license.

A commission can be earned even if the sale is not finalized. The broker is entitled to a commission if all the terms of the listing agreement are met, provided the buyer is **ready, willing** and **able** to complete the transaction. This is true even if the seller changes his or her mind and refuses to sell. If there is a valid listing agreement, the seller is still responsible for the commission.

See Figure 4-9 for facts about commissions from auctions.

FIGURE 4-9

Real Estate Auction ... is another way to sell and receive commissions.

A *REAL ESTATE AUCTION is a meeting where interested parties come together and continue to offer higher bids (purchase prices) until only one bidder is left, to whom the property is sold.* The person making the highest bid buys the property. The time and place are always stated on the announcement, but the amount of advertising depends on the type of auction.

An auction is one of the quickest ways to unload a piece of property. Auctions are very popular with government agencies and builders in over-built or economically depressed communities. This can be a great way to pick up a real bargain property, as long as you bid using your head, not your heart. Auctions are emotional events where the excitement keeps rising until the property is sold. The best buys are at foreclosure sales, which are put on by public agencies, banks or savings banks.

But be forewarned: you will be bidding against seasoned professionals at most of these auctions. Be careful!

An *ABSOLUTE AUCTION is an auction where the property must be sold to the highest bidder no matter how low the final bid.* A *NO-SALE AUCTION is where there is a minimum bid underlying each property so that a certain price must be reached before the property will be sold.* In legitimate auctions, the starting bid is the minimum bid. But if that fact is not stated, make sure the minimum bid is stated clearly before the auction starts, or do not bid.

Do not attend a real property auction if you have not first seen the property and decided what you would be willing to pay for it. The broker auctioneers will be glad to give you maps or help you view the properties. Remember, don't get caught up in auction fever, because you should never go beyond your maximum bid price established well in advance of the auction.

An auction salesperson is also required to have a real estate license.

If an offer meets the exact terms of the listing, the agent has earned the commission even if the owner refuses to sell to the buyer.

A broker or his or her salesperson must be the procuring cause of a sale to earn a commission. *PROCURING CAUSE is defined as a series of unbroken events that lead to an acceptable agreement with the seller.* If there are several brokers trying to sell the same property, the one who is the procuring cause of the sale is entitled to the selling broker's portion of the commission.

TRANSFER DISCLOSURE STATEMENT

EASTON VS. STRASSBURGER

The agent has a duty to inspect and disclose. Both the listing and selling agents must conduct a reasonable, competent and diligent inspection of residential property. They must disclose, on the Transfer Disclosure Statement, any relevant facts that materially affect the value or desirability of the property.

A 1984 California Court of Appeals ruling in the case of **Easton versus Strassburger** greatly extended the liability of brokers engaged in real estate sales. **Be warned:** Brokers are required to be aware of all material facts negatively influencing the value of a property, whether they are obvious or not, and must disclose these facts to all prospective buyers.

TRANSFER DISCLOSURE STATEMENT
(SELLER & SELLING BROKER MUST PROVIDE THIS FORM)

The law requires sellers of residential property of from one to four units to provide prospective buyers with a Real Estate Transfer Disclosure Statement. This statement (Figures 4-10 and 4-11) identifies items of value attached to the structure or land and states whether these items are operational. It also asks the seller to identify any structural or material defects. This form provides an opportunity for the seller to completely disclose any problems of any kind that might adversely affect the value of the property. The obligation to prepare and deliver the Transfer Disclosure Statement to the prospective buyer is imposed upon the **seller and the seller's broker**. (See Civil Code 1102.6 for exemptions.)

Legally, the listing (selling) broker and the buyer's broker must conduct a reasonably competent, diligent and visual inspection of accessible areas of the property and disclose to a prospective buyer all material facts affecting value and desirability.

FIGURE 4-10

CALIFORNIA
ASSOCIATION
OF REALTORS®

REAL ESTATE TRANSFER DISCLOSURE STATEMENT
(CALIFORNIA CIVIL CODE 1102, ET SEQ.)

THIS DISCLOSURE STATEMENT CONCERNS THE REAL PROPERTY SITUATED IN THE CITY OF _____
_____, COUNTY OF _____, STATE OF CALIFORNIA,
DESCRIBED AS _____.
THIS STATEMENT IS A DISCLOSURE OF THE CONDITION OF THE ABOVE DESCRIBED PROPERTY IN COMPLIANCE
WITH SECTION 1102 OF THE CIVIL CODE AS OF _____, 19 _____. IT IS NOT A WARRANTY
OF ANY KIND BY THE SELLER(S) OR ANY AGENT(S) REPRESENTING ANY PRINCIPAL(S) IN THIS TRANSACTION,
AND IS NOT A SUBSTITUTE FOR ANY INSPECTIONS OR WARRANTIES THE PRINCIPAL(S) MAY WISH TO OBTAIN.

I
COORDINATION WITH OTHER DISCLOSURE FORMS

This Real Estate Transfer Disclosure Statement is made pursuant to Section 1102 of the Civil Code. Other statutes require disclosures, depending upon the details of the particular real estate transaction (for example: special study zone and purchase-money liens on residential property).

Substituted Disclosures: The following disclosures have or will be made in connection with this real estate transfer, and are intended to satisfy the disclosure obligations on this form, where the subject matter is the same:

☐ Inspection reports completed pursuant to the contract of sale or receipt for deposit.

☐ Additional inspection reports or disclosures: _____
_____

II
SELLER'S INFORMATION

The Seller discloses the following information with the knowledge that even though this is not a warranty, prospective Buyers may rely on this information in deciding whether and on what terms to purchase the subject property. Seller hereby authorizes any agent(s) representing any principal(s) in this transaction to provide a copy of this statement to any person or entity in connection with any actual or anticipated sale of the property.

THE FOLLOWING ARE REPRESENTATIONS MADE BY THE SELLER(S) AND ARE NOT THE REPRESENTATIONS OF THE AGENT(S), IF ANY. THIS INFORMATION IS A DISCLOSURE AND IS NOT INTENDED TO BE PART OF ANY CONTRACT BETWEEN THE BUYER AND SELLER.

Seller ☐ is ☐ is not occupying the property.

A. The subject property has the items checked below (read across):

☐ Range	☐ Oven	☐ Microwave
☐ Dishwasher	☐ Trash Compactor	☐ Garbage Disposal
☐ Washer/Dryer Hookups		☐ Rain Gutters
☐ Burglar Alarms	☐ Smoke Detector(s)	☐ Fire Alarm
☐ T.V. Antenna	☐ Satellite Dish	☐ Intercom
☐ Central Heating	☐ Central Air Conditioning	☐ Evaporator Cooler(s)
☐ Wall/Window Air Conditioning	☐ Sprinklers	☐ Public Sewer System
☐ Septic Tank	☐ Sump Pump	☐ Water Softener
☐ Patio/Decking	☐ Built-in Barbecue	☐ Gazebo
☐ Sauna		
☐ Hot Tub ☐ Locking Safety Cover*	☐ Pool ☐ Child Resistant Barrier*	☐ Spa ☐ Locking Safety Cover*
☐ Security Gate(s)	☐ Automatic Garage Door Opener(s)*	☐ Number Remote Controls _____
Garage: ☐ Attached	☐ Not Attached	☐ Carport
Pool/Spa Heater: ☐ Gas	☐ Solar	☐ Electric
Water Heater: ☐ Gas	☐ Water Heater Anchored, Braced, or Strapped*	
Water Supply: ☐ City	☐ Well	☐ Private Utility or
Gas Supply: ☐ Utility	☐ Bottled	Other _____
☐ Window Screens	☐ Window Security Bars ☐ Quick Release Mechanism on Bedroom Windows*	

Exhaust Fan(s) in _____ 220 Volt Wiring in _____ Fireplace(s) in _____
☐ Gas Starter _____ ☐ Roof(s): Type: _____ Age: _____ (approx.)
☐ Other: _____

Are there, to the best of your (Seller's) knowledge, any of the above that are not in operating condition? ☐ Yes ☐ No. If yes, then describe. (Attach additional sheets if necessary.): _____
_____

B. Are you (Seller) aware of any significant defects/malfunctions in any of the following? ☐ Yes ☐ No. If yes, check appropriate space(s) below.

☐ Interior Walls ☐ Ceilings ☐ Floors ☐ Exterior Walls ☐ Insulation ☐ Roof(s) ☐ Windows ☐ Doors ☐ Foundation ☐ Slab(s)
☐ Driveways ☐ Sidewalks ☐ Walls/Fences ☐ Electrical Systems ☐ Plumbing/Sewers/Septics ☐ Other Structural Components
(Describe: _____
_____)

If any of the above is checked, explain. (Attach additional sheets if necessary): _____
_____

*This garage door opener or child resistant pool barrier may not be in compliance with the safety standards relating to automatic reversing devices as set forth in Chapter 12.5 (commencing with Section 19890) of Part 3 of Division 13 of, or with the pool safety standards of Article 2.5 (commencing with Section 115920) of Chapter 5 of Part 10 of Division 104 of, the Health and Safety Code. The water heater may not be anchored, braced, or strapped in accordance with Section 19211 of the Health and Safety Code. Window security bars may not have quick release mechanisms in compliance with the 1995 Edition of the California Building Standards Code.

Buyer and Seller acknowledge receipt of copy of this page, which constitutes Page 1 of 2 Pages.
Buyer's Initials (_____) (_____) Seller's Initials (_____) (_____)

The copyright laws of the United States (17 U.S. Code) forbid the unauthorized reproduction of this form by any means, including facsimile or computerized formats.
Copyright © 1990-1997, CALIFORNIA ASSOCIATION OF REALTORS®. In compliance with Civil Code Section 1102.6 Effective July 1, 1997.

Published and Distributed by:
REAL ESTATE BUSINESS SERVICES, INC.
a subsidiary of the CALIFORNIA ASSOCIATION OF REALTORS®
525 South Virgil Avenue, Los Angeles, California 90020

┌ OFFICE USE ONLY ┐
Reviewed by Broker
or Designee _____
Date _____

EQUAL HOUSING
OPPORTUNITY

REAL ESTATE TRANSFER DISCLOSURE STATMENT (TDS-14 PAGE 1 OF 2) REVISED 3/97

FIGURE 4-11

Subject Property Address: _____ Date _____

C. Are you (Seller) aware of any of the following:

1. Substances, materials, or products which may be an environmental hazard such as, but not limited to, asbestos, formaldehyde, radon gas, lead-based paint, fuel or chemical storage tanks, and contaminated soil or water on the subject property .... ☐ Yes ☐ No
2. Features of the property shared in common with adjoining landowners, such as walls, fences, and driveways, whose use or responsibility for maintenance may have an effect on the subject property................................ ☐ Yes ☐ No
3. Any encroachments, easements or similar matters that may affect your interest in the subject property............... ☐ Yes ☐ No
4. Room additions, structural modifications, or other alterations or repairs made without necessary permits .... ☐ Yes ☐ No
5. Room additions, structural modifications, or other alterations or repairs not in compliance with building codes .... ☐ Yes ☐ No
6. Fill (compacted or otherwise) on the property or any portion thereof .... ☐ Yes ☐ No
7. Any settling from any cause, or slippage, sliding, or other soil problems.. ☐ Yes ☐ No
8. Flooding, drainage or grading problems .... ☐ Yes ☐ No
9. Major damage to the property or any of the structures from fire, earthquake, floods, or landslides..................... ☐ Yes ☐ No
10. Any zoning violations, nonconforming uses, violations of "setback" requirements.................................. ☐ Yes ☐ No
11. Neighborhood noise problems or other nuisances .... ☐ Yes ☐ No
12. CC&R's or other deed restrictions or obligations.. ☐ Yes ☐ No
13. Homeowners' Association which has any authority over the subject property .... ☐ Yes ☐ No
14. Any "common area" (facilities such as pools, tennis courts, walkways, or other areas co-owned in undivided interest with others). .... ☐ Yes ☐ No
15. Any notices of abatement or citations against the property... ☐ Yes ☐ No
16. Any lawsuits by or against the seller threatening to or affecting this real property, including any lawsuits alleging a defect or deficiency in this real property or "common areas" (facilities such as pools, tennis courts, walkways, or other areas, co-owned in undivided interest with others)... ☐ Yes ☐ No

If the answer to any of these is yes, explain. (Attach additional sheets if necessary.): _____
_____
_____

Seller certifies that the information herein is true and correct to the best of the Seller's knowledge as of the date signed by the Seller.

Seller _____ Date _____

Seller _____ Date _____

III
AGENT'S INSPECTION DISCLOSURE

(To be completed only if the Seller is represented by an agent in this transaction.)

THE UNDERSIGNED, BASED ON THE ABOVE INQUIRY OF THE SELLER(S) AS TO THE CONDITION OF THE PROPERTY AND BASED ON A REASONABLY COMPETENT AND DILIGENT VISUAL INSPECTION OF THE ACCESSIBLE AREAS OF THE PROPERTY IN CONJUNCTION WITH THAT INQUIRY, STATES THE FOLLOWING:

☐ Agent notes no items for disclosure.
☐ Agent notes the following items: _____
_____
_____
_____

Agent (Broker Representing Seller)_____ By _____ Date_____
                        (Please Print)   (Associate Licensee or Broker Signature)

IV
AGENT'S INSPECTION DISCLOSURE

(To be completed only if the agent who has obtained the offer is other than the agent above.)

THE UNDERSIGNED, BASED ON A REASONABLY COMPETENT AND DILIGENT VISUAL INSPECTION OF THE ACCESSIBLE AREAS OF THE PROPERTY, STATES THE FOLLOWING:

☐ Agent notes no items for disclosure.
☐ Agent notes the following items: _____
_____
_____

Agent (Broker Obtaining the Offer)_____ By _____ Date_____
                        (Please Print)   (Associate Licensee or Broker Signature)

V

BUYER(S) AND SELLER(S) MAY WISH TO OBTAIN PROFESSIONAL ADVICE AND/OR INSPECTIONS OF THE PROPERTY AND TO PROVIDE FOR APPROPRIATE PROVISIONS IN A CONTRACT BETWEEN BUYER AND SELLER(S) WITH RESPECT TO ANY ADVICE/INSPECTIONS/DEFECTS.

I/WE ACKNOWLEDGE RECEIPT OF A COPY OF THIS STATEMENT.

Seller _____ Date _____   Buyer _____ Date _____

Seller _____ Date _____   Buyer _____ Date _____

Agent (Broker Representing Seller)_____ By _____ Date_____
                                                        (Associate Licensee or Broker Signature)

Agent (Broker Obtaining the Offer) _____ By _____ Date_____
                                                        (Associate Licensee or Broker Signature)

SECTION 1102.3 OF THE CIVIL CODE PROVIDES A BUYER WITH THE RIGHT TO RESCIND A PURCHASE CONTRACT FOR AT LEAST THREE DAYS AFTER THE DELIVERY OF THIS DISCLOSURE IF DELIVERY OCCURS AFTER THE SIGNING OF AN OFFER TO PURCHASE. IF YOU WISH TO RESCIND THE CONTRACT, YOU MUST ACT WITHIN THE PRESCRIBED PERIOD.

A REAL ESTATE BROKER IS QUALIFIED TO ADVISE ON REAL ESTATE. IF YOU DESIRE LEGAL ADVICE, CONSULT YOUR ATTORNEY.

This form is available for use by the entire real estate industry. It is not intended to identify the user as a REALTOR®. REALTOR® is a registered collective membership mark which may be used only by members of the NATIONAL ASSOCIATION OF REALTORS® who subscribe to its Code of Ethics.

┌─ OFFICE USE ONLY ─┐
Reviewed by Broker
or Designee _____
Date _____

Page 2 of 2 Pages.

REAL ESTATE TRANSFER DISCLOSURE STATMENT (TDS-14 PAGE 2 OF 2) REVISED 3/97

The following sequence of events may help explain how the four parties (seller, seller's agent, buyer and buyer's agent) fill-in and sign the Transfer Disclosure Statement form:

1) The Transfer Disclosure Statement form should be filled out and signed completely by the seller at the time of listing the property. Since the seller is the one most familiar with the property, he or she must be encouraged to be forthright and honest about all known defects.

2) The seller's agent makes a visual, diligent inspection of the property, fills out the Transfer Disclosure Statement and signs at the same time the seller lists the property for sale.

3) The buyer should receive a copy of the Transfer Disclosure Statement and sign that he or she has received it before making a written offer.

4) The buyer's agent must also visually inspect the property, fill out the appropriate section of the statement and sign it.

5) If the buyer fails to receive the Transfer Disclosure Statement form prior to signing the contractual offer (Deposit Receipt), he or she has the right to cancel, after receipt, for any reason (three days if delivered by hand or five days if mailed). A written notice of termination must be delivered to the seller or to the seller's broker.

The Transfer Disclosure Statement (or amended Disclosure Statement) must be given to the prospective buyer as soon as practicable before the offer (Deposit Receipt) is signed.

AGENTS' OTHER RESPONSIBILITIES

TRUST ACCOUNTS (OTHER PEOPLE'S MONEY)

A broker, when receiving a buyer's money deposit (and instructions), either opens an escrow, gives it to the principal, or puts it in the broker's trust fund account. If not instructed otherwise, the money must go into the broker's trust fund account by the next business day.

A broker accepting a money deposit (and instructions) is required to give it to the principal, place it in a trust account or with an escrow company by the next business day. **Deposits are never the personal property of the broker.** Any moneys accepted should go, by the next business day, into an independent bank trust account in the name of the broker as trustee. Most trust accounts are non-interest bearing because all overages must be explained. Placing a buyer's cash or check in the broker's personal account is called commingling.

COMMINGLING *is the mixing together of the funds of a principal and a licensee.* Commingling is a violation of the Commissioner's Regulations.

> *Commingling is the illegal practice of mixing a client's money with private funds. By law, each entry in the broker's trust fund account (bank) must be identified.*

CONVERSION *is the unlawful misappropriation and use of a client's funds by a licensee.* A broker, who upon receipt spends his or her principal's deposit without the principal's authorization, has not commingled in a technical sense, but has converted. This is a much more serious violation with heavy criminal penalties.

A TRANSACTION FILE (KEEP FOR THREE YEARS)

A **TRANSACTION FILE** *is the file or folder* (**all** documents) *kept for three years by the broker for each real estate transaction in which the broker or his or her salespeople participated.* The commissioner of real estate has the right to inspect this file. Maintaining a complete, up-to-date transaction file is not only good business practice, **it is the law**.

A licensed broker must retain for three years copies of all listings, deposit receipts, canceled checks, trust fund records and other documents executed by the broker or obtained by him or her in connection with any real estate transaction. The retention period shall run from the date of the closing of the transaction or from the date of the listing, if the transaction is not consummated.

> *The Real Estate Commissioner requires that all records of a broker or salesperson be kept a minimum of three years, except the mortgage disclosure form (four years).*

AGENTS WHO BUY & SELL FOR THEIR OWN ACCOUNT (DISCLOSE YOU HAVE A REAL ESTATE LICENSE)

Many real estate professionals buy and sell property for themselves as part of their own personal investments (acting as a principal and not as an agent). The Real Estate Commissioner created a regulation requiring disclosure of license status (buyer and seller) which has the full force and effect of law. The commissioner has strongly suggested that it would be in the licensee's best interest to disclose this fact, in writing, as soon as possible. This protects the purchasers and others involved. Everyone should be aware that they are dealing with a person knowledgeable in real estate and that he or she is representing his or her own interests.

The most confusing situation is where a real estate agent, acting as an agent, decides to become a buyer or seller. In this case, the agent must tell everyone involved of the change in status, and make sure they understand all the implications of this change. It is up to the agent to prove that everyone understands this new position and how it will affect them. This should also be in writing.

POWER OF ATTORNEY

POWER OF ATTORNEY is acknowledged, written authorization of one person to act for another. There are two categories under power of attorney; 1) a general power of attorney and 2) a special power of attorney.

A *GENERAL POWER OF ATTORNEY allows the person so authorized to perform any act the principal could perform.* The person thus authorized to act on behalf of the principal is called the general attorney in fact.

A *GENERAL ATTORNEY IN FACT is an agent who may have the power to transact all of a principal's business.* The specific powers conferred must be set down in writing, duly acknowledged and recorded with the county recorder's office, in the county where the property is located, in order for the agency to take effect. **Death of either party, or an acknowledged declaration from the principal, may revoke this power.**

The power of attorney must be recorded in the county where the property is located in order to be properly exercised.

A *SPECIAL POWER OF ATTORNEY allows the person so authorized to perform only a specific act (for example, sell your house).* The *SPECIAL ATTORNEY IN FACT has the authorization to perform only a specific act.*

A real estate agent is a "special attorney in fact" who is usually authorized to find a ready, willing and able buyer.

A listing agreement makes the broker a special agent to perform the authorized act of selling, exchanging or otherwise transferring real property. Usually an agent is given expressed authority, by written agreement (listing), to sell a home. If not otherwise expressed in writing, the agent is allowed to delegate parts of that authority under three circumstances:

1. If the act to be performed is purely mechanical, such as typing out a standard form.

2. If the agent is not legally qualified to do something, such as notarizing a document that requires a state license.

3. If it is customary to delegate authority for that task in that business or locality.

Agency & Its Responsibilities

TORTS

A **TORT** *is any civil injury or wrong committed upon a person or that person's property.* Fraud, misrepresentation, negligence and secret profit all stem from a breach of an agent's duty. In some cases they can even be considered criminal acts. The broker and his or her salespeople, as professionals, are expected to maintain a high standard of ethics. They are responsible for their own acts and representations even when following the seller's directions.

MISREPRESENTATION OF A MATERIAL FACT

A misrepresentation by a broker or salesperson may be material or immaterial. If the representation is slight, or would not have a measurable effect on the people relying on it, it is not a material fact. When a broker misrepresents his or her authority to act as an agent for someone else, he or she may be liable to the person who relies on the misrepresentation. A statement such as "I think this is the best house on the street" is a statement of opinion and is not considered a misrepresentation.

> *"Puffing" is a statement that exaggerates a property's benefits. It is expected. But an agent should never misrepresent a material fact.*

A misrepresentation of a material fact can financially injure someone, and may be punishable under the Civil Code or the Commissioner's Regulations.

There are three types of misrepresentations:

1. Innocent Misrepresentations
2. Negligent Misrepresentations
3. Fraudulent Misrepresentations (nondisclosure)

The first misrepresentation usually has no broker liability. The second and third are subject to civil penalties and the real estate commissioner's actions. **INNOCENT MISREPRESENTATIONS** *are false statements that are not known to be false at the time they are made.* These statements do not usually warrant legal liability for the broker, but can cause a rescission of any contract. Everyone involved would then be reinstated to their original positions.

> *An agent who sells the wrong condo because a prankster switched the condo unit's number is an example of an innocent misrepresentation.*

Chapter 4

NEGLIGENT MISREPRESENTATIONS are statements believed to be true but made without reasonable grounds and are, in fact, false. This is breach of duty without fraudulent intent. The broker is liable for any negligent statements made to a buyer or seller. Such statements are in effect a form of deceit.

> *A room was added without a building permit, but the agent stated that there was a building permit without first checking. This would be negligent misrepresentation.*

FRAUDULENT MISREPRESENTATIONS are statements made at a time when the broker knows the statement to be false or does not disclose material facts. This is actual fraud. Any contract made under the influence of fraudulent information may become void, and the person making the fraudulent statements may be liable for civil or even criminal fraud.

> *Intentional deceptions or the concealment of material facts are fraudulent misrepresentations.*

SECRET PROFITS

An agent may not make any secret profit. This would be a violation or breach of the fiduciary relationship between the principal and the real estate agent. All financial offers, whether legitimate or not, must be presented to the seller. So, if a real estate agent is offered a secret profit, he or she has a duty to let the principal know of the bribe. In addition, the broker may not allow others (friends and relatives) to make a secret profit with his or her knowledge.

WARRANTY OF AUTHORITY

As an agent, the broker warrants that he or she has the authority to represent another person. If there is a written listing between the seller and the broker, he or she has an expressed warranty of authority to offer the property for sale. The problem arises when the broker, without a listing, offers to sell a property to an unsuspecting buyer, who relies on the fact that the agent has certain authority. In such cases, the broker could be liable for this untrue representation. A broker gives implied warranty of authority to act for a seller by the mere fact that he or she shows the seller's property.

When a broker represents a seller, he or she does not warrant that the seller has the capacity to sell. If in fact the seller does not have the capacity to contract, then the broker is not liable as long as he or she did not have knowledge of the fact. However, if the broker has knowledge that the seller could not contract, then the broker could be liable to the buyer.

100

TERMINATING AN AGENCY RELATIONSHIP

TERMINATION OF AGENCY

An agency relationship between a seller and a real estate broker can be terminated by operation of law or by the acts of either the broker or the seller. Figure 4-12 shows the six subcategories of these methods.

FIGURE 4-12

1. Expiration of the agency (listing) agreement

The Exclusive Agency Listing Agreement and the Exclusive Authorization and Right to Sell Listing Agreement have a definite termination date. These listings will end automatically on the stated date if not terminated in some other way before that date. The other type of listing, an open listing, does not require a termination date because it can be terminated at any time.

2. Destruction of the property

If the property is destroyed or damaged by certain causes, such as earthquake or fire, the listing agreement is terminated.

3. Death or incapacity of the broker or seller

If either the agent or seller is not mentally or physically able to complete the agency relationship (personal service contract) it is terminated.

4. Agreement by both the broker and seller

If both parties to a contract want to end it, it is considered terminated by mutual agreement.

5. Renouncement of the listing agreement by the broker

The broker can refuse to fulfill the listing agreement but may be subject to damages for breach of contract.

6. Revocation of the listing agreement by the seller

The seller can refuse to sell the listed property but may be liable for the commission if the broker has found a buyer who is ready, willing and able to purchase the property.

LISTING AGREEMENT COPIES
(GIVE COPY WHEN SIGNED)

Always give the buyer and seller a copy of any agreement when signed. Couples who are considered "one legal person" receive one copy; so if there are six couples, give six copies.

A copy of the listing agreement or any other real estate agreement, including the agency relationship and the transfer disclosure statements, **must** be given to the signing party immediately after they are signed. This is a requirement of the Commissioner's Regulations and a violation could result in license suspension or revocation.

DISCLOSURE OF AIDS AND DEATH

An occupant's death from AIDS or AIDS related illness, or any other contagious disease, is a highly emotional issue. Brokers must strive to balance the principle of full disclosure against the right to privacy of an AIDS victim. Disclosing casually that a tenant or former tenant (owner or occupant) died, or is dying, from AIDS might very well be in violation of that person's civil rights and might expose the broker to civil or criminal penalties. By law sellers, brokers and landlords have no liability for failure to disclose a prior occupant's death or its cause after three years. On the other hand, intentional misrepresentation concerning an occupant's death on the property, in response to direct inquiry, is illegal.

The broker does not have to disclose cause of death unless there is a direct inquiry.

A BROKERAGE MUST BE RUN LIKE A BUSINESS

A "company dollar" is the dollar (income and commissions) a broker receives after all commissions have been paid.

A **GROSS DOLLAR** *is all the income that is received by the office before commissions.* A **COMPANY DOLLAR** *is the amount left to management after payment of all commissions, including in-house salespeople and other multiple listings brokers and salespeople.* See Figure 4-13. The concept of the company dollar allows the brokerage to examine and focus on how their after-commission income is spent.

FIGURE 4-13

The following is a general list of how a brokerage spends its company dollar after paying commissions:

1.	**15 to 21** %	**Advertising** - Newspapers, signs
2.	**10 to 15** %	**Staff Salaries** - Secretary and receptionist
3.	**10 to 15** %	**Entertainment and Travel**
4.	**7 to 10** %	**Facilities** - Interest, property taxes and maintenance
5.	**7 to 10** %	**Sales Manager Salary**
6.	**5 to 9** %	**Telephone**
7.	<u>**24 to 41**</u> %	<u>**Return to Owners**</u> - <u>profit, training, and income taxes</u>

"TOE" is the acronym for Total Operating Expense.

T   Total

O   Operating

E   Expense

*The **DESK COST** is the total operating expense divided by the number of salespeople. The desk cost tells the broker the financial loss caused by an empty desk or an unproductive salesperson.*

A NEW BROKERAGE TREND: ONE-STOP SHOPPING

The soft real estate markets of the last few years have meant shrinking profit margins and fewer company dollars. Some brokerages have responded to this by offering one-stop shopping. ***ONE-STOP SHOPPING*** *means the brokerage is involved in multiple facets of property transactions, including escrow and title services, property management and mortgage brokerage.*

A recent trend has shown significant increases in large real estate brokerages providing mortgages and trust deeds to buyers. Often, though, sales agents would prefer not to use an in-house lender. The reason? If something goes wrong in-house, it will reflect on the sales agent. Brokerages are countering this by hiring experienced mortgage executives and top-notch processing and closing staff.

ALLIANCE ASSOCIATION (NEW ASSOCIATIONS)

*An **ALLIANCE** is an association (cooperative) of members who seek to reduce their costs by negotiating service discounts with a company and then referring their members to that company.* For example, a large retail discount chain may charge their members $100 to refer them to real estate brokers who in turn reduce their commissions by 35%. A real estate broker may refer his or her clients to a good carpet cleaner if their clients receive a genuine discount.

INTERNET SITES:
REAL ESTATE LISTINGS & FRANCHISES

Listing Sites

http://www.prnewswire.com (Listings in Spanish)
http://sucase.net (Listings in Spanish)
http://db.inman.com/inman/inf/inman (Independent Broker)
http://www.homeseekers.com (Independent Listings)
http://www.baynet.com (San Francisco Area Listings)
http://listinglink.com (Listing Link, LLC - Internet Listing Service)
http://www.us-digital.com (Listings-Homeweb)
http://realestatenet.com (Remax of California-Listings)
(Others) _____

_____
_____
_____

Franchise Sites

http://www.remax.com (Remax Real Estate)
http://www.lyonrealty.com (Independent Broker)
http://www.century 21.com (Century 21)
http://www.sevilleprop.com (Independent Broker)
http://www.mcguirere.com (Regional Franchise)
http://www.fredsands.com (Regional Franchise)
http://www.mm4re.com (Mason-Duffie Regional Franchise)
http://www.tarbellrealtors.com (Large Independent)
(Others) _____

_____
_____
_____

TERMINOLOGY - CHAPTER 4

A. Agency	**K.** Secret Profit	**U.** Multiple Listing Service
B. Fiduciary Relationship	**L.** Easton Decision	**V.** Transfer Disclosure Statement
C. Agency Disclosure Form	**M.** Principal	**W.** Commingling
D. Estoppel	**N.** General Attorney in Fact	**X.** Conversion
E. Ratification	**O.** Special Attorney in Fact	**Y.** Tort
F. Third Party	**P.** Subagent	**Z.** Innocent Misrepresentation
G. Employee	**Q.** Open Listing	**AA.** Negligent Misrepresentation
H. Independent Contractor	**R.** Exclusive Agency Listing	**BB.** Fraudulent Misrepresentation
I. Dual Agency	**S.** Exclusive Right to Sell Listing	
J. Policy Manual	**T.** Net Listing	

1.____ To mixing of funds held in trust with personal funds.

2.____ Authorization from a property owner giving a real estate agent the non-exclusive right to secure a purchaser. Other brokers, or the owners themselves, may also solicit a purchaser.

3.____ The unlawful taking and use of another's property placed in your trust, as an agent, by that person.

4.____ The person (s) who employs a real estate agent, usually through a listing agreement.

5.____ The relationship between the principal and the principal's agent that arises out of a contract, either expressed or implied, written or oral, wherein the agent is employed by the principal to do certain acts dealing with a third party.

6.____ A person upon whom the powers of an agent have been conferred, not by the principal, but by an agent as authorized by the principal.

7.____ A civil wrong committed against a person or property, independent of any contractual agreement.

8.____ The theory of law that states a person cannot suddenly assert a legal right when that person has neglected to assert it previously. For example: If someone claims to be your agent and you know about it and don't stop that person, you can't later claim that person was they were not acting on your behalf.

9.____ A person who acts for another, selling final results and using his or her own judgment to achieve those results.

10.____ The approval of an act performed on behalf of a person without previous authorization, such as the approval by a principal of a previously unauthorized act of an agent.

11.____ An agency relationship in which the agent acts concurrently for both of the principals (buyer and seller), with their consent, in a transaction.

12.____ An association of real estate agents that provides a pooling of listings and the sharing of commissions.

13.____ Any party to a transaction other than the principal with whom you have an agency relationship.

14.____ One who is authorized to perform many acts for another under a power of attorney.

15.____ A listing agreement employing a broker as the sole agent for the seller of real property, under the terms of which the broker is entitled to a commission unless the homeowner sells the property.

16.____ A listing agreement employing a broker to act as an agent for the seller of real property. Under the terms of this agreement, the broker is entitled to a commission if the property is sold during the duration of the listing by the broker or by the owner without an agent.

17.____ A listing that provides for the agent to retain, as compensation for his or her services, all sums received over and above a net price to the owner.

18.____ The major court decision which requires an agent to disclose any physical defects or evidence of defects that could affect the value of real property.

19.____ An agent's making of additional money in a real estate transaction without disclosing it to the principal and third party.

20.____ Knowingly making false and deceptive statements to help sell a property.

21.____ Making false statements about a property, without realizing it.

22.____ Making false statements regarding a property that could have been checked out or verified.

23.____ A form that notifies buyers of any physical defects to a property by requires the seller and the agent to list any evidence of defects of which they are aware.

24.____ A form presented to the principal (s) in a transaction stating exactly who the agent is working for, the buyer, the seller, or both.

25.____ The relationship between the agent and the principal which requires the highest level of trust and good faith.

26.____ One who works directly for another person and is told what to do and is controlled in how they do it.

27.____ A written book of procedures explaining how a broker expects the agents working under him or her to conduct business and handle routine problems.

28.____ Someone authorized to represent a principal in a specific task, such as selling a property.

MULTIPLE CHOICE

1. The Real Estate Commissioner's regulations require a broker to have a signed employment agreement for each of his or her salespeople. A copy of this agreement must be kept by both parties for:

   A. one year from the date of termination
   B. two years from the date of termination
   C. three years from the date of termination
   D. the parties do not have to keep copies

2. A broker is required, by law, to make certain representations about the property he or she is selling. These requirements are spelled out in the:

   A. Agency Disclosure Form
   B. Listing Agreement
   C. Transfer Disclosure Statement
   D. Business and Professional Code

3. The Agency Disclosure Law went into effect in:

   A. 1986
   B. 1988
   C. 1990
   D. 1991

4. Real estate law (Section 2013) requires that an exclusive listing:

   A. must have a definite starting time
   B. be unilateral in nature
   C. be printed in ten point bold
   D. must have a definite termination date

5. The unethical practice of NOT giving a new listing to an MLS until the listing broker first tries to sell it within the company is called a (an):

   A. negligent misrepresentation
   B. secret profit
   C. pocket listing
   D. illegal conversion

6. In any real estate transaction, the salesperson would receive his or her commission from:

   A. the listing agent
   B. his or her broker
   C. the selling agent
   D. the buyer's broker

7. A statement that exaggerates a property's benefits is called:

   A. innocent misrepresentations
   B. steering
   C. negligent misrepresentations
   D. puffing

8. The salesperson, who is required to work for a broker by law, is technically called a:

   A. subagent
   B. principal
   C. third party
   D. all of the above

9. Real estate salespeople are:

   A. employees of the seller
   B. employees of the buyer
   C. agents of the buyer or seller
   D. agents of the title company

10. The proper way to create an agency relationship is by:

    A. estoppel
    B. written agreement
    C. ratification
    D. implication

CHAPTER 5
Contracts

http://www.calbar.org (State Bar of California)
http://www.leginfo.ca.gov/calaw.html (California Law)
http://www.leginfo.ca.gov/statute.html (State Statutes)
http://www.courtinfo.ca.gov (California Courts)
http://www.law.vill.edu/fed-Ct/ca09.html (9th Circuit Court)

Nothing is as important to the real estate broker and his or her salespeople than the law of contracts. Because every phase of a real estate transaction involves one or more contracts, it is important to understand the basic rules that govern the creation and life of a contract. This chapter will explain the elements of contracts and illustrate, in detail, the important parts of a deposit receipt (the Residential Purchase Agreement).

CONTRACTS IN GENERAL

A **CONTRACT** *is an agreement to perform or not to perform a certain act or service.* Every contract consists of a promise or a set of promises that are enforceable by law. These promises may be created in two ways, either in an expressed manner or in an implied manner. An **EXPRESSED CONTRACT** *is an agreement that is made either orally or in writing.* Listings, deposit receipts and leases are all expressed contracts.

> *Contracts may be either oral (rare) or in writing, but any important contract should be written, even if not required by law.*

109

On the other hand, an *IMPLIED CONTRACT is created when an agreement is made by acts and conduct (implication) rather than by words*. For example, suppose you entered a hardware store where you had an account, picked up an $8 paint brush, and waved it at the clerk as you left. The clerk, judging from your conduct, would assume that you wanted the paint brush charged to your account and would bill you accordingly. An implied contract would have been formed. Implied contracts are not used in the practice of real estate.

> *Contracts are expressed in words or implied (but not in real estate) by actions.*

A *BILATERAL CONTRACT is a promise made by one party in exchange for the promise of another party*. It is a promise for a promise. For instance, if a homeowner offers a painter $400 to paint his or her garage, and the painter agrees to do it, a bilateral contract is formed: The painter promises to paint the garage, while the homeowner promises to give the painter $400. *When only one party makes a promise for an act of another, the agreement is called a UNILATERAL CONTRACT.* It is a promise for an act. If someone acts upon an offer, the one making the offer is obligated to complete his or her promise. Suppose Mr. Bentley offers a reward to any person who can identify the arsonist who set his home on fire. Because this is a unilateral contract, Mr. Bentley is required to give the reward to any person who can fulfill the obligation.

> *A contract can be either bilateral (two promises) or unilateral (one promise).*

Contracts may be classified in any of these four ways:

> **(1) VALID** — A contract that is binding and enforceable in a court of law.

> *Performance is expected or legal action can be filed.*

> **(2) VOIDABLE** — Valid on its face, but one or more of the parties may reject it.

> *Victim can rescind, cancel or annul.*

> **(3) VOID** — No contract exists, and therefore it has no legal effect.

> *Lacks one of the essential elements of a contract.*

> **(4) UNENFORCEABLE** — Valid, but for some reason cannot be proved or sued upon.

> *Laws have changed making the performance illegal.*

LIFE OF A CONTRACT
(A CONTRACT HAS THREE BASIC PHASES)

Phase 1 - Negotiation

This is the negotiation period. During this period the buyer and seller discuss the possibility of a contract. If there is mutual interest between the parties, then an offer, or perhaps several offers, can be made. The offer becomes a contract when accepted by both parties, provided that all the other elements necessary for the creation of a contract are present.

Phase 2 - Performance

This is the performance stage of the contract. An *EXECUTORY CONTRACT is a legal agreement, the provisions of which have yet to be completely fulfilled.* A deposit receipt is executory until payment is made and title is transferred. Then it becomes executed. A land contract might be executory for years.

Phase 3 - Completion

This stage occurs after a contract has been completed. An *EXECUTED CONTRACT is one that has either been discharged or performed.* After a contract has been completed, there is the warranty that every aspect of the contract has been properly performed. The contract lives on until the legal right to bring legal action is over; this is called the statute of limitations. After this, the recorded real estate transaction becomes history.

This term should not be confused with the execution of a contract. To **EXECUTE** *a contract is to sign a contract,* while the **EXECUTION** *of a contract is the* **act** *of performing or carrying out the contract.*

A contract to be performed is called "executory"; a completely performed contract has been "executed." The contract lives on until legal right to bring legal action has expired. This is called the "statute of limitations."

ELEMENTS OF A CONTRACT

ELEMENTS OF A CONTRACT

According to the California Civil Code there must be four elements to any valid contract whether it involves real estate or not. However in real estate, contracts generally must be in writing. See Figure 5-1.

FIGURE 5-1

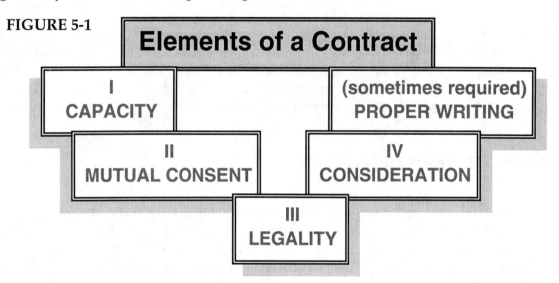

These are the four elements of any contract; if it involves real estate there is a fifth element (proper written). The following are NOT essential elements of a valid contract:

> *1) money (there can be other consideration)*
> *2) writing (but real estate contracts require it)*
> *3) performance (but failure of performance is a breach)*

1. Capacity

For a contract to be valid there must be two or more parties who have the legal capacity to contract. Everyone, **except** for the following, is capable of contracting: 1) minors, 2) incompetents and 3) convicts.

MINOR

A *MINOR is a person under the age of eighteen.* A minor cannot make contracts relating to real property or property not in his or her immediate possession or control, and does not have the right to employ an agent, **unless the minor is emancipated**. An *EMANCIPATED minor is one who has the contractual rights of an adult.* The three ways that a minor becomes emancipated are:

1. Through marriage
2. Member or former member of the armed forces
3. Declared to be self-supporting by the courts.

A minor who has been (emancipated) has legal capacity. Once emancipated, always emancipated. Otherwise, a contract or deed signed by a minor would be void. Any minor can acquire property by gift or inheritance.

A contract with a minor is void since a minor cannot delegate authority. A minor may, however, buy and sell real estate through a guardian if the action is given court approval.

INCOMPETENT

An **INCOMPETENT** *is a person who is judged to be of unsound mind.* Such a person has no power to contract; any contract made is void. In real estate transactions with incompetents, it is necessary to have the guardian's decision approved by the court. However, both minors and incompetents may acquire real property by gift or inheritance.

CONVICTS

CONVICTS *are persons who have lost their civil rights during their imprisonment.* Convicts usually do not have the right to contract, but they do not forfeit any property in their possession. They may acquire property by gift, inheritance or will, but can only convey property if the action is ratified by the California Adult Authority.

Criminal acts (illegal acts) are prosecuted by the city or county prosecutor.

ALIENS *are not citizens of the United States but they have the right to own property in California.* This surprises many people, but it is true that any person, whether he or she is a U.S. citizen or not, may buy, hold or transfer real property.

2. Mutual Consent

Mutual consent is an offer by one party and acceptance by the other party.

This is the second major requirement of a valid contract. *MUTUAL CONSENT is an offer of one party and acceptance of that offer by the other party.* This acceptance need not be a true "meeting of the minds" of the parties because they are bound only by their apparent intentions as evidenced by words or acts. Since courts cannot read minds, any secret or unexpressed intentions are immaterial. The consent must be genuine and free from fraud or mistake, and there must be a true intention to be obligated or it may be voidable by one or both of the parties.

Death does not cancel most contracts; they are binding on the estate, except a listing agreement, which is an employment (personal service) contract.

THE OFFER

An *OFFER expresses a person's willingness to enter into a contract.* The *OFFEROR is the person (buyer) who has made the offer,* and the *OFFEREE is the person (seller) to whom the offer has been made.* The offer made by the offeror must be communicated to the offeree. Every offer must have contractual intent. *CONTRACTUAL INTENT exists when a party communicates an offer to another with the intention of forming a binding contract.* For example, a social invitation to attend a party is not meant to be a contract and therefore lacks contractual intent. Likewise, an advertisement in the newspaper is not an offer, but merely an invitation to deal. In real estate, a condition must often be met before a contract becomes binding. If the condition is not satisfied, there is no contractual intent and no binding agreement.

Finally, an offer must be definite and certain in its terms. *DEFINITE AND CERTAIN means that the precise acts to be performed must be clearly stated.* A court can neither create contracts for parties nor fix the terms and conditions of any contract. An *ILLUSORY CONTRACT is one in which the terms are uncertain, therefore the contract is unenforceable.*

An "illusory contract" appears to be a contract but it is not definite and certain, so it is unenforceable.

A buyer can withdraw his or her offer anytime prior to receiving communication of its acceptance and receive a refund of the money deposited.

ACCEPTANCE

ACCEPTANCE is the consent to the terms by the offeree. The person to whom the offer is made must know he or she has been made an offer before that person can accept the offer. Normally, when the requested act is performed, the offer is automatically accepted. If the offeree, however, does not intend his or her act to be an acceptance, or has no knowledge of the offer, there can be no real acceptance. Acceptance of an offer must be in the manner specified in the offer, but if no particular manner of acceptance is specified, then acceptance may be made by any reasonable or usual mode.

Silence cannot be interpreted as an acceptance of an offer because a party cannot be forced to express rejection of an offer. One cannot say "If I do not hear from you in 10 days the offer is considered accepted." There must be a communicated acceptance of an offer, in writing, personally or by registered mail.

The broker most likely to have earned a commission is the one who has communicated acceptance of the offer.

The acceptance must be absolute and unqualified, because if it modifies the terms of the offer, it becomes a counter offer. A *COUNTER OFFER is the rejection of an original offer and the proposal of a new offer.* The offeree rejects the offer then becomes the offeror of the counter offer. Any offer after the original offer is a counter offer. **Once there is a counter offer, the previous offer is automatically terminated**. (See Counter Offer form, Figure 5-12.)

TERMINATION OF AN OFFER

The hope of the offeror is that the other party will accept and that a contract will be formed, but most initial offers are rejected. Here are six ways an offer can be terminated:

Lapse of Time - The offer is terminated if the offeree fails to accept within a prescribed period.

Communication of Revocation - An offer can be withdrawn anytime before the other party has communicated his or her acceptance.

Failure of Offeree to Fulfill a Condition — A specified condition must be accepted in a prescribed manner or the offer is terminated.

Rejection — If the offer is rejected, it is terminated.

Death or Insanity of the Offeror or Offeree — This would void the offer. The death of the offeror or offeree constitutes a revocation of the offer — the offer died with the death of the offeror.

Illegality of Purpose — If a condition or the purpose of a contract is illegal, then the contract is terminated.

GENUINE CONSENT (CONTRACT IS VOID OR VOIDABLE BY VICTIM)

The final requirement for mutual consent is that the offer and acceptance must be real or genuine. If not, the contract is void or voidable by the victim. Genuine consent does not exist if any of the following conditions are present:

FRAUD — *Occurs when a person misrepresents a material fact, knowing it is not true, or is carelessly indifferent to the truth of the stated facts.* The contract is void or voidable, depending on the degree of fraud.

MISREPRESENTATION — *Occurs when one makes false statements.*

MISTAKE — *Exists when both parties are mistaken as to the matter of the agreement, or where the subject matter of the contract ceases to exist.* A mistake is also void or voidable.

> **Example**: I offer to buy your mountain cabin but neither of us knows it has burned down.

DURESS — *Is the unlawful detention of a person and/or that person's property.*

MENACE — *Is a threat to commit duress*, but it also can be a threat of unlawful violent injury to a person and/or his or her character as a party to the contract.

UNDUE INFLUENCE — *Occurs when a person in a position of authority uses that authority to an unfair advantage.* This is usually found in a confidential relationship.

Duress, menace and undue influence are voidable because the contract was entered into under pressure.

All or any of the above acts make the contract voidable.

3. Legality

A contract that forces one to break the law is void.

A contract must be legal in its formation and operation. Both the consideration and its objective must also be lawful. The objective refers to what the contract requires the parties to do or not to do. If the contract consists of a single objective, which is unlawful in whole or in part, then the contract is void. If there are several objectives, the contract is normally valid as to those parts that are lawful.

The law will not enforce an illegal contract. If an illegal contract is not completed, the courts will not force its completion. Even if an illegal contract is completed, the courts will rarely enforce it unless the law violated was designed to protect one of the parties.

> **Example**: A contract to bribe a city building inspector to accept substandard work for $5,000 is illegal and void.

4. Consideration (Anything Of Value)

VALUABLE CONSIDERATION in a contract is anything of value given by one party to another party to make the agreement binding. A valid contract must have sufficient consideration. Consideration need not be money. It may: (1) benefit the person making the contract or another person, (2) be a loss suffered or agreed to be suffered or (3) be an agreement not to bring a legal suit. If the price paid is a promise, consideration may be a promise for a promise. The important point is that the consideration must be of some value.

Payment of money is not necessary as consideration. It can also be a benefit, like the performance of an act or the nonperformance (forbearance) of an act.

Some rare types of contracts require that consideration be adequate. In such contracts the condition of adequate consideration must be met for those contracts to be enforceable. Other contracts, without such a condition, are enforceable no matter what the consideration is, as long as it is agreed on by all parties.

Proper Writing (Real Estate Contracts)

Sometimes (mistakenly) referred to as the "fifth" element of a contract because it is so important.

A contract for personal property can be oral or written, but the Statute of Frauds requires that most real estate contracts be in writing. By law, all contracts may be oral except those specifically required by the Statute of Frauds to be in writing. See Figure 5-2.

In real estate, a contract usually must be in writing, but not always. A listing agreement must be in writing to enforce the payment of a commission. Oral agreements between brokers to share commissions are binding. Personal property contracts, like rental agreements, for one year or less, need not be in writing. Any contract that can't be performed within a year from the date of signing must be in writing.

Parol Evidence Rule

***PAROL EVIDENCE** refers to prior oral or written agreements of the parties, or even oral agreements concurrent (contemporaneous) with a written contract.* Under the "parol evidence rule," a contract expressed in writing is intended to be complete and final as an expression of the rights and duties of the contracting parties. Parol evidence means that prior oral or written agreements of the parties **cannot** be introduced as evidence. The courts will permit such outside evidence to be introduced only when the written contract is incomplete, ambiguous or when it is necessary to show that the contract is not enforceable because of mistake or fraud.

Rarely will the courts allow prior "oral parts or an entire oral contract" to be substituted for a later written contract. The courts would be jammed with people who wanted to change their contracts. So do it properly. Make only written real estate contracts.

FIGURE 5-2

STATUTE OF FRAUDS

Most contracts, which by statute are required to be in writing, are found under the Statute of Frauds. The Statute of Frauds was first adopted in England in 1677 and became part of English common law. Subsequently, it was introduced into this country and has become part of California's law. The main purpose of this law is to prevent forgery, perjury and dishonest conduct by unscrupulous people, thus improving the existence and terms of certain important types of contracts.

The statute provides that certain contracts are invalid unless those contracts are in writing and signed by either the parties to be charged or their agents. Under California's Civil Code, the following contracts must be in writing:

1. Any agreement where the terms will not be performed within one year following the making of the contract.

2. A special promise to answer for the debt, default or nonperformance of another, except in cases provided for by the Civil Code.

3. Agreement made upon the consideration of marriage, other than a mutual promise to marry.

4. An agreement for the leasing of real property for a period longer than one year (one year and one day), or for the sale of real property or of interest therein. It also applies to any agreement authorizing an agent to perform the above acts.

5. An agreement employing an agent, broker or any other person to purchase, sell or lease real estate for more than one year. It is also an agreement to find a buyer, seller or lessee for more than one year, in return for compensation.

6. An agreement, which by its terms is not to be performed during the lifetime of the promisor, or an agreement that devises or bequeaths any property, or makes provision for any reason by will.

7. An agreement by a purchaser of real estate to pay a debt secured by a trust deed or mortgage upon the property purchased, unless assumption of that debt by the purchaser is specifically provided for in the conveyance of such property.

The Statute of Frauds also applies to personal property. If the sales price of an item is more than $500, the contract must be in writing. Furthermore, if several items are purchased with the intent that the agreement be a single contract, the contract should be in writing if the total sales price is $500 or more.

PERFORMANCE, DISCHARGE & BREACH OF CONTRACT

Acts described in a contract must be performed in a TIMELY MANNER (within time limits described in the contract). Most contracts are properly performed and discharged without any legal complications. If difficulties do arise, the parties, either by themselves or with the aid of legal counsel, usually work out an agreeable settlement. If there is no settlement, the courts are available for the resolution of any contractual conflicts.

PERFORMANCE OF A CONTRACT

Sometimes with performance of a contract, one of the parties would prefer to drop out of the picture without terminating the contract. He or she may, under proper circumstances, accomplish this by assignment. An *ASSIGNMENT is the transfer of a person's right in a contract to another party.* An assignment happens when the *ASSIGNOR, the party to the original contract, transfers his or her rights in the contract to another party, called an ASSIGNEE.* Any contract, unless it calls for some personal service, can be assigned if the contract does not state otherwise. For example, listings are not assignable because they are personal service contracts. If the assignee does not perform, the assignor remains liable (secondary liability) for the contract.

In some cases, the original contracting party may want to drop out of the contract completely. This can be done by novation. A *NOVATION is the substitution or exchange (by mutual agreement of the parties) of a new obligation or contract for an existing one with intent to cancel the old contract.* Since it is a new contract, it requires consideration and the other essentials of a valid contract.

Novation replaces the old contract with a new contract.

Time is often significant in a contract and is usually stated in the contract. By statute, if no time is specified for the performance of an act, a reasonable time is allowed. If an act, by its nature, can be done instantly (such as the payment of money) it must be done. If the last day for the performance of an act falls upon a holiday or weekend, the period is extended to include the next business day. *REVOCATION is the cancelling of an offer to contract by the original offeror.*

DISCHARGE OF A CONTRACT

The *DISCHARGE OF A CONTRACT occurs when the contract has been terminated.* Contracts can be discharged in many ways, from the extreme of full performance (which is the usual pattern) to breach of contract (nonperformance). Figure 5-3 illustrates these extremes and the variety of possibilities that may exist between them. A brief description of these possibilities follows Figure 5-3.

FIGURE 5-3

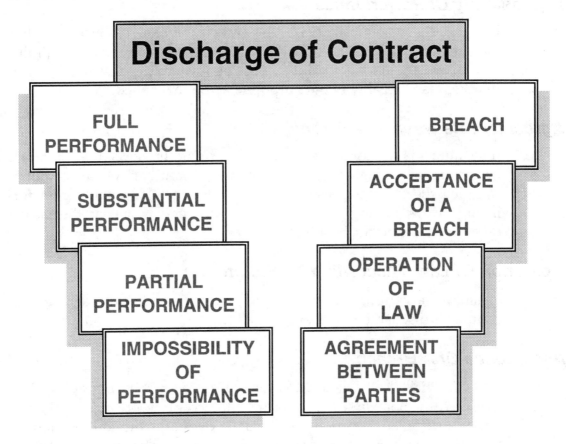

Full Performance

The contract is completed according to the terms specified in the original agreement.

Substantial Performance

Sometimes one party attempts to discharge a contract when the contract has almost, but not entirely, been completed. In certain cases the courts will accept this as a discharge of the contract. Otherwise there are usually slight monetary charges for damages.

Partial Performance

If both parties agree to the value of the work partially completed, the contract is discharged. This agreement should be in writing. However if a dispute arises, the courts will determine the obligations of the defaulting party. Damages are one of the hardest things to prove and the courts usually lean towards the non-defaulting party. A judge will most likely award the non-defaulting party any amount necessary to complete the contract.

Impossibility Of Performance

Under certain circumstances, the contract, for one reason or another, may be impossible to perform. An obvious example is where a painting contractor can no longer paint a house because it was destroyed by fire. In other cases, legality of the purpose may be challenged.

Agreement Between The Parties

If a contract is not completed, the usual way to discharge the contract is by mutual agreement (agree to disagree). A mutual agreement not to complete the contract is also a contract. Most knowledgeable contractors include ways for the contract to be discharged if one of the parties defaults on the original contract.

Operation Of Law (According To Statutes)

Whenever a contract, or parts of a contract, become illegal, then the contract is discharged by operation of law.

Acceptance Of A Breach

A *BREACH is the failure to perform a contract, in part or in whole, without legal excuse.* Sometimes a person will accept a breach. If time is important, the anxious party will usually discharge the contract and try to find a new party to perform the task. Contesting the contract sometimes only creates more problems, such as expensive interruption of work in progress and postponement of other contracts.

Breach (Nonperformance)

This is the nonperformance by one of the contracting parties. The performing party has his or her choice of several legal remedies.

The most common breaches, from the agent's point of view, are: (1) the buyers who decide not to buy after signing the deposit receipt or (2) the seller who decides not to sell after signing the listing and/or deposit receipt.

Statute Of Limitations (For Breach Of Contract)

According to the Statute of Limitations, a civil action for a breach of contract must be started within a certain period of time. If the civil action has not been started within that given time, no legal recourse will be possible. This policy of law states that a person who "sleeps upon his rights" may find himself barred from any legal action. See Figure 5-4.

FIGURE 5-4

STATUTE OF LIMITATIONS

Actions Which Must Be Brought Within 90 Days

CIVIL ACTION FOR THE RECOVERY OF PERSONAL PROPERTY, such as trunks or baggage left in a hotel or other furnished establishment, must be started within 90 days after being left by the owner of the personal property.

Within Six Months

AN ACTION AGAINST AN OFFICER TO RECOVER ANY GOODS, WAGES, MERCHANDISE OR OTHER PROPERTY seized by any officer in his or her official capacity as tax collector. To recover the value of such goods, as well as compensation for damage done to the property seized, and further actions against the county, an action must be started within six months of the seizure.

Within One Year

AN ACTION FOR LIBEL, SLANDER, INJURY OR DEATH caused by the neglect of another or against a bank for the payment of a forged check, must be started within one year of the alleged wrong.

Within Two Years

ACTION MUST BE TAKEN WITHIN TWO YEARS AGAINST CONTRACTS OR OBLIGATIONS THAT WERE NOT MADE IN WRITING. Actions against contracts that have been founded on title insurance policies, certificates or abstracts of title for real property must be made within two years from the date the cause of these actions is discovered. This does not include contracts made for accounts receivable.

Within Three Years (Attachments)

ACTIONS UPON LIABILITIES CREATED BY STATUTE (other than penalties) for trespass upon, or damage to, real property; for taking or damaging goods (including action for the recovery of specific personal property) and actions on the grounds of fraud or mistake caused before discovery by the injured party, must be brought within three years.

Within Four Years (Listings & deposit receipts)

ACTIONS WHICH MUST BE MADE ON ANY WRITTEN CONTRACT WITHIN FOUR YEARS include most real estate contracts such as deposit receipts and listings, except for notes or obligations of publicly held corporations (where the limit is specified as being six years). Other exceptions exist when specific limitations are written into a contract. These exceptions include actions on a money judgment for the balance due upon a trust deed or mortgage, actions following the exercise of the power of sale (which may not be brought later than three months after the sale) and actions to recover upon accounts receivable.

Within Five Years

ANY ACTION FOR INTERMEDIATE PROFITS OF REAL ESTATE from wrongful occupancy and any action for the recovery of real property may be started anytime within five years.

Within Ten Years (Judgments)

AN ACTION UPON A JUDGMENT OF ANY COURT OF THE UNITED STATES, or any state within the United States, must be brought within ten years.

REMEDIES FOR BREACH OF A CONTRACT

A breach of contract occurs when one party fails to perform his or her contractual obligations. By law, the party who has been wronged has only four choices. Action for dollar damages is the most common remedy for breach of a contract because most people prefer to receive money (cash) for their damages. Figure 5-5 illustrates the four alternatives.

FIGURE 5-5

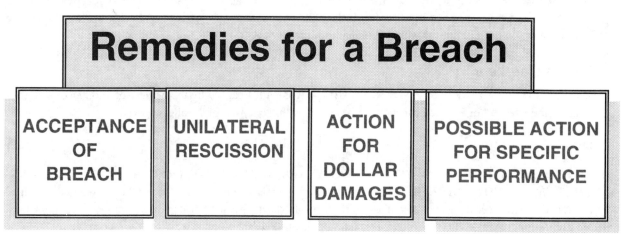

ACCEPTANCE OF BREACH

A discharge of a contract may be simply the acceptance of the breach. In an *ACCEPTANCE OF BREACH the wronged party does not pursue legal action.* Sometimes he or she may feel that the damages recoverable are too limited to justify litigation. Perhaps the person considers the other party judgment-proof, which means that the other party does not have enough assets available to satisfy a judgment. Moreover, the legal cost of a lawsuit, the time, the effort and the psychological effect may not be worth the possible outcome.

UNILATERAL RESCISSION

In a **UNILATERAL RESCISSION** *the wronged party (1) discloses the wrong and (2) restores everything of value to the other offending party.* The legal grounds for a rescission are: fraud, mistake, duress, menace, undue influence and faulty consideration. Rescission is possible when the contract is unlawful for causes not apparent on its face, when the parties are not equally at fault or when the public interest would be hurt. Minors or incompetents may generally rescind their contracts.

ACTION FOR DOLLAR DAMAGES

An *ACTION FOR DOLLAR DAMAGES occurs when a court suit for a breach requests payment of a fixed amount of money as compensation.* If a party to a contract causes you to lose money, it is only fair for you to receive compensation. In most deposit receipts (contract to purchase), there is usually a liquidated damages agreement. A *LIQUIDATED DAMAGES AGREEMENT sets, in advance, a specified amount of money as a penalty if there is a breach.* This clause is used because it is usually impractical or difficult to determine the actual damages caused by a breach.

The current award for liquidated damages on a deposit receipt form is a maximum of 3% (by law) of the home purchase price. Any deposit amount in excess of 3% must be refunded to the offeror. The damages are usually split 50%-50% between the seller and listing agent.

SPECIFIC PERFORMANCE

The final remedy for a breach of contract is specific performance. *SPECIFIC PERFORMANCE means that the party causing the breach is, through court action, forced to perform.* For the most part, courts are skeptical of forcing a person to sell their real property and, as a result, this type of remedy is seldom used. Courts of equity will only consider this action if dollar damages cannot provide an adequate remedy. If a specific performance is ordered, the remedy must be mutual. That is, neither party to a contract can be compelled specifically to perform unless the other party has performed, or is also specifically compelled to perform.

As discussed in Chapter 2, community real property must be transferred by both husband and wife. A buyer who does not realize the existence of a marriage relationship, where the husband alone holds all titles, may have his or her rights enforced through specific performance without the wife's signature. This, however, requires court action. An agreement to obtain a spouse's consent cannot be specifically enforced until one year's spousal silence on the matter has passed. So it is extremely important for a **salesperson** to acquire the signatures of both husband and wife. In fact, the signatures of both spouses should always be obtained if the contract relates to community real property.

To obtain specific performance, the plaintiff must show that the contract was just and reasonable. The contract must have been based on adequate consideration, meaning that the price received for the property must have been fair and reasonable. In addition, specific performance cannot be forced against a party if the contract was obtained by misrepresentation, concealment, circumvention or any other unfair practice.

THE DEPOSIT RECEIPT

THE OFFER & ACCEPTANCE (WITH DEPOSIT)

A deposit of money or items of value must accompany a deposit receipt to be a valid offer. If a postdated check or promissory note is given as consideration for a deposit with an offer (deposit receipt), the agent must disclose this fact to the seller.

The deposit receipt is the most important contract in the real estate field! A **DEPOSIT RECEIPT** *is an offer and deposit to purchase a specific property on certain terms and conditions.* When acceptance is communicated, this becomes a binding contract on the buyer and seller. Acceptance is communicated:

        1. in writing
        2. in person
        3. or by registered mail.

In addition, the deposit receipt discloses (as in the listing agreement) the percentage of commission to be paid to the brokers involved. (See Figures 5-6 through 5-10.)

The Deposit Receipt is also referred to as: "The Contract" or "Residential Purchase Agreement," but it is most commonly referred to as the "Deposit Receipt."

The deposit receipt is neater and more polished if it is typed, but there is nothing wrong with filling it in with a pen. Each form has four copies: one for the buyer, one for the seller, one for the escrow company and one for the broker's file.

As an agent, always give a copy of a contract to the parties involved when it is signed.

NOTE: **When using preprinted forms, the handwritten parts have control over the printed parts, and all corrections must be initialed by both parties.**

THE DEPOSIT (CONSIDERATION FOR DEPOSIT RECEIPT)

The deposit is collected as consideration, from a prospective buyer on behalf of the seller, for the deposit receipt contract. Suppose the seller accepts the offer on the CAR® Deposit Receipt form and the buyer later defaults on the transaction. If the liquidated damages clause is initialed by both the buyer and seller, the seller may retain the deposit (up to three percent of the sale's price). This would then be split 50-50 between the seller and the listing broker, unless otherwise stated in the deposit receipt. **Deposits are always the property of the seller (after the removal of contingencies on the binding Deposit Receipt contract); never the broker.**

FIGURE 5-6

CALIFORNIA ASSOCIATION OF REALTORS®

RESIDENTIAL PURCHASE AGREEMENT
(AND RECEIPT FOR DEPOSIT)
For Use With Single Family Residential Property— Attached or Detached

Date: _SEPTEMBER 9, 2000_ , at _COSTA MESA_ , California,
Received From _WALTER AND DEBBIE BUYER_ ("Buyer"),
A Deposit Of _TEN THOUSAND AND_————— xx/100, Dollars $ _10,000_——, toward the
Purchase Price Of _FOUR HUNDRED THOUSAND_ No/100 Dollars $ _400,000_ .
For Purchase Of Property Situated In _COSTA MESA_ , County Of _ORANGE_
California, Described As _264 BEACH LANE, COSTA MESA, CALIFORNIA 92627_ , ("Property").

1. **FINANCING:** Obtaining the loans below is a contingency of this Agreement. Buyer shall act diligently and in good faith to obtain the designated loans. Obtaining deposit, down payment and closing costs is not a contingency.
   A. **BUYER'S DEPOSIT** shall be held uncashed until Acceptance and then deposited within **3 business days** after Acceptance or ☐ _ABC ESCROW_ , ☒ with Escrow Holder, ☐ into Broker's trust account or ☐ _____ , by Personal Check ☐ Cashier's Check ☐ Cash or ☐ _____ .... $ _10,000_——
   B. **INCREASED DEPOSIT** shall be deposited with _____ within ____ Days After Acceptance, or ☐ _____ .... $ _—0—_
   C. **FIRST LOAN IN THE AMOUNT OF** .... $ _320,000_——
      NEW First Deed of Trust in favor of LENDER, encumbering the Property, securing a note payable at maximum interest of _9_ % fixed rate, or _____ % initial adjustable rate with a maximum interest rate cap of _____ %, balance due in _25_ years. Buyer shall pay loan fees/points not to exceed _Two POINTS_ . If FHA/VA, Seller shall pay _____% discount points, other fees not allowed to be paid by Buyer, not to exceed $_____ , and the cost of lender required repairs not otherwise provided for in this Agreement, not to exceed $_____ .
   D. **ADDITIONAL FINANCING TERMS:** _____ .... $ _—0—_
      ☐ seller financing, (C.A.R. Form SFA-14); ☐ junior or assumed financing, (C.A.R. Form PAA-14, paragraph 5)
   E. **BALANCE OF PURCHASE PRICE** (not including costs of obtaining loans and other closing costs) to be deposited .. $ _70,000_—— with escrow holder within sufficient time to close escrow
   F. **TOTAL PURCHASE PRICE** .... $ _400,000_——
   G. **LOAN CONTINGENCY** shall remain in effect until the designated loans are funded (or ☐ _____ Days After Acceptance, by which time Buyer shall give Seller written notice of Buyer's election to cancel this Agreement if Buyer is unable to obtain the designated loans. If Buyer does not give Seller such notice, the contingency of obtaining the designated loans shall be removed by the method specified in paragraph 16B.)
   H. **LOAN APPLICATIONS; PREQUALIFICATION:** For NEW financing, within 5 (or ☐ _____) Days After Acceptance, Buyer shall provide Seller a letter from lender or mortgage loan broker stating that, based on a review of Buyer's written application and credit report, Buyer is prequalified for the NEW loan indicated above. If Buyer fails to provide such letter within that time, Seller may cancel this Agreement in writing.
   I. ☐ **APPRAISAL CONTINGENCY:** (If checked) This Agreement is contingent upon Property appraising at no less than the specified total purchase price. The Appraisal contingency shall remain in effect for the same period as specified for the Loan Contingency in paragraph 1G.
   J. **ALL CASH OFFER:** If this is an all cash offer, Buyer shall, within 5 (or ☐ _____) Days After Acceptance, provide Seller written verification of sufficient funds to close this transaction. Seller may cancel this Agreement in writing within **5 Days After**: (1) time to provide verification expires, if Buyer fails to provide verification; or (2) receipt of verification, if Seller reasonably disapproves it.

2. **ESCROW:** Close Of Escrow shall occur _70_ Days After Acceptance (or ☐ on _____ (date)). Buyer and Seller shall deliver signed escrow instructions consistent with this Agreement ☒ within _10_ Days After Acceptance, ☐ at least _____ Days before Close Of Escrow, or ☐ _____ . Seller shall deliver possession and occupancy of the Property to Buyer at _10_ (AM/PM, ☒ on the date of Close Of Escrow, or ☐ no later than _____ Days After date of Close Of Escrow, or ☐ _____ . Property shall be vacant, unless otherwise agreed in writing. If transfer of title and possession do not occur at the same time, Buyer and Seller are advised to (a) consult with their insurance advisors, and (b) enter into a written occupancy agreement. Escrow instructions may include matters required to close this transaction which are not covered by this Agreement. The omission from escrow instructions of any provision in this Agreement shall not constitute a waiver of that provision.

3. **OCCUPANCY:** Buyer ☒ does, ☐ does not, intend to occupy Property as Buyer's primary residence.

4. **ALLOCATION OF COSTS:** (Check boxes which apply. If needed, insert additional instructions in blank lines.)
   TRANSFER FEES:
   A. ☐ Buyer ☐ Seller shall pay County transfer tax or transfer fee. _____
   B. ☐ Buyer ☐ Seller shall pay City transfer tax or transfer fee. _____
   C. ☐ Buyer ☐ Seller shall pay Homeowners' Association transfer fee. _____
   TITLE AND ESCROW COSTS:
   D. ☐ Buyer ☒ Seller shall pay for owner's title insurance policy, issued by _GOOD TITLE_ company.
   E. ☐ Buyer ☐ Seller shall pay escrow fee. _____ Escrow holder shall be _____ .
   SEWER/SEPTIC/WELL COSTS:
   F. ☐ Buyer ☐ Seller shall pay for sewer connection, if required by Law prior to Close Of Escrow. _____
   G. ☐ Buyer ☐ Seller shall pay to have septic or private sewage disposal system inspected. _____
   H. ☐ Buyer ☐ Seller shall pay to have wells tested for water quality, potability, productivity, and recovery rate. _____
   OTHER COSTS:
   I. ☐ Buyer ☐ Seller shall pay for zone disclosure reports, if any (paragraph 7). _____
   J. ☐ Buyer ☐ Seller shall pay for Smoke Detector Installation and/or Water Heater bracing. _____ Seller, prior to close of escrow, shall provide Buyer a written statement of compliance in accordance with state and local Law, unless exempt.
   K. ☐ Buyer ☐ Seller shall pay the cost of compliance with any other minimum mandatory government retrofit standards and inspections required as a condition of closing escrow under any Law. _____
   L. ☐ Buyer ☐ Seller shall pay the cost of a one-year home warranty plan, issued by _____ with the following optional coverage: _____ . Policy cost not to exceed $ _____ .
   PEST CONTROL REPORT:
   M. ☐ Buyer ☒ Seller shall pay for the Pest Control Report ("Report"), which shall be prepared by _XXX PEST CONTROL_ , a registered structural pest control company.
   N. ☐ Buyer ☐ Seller shall pay for work recommended to correct conditions described in the Report as "Section 1,".
   O. ☐ Buyer ☐ Seller shall pay for work recommended to correct conditions described in the Report as "Section 2," if requested by Buyer.

Buyer and Seller acknowledge receipt of copy of this page, which constitutes Page 1 of _5_ Pages.
Buyer's Initials _(WB) (db)_ Seller's Initials _(JS) (vp)_

Published and Distributed by:
REAL ESTATE BUSINESS SERVICES, INC.
a subsidiary of the CALIFORNIA ASSOCIATION OF REALTORS®
525 South Virgil Avenue, Los Angeles, California 90020

OFFICE USE ONLY
Reviewed by Broker or Designee _AL_
Date _9.9.00_

RESIDENTIAL PURCHASE AGREEMENT AND RECEIPT FOR DEPOSIT (RPA-14 PAGE 1 OF 5) REVISED 5/97

FIGURE 5-7

Property Address: 264 BEACH LANE, COSTA MESA, CA 92627   Date: SEPT. 9 2000

5. PEST CONTROL TERMS:

A. The Report shall cover the main building and attached structures and, if checked: ☐ detached garages and carports, ☐ detached decks, ☐ the following other structures on the Property: _____

B. If Property is a unit in a condominium, planned development, or residential stock cooperative, the Report shall cover only the separate interest and any exclusive-use areas being transferred, and shall not cover common areas, unless otherwise agreed.

C. If inspection of inaccessible areas is recommended in the Report, Buyer has the option, within 5 Days After receipt of the Report, either to accept and approve the Report by the method specified in paragraph 16B, or to request in writing that further inspection be made. If further inspection recommends "Section 1" and/or "Section 2" corrective work, such work, and the cost of inspection, entry, and closing of the inaccessible areas shall be paid for, respectively, by the party designated in paragraph 4N or 4O. If no infestation or infection is found in the inaccessible areas, the cost of the inspection, entry, and closing of those areas shall be paid for by Buyer.

D. If no infestation or infection by wood destroying pests or organisms is found, the Report shall include a written Pest Control Certification. Certification shall be issued prior to Close Of Escrow unless otherwise agreed in writing.

E. Inspections, corrective work and Pest Control Certification in this paragraph refers only to the presence or absence of wood destroying pests or organisms, and does not include the condition of roof coverings. Read paragraphs 9 and 12 concerning roof coverings.

F. Nothing in paragraph 5 shall relieve Seller of the obligation to repair or replace shower pans and shower enclosures due to leaks, if required by paragraph 9B(3). Water test of shower pans on upper level units may not be performed unless the owners of property below the shower consent.

6. TRANSFER DISCLOSURE STATEMENT; SUBSEQUENT DISCLOSURES; MELLO-ROOS NOTICE:

A. Within 5 (or ☐ _____) Days After Acceptance, unless exempt, a Real Estate Transfer Disclosure Statement ("TDS") shall be completed and delivered to Buyer, who shall sign and return a copy of it to Seller.

B. In the event Seller, prior to Close Of Escrow, becomes aware of adverse conditions materially affecting the Property, or any material inaccuracy in disclosures, information, or representations previously provided to Buyer (including those made in a TDS) of which Buyer is otherwise unaware, Seller shall promptly provide a subsequent or amended disclosure, in writing, covering those items **except for those conditions and material inaccuracies disclosed in reports obtained by Buyer.**

C. Seller shall make a good faith effort to obtain a disclosure notice from any local agencies which levy a special tax on the Property pursuant to the Mello-Roos Community Facilities Act, and shall promptly deliver to Buyer any such notice made available by those agencies.

D. If the TDS, the Mello-Roos disclosure notice, or a subsequent or amended disclosure is delivered to Buyer after the offer is signed, Buyer shall have the right to terminate this Agreement within **3 days** after delivery in person, or **5 days** after delivery by deposit in the mail, by giving written notice of termination to Seller or Seller's agent.

7. DISCLOSURES: Within the time specified in paragraph 16, Seller shall provide to Buyer the following disclosures and information, take the following actions, and disclose material facts pertaining to the following conditions. Buyer shall then, within the time specified in paragraph 16, investigate the disclosures and information, and provide written notice to Seller of any item disapproved.

A. **PROPERTY DISCLOSURES:** Earthquake Fault Zones, Seismic Hazard Zones (when available), Special Flood Hazard Areas, State Fire Responsibility Areas, Earthquake Guides, Lead-Based Paint Disclosures, Environmental Hazards Booklet, and Energy Efficiency Booklet (when published), or any other federal, state, or locally designated zone for which disclosure is required by Law.

B. **CONDOMINIUM/COMMON INTEREST SUBDIVISION:** If Property is a unit in a condominium, planned development, or other common interest subdivision, Seller shall request from the Homeowners' Association ("HOA"), and upon receipt provide to Buyer, a statement indicating any current regular dues and assessments; known pending regular or special assessments, claims, or litigation and the location and number of parking and storage spaces; copies of covenants, conditions, and restrictions; articles of incorporation; "by-laws"; other governing documents; most current financial statement distributed; statement regarding limited enforceability of age restrictions, if applicable; current HOA statement showing any unpaid assessments; any other documents required by Law; and the most recent 12 months of HOA minutes for regular and special meetings, if available.

C. **NOTICE OF VIOLATION:** If, prior to Close Of Escrow, Seller receives notice or is made aware of any notice filed or issued against the Property, of violations of city, county, state, or federal building, zoning, fire or health Laws, Seller shall immediately notify Buyer in writing. Buyer shall, within the time specified in paragraph 16, provide written notice to Seller of any items disapproved.

8. TITLE AND VESTING:

A. Within the time specified in paragraph 16A, Buyer shall be provided a current preliminary (title) report (which is only an offer by the title insurer to issue a policy of title insurance, and may not contain every item affecting title). Buyer shall, within the time specified in paragraph 16, provide written notice to Seller of any items reasonably disapproved.

B. At Close Of Escrow, Buyer shall receive a grant deed conveying title (or, for stock cooperative, an assignment of stock certificate), including oil, mineral and water rights if currently owned by Seller. Title shall be subject to all encumbrances, easements, covenants, conditions, restrictions, rights, and other matters which are of record or disclosed to Buyer prior to Close Of Escrow, unless disapproved in writing by Buyer within the time specified in paragraph 16. However, title shall not be subject to any liens against the Property, except for those specified in the Agreement. Buyer shall receive an ALTA-R owner's title insurance policy, if reasonably available. If not, Buyer shall receive a standard coverage owner's policy (e.g. CLTA or ALTA with regional exceptions). Buyer shall pay for Lender's title insurance policy. Title shall vest as designated in Buyer's escrow instructions. The title company at Buyer's request, can provide information, about availability, desirability and cost of various title insurance coverages. THE MANNER OF TAKING TITLE MAY HAVE SIGNIFICANT LEGAL AND TAX CONSEQUENCES.

9. NO WARRANTIES EXCEPT AS SPECIFIED:

A. EXCEPT AS SPECIFIED BELOW, AND ELSEWHERE IN THIS AGREEMENT, Property is sold "AS IS", in its present physical condition.

B. (IF CHECKED) SELLER WARRANTS THAT AT THE TIME POSSESSION IS MADE AVAILABLE TO BUYER:

☒ (1) Roof shall be free of leaks KNOWN to Seller or DISCOVERED during escrow.

☒ (2) Built-in appliances (including free-standing oven and range, if included in sale), heating, air conditioning, electrical, water, sewer and pool/spa systems, if any, shall be repaired, if KNOWN by Seller to be inoperative or DISCOVERED to be so during escrow. (Septic/Well systems are not covered in this paragraph. Read paragraphs 4G and H.)

☒ (3) Plumbing systems, shower pans and shower enclosures shall be free of leaks KNOWN to Seller or DISCOVERED during escrow.

☒ (4) All fire, safety, and structural defects in chimneys and fireplaces KNOWN to Seller or DISCOVERED during escrow shall be repaired.

☒ (5) All broken or cracked glass, torn existing window and door screens, and broken seals between multi-pane windows shall be replaced.

☒ (6) All debris and all personal property not included in the sale shall be removed.

☐ (7) _____

C. **PROPERTY MAINTENANCE:** Unless otherwise agreed, Property, including pool, spa, landscaping and grounds, is to be maintained in substantially the same condition as on the date of Acceptance.

D. **PROPERTY IMPROVEMENTS** may not (a) be built according to codes or in compliance with Law, or (b) have had permits issued.

E. **INSPECTIONS AND DISCLOSURES:** Items discovered in Buyer's Inspections which are not covered by paragraph 9B, shall be governed by the procedure in paragraphs 12 and 16. Buyer retains the right to disapprove the condition of the Property based upon items discovered in Buyer's Inspections. Disclosures in the TDS and items discovered in Buyer's Inspections do NOT eliminate Seller's obligations under paragraph 9B, unless specifically agreed in writing. WHETHER OR NOT SELLER WARRANTS ANY ASPECT OF THE PROPERTY, SELLER IS OBLIGATED TO DISCLOSE KNOWN MATERIAL FACTS AND TO MAKE OTHER DISCLOSURES REQUIRED BY LAW.

Buyer and Seller acknowledge receipt of copy of this page, which constitutes Page 2 of ___5___ Pages.

Buyer's Initials (NB) (W)   Seller's Initials (J) (NP)

OFFICE USE ONLY
Reviewed by Broker
or Designee _____
Date 9/9/00

RESIDENTIAL PURCHASE AGREEMENT AND RECEIPT FOR DEPOSIT (RPA-14 PAGE 2 OF 5) REVISED 5/97

FIGURE 5-8

Property Address: <u>264 BEACH LANE, COSTA MESA, CA 92627</u>   Date: <u>SEPT. 9, 2000</u>

10. **FIXTURES:** All EXISTING fixtures and fittings that are attached to the Property, or for which special openings have been made, are INCLUDED IN THE PURCHASE PRICE (unless excluded below), and shall be transferred free of liens and "AS IS," unless specifically warranted. Fixtures shall include, but are not limited to, existing electrical, lighting, plumbing and heating fixtures, fireplace inserts, solar systems, built-in appliances, window and door screens, awnings, shutters, window coverings, attached floor coverings, television antennas, satellite dishes and related equipment, private integrated telephone systems, air coolers/conditioners, pool/spa equipment, water softeners (if owned by Seller), security systems/alarms (if owned by Seller), garage door openers/remote controls, attached fireplace equipment, mailbox, in-ground landscaping including trees/shrubs, and _____ .

FIXTURES EXCLUDED: _____

11. **PERSONAL PROPERTY:** The following items of personal property, free of liens and "AS IS," unless specifically warranted, are INCLUDED IN THE PURCHASE PRICE: <u>REFRIGERATOR</u> _____ .

12. **BUYER'S INVESTIGATION OF PROPERTY CONDITION:** Buyer's Acceptance of the condition of the Property is a contingency of this Agreement, as specified in this paragraph and paragraph 16. Buyer shall have the right, at Buyer's expense, to conduct inspections, investigations, tests, surveys, and other studies ("Inspections"), including the right to inspect for lead-based paint and other lead hazards. No Inspections shall be made by any governmental building or zoning inspector or government employee without Seller's prior written consent, unless required by Law. Buyer shall, within the time specified in Paragraph 16, complete these Inspections and notify Seller in writing of any items reasonably disapproved. Seller shall make Property available for all Inspections. Buyer shall: keep Property free and clear of liens; indemnify and hold Seller harmless from all liability, claims, demands, damages and costs; and repair all damages arising from Inspections. Buyer shall carry, or Buyer shall require anyone acting on Buyer's behalf to carry, policies of liability, worker's compensation, and other applicable insurance, defending and protecting Seller from liability for any injuries to persons or property occurring during any work done on the Property at Buyer's direction, prior to Close Of Escrow. Seller is advised that certain protections may be afforded Seller by recording a notice of non-responsibility for work done on the Property at Buyer's direction. At Seller's request Buyer shall give Seller, at no cost, complete copies of all Inspection reports obtained by Buyer concerning the Property. Seller shall have water, gas, and electricity on for Buyer's Inspections, and through the date possession is made available to Buyer.

13. **FINAL WALK-THROUGH; VERIFICATION OF CONDITION:** Buyer shall have the right to make a final inspection of the Property within 5 (or ☐ _____) Days prior to Close Of Escrow, NOT AS A CONTINGENCY OF THE SALE, but solely to confirm that Repairs have been completed as agreed in writing, and that Seller has complied with Seller's other obligations.

14. **PRORATIONS AND PROPERTY TAXES:** Unless otherwise agreed in writing, real property taxes and assessments, interest, rents, HOA regular dues and regular assessments, premiums on insurance assumed by Buyer, payments on bonds and assessments assumed by Buyer, payments on Mello-Roos and other Special Assessment District bonds and assessments which are now a lien, and payments on HOA bonds and special assessments which have been imposed prior to Close Of Escrow, shall be PAID CURRENT and prorated between Buyer and Seller as of Close Of Escrow, except: _____
Prorated payments on Mello-Roos and other Special Assessment District bonds and assessments and HOA special assessments that are now a lien but not yet due, shall be assumed by Buyer WITHOUT CREDIT toward the purchase price. Property will be reassessed upon change of ownership. Any supplemental tax bills shall be paid as follows: (1) For periods after Close Of Escrow, by Buyer; and, (2) For periods prior to Close Of Escrow, by Seller. TAX BILLS ISSUED AFTER CLOSE OF ESCROW SHALL BE HANDLED DIRECTLY BETWEEN BUYER AND SELLER.

15. **SALE OF BUYER'S PROPERTY:**
    A. This Agreement is NOT contingent upon the sale of Buyer's property, unless paragraph 15B is checked.
OR B. ☐ (If checked) This Agreement IS CONTINGENT on the Close Of Escrow of Buyer's property, described as (address) _____
    _____ ("Buyer's Property"), which is
    (if checked) ☐ listed for sale with _____ Company, and/or
    (if checked) ☐ in Escrow No. _____ with _____ Escrow Holder, scheduled to
    Close Escrow on _____ (date). Buyer shall deliver to Seller, within 5 Days After Seller's request, a copy of the contract for the sale
    of Buyer's Property, escrow instructions, and all amendments and modifications thereto. If Buyer's Property does not close escrow by the date
    specified for Close Of Escrow in this paragraph, then either Seller or Buyer may cancel this Agreement in writing.
    (Check ONLY 1 or 2; do NOT check both.) After Acceptance:
    ☐ (1) Seller SHALL have the right to continue to offer the Property for sale. If Seller accepts another written offer, Seller shall give Buyer written
    notice to (a) remove this contingency in writing, (b) provide written verification of sufficient funds to close escrow on this sale without the sale
    of Buyer's Property, and (c) comply with the following additional requirement(s) _____
    _____ .
    If Buyer fails to complete those actions within _____ hours or _____ Days After receipt of such notice, Seller may cancel this Agreement in writing.
    ☐ (2) Seller shall not have the right to continue to offer the Property for sale, except for back-up offers.

16. **TIME PERIODS; INSPECTIONS; SATISFACTION/REMOVAL OF CONTINGENCIES; DISAPPROVAL/CANCELLATION RIGHTS:**
    A. **TIME PERIODS:** The following time periods shall apply, unless changed by mutual written agreement:
        (1) **SELLER HAS:** 5 (or ☐ _____) Days After Acceptance (a) to deliver to Buyer all reports, disclosures, and information for which Seller is responsible under paragraphs 4G, 4H, 4M and 7A; and, (b) to request and 2 Days After receipt to provide to Buyer all reports, disclosures, and information for which Seller is responsible under paragraphs 7B and 8.
        (2) **BUYER HAS:** (a) 10 (or ☐ _____) Days After Acceptance to complete all Inspections (including, if applicable, Inspections for wood destroying pests or organisms under paragraph 4M and lead-based paint and lead hazards under paragraph 12), investigations and review of reports and other applicable information, with an additional 7 Days to complete geologic Inspections. WITHIN THIS TIME, Buyer must either disapprove in writing any items which are unacceptable to Buyer or remove the contingency associated with such disapproval right, by the active or passive method, as specified below; (b) 5 (or ☐ _____) Days After receipt of (I) each of the items in paragraph 16A(1); and (II) notice of code and legal violations under paragraph 7C, to either disapprove in writing any items which are unacceptable to Buyer, or remove the contingency associated with such disapproval right by the active or passive method as specified below.
        (3) **SELLER'S RESPONSE TO BUYER'S DISAPPROVALS:** Seller shall have 5 (or ☐ _____) Days After receipt of Buyer's written notice of items reasonably disapproved to respond in writing. If Seller refuses or is unable to make repairs to, or correct, any items reasonably disapproved by Buyer, or if Seller does not respond within the time period specified, Buyer shall have 5 (or ☐ _____) Days After receipt of Seller's response, or after the expiration of the time for Seller to respond, whichever occurs first, to cancel this Agreement in writing.
    B. **ACTIVE OR PASSIVE REMOVAL OF BUYER'S CONTINGENCIES:**
        (1) ☐ **ACTIVE METHOD (APPLIES IF CHECKED):** If Buyer does not give Seller written notice of items reasonably disapproved, removal of contingencies, or cancellation, within the time periods specified, Seller shall have the right to cancel this Agreement by giving written notice to Buyer.
        (2) **PASSIVE METHOD (Applies UNLESS Active Method is checked):** If Buyer does not give Seller written notice of items reasonably disapproved, or of removal of contingencies or cancellation within the time periods specified, Buyer shall be deemed to have removed the contingency associated with the disapproval right, or waived the contingency and the right to take those actions or to cancel.
    C. **EFFECT OF CONTINGENCY REMOVAL:** If Buyer removes any contingency or cancellation right by the active or passive method, as applicable, Buyer shall conclusively be deemed to have: (1) Completed all Inspections, investigations, and review of reports and other applicable information and disclosures pertaining to that contingency or cancellation right; (2) Elected to proceed with the transaction; and, (3) Assumed all liability, responsibility, and expense for repairs or corrections pertaining to that contingency or cancellation right, or for inability to obtain financing if the contingency pertains to financing, except for items which Seller has agreed in writing to repair or correct.

Buyer and Seller acknowledge receipt of copy of this page, which constitutes Page 3 of <u>5</u> Pages.
Buyer's Initials (WB) (JN)   Seller's Initials (TS) (NP)

<table>
<tr><td>OFFICE USE ONLY</td></tr>
<tr><td>Reviewed by Broker or Designee ____</td></tr>
<tr><td>Date 9/9/00</td></tr>
</table>

EQUAL HOUSING OPPORTUNITY

RESIDENTIAL PURCHASE AGREEMENT AND RECEIPT FOR DEPOSIT (RPA-14 PAGE 3 OF 5) REVISED 5/97

FIGURE 5-9

Property Address: _264 BEACH LANE, COSTA MESA, CA 92627_ Date: _SEPT. 9, 2000_

D. **CANCELLATION OF SALE/ESCROW; RETURN OF DEPOSITS:** If Buyer or Seller gives written NOTICE OF CANCELLATION pursuant to rights duly exercised under the terms of this Agreement, Buyer and Seller agree to sign mutual instructions to cancel the sale and escrow and release deposits, less fees and costs, to the party entitled to the funds. Fees and costs may be payable to service providers and vendors for services and products provided during escrow. Release of funds will require mutual, signed release instructions from both Buyer and Seller, judicial decision, or arbitration award. A party may be subject to a civil penalty of up to $1,000 for refusal to sign such instructions, if no good faith dispute exists as to who is entitled to the deposited funds (Civil Code §1057.3).

17. **REPAIRS:** Repairs under this Agreement shall be completed prior to Close Of Escrow, unless otherwise agreed in writing. Work to be performed at Seller's expense may be performed by Seller or through others, provided that work complies with applicable laws, including governmental permit, inspection, and approval requirements. Repairs shall be performed in a skillful manner with materials of quality comparable to existing materials. It is understood that exact restoration of appearance or cosmetic items following all Repairs may not be possible.

18. **WITHHOLDING TAXES:** Seller and Buyer agree to execute and deliver any instrument, affidavit, statement, or instruction reasonably necessary to comply with state and federal withholding Laws, if required.(For example, C.A.R. FIRPTA and California compliance Forms AS-14 and AB-11.)

19. **KEYS:** At the time possession is made available to Buyer, Seller shall provide keys and/or means to operate all Property locks, mailboxes, security systems, alarms, and garage door openers. If the Property is a unit in a condominium or subdivision, Buyer may be required to pay a deposit to the HOA to obtain keys to accessible HOA facilities.

20. **LIQUIDATED DAMAGES: If Buyer fails to complete this purchase by reason of any default of Buyer, Seller shall retain, as liquidated damages for breach of contract, the deposit actually paid. However, if the Property is a dwelling with no more than four units, one of which Buyer intends to occupy, then the amount retained shall be no more than 3% of the purchase price. Any excess shall be returned to Buyer. Buyer and Seller shall also sign a separate liquidated damages provision for any increased deposit. (C.A.R. Form RID-11 shall fulfill this requirement.)**   Buyer's Initials _NB / db_   Seller's Initials _TC / NA_

21. **DISPUTE RESOLUTION:**
    A. **MEDIATION:** Buyer and Seller agree to mediate any dispute or claim arising between them out of this Agreement, or any resulting transaction, before resorting to arbitration or court action, subject to paragraphs 21C and D below. Mediation fees, if any, shall be divided equally among the parties involved. If any party commences an action based on a dispute or claim to which this paragraph applies, without first attempting to resolve the matter through mediation, then that party shall not be entitled to recover attorney's fees, even if they would otherwise be available to that party in any such action. THIS MEDIATION PROVISION APPLIES WHETHER OR NOT THE ARBITRATION PROVISION IS INITIALED.

    B. **ARBITRATION OF DISPUTES: Buyer and Seller agree that any dispute or claim in Law or equity arising between them out of this Agreement or any resulting transaction, which is not settled through mediation, shall be decided by neutral, binding arbitration, subject to paragraphs 21C and D below. The arbitrator shall be a retired judge or justice, unless the parties mutually agree to a different arbitrator, who shall render an award in accordance with substantive California Law. In all other respects, the arbitration shall be conducted in accordance with Part III, Title 9 of the California Code of Civil Procedure. Judgment upon the award of the arbitrator(s) may be entered in any court having jurisdiction. The parties shall have the right to discovery in accordance with Code of Civil Procedure §1283.05.**

    "NOTICE: BY INITIALING IN THE SPACE BELOW YOU ARE AGREEING TO HAVE ANY DISPUTE ARISING OUT OF THE MATTERS INCLUDED IN THE 'ARBITRATION OF DISPUTES' PROVISION DECIDED BY NEUTRAL ARBITRATION AS PROVIDED BY CALIFORNIA LAW AND YOU ARE GIVING UP ANY RIGHTS YOU MIGHT POSSESS TO HAVE THE DISPUTE LITIGATED IN A COURT OR JURY TRIAL. BY INITIALING IN THE SPACE BELOW YOU ARE GIVING UP YOUR JUDICIAL RIGHTS TO DISCOVERY AND APPEAL, UNLESS THOSE RIGHTS ARE SPECIFICALLY INCLUDED IN THE 'ARBITRATION OF DISPUTES' PROVISION. IF YOU REFUSE TO SUBMIT TO ARBITRATION AFTER AGREEING TO THIS PROVISION, YOU MAY BE COMPELLED TO ARBITRATE UNDER THE AUTHORITY OF THE CALIFORNIA CODE OF CIVIL PROCEDURE. YOUR AGREEMENT TO THIS ARBITRATION PROVISION IS VOLUNTARY."

    "WE HAVE READ AND UNDERSTAND THE FOREGOING AND AGREE TO SUBMIT DISPUTES ARISING OUT OF THE MATTERS INCLUDED IN THE 'ARBITRATION OF DISPUTES' PROVISION TO NEUTRAL ARBITRATION."   Buyer's Initials _NB / db_   Seller's Initials _TC / NA_

    C. **EXCLUSIONS FROM MEDIATION AND ARBITRATION:** The following matters are excluded from Mediation and Arbitration hereunder: (a) A judicial or non-judicial foreclosure or other action or proceeding to enforce a deed of trust, mortgage, or installment land sale contract as defined in Civil Code §2985; (b) An unlawful detainer action; (c) The filing or enforcement of a mechanic's lien; (d) Any matter which is within the jurisdiction of a probate, small claims, or bankruptcy court; and (e) An action for bodily injury or wrongful death, or for latent or patent defects to which Code of Civil Procedure §337.1 or §337.15 applies. The filing of a court action to enable the recording of a notice of pending action, for order of attachment, receivership, injunction, or other provisional remedies, shall not constitute a violation of the mediation and arbitration provisions.

    D. **BROKERS:** Buyer and Seller agree to mediate and arbitrate disputes or claims involving either or both Brokers, provided either or both Brokers shall have agreed to such mediation or arbitration, prior to, or within a reasonable time after the dispute or claim is presented to Brokers. Any election by either or both Brokers to participate in mediation or arbitration shall not result in Brokers being deemed parties to the purchase and sale Agreement.

22. **DEFINITIONS:** As used in this Agreement:
    A. **"Acceptance"** means the time the offer or final counter offer is accepted by the other party, in accordance with paragraph 30 of the Agreement or the terms of the final counter offer.
    B. **"Agreement"** means the terms and conditions of this Residential Purchase Agreement and any counter offer.
    C. **"Days"** means calendar days, unless otherwise required by Law.
    D. **"Days After .."** means the specified number of calendar days after the occurrence of the event specified, not counting the calendar date on which the specified event occurs.
    E. **"Close Of Escrow"** means the date the grant deed, or other evidence of transfer of title, is recorded.
    F. **"Law"** means any law, code, statute, ordinance, regulation, or rule, which is adopted by a controlling city, county, state or federal legislative or judicial body or agency.
    G. **"Repairs"** means any repairs, alterations, replacements, or modifications, (including pest control work) of the Property.
    H. **"Pest Control Certification"** means a written statement made by a registered structural pest control company that on the date of inspection or re-inspection, the Property is "free" or is "now free" of "evidence of active infestation in the visible and accessible areas".
    I. **Singular and Plural** terms each include the other, when appropriate.

23. **MULTIPLE LISTING SERVICE ("MLS"):** Brokers are authorized to report the terms of this transaction to any MLS, to be published and disseminated to persons authorized to use the information on terms approved by the MLS.

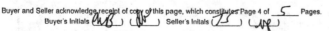 Buyer and Seller acknowledge receipt of copy of this page, which constitutes Page 4 of _5_ Pages.
Buyer's Initials (_NB_) (_db_) Seller's Initials (_TC_) (_NA_)

OFFICE USE ONLY
Reviewed by Broker or Designee
Date _9/9/00_

RESIDENTIAL PURCHASE AGREEMENT AND RECEIPT FOR DEPOSIT (RPA-14 PAGE 4 OF 5) REVISED 5/97

FIGURE   5-10

Property Address: __264 BEACH LANE, COSTA MESA, CA 92627__   Date: __SEPT. 9, 2000__

24. **EQUAL HOUSING OPPORTUNITY:** The Property is sold in compliance with federal, state, and local anti-discrimination Laws.
25. **ATTORNEY'S FEES:** In any action, proceeding, or arbitration between Buyer and Seller arising out of this Agreement, the prevailing Buyer or Seller shall be entitled to reasonable attorney's fees and costs from the non-prevailing Buyer or Seller, except as provided in paragraph 21A.
26. **SELECTION OF SERVICE PROVIDERS:** If Brokers give Buyer or Seller referrals to persons, vendors, or service or product providers ("Providers"), Brokers do not guarantee the performance of any of those Providers. Buyer and Seller may select ANY Providers of their own choosing.
27. **TIME OF ESSENCE; ENTIRE CONTRACT; CHANGES:** Time is of the essence. All understandings between the parties are incorporated in this Agreement. Its terms are intended by the parties as a final, complete, and exclusive expression of their agreement with respect to its subject matter, and may not be contradicted by evidence of any prior agreement or contemporaneous oral agreement. This Agreement may not be extended, amended, modified, altered, or changed, except in writing signed by Buyer and Seller.
28. **OTHER TERMS AND CONDITIONS,** including ATTACHED SUPPLEMENTS:

    ☑ Buyer Inspection Advisory (C.A.R. Form BIA-14)
    ☐ Purchase Agreement Addendum (C.A.R. Form PAA-14, paragraph number(s)   )

29. **AGENCY CONFIRMATION:** The following agency relationships are hereby confirmed for this transaction:
    Listing Agent: __SAIL REALTY__   (Print Firm Name) is the agent of (check one):
    ☒ the Seller exclusively; or ☐ both the Buyer and Seller.
    Selling Agent: __RAMOS REALTY__   (Print Firm Name) (if not same as Listing Agent) is the agent of (check one):
    ☒ the Buyer exclusively; or ☐ the Seller exclusively; or ☐ both the Buyer and Seller.
    Real Estate Brokers are not parties to the Agreement between Buyer and Seller.
30. **OFFER:** This is an offer to purchase the Property on the above terms and conditions. All paragraphs with spaces for initials by Buyer and Seller are incorporated in this Agreement only if initialed by all parties. If at least one but not all parties initial, a counter offer is required until agreement is reached. Unless Acceptance of Offer is signed by Seller, and a signed copy delivered in person, by mail, or facsimile, and personally received by Buyer, or by _____, who is authorized to receive it, by __SEPTEMBER 11, 2000__(date), at __11__ AM/PM, the offer shall be deemed revoked and the deposit shall be returned. Buyer has read and acknowledges receipt of a copy of the offer and agrees to the above confirmation of agency relationships. If this offer is accepted and Buyer subsequently defaults, Buyer may be responsible for payment of Brokers' compensation. This Agreement and any supplement, addendum, or modification, including any photocopy or facsimile, may be signed in two or more counterparts, all of which shall constitute one and the same writing.

> **Buyer and Seller acknowledge and agree that Brokers: (a) Do not decide what price Buyer should pay or Seller should accept; (b) Do not guarantee the condition of the Property; (c) Shall not be responsible for defects that are not known to Broker(s) and are not visually observable in reasonably accessible areas of the Property; (d) Do not guarantee the performance or Repairs of others who have provided services or products to Buyer or Seller; (e) Cannot identify Property boundary lines; (f) Cannot verify inspection reports or representations of others; (g) Cannot provide legal or tax advice; (h) Will not provide other advice or information that exceeds the knowledge, education and experience required to obtain a real estate license. Buyer and Seller agree that they will seek legal, tax, insurance, and other desired assistance from appropriate professionals.**

BUYER _Walter Buyer_   BUYER _Debbie Buyer_

31. **BROKER COMPENSATION:** Seller agrees to pay compensation for services as follows:
    ___THREE PERCENT___, to ___LISTING___, Broker, and
    ___THREE PERCENT___, to ___SELLING___, Broker,
    payable: (a) On recordation of the deed or other evidence of title; or (b) If completion of sale is prevented by default of Seller, upon Seller's default; or, (c) If completion of sale is prevented by default of Buyer, only if and when Seller collects damages from Buyer, by suit or otherwise, and then in an amount equal to one-half of the damages recovered, but not to exceed the above compensation, after first deducting title and escrow expenses and the expenses of collection, if any. Seller hereby irrevocably assigns to Brokers such compensation from Seller's proceeds, and irrevocably instructs Escrow Holder to disburse those funds to Brokers at close of escrow. Commission instructions can be amended or revoked only with the consent of Brokers. In any action, proceeding or arbitration relating to the payment of such compensation, the prevailing party shall be entitled to reasonable attorney's fees and costs, except as provided in paragraph 21A.
32. **ACCEPTANCE OF OFFER:** Seller warrants that Seller is the owner of this Property or has the authority to execute this Agreement. Seller accepts the above offer, agrees to sell the Property on the above terms and conditions, and agrees to the above confirmation of agency relationships. Seller has read and acknowledges receipt of a copy of this Agreement, and authorizes Broker to deliver a signed copy to Buyer.

If checked: ☐ SUBJECT TO ATTACHED COUNTER OFFER, DATED _____.

SELLER _Tony Seller_   Date _9/10/00_
SELLER _Yolanda Seller_   Date _9/10/00_

(WB/db) ACKNOWLEDGMENT OF RECEIPT: Buyer or authorized agent acknowledges receipt of signed Acceptance on (date) _9/10/00_.
(Initials)   at __11__ AM/PM.

Agency relationships are confirmed as above. Real Estate Brokers are not parties to the Agreement between Buyer and Seller. Receipt for deposit is acknowledged:
Real Estate Broker (Selling Firm Name) __RAMOS REALTY__   By _Joseph Ramos_ Date _9/9/2000_
Address __777 NEWPORT BLVD, NEWPORT BEACH, CA__   Telephone _714-647-0000_ Fax _714-647-0001_

Agency relationships are confirmed as above. Real Estate Brokers are not parties to the Agreement between Buyer and Seller.
Real Estate Broker (Listing Firm Name) __SAIL REALTY__   By _Carmen Cano_ Date _9/10/2000_
Address __222 HARBOR BLVD, COSTA MESA, CA 92627__   Telephone _714-646-2828_ Fax _714-646-2829_

This form is available for use by the entire real estate industry. It is not intended to identify the user as a REALTOR®. REALTOR® is a registered collective membership mark which may be used only by members of the NATIONAL ASSOCIATION OF REALTORS® who subscribe to its Code of Ethics.   Page 5 of __5__ Pages.

OFFICE USE ONLY
Reviewed by Broker
or Designee ____
Date _9/9/00_

RESIDENTIAL PURCHASE AGREEMENT AND RECEIPT FOR DEPOSIT (RPA-14 PAGE 5 OF 5) REVISED 5/97

FIGURE 5-11

CALIFORNIA
ASSOCIATION
OF REALTORS®

PURCHASE AGREEMENT ADDENDUM
MAY ALSO BE USED WITH COUNTER OFFER

This is an addendum to the ☐ Residential Purchase Agreement, ☐ Counter Offer, or ☐ Other _____

_____ , ("Agreement"), dated _____ ,

On property known as _____ ("Property"),

In which _____ is referred to as Buyer,

And _____ is referred to as Seller.

1. ☐ **CANCELLATION OF PRIOR SALE; BACK-UP OFFER:** (If checked) This Agreement is in back-up position number _____, and is contingent upon written cancellation of any prior contracts and related escrows ("Prior Contracts") between Seller and other buyers. Seller and other buyers may mutually agree to modify or amend the terms of Prior Contracts. Buyer may cancel this Agreement in writing at any time before Seller provides Buyer copies of written cancellations of Prior Contracts signed by all parties to those contracts. If Seller is unable to provide such written signed cancellations to Buyer by _____ (date), then either Buyer or Seller may cancel the Agreement in writing.
   A. **BUYER'S DEPOSIT CHECK SHALL BE** held uncashed until copies of the written cancellations signed by all parties to the prior contracts are provided to Buyer, (OR if checked ☐ immediately handled as provided in the Agreement).
   B. **TIME PERIODS** in the Agreement for inspections, contingencies, covenants and other obligations, shall begin on the Day After Seller provides Buyer copies of signed cancellations of Prior Contracts, (OR, if checked, ☐ all time periods shall begin as provided in this Agreement). However, if the **date for close of escrow** is a specific calendar date, that date shall NOT be extended, unless agreed to in writing by Buyer and Seller.

2. ☐ **SHORT PAY:** (If checked) This Agreement is contingent upon Seller's receipt of written consent from all existing secured lenders and lienholders ("Short-Pay Lenders"), no later than 5:00 p.m. on _____ (date) ("Short-Pay Contingency Date"), to reduce their respective loan balances by an amount sufficient to permit the proceeds from the sale of the Property, without additional funds from Seller, to pay the existing balances on loans, real estate taxes, brokerage commissions, closing costs, and other monetary obligations the Agreement requires Seller to pay at Close Of Escrow (including, but not limited to, escrow charges, title charges, documentary transfer taxes, prorations, retrofit costs, and pest control inspection costs and repairs). If Seller fails to give Buyer written notice of all existing Short-Pay Lenders' consent by the Short-Pay Contingency Date, either Seller or Buyer may cancel the Agreement in writing. Seller shall reasonably cooperate with existing Lenders in the short pay-off process. Buyer and Seller understand that Lenders are not obligated to accept a short pay-off, and that Seller, Buyer and Broker(s) do not have any control over whether or not Short-Pay Lenders will accept a "short pay-off," or any act, omission, or decision by any Short-Pay Lender in the short pay-off process. Seller is informed that a short-pay may create credit or legal problems, or may result in taxable income to Seller. **Seller is advised to seek advice from an attorney, certified public accountant, or other expert regarding such potential consequences.**

3. ☐ **COURT CONFIRMATION:** (If checked) This Agreement is contingent upon court confirmation on or before _____ (date). If court confirmation is not obtained by that date, Buyer may cancel this Agreement in writing. Court confirmation may be required in probate, conservatorship, guardianship, receivership, bankruptcy, or other proceedings. The court may allow open, competitive bidding, resulting in Property being sold to the highest bidder. Buyer is advised to be in court when the offer is considered for confirmation. Buyer understands that (a) Broker and others may continue to market the Property, and (b) Broker may represent other competitive bidders prior to and at the court confirmation.

4. ☐ **TENANT OCCUPIED PROPERTY:** (This paragraph applies only if A or B is checked. Do not check both.)
   A. ☐ **TENANT TO VACATE:** Seller shall deliver Property vacant as of the date specified in the Agreement.
OR B. ☐ **TENANT TO REMAIN IN POSSESSION:** Buyer shall take Property subject to the rights of existing tenants. Seller shall, within **5 (or ☐ _____) Days** After Acceptance, deliver to Buyer copies of all leases, rental agreements, outstanding notices sent to tenants, and current income and expense statements ("Rental Documents"). Buyer shall, within **5 (or ☐ _____) Days** After receipt of Rental Documents, provide written notice to Seller of any items reasonably disapproved, by the method specified in the Agreement. Seller shall make no changes in leases and tenancies, and shall enter into no new leases or rental agreements during the pendency of this transaction without Buyer's prior written consent. Seller shall transfer to Buyer, through escrow, all unused tenant deposits. No warranty is made concerning compliance with governmental restrictions, if any, limiting the amount of rent that can lawfully be charged, and/or the maximum number of persons who can lawfully occupy the Property, unless otherwise agreed in writing.

5. ☐ **JUNIOR OR ASSUMED FINANCING:** (If checked) Obtaining the following loan or assumption **is a contingency** of this Agreement. Buyer shall act in good faith to obtain the designated financing.
   A. Either: ☐ NEW Second Deed of Trust in favor of LENDER; or ☐ ASSUMPTION of Existing Deed of Trust; encumbering the Property, securing a note payable at maximum interest of _____% fixed rate, or _____% initial adjustable rate, with a maximum lifetime interest rate cap of of _____%, balance due in _____ years. Buyer shall pay loan fees/points not to exceed _____.
   B. This loan contingency shall remain in effect until the designated loan is funded or assumption of existing financing is approved by Lender and completed, **(or ☐ _____ Days** After Acceptance, by which time Buyer shall give Seller written notice of Buyer's election to cancel this Agreement because of Buyer's inability to obtain the designated loan or assumption. If Buyer does not give Seller such notice, the contingency of obtaining the loan or assumption shall be removed by the method specified in the Agreement.).
   C. For assumption, Seller shall, within **5 (or ☐ _____) Days** After Acceptance, request from Lender, and upon receipt provide to Buyer, copies of all applicable notes and deeds of trust, loan balances and current interest rates. Buyer shall, within **5 (or ☐ _____) Days** After receipt, provide written notice to Seller of any items reasonably disapproved by the method specified in the Agreement. Differences between estimated and actual loan balances shall be adjusted at close of escrow by cash down payment. Impound accounts, if any, shall be assigned and charged to Buyer and credited to Seller. If this is an assumption of a VA Loan, the sale is contingent upon Seller being provided a release of liability and substitution of eligibility, unless otherwise agreed in writing.

Date _____ Date _____

Buyer _____ Seller _____

Buyer _____ Seller _____

THIS FORM HAS BEEN APPROVED BY THE CALIFORNIA ASSOCIATION OF REALTORS® (C.A.R.). NO REPRESENTATION IS MADE AS TO THE LEGAL VALIDITY OR ADEQUACY OF ANY PROVISION IN ANY SPECIFIC TRANSACTION. A REAL ESTATE BROKER IS THE PERSON QUALIFIED TO ADVISE ON REAL ESTATE TRANSACTIONS. IF YOU DESIRE LEGAL OR TAX ADVICE, CONSULT AN APPROPRIATE PROFESSIONAL.

This form is available for use by the entire real estate industry. It is not intended to identify the user as a REALTOR®. REALTOR® is a registered collective membership mark which may be used only by members of the NATIONAL ASSOCIATION OF REALTORS® who subscribe to its Code of Ethics.
The copyright laws of the United States (17 U.S. Code) forbid the unauthorized reproduction of this form by any means, including facsimile or computerized formats. Copyright © 1997, CALIFORNIA ASSOCIATION OF REALTORS®

Published and Distributed by:
REAL ESTATE BUSINESS SERVICES, INC.
a subsidiary of the CALIFORNIA ASSOCIATION OF REALTORS®
525 South Virgil Avenue, Los Angeles, California 90020   Page _____ of _____ Pages.

OFFICE USE ONLY
Reviewed by Broker
or Designee _____
Date _____

EQUAL HOUSING OPPORTUNITY

PURCHASE AGREEMENT ADDENDUM (PAA-14 PAGE 1 OF 1) REVISED 5/97

THE PURCHASE AGREEMENT ADDENDUM

The **PURCHASE AGREEMENT ADDENDUM** *form is used as an addendum to either the Residential Purchase Agreement, another offer form or the counter offer form.* Only the paragraphs that are checked are included as part of the contract. The one-page addendum (Figure 5-11) covers five separate topics that are occasionally relevant to a transaction:

1) The cancellation of prior sale/back-up offers
2) "Short-pay" lenders (secured lenders and lienholders)
3) Court confirmation (for probate, guardianship, receivership, bankruptcy, etc.)
4) Tenant-occupied properties
5) Junior or assumed financing.

ERRORS AND OMISSIONS INSURANCE *is the liability insurance that brokers and salespeople are required to carry in order to pay for any costly lawsuits.*

THE COUNTER OFFER
(REPLACES ORIGINAL OFFER WITH CHANGES IN TERMS)

If the original offer is rejected, a new offer, with only a few different terms (sales price, down payment, etc.), is called a counter offer.

Rather than preparing a whole new deposit receipt when presenting a counter offer, most sellers prefer to use a standard counter offer form like the sample CAR® form shown in Figure 5-12. This form is used to change some of the terms of the original deposit receipt and allows the seller and buyer to accept the remaining agreed to terms and conditions of the original agreement. Plenty of blank space is provided to list these exceptions that formally amend the deposit receipt without the necessity of completing an entirely new contract.

A contract negotiation may involve several counter offers.

If there is only a minor change in a term (like sale's price), the counter offer can be written on the back of the original deposit receipt and signed by the buyer and seller. The seller can never change the deposit receipt on its face by crossing out sections or adding new information. The counter offer must contain a clause stating that all of the conditions of the original deposit receipt are acceptable except for the listed new terms. If there are major changes, the formal counter offer form may be required. Finally, if there are several changes it may be better to start the process again by filling out a new deposit receipt.

FIGURE 5-12

CALIFORNIA
ASSOCIATION
OF REALTORS®

COUNTER OFFER No. _____
(For use by Seller or Buyer. May be used for Multiple Counter.)

This is a counter offer to the: ☐ Offer, ☐ Counter Offer, ☐ Other _____, dated _____,
regarding (property address): _____
between _____, "Buyer," and _____, "Seller."

1. **TERMS:** The terms and conditions of the above referenced document are **accepted subject to the following:**

   A. Paragraphs in the purchase contract (offer) which require initials by all parties, but are not initialed by all parties, are excluded from the final agreement unless specifically referenced for inclusion in paragraph 1C of this or another Counter Offer.

   B. Unless otherwise specified in writing, down payment and loan amount(s) will be adjusted in the same proportion as in the original offer.

   C. _____
   _____
   _____
   _____
   _____
   _____
   _____
   _____
   _____
   _____
   _____
   _____
   _____
   _____
   _____
   _____
   _____
   _____
   _____
   _____
   _____
   _____
   _____

   D. The following attached supplements are incorporated in this Counter Offer:
   ☐ _____ ☐ _____
   ☐ _____ ☐ _____

2. ☐ **(If Checked:) MULTIPLE COUNTER OFFER:** Seller is making a Counter Offer(s) to another prospective buyer(s) on terms which may or may not be the same as in this Counter Offer. Acceptance of this Counter Offer by Buyer shall **not** be binding unless and until it is subsequently re-signed by Seller in paragraph 7 below. Prior to the completion of all of these events, Buyer and Seller shall have no duties or obligations for the purchase or sale of the Property.

3. **RIGHT TO ACCEPT OTHER OFFERS:** Seller reserves the right to continue to offer the Property for sale or for other transaction, and to accept any other offer at any time prior to communication of acceptance, as described in paragraph 4. Seller's acceptance of another offer prior to Buyer's acceptance and communication of acceptance of this Counter Offer shall revoke this Counter Offer.

4. **EXPIRATION:** Unless acceptance of this Counter Offer is signed by the person receiving it, and communication of acceptance is made by delivering a signed copy in person, by mail, or by facsimile which is personally received, to the person making this Counter Offer or to _____, by 5:00 PM on the third calendar day after this Counter Offer is written (or, if checked, ☐ date: _____, time _____ AM/PM), this Counter Offer shall be deemed revoked and the deposit shall be returned to Buyer. This Counter Offer may be executed in counterparts.

   As the person(s) making this Counter Offer on the terms above, receipt of a copy is acknowledged.

   _____ Date: _____ Time: _____ AM/PM

   _____ Date: _____ Time: _____ AM/PM

5. **ACCEPTANCE:** I/WE accept the above Counter Offer (If checked: ☐ **SUBJECT TO THE ATTACHED COUNTER OFFER**) and acknowledge receipt of a copy.

   _____ Date: _____ Time: _____ AM/PM

   _____ Date: _____ Time: _____ AM/PM

6. **ACKNOWLEDGMENT OF RECEIPT:** Receipt of signed acceptance on (date) _____, at _____ AM/PM, by the maker of the Counter Offer, or other person designated in paragraph 4, is acknowledged. (_____/_____) (Initials)

7. **MULTIPLE COUNTER OFFER SIGNATURE LINE:** (Paragraph 7 applies only if paragraph 2 is checked.) By signing below, Seller accepts this Multiple Counter Offer, and creates a binding contract. (NOTE TO SELLER: Do NOT sign in this paragraph until after Buyer signs the acceptance in paragraph 5, and returns to Seller for re-signing.)

   _____ Date: _____ Time: _____ AM/PM

   _____ Date: _____ Time: _____ AM/PM

Published and Distributed by:
REAL ESTATE BUSINESS SERVICES, INC.
a subsidiary of the CALIFORNIA ASSOCIATION OF REALTORS®
525 South Virgil Avenue, Los Angeles, California 90020

Page _____ of _____ Pages.

OFFICE USE ONLY
Reviewed by Broker
or Designee _____
Date _____

COUNTER OFFER (CO-14 PAGE 1 OF 1) REVISED 9/95

INSPECTION ADVISORY FOR BUYERS (ENVIRONMENTAL HAZARDS)

Property inspection is important. The physical condition of the land and improvements being purchased are not guaranteed by either Sellers or Brokers, except as specifically set forth in the purchase agreement. For this reason, buyer should conduct a thorough inspection of the property personally and with professionals, who should provide a written report of their inspections. If the professionals recommend further investigation or inspections, the buyer should contact the necessary qualified experts.

Figure 5-13 shows the CAR® Buyer's Inspection Form that covers the following:

1. General condition of the property;
2. Square footage, age, boundaries;
3. Soil stability/geologic conditions;
4. Roof;
5. Pool/spa;
6. Waste disposal;
7. Water and utilities;
8. Environmental hazards;
9. Earthquake and flood;
10. Governmental requirements;
11. Rent and occupancy control;
12. Neighborhood.

HOMEOWNER'S GUIDE TO EARTHQUAKE SAFETY

Earthquakes pose a serious threat to some California homes, and many older homes are not built to modern earthquake codes. California's real estate disclosure laws require sellers of real property to disclose known defects (including earthquake weakness and hazards) to prospective purchasers. CAR® has a booklet entitled <u>Environmental Hazards: Guide for Homeowners and Buyers/ The Homeowners Guide to Earthquakes</u>.

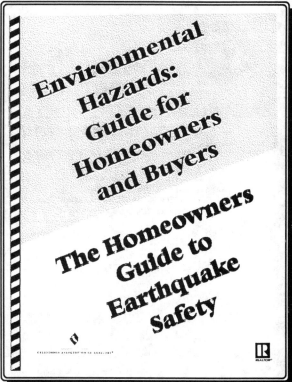

FIGURE 5-13

CALIFORNIA
ASSOCIATION
OF REALTORS®

BUYER'S INSPECTION ADVISORY

Property Address: _____ ("Property")

IMPORTANCE OF PROPERTY INSPECTION: The physical condition of the land and improvements being purchased are not guaranteed by either Seller or Brokers, except as specifically set forth in the purchase agreement. For this reason, Buyer should conduct a thorough inspection of the Property personally and with professionals, who should provide a written report of their inspections. If the professionals recommend further investigation, tests, or inspections, Buyer should contact qualified experts to conduct such additional investigations, tests, or inspections. **Disclosure duties:** The law requires Seller and Brokers to disclose to Buyer all material facts known to them which affect the value or desirability of the Property. In sales involving residential dwellings with no more than four units, Brokers have a duty to make a diligent visual inspection of the accessible areas of the Property, and to disclose the results of that inspection. However, as some Property defects or conditions may not be discoverable from a visual inspection, it is possible neither Seller nor Brokers are aware of them. **Buyer duties:** Buyer has an affirmative duty to exercise reasonable care to protect himself or herself, including discovery and investigation of information and facts which are known to Buyer, or are within the diligent attention and observation of Buyer. **Property Inspections:** Brokers do not have expertise, and therefore cannot advise Buyer on many items, such as soil stability, geologic conditions, hazardous substances, structural conditions of the foundation or other improvements, or the condition of the roof, heating, air conditioning, plumbing, electrical, sewer, septic, waste disposal or other systems. The only way to accurately determine the condition of the Property is through an inspection by an appropriate professional selected by Buyer.

YOU ARE ADVISED TO CONDUCT INSPECTIONS OF THE ENTIRE PROPERTY, INCLUDING BUT NOT LIMITED TO THE FOLLOWING:

1. **GENERAL CONDITION OF THE PROPERTY, ITS SYSTEMS AND COMPONENTS:** Foundation, roof, plumbing, heating, air conditioning, electrical, mechanical, security, pool/spa, and other structural and non-structural systems and components, built-in appliances, any personal property included in the sale, and energy efficiency of the Property. (Structural engineers are best suited to determine possible design or construction defects, and whether improvements are structurally sound.)
2. **SQUARE FOOTAGE, AGE, BOUNDARIES:** Square footage, room dimensions, lot size, age of improvements, and boundaries. Any numerical statements regarding these items are APPROXIMATIONS ONLY, and have not been and cannot be verified by Brokers. Fences, hedges, walls, retaining walls, and other natural or constructed barriers or markers do not necessarily identify true Property boundaries. (An appraiser, architect, surveyor, or civil engineer is best suited to determine respectively square footage, dimensions and boundaries of the Property.)
3. **SOIL STABILITY/GEOLOGIC CONDITIONS:** Existence of fill or compacted soil, or expansive or contracting soil, susceptibility to slippage, settling or movement, and the adequacy of drainage. These types of inspections are particularly important for hillside or sloped properties, but the referenced conditions may also exist on flat land. (Geotechnical engineers are best suited to determine such conditions, causes, and remedies.)
4. **ROOF:** Present condition, approximate age, leaks, and remaining useful life. (Roofing contractors are best suited to determine these conditions.)
5. **POOL/SPA:** Whether there are any cracks, leaks or operational problems. (Pool contractors are best suited to determine these conditions.)
6. **WASTE DISPOSAL:** Type, size, adequacy, capacity and condition of sewer and septic systems and components, connection to sewer, and applicable fees.
7. **WATER AND UTILITIES; WELL SYSTEMS AND COMPONENTS:** Water and utility availability, use restrictions, and costs. Adequacy, condition, and performance of well systems and components.
8. **ENVIRONMENTAL HAZARDS:** Potential environmental hazards, including asbestos, lead-based paint and other lead contamination, methane, other gases, fuel, oil or chemical storage tanks, contaminated soil or water, hazardous waste, waste disposal sites, electromagnetic fields, nuclear sources, and other substances, materials, products, or conditions. (For further information, read the booklet "Environmental Hazards: A Guide for Homeowners and Buyers," or consult an appropriate professional.)
9. **EARTHQUAKE AND FLOOD; INSURANCE AVAILABILITY:** Susceptibility of the Property to earthquake hazards and propensity of the Property to flood. These and other conditions may affect the availability and need for certain types of insurance. (Geologist, Geotechnic Engineer and insurance agents are best suited to provide information on these conditions.)
10. **GOVERNMENTAL REQUIREMENTS AND LIMITATIONS:** Permits, inspections, certificates, zoning, other governmental limitations, restrictions, and requirements affecting the current or future use of the Property, its development or size. (Such information is available through appropriate governmental agencies and private information providers. Brokers are not qualified to obtain, review, or interpret any such information.)
11. **RENT AND OCCUPANCY CONTROL:** Some cities and counties impose restrictions which may limit the amount of rent that can be charged, the maximum number of persons who can occupy the Property, and the circumstances in which tenancies can be terminated. (Information about such restrictions can be obtained from local governmental agencies.)
12. **NEIGHBORHOOD, AREA, SUBDIVISION CONDITIONS; PERSONAL FACTORS:** Neighborhood or area conditions, including schools, proximity and adequacy of law enforcement, crime statistics, registered felons or offenders, fire protection, other governmental services, proximity to commercial, industrial or agricultural activities, existing and proposed transportation, construction and development which may affect noise, view, or traffic, airport noise, noise or odor from any source, wild and domestic animals, other nuisances, hazards, or circumstances, facilities and condition of common areas of common interest subdivisions, and possible lack of compliance with any governing documents or Homeowners' Association requirements, conditions and influences of significance to certain cultures and/or religions, and personal needs, requirements and preferences of Buyer.

> Buyer acknowledges and agrees that Brokers: (a) Do not guarantee the condition of the Property; (b) Shall not be responsible for defects that are not known to Broker(s) or are not visually observable in reasonably and normally accessible areas of the Property; (c) Cannot verify information contained in inspection reports or representations made by others; (d) Do not guarantee the performance of others who have provided services or products to Buyer or Seller; (e) Do not guarantee the adequacy or completeness of repairs made by Seller or others; (f) Cannot identify Property boundary lines; and (g) Do not decide what price a buyer should pay or a seller should accept. Buyer agrees to seek desired assistance from appropriate professionals.

YOU ARE STRONGLY ADVISED TO INVESTIGATE THE CONDITION AND SUITABILITY OF ALL ASPECTS OF THE PROPERTY. IF YOU DO NOT DO SO, YOU ARE ACTING AGAINST THE ADVICE OF BROKERS.

By signing below, Buyer acknowledges receipt of a copy of this document. Buyer is encouraged to read it carefully.

_____   _____   _____   _____
Buyer Signature   Date   Buyer Signature   Date

Buyer(s) (Print Name(s)) _____

Current Address _____

REBS | Published and Distributed by:
REAL ESTATE BUSINESS SERVICES, INC.
a subsidiary of the CALIFORNIA ASSOCIATION OF REALTORS®
525 South Virgil Avenue, Los Angeles, California 90020

OFFICE USE ONLY
Reviewed by Broker
or Designee _____
Date _____

EQUAL HOUSING OPPORTUNITY

Page _____ of _____ Pages.

BUYER'S INSPECTION ADVISORY (BIA-14 PAGE 1 OF 1) REVISED 5/97

(1) The Homeowner's Guide to Earthquake Safety must be given to all buyers of one to four dwelling units built before 1960 and (2) the disclosure form must be filled out by the seller.

Figure 5-14 is the disclosure form to be used for this disclosure. See Chapter 12 for more details about earthquake zones.

Before you agree to buy a house, review the information disclosed by the seller. Pay special attention to any items that indicate earthquake weakness. Consider the house's location: Is it in or near a fault rupture zone or in an area where it might be damaged by a landslide? You may wish to discuss the cost of strengthening with the seller. The law does not require that either you or the seller strengthen the home, but failure to fix any weakness before a damaging earthquake could lead to repair costs that exceed your equity in the home.

The law requires the seller to certify to the buyer that the water heaters are strapped or braced to the building according to the minimum standards of the Uniform Plumbing Code.

FIGURE 5-14

RESIDENTIAL EARTHQUAKE HAZARDS REPORT

Refer to Section 8897 *et seq.*, California Government Code

Name	Assessor's Parcel No.
Street Address	Year Built
City and County	Zip Code

Answer these questions to the best of your knowledge. If you do not have actual knowledge as to whether the weakness exists or not, answer "Don't Know:" If your house does not have the feature, answer "Doesn't Apply." The page numbers in the right-hand column indicate where in this guide you can find information on each of these features.

		Yes	No	Doesn't Apply	Don't Know	See Page
1.	Is the water heater braced, strapped, or anchored to resist falling during an earthquake?	☐	☐	☐	☐	6
2.	Is the house anchored or bolted to the foundation?	☐	☐	☐	☐	7
3.	If the house has cripple walls:					
	° Are the exterior cripple walls braced?	☐	☐	☐	☐	8
	° If the exterior foundation consists of unconnected concrete piers and posts, have they been strengthened?	☐	☐	☐	☐	9
4.	If the exterior foundation, or part of it, is made of unreinforced masonry, has it been strengthened?	☐	☐	☐	☐	10
5.	If the house is built on a hillside, answer the following:					
	° Are the exterior tall foundation walls braced?	☐	☐	☐	☐	11
	° Were the tall posts or columns either built to resist earthquakes or have they been strengthened?	☐	☐	☐	☐	11
6.	If the exterior walls of the house, or part of them, are made of unreinforced masonry, have they been strengthened?	☐	☐	☐	☐	12
7.	If the house has a living area over the garage, was the wall around the garage door opening either built to resist earthquakes or has it been strengthened?	☐	☐	☐	☐	13

If any of the questions are answered "No," the house is likely to have an earthquake weakness. Questions answered "Don't Know" may indicate a need for further evaluation. If you corrected one or more of these weaknesses, describe the work on a separate page.

As Seller of the property described herein, I have answered the questions above to the best of my knowledge in an effort to fully disclose any potential earthquake weaknesses it may have.

EXECUTED BY

_____   _____   _____
(Seller)   (Seller)   Date

I acknowledge receipt of this form, completed and signed by the Seller. I understand that if the Seller has answered "No" to one or more questions, or if Seller has indicated a lack of knowledge, there may be one or more earthquake weaknesses in this house.

_____   _____   _____
(Buyer)   (Buyer)   Date

This earthquake disclosure is made in addition to the standard real estate transfer disclosure statement also required by law.

Keep your copy of this form for future reference.

COVENANTS (A PROMISE IN THE DEPOSIT RECEIPT)

COVENANTS *are promises between the parties to a contract.* Covenants represent promises, obligations and considerations exchanged to fulfill a contract.

If you break a contractual promise, you can be sued for damages.

Failure to perform a stipulated covenant does not release either party from his or her responsibility. The contract is still in effect, although the offended party may sue for damages.

CONTINGENCIES, CONDITIONS OR SUBJECT TO (AN "IF" CLAUSE IN THE DEPOSIT RECEIPT)

CONTINGENCIES, CONDITIONS OR SUBJECT TO *are provisions by which all parties are released from any obligations of a contract if some stated condition fails to materialize.* For example, purchase offers may be made contingent upon the availability of financing, or subject to the successful sale of another property. If the contingency falls through, the contract is voidable by the buyer.

A contingency clause is an "if" situation, so it should be used sparingly. Example: Only if I qualify for the loan will I purchase the property. They are also referred to as conditions or "subject to" provisions.

Items that are usually found in contingency clauses include:

1. Obtaining financing at a certain interest rate or less.
2. Subject to the approval of my CPA and attorney within 20 days.
3. Conditional upon inspection and approval of each apartment.

PURCHASE OPTIONS

OPTIONS (A UNILATERAL CONTRACT)

An **OPTION** is *a right to purchase a property upon specified terms within a specific time period, which is granted in exchange for money* (see Figure 5-15, only page 1 of 3). An option is normally purchased to take a property off the open market. The prospective purchaser holds an exclusive right to buy during the option period.

FIGURE 5-15

CALIFORNIA ASSOCIATION OF REALTORS®

☐

RESIDENTIAL PURCHASE OPTION

THIS IS INTENDED TO BE A LEGALLY BINDING CONTRACT. READ IT CAREFULLY.
CALIFORNIA ASSOCIATION OF REALTORS® (C.A.R.) STANDARD FORM

_____, California _____, 19_____
_____, Optionor,
and _____, Optionee, agree as follows:

1. **PROPERTY:** Optionor grants to Optionee the option to purchase the real property and improvements described as:
   _____
   (Street address or other description)
   _____ ("Premises").
   (City, County, State)

2. **OPTION TO PURCHASE:** In consideration of the payment of $_____ as option consideration,
   ☐ receipt of $_____ is acknowledged by Optionor, evidenced by ☐ cash, ☐cashier's check, ☐ personal check,
   or ☐ _____,
   ☐ payable as follows: _____
   _____.

   Optionor grants to Optionee the option to purchase the Premises on the terms and conditions set forth in the attached:
   ☐ Real Estate Purchase Contract and Receipt for Deposit,
   ☐ Mobile Home Purchase Contract and Receipt for Deposit,
   ☐ Other _____,
   which are incorporated by this reference as a part of this Agreement. **All of the time limits contained in the attached agreement shall begin to run on the date the option is exercised. If any contingency in the attached agreement, including but not limited to any right of inspection or financing provision, is not satisfied or is disapproved by Optionee at any time, all option consideration paid, rent paid, services rendered to Optionor, and improvements to the Premises, if any, by Optionee, shall be retained by Optionor in consideration of the granting of the option.**

3. **SUPPLEMENTS:** The ATTACHED supplements below are incorporated as part of this Agreement:
   ☐ _____ ☐ _____
   ☐ _____ ☐ _____
   ☐ _____ ☐ _____

4. **TERM OF OPTION:** The Option shall begin on _____, 19_____, and shall end at 11:59 p.m. on
   _____, 19_____.

5. **MANNER OF EXERCISE:** Optionee may exercise the Option **only** by:
   (a) delivering to Optionor, no earlier than _____ and no later
       than _____, a written, unconditional notice of exercise, signed by Optionee, and
   (b) ☐ [If checked] opening escrow with the escrow holder named in the attached agreement, and
   (c) ☐ [If checked] delivering to the named escrow holder
          ☐ a copy of the notice of exercise,
          ☐ signed escrow instructions, and
   (d) ☐ [If checked] Other: _____
       _____

6. **EFFECT OF DEFAULT ON OPTION:**
   (a) Optionee shall have no right to exercise the Option during the time period any monetary or non-monetary obligation of Optionee then due is unpaid or unperformed (whether or not notice of default is given to Optionee).
   (b) All of Optionee's rights under the Option shall terminate, even if the Option is timely exercised if, after exercise and before the close of the sale, Optionee fails to pay or perform any monetary or non-monetary obligation under the terms of this Agreement, for a period of 30 days after the obligation becomes due or before the scheduled close of the sale, whichever occurs first (whether or not Optionor gives notice of default to Optionee).

7. **NON-EXERCISE:** If the Option is not exercised in the manner specified, within the option period or any written extension thereof, or if it is terminated under any provision of this Agreement, then:
   (a) The Option and all rights of Optionee to purchase the Premises shall immediately terminate without notice.
   (b) All Option consideration paid, rent paid, services rendered to Optionor, and improvements to the Premises, if any, by Optionee, shall be retained by Optionor in consideration of the granting of the Option.
   (c) If requested by Optionor, Optionee shall execute, acknowledge, and deliver to Optionor within _____ calendar days of Optionor's request, a release, quitclaim deed, or any other document reasonably required by Optionor or a title insurance company to verify the termination of the Option.

8. **ASSIGNMENT OF OPTION:** Optionee shall not assign the Option or any interest therein
   ☐ [If checked] except upon Optionor's review and approval of financial statements, tax returns, and credit history of the proposed assignee(s). Any assignment in violation of this paragraph shall be void.

9. **NOTICES:** Unless otherwise provided in this Agreement, any notice, tender, or delivery to be given by either party to the other may be effected by personal delivery, or by registered or certified mail, postage prepaid, return receipt requested, and shall be deemed delivered when mailed (except for acceptance of the offer to enter into this Agreement, which must be done in the manner specified in paragraph 23). Mailed notices shall be addressed as shown below, but each party may designate a new address by written notice to the other.

10. **TRANSFER DISCLOSURE STATEMENT:** Unless exempt, if the Premises contain one-to-four residential dwelling units, Optionor must comply with Civil Code §§1102 et seq., by providing Optionee with a Real Estate Transfer Disclosure Statement.

Optionee and Optionor acknowledge receipt of copy of this page, which constitutes Page 1 of _____ Pages.
Optionee's Initials (_____) (_____) Optionor's Initials (_____) (_____)

OFFICE USE ONLY
Reviewed by Broker or Designee _____
Date _____

EQUAL HOUSING OPPORTUNITY

RESIDENTIAL PURCHASE OPTION (O-14 PAGE 1 OF 3)

An *OPTIONOR* is a property owner who gives an interested buyer an exclusive right to purchase a property. An *OPTIONEE* is a potential buyer who purchases an agreed to amount of time to buy a specific property upon set terms. The optionee does not have to go through with the purchase.

> *It is a good practice to approve a preliminary title report (verify title) on the property before purchasing an option.*

If the optionee decides to buy the property during his or her option period, the optionor must sell. In this case, the option will become a sales contract and both parties are bound by its terms.

The optionee may also secure another buyer for the property (sell his or her option to another party) during its term. Thus, all rights and interests may be transferred without the consent of the optionor, unless stated otherwise.

If an optionee has, for example, a one year recorded option and, after six months decides not to exercise his or her option, the property owner should see to it that a quitclaim deed is recorded so that the option might be removed from the records.

> *An agent who exercises an option to buy his own listing has a conflict of interest. He or she must disclose the full amount of his or her commission and profit and obtain the seller's approval before buying the property.*

TERMINOLOGY - CHAPTER 5

A. Contract
B. Expressed Contract
C. Implied Contract
D. Bilateral Contract
E. Unilateral Contract
F. Executory Contract
G. Execute
H. Valid Contract
I. Minors
J. Incompetent
K. Fraud Duress, Menace
L. Undue Influence
M. Mutual Consent

N. Offer
O. Offeror
P. Offeree
Q. Void, Voidable, Unenforceable
R. Definite and Certain
S. Acceptance
T. Counteroffer
U. Consideration
V. Assignment
W. Assignor
X. Assignee
Y. Novation
Z. Breach

AA. Rescission
BB. Dollar Damages
CC. Liquidated Damages
DD. Specific Performance
EE. Deposit Receipt
FF. Covenant
GG. Contingencies
HH. Pest Control Report
II. Option
JJ. Optionor
KK. Optionee
LL. Capable Parties

1.____ A court action to compel the performance of an agreement, e.g., sale of land.

2.____ Anything given or promised by a party to induce another to enter into a contract.

3.____ A contract in which something remains to be done by one or both the parties.

4.____ A right given, for consideration, to purchase a property upon specified terms within a specified time period, without obligating the party to purchase the property.

5.____ A written offer to purchase real property upon stated terms and conditions, accompanied by a deposit toward the purchase price, which becomes the contract for the sale of the property upon acceptance.

6.____ All persons under 18 years of age.

7.____ The act of agreeing or consenting to the terms of an offer, thereby establishing "the meeting of the minds" that is an essential element of a contract; genuine assent from both parties.

8.____ One who assigns his or her right in a contract.

9.____ A person to whom property or interests therein shall have been assigned.

10.____ One who is mentally incapable of managing or taking care of self or property and therefore cannot enter into a contract without a guardian.

11.____ A promise to do or not to do a particular act.

12.____ The substitution or exchange of a new contract for an old one by the mutual agreement of the parties.

13.____ A transfer by a person of that person's rights under a contract.

14.____ An agreement to do or not to do a certain thing. It must have four essential elements: parties capable of contracting, consent of the parties, a lawful object, and consideration.

15.____ The terms and provisions of a contract, which are clear, definite and set forth, as opposed to implied.

16.____ A binding contract created by the actions of the principals rather than by written or oral agreement.

17.____ A contract under which the parties expressly enter into mutual promises, such as sales contracts.

18.____ A contract under which only one party expressly makes a promise.

19.____ Having no legal force or binding effect, or cannot be enforced for one reason or another.

20.____ One making an offer.

21.____ One to whom an offer is made.

22.____ A proposal for acceptance, in order to form a contract. It must be definite as to price and terms.

23.____ Voluntarily agreeing to the price and terms of an offer. Offer and acceptance create a contract.

24.____ An offer in response to an offer.

25.____ Failure to perform a contract, in whole or part, without legal excuse.

26.____ Annulling a contract and placing the parties to it in a position as if there had not been a contract.

27.____ A definite amount of damage, set forth in a contract, to be paid by the party breaching the contract. A predetermined estimate of actual damages from a breach.

28.____ An inspection report required, in the sale of property, to determine if termites are present within a building.

29.____ One who, for consideration, receives an option.

30.____ One who, for consideration, gives an option.

31.____ A contract under which the parties expressly enter into mutual promises.

32.____ The dependence upon a stated event before a contract becomes binding.

33.____ An action that abandons all other remedies and simply asks for money.

34.____ Influence used to destroy the will of another so that any decision is not his or her free act.

35.____ To complete a contract by signing it.

36.____ Legally binding, the terms of which can be sued for in a court of law.

37.____ Deceptive statements or acts used to wrongfully obtain money or property.

38.____ Individuals who have a legal capacity to contract, as opposed to minors, convicts and incompetents.

MULTIPLE CHOICE

1. An agreement that is created by acts and conduct, rather than by words, is known as a (an):

    A. bilateral contract
    C. expressed contract

    B. unilateral contract
    D. implied contract

2. When using pre-printed forms, what is the order of control over the parts?

    A. Typed, handwritten, printed
    C. Printed, typed, handwritten

    B. Handwritten, typed, printed
    D. None of the above

3. Misrepresentation of a material fact that is known to be false is called:

    A. mistake
    C. fraud

    B. duress
    D. undue influence

4. What restrictions are placed on aliens with regards to buying real property in California?

    A. Must be at least 21 years of age
    C. Cannot transfer property for at least 1 year

    B. Must live in California for at least 10 years
    D. There are no unusual restrictions

5. An initial counteroffer has the effect of:

    A. amending the original offer
    C. modifying the original offer

    B. terminating the original offer
    D. no effect on the original offer

6. Which of the following can terminate an original offer?

    A. Counteroffer
    C. Withdrawal before acceptance

    B. Lapse of time
    D. All of the above

7. A bilateral contract is a (an):

    A. promise for an act
    C. implied contract

    B. promise for a promise
    D. contract made in writing

8. What is the most commonly requested court action for the remedy of breach?

    A. Action for dollar damages
    C. Specific performance

    B. Unilateral rescission
    D. Acceptance of breach

9. A contract that is NOT definite and certain and therefore unenforceable is a (an):

    A. implied contract
    C. partially completed contract

    B. illusory contract
    D. emancipated contract

10. Which of the following do the courts consider to be grounds for emancipation?

    A. Married minors
    C. Court-declared self-supporting minors

    B. Minors serving in the armed forces
    D. All of the above

CHAPTER 6
Landlord and Tenant
(Lessor and Lessee)

http://www.ca-apartment.org (Apartment Owners Association)
http://search.yahoo.com/search?p=California+rental (Rental Group)
http://tenant.net/Other_Areas/Calif (Tenant Association)

A landlord and tenant relationship is created when the owner gives the possession and use of his or her property to another for rent or other consideration. The *LANDLORD* is the owner of the property being rented or leased. The landlord, or his or her agent, may lease only the land, the land and buildings or only the buildings or parts of the buildings. The *TENANT* is the person or persons renting or leasing the property.

A lease is a contract for a set time, typically one year or longer. A rental agreement is different in that it is usually made on a monthly basis and is renewable at the end of each period (week-to-week, month-to-month or any period-to-period up to one year). Because a rental agreement is a type of lease, the principles are the same as those of the lease, except for the time periods involved.

LEASEHOLD ESTATES
(Less-than-Freehold)

TYPES OF LEASEHOLD ESTATES

A leasehold is a personal property right in real property.

As discussed before, with **less-than-freehold** estates, there is no direct ownership of real estate. They are chattel real estates. A *CHATTEL REAL ESTATE is a personal property estate (in real property), such as a lease.* We call this type of interest in a property a **lease** or leasehold. A *LEASEHOLD is an exclusive right to occupy and use the property on a temporary basis.* There are no ownership rights in real property. The owner has reversionary interest, which means that he or she can regain possession at the end of the leasehold period. Figure 6-1 shows the four types of leasehold estates.

FIGURE 6-1

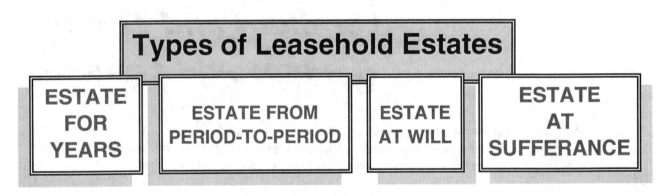

ESTATE FOR YEARS

(A LEASE - PREDETERMINED AMOUNT OF TIME)

With a lease, you know ahead of time when to move in and when to move out. A lease is usually for a year or more but can be for any predetermined time, agreed to in advance, up to 99 years.

A *conveyance of an estate in real property, such as a lease, to someone for a certain length of time is called a* **DEMISE.** *An* **ESTATE FOR YEARS** *is an agreement, in advance, between a lessee and a lessor for use of a property for a fixed (predetermined) period of time.* A **LEASE** *is a contractual agreement to possess and use a property for an agreed to (predetermined) period of time.* If the lease period is longer than one year from the date of the signing, then it must be in writing and signed by the lessor. The **LESSOR** *is the owner, sometimes referred to as the landlord, and the* **LESSEE** *is the tenant.*

> *The lessor is the owner of a fee estate or a holder of a life estate who gives up possession to all or part of his or her estate and holds a reversionary interest.*

ESTATE FROM PERIOD-TO-PERIOD

(RENEWABLE - EACH PERIOD)

An **ESTATE FROM PERIOD-TO-PERIOD** *is periodic tenancy that continues from year-to-year, month-to-month, week-to-week or from any other designated period-to-period.* This period-to-period estate, which is automatically renewable, is called a rental agreement. A **RENTAL AGREEMENT** *is an agreement between a tenant and landlord for continuing periods of time, usually from month-to-month.* Rental agreements do not expire; notice must be given by one of the parties. Written rental agreements have become the most commonly used real estate agreements in the United States. They are used frequently when renting apartments, duplexes, houses, condominiums and other types of residential property. The California Association of Realtors® (CAR) has a standard residential rental agreement that covers all the basic conditions desired in such a contract. Figure 6-2 is a copy of the first page of that form. The reverse side of the form, as seen in Figure 6-3, is a credit application to be filled out by the prospective tenant.

> *If no expiration date is given on a rental agreement and, unless stated otherwise, a 30-Day Notice by either party is required to terminate a month-to-month tenancy.*

A landlord holds a reversionary right to the property. A **REVERSIONARY RIGHT** *means the landlord grants the tenant the right to occupy (possess) the property, but he or she retains the right to retake possession after the lease or rental term has expired.* Periodic tenancy is usually terminated when either party gives 30 day's notice, because most rental agreements are month-to-month. If the rental period is less than one month, then only one period (that is, agreed length of the tenancy) notice is required. For example, if tenancy was from week-to-week, only seven days notice would be necessary.

FIGURE 6-2

CALIFORNIA ASSOCIATION OF REALTORS®

RESIDENTIAL LEASE OR MONTH-TO-MONTH RENTAL AGREEMENT

_____, California _____ 19, _____

_____, Landlord and

_____, Tenant, agree as follows:

1. **PROPERTY:** Landlord rents to Tenant and Tenant rents from Landlord the real property and improvements described as:
   _____
   (Street address or other description)
   _____ ("Premises"). The following personal property
   (City, County, State)
   is included: _____

2. **RENT; TERM:** Tenant agrees to pay rent monthly, at the rate of $ _____, in advance, on the _____ day
   of each calendar month. The term begins on _____, 19 _____, ("Commencement Date"), as a:
   - ☐ **A.** month-to-month tenancy, which may be terminated by either party, by giving written notice to the other at least 30 days prior to the intended termination date; or,
   - ☐ **B.** lease ending _____, 19 _____, with a total rent of $ _____, monthly installments as above; or,
   - ☐ **C.** _____

3. **LATE CHARGE:** Tenant acknowledges that late payment of rent may cause Landlord to incur costs and expenses, the exact amount of which are extremely difficult and impractical to determine. These costs may include, but are not limited to, processing and accounting expenses, late charges that may be imposed on Landlord by terms of any loan secured by the Premises, costs for additional attempts to collect rent, and preparation of notices. Therefore, if any installment of rent due from Tenant is not received by Landlord within _____ calendar days after date due, Tenant shall pay to Landlord an additional sum of $ _____ as a late charge which shall be deemed additional rent. Landlord and Tenant agree that this late charge represents a fair and reasonable estimate of the costs that Landlord may incur by reason of Tenant's late payments. Any late charge due shall be paid with the current installment of rent. Landlord's acceptance of any late charge shall not constitute a waiver as to any default of Tenant, or prevent Landlord from exercising any other rights and remedies under this Agreement, and as provided by law.

4. **PAYMENT:** The rent shall be paid to _____, at _____
   (Name)
   _____, or
   (Address, City, State, Zip Code)
   at any other location specified by Landlord.

5. **SECURITY DEPOSIT:** $ _____ shall be given by Tenant as a security deposit. Landlord may use all or any portion of the security deposit reasonably necessary to: (a) cure Tenant's default in payment of rent, late charges or other sums due; (b) repair damages caused by Tenant, or by a guest or a licensee of Tenant; (c) clean the Premises, if necessary, upon termination of tenancy; and (d) replace or return personal property or appurtenances, excluding ordinary wear and tear. If used during the tenancy, Tenant agrees to reinstate the total security deposit within five days after written notice delivered to Tenant in person or by mail. No later than three weeks after Tenant vacates the Premises, Landlord shall furnish to Tenant an itemized written statement of the basis for, and the amount of, any security received and the disposition of the security, and shall return any remaining portion of the security to Tenant. The return of the security deposit at the end of the tenancy, if otherwise due, will be handled directly between Landlord and Tenant and will not involve any broker who releases the security deposit to Landlord. Landlord and Tenant each indemnify and release any broker from any liability relating to return of the security deposit.

6. **UTILITIES:** Tenant agrees to pay for all utilities and services based upon occupancy of the Premises, and the following charges: _____
   _____, except
   _____ which shall be paid for by Landlord. If any utilities
   (Specify exceptions or write "none")
   are not separately metered, Tenant shall pay Tenant's proportional share thereof as reasonably determine by Landlord.

7. **CONDITION:** Tenant has examined the Premises, all furniture, furnishings, and appliances, if any, and fixtures, including smoke detector(s). Tenant acknowledges that those items are clean and in operative condition, with the following exceptions: _____
   _____.

8. **OCCUPANTS:** The Premises are for the sole use as a personal residence by the following named persons **only:** _____
   _____.

9. **PETS:** No animal or pet shall be kept on or about the Premises without Landlord's prior written consent, except _____
   _____.

10. **LIQUID-FILLED FURNITURE:** Tenant shall not use or have liquid-filled furniture on the Premises unless Tenant first gives proof of compliance to Landlord's reasonable satisfaction, including increased security deposit, under Civil Code section 1940.5.

11. **RULES/REGULATIONS:** Tenant agrees to comply with all covenants, conditions and restrictions, bylaws, rules, regulations, and decisions of owners' association, or Landlord, which are at any time posted on the Premises or delivered to Tenant. Tenant shall pay any fines or charges imposed by owners' association, or other authorities, due to any violation by Tenant, or the guests or licensees of Tenant. Tenant shall not, and shall ensure that guests and licensees of Tenant shall not, disturb, annoy, endanger, or interfere with other tenants of the building or neighbors, or use the Premises for any unlawful purposes, including, but not limited to, using, manufacturing, selling, storing, or transporting illicit drugs or other contraband, or violate any law or ordinance, or commit waste or a nuisance upon or about the Premises.

Landlord and Tenant acknowledge receipt of copy of this page, which constitutes Page 1 of _____ Pages.
Landlord's Initials (_____) (_____)   Tenant's Initials (_____) (_____)

Published and Distributed by:
REAL ESTATE BUSINESS SERVICES, INC.
a subsidiary of the CALIFORNIA ASSOCIATION OF REALTORS®
525 South Virgil Avenue, Los Angeles, California 90020

OFFICE USE ONLY
Reviewed by Broker
or Designee _____
Date _____

EQUAL HOUSING OPPORTUNITY

RESIDENTIAL LEASE OR MONTH-TO-MONTH RENTAL AGREEMENT (LR-14 PAGE 1 OF 2) REVISED 3/95

FIGURE 6-3

Subject Property Address: _____ Date _____

12. **MAINTENANCE/DAMAGE/INSURANCE:** Tenant shall properly use, operate, and safeguard the Premises, all furniture, furnishings, and appliances, and all electrical, gas, and plumbing fixtures, and shall keep them as clean and sanitary as their condition permits. Tenant shall immediately notify Landlord of any damage, and shall pay for all repairs or replacements caused by Tenant, or the guests or invitees of Tenant, excluding ordinary wear and tear. **Tenant's personal property is not insured by Landlord.**

13. **ALTERATIONS:** Tenant shall not paint, wallpaper, add or change locks, or make any other alterations to the Premises without Landlord's prior written consent. Tenant acknowledges receipt of:

☐ _____ key(s) to Premises, ☐ _____

☐ _____ key(s) to mailbox, ☐ _____

☐ _____ key(s) to common area(s), ☐ _____

☐ _____ remote control device(s) for garage door opener(s).

Tenant may not re-key existing locks or opening devices unless Tenant immediately delivers copies of all keys to Landlord. Tenant shall pay all costs related to loss of any keys or devices, including charges imposed by any owners' association.

14. **ENTRY:** Tenant shall make the Premises available to Landlord, authorized agent, or representative, for the purpose of entering to make necessary or agreed repairs, decorations, alterations, or improvements, or to supply necessary or agreed services, or to show the Premises to prospective or actual purchasers, tenants, mortgagees, lenders, appraisers, or contractors. **Landlord and Tenant agree that four hours notice (oral or written) shall be reasonable and sufficient notice.** In an emergency, Landlord, authorized agent, or representative may enter the Premises, at any time, without prior notice.

15. **ASSIGNMENT/SUBLETTING:** Tenant shall not let or sublet all or any part of the Premises, or assign this Agreement or any interest in it. Any assignment, letting, or subletting that violates this paragraph shall be void. Landlord's acceptance of rent from a person other than the named Tenant shall not be a waiver of this paragraph.

16. **POSSESSION:** If Tenant abandons or vacates the Premises, Landlord may terminate this Agreement and regain lawful possession. If Landlord is unable to deliver possession of the Premises on the Commencement Date, the Commencement Date shall be extended to the date on which possession is made available to Tenant. If Landlord is unable to deliver possession with 10 (or ☐ _____) calendar days after the agreed Commencement Date, Tenant may terminate this Agreement by giving written notice to Landlord, and shall receive a refund of all rent and security deposit paid.

17. **HOLDING OVER:** Any holding over after the term of this Agreement expires, with Landlord's consent, shall create a month-to-month tenancy, which may be terminated by either party, by giving written notice to the other, at least 30 days prior to the intended termination date. Rent shall be at a rate equal to the rent for the immediately preceding month, payable in advance. All other terms and conditions of this Agreement shall remain in full force and effect.

18. **ATTORNEY'S FEES:** In any action or proceeding arising out of this Agreement, the prevailing party shall be entitled to reasonable attorney's fees and costs.

19. **WAIVER:** The waiver of any breach shall not be construed as a continuing waiver of the same or any subsequent breach.

20. **NOTICE:** Notices to Landlord or Manager may be served at _____.
    Notices to Tenant may be served at _____.

21. **TENANCY STATEMENT (ESTOPPEL CERTIFICATE):** Tenant shall execute and deliver a tenancy statement (estoppel certificate) submitted by Landlord, within 24 hours after receipt, acknowledging that this Agreement is unmodified and in full force, or in full force as modified, and stating the modifications. Failure to comply shall be deemed Tenant's acknowledgement that the certificate submitted by Landlord is true and correct and may be relied upon by a lender or purchaser. (C.A.R. Form TS-14 SHALL SATISFY THIS REQUIREMENT.)

22. **JOINT AND INDIVIDUAL OBLIGATIONS:** If there is more than one Tenant, each one shall be individually and completely responsible for the performance of all obligations of Tenant under this Agreement, jointly with every other Tenant, and individually.

23. **SUPPLEMENTS/OTHER TERMS AND CONDITIONS:** _____
    _____
    _____
    _____
    _____
    _____
    _____
    _____
    _____

    The following ATTACHED supplements are incorporated in this Agreement: _____
    _____
    _____.

24. **TENANT REPRESENTATIONS; CREDIT:** Tenant warrants that all statements in Tenant's rental application are accurate. Tenant authorizes Landlord and Broker(s) to obtain Tenant's credit report at the time of the application and periodically during the tenancy, in connection with approval, modification, or enforcement of this Agreement. Landlord may cancel this Agreement, (a) before occupancy begins, upon disapproval of the credit report(s), or (b) at any time, upon discovering that information in Tenant's application is false. A negative credit report reflecting on Tenant's record may be submitted to a credit reporting agency if Tenant fails to fulfill the terms of payment and other obligations under this Agreement.

25. **ENTIRE CONTRACT:** Time is of the essence. All prior agreements between Landlord and Tenant are incorporated in this Agreement which constitutes the entire contract. It is intended as a final expression of the parties' agreement with respect to the general subject matter covered, and may not be contradicted by evidence of any prior agreement or contemporaneous oral agreement. The parties further intend that this Agreement constitutes the complete and exclusive statement of its terms and that no extrinsic evidence whatsoever may be introduced in any judicial or other proceeding, if any, involving this Agreement.

26. **AGENCY CONFIRMATION:** The following agency relationship(s) are hereby confirmed for this transaction:
    Listing Agent: _____ is the agent of (check one):
                    (Print Firm Name)

    ☐ the Landlord exclusively; or ☐ both the Tenant and Landlord.
    Leasing Agent: _____ (if not same as Listing Agent) is the agent of (check one):
                    (Print Firm Name)

    ☐ the Tenant exclusively; or ☐ the Landlord exclusively; or ☐ both the Tenant and Landlord.

27. **ACKNOWLEDGEMENT:** The undersigned have read the forgoing prior to the execution and acknowledge receipt of a copy.

Landlord _____ Date _____   Tenant _____ Date _____
(or authorized agent)

Landlord _____ Date _____   Tenant _____ Date _____
(or authorized agent)

OFFICE USE ONLY
Reviewed by Broker
or Designee _____
Date _____

Page 2 of 2 Pages.

RESIDENTIAL LEASE OR MONTH-TO-MONTH RENTAL AGREEMENT (LR-14 PAGE 2 OF 2) REVISED 3/95

ESTATE AT WILL (NOT COMMON)

An **ESTATE AT WILL** *can be terminated at the will of either the lessor or the lessee, and has no fixed duration period.* By California statute, 1) the parties involved must give at least a 30-day notice of termination and 2) since a periodic tenancy is automatically created when a landlord accepts rent, there is no true estate at will in California.

ESTATE AT SUFFERANCE

An **ESTATE AT SUFFERANCE** *occurs when a lessee, who has rightfully come into possession of the land, retains possession after the expiration of his or her term.* (In other words, the tenant will not leave after expiration of the lease.) An estate at sufferance does not require a notice of termination because the expiration of the lease is an automatic termination. If the landlord accepts any payment of rent, the lease reverts to periodic tenancy.

To evict a tenant who stays past the expiration of his or her lease, you would bring a court action called an "unlawful detainer." This is not the same as dealing with a trespasser.

MINIMUM REQUIREMENTS OF A LEASE (OR RENTAL AGREEMENT)

As long as there is intent to rent property, the creation of a lease requires no particular language and can be either a written or an oral agreement. A lease or rental agreement must, at a minimum, include these four items:

> 1. the **names** of the parties
> 2. a **description** of the property
> 3. the **amount** of the rent payments
> 4. the **time period** or periods of the lease (duration).

Leases for one year or less do not need to be in writing, but it makes good business sense to have all real estate agreements in writing. According to the Statute of Frauds, any lease lasting longer than one year from the date of signing must be in writing. The California courts have held that in the event the lease is written, it must be signed by the lessor. It is not necessary for the lessee to sign if the lease has been delivered to, and accepted by, the lessee. The payment of rent and possession of the property is sufficient acceptance. Hotels, motels and other types of lodging fall into the category of leases, even though the duration of use may be for a much shorter time and eviction or termination is handled differently for these daily or weekly rentals.

A lease for more than one year must be in writing and signed by the lessor; but if the lessee does not sign, moves in and pays rent, he or she is bound to the terms of the lease.

RIGHTS AND OBLIGATIONS OF THE PARTIES

In addition to the minimum requirements, a number of contractual factors between a landlord and tenant should be considered before entering into a lease. The importance of these factors increases as the time period covered by the contract increases. Certain points that should be covered are:

1. duration of lease
2. amount of rent
3. security deposits
4. assignment and subleasing provisions
5. liabilities for injuries and repairs
6. conditions and provisions of a lease
7. termination of a lease or rental agreement.

Duration Of Lease

There are certain statutory restrictions on the terms of certain leases:

1. Agricultural lands cannot be leased for more than 51 years
2. Property situated in a city or town cannot be leased for more than 99 years
3. A mineral, oil, or gas lease cannot be longer than 99 years after work begins
4. A minor or incompetent can possess property only for the time a court has approved.

Amount Of Rent

RENT is the amount of money paid for the use of a property. It is important to state both the specific amount of rent and when the rent is to be paid to the landlord. With a periodic tenancy, if the rent is to be paid in advance, or any time other than the end of the term, it should be stated in the agreement. By law, rent becomes due only at the end of the term, unless the lease agreement states otherwise or if it is customary to make payments at a different time.

Warning: With an estate for years, if the due date is not stated in the agreement, it is due on the last business day of the calendar year.

The actual amount of rent to be paid is called contract rent. *CONTRACT RENT is the payment designated in a lease contract, at the time the lease is signed, for the use of the property.* This amount must be distinguished from the economic rent. *ECONOMIC RENT is the amount of rent that a property might be expected to yield if it was available for lease in the current market.* The economic rent and contract rent of a given property might differ if the lessor is receiving more or less rent than the property should reasonably yield.

> *If a rental property is sold, the rents of the tenants are prorated in escrow.*

For income tax purposes, the amount of rent paid in advance must be included in the landlord's income for that year. If the landlord collects first and last months' rent, both are considered current year income.

Security Deposits

A *SECURITY DEPOSIT provides the landlord with funds to pay for damages or unpaid rent when the tenant vacates.* It is in the landlord's and tenant's best interests to have an inspection of the premises before the tenant moves in and before the tenant moves out.

A *STATEMENT OF PROPERTY CONDITION is a report filled out by the landlord, in the presence of the tenant, that states the condition of the premises on moving in and moving out.* If both parties to a lease or rental agreement complete this form together, the chances of any disputes arising, with regards to damages and the security deposit, are greatly reduced.

Maximum rental agreement deposits for residential properties are:

Unfurnished = 2 months rent
Furnished = 3 months rent

Security (and "cleaning") deposits for residential leases **in California must be refunded, in full, within twenty-one days of the tenant vacating the premises unless there is damage to the property or required cleaning.** If part (or all) of the security deposit is to be withheld from the tenant, the landlord must furnish the tenant, within the same twenty-one day period, an itemized, written statement. There are a limited number of areas in California that require a minimal amount of interest to be paid on deposits.

Assignment And Subleasing Provisions

The tenant, without a clause to the contrary, may assign or sublease the property. An *ASSIGNMENT* *is a transfer of the entire lease*, whereas a *SUBLEASE* *is a transfer of less than the entire time or space of the lease.* For example, if there is a two year lease, then an assignment could be for those two years, or a sublease could be for one year of the two year lease.

A sublease transfers "possession," but not "ownership" of real property.

When a lessee or sublessee subleases a property, he or she holds a sandwich lease. A *SANDWICH LEASE* *is a leasehold interest in a property that lies between the primary (ownership) interest and the possessory (tenancy) interest.* The holder of a sandwich lease is both a tenant and landlord to the same property.

If a developer leases land for 70 years, builds apartments and then leases the units out individually, the developer has a "sandwich lease."

Liabilities For Injuries And Repairs

Generally, when the entire premises are leased, the landlord is not liable for injuries to the tenant or any guests that resulted from a defective condition on the premises. This is true even if reasonable care would have disclosed the defects. In apartments or situations where the tenant does not lease the entire property, the liability for injury in the common areas belongs to the landlord. Therefore, it is the landlord's responsibility to either repair defective conditions in the common areas or be liable for injuries resulting from them. If a landlord has knowledge of such defects or disrepair, but conceals the fact from the tenant, the landlord is liable for any resulting injuries.

It's easy to see why landlords should carry a large amount of liability insurance. Building defects may cause serious injury that could result in a lawsuit against the landlord. The tenant may also carry a renter's liability policy to protect against injuries sustained by others while visiting his or her apartment. This type of protection is usually contained in a "renter's" or "contents" policy, which protects the tenants from most losses, including liability and personal property damages.

Conditions And Provisions Of A Lease

The California State Bar Association, in conjunction with CAR, has developed a standard combination lease and rental agreement form (Figures 6-2 and 6-3). This lease contains a number of conditions and provisions that both groups believe provide a good lease contract. As well as explaining who is responsible for any breach, this lease covers most of the common problems that may arise. Figure 6-5 is an Application to Rent and Receipt for Rental Deposit and Application Screening Fee form.

Possessory rights belong to the lessee, while reversionary rights belong to the lessor. A lease form, just like any other contract, is very important. Therefore, you should take time to carefully read each of its provisions.

TERMINATION OF A LEASE (OR RENTAL AGREEMENT)

A lease or rental agreement can be terminated for a variety of reasons. Figure 6-4 lists the seven most common reasons for termination. A lease ends at the expiration of the term and without notice. Rental agreements terminate by a written notice that must be at least one rental period in length. For example, if a tenancy is on a two-week basis, and the rent is paid for that period, then two week's notice is required.

FIGURE 6-4

FIGURE 6-5

CALIFORNIA ASSOCIATION OF REALTORS®

APPLICATION TO RENT AND RECEIPT FOR
RENTAL DEPOSIT AND APPLICATION SCREENING FEE

Application to rent property at _____

Full name of applicant _____	**Co-applicant/spouse** _____
Phone _____ Date of birth ___/___/___	Phone _____ Date of birth ___/___/___
Present address _____	Present address _____
City/State/Zip _____	City/State/Zip _____
Name of current landloard/manager _____	Name of current landlord/manager _____
Landloard/manager's phone _____	Landloard/manager's phone _____
How long at present address _____	How long at present address _____
Reason for leaving _____	Reason for leaving _____

List prior address(es), landlord/manager's name(s), phone number(s), and length of tenancy _____

Name(s) of all other occupant(s) and relationship to applicant _____
_____ Pet(s) (number and type) _____

An application to rent is required for any occupant 18 years of age or over.

Applicant: Soc. Sec. No. _____ Driver's license no. _____ State _____ Expires _____
Present employer _____ Supervisor _____ How long with this employer _____
Employer's address _____ City _____ Zip _____ Phone _____
Position or title _____ Gross income $ _____ per _____
Other income $ _____ per _____ Source _____
Auto make _____ Model _____ Year _____ License no. _____ State _____ Color _____
If present employment is less than one year, list immediate prior employment information _____

In case of emergency, person to notify _____ Relationship _____
Address _____ City _____ Zip _____ Phone _____

Co-applicant: Soc. Sec. No. _____ Driver's license no. _____ State _____ Expires _____
Present employer _____ Supervisor _____ How long with this employer _____
Employer's address _____ City _____ Zip _____ Phone _____
Position or title _____ Gross income $ _____ per _____
Other income $ _____ per _____ Source _____
Auto make _____ Model _____ Year _____ License no. _____ State _____ Color _____
If present employment is less than one year, list immediate prior employment information _____

In case of emergency, person to notify _____ Relationship _____
Address _____ City _____ Zip _____ Phone _____
Does either applicant plan to use liquid filled furniture? No ☐ Yes ☐ Type _____
Has either applicant been a party to an unlawful detainer action or filed bankruptcy within the last seven years? No ☐ Yes ☐
If yes, explain _____

Credit Information

Appl./Co-appl.	Name of creditor	Account number	Monthly payment	Balance due

Bank Account Information

Appl./Co-appl.	Name of bank	Address/branch	Account number	Type of account

The property shall be occupied only by the person(s) named in this application. Applicant(s) represent(s) the above information to be true and complete, and hereby authorize(s) verification of the information provided. Applicant(s) agree(s) to execute a lease or rental agreement and understand(s) that the landlord may terminate any such agreement for any misrepresentation made above.

Date _____ Time _____ Applicant _____ Date _____ Time _____ Co-applicant _____
Phone (day) _____ (eve) _____ Phone (day) _____ (eve) _____

Applicant(s) has/have deposited the sum of _____ Dollars $ _____
evidenced by: ☐ Cash, ☐ Cashier's Check, ☐ Personal Check, ☐ or _____ payable
to _____, to be held uncashed until approval of the application to rent, as deposit
on the property located at _____ at a monthly rent of $ _____
In the event the application to rent is not approved within _____ days, this deposit shall be returned to applicant(s). If approved, the ☐ month-to-
month rental, ☐ _____ month lease, or ☐ other _____, shall commence on _____ (date).
Additional Terms _____

TOTAL SUMS DUE PRIOR TO OCCUPANCY:
Rent for the period _____ to _____ $ _____
Security deposit (not applicable toward last month's rent) .... $ _____
Other _____ $ _____
Other _____ $ _____
Total .... $ _____
Less amount received above .... $ _____
Balance due, on or before _____ (date) $ _____

In addition, applicant(s) has/have paid a screening fee of $ _____, applied as follows: $ _____ for credit report(s);
$ _____ for _____ (other out-of-pocket expenses) and $ _____ for processing. The undersigned has/have read
the foregoing and acknowledge(s) receipt of a copy.

_____ _____ _____ _____
Applicant   Date   Co-Applicant   Date

─ OFFICE USE ONLY ─
Reviewed by Broker
or Designee _____
Date _____

APPLICATION TO RENT AND RECEIPT FOR RENTAL DEPOSIT (LRA-14 PAGE 1 OF 1) REVISED 1/97

TERMINATION: EXPIRATION OF THE TERM

A lease ends, without notice, at the expiration of the term. Rental agreements are usually terminated by either party with a 30-day written notice, unless a longer period is agreed to by both parties. As stated before, if the rental period is less than a month, only that much time is required. "Tenancies at Will" require no less than a 30-day written "notice to vacate" to be served upon the tenant, or a 30-day notice given to the landlord by a vacating tenant. The 30-day notice may be made at any time during the rental period, with the balance of the rent due prorated. **Any condition in a rental agreement may be changed with a 30-day written notice.**

TERMINATION: LACK OF QUIET POSSESSION

A tenant is entitled to the quiet possession and enjoyment of the premises. The lease or rental agreement is made with the assumption that the tenant will have use of the premises and enjoy a quiet, uninterrupted stay. The landlord has the responsibility to maintain reasonable quiet on the premises for his or her tenants, and must not harass them unduly. Failure in either responsibility can give a tenant grounds for terminating a lease.

A lessor (landlord) gives quiet enjoyment to the lessee (tenant). This means without disturbance from holder of the paramount title (owner).

The California Civil Code permits the landlord to enter a tenant's unit under the following conditions:

1. Emergencies
2. Necessary repairs
3. To show premises to prospective tenants, buyers or appraisers
4. If the tenant has abandoned the premises
5. With a court order to enter.

No notice to the tenant is required if the landlord believes the tenant has abandoned the premises or it is an emergency. Otherwise, 24 hours is considered sufficient notice.

TERMINATION: REPAIRS FOR HABITABILITY

The landlord of a rented home, whether the home is a house, a condominium or an apartment, has the implied responsibility to keep the premises maintained in a condition that meets at least bare living requirements: Hazardous conditions cannot exist that threaten the tenant's health or safety. See Figure 6-6.

FIGURE 6-6

HABITABILITY OBLIGATIONS
(CIVIL CODE SECTION 1941.1)

LANDLORD'S LEGAL MINIMUM OBLIGATIONS

The landlord's minimum habitability obligations are:

1. Effective waterproofing of roof and exterior walls, including unbroken windows and doors.
2. Plumbing and gas facilities installation maintained in good working order.
3. A water supply capable of hot and cold running water, fixtures and connection to a sewage disposal system.
4. Heating facilities maintained in good working order.
5. Electrical lighting maintained in good working order.
6. Building and grounds kept clean, sanitary free from all accumulations of debris, filth, rubbish, garbage and rodents.
7. An adequate number of rubbish receptacles.
8. Floors, stairways and railings maintained in good repair.

TENANT'S LEGAL OBLIGATIONS

Tenant's Legal Obligations for Care of Premises. A tenant's affirmative obligations to a landlord for reasonable care and habitability are:

1. Keep his or her part of the premises as clean and sanitary as possible.
2. Dispose of garbage and trash in a clean and sanitary manner.
3. Properly use the plumbing, electrical and gas fixtures and keep them as clean as their condition permits.
4. Not permit any person on the premises to willfully destroy, deface, damage, impair or remove any part of the structure, facilities or equipment.
5. Occupy the premises for sleeping, cooking, dining or other purposes for which they were designed or intended.

If the landlord does not live up to this implied warranty of habitability, the tenant is not obligated to pay all the rent. However, a tenant must give notice of any necessary repairs to the landlord. The landlord has a reasonable amount of time to make any necessary repairs. A "reasonable amount of time" is determined by the type of repair needed. If the landlord, after a reasonable amount of time, has failed to make the necessary repairs, the tenant has two methods of recourse:

1. Spend up to 1 month's rent (cannot exceed 1 month's rent) in repairs **(max. twice in a 12 consecutive month period)**.

2. Abandon the premises, which terminates the lease or rental agreement.

TERMINATION: EVICTION OR OPERATION OF LAW

If a tenant does not pay the rent, or the tenant does illegal acts on the premises, legal action is available to the landlord. *EVICTION is the legal process of removing a tenant because there is a breach of the lease or rental agreement.* An alternative would be for the landlord to sue for each payment (installment) as it becomes due. This is true whether the tenant remains in possession or abandons the premises. But at this point most landlords elect to evict the lessee. If the tenant moves and the landlord leases the property, the landlord can only sue for the rent lost while the property was vacant. A *RETALIATORY EVICTION is the unlawful process whereby a landlord evicts a tenant in response to a complaint lodged by the tenant.*

FIGURE 6-7

Life of an Eviction Process

3 Days	1 Day	5 Days	1 Day	5 Days
3 Day Notice to Pay or Quit	Grace Period	Unlawful Detainer	Grace Period	Writ of Possession

Minimum Time Span

Remember; it is unlawful for the landlord to lock out tenants, take the tenants property, remove doors, shut off utilities or trespass. The landlord must protect the health and safety of tenants, obey fair housing laws and give 24 hours notice before entering a rental.

When the tenant refuses to give up possession but does not pay the rent, the landlord normally serves a "three-day notice" and, if necessary, files an "unlawful detainer" action. Figure 6-7 shows the life of an eviction process. A *THREE-DAY NOTICE TO PAY is a legal document that informs the tenant that he or she has three business days to pay all past due rent or vacate the property. A **THREE-DAY NOTICE TO QUIT** states that the tenant has breached the lease or rental agreement and has three business days to surrender (quit) the premises or face an unlawful detainer court action.* (See Figure 6-8.) It is referred to as an eviction notice. After serving the three-day notice, a minimum one-day grace period is recommended to ensure proper service.

FIGURE 6-8

Notice to Pay Rent or Quit

STATE OF CALIFORNIA }

COUNTY OF_____ } ss

TO_____, John Doe, Jane Doe, and to all others in possession of the accommodations described below.

PLEASE TAKE NOTICE that you are hereby required to pay rent for the accommodations described below in the amount stated below or you are hereby required to QUIT and DELIVER UP POSSESSION of the said accommodations within three (3) days after service upon you of this notice.

The undersigned, as landlord, hereby elects to declare a forfeiture of the lease or agreement under which you occupy the said accommodations and, unless you pay the rent or vacate the premises as required by this notice, will institute legal proceedings against you to recover possession of the premises plus court costs and three times the amount of rent and damages due as provided by California Law*.

Description of Accommodations

Address_____, _____, Calif.

Unit No_____Rental Due Date_____Rental Rate per_____$_____

Amount Due $_____From_____, 19____Through_____, 19____

_____

Date_____, 19____.

_____
Landlord/Agent

*Code of Civil Procedure Annotated, State of California, Section 1174.

FORM NO. 110 - NOTICE TO PAY RENT OR QUIT - COPYRIGHT 1976 - APARTMENT SERVICE CO. 3921 WILSHIRE BLVD. SUITE 402. LOS ANGELES, CALIFORNIA 388-6136

An **UNLAWFUL DETAINER** *is a document, filed with the court, that asserts the charges against the tenant.* After it is served, the tenant has five days to surrender possession or answer the complaint. Once again, it is suggested that at least a one-day grace period be allowed.

> *An unlawful detainer action is used by the offended lessor (landlord) to gain possession.*

If the tenant loses or does not answer the unlawful detainer complaint, a judge may issue a writ of possession. A **WRIT OF POSSESSION** *is a court order directing the sheriff to remove the tenant from the premises within five days.* Often, the landlord will have to account for the storage of the tenant's personal property. This can be complicated, so a landlord should consult an attorney before obtaining an unlawful detainer or writ of possession. Although an entire eviction process could take only fifteen working days, it will most likely take a longer period of time. If the tenant answers the complaint, the matter could take several months.

> *A lessor goes to court to get possession.*

TERMINATION: SURRENDER

SURRENDER *is the giving up of a lease or other estate, thus terminating any further obligations.* Leases may be surrendered either by mutual agreement of the parties or through operation of law.

A lease or rental agreement may be terminated, at any time, by the mutual agreement of both parties. In fact, if you are thinking about breaking a lease, it is a good idea to talk to the landlord first. He or she may want to terminate the agreement just as much as you do, or at least suggest a way to sublease the unit.

> *It is generally considered a good idea to try to negotiate your way out of a rental contract instead of creating hard feelings with a breach of the contract. It is only natural to feel guilty about breaking a lease or rental agreement. If you do not try to communicate your problems or circumstances to the landlord, he or she cannot help feeling that you do not care. Most people will be more sympathetic if you explain the situation to them. This will give them a chance to help you. Allow the landlord a chance to minimize any loss either of you might suffer.*

If a tenant abandons a property without cause, he or she has, by "operation of law," surrendered the property back to the landlord. Any cost for legal action by the landlord, plus the cost of any rental loss, may be charged to the tenant. The losses will be minimized if the landlord recovers possession and re-leases the premises quickly. A landlord can bring a lawsuit against the tenant for the lost rents, advertising expenses and repairs or cleaning.

If a tenant's rent is 14 days delinquent and the landlord has reasonable cause to believe that the lessee has abandoned the premises, the lessor may bring action to reclaim the property. The lease is terminated 15 to 18 days after the lessor posts a **Notice of Belief of Abandonment** in a conspicuous place (door, window) on the premises. This will occur unless the lessee pays the rent or notifies the landlord that the premises has not been abandoned and he or she does not wish to surrender the leasehold estate.

TERMINATION: BREACH OF CONDITIONS

The violation of any conditions of the lease is a breach of contract and may terminate the agreement. Both the lessee and lessor have the responsibility of being informed of all contractual conditions and understand that violation of the conditions may cause termination.

TERMINATION: DESTRUCTION OF THE PREMISES

If a structure is destroyed, there is usually a clause in the contract that automatically terminates the lease. If the damage is light, the tenant may stay while the landlord makes repairs. The lessee has the right to vacate the lease if the property is condemned.

Selling an apartment is "subject to the rights of tenants in possession." It does NOT terminate leases.

SPECIAL PURPOSE LEASES

In this section we will cover several unique types of leases designed to meet specific needs.

SALE-LEASEBACK

A *SALE-LEASEBACK occurs when an owner sells his or her property to another party and leases it back for a stated period of time; the original owner becomes the lessee.* This is also a financing device, but it is used mostly for commercial buildings where large business concerns are involved. The main reason for this type of lease is that a large company usually builds structures to its specifications. A large amount of money is required, therefore the company sells the building to get back most of its invested capital. By doing this, the company increases its working capital.

Large investors, such as insurance companies and pension funds, will purchase or build such a property, provided they get a well written, long-term lease. Of course the credit rating and financial position of the lessee must be outstanding. This is one device that nets a high rental income to the investor and allows the business concern a better cash flow. Chain stores, such as department stores and discount stores, use this device frequently.

The original owner of property in a sale-leaseback becomes the lessee. All lease payments are deductible from taxable income if it is business property (nonresidential).

LEASE-PURCHASE OPTION

A **LEASE-PURCHASE OPTION** *exists only when a tenant leases a property with the option to purchase it at some future date*. This gives the lessee the chance to occupy the property and to decide if it suits his or her needs before purchasing it. This is the "try before you buy" idea.

This type of option can also be used as a financing device. If current interest rates for financing are high, it gives the tenant an additional period of time during which interest rates may decrease. Time may also be needed to raise enough money for the down payment. This option must be carefully written and all terms must be clear and definite to be legally enforceable. See Chapter 5 for more details on options.

GROUND LEASE

Large business concerns have several different kinds of leases designed to conform to specific purposes. A **GROUND LEASE** *is for the exclusive use and possession of a specific parcel of land*. The ground lease allows a company to build on a parcel of land without investing a large amount of money for the purchase of the land, because the lessor retains ownership of the land. Ground leases can run for 99 years. In other instances, the land may be used for parking spaces, trailer parks, farming or as recreational land, such as a golf course or motorcycle park.

GRADUATED LEASE

A **GRADUATED LEASE** *provides for a varying rental rate*. It is often based upon future determination, such as periodic appraisals. Also called a "stair-step" lease.

GROSS LEASE (INCOME PROPERTY)

A *GROSS LEASE is a lease where the lessee pays only a rental fee for the use of the property.* The lessor is responsible for property taxes, insurance and other property expenses.

NET LEASE (INCOME PROPERTY)

A *NET LEASE is one where the lessee pays the property taxes, insurance and other operating costs in addition to rental payments.* The lessor receives only a net amount and does not pay for the other related property expenses. Sometimes the net lease is referred to as a "triple net lease" because the lessee pays: (1) property taxes, (2) fire and hazard insurance and (3) assessments or other operating expenses.

PERCENTAGE LEASE (RETAIL SALES PROPERTY)

A *PERCENTAGE LEASE is a commercial (retail sales) lease in which the lessee pays, or may pay, a certain percentage of the gross sales to the lessor.* The idea is that if the lessee has a good or excellent location, the lessor will also benefit. Most percentage leases are written for a base rental amount, paid in advance, with an additional amount due if a predetermined percentage of the gross income receipts exceeds the base rental amount.

Percentage lease payments are based upon gross income receipts.

PROPERTY MANAGER
(MUST HAVE A REAL ESTATE LICENSE)

In ever growing numbers, real estate brokers are now functioning as real property managers. A *PROPERTY MANAGER is a licensed real estate person who is paid to oversee the proper management and operations of rental and commercial property.* A property management company in California must be run by a licensed real estate broker and may include licensed salespeople working as property managers. Property managers include, for example, those who only engage in the management of one and two-family homes as well as agents who oversee large projects such as office and industrial complexes, apartment buildings and condominiums.

Property managers must also be familiar with rent control laws in their city. See Figure 6-9 for an explanation of rent control.

FIGURE 6-9

RENT CONTROL

Residential

RENT CONTROL *is government regulation of the amount of rent a landlord may charge tenants.* In its usual form the government restricts, by percentage, annual increases in rental payments. Such restrictions may be applied at the city, county and even the state level. Commercial, industrial and luxury rentals are generally exempt from this control.

In the opinion of many informed real estate analysts, rent control is a form of economic suicide. It discourages new construction by removing economic incentives for developers. This results in a limited supply of new units available to deserving renters.

Landlords, victimized by this profit squeeze, are often forced to convert their apartments into condominiums. This further reduces the number of units available in the open market.

Rent control was originated by well-meaning politicians to relieve an inflated rental market. However, it has, in effect, worsened the situation by reducing the supply in the face of an ever increasing demand.

The real solution to the rental crunch will not involve more government regulation. **The answer lies in the government providing more incentives and increased profits to developers, thereby increasing availability and allowing rents to settle at their natural level on the open market.**

COMMERCIAL RENT CONTROL PROHIBITED

Commercial

By California law, no governmental agency can adopt any rent control restrictions on nonresidential property. Nonresidential property is defined as all rental space except dwelling units, mobilehome parks and residential hotels. However, public entities can establish requirements for notice relating to the termination of a nonresidential lease.

MANAGEMENT CONTRACT

It is good business practice for a property manager, managing properties for an owner, to have a well written contract with the property owner that sets forth the responsibilities of both parties. (See Figures 6-10 and 6-11.) This should include the terms and period of the contract, policies pertaining to the management of the premises, management fees and the powers granted the agent by the owner.

RESIDENTIAL MANAGER

California law requires that rental unit buildings of 16 units or more must have a resident manager in the employ of the owner or property management company living on the premises. *RESIDENTIAL MANAGERS are tenants of the property who rent units, handle tenants' complaints and maintain the premises.* They are not required to have a real estate license.

A residential manager does not need a real estate license to manage property where he or she is living, but does need one if he or she manages other properties.

PROFESSIONAL ASSOCIATIONS

http://www.irem.org (Institute of Real Estate Management)

The Institute of Real Estate Management® (IREM) was created by the National Association of Realtors® as a professional society for real property managers. To bolster professionalism within the industry, they offer the designation Certified Property Manager® (CPM) to qualified candidates who can demonstrate a high standard of competence, ethics and experience. Property management companies may apply for the Accredited Management Organization® (AMO) designation, while residential on-site managers, who live up to the education and experience guidelines, are bestowed with the Accredited Resident Managers® (ARM) designation.

The California Apartment Association® has many local associations to assist property owners with forms and credit checks. Their professional designation for resident managers is Certified Apartment Manager® (CAM) for on-site managers.

FIGURE 6-10

CALIFORNIA ASSOCIATION OF REALTORS®

PROPERTY MANAGEMENT AGREEMENT

_____ ("Owner"), and
_____ ("Broker") agree as follows:

1. **APPOINTMENT OF BROKER:** The Owner hereby appoints and grants Broker the exclusive right to rent, lease, operate, and manage the property (ies) known as _____

_____ and any additional property which may later be added to this Agreement (collectively "Property"), upon the terms below, for the period beginning _____, 19 _____ and ending _____, 19 _____ at 11:59 p.m. However, either Owner or Broker may terminate this Agreement on at least 30 days written notice after the expiration of _____ months of the original term. After the original term this Agreement shall become a Non-Exclusive Agreement.

2. **BROKER ACCEPTANCE:** Broker accepts the appointment and grant and agrees to:
   (a) Use due diligence in the performance of this Agreement.
   (b) Furnish the services of its organization for the rental, leasing, operating, and management of the Property.

3. **AUTHORITY AND POWERS:** Owner grants to Broker the authority and power, at Owner's expense, to:
   (a) Advertising: Display "for rent," "for lease," and similar signs on the Property; advertise the availability for rental or lease of the Property or any part of it.
   (b) Rental/Leasing: Initiate, sign, renew, or cancel rental agreements and leases for the Property or any part of it; collect and give receipts for rents, other charges, and security deposits. Any lease executed by Broker for Owner shall not exceed _____ year(s). Rent shall be at least ☐

   $ _____

   per _____, or ☐ see attachment, unless Owner authorizes a lower amount.
   (c) Tenancy Termination: Sign and serve in Owner's name notices which are required or appropriate; commence and prosecute actions to evict tenants; recover possession of the Property in Owner's name; recover rents and other sums due; and when expedient, settle, compromise, and release claims, actions and suits and/or reinstate tenancies.
   (d) Repair/Maintenance: Make, cause to be made, and/or supervise repairs, improvements, alterations, and decorations to the Property; purchase and pay bills for services and supplies. Broker shall obtain prior approval of Owner on all expenditures over $ _____ for any one item. Prior approval shall not be required for monthly or recurring operating charges, or if in Broker's opinion emergency expenditures over the maximum are needed to protect the Property, or other property(ies) from damage, prevent injury to persons, avoid suspension of necessary services, avoid penalties, fines, or suspension of services to tenants called for in a lease or rental agreement or by law. Broker shall not be required to advance Broker's own funds in connection with the Property or this Agreement. However, if Broker elects to advance any funds, Owner shall promptly repay to Broker, on request, the amount advanced.
   (e) Contracts/Services: Contract, hire, supervise, and/or discharge firms and persons, including utilities, required for the operation and maintenance of the Property. Broker may perform any of Broker's duties through attorneys, agents, employees, and independent contractors, and shall not be responsible for their acts, omissions, defaults, negligence, and/or costs of same, except for persons working in Broker's firm.
   (f) Expense Payments: Pay expenses and costs for the Property from Owner's funds held by Broker, unless directed otherwise by Owner, including but not limited to property management fees and charges, expenses for goods and services, property and other taxes, Association dues, assessments, loan payments, and insurance premiums.
   (g) Trust Funds: Deposit all receipts collected for Owner, less any sums properly deducted or disbursed, in a financial institution whose deposits are insured by an agency of the United States government. The funds shall be held in a trust account separate from Broker's personal accounts. Broker shall not be liable in event of bankruptcy or failure of a financial institution.
   (h) Tenant Deposits: Handle tenant security deposits as follows:
   ☐ Hold such deposits in Broker's trust account; account for and return them to tenants, as required by law; OR
   ☐ Forward such deposits to Owner; OR
   ☐ _____
   _____
   _____.
   Owner shall be responsible to Broker and tenants for the refund of all security deposits held by Owner, unless forwarded to Broker.
   (i) Reserves: Maintain as a reserve in Broker's trust account: _____
   _____
   _____.
   (j) Owner Statements: Render ☐ monthly, ☐ _____, statements of receipts, expenses and charges for each Property.
   (k) Owner Distribution: Remit funds ☐ monthly, ☐ _____, to Owner, in accordance with Paragraph 3(l).
   (l) Disbursements: Disburse Owner's funds in the following order:
   (1) Fees, charges, and reimbursements due under this Agreement.
   (2) All other operating expenses, costs, and disbursements payable from Owner's funds held by Broker.
   (3) Reserves.
   (4) Balance to Owner.

4. **OWNER RESPONSIBILITIES:** Owner shall:
   (a) Provide all documentation and records required by Broker to manage and operate the Property.
   (b) Indemnify and hold harmless Broker and all persons in Broker's firm, from all costs, expenses, suits, liabilities, damages, and claims of every type, including but not limited to those arising out of injury or death of any person(s), or damage to any real or personal property of any person(s), including Owner, in any way relating to the management, rental, or operation of the Property by Broker or any person in Broker's firm, or the performance or exercise of any of the duties, powers, or authorities herein or hereafter granted to Broker, except to the extent due to the negligence of Broker or any person in Broker's firm.
   (c) Carry and pay for public and premises liability, property damage, and worker's compensation insurance adequate to protect the interests of Owner and Broker, and shall name both as insured parties.
   (d) Pay any late charges, penalties, and/or interest imposed by lenders or other parties caused by a lack of Owner's funds held by Broker and available for payment to same parties.

Broker and Owner acknowledge receipt of copy of this page, which constitutes Page 1 of _____ Pages.
Broker's Initials (_____) (_____) Owner's Initials (_____) (_____)

Published and Distributed by:
REAL ESTATE BUSINESS SERVICES, INC.
a subsidiary of the CALIFORNIA ASSOCIATION OF REALTORS®
525 South Virgil Avenue, Los Angeles, California 90020

OFFICE USE ONLY
Reviewed by Broker
or Designee _____
Date _____

EQUAL HOUSING OPPORTUNITY

PROPERTY MANAGEMENT AGREEMENT (PMA-14 PAGE 1 OF 3) REVISED 1/94

FIGURE 6-11

5. **COMPENSATION:**
    (a) Owner agrees to pay Broker fees as indicated for:
        (1) Management: _____.
        (2) Renting or Leasing: _____.
        (3) Evictions: _____.
        (4) Preparing Property for rental, lease, or sale: _____.
        (5) Managing Property during extended periods of vacancy: _____.
        (6) An overhead and service fee added to the cost of all work performed by or at the direction of Broker: _____.
        (7) Other: _____.
    (b) Normal property management does not include providing on-site management services, property sales, refinancing, preparing Property for sale or refinancing, modernization, fire or major damage restoration, rehabilitation, obtaining income tax, accounting, or legal advice, representation before public agencies, advising on proposed new construction, debt collection, counseling, attending Owner's Association meetings, or
        _____
        If Owner requests Broker to perform services not included in normal property management or specified above, a fee shall be agreed upon for these services before the work begins.
    (c) Owner further agrees that:
        (1) Broker may receive fees and charges from tenants for: (i) requesting an assignment of lease or sublease of the Property, (ii) processing credit applications, (iii) returned checks, (iv) other services that are not in conflict with this Agreement.
        (2) Broker may perform any of its duties, and obtain necessary products and services, through affiliated companies or organizations in which Broker may own an interest, and may receive fees, commissions, and/or profits from these affiliated companies or organizations. Broker shall disclose to Owner any such relationship. Broker shall not, however, receive fees, commissions, or profits from unaffiliated companies in the performance of this Agreement without prior disclosure to and agreement of Owner.
        (3) Broker may divide compensation, fees, and charges due under this Agreement, in any manner acceptable to Broker.
        (4) Other: _____.
6. **AGENCY RELATIONSHIPS:** Broker agrees to act as the agent of Owner in any resulting lease or rental transaction involving any Property covered by this Agreement. It may be necessary or appropriate for Broker to act as agent of both Owner and tenants, or one or more additional parties, in any resulting lease transaction, in which case Broker will seek Owner's consent to Broker's representation of additional parties as soon as practicable. However, if Broker is the listing Broker and/or property manager for a different property in which a tenant is interested, Owner understands that Broker may act as agent of that tenant and/or other property owner with respect to a transaction involving that other property. For one-to-four unit residential property, Broker shall provide agency relationships disclosure as required by law.
7. **NOTICES:** Any written notice to Owner or Broker required under this Agreement shall be served by sending such notice by first class mail to that party at the address below, or at any different address which the parties may later designate for this purpose, and shall be deemed received three business days after deposit into the United States mail.
8. **BINDING AGREEMENT:** This Agreement shall be binding upon and shall inure to be benefit of Owner and Broker and their respective heirs, administrators, executors, successors, and assigns.
9. **ADDITIONAL TERMS:** _____
10. **EQUAL HOUSING OPPORTUNITY:** The Property is offered in compliance with federal, state, and local anti-discrimination laws.
11. **MEDIATION:** Broker and Owner agree to mediate any dispute or claim arising between them out of this Agreement, or any resulting transaction, before resorting to arbitration or court action, subject to paragraph 11C below. Mediation fees, if any, shall be divided equally among the parties involved. If any party commences an action based on a dispute or claim to which this paragraph applies, without first attempting to resolve the matter through mediation, then that party shall not be entitled to recover attorney's fees, even if they would otherwise be available to that party in any such action. THIS MEDIATION PROVISION APPLIES WHETHER OR NOT THE ARBITRATION PROVISION IS INITIALED.
12. **ARBITRATION OF DISPUTES:** Broker and Owner agree that any dispute or claim in Law or equity arising between them out of this Agreement or any resulting transaction, which is not settled through mediation, shall be decided by neutral, binding arbitration, subject to paragraph 11C below. The arbitrator shall be a retired judge or justice, unless the parties mutually agree to a different arbitrator, who shall render an award in accordance with substantive California Law. In all other respects, the arbitration shall be conducted in accordance with Part III, Title 9 of the California Code of Civil Procedure. Judgment upon the award of the arbitrator(s) may be entered in any court having jurisdiction. The parties shall have the right to discovery in accordance with Code of Civil Procedure §1283.05.

    "NOTICE: BY INITIALING IN THE SPACE BELOW YOU ARE AGREEING TO HAVE ANY DISPUTE ARISING OUT OF THE MATTERS INCLUDED IN THE 'ARBITRATION OF DISPUTES' PROVISION DECIDED BY NEUTRAL ARBITRATION AS PROVIDED BY CALIFORNIA LAW AND YOU ARE GIVING UP ANY RIGHTS YOU MIGHT POSSESS TO HAVE THE DISPUTE LITIGATED IN A COURT OR JURY TRIAL. BY INITIALING IN THE SPACE BELOW YOU ARE GIVING UP YOUR JUDICIAL RIGHTS TO DISCOVERY AND APPEAL, UNLESS THOSE RIGHTS ARE SPECIFICALLY INCLUDED IN THE 'ARBITRATION OF DISPUTES' PROVISION. IF YOU REFUSE TO SUBMIT TO ARBITRATION AFTER AGREEING TO THIS PROVISION, YOU MAY BE COMPELLED TO ARBITRATE UNDER THE AUTHORITY OF THE CALIFORNIA CODE OF CIVIL PROCEDURE. YOUR AGREEMENT TO THIS ARBITRATION PROVISION IS VOLUNTARY."

    "WE HAVE READ AND UNDERSTAND THE FOREGOING AND AGREE TO SUBMIT DISPUTES ARISING OUT OF THE MATTERS INCLUDED IN THE 'ARBITRATION OF DISPUTES' PROVISION TO NEUTRAL ARBITRATION."

    Buyer's Initials ____/____   Seller's Initials ____/____

13. **ATTORNEY'S FEES:** In any action, proceeding, or arbitration arising out of this Agreement, the prevailing party shall be entitled to reasonable attorney's fees and costs, except as provided in paragraph 11A.
    We have read the foregoing prior to execution and have received a copy this _____ day of _____ 19 _____

_____   _____
             OWNER(S)   BROKER

_____   _____
          OFFICE ADDRESS   BY

_____   _____
          HOME ADDRESS   ADDRESS

_____   _____
     TELEPHONE   FAX   TELEPHONE   FAX

Page 3 of _____ Pages.

PROPERTY MANAGEMENT AGREEMENT (PMA-14 PAGE 3 OF 3) REVISED 1/94

TERMINOLOGY - CHAPTER 6

A. Landlord
B. Tenant
C. Estate for Years
D. Lease
E. Lessor
F. Lessee
G. Estate From Period-to-Period
H. Rental Agreement
I. Estate at Will

J. Estate at Sufferance
K. Rent
L. Contract Rent
M. Economic Rent
N. Assignment
O. Sublease
P. Sandwich Lease
Q. Eviction Process
R. Unlawful Detainer or Notice to Quit

S. Writ of Possession
T. Surrender
U. Sale-Lease Back
V. Lease Purchase Option
W. Ground Lease
X. Net Lease
Y. Percentage Lease
Z. Rent Control

1.____ A financial arrangement where at the time of sale the seller retains occupancy by concurrently agreeing to lease the property back from the purchaser.

2.____ One who pays rent under a lease agreement.

3.____ Lease on the property, the rental payment for which is determined by a percentage of gross receipts from the business.

4.____ The amount of rent expected if the property were currently available for renting.

5.____ One who rents his or her property to another under a lease or rental agreement.

6.____ An owner who enters into a lease agreement with a tenant.

7.____ A lease requiring a lessee to pay charges against the property such as taxes, insurance and maintenance costs in addition to rental payments.

8.____ The party who pays rent for a lease or rental agreement.

9.____ An agreement for the use of the land only.

10.____ The occupation of property by a tenant for an indefinite period, terminable by one or both parties (not common in California).

11.____ The general name of the process, from beginning to end, that serves to remove a person from the possession of real property.

12.____ A lease given by a lessee.

13.____ A leasehold interest that lies between the primary lease and the operating lease.

14.____ The concept of possessing an interest in real property by virtue of a contract for a fixed and definite period of time.

15.____ A transfer by a person of that person's entire rights under a contract.

16.____ An estate contract between owner and tenant, setting forth conditions of a period-to-period tenancy.

17.____ A contract between an owner and tenant, setting forth conditions of tenancy for a fixed period of time.

18.____ An estate arising when the tenant wrongfully holds over after the expiration of the term.

19.____ A contract for the monthly rental of residential property.

20.____ Consideration paid for the occupancy and use of real property.

21.____ Rent paid under a lease. The actual rent as opposed to the market rental value of the property.

22.____ The name of the legal process to initiate the removal of a tenant.

23.____ The giving up of an estate, such as a lease. A contractual agreement, having the consent of both parties, such as lessor and lessee, as opposed to abandonment.

24.____ A legal maximum on rental price.

25.____ The court order physically expelling a tenant.

26.____ A lease that includes the right to purchase later.

MULTIPLE CHOICE

1. The lessor is more commonly known as the:

   A. tenant
   C. renter
   B. landlord
   D. agent

2. Whatever remains of a lessee's (tenant's) security and cleaning deposit must be refunded within how many days after he or she vacates the premises?

   A. 21
   C. 45
   B. 30
   D. 60

3. A transfer of less than the entire time or space of a lease is called a (an):

   A. assignment
   C. estate from period-to-period
   B. sublease
   D. defeasable transfer

4. What document, filed with the court, asserts nonpayment of rent or other illegal acts by the tenant?

   A. Writ of possession
   C. Notice to vacate
   B. Three-day notice
   D. Unlawful detainer

5. With a sale-leaseback, the original owner assumes the role of:

   A. landlord
   C. lessor
   B. lessee
   D. seller

6. Percentage lease payments are based upon:

   A. gross income receipts
   C. an amount due after taxes and other
      expenses have been deducted
   B. a predetermined lease amount
   D. an amount due including all taxes and
      operating expenses

7. Can a landlord check the credit rating of a prospective tenant?

   A. No
   C. Yes
   B. If a prospect is from out of state
   D. Only with prospect's approval

8. If a large investment group leases a regional shopping center from the developer and subleases to retailers, this second lease is called a (an):

   A. sandwich lease
   C. assignment
   B. blanket lease
   D. double lease

9. California law requires that an apartment building have a residential manager when it consists of:

   A. 4 units or more
   C. 20 units or more
   B. 16 units or more
   D. 50 units or more

10. Rent control in California CANNOT be imposed on which of the following?

    A. Retail stores
    C. Manufacturing sites
    B. Office buildings
    D. All of the above

CHAPTER 7
Escrows and Title Insurance

An escrow is the processing of the paperwork and money involved in a sale or other real estate transaction. The purpose of an escrow is meet the terms of the contract.

ESCROWS

An **ESCROW** *is created when a new written agreement instructs a neutral third party to hold funds and only proceed when all the agreed to conditions have been performed.* In California, an escrow is usually a requirement for the sale of a home or any other real estate. Although it is not always required by law, it is an indispensable process by which an independent third party handles the legal paperwork of a real estate sale. An escrow is not only an effective tool for handling normal real estate transactions like sales or refinancing, but also for the sale of trust deeds, exchanges and transfer of liquor licenses, businesses, securities and court required transfers. The legally required and recommended uses of an escrow are illustrated in Figure 7-1.

FIGURE 7-1

Highly Recommended	Required By Law
1. Sales of real property	1. Liquor license transfers
2. Loans	2. Security sales, (impound accounts)
3. Exchanges	3. Court ordered transfers (Probate sales)

The three requirements for a valid escrow are:

1. Signed escrow instructions, forming a binding contract between two or more parties; usually a buyer and seller.

2. A neutral party, which is the escrow company, acting as a dual agent of the buyer and seller.

3. Conditional delivery of funds and documents when all the conditions in the escrow are met.

When escrow closes, dual agency (representing both parties, usually buyers and sellers, at once) changes to separate agency (handling each party's separate paperwork requirements).

An escrow may be initiated with a written contract, such as a deposit receipt, or through oral instructions. It is important to have agreed upon the written instructions drawn by the escrow company. Since this may be a new experience for most people, the escrow agent will, when necessary, explain each step to a buyer or seller. A helpful escrow officer can point out possible problems, suggest alternatives, but cannot give legal advice.

ESCROW OFFICER

An escrow holder can be: 1) a corporation, 2) an attorney or 3) a real estate broker, who also acts as a real estate agent in the transaction.

A *NEUTRAL DEPOSITORY* is an escrow business conducted by a licensed escrow holder. An *ESCROW OFFICER, HOLDER OR AGENT*, though not licensed by the state, is an employee of a licensed escrow company that acts as the agent. Escrow law is found in the California Financial Code. An independent escrow corporation must be licensed by the Department of Corporations to handle escrows. Corporations that are exempt from the escrow law but can handle escrows include: banks, savings banks and title insurance companies because they are under the supervision of their respective authorizing agencies.

There are two other types of escrow holders. They are attorneys who perform escrow duties as a part of their practice and brokers who handle their own escrows (must be an agent in the transaction). Regardless of the type of escrow company, each performs three essential duties. (Diagrammed in Figure 7-2.)

FIGURE 7-2

Conditional	Confidentiality	Deposit Holder
Delivery of all funds and documents when the conditions of the escrow have been met.	All escrow instructions are confidential and disclosure can be authorized only by the buyer or seller.	The escrow company can disburse funds and documents only when all conditions have been met and both parties have reached an agreement.

The complete sequence of events in an escrow is:

1. Preliminary title search and report
2. Lender's demand (amount owed, pay-off statement)
3. Request for new loan documents
4. Completion of conditions and depositing of funds
5. Adjustments and prorations
6. Transfer of existing fire policies or creation of new ones
7. Recording and issuing of title policy
8. Disbursement of funds
9. Escrow statement sent to each party

After these steps have been completed and all other escrow conditions have been met, the closing of an escrow is usually routine. See Figure 7-3.

The escrow agent is authorized to call for buyer's documents and funds.

FIGURE 7-3

California Customs (North vs. South) for Escrow Services and Title Insurance

When are signed escrow instructions delivered?

Customarily in Southern California, the (bilateral) escrow instructions are signed by both the buyer and seller just after the **start of escrow.**

Customarily in Northern California, the (unilateral) escrow instructions are given to the escrow officer just before the **close of escrow.**

Who performs the escrow services?

Escrow services in Southern California are traditionally performed by **independent escrow companies (corporations) or financial institutions.**

Escrow services in Northern California are traditionally performed by **title insurance companies.**

Who pays the escrow fees?

Escrow service fees in Southern California are usually **split 50-50 between the buyer and the seller.**

Escrow service fees in Northern California are usually **paid for by the buyer.**

Who traditionally pays title insurance fees?

Customarily in Southern California, the **seller pays for the California Standard Title Insurance (CLTA) policy.**

Customarily in Northern California, the **buyer pays for the California Standard Title Insurance (CLTA) policy.**

In both the North and the South, the buyers pay for any coverage above the California Standard Title Insurance (CLTA) policy.

REAL ESTATE BROKERS CAN CONDUCT ESCROWS

A broker can handle escrows, for a fee, only if the broker is acting as a real estate agent in that transaction.

A licensed broker can handle an escrow for a fee only if he or she is acting as a broker in that real estate transaction. This right is personal to the broker and the broker shall not delegate any duties other than escrow duties normally performed under the direct supervision of the broker.

All written escrow instructions executed by a buyer or seller must contain a statement, in not less than 10-point type, that includes the licensee's name and the fact that he or she is licensed by the Department of Real Estate.

HOW ESCROWS WORK

Escrow amendments must be signed by the parties to change the escrow.

ESCROW RULES

Once the escrow instructions have been drawn from the original contract (deposit receipt) and signed by each party, neither party may change the escrow instructions without the agreement of the other. The escrow is complete when 1) all conditions of the escrow have been met and 2) all conditions of the parties have been met and 3) the parties have received an accounting of the procedure. If both parties mutually agree to change the instructions, the change can be put into effect at any time. However, if a dispute should arise, the escrow company will not proceed until both parties come to terms. If the parties cannot agree to terms, an escrow company will settle a dispute by bringing an interpleader action (court action) to determine where the money or consideration goes. Figure 7-4 illustrates the three ways in which an escrow can be terminated.

If the seller thinks he or she can obtain more money and wants to rescind an escrow, remember: the seller cannot rescind an escrow without the consent of the buyer.

FIGURE 7-4

Three Ways to Terminate an Escrow

COMPLETE ESCROW **MUTUAL AGREEMENT** **COURT ACTION "INTERPLEADER"**

WHO SELECTS THE ESCROW COMPANY?

Selection of an escrow company and an escrow officer are part of the negotiation between buyer and seller. Like any other item in a real estate transaction, it is part of the negotiated agreement. Either one of the parties may choose the escrow company, which should be explained when completing the deposit receipt. The salesperson may certainly make suggestions as to a preferred escrow company for both the buyer and seller. When the escrow company is named in the listing agreement, the real estate listing agent cannot change the escrow company without the consent of the seller or the seller's agent. If the buyer and seller each desire a different escrow company, then the salesperson must work for a mutual agreement before there can be an offer and acceptance of the sale.

Death does not cancel an escrow; it is binding on the heirs (estate) due to the prior agreed to contract.

It is imperative that the salesperson disclose, in writing, any interest that salesperson or his or her broker share with the selected escrow company. This disclosure must be made either at the time of listing or whenever the escrow company is selected. Disciplinary action will be taken against any salesperson or broker who, in bad faith and against the wishes of the buyer and seller, attempts to force the use of a particular escrow company. Furthermore, a real estate licensee is prohibited by law from receiving any "kickback" for solicitation of escrow business.

ESCROW INSTRUCTIONS

A conflict between escrow instructions and the deposit receipt contract will be controlled by the escrow instructions.

ESCROW INSTRUCTIONS *are formal instructions that are drawn from the information contained in the original agreement, usually the signed deposit receipt.* When these instructions are drawn and signed, they become an enforceable contract binding on all parties.

Since the escrow instructions supplement the original contract, both are interpreted together whenever possible. If a conflict should arise between the content of the instructions and the original contract, the instructions will usually prevail.

Therefore, all parties to the escrow should read the escrow instructions very carefully, and sign only after every detail is absolutely correct and the terms meet with their approval.

FINANCING IS AN IMPORTANT ASPECT OF THE ESCROW

Most escrows for the sale of a home include obtaining a new loan and the payoff or assumption of an old loan. The brokers and their salespeople can be helpful to the buyer obtaining new financing by providing the necessary loan documentation to the escrow company in a timely manner. Keeping the buyer and seller informed about the progress of the financing and escrow helps to maintain good client-agent communication and trust.

The **PAYOFF DEMAND STATEMENT** *is a formal demand statement from the lender that details the amounts owed, as calculated by the lender, for purposes of paying off the loan in full.* The failure to obtain a payoff or beneficiary statement in a timely manner could hold up the escrow. A payoff demand statement is different from a beneficiary's statement. A **BENEFICIARY'S (LENDER'S) STATEMENT** *is a demand statement by a lender, under a deed of trust, that provides information, such as the unpaid balance, monthly payment and interest rate, necessary if the loan is to be assumed.* The lender may charge up to $60 for furnishing the payoff or beneficiary statement, except when the loan is insured by the FHA or guaranteed by the VA.

AN ESCROW EXAMPLE

To help illustrate the closing statements used in a simple escrow, let's assume the following facts:

An Escrow Example

BUYER	John Buyer and Jane Buyer	
SELLER	John Seller and Jane Seller	
SALES PRICE	....	$800,000
1ST TRUST DEED	....	$640,000
2ND TRUST DEED	....	$ 80,000
DOWN PAYMENT	....	$ 80,000
BROKER	J. Q. Smart	$ 48,000
EXISTING LIENS		
1) 1ST TRUST DEED		$290,000
2) STREET ASSESSMENT BOND		$ 1,300
CLTA TITLE POLICY PAID BY SELLER		$ 2,165

DATE of Closing is June 1, 2020

Figure 7-5 illustrates the buyer's escrow statement, and Figure 7-6 illustrates the seller's statement. These statements include many other miscellaneous costs that are a usual part of the escrow.

CLOSING IS THE DATE OF RECORDATION

Closing, in a broad sense, is the process of signing, transfer of documents and distribution of funds. When time is not specified, the escrow will close by mutual consent or within a reasonable period.

The **CLOSING DATE** *is the date that the documents are recorded.* Escrow usually approximates the closing date but the actual date is when all the conditions of the escrow have been completed, the buyer's remaining money (cashier's checks) is received and when all the documents are recorded. Most escrows are for handling the paperwork of property sale and loan financing, but escrows can be for almost any purpose.

Note: In closing statements, the buyer's and seller's totals are different. However, each closing statement must balance within itself. In the "buyer's closing statement, the purchase price is debited."

COLONIAL *Escrow, Inc.*

601 East Glenoaks Blvd. Suite 210
Glendale, CA 91207
P.O. Box 433 Glendale, CA 91209-0433
Tel: (818) 500-1633
Fax: (818) 500-0862

BUYER FINAL SETTLEMENT STATEMENT

PROPERTY: 123 Purchase Lane   CLOSING DATE: 06/01/20
          Glendale, CA   ESCROW NO.:   1-10533
BUYER: John Buyer and Jane Buyer

	DEBITS	CREDITS
FINANCIAL		
Total Consideration	$ 800,000.00	$
Cash Deposit		5,000.00
Cash Deposit		86,000.00
New 1st Trust Deed		640,000.00
New 2nd Trust Deed		80,000.00
PRORATIONS AND ADJUSTMENTS		
Taxes at 4000.00/6 mo. from 06/01/20 to 07/01/20	666.67	
OTHER DISBURSEMENTS		
Property Insurance, Inc. for Fire Insurance	1,000.00	
TITLE CHARGES TO AMERICAN COAST TITLE		
Title Policy Premium	628.50	
Sub Escrow Fee	75.00	
Recording Grant Deed	8.00	
Recording Trust Deed(s)	20.00	
Title Endorsement Fee(s)	50.00	
ESCROW CHARGES TO COLONIAL ESCROW, INC.		
Escrow Fee	900.00	
Messenger Fee	50.00	
Loan Tie In Fee	125.00	
NEW 1ST TRUST DEED TO GET SMART SAVINGS AND LOAN		
Loan Fees	6,400.00	
Credit Report	45.00	
Appraisal	350.00	
Tax Service	89.00	
Document Fee	250.00	
Interest at 7.5000% from 05/31/20 to 06/01/20	131.51	
REFUND	211.32	
TOTALS	811,000.00	811,000.00

SAVE FOR INCOME TAX PURPOSES

FIGURE 7-6   **SELLER**

COLONIAL
Escrow, Inc.

601 East Glenoaks Blvd. Suite 210
Glendale, CA   91207
P.O. Box 433 Glendale, CA 91209-0433
Tel: (818) 500-1633
Fax: (818) 500-0862

SELLER FINAL SETTLEMENT STATEMENT

PROPERTY: 123 Purchase Lane   CLOSING DATE: 06/01/20
          Glendale, CA   ESCROW NO.:   1-10533
SELLER: John Seller and Jane Seller

	DEBITS	CREDITS
FINANCIAL		
Total Consideration	$	$ 800,000.00
New 2nd Trust Deed	**80,000.00**	
PRORATIONS AND ADJUSTMENTS		
Taxes at 4000.00/6 mo. from 06/01/20 to 07/01/20		666.67
PAYOFF CHARGES TO MOST SUPERIOR		
SAVINGS AND LOAN		
Principal Balance	490,000.00	
Interest on Principal Balance at 10.0000% from 05/01/20 to 06/01/20	4,161.64	
Forwarding Fee	50.00	
Reconveyance Fee	60.00	
OTHER DISBURSEMENTS		
Pest Control, Inc. for Termite Report/Work	1,000.00	
Home Warranty, Inc. for Home Protection Policy	400.00	
COMMISSION		
Listing Broker: J. Q. Smart	48,000.00	
TITLE CHARGES TO AMERICAN COAST		
TITLE		
Title Policy Premium	2,165.00	
Sub Escrow Fee	75.00	
Documentary Transfer Tax	880.00	
Recording Reconveyance	5.00	
Street Assessment Bond	1,300.00	
ESCROW CHARGES TO COLONIAL ESCROW,		
INC.		
Escrow Fee	900.00	
Processing Demands	35.00	
Document Fee	85.00	
NET PROCEEDS	171,550.03	
TOTALS	**800,666.67**	**800,666.67**

SAVE FOR INCOME TAX PURPOSES

PRORATION

*Property taxes, interest, fire insurance and rents are prorated,
but not interest on unsecured loans.*

PRORATION is the process of proportionately dividing expenses or income to the precise date that escrow closes, or any other date previously agreed upon. It enables the buyer and seller to pay or receive their proportionate share of expenses or income. Items that are commonly prorated include:

1. property taxes
2. fire insurance
3. interest
4. rents.

30 DAYS IS THE BASIS FOR PRORATION

All escrow companies use 30 days as a base month. For example, if an escrow closes on the 10th day of the month, all prepaid rents for that month would constitute 9/30 of the rent left for the seller, and 21/30 of the rent would go to the buyer. If the rent is $2,000, the seller's portion would be 9/30 of $2,000, or $600, and the buyer's portion would be 21/30 of $2,000 or $1,400. (Rents belong to the buyer as of the closing date.)

*The two rules of proration: (1) date escrow closes and (2)
date item is paid.*

The date used in calculating proration is usually assumed to be the date of closing, but any date may be used if agreed upon by all parties. This is the case when the possession date differs from the closing date.

*Property tax prorations are based on the amount the seller is
paying. Escrow uses the old assessed valuation when
prorating.*

Taxes are prorated either from July 1, which marks the beginning of the county fiscal year, or January 1, the middle of the fiscal year. If the property taxes on a home, amounting to $2,400 per year, have been paid up to July 1, what is the proration if escrow is to be closed on June 1? In this case, the buyer would reimburse the seller for one month's taxes (or $2,400 divided by twelve months, equaling $200 per month). The seller would then be credited for the $200 in property taxes that he or she had already paid in advance.

TERMITES AND OTHER PROBLEMS

PEST CONTROL INSPECTION REPORT (REPORT & CLEARANCE)

> *A Structural Pest Control Report is usually a condition of the escrow.*

Pest control inspection reports are not required by law in California, but many lenders will require this report. A **PEST CONTROL INSPECTION REPORT** *is a written report, given by a licensed pest control company, identifying any wood destroying pests or conditions likely to cause pest infestation. The report states the condition and correction cost of any pest, dry rot, excessive moisture, earth-wood contacts or fungus damage in accessible areas of a structure.* Who pays for the (1) pest control inspection report and (2) any required or recommended repair work is up to the buyer and seller, but is usually paid for by the seller. There may sometimes be a local custom that dictates who will pay, while in other instances financial institutions or financing agencies will decide which one of the parties will pay.

> *Escrow accepts and holds the pest control report and awaits further instructions from both parties. If there is infestation damage (required work), it is usually paid for by the seller. If there is only non-infestation (recommended work), the extent of repairs is up to the parties.*

Most lenders require a pest control inspection report before making a loan, and every VA & FHA loan application requires an inspection report. The usual cost for an inspection report is about $65.00. The cost, in some areas, may be as high as $175 to $195. The California Association of Realtors® has developed a Request (and Receipt) For Structural Pest Control Certificate Report form. See Figure 7-7.

> *If escrow holds two pest control reports, escrow will notify broker and get instructions from both buyer and seller.*

The question of which party pays for any necessary repairs to obtain a "Notice of Work Completed" report is also a matter of local custom. In most areas the seller usually pays, whereas in some localities it is the opposite. However, all FHA and VA termite certificates and repairs are paid for by the seller. The seller is allowed to include a clause stating what the maximum cost of repairs will be as a condition of the sale.

FIGURE 7-7

CALIFORNIA ASSOCIATION OF REALTORS

REQUEST FOR STRUCTURAL PEST CONTROL CERTIFICATION REPORT

To _____
　　　NAME OF OPERATOR　　　　　　　　　　　　　　　　　ADDRESS OF OPERATOR

You are instructed to make a Structural Pest Control Inspection of the main building, ☐ detached garage(s) or carport(s), if any, and the following other structures on the property: _____

Located at _____

For purposes of clarification you are requested to furnish a "Separated Report" in accordance with Business and Professions Code § 8516 (c) setting forth your findings and recommendations for work as follows:

SECTION 1)　　infestation or infection which is evident.

SECTION 2)　　Conditions that are present which are deemed likely to lead to infestation or infection.

Your quotations for cost of any recommended work should be segregated as above and be as itemized as possible. Inspection of inaccessible areas, if any, shall not be made without specific authorization.

If your report discloses no infestation or infection, you shall issue a CERTIFICATION to that effect in accordance with Business and Professions Code § 8519 (a).

If your report discloses infestation and infection and you subsequently are requested to perform recommended work in whole or in part your NOTICE OF WORK COMPLETED shall contain a CERTIFICATION to that effect in accordance with Business and Professions Code § 8519 (b) or (c), whichever is applicable.

The undersigned agrees to pay $ _____ for your inspection and report in the above form, providing you deliver said report as indicated below on or before _____ 19_____ .

Date _____　　　_____
　　　　　　　　　　　　　　　　　　　　PERSON ORDERING THE REPORT (PRINTED)

　　　　　　　　　　　　　　　　　　　_____
　　　　　　　　　　　　　　　　　　　　PERSON ORDERING THE REPORT (SIGNATURE)

_____
ADDRESS　　　　　　　　　　　　CITY　　　　　　STATE　　　　　　ZIP　　　　　　PHONE

Copies to:

_____
NAME OF LISTING BROKER　　　　　　　　　　　　　　ADDRESS

_____
NAME OF SELLING BROKER　　　　　　　　　　　　　　ADDRESS

_____
NAME OF ESCROW HOLDER (ESCROW #)　　　　　　　　ADDRESS

SPC-2　　　　　　　　　　　　　　　　　　　　　　　　M-SC-JAN-93

CALIFORNIA ASSOCIATION OF REALTORS

RECEIPT FOR STRUCTURAL PEST CONTROL DOCUMENTS

(In compliance with Cal. Civil Code Section 1099)

Receipt is hereby acknowledged of delivery of the following documents:

☐　　Copy of Structural Pest Control Inspection Report dated _____ 19____ , issued by

　　　_____
　　　　　　　　　　　　　　　　　(Name of Operator)

　　　pertaining to the property located at _____

　　　_____

☐　　Copy of Certification

☐　　Copy of "Notice of Work Completed" with Certification endorsed or attached thereto.

Buyer hereby acknowledges receipt of a copy hereof.

DATED _____　　19_____　　_____
　　　　　　　　　　　　　　　　　　　　　　　　Buyer or transferee

　　　　　　　　　　　　　　　　　　　　　　　_____
　　　　　　　　　　　　　　　　　　　　　　　　Buyer or transferee

SPC-3　　　　　　　　　　　　　　　　　　　　　　　　M-SC-AUG-92

California law requires that the seller must receive a copy of the pest control certificate before the close of escrow. For a **two dollar fee**, any person may request certified copies of any certificate inspection report, filed during the preceding two years, from the State Structural Pest Control Board.

Structural Pest Control Board
1430 Howe Avenue
Sacramento, Calif. 95825
http://www.dca.ca.gov (DCA/Strructural Pest Control Board)

BROKER MAINTAINS PEST CONTROL DOCUMENTATION

The Civil Code requires that the broker shall deliver a copy of the Structural Pest Control Inspection Report, and any Notice of Work Completed, to the buyer, if such a report is a condition of the deposit receipt or is a requirement imposed as a condition of financing. If more than one broker is acting as an agent in the transaction, the broker who obtained the offer (selling broker) made by the buyer shall deliver the required documents to the buyer. See Figure 7-7.

FIRE INSURANCE

FIRE INSURANCE . . . A MUST!

Fire insurance is very inexpensive compared to the possible dollar loss due to fire, and all property owners should have this financial protection. A lending institution will require coverage for the amount of its loan. However, it is in the owner's best interest to carry sufficient fire insurance to replace the structure if it is totally destroyed. It is only necessary to insure the current replacement value of the dwelling, since the land itself cannot be destroyed by fire.

The *CALIFORNIA STANDARD FORM FIRE INSURANCE POLICY insures the dwelling against (1) fire and (2) lightning.* If you so desire, you may procure an *EXTENDED COVERAGE ENDORSEMENT that will insure you against the additional perils of windstorm, explosion, hail, aircraft, smoke, riot and vehicles not attributed to a strike or civil commotion.* Other types of endorsements may insure you against vandalism, malicious mischief, floods and other damage. Coverage depends on your needs and the perils common to your area.

FIRE INSURANCE PRORATION

When purchasing property, you as a buyer may assume the existing fire insurance policy or obtain a new policy. If the old policy is canceled the seller is charged a higher rate; it is said to be "short-rated." If the old policy is assumed, an endorsement designating you as the new owner is forwarded to you and the premium amount will be prorated in escrow. You will then be assessed for the unused premium. It is always the buyer's choice to select his or her own house insurance (condo insurance is chosen by the association) or assume the seller's policy.

Whenever you are buying insurance, review the policy carefully to determine if you are carrying an adequate amount of insurance, and that you have the correct type of coverage.

COINSURANCE

COINSURANCE is a clause in a policy that requires you to insure 80% of the value of the dwelling or you will receive only a percentage of the insurance benefits. The percentage paid represents the actual percentage of insurance carried (up to 80%), which is then divided by the required 80%. Figure 7-8 illustrates this for you.

Coinsurance usually applies to nonresidential property.

FIGURE 7-8

HOW NONRESIDENTIAL COINSURANCE WORKS

1) Actual value of your improvements	=	$200,000
2) 80% coinsurance clause requires you to carry fire insurance on 80% of the actual value of the dwelling (80% of $200,000)	=	$160,000
3) Amount of fire insurance carried (Face amount on your policy)	=	$120,000
4) Ratio of loss payment $120,000 (actual amount) $160,000 (required amount)	=	75%
5) If your actual fire loss is	=	$80,000
6) Your insurance would pay 75% of actual loss (75% of $80,000)	=	$60,000
7) Your out-of-pocket cost would be the loss less insurance payments ($80,000 - $60,000)	=	$20,000

ESCROW REPORTS INFORMATION TO THE I.R.S.

All real estate transactions must be reported to the Internal Revenue Service. This is done by the escrow company or whoever handles the closing. A 1099 Form is required for any sale or exchange.

The 1099 Form must contain the following information:

1. Name of the taxpayer.
2. Address of the taxpayer.
3. Social Security number of the taxpayer.
4. Legal description of the property.
5. Address of the property.
6. Assessor's parcel number.
7. Agent's name, address and social security number.

Escrow reports real estate transactions to the I.R.S.

TITLE INSURANCE

CHAIN OF TITLE (RECORDED PUBLIC HISTORY)

Abstract of title: a written summary of a property's documents.

If one person sells a property to another person, *a recorded public history of a specific property, called the* **CHAIN OF TITLE**, is compiled. These public records include files at the county recorder's office, various tax agencies, federal court clerk and the Secretary of State. *All such information about people and their real property is stored in computers and is referred to as a* **TITLE PLANT.**

A title insurance company is primarily concerned with a search of the public records, which includes: the Federal Land's Office, the County Clerk's Office, the County Recorder's Office and other sources. This search establishes what is called the "chain of title."

TITLE INSURANCE (HAS FOUR FUNCTIONS)

Title insurance companies are regulated by the California Insurance Commissioner. Fee schedules must be available to the general public upon request. To guarantee solvency, each title insurance company must set aside reserves.

Because many things outside the public record can affect the legality of title, title insurance performs four important functions to protect the insured.

TITLE INSURANCE also insures a lender (and property owner for an additional fee) against losses that result from imperfections in title. Title insurance companies examine the records documenting chain of title, review any risks that might not be found in the public records, seek legal interpretation, help the seller correct any defects and insure marketable title to the property. Title insurance is only paid once, unlike auto or fire insurance, which must be paid annually. Figure 7-9 emphasizes the four most important functions of title insurance.

FIGURE 7-9

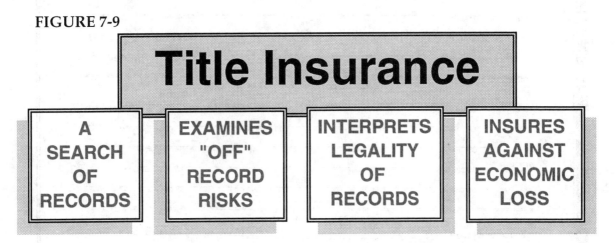

PRELIMINARY TITLE REPORT (ORDERED FIRST)

The first event to occur in a title search is the ordering of the preliminary title report by the escrow officer (after the buyer or borrower completes the statement of information). See Figure 7-10. A *PRELIMINARY TITLE REPORT is a report showing the condition of title before a sale or loan transaction.* After completion of the transaction, a title insurance policy is issued. The preliminary title report consists of the following items:

1. The name of the owner and a description of the property.
2. A list of any outstanding taxes, bonds or other assessments.
3. The identity of any covenants, conditions or restrictions.
4. Shows any recorded liens or other encumbrances that must be eliminated before any loan is made.

A "preliminary title report" gives the current status of items (from the county records) that affect the property's title.

FIGURE 7-10

NORTH AMERICAN TITLE COMPANY

Complete, Sign and Return
STATEMENT OF INFORMATION

Order No. 5278

To expedite the completion of your escrow, please fill out and return this form at your earliest convenience. This information is for confidential use by North American Title Company in searching the land records in connection with the order number shown above. Further explanation of the need for this information is printed on the reverse side of this form.

Please Print all information

PERSONAL IDENTIFICATION

Name

_____
FIRST NAME · FULL MIDDLE NAME—IF NONE, INDICATE · LAST NAME

Year of Birth _____ Birthplace _____ Social Security No. _____

Full name of Wife / Husband _____

_____
FIRST NAME · FULL MIDDLE NAME—IF NONE, INDICATE · LAST NAME

Year of Birth _____ Birthplace _____ Social Security No. _____

We were married on _____ at _____
DATE · CITY AND STATE

Wife's maiden name _____

RESIDENCES DURING PAST 10 YEARS

NUMBER AND STREET	CITY	FROM (DATE)	TO (DATE)
NUMBER AND STREET	CITY	FROM (DATE)	TO (DATE)
NUMBER AND STREET	CITY	FROM (DATE)	TO (DATE)

(If more space is needed, use reverse side of form)

OCCUPATIONS DURING PAST 10 YEARS

Husband's

OCCUPATION	FIRM NAME	STREET AND CITY	FROM (DATE) TO (DATE)
OCCUPATION	FIRM NAME	STREET AND CITY	FROM (DATE) TO (DATE)
OCCUPATION	FIRM NAME	STREET AND CITY	FROM (DATE) TO (DATE)

Wife's

OCCUPATION	FIRM NAME	STREET AND CITY	FROM (DATE) TO (DATE)
OCCUPATION	FIRM NAME	STREET AND CITY	FROM (DATE) TO (DATE)

(If more space is needed, use reverse side of form)

FORMER MARRIAGE(S), IF ANY

If no former marriages, write "None" _____ Otherwise, please complete the following:

Name of former wife _____

Deceased ☐   Divorced ☐   When _____ Where _____

Name of former husband _____

Deceased ☐   Divorced ☐   When _____ Where _____

(If more space is needed, use reverse side of form)

Buyer intends to reside on the property in this transaction   Yes ☐   No ☐

THIS PORTION IS TO BE COMPLETED BY THE SELLER

The Street Address of the property in this transaction is _____
(LEAVE BLANK IF NONE)

The land is unimproved ☐ or improved with a structure of the following type;

IMPROVEMENTS: ☐ SINGLE RESIDENCE OR 1-4 FAMILY   ☐ MULTIPLE RESIDENCE   ☐ COMMERCIAL

OCCUPIED BY: ☐ OWNER   ☐ LESSEE   ☐ TENANTS

ANY PORTION OF NEW LOAN FUNDS TO BE USED FOR CONSTRUCTION

IMPROVEMENTS, REMODELING OR REPAIRS TO THIS PROPERTY HAVE BEEN MADE WITHIN THE PAST SIX MONTHS   ☐ YES   ☐ NO

IF YES,

HAVE ALL COSTS FOR LABOR AND MATERIALS ARISING IN CONNECTION THEREWITH BEEN PAID IN FULL?   ☐ YES   ☐ NO

The undersigned declare, under penalty of perjury, that the foregoing is true and correct.

DATE _____   _____

HOME PHONE _____   BUSINESS PHONE _____   _____
(IF MARRIED, BOTH HUSBAND AND WIFE SHOULD SIGN)

NAT 44 (5/88)

TYPES OF TITLE INSURANCE POLICIES

*All title insurance policies in California cover policyholders
as of the date of the policy.*

CALIFORNIA LAND TITLE ASSOCIATION (STANDARD COVERAGE POLICY)

 http://www.clta.org (California Land Title Association)

In California, the standard title insurance policy is the CLTA. The *CALIFORNIA LAND TITLE ASSOCIATION (CLTA) policy is the basic title insurance policy.* It may be issued to insure a lender only, or an owner only, or it may insure both the lender and the owner (a joint-protection standard coverage policy). This standard policy insures the lender only unless the owner requests and pays for owner coverage.

CLTA is the acronym for the state trade association, California Land Title Association®.

Figures 7-11 through 7-14 are samples of a standard CLTA policy form.

Besides insuring against all items of record, the CLTA policy offers protection against many off-record risks. Some of these off-record risks include forgeries, acts of minors and incompetents, acts of an agent whose authority has terminated, invalid deed delivery, unrecorded federal estate tax liens, undisclosed rights of husband and wife when the chain of title states "unmarried" and the expenses (including attorneys' fees) incurred in defending title.

The "standard," and most common title insurance policy in California, is the CLTA policy (no survey). The CLTA policy protects against: 1) lack of capacity of a party in the chain of title, 2) deeds not properly delivered and 3) forgery.

It is very important to note those items not included in the standard policy. The items **not** included are:

1. Easements and liens that are not shown by the public record.
2. Rights or claims of persons in physical possession of the land.
3. Unrecorded claims not shown by the public record that could be ascertained by physical inspection or correct survey.
4. Mining claims, reservations in patents, water rights and government actions such as zoning ordinances.

FIGURE 7-11

POLICY OF TITLE INSURANCE

ISSUED BY

NORTH AMERICAN TITLE INSURANCE COMPANY

SUBJECT TO THE EXCLUSIONS FROM COVERAGE, THE EXCEPTIONS FROM COVERAGE CONTAINED IN SCHEDULE B AND THE CONDITIONS AND STIPULATIONS, NORTH AMERICAN TITLE INSURANCE COMPANY, a California corporation, herein called the Company, insures, as of Date of Policy shown in Schedule A, against loss or damage, not exceeding the Amount of Insurance stated in Schedule A, sustained or incurred by the insured by reason of:

1. Title to the estate or interest described in Schedule A being vested otherwise than as stated therein;
2. Any defect in or lien or encumbrance on such title;
3. Unmarketability of the title;
4. Lack of a right of access to and from the land;
5. The invalidity or unenforceability of the lien of the insured mortgage upon the title;
6. The priority of any lien or encumbrance over the lien of the insured mortgage;
7. Lack of priority of the lien of the insured mortgage over any statutory lien for services, labor or material:
   (a) arising from an improvement or work related to the land which is contracted for or commenced prior to Date of Policy; or
   (b) arising from an improvement or work related to the land which is contracted for or commenced subsequent to Date of Policy and which is financed in whole or in part by proceeds of the indebtedness secured by the insured mortgage which at Date of Policy the insured has advanced or is obligated to advance.
8. Any assessments for street improvements under construction or completed at Date of Policy which now have gained or hereafter may gain priority over the insured mortgage; or
9. The invalidity or unenforceability of any assignment of the insured mortgage, provided the assignment is shown in Schedule A, or the failure of the assignment shown in Schedule A to vest title to the insured mortgage in the named insured assignee free and clear of all liens.

The Company will also pay the costs, attorneys' fees and expenses incurred in defense of the title or the lien of the insured mortgage, as insured, but only to the extent provided in the Conditions and Stipulations.

NORTH AMERICAN TITLE INSURANCE COMPANY

BY _Gerald B Beery_   PRESIDENT

ATTEST _____ SECRETARY

NORTH AMERICAN TITLE INSURANCE COMPANY
INCORPORATED
— • —
SEPT 18, 1958
CALIFORNIA

FIGURE 7-12

```
FORM NO. 6056-87 (4-6-90)
ALTA LOAN POLICY          SCHEDULE A
FORM 1
```

POLICY NO. 116823   FILE NO.: 14-15360-63

AMOUNT OF INSURANCE: $296,800.00   PREMIUM: $1,161.75

   DATE OF POLICY: JULY 22, 1992 AT 8:00 A.M.

1. **NAME OF INSURED:**

   SYCAMORE FINANCIAL GROUP, INC., A CALIFORNIA CORPORATION

2. **THE ESTATE OR INTEREST IN THE LAND WHICH IS ENCUMBERED BY THE INSURED MORTGAGE IS:**

   A CONDOMINIUM, AS DEFINED IN SECTION 783 OF THE CALIFORNIA CIVIL CODE, IN FEE

3. **TITLE TO THE ESTATE OR INTEREST IN THE LAND IS VESTED IN:**

   WALTER ROY HUBER AND DEBBIE R. HUBER, HUSBAND AND WIFE AS COMMUNITY PROPERTY

4. **THE INSURED MORTGAGE AND ASSIGNMENTS THEREOF, IF ANY, ARE DESCRIBED AS FOLLOWS:**

A DEED OF TRUST TO SECURE AN INDEBTEDNESS IN THE AMOUNT SHOWN BELOW AND ANY OTHER OBLIGATIONS SECURED THEREBY:

```
RECORDED:      JULY 22, 1992 AS  INSTRUMENT  NO.  92-1329290 OF
               OFFICIAL RECORDS
AMOUNT:        $296,800.00
DATED:         JULY 13, 1992
TRUSTOR:       WALTER ROY HUBER AND DEBBIE R. HUBER,  HUSBAND  AND
               WIFE AS COMMUNITY PROPERTY
TRUSTEE:       UTICA ESCROW INC., A CALIFORNIA CORPORATION
BENEFICIARY:   SYCAMORE  FINANCIAL  GROUP,  INC.,  A   CALIFORNIA
               CORPORATION
```

5. **THE LAND REFERRED TO IN THIS POLICY IS DESCRIBED AS FOLLOWS:**

PARCEL 1:

THAT PORTION OF PARCEL A OF PARCEL MAP L.A. NO. 3111, IN THE CITY OF LOS ANGELES, COUNTY OF LOS ANGELES, STATE OF CALIFORNIA, AS PER MAP FILED IN BOOK 72 PAGE 26 OF PARCEL MAPS, IN THE OFFICE OF THE COUNTY RECORDER OF SAID COUNTY, SHOWN AND DEFINED AS UNIT 1 AND AIR SPACE A ON THE CONDOMINIUM PLAN, RECORDED DECEMBER 17, 1976 AS INSTRUMENT NO. 5334, OF OFFICIAL RECORDS OF SAID COUNTY.

PARCEL 2:

AN UNDIVIDED 1/4 INTEREST IN AND TO PARCEL A OF SAID PARCEL MAP LOS ANGELES NO. 3111.

EXCEPT THEREFROM THOSE PORTIONS SHOWN AND DEFINED AS UNITS 1 TO 4 AND AIR SPACE A AND B ON SAID CONDOMINIUM PLAN.

FIGURE 7-13

EXCLUSIONS FROM COVERAGE

The following matters are expressly excluded from the coverage of this policy and the Company will not pay loss or damage, costs, attorneys' fees or expenses which arise by reason of:

1. (a) Any law, ordinance or governmental regulation (including but not limited to building and zoning laws, ordinances, or regulations) restricting, regulating, prohibiting or relating to (i) the occupancy, use, or enjoyment of the land; (ii) the character, dimensions or location of any improvement now or hereafter erected on the land; (iii) a separation in ownership or a change in the dimensions or area of the land or any parcel of which the land is or was a part; or (iv) environmental protection, or the effect of any violation of these laws, ordinances or governmental regulations, except to the extent that a notice of the enforcement thereof or a notice of a defect, lien or encumbrance resulting from a violation or alleged violation affecting the land has been recorded in the public records at Date of Policy.

   (b) Any governmental police power not excluded by (a) above, except to the extent that a notice of the exercise thereof or a notice of a defect, lien or encumbrance resulting from a violation or alleged violation affecting the land has been recorded in the public records at Date of Policy.

2. Rights of eminent domain unless notice of the exercise thereof has been recorded in the public records at Date of Policy, but not excluding from coverage any taking which has occurred prior to Date of Policy which would be binding on the rights of a purchaser for value without knowledge.

3. Defects, liens, encumbrances, adverse claims or other matters:
   (a) created, suffered, assumed or agreed to by the insured claimant;
   (b) not known to the Company, not recorded in the public records at Date of Policy, but known to the insured claimant and not disclosed in writing to the Company by the insured claimant prior to the date the insured claimant became an insured under this policy;
   (c) resulting in no loss or damage to the insured claimant;
   (d) attaching or created subsequent to Date of Policy (except to the extent that this policy insures the priority of the lien of the insured mortgage over any statutory lien for services, labor or material or the extent insurance is afforded herein as to assessments for street improvements under construction or completed at Date of Policy); or
   (e) resulting in loss or damage which would not have been sustained if the insured claimant had paid value for the insured mortgage.

4. Unenforceability of the lien of the insured mortgage because of the inability or failure of the insured at Date of Policy, or the inability or failure of any subsequent owner of the indebtedness, to comply with applicable doing business laws of the state in which the land is situated.

5. Invalidity or unenforceability of the lien of the insured mortgage, or claim thereof, which arises out of the transaction evidenced by the insured mortgage and is based upon usury or any consumer credit protection or truth in lending law.

6. Any statutory lien for services, labor or materials (or the claim of priority of any statutory lien for services, labor or materials over the lien of the insured mortgage) arising from an improvement or work related to the land which is contracted for and commenced subsequent to Date of Policy and is not financed in whole or in part by proceeds of the indebtedness secured by the insured mortgage which at Date of Policy the insured has advanced or is obligated to advance.

7. Any claim, which arises out of the transaction creating the interest of the mortgagee insured by this policy, by reason of the operation of federal bankruptcy, state insolvency, or similar creditors' rights laws.

CONDITIONS AND STIPULATIONS

1. DEFINITION OF TERMS.
The following terms when used in this policy mean:

(a) "insured": the insured named in Schedule A. The term "insured" also includes

(i) the owner of the indebtedness secured by the insured mortgage and each successor in ownership of the indebtedness except a successor who is an obligor under the provisions of Section 12(c) of these Conditions and Stipulations (reserving, however, all rights and defenses as to any successor that the Company would have had against any predecessor insured, unless the successor acquired the indebtedness as a purchaser for value without knowledge of the asserted defect, lien, encumbrance, adverse claim or other matter insured against by this policy as affecting title to the estate or interest in the land);

(ii) any governmental agency or governmental instrumentality which is an insurer or guarantor under an insurance contract or guaranty insuring or guaranteeing the indebtedness secured by the insured mortgage, or any part thereof, whether named as an insured herein or not;

(iii) the parties designated in Section 2(a) of these Conditions and Stipulations.

(b) "insured claimant": an insured claiming loss or damage.

(c) "knowledge" or "known": actual knowledge, not constructive knowledge or notice which may be imputed to an insured by reason of the public records as defined in this policy or any other records which impart constructive notice of matters affecting the land.

(d) "land": the land described or referred to in Schedule (A), and improvements affixed thereto which by law constitute real property. The term "land" does not include any property beyond the lines of the area described or referred to in Schedule (A), nor any right, title, interest, estate or easement in abutting streets, roads, avenues, alleys, lanes, ways or waterways, but nothing herein shall modify or limit the extent to which a right of access to and from the land is insured by this policy.

(e) "mortgage": mortgage, deed of trust, trust deed, or other security instrument.

(f) "public records": records established under state statutes at Date of Policy for the purpose of imparting constructive notice of matters relating to real property to purchasers for value and without knowledge. With respect to Section 1(a)(iv) of the Exclusions From Coverage, "public records" shall also include environmental protection liens filed in the records of the clerk of the United States district court for the district in which the land is located.

(g) "unmarketability of the title": an alleged or apparent matter affecting the title to the land, not excluded or excepted from coverage, which would entitle a purchaser of the estate or interest described in Schedule A or the insured mortgage to be released from the obligation to purchase by virtue of a contractual condition requiring the delivery of marketable title.

2. CONTINUATION OF INSURANCE.
(a) **After Acquisition of Title.** The coverage of this policy shall continue in force as of Date of Policy in favor of (i) an insured who acquires all or any part of the estate or interest in the land by foreclosure, trustee's sale, conveyance in lieu of foreclosure, or other legal manner which discharges the lien of the insured mortgage; (ii) a transferee of the estate or interest so acquired from an insured corporation, provided the transferee is the parent or wholly-owned subsidiary of the insured corporation, and their corporate successors by operation of law and not by purchase, subject to any rights or defenses the Company may have against any predecessor insureds; and (iii) any governmental agency or governmental instrumentality which acquires all or any part of the estate or interest pursuant to a contract of insurance or guaranty insuring or guaranteeing the indebtedness secured by the insured mortgage.

settlement, and (ii) in any other lawful act which in the opinion of the Company may be necessary or desirable to establish the title to the estate or interest or the lien of the insured mortgage, as insured. If the Company is prejudiced by the failure of the insured to furnish the required cooperation, the Company's obligations to the insured under the policy shall terminate, including any liability or obligation to defend, prosecute, or continue any litigation, with regard to the matter or matters requiring such cooperation.

5. PROOF OF LOSS OR DAMAGE.
In addition to and after the notices required under Section 3 of these Conditions and Stipulations have been provided the Company, a proof of loss or damage signed and sworn to by the insured claimant shall be furnished to the Company within 90 days after the insured claimant shall ascertain the facts giving rise to the loss or damage. The proof of loss or damage shall describe the defect in, or lien or encumbrance on the title, or other matter insured against by this policy which constitutes the basis of loss or damage and shall state, to the extent possible, the basis of calculating the amount of the loss or damage. If the Company is prejudiced by the failure of the insured claimant to provide the required proof of loss or damage, the Company's obligations to the insured under the policy shall terminate, including any liability or obligation to defend, prosecute, or continue any litigation, with regard to the matter or matters requiring such proof of loss or damage.

In addition, the insured claimant may reasonably be required to submit to examination under oath by any authorized representative of the Company and shall produce for examination, inspection and copying, at such reasonable times and places as may be designated by any authorized representative of the Company, all records, books, ledgers, checks, correspondence and memoranda, whether bearing a date before or after Date of Policy, which reasonably pertain to the loss or damage. Further, if requested by any authorized representative of the Company, the insured claimant shall grant its permission, in writing, for any authorized representative of the Company to examine, inspect and copy all records, books, ledgers, checks, correspondence and memoranda in the custody or control of a third party, which reasonably pertain to the loss or damage. All information designated as confidential by the insured claimant provided to the Company pursuant to this Section shall not be disclosed to others unless, in the reasonable judgment of the Company, it is necessary in the administration of the claim. Failure of the insured claimant to submit for examination under oath, produce other reasonably requested information or grant permission to secure reasonably necessary information from third parties as required in this paragraph, unless prohibited by law or governmental regulation, shall terminate any liability of the Company under this policy as to that claim.

the insured was and continued to be obligated to advance at and after Date of Policy.

9. REDUCTION OF INSURANCE; REDUCTION OR TERMINATION OF LIABILITY.
(a) All payments under this policy, except payments made for costs, attorneys' fees and expenses, shall reduce the amount of the insurance pro tanto. However, any payments made prior to the acquisition of title to the estate or interest as provided in Section 2(a) of these Conditions and Stipulations shall not reduce pro tanto the amount of the insurance afforded under this policy except to the extent that the payments reduce the amount of the indebtedness secured by the insured mortgage.

(b) Payment in part by any person of the principal of the indebtedness, or any other obligation secured by the insured mortgage, or any voluntary partial satisfaction or release of the insured mortgage, to the extent of the payment, satisfaction or release, shall reduce the amount of insurance pro tanto. The amount of insurance may thereafter be increased by accruing interest and advances made to protect the lien of the insured mortgage and secured thereby, with interest thereon, provided in no event shall the amount of insurance be greater than the amount of insurance stated in Schedule A.

(c) Payment in full by any person or the voluntary satisfaction or release of the insured mortgage shall terminate all liability of the Company except as provided in Section 2(a) of these Conditions and Stipulations.

10. LIABILITY NONCUMULATIVE.
If the insured acquires title to the estate or interest in satisfaction of the indebtedness secured by the insured mortgage, or any part thereof, it is expressly understood that the amount of insurance under this policy shall be reduced by any amount the Company may pay under any policy insuring a mortgage to which exception is taken in Schedule B or to which the insured has agreed, assumed, or taken subject, or which is hereafter executed by an insured and which is a charge or lien on the estate or interest described or referred to in Schedule A, and the amount so paid shall be deemed a payment under this policy.

11. PAYMENT OF LOSS.
(a) No payment shall be made without producing this policy for endorsement of the payment unless the policy has been lost or destroyed, in which case proof of loss or destruction shall be furnished to the satisfaction of the Company.

(b) When liability and the extent of loss or damage has been definitely fixed in accordance with these Conditions and Stipulations, the loss or damage shall be payable within 30 days thereafter.

FIGURES 7-14

(b) After Conveyance of Title. The coverage of this policy shall continue in force as of Date of Policy in favor of an insured only so long as the insured retains an estate or interest in the land, or holds an indebtedness secured by a purchase money mortgage given by a purchaser from the insured, or only so long as the insured shall have liability by reason of covenants of warranty made by the insured in any transfer or conveyance of the estate or interest. This policy shall not continue in force in favor of any purchaser from the insured of either (i) an estate or interest in the land, or (ii) an indebtedness secured by a purchase money mortgage given to the insured.

(c) Amount of Insurance: The amount of insurance after the acquisition or after the conveyance shall in neither event exceed the least of:

(i) the amount of insurance stated in Schedule A;

(ii) the amount of the principal of the indebtedness secured by the insured mortgage as of Date of Policy, interest thereon, expenses of foreclosure, amounts advanced pursuant to the insured mortgage to assure compliance with laws or to protect the lien of the insured mortgage prior to the time of acquisition of the estate or interest in the land and secured thereby and reasonable amounts expended to prevent deterioration of improvements, but reduced by the amount of all payments made; or

(iii) the amount paid by any governmental agency or governmental instrumentality, if the agency or instrumentality is the insured claimant, in the acquisition of the estate or interest in satisfaction of its insurance contract or guaranty.

3. NOTICE OF CLAIM TO BE GIVEN BY INSURED CLAIMANT.

The insured shall notify the Company promptly in writing (i) in case of any litigation as set forth in Section 4(a) below, (ii) in case knowledge shall come to an insured hereunder of any claim of title or interest which is adverse to the title to the estate or interest or the lien of the insured mortgage, as insured, and which might cause loss or damage for which the Company may be liable by virtue of this policy, or (iii) if title to the estate or interest or the lien of the insured mortgage, as insured, is rejected as unmarketable. If prompt notice shall not be given to the Company, then as to the insured all liability of the Company shall terminate with regard to the matter or matters for which prompt notice is required; provided, however, that failure to notify the Company shall in no case prejudice the rights of any insured under this policy unless the Company shall be prejudiced by the failure and then only to the extent of the prejudice.

4. DEFENSE AND PROSECUTION OF ACTIONS; DUTY OF INSURED CLAIMANT TO COOPERATE.

(a) Upon written request by the insured and subject to the options contained in Section 6 of these Conditions and Stipulations, the Company, at its own cost and without unreasonable delay, shall provide for the defense of an insured in litigation in which any third party asserts a claim adverse to the title or interest as insured, but only as to those stated causes of action alleging a defect, lien or encumbrance or other matter insured against by this policy. The Company shall have the right to select counsel of its choice (subject to the right of the insured to object for reasonable cause) to represent the insured as to those stated causes of action and shall not be liable for and will not pay the fees of any other counsel. The Company will not pay any fees, costs or expenses incurred by the insured in the defense of those causes of action which allege matters not insured against by this policy.

(b) The Company shall have the right, at its own cost, to institute and prosecute any action or proceeding or to do any other act which in its opinion may be necessary or desirable to establish the title to the estate or interest or the lien of the insured mortgage, as insured, or to prevent or reduce loss or damage to the insured. The Company may take any appropriate action under the terms of this policy, whether or not it shall be liable hereunder, and shall not thereby concede liability or waive any provision of this policy. If the Company shall exercise its rights under this paragraph, it shall do so diligently.

(c) Whenever the Company shall have brought an action or interposed a defense as required or permitted by the provisions of this policy, the Company may pursue any litigation to final determination by a court of competent jurisdiction and expressly reserves the right, in its sole discretion, to appeal from any adverse judgment or order.

(d) In all cases where this policy permits or requires the Company to prosecute or provide for the defense of any action or proceeding, the insured shall secure to the Company the right to so prosecute or provide defense in the action or proceeding, and all appeals therein, and permit the Company to use, at its option, the name of the insured for this purpose. Whenever requested by the Company, the insured, at the Company's expense, shall give the Company all reasonable aid (i) in any action or proceeding, securing evidence, obtaining witnesses, prosecuting or defending the action or proceeding, or effecting

6. OPTIONS TO PAY OR OTHERWISE SETTLE CLAIMS; TERMINATION OF LIABILITY.

In case of a claim under this policy, the Company shall have the following options:

(a) To Pay or Tender Payment of the Amount of Insurance or to Purchase the Indebtedness.

(i) to pay or tender payment of the amount of insurance under this policy together with any costs, attorneys' fees and expenses incurred by the insured claimant, which were authorized by the Company, up to the time of payment or tender of payment and which the Company is obligated to pay; or

(ii) to purchase the indebtedness secured by the insured mortgage for the amount owing thereon together with any costs, attorneys' fees and expenses incurred by the insured claimant which were authorized by the Company up to the time of purchase and which the Company is obligated to pay.

If the Company offers to purchase the indebtedness as herein provided, the owner of the indebtedness shall transfer, assign, and convey the indebtedness and the insured mortgage, together with any collateral security, to the Company upon payment therefor.

Upon the exercise by the Company of either of the options provided for in paragraphs a(i) or (ii), all liability and obligations to the insured under this policy, other than to make the payment required in those paragraphs, shall terminate, including any liability or obligation to defend, prosecute, or continue any litigation, and the policy shall be surrendered to the Company for cancellation.

(b) To Pay or Otherwise Settle With Parties Other than the Insured or With the Insured Claimant.

(i) to pay or otherwise settle with other parties for or in the name of an insured claimant any claim insured against under this policy, together with any costs, attorneys' fees and expenses incurred by the insured claimant which were authorized by the Company up to the time of payment and which the Company is obligated to pay; or

(ii) to pay or otherwise settle with the insured claimant the loss or damage provided for under this policy, together with any costs, attorneys' fees and expenses incurred by the insured claimant which were authorized by the Company up to the time of payment and which the Company is obligated to pay.

Upon the exercise by the Company of either of the options provided for in paragraphs b(i) or (ii), the Company's obligations to the insured under this policy for the claimed loss or damage, other than the payments required to be made, shall terminate, including any liability or obligation to defend, prosecute or continue any litigation.

7. DETERMINATION AND EXTENT OF LIABILITY.

This policy is a contract of indemnity against actual monetary loss or damage sustained or incurred by the insured claimant who has suffered loss or damage by reason of matters insured against by this policy and only to the extent herein described.

(a) The liability of the Company under this policy shall not exceed the least of:

(i) the amount of insurance stated in Schedule A, or, if applicable, the amount of insurance as defined in Section 2 (c) of these Conditions and Stipulations;

(ii) the amount of the unpaid principal indebtedness secured by the insured mortgage as limited or provided under Section 8 of these Conditions and Stipulations or as reduced under Section 9 of these Conditions and Stipulations, at the time the loss or damage insured against by this policy occurs, together with interest thereon; or

(iii) the difference between the value of the insured estate or interest as insured and the value of the insured estate or interest subject to the defect, lien or encumbrance insured against by this policy.

(b) In the event the insured has acquired the estate or interest in the manner described in Section 2(a) of these Conditions and Stipulations or has conveyed the title, then the liability of the Company shall continue as set forth in Section 7(a) of these Conditions and Stipulations.

(c) The Company will pay only those costs, attorneys' fees and expenses incurred in accordance with Section 4 of these Conditions and Stipulations.

8. LIMITATION OF LIABILITY.

(a) If the Company establishes the title, or removes the alleged defect, lien or encumbrance, or cures the lack of a right of access to or from the land, or cures the claim of unmarketability of title, or otherwise establishes the lien of the insured mortgage, all as insured, in a reasonably diligent manner by any method, including litigation and the completion of any appeals therefrom, it shall have fully performed its obligations with respect to that matter and shall not be liable for any loss or damage caused thereby.

(b) In the event of any litigation, including litigation by the Company or with the Company's consent, the Company shall have no liability for loss or damage until there has been a final determination by a court of competent jurisdiction, and disposition of all appeals therefrom, adverse to the title or to the lien of the insured mortgage, as insured.

(c) The Company shall not be liable for loss or damage to any insured for liability voluntarily assumed by the insured in settling any claim or suit without the prior written consent of the Company.

(d) The Company shall not be liable for:

(i) any indebtedness created subsequent to Date of Policy except for advances made to protect the lien of the insured mortgage and secured thereby and reasonable amounts expended to prevent deterioration of improvements; or

(ii) construction loan advances made subsequent to Date of Policy, except construction loan advances made subsequent to Date of Policy for the purpose of financing in whole or in part the construction of an improvement to the land which at Date of Policy were secured by the insured mortgage and which

12. SUBROGATION UPON PAYMENT OR SETTLEMENT.

(a) The Company's Right of Subrogation.

Whenever the Company shall have settled and paid a claim under this policy, all right of subrogation shall vest in the Company unaffected by any act of the insured claimant.

The Company shall be subrogated to and be entitled to all rights and remedies which the insured claimant would have had against any person or property in respect to the claim had this policy not been issued. If requested by the Company, the insured claimant shall transfer to the Company all rights and remedies against any person or property necessary in order to perfect this right of subrogation. The insured claimant shall permit the Company to sue, compromise or settle in the name of the insured claimant and to use the name of the insured claimant in any transaction or litigation involving these rights or remedies.

If a payment on account of a claim does not fully cover the loss of the insured claimant, the Company shall be subrogated to all rights and remedies of the insured claimant after the insured claimant shall have recovered its principal, interest, and costs of collection.

(b) The Insured's Rights and Limitations.

Notwithstanding the foregoing, the owner of the indebtedness secured by the insured mortgage, provided the priority of the lien of the insured mortgage or its enforceability is not affected, may release or substitute the personal liability of any debtor or guarantor, or extend or otherwise modify the terms of payment, or release a portion of the estate or interest from the lien of the insured mortgage, or release any collateral security for the indebtedness.

When the permitted acts of the insured claimant occur and the insured has knowledge of any claim of title or interest adverse to the title to the estate or interest or the priority or enforceability of the lien of the insured mortgage, as insured, the Company shall be required to pay only that part of any losses insured against by this policy which shall exceed the amount, if any, lost to the Company by reason of the impairment by the insured claimant of the Company's right of subrogation.

(c) The Company's Rights Against Non-insured Obligors.

The Company's right of subrogation against non-insured obligors shall exist and shall include, without limitation, the rights of the insured to indemnities, guaranties, other policies of insurance or bonds, notwithstanding any terms or conditions contained in those instruments which provide for subrogation rights by reason of this policy.

The Company's right of subrogation shall not be avoided by acquisition of the insured mortgage by an obligor (except an obligor described in Section 1(a)(ii) of these Conditions and Stipulations) who acquires the insured mortgage as a result of an indemnity, guarantee, other policy of insurance, or bond and the obligor will not be an insured under this policy, notwithstanding Section 1(a)(i) of these Conditions and Stipulations

13. ARBITRATION.

Unless prohibited by applicable law, either the Company or the insured may demand arbitration pursuant to the Title Insurance Arbitration Rules of the American Arbitration Association. Arbitrable matters may include, but are not limited to, any controversy or claim between the Company and the insured arising out of or relating to this policy, any service of the Company in connection with its issuance or the breach of a policy provision or other obligation. All arbitrable matters when the Amount of Insurance is $1,000,000 or less shall be arbitrated at the option of either the Company or the insured. All arbitrable matters when the Amount of Insurance is in excess of $1,000,000 shall be arbitrated only when agreed to by both the Company and the insured. Arbitration pursuant to this policy and under the Rules in effect on the date the demand for arbitration is made or, at the option of the insured, the Rules in effect at Date of Policy shall be binding upon the parties. The award may include attorneys' fees only if the laws of the state in which the land is located permit a court to award attorneys' fees to a prevailing party. Judgment upon the award rendered by the Arbitrator(s) may be entered in any court having jurisdiction thereof.

The law of the situs of the land shall apply to an arbitration under the Title Insurance Arbitration Rules.

A copy of the Rules may be obtained from the Company upon request.

14. LIABILITY LIMITED TO THIS POLICY; POLICY ENTIRE CONTRACT.

(a) This policy together with all endorsements, if any, attached hereto by the Company is the entire policy and contract between the insured and the Company. In interpreting any provision of this policy, this policy shall be construed as a whole.

(b) Any claim of loss or damage, whether or not based on negligence, and which arises out of the status of the lien of the insured mortgage or of the title to the estate or interest covered hereby or by any action asserting such claim, shall be restricted to this policy.

(c) No amendment of or endorsement to this policy can be made except by a writing endorsed hereon or attached hereto signed by either the President, a Vice President, the Secretary, an Assistant Secretary, or validating officer or authorized signatory of the Company.

15. SEVERABILITY.

In the event any provision of this policy is held invalid or unenforceable under applicable law, the policy shall be deemed not to include that provision and all other provisions shall remain in full force and effect.

16. NOTICES, WHERE SENT.

All notices required to be given the Company and any statement in writing required to be furnished the Company shall include the number of this policy and shall be addressed to the Company at 114 East Fifth Street, Santa Ana, California 92701, or to the office which issued this policy.

AMERICAN LAND TITLE ASSOCIATION
(EXTENDED COVERAGE POLICY - SURVEY INCLUDED)

Most lenders require more protection than provided for by the standard coverage (CLTA) policy; they require the extended coverage (ALTA) policy, which includes a "competent survey or inspection" that determines the correct property lines. ALTA is the acronym for the national trade association, American Land Title Association®.

The **AMERICAN LAND TITLE ASSOCIATION POLICY (ALTA)** *is an extended coverage policy that insures against many exclusions of the standard coverage (CLTA) policy.* The ALTA policy (which includes a competent survey or physical inspection) is usually required by California lenders and by out-of-state lenders who are not able to make a personal, physical inspection of the property.

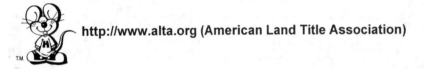

http://www.alta.org (American Land Title Association)

An extended ALTA title insurance policy is a lender's policy. It only protects the lender. If an owner wants this kind of protection, he or she should request the extended ALTA Owner's Policy.

Purchasers should note that there are still certain exceptions to the CLTA standard policy and even to the ALTA extended policy. There is no insurance coverage for the following: 1) Defects known to the insured at the time the policy was issued but not designated in writing and 2) government regulations regarding occupancy and use (zoning).

No title insurance protects you against governmental regulations (zoning changes) or defects known to insured.

ALTA-R (ONE TO FOUR RESIDENTIAL UNITS)

The **ALTA-R POLICY** *is recommended, by title companies, for one-to-four owner-occupied residential dwellings.* It doesn't include a survey because the property lines are already established by a recorded subdivision map. Since the title company does not have to do a survey, it gives the buyer more coverage for the same price. The CAR® deposit receipt includes the ALTA-R as the preferred residential title policy choice.

WHO PAYS TITLE INSURANCE FEES?

Title insurance fees are a part of the escrow closing costs. Title insurance companies are required to publish rate schedules and charge according to the published rates. Who assumes payment of the fees, however, varies depending upon the area in which one lives.

In Southern California it is customary for the seller to pay the title fees, whereas in Northern California it is usually the buyer who assumes the cost. Because there is no law determining who must pay, it should be stated in the deposit receipt to prevent any misunderstanding. This, however, covers only the standard CLTA policy. The additional cost of the ALTA extended policy is usually charged to the party purchasing the property (the buyer).

TITLE INSURANCE DISCLOSURE

In any escrow transaction for the purchase or exchánge of real property where a title insurance policy will not be issued to the buyer (or exchanger), the buyer (or exchanger) must sign and acknowledge a disclosure statement stating that it may be advisable to obtain title insurance.

REAL ESTATE SETTLEMENT PROCEDURES ACT (RESPA)

RESPA provides borrowers the opportunity to shop for settlement services. The law covers first loans on one-to-four unit residential dwellings.

THE REAL ESTATE SETTLEMENT PROCEDURES ACT (RESPA) is a law for the sale or transfer of one-to-four residential units requiring: 1) specific procedures and; 2) forms for settlements (closing costs) involving most home loans from financial institutions with federally insured deposits, including FHA and VA loans.

This law, although amended several times, states that the closing settlement cost of a real estate transaction must be made known to the borrower, at his or her request, one business day before escrow closes. Until this law was passed, buyers were unaware of the exact amount needed until the actual escrow closing day. Sometimes the buyers were surprised to find that more money than expected was needed to complete the procedure. The current law alleviates this problem.

RESPA disclosure requirements are for federally related lenders - this means almost all lenders.

Other provisions required by the Real Estate Settlement Procedures Act include the following:

1. At the time of loan application, or within three business days, the lender must give a good faith estimate of the total closing charges to the borrower.

2. At the same time, the lender must furnish the buyer with an information booklet.

3. The escrow agent must give a uniform settlement statement to the borrower, the seller and the lender. **Figures 7-15 and 7-16 illustrate the settlement statement**. It must be furnished by the time of settlement, except when the borrower waives it, or in areas where the HUD (Department of Housing and Urban Development) permits a later date for supplying it.

The settlement statement must be delivered at or before the date of settlement, at no charge. The buyer can request it one business day before closing.

4. Individuals are prohibited from receiving kickbacks and unearned fees. Payments to cooperating brokerages and referral agreements between brokers are exempt.

5. No seller may require a buyer to purchase title insurance from any particular company as a condition of sale.

There are penalties for kickbacks and unearned fees. The seller may request a specific title insurer, but only the buyer can require a specific insurance company.

CALIFORNIA ESCROW ASSOCIATION

The California Escrow Association has developed a statewide program to promote professional service and educational opportunities for its members. Many community colleges have also adopted certificate courses for escrow personnel and real estate brokers to provide a better understanding of the highly technical escrow field.

http://www.ec-dicom/escrow/whatis.htm (Trade organization via independent)

California Escrow Association
530 Bercut Drive, Suite G
Sacramento, CA 95814

FIGURE 7-15

A. U.S. DEPARTMENT OF HOUSING AND URBAN DEVELOPMENT SETTLEMENT STATEMENT	B. TYPE OF LOAN
	1. [ ] FHA 2. [ ] FmHA 3. [X] Conv. unis 4. [ ] VA 5. [ ] Conv. ins

6. ESCROW NUMBER: 1-10533	7. LOAN NUMBER:
8. MORTGAGE INSURANCE NUMBER:	

THIS NOTE IS FURNISHED TO GIVE YOU A STATEMENT OF THE ACTUAL SETTLEMENT COSTS. AMOUNTS PAID TO AND BY THE SETTLEMENT AGENT ARE SHOWN. ITEMS MARKED "(P.O.C.)" WERE PAID OUTSIDE OF THE CLOSING; THEY ARE SHOWN HERE FOR INFORMATIONAL PURPOSES AND ARE NOT INCLUDED IN THE TOTALS.

D. NAME OF BORROWER: JOHN BUYER JANE BUYER 123 Purchase Lane Glendale, CA	E. NAME OF SELLER: JOHN SELLER JANE SELLER	F. NAME OF LENDER: GET SMART SAVINGS AND LOAN 123 Lending Lane Beverly Hills, CA 91020
G. PROPERTY LOCATION: 123 PURCHASE LANE GLENDALE, CA	H. SETTLEMENT AGENT:COLONIAL ESCROW, INC. PLACE OF SETTLEMENT: 601 EAST GLENOAKS BLVD. SUITE 210 GLENDALE, CA 91207 P.O. BOX 433 GLENDALE, CA 91209-0433	I. SETTLEMENT DATE: 06/01/20

J. SUMMARY OF BORROWER'S TRANSACTIONS		K. SUMMARY OF SELLER'S TRANSACTIONS	
100. GROSS AMOUNT DUE FROM BORROWER		**400. GROSS AMOUNT DUE TO SELLER**	
101.CONTRACT SALES PRICE	800,000.00	401.CONTRACT SALES PRICE	800,000.00
102.PERSONAL PROPERTY		402.PERSONAL PROPERTY	
103.SETTL. CHRGS. TO BORROWER (LINE 1400)	10,122.01	403.DEPOSITS	
104.		404.	
105.		405.	
Adjustments: items paid by seller in advance		Adjustments: items paid by seller in advance	
106.CITY/TOWN TAXES		406.CITY/TOWN TAXES	
107.COUNTY TAXES		407.COUNTY TAXES	
108.ASSESSMENTS		408.ASSESSMENTS	
109.TAXES : 06/01/20 TO 07/01/20	666.67	409.TAXES : 06/01/20 TO 07/01/20	666.67
110.		410.	
111.		411.	
112.		412.	
120. GROSS AMOUNT DUE FROM BORROWER	810,788.68	420. GROSS AMOUNT DUE TO SELLER	800,666.67
200. AMOUNTS PAID BY OR IN BEHALF OF BORROWER		**500. REDUCTIONS IN AMOUNT DUE TO SELLER**	
201.DEPOSITS	91,000.00	501.EXCESS DEPOSIT	
202.PRINCIPAL AMOUNT OF NEW LOAN(S)	640,000.00	502.SETTL. CHRGS. TO SELLER (LINE 1400)	54,845.00
203.EXISTING LOAN(S) TAKEN SUBJECT TO		503.EXISTING LOAN(S) TAKEN SUBJECT TO	
204.NEW 2ND TRUST DEED	80,000.00	504.PAYOFF TO MOST SUPERIOR SAVINGS AND L	490,000.00
205.		505.INTEREST FROM 05/01/20 TO 06/01/20	4,161.64
206.		506.FORWARDING FEE	50.00
207.		507.RECONVEYANCE FEE	60.00
208.		508.NEW 2ND TRUST DEED	80,000.00
209.		509.	
Adjustments: Items unpaid by seller		Adjustments: Items unpaid by seller	
210.CITY/TOWN TAXES		510.CITY/TOWN TAXES	
211.COUNTY TAXES		511.COUNTY TAXES	
212.ASSESSMENTS		512.ASSESSMENTS	
213.		513.	
214.		514.	
215.		515.	
216.		516.	
217.		517.	
218.		518.	
219.		519.	
220. TOTAL PAID BY/FOR BORROWER	811,000.00	520. TOTAL REDUCTION AMOUNT DUE SELLER	629,116.64
300. CASH AT SETTLEMENT FROM/TO BORROWER		**600. CASH AT SETTLEMENT TO/FROM SELLER**	
301. Gross amounts due from borrower (line 120)	810,788.68	601. Gross amount due to seller (line 420)	800,666.67
302. Less amounts paid by/for borrower (line 220)	811,000.00	602. Less reductions in amount due seller (line 520)	629,116.64
303. CASH FROM[ ] TO[X] BORROWER	211.32	603. CASH FROM[ ] TO[X] SELLER	171,550.03

FIGURE 7-16

L. SETTLEMENT STATEMENT

	PAID FROM BORROWER'S FUNDS AT SETTLEMENT	PAID FROM SELLER'S FUNDS AT SETTLEMENT
700. TOTAL SALES/BROKER'S COMMISSION		
BASED ON PRICE $ 800,000.00 @ 6.00%		
701. BROKER: J. Q. SMART 48,000.00		
702.		
703.		
704. COMMISSIONS PAID AT SETTLEMENT		48,000.00
800. ITEMS PAYABLE IN CONNECTION WITH LOAN		
801. LOAN FEE	6,400.00	
802. LOAN DISCOUNT		
803. APPRAISAL	350.00	
804. CREDIT REPORT	45.00	
805. LENDER'S INSPECTION FEE		
806. MORTGAGE INSURANCE APPLICATION FEE		
807. ASSUMPTION FEE		
808. TAX SERVICE	89.00	
809. DOCUMENT FEE	250.00	
810.		
811.		
900. ITEMS REQUIRED BY LENDER TO BE PAID IN ADVANCE		
901. INTEREST AT 7.5000% FROM 05/31/20 TO 06/01/20	131.51	
902. MORTGAGE INSURANCE		
903. PROPERTY INSURANCE, INC. FOR FIRE INSURANCE	1,000.00	
904.		
905.		
1000. RESERVES DEPOSITED WITH LENDER		
1001. HAZARD INSURANCE		
1002. MORTGAGE INSURANCE		
1003. CITY PROPERTY TAXES		
1004. COUNTY PROPERTY TAXES		
1005. ANNUAL ASSESSMENTS		
1006.		
1007.		
1008.		
1100. ESCROW AND TITLE CHARGES		
1101. ESCROW FEE TO COLONIAL ESCROW, INC.	900.00	900.00
1102. ABSTRACT OR TITLE SEARCH		
1103. TITLE EXAMINATION		
1104. TITLE INSURANCE BINDER		
1105. DOCUMENT PREPARATION TO COLONIAL ESCROW, INC.		
1106. MESSENGER FEE TO COLONIAL ESCROW, INC.	50.00	
1107. ATTORNEY'S FEES		
1108. TITLE POLICY TO AMERICAN .COAST TITLE	628.50	2,165.00
1109. LENDERS COVERAGE $ 640,000.00		
1110. OWNERS COVERAGE $ 800,000.00		
1111. PROCESSING DEMANDS TO COLONIAL ESCROW, INC.		35.00
1112. DOCUMENT FEE TO COLONIAL ESCROW, INC.		85.00
1113. LOAN TIE IN FEE TO COLONIAL ESCROW, INC.	125.00	
1200. GOVERNMENT RECORDING AND TRANSFER CHARGES		
1201. RECORDING FEES: DEED $8.00; MORTGAGE $20.00; RELEASES $5.00	28.00	5.00
1202. DOCUMENTARY TRANSFER TAX		880.00
1203. STATE TAX/STAMPS		
1204.		
1205.		
1300. ADDITIONAL SETTLEMENT CHARGES		
1301. SURVEY		
1302. PEST CONTROL, INC. FOR TERMITE REPORT/WORK		1,000.00
1303. SUB ESCROW FEE TO AMERICAN COAST TITLE	75.00	75.00
1304. TITLE ENDORSEMENT FEE(S) TO AMERICAN COAST TITLE	50.00	
1305. STREET ASSESSMENT BOND TO AMERICAN COAST TITLE		1,300.00
1306. HOME WARRANTY, INC. FOR HOME PROTECTION POLICY		400.00
1307.		
1400. TOTAL SETTLEMENT CHARGES		
(ENTER ON LINES 102 SECTION J AND 501, SECTION k)	10,122.01	54,845.00

Escrows and Title Insurance

TERMINOLOGY - CHAPTER 7

A. Escrow

B. Escrow Officer

C. Escrow Instruction

D. Proration

E. Pest Control Report

F. Coinsurance

G. Chain of Title

H. Title Plant

I. Title Insurance

J. CLTA

K. ALTA

L. Payoff Demand Statement

M. Date of Closing

N. Preliminary Title Report

O. RESPA

1.____ Insurance to protect a real property owner or lender up to a specified amount against certain types of loss, e.g., defective or unmarketable title.

2.____ The process of depositing instruments, funds and instructions, with a third neutral party who finalizes the transaction.

3.____ A history of conveyances and encumbrances affecting the title from the time the original patent was granted, or as far back as records are available; used to determine how title came to be vested in current owner.

4.____ Adjustments of interest, taxes and insurance, etc., on a prorated basis as of the closing or agreed upon date.

5.____ The person at the escrow company who handles the paperwork of the escrow.

6.____ The written instructions of the escrow, prepared by the escrow officer and approved by both the buyer and the seller.

7.____ The most all inclusive title insurance policy. It requires a property survey and is usually required by most lenders.

8.____ The minimum standard title insurance policy in California that does NOT require a property survey.

9.____ The requirement by a lender that a property be insured up to its full value, or only a proportion of any loss will be reimbursed.

10.____ A report from a structural pest control company stating the termite or other type of pest damage found and the cost of repairing it.

11.____ The date documents are recorded and title insurance is written.

12.____ A federal statute requiring disclosure of certain costs in the sale of residential property.

13.____ A report showing the condition of title before a sale or loan transaction.

14.____ Written instructions by a lender stating and demanding the amount necessary to payoff a loan.

15.____ A filing of all recorded information to real property.

MULTIPLE CHOICE

1. When a trust deed is sold, the parties often use an escrow (agent) in order to:

   A. obey the civil code
   C. assure conditions are met
   B. serve as a witness
   D. provide a legal service

2. Which of the following is NOT a requirement of a valid escrow?

   A. Escrow officer must be licensed
   C. Neutral third party
   B. Signed instructions
   D. Conditional delivery

3. Of the following, which would be the last function in an escrow sequence of events?

   A. Recording and issuing of title policy
   C. Request of new loan documents
   B. Lender's demand (amount owed on property)
   D. Adjustments and prorations

4. The decision to assume an existing fire insurance policy or buy a new one is made by the:

   A. buyer and seller
   C. seller
   B. buyer
   D. escrow officer

5. The only way that escrow instructions can be changed, once they have been drawn and signed by each party, is by:

   A. the escrow officer
   C. the listing broker
   B. mutual consent of the parties
   D. operation of law

6. The California Standard Form Fire Insurance Policy would NOT insure your property against:

   A. fire
   C. lightning
   B. windstorm
   D. none of the above

7. Escrow companies use what base period when calculating prorations?

   A. 31 days
   C. 28 days
   B. 30 days
   D. Depends on the month being prorated

8. What title policy would cover most of the exclusions of a standard policy?

   A. ALTA
   C. CLTA
   B. MLTA
   D. BLTA

9. Who selects the escrow company?

   A. Agent only
   C. Seller only
   B. Buyer only
   D. Buyer and seller

10. Which of the following is NOT a one-time fee but is in fact a recurrring charge?

    A. Property tax fees
    C. Escrow fees
    B. Title insurance fees
    D. County recording fees

CHAPTER 8
Real Estate Finance

http://www.knsd.com (Careers in Finance)
http://www.careermosaic.com (Careers in Finance and Accounting)

Real estate is expensive compared to most other possessions. A person or business seldom has enough cash to buy the real estate outright, and therefore must borrow the necessary money to help finance the transaction. A buyer usually makes a cash down payment of 20% and must obtain a loan for the remaining 80% of the purchase price. Most buyers must finance at least part of the purchase, so a good rule to remember is, "If you can't finance a property, you probably can't sell it later." If a property can't be easily financed, don't waste time with it: find another, more easily financed, property.

Even buyers with large amounts of cash rarely purchase real estate outright. An investment principle known as "leverage" favors buying real estate using borrowed funds. *LEVERAGE is the practice of purchasing real estate using a small amount of your own money and a larger proportion of borrowed funds.* The more money borrowed to buy a property, the greater the leverage.

Example: If you buy a $300,000 house with 20% down, the down payment is $60,000. If inflation increases the value by 30% over 10 years, you have increased the market value by $90,000 on a $60,000 investment.

As you can see, employing leverage makes it possible for real estate investors to reap the same profits as those buying entirely with their own funds without having to tie up as much cash. This chapter explores the different ways in which real estate can be financed. Each type of financing instrument will be discussed, including the many clauses in the note and trust deed.

HYPOTHECATION (PROPERTY AS COLLATERAL)

Real estate finance is based on the principle of hypothecation. To **HYPOTHECATE** *is to provide title to a property as security for a loan without the necessity of giving up possession.* Although one can hypothecate, or "put up," stocks as security for a bank loan, most real property buyers hypothecate their property as security for a real estate loan. In neither case does the person surrender the use or possession of the property. The hypothecation principle is fundamental to the major instruments of real estate finance; the **trust deed** in California and the less common **mortgage**. Each of these instruments uses the promissory note as the primary evidence of debt, which creates a lien on the property.

THE PROMISSORY NOTE
(Negotiable Instrument)

A **PROMISSORY NOTE** *is the basic instrument used to evidence the obligation or debt.* It is an unconditional promise, in writing, by one person to another, promising to pay on demand, or over a fixed determinable time, a certain sum of money. Borrowers hypothecate real property as security for payment of the promissory note. The trust deed or mortgage is used with the promissory note to hypothecate the property as security for the note.

> *Co-borrowers responsible for each others debts sign the promissory note as "jointly and severally."*

A loan payment on a note is made up of principal and interest. **PRINCIPAL** *is the dollar amount of the loan.* Commonly we call it the amount of money remaining to be paid off on a promissory note (the loan balance). **INTEREST** *is the rent charged for the use of money.*

> *Interest on most real estate loans is "simple interest." Simple interest is interest paid only on the principal amount owed.*

Figure 8-1 illustrates the three basic kinds of promissory notes that affect real estate financing. The three types of notes are explained below.

FIGURE 8-1

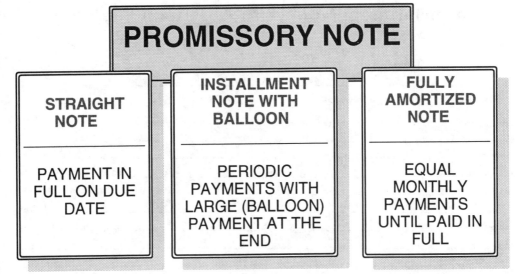

STRAIGHT NOTE (INTEREST ONLY)

A *STRAIGHT NOTE is a promissory note in which a borrower repays the principal in one lump sum, at maturity, while interest is paid in installments or at maturity.* The parties could agree that interest be paid monthly, quarterly, annually or any agreed to term, but the principal is a lump sum payment. In real estate, this type of note is usually for relatively small amounts of money being borrowed for a short time.

INSTALLMENT NOTE WITH BALLOON PAYMENT

An *INSTALLMENT NOTE WITH A BALLOON PAYMENT (PARTIALLY AMORTIZED NOTE) is a promissory note with periodic payments of principal and interest and a large payment at the end (maturity date or due date).* This type of note and the straight note are usually in the form of secondary financing (second trust deeds). See Figure 8-2.

FULLY AMORTIZED INSTALLMENT NOTE

A *FULLY AMORTIZED INSTALLMENT NOTE is a promissory note where both the principal and interest are paid in equal installments until the debt is paid in full.* Installments make it easy to pay off a note and there is no balloon payment at the end of the loan period.

FIGURE 8-2

An Installment Note With A Balloon Payment

$_____ _____, California_____, 19____

In installments as herein stated, for value received, I promise to pay to_____

_____, or order,

at_____

the sum of _____ DOLLARS,

with interest from_____on unpaid principal at the

rate of_____per cent per annum; principal and interest payable in installments of

_____ Dollars

or more on the_____day of each _____month, beginning

on the_____ day of _____, 19____ . _____

_____

_____

_____

_____ and continuing until said principal and interest have been paid.

Each payment shall be credited first on interest then due and the remainder on principal; and interest shall thereupon cease upon the principal so credited. Should default be made in payment of any installment when due the whole sum of principal and interest shall become immediately due at the option of the holder of this note. Principal and interest payable in lawful money of the United States. If action be instituted on this note I promise to pay such sum as the Court may fix as attorney's fees. I promise to pay Servicing Agent a late payment charge of $5 or 10% of installment due of principal and interest, which-ever is greater. For First Trust Deed loans of $16,000 or more; and for Junior Lien loans of $8,000 or more, the following clause governs: $5 or 6% of installment due of principal and interest, whichever is greater. For all loans, regardless of principal amount, no late payment charge will be made if the installment is paid or tendered in full within 10 days after its scheduled

due date. This note is secured by a DEED OF TRUST to _____

_____   _____

_____   _____

DEED OF TRUST NOTE-INSTALLMENT NOTE-WOLCOTTS FORM 1458 REV.

For real estate financing in California, the fully amortized installment note is the most commonly used type of note. Loan payments are either fixed or adjustable.

To amortize is to slowly reduce the principal owed. Fully amortized loans are seldom foreclosed on because the principal is reduced with each payment.

A fully amortized loan has equal monthly payments except for the last payment, which is slightly higher or lower. With *EQUAL MONTHLY PAYMENTS, the monthly payment amount including principal and interest is constant, but as the loan is paid-off the amount of the payment attributed to interest decreases, and the amount attributed to principal increases.*

NEGOTIABLE INSTRUMENTS
(PROMISSORY NOTES, CHECKS, OTHERS)

Negotiable instruments are easily transferable from one person to another. Promissory notes are negotiable. The most common example is a personal check.

A **NEGOTIABLE INSTRUMENT** *is any financial document (promissory note, check or other) that can be passed easily, from one person to another, if it meets certain legal requirements.* Any promissory note may be a negotiable instrument that is freely transferable. A negotiable instrument must be:

     1. an unconditional promise
     2. in writing
     3. made by one person to another
     4. signed by the maker
     5. payable on demand or on a set date
     6. for a set amount of money.

HOLDER IN DUE COURSE (NO KNOWLEDGE OF DEFECT)

The new owner of the check or note has become an innocent third party.

A **HOLDER IN DUE COURSE** *is one who has taken a negotiable instrument from another.* The holder in due course must have obtained the note under the following conditions:

     1. The note itself must be complete and regular.
     2. It must not have been overdue or uncollectible.
     3. Note must be taken in good faith for valuable consideration.
     4. The person receiving the note must not have had any knowledge of any defect in title or anything wrong in the note.

This means that the holder in due course has a better position because the maker of the note has fewer grounds for refusing to make payment. **Warning:** Many banks and other financial institutions do not like to take holder in due course checks (second or third party checks). Since they do not know the one who wrote the check, they may find it difficult to collect.

IMPORTANT CLAUSES IN FINANCING INSTRUMENTS

The following financial instrument clauses are more than commonly used terms, they have definite meanings that affect the financial obligations of both a lender and borrower.

ACCELERATION CLAUSE (ENTIRE AMOUNT DUE)

In an *ACCELERATION CLAUSE, upon the occurrence of a **specific event**, the lender has the right to demand immediate payment of the entire note.* An acceleration clause is used to demand immediate payment in full because of a default in loan payments, property taxes, fire insurance or upon the transfer of property. The main purpose of an acceleration clause is to make the entire balance of the loan due and payable at once. A *LATE PAYMENT is a payment that is, unless otherwise stated, more than ten days past due.*

> *An acceleration clause speeds up the "balance due" based on the occurrence of a specific event.*

ALIENATION CLAUSE (DUE ON SALE)

An *ALIENATION CLAUSE is a form of the acceleration clause, stating that the entire loan becomes due and payable when the property is sold, assigned, transferred or otherwise alienated.* The lender, whether a financial institution or a private party, is given the right to full payment when the original borrower transfers the property. This is also commonly referred to as a **"due on sale"** clause.

> *With an alienation clause, the lender demands that the entire balance of the loan is due when the owner is alienating, transferring or "conveying" the property.*

ASSUMPTION

If a buyer *ASSUMES a loan on a property that is already encumbered, he or she accepts responsibility, with the lender's consent, for the full payment of the loan.* The name on the loan is changed to that of the buyer. With a true assumption, the seller has **secondary responsibility**. To end his or her liability and put the loan in the name of the buyer, the seller files a Substitution of Liability form.

> *Relieves seller of primary responsibility.*

When a buyer purchases a property "subject to," he or she has no responsibility in the event of a default: the seller retains responsibility. "Subject to" benefits the buyer.

Taking title **SUBJECT TO** *a prior loan constitutes an agreement to take over and make the payments or lose the property.* The seller (to whom the loan was originally made) remains legally responsible for the note, but the buyer makes the payments.

SUBORDINATION CLAUSE (CURRENT LOAN STANDS STILL - NEW LOAN MOVES AHEAD)

Subordination allows subsequent loans (future loans) to have priority over previously recorded loans.

A **SUBORDINATION CLAUSE** *is part of a trust deed or mortgage that allows for a future change in the priority of financial liens.* It is used when the buyer wants future financial liens to have priority over a lien he or she is now acquiring. The seller of vacant land will sometimes lend money to the buyer as part of the transaction and will allow the subordination of that loan to any new construction loans.

The subordination clause is used to change the priority on one or more financial liens, but the terms of a subordination clause must be clear and definite. The courts are skeptical about loosely written subordination clauses. Subordination clauses are not used that often, but a salesperson must know and understand them.

PREPAYMENT PENALTIES (FEE FOR EARLY PAYMENT)

A **PREPAYMENT PENALTY** *is a charge to the borrower for paying off all or part of a loan balance before the due date.*

Most financial institutions use a prepayment penalty clause on fixed rate loans, but they are rarely employed with the adjustable rate loans. California law prohibits lenders from charging prepayment penalties on fixed rate loans, after the first seven years, if they are owner-occupied home loans. A prepayment penalty is only enforceable during the first seven years of a (1-to-4 unit) home loan. The penalty is usually six months' interest on the amount prepaid (each year) that exceeds 20% of the original principal amount of the loan. However, penalties do vary among lenders. After negotiating, a lender may sometimes waive the prepayment penalty if the borrower obtains a new loan from that institution.

A prepayment penalty is only enforceable during the first seven years of a one-to-four unit home loan.

IMPOUND ACCOUNTS (RESERVES)

IMPOUND ACCOUNTS (RESERVES) are moneys collected in advance from borrowers to assure the payment of recurring costs, such as property taxes and fire insurance. Some lenders require impound accounts. Impound accounts are especially appropriate when there is a relatively low down payment.

Impounds are reserves (money) on hand for recurring costs, such as taxes and insurance. Impounds can NOT be used to pay interest.

ASSIGNMENT OF RENTS (TAKE POSSESSION)

An *ASSIGNMENT OF RENTS* clause allows a lender, upon default of the borrower, to take possession of the property, collect rents and pay expenses.

INTEREST & TYPES OF LOANS

INTEREST (SIMPLE INTEREST)

INTEREST is the charge for borrowing money. In real estate we use simple interest, not compound interest. Interest can be thought of as a rental charge for the use of money.

The "Nominal Interest Rate" is the rate stated in the note. The "Effective Interest Rate" is the rate the borrower is actually paying (including interest, points and loan fees).

The formula for calculating interest is:

$$I = P \times R \times T$$
or
Interest = Principal x Rate x Time

To find the interest on an $80,000 loan at 12 percent interest for 3 years, we would make the following calculation:

$$I = P \times R \times T$$
$28,800 = $80,000 x .12 x 3 years

(See Chapter 15 for a more detailed discussion of interest calculations.)

FIXED INTEREST RATES (FIXED RATE)

A **FIXED INTEREST RATE LOAN** *is a loan where the payments are the same each month for the life of the loan.* The equal monthly payment includes both the principal and the interest. A loan with this kind of fixed rate of interest is said to be a "fully amortized fixed rate loan."

http://www.bankrate.com (Current interest rates)

AMORTIZATION PAYMENTS

Amortization is the liquidation of a note including principal and interest.

AMORTIZATION *is the repaying of a loan (principal and interest), in regular payments, over the term of the loan.* This repayment is usually in monthly payments but can be paid quarterly or semi-annually.

NEGATIVE AMORTIZATION *means the interest rate charges are higher than the monthly payment.* Negative amortization means that the loan payment does not cover the interest charges and the amount of unpaid interest is added to the unpaid loan balance.

Real estate salespeople should always have amortization books handy so that they can figure out the monthly payment on any loan. The **AMORTIZATION (SCHEDULE) BOOK** *shows the monthly payments necessary to amortize a loan, over a given number of years, at different interest rates and for different loan amounts.* This amortization table book is usually given free, upon request, to salespeople by title insurance companies or financial institutions. Salespeople can also use specially programmed, hand-held calculators to instantly determine the monthly payment amount.

Figure 8-3 is an example of an amortization table at 12.5% interest per annum for 20, 25, 30 and 40 years at different loan amounts. The loan amounts range from $100 to $100,000, but any loan amount can be obtained by adding the necessary increments. For example, if we want to determine the monthly payments for a $155,700 loan at 12.5% interest for 30 years, this is what we would do:

1. Check the 30 year's column for the monthly payment on $100,000.

2. Next, determine the monthly payment for $50,000, $5,000 and $700 using the same method.

3. Lastly, add the monthly payment amounts together.

Amount	Payment
$100,000	$1,067.26
50,000	533.63
5,000	53.37
700	7.48

TOTAL LOAN $155,700   **$1,661.74 Monthly Payment**

The use of an amortization table or mortgage calculator enables the salesperson to determine monthly payments.

http://www.latimes.com/home/news/realest (Mortgage calculator)
http://www.relist.com/mortcalc.html (Mortgage calculator)

AMORTIZATION BOOK

FIGURE 8-3

	MONTHLY PAYMENTS NECESSARY TO AMORTIZE A LOAN		12½%	
TERM **AMOUNT**	**20** **YEARS**	**25** **YEARS**	**30** **YEARS**	**40** **YEARS**
$ 100	1.14	1.10	1.07	1.05
200	2.28	2.19	2.14	2.10
300	3.41	3.28	3.21	3.15
400	4.55	4.37	4.27	4.20
500	5.69	5.46	5.34	5.25
600	6.82	6.55	6.41	6.30
700	7.96	7.64	7.48	7.35
800	9.09	8.73	8.54	8.40
900	10.23	9.82	9.61	9.45
1,000	11.37	10.91	10.68	10.49
2,000	22.73	21.81	21.35	20.98
3,000	34.09	32.72	32.02	31.47
4,000	45.45	43.62	42.70	41.96
5,000	56.81	54.52	53.37	52.45
6,000	68.17	65.43	64.04	62.94
7,000	79.53	76.33	74.71	73.43
8,000	90.90	87.23	85.39	83.92
9,000	102.26	98.14	96.06	94.41
10,000	113.62	109.04	106.73	104.90
20,000	227.23	218.08	213.46	209.79
30,000	340.85	327.11	320.18	314.68
40,000	454.46	436.15	426.91	419.57
50,000	568.08	545.18	533.63	524.46
100,000	1,136.15	1,090.36	1,067.26	1,048.92

ADJUSTED RATE MORTGAGES (ARMS)

Many lenders will allow the borrower a choice of either 1) a fixed interest rate loan or 2) an adjustable rate mortgage (ARM) loan. An ARM allows the interest rate to fluctuate (go up or down) depending on money market conditions. Rather than making equal monthly payments, as with a fixed rate loan, the ARM payments will vary over the term of the loan.

An *ADJUSTED RATE MORTGAGE "ARM" (OR TRUST DEED) is a loan where the interest rate fluctuates periodically based on a specific index, which makes the payment amount also change.* Each lending institution has its own ARM terms and provisions. Figure 8-4 illustrates how an adjusted rate mortgage (ARM) works. The interest rate, and therefore the payments, will change often over the term of the loan. ARM lenders attempt to make this type of loan more attractive to a potential borrower by offering the loan at a much lower starting interest rate than with a fixed interest rate loan.

http://www.loanpage.com (Independent loan information)
http://www.loanshop.com (Independent loan information)

SOME SPECIAL PURPOSE TYPES OF LOANS

Graduated Payment Mortgage (For First Time Buyers)

A *GRADUATED PAYMENT MORTGAGE (TRUST DEED) is a type of fixed interest rate loan where the monthly payments start out lower and then gradually increase (for example, after five years it levels off for the remainder of the loan payment).* Although the final level of payments is higher than the payments would have been had the loan been fully amortized, the initial payments are much lower than the fully amortized rate.

Biweekly Mortgage (26 Payments)

A *BIWEEKLY MORTGAGE (TRUST DEED) is a fixed interest rate loan where the payments are made every two weeks, but the payment is one-half the amount of a regular monthly payment.* Since there are 52 weeks in a year the borrower pays a total of 26 payments, which is the equivalent of 13 monthly payments.

15-Year Fixed & Adjustable Rate Loans

Fifteen-year fixed-rate loans are gaining in popularity because, for a slight increase in the monthly payment, the loan can be paid off in only 15 years.

FIGURE 8-4

How ARM's Work

THE INDEX

The *INDEX is the starting interest rate used as the indicator so that changes from it can be calculated.* If the index rises 1%, the ARM interest rate you pay goes up 1%. The index must be: 1) beyond the control of the lender and 2) available and verifiable by the public. Examples of indexes used are the Cost of Living Index, the San Francisco District 12 Cost of Funds, the One Year T-Bill and the London Interbank Offered Rate (LIBOR).

THE ADJUSTABLE INTERVAL

The *ADJUSTABLE INTERVAL is the frequency with which interest rates are reset.* This period can be monthly, quarterly, every six months or even once a year. If the index has risen .3% by the end of the interval period, the interest rate you pay goes up .3%.

THE CAP

The *CAP is a percentage rate ceiling or restriction on the 1) periodic (adjustable interval); and 2) lifetime change in interest rates or payments.* An adjustable interval cap limits the percentage of change upward or downward to, for example, 1/2% every quarter. The lifetime cap is often around a maximum of 5% above or below the initial agreed to contract rate.

THE MARGIN

The *MARGIN is the spread between the index rate and the initial contract rate from which the lender will make a profit and cover its costs.* It is the agreed to, in advance, amount of profit for the lender. If the index rate is 4% and the margin is 3%, then the current APR rate paid by the borrower is 7%. Even if the index rate moves up to 5%, the margin will always remain at 3% and the new APR will be 8%.

ADVANTAGES OF ARMS

The main advantage of an ARM is a lower interest rate than can be found with a fixed rate loan because the lender is protected if interest rates rise over the loan period. This makes an ARM more affordable, thus more people can qualify for it. Generally there are no prepayment penalties and an assumption is usually permitted, if the new buyer meets credit standards. ARM's benefit first time buyers, because interest rates are initially lower, and short-term investors who just want a lower interest rate.

Reverse Annuity Loans (Seniors Who Need Income)

REVERSE ANNUITY LOANS are loans where the lender pays the borrower a fixed monthly payment based on the value of the property. The loan is not repaid until the last owner dies, at which time it is paid back through probate. This type of loan is good for senior citizens who need a monthly income and have a large amount of equity in their homes. The senior citizens can pay off the loans earlier if they so desire.

POINTS, LOAN FEES & USURY

POINTS (1 POINT = 1% OF THE LOAN AMOUNT)

A point is one percent of the loan amount. Five points on a $300,000 loan is $15,000. It is also called an origination fee.

A **POINT** *is a fee (origination fee) of 1% of the amount borrowed, charged by the lender.* Most financial institutions charge the borrower points when he or she obtains a new loan. Points vary, but generally range from 1% to 7% of the loan amount. They are usually paid by the buyer but, if so negotiated, the seller may also pay.

If you purchase a home for $150,000 and obtain a loan for $120,000 plus two points, the loan points will cost you $2,400 ($120,000 x .02). These points are an additional cost and are added to the down payment and other closing costs required to complete the transaction at the time of purchase.

Points paid are usually adjustments to the interest rate. If the interest rate quoted is lower than what is currently being charged, more points are charged to make up the difference, which is paid to the lender. If a savings bank wants to quote a lower interest rate, the borrower can expect a larger point charge.

LOAN FEES

In addition to points, there is usually a loan fee. A **LOAN FEE** *is the fee charged by the lender in order to apply for a loan.* This charge runs about $250 to $400. Other charges may include the appraisal and credit report.

USURY

USURY *is charging more than the legally allowed percentage of interest.* In California the maximum interest rate charged for various loans is set by law. Anyone charging more than the designated rate is committing usury and is breaking the law. In determining whether an interest charge is usurious or not, all loan fees and points are added to the interest rate. Prepayment penalties are not included in the usury law test.

The constitutional usury rate in California is ten percent, or five percent above the discount rate charged by the Federal Reserve Bank of San Francisco, whichever is higher. This limit only applies to lenders who are not exempt from the law. Nearly every conventional source of real estate financing, however, has been exempted from the usury limit. Banks, savings banks and other institutional lenders are all exempt. Sellers carrying back a purchase money trust deed as part of their equity in a real estate sale are exempt. Any transaction made through a licensed broker is also exempt from usury laws. The problem arises when a private individual lends money to another private individual. Check with an attorney first.

 http://www.frbsf.org (Federal Reserve Bank of San Francisco, 12th District)
http://www.fdic.gov (Federal Deposit Insurance Corporation - FDIC)

MORTGAGES

SECURITY DEVICES (FINANCIAL INSTRUMENTS) are written documents that pledge real property as security for a promissory note.

> *The three financial instruments (security devices to collateralize real property) used in California are:*
>
> *1) mortgages (rare)*
> *2) trust deeds (1st and 2nd are common)*
> *3) land contracts (not common).*

In California we have three common types of security devices (financing instruments). See Figure 8-5. Any of the three previously mentioned notes may be used in conjunction with these financial instruments.

FIGURE 8-5

A **MORTGAGE** *is a financial instrument, in the form of a lien, that secures a property for payment of a promissory note.* It is not common in California. The **MORTGAGOR** *is the buyer/owner who is borrowing*, and the **MORTGAGEE** *is the lender*. If the mortgagor defaults in his or her payments, a foreclosure action may be started. After the foreclosure sale, the borrower has one year to redeem (buy back) the property, pay all the accumulated charges or pay the mortgagee rent. Figure 8-6 is a two-page comparison of the differences between mortgages and trust deeds.

> *Mortgagee = Lender*
> *Mortgagor = Owner/Borrower*

POWER OF SALE CLAUSE

Some mortgages have a power of sale clause. A **POWER OF SALE CLAUSE** *allows the mortgagee to sell the property without a court proceeding (much like a trustee's sale) if the mortgagor is in default.* But it still requires a lengthy proceeding. If there is no power of sale clause, court (judicial) action is required for a foreclosure.

MORTGAGES COMPARED TO TRUST DEEDS

Parties

In the mortgage there are two parties: the **mortgagor** (borrower) and the **mortgagee** (lender). The deed of trust has three: **trustor** (borrower), **trustee** (third party) and **beneficiary** (lender).

Title

A mortgage does not convey title, it creates a lien. In a deed of trust the title is conveyed to a trustee (third party) for the benefit of the lender (beneficiary) and is in effect a lien.

Statute Of Limitations

In a mortgage, an action to foreclose is subject to the statute of limitations. Since it is a promissory note, the mortgagee has four years from the date of the last payment to start foreclosure. With a trust deed, there is no time limit because the third party (trustee) has title and power of sale.

Remedy For Default

In a mortgage, the only remedy of the mortgagee (lender) is judicial (court) foreclosure, unless the mortgage contains a power of sale clause. Although the actual mortgage foreclosure takes a short period of time, the redemption period is very long (1 year). The **REDEMPTION PERIOD** *is the legally acceptable time period for buying back one's property after a judicial sale.* In a deed of trust the entire process, including any redemption or sale, requires a short period of time (4 months).

FIGURE 8-6

TRUST DEED

1. **Parties:**

    a. **Trustor** - Borrower who conveys title to trustee who holds as security for debt.

    b. **Trustee** - Receiver of naked legal title who will reconvey it when debt is paid or will sell if foreclosure necessary.

    c. **Beneficiary -** Lender who holds note and trust deed.

2. **Title -** Conveyed to trustee with trustor retaining possession of the property.

3. **Statute of Limitations -** Since security for debt (title) is held by trustee, rights of creditor are not ended when statute has run out on note.

4. **Remedy for Default -** Foreclosure can be instituted through:

    a. Trustee's Sale, or
    b. Court Foreclosure.

5. **Right of Redemption -** When title has been sold by trustee at Trustee's Sale, no right of redemption previously existed, but in rare cases the courts now say it does.

6. **Satisfaction -** Trustor has beneficiary send original note and trust deed to trustee with request for full reconveyance. Upon payment of fees, trustee issues reconveyance deed which must be recorded.

7. **Foreclosure** by Trustee's Sale:

    a. **Beneficiary notifies trustee of default** who in turn notifies trustor and also records notice. Anyone with recorded "Request for Notice of Default" must also be notified.

    b. **Trustee waits at least three months.** During three month period trustor can reinstate loan.

    c. **Trustee advertises "Notice of Sale"** once a week for three weeks and posts notice on property.

    d. Trustee conducts sale and issues Trustee's Deed to highest bidder.

8. **Deficiency Judgment -** No judgment available:

    a. If foreclosure by Trustee's Sale.

    b. On purchase money trust deeds, even if by court foreclosure.

FIGURE 8-6 CONTINUED

MORTGAGE

1. **Parties:**

    a. **Mortgagor -** Borrower who retains title but gives lender a lien on the property as the security for debt.

    b. **Mortgagee -** Lender who holds the mortgage.

2. **Title -** Retained by mortgagor together with possession.

3. **Statute of Limitations -** Foreclosure is barred if no action is taken within four years of delinquency. Mortgage is said to have "outlawed."

4. **Remedy for Default -** Court foreclosure is usually only remedy.

5. **Right of Redemption -** Mortgagor has one year to redeem following court foreclosure; called "Equity of Redemption."

6. **Satisfaction of Mortgage -** Upon final payment and on demand, mortgagee signs certificate that debt is satisfied. Certificate or release is recorded.

7. **Foreclosure by Court:**

    a. **Court action commenced by mortgagee.** Court issues decree of foreclosure and order of sale.

    b. **Commissioner appointed by court sells** to highest bidder after publication and posting of sale notice.

    c. **Certificate of Sale issued by Commissioner.** Mortgagor has one year to redeem property and to remain in possession.

    d. **Sheriff's Deed issued after one year.**

8. **Deficiency Judgment -** Available in court foreclosure unless mortgage was purchase money mortgage as noted below.

Note: Purchase money is defined as:

    1. Mortgage or trust deed or real property sales contract given to seller as part of purchase price, or

    2. Mortgage or trust deed given to lender to finance purchase of owner-occupied dwelling of four or less units.

TRUST DEEDS ARE PREFERRED TO MORTGAGES

In California, the trust deed is preferred to the mortgage as the usual financing device. The lender has fewer restrictions when using a trust deed. There is: 1) A short period of redemption prior to the sale and the fact that the sale, once made, is usually absolute. The purchaser can take possession at once, which is not true for a mortgage; 2) The ease and convenience, without having to resort to court action, with which the property may be sold to satisfy the debt if the borrower defaults. California laws favor lenders who use the trust deed, which allows them more freedom in granting loans to deserving buyers.

MORTGAGE: A GENERAL TERM

Although mortgages are rarely used in California, the term "mortgage" is so ingrained in the tradition of lending that often trust deeds and other loans are referred to as "mortgages." Adjusted Rate Mortgages and Fixed Rate Mortgages, for example, are deeds of trust. **We will use the general words mortgage and deed of trust interchangeably**, but mortgagee or mortgagor refer only to mortgages and trustee, trustor and beneficiary refer only to trust deeds.

TRUST DEEDS

TRUST DEEDS ARE USED IN CALIFORNIA

> *Trust deeds (deeds of trust loans) are personal property.*

In California the trust deed, sometimes called a deed of trust, is the usual financing instrument. The **TRUST DEED** *is a security device that makes the real property collateral for the promissory note.* Figures 8-7 and 8-8 show a copy of a trust deed.

> *A trust deed needs a note for security, but a note does NOT need a trust deed. A trust deed is not a negotiable instrument; the note is. If the conditions of a note and the trust deed are in conflict, the note prevails.*

In a trust deed there are three parties. The **TRUSTOR** *is the party that is borrowing the money.* This is usually the buyer, but may also be the owner if the property is being refinanced. The **BENEFICIARY** *is the lender who is loaning money for the purchase of real property.* Home lenders in California are usually savings banks, but may also be banks. The **TRUSTEE** *is the third, disinterested party (usually a corporation) who holds title to the property, but only in so far as the trustee may have to sell the property, for the beneficiary, should the trustor default.* This is normally a title insurance company. Figure 8-9 illustrates this three-party relationship.

FIGURE 8-7

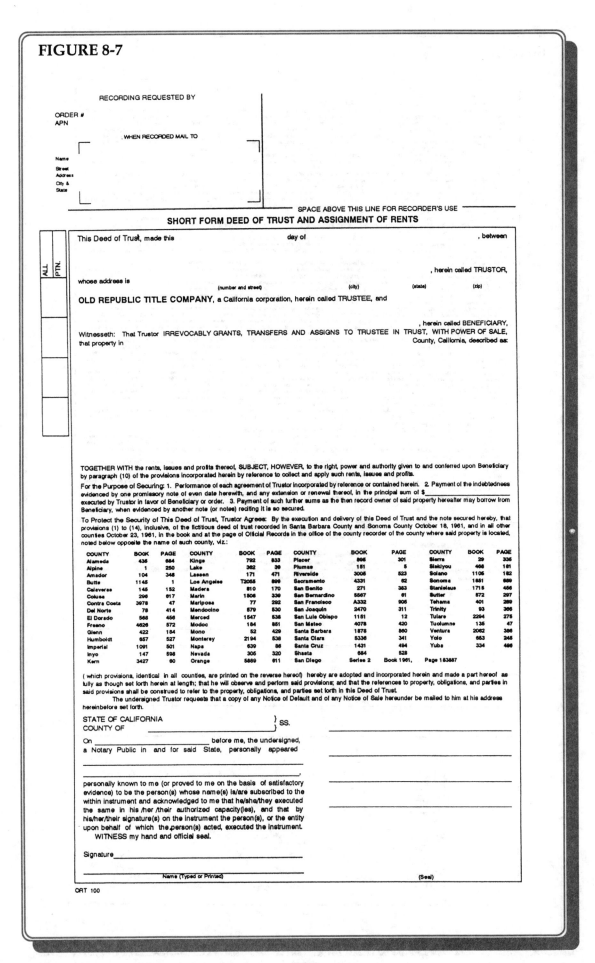

RECORDING REQUESTED BY

ORDER #
APN

.WHEN RECORDED MAIL TO

Name
Street
Address
City &
State

SPACE ABOVE THIS LINE FOR RECORDER'S USE

SHORT FORM DEED OF TRUST AND ASSIGNMENT OF RENTS

This Deed of Trust, made this   day of   , between

, herein called TRUSTOR,

whose address is

(number and street)   (city)   (state)   (zip)

OLD REPUBLIC TITLE COMPANY, a California corporation, herein called TRUSTEE, and

, herein called BENEFICIARY,

Witnesseth: That Trustor IRREVOCABLY GRANTS, TRANSFERS AND ASSIGNS TO TRUSTEE IN TRUST, WITH POWER OF SALE,
that property in   County, California, described as:

TOGETHER WITH the rents, issues and profits thereof, SUBJECT, HOWEVER, to the right, power and authority given to and conferred upon Beneficiary
by paragraph (10) of the provisions incorporated herein by reference to collect and apply such rents, issues and profits.

For the Purpose of Securing: 1. Performance of each agreement of Trustor incorporated by reference or contained herein. 2. Payment of the indebtedness
evidenced by one promissory note of even date herewith, and any extension or renewal thereof, in the principal sum of $_____
executed by Trustor in favor of Beneficiary or order. 3. Payment of such further sums as the then record owner of said property hereafter may borrow from
Beneficiary, when evidenced by another note (or notes) reciting it is so secured.

To Protect the Security of This Deed of Trust, Trustor Agrees: By the execution and delivery of this Deed of Trust and the note secured hereby, that
provisions (1) to (14), inclusive, of the fictitious deed of trust recorded in Santa Barbara County and Sonoma County October 18, 1961, and in all other
counties October 23, 1961, in the book and at the page of Official Records in the office of the county recorder of the county where said property is located,
noted below opposite the name of such county, viz.:

COUNTY	BOOK	PAGE	COUNTY	BOOK	PAGE	COUNTY	BOOK	PAGE	COUNTY	BOOK	PAGE
Alameda	435	684	Kings	792	833	Placer	895	301	Sierra	29	335
Alpine	1	250	Lake	362	39	Plumas	151	5	Siskiyou	468	181
Amador	104	348	Lassen	171	471	Riverside	3005	523	Solano	1105	182
Butte	1145	1	Los Angeles	T2055	899	Sacramento	4331	62	Sonoma	1851	689
Calaveras	145	152	Madera	810	170	San Benito	271	383	Stanislaus	1715	456
Colusa	296	617	Marin	1508	339	San Bernardino	5567	61	Sutter	572	297
Contra Costa	3978	47	Mariposa	77	292	San Francisco	A332	905	Tehama	401	289
Del Norte	78	414	Mendocino	579	530	San Joaquin	2470	311	Trinity	93	366
El Dorado	568	456	Merced	1547	538	San Luis Obispo	1151	12	Tulare	2294	275
Fresno	4626	572	Modoc	184	851	San Mateo	4078	420	Tuolumne	135	47
Glenn	422	184	Mono	52	429	Santa Barbara	1878	860	Ventura	2062	386
Humboldt	657	527	Monterey	2194	538	Santa Clara	5336	341	Yolo	653	245
Imperial	1091	501	Napa	639	86	Santa Cruz	1431	494	Yuba	334	486
Inyo	147	598	Nevada	305	320	Shasta	684	528			
Kern	3427	60	Orange	5889	611	San Diego	Series 2	Book 1961,	Page 183887		

(which provisions, identical in all counties, are printed on the reverse hereof) hereby are adopted and incorporated herein and made a part hereof as
fully as though set forth herein at length; that he will observe and perform said provisions; and that the references to property, obligations, and parties in
said provisions shall be construed to refer to the property, obligations, and parties set forth in this Deed of Trust.

      The undersigned Trustor requests that a copy of any Notice of Default and of any Notice of Sale hereunder be mailed to him at his address
hereinbefore set forth.

STATE OF CALIFORNIA   } SS.
COUNTY OF _____

On _____ before me, the undersigned,
a Notary Public in and for said State, personally appeared

_____

_____ ,

personally known to me (or proved to me on the basis of satisfactory
evidence) to be the person(s) whose name(s) is/are subscribed to the
within instrument and acknowledged to me that he/she/they executed
the same in his /her /their authorized capacity(ies), and that by
his/her/their signature(s) on the instrument the person(s), or the entity
upon behalf of which the person(s) acted, executed the instrument.
    WITNESS my hand and official seal.

Signature_____

_____
Name (Typed or Printed)

(Seal)

ORT 100

FIGURE 8-8

The following is a copy of provisions (1) to (14) inclusive, of the fictitious Deed of Trust, recorded in each county in California, as stated in the foregoing Deed of Trust and incorporated by reference in said Deed of Trust as being a part thereof as if set forth at length therein.

To Protect the Security of This Deed of Trust, Trustor Agrees:

1. To keep said property in good condition and repair; not to remove or demolish any building thereon; to complete or restore promptly and in good and workmanlike manner any building which may be constructed, damaged or destroyed thereon and to pay when due all claims for labor performed and materials furnished therefor; to comply with all laws affecting said property or requiring any alterations or improvements to be made thereon, not to commit or permit waste thereof; not to commit, suffer or permit any act upon said property in violation of law; to cultivate, irrigate, fertilize, fumigate, prune and do all other acts which from the character or use of said property may be reasonably necessary, the specific enumerations herein not excluding the general.

2. To provide, maintain and deliver to Beneficiary fire insurance satisfactory to and with loss payable to Beneficiary. The amount collected under any fire or other insurance policy may be applied by Beneficiary upon any indebtedness secured hereby and in such order as Beneficiary may determine, or at option of Beneficiary the entire amount so collected or any part thereof may be released to Trustor. Such application or release shall not cure or waive any default or notice of default hereunder or invalidate any act done pursuant to such notice.

3. To appear in and defend any action or proceeding purporting to affect the security hereof or the rights or powers of Beneficiary or Trustee, and to pay all costs and expenses, including cost of evidence of title and attorney's fees in a reasonable sum, in any such action or proceeding in which Beneficiary or Trustee may appear, and in any suit brought by Beneficiary to foreclose this Deed.

4. To pay: at least ten days before delinquency all taxes and assessments affecting said property, including assessments on appurtenant water stock; when due, all encumbrances, charges and liens, with interest, on said property or any part thereof, which appear to be prior or superior hereto, all costs, fees and expenses of this Trust. Should Trustor fail to make any payment or to do any act as herein provided, then Beneficiary or Trustee, but without obligation so to do and without notice to or demand upon Trustor and without releasing Trustor from any obligation hereof, may: make or do the same in such manner and to such extent as either may deem necessary to protect the security hereof, Beneficiary or Trustee being authorized to enter upon said property for such purposes; appear in and defend any action or proceeding purporting to affect the security hereof or the rights or powers of Beneficiary or Trustee; pay, purchase, contest or compromise any encumbrance, charge or lien which in the judgment of either appears to be prior or superior hereto; and, in exercising any such powers, pay necessary expenses, employ counsel and pay his reasonable fees.

5. To pay immediately and without demand all sums so expended by Beneficiary or Trustee, with interest from date of expenditure at the amount allowed by law in effect at the date hereof, and to pay for any statement provided for by law in effect at the date hereof regarding the obligation secured hereby any amount demanded by the Beneficiary not to exceed the maximum allowed by law at the time when said statement is demanded.

6. That any award of damages in connection with any condemnation for public use of or injury to said property or any part thereof is hereby assigned and shall be paid to beneficiary who may apply or release such moneys received by him in the same manner and with the same effect as above provided for disposition of proceeds of fire or other insurance.

7. That by accepting payment of any sum secured hereby after its due date, Beneficiary does not waive his right either to require prompt payment when due of all other sums so secured or to declare default for failure so to pay.

8. That at any time or from time to time, without liability therefor and without notice, upon written request of Beneficiary and presentation of this Deed and said note for endorsement, and without affecting the personal liability of any person for payment of the indebtedness secured hereby, Trustee may: reconvey any part of said property; consent to the making of any map or plat thereof; join in granting any easement thereon; or join in any extension agreement or any agreement subordinating the lien or charge thereof.

9. That upon written request of Beneficiary stating that all sums secured hereby have been paid and upon surrender of this Deed and said note to Trustee for cancellation and retention and upon payment of its fees, Trustee shall reconvey, without warranty the property then held hereunder. The recitals in such reconveyance of any matters or facts shall be conclusive proof of the truthfulness thereof. The Grantee in such reconveyance may be described as "the person or persons legally entitled thereto." Five years after issuance of such full reconveyance, Trustee may destroy said note and this Deed (unless directed in such request to retain them).

10. That as additional security, Trustor hereby gives to and confers upon Beneficiary the right, power and authority, during the continuance of these trusts, to collect the rents, issues and profits of said property, reserving unto Trustor the right, prior to any default by Trustor in payment of any indebtedness secured hereby or in performance of any agreement hereunder, to collect and retain such rents, issues and profits as they become due and payable. Upon any such default, Beneficiary may at any time without notice, either in person, by agent or by a receiver to be appointed by a court, and without regard to the adequacy of any security for the indebtedness hereby secured, enter upon and take possession of said property or any part thereof in his own name sue for or otherwise collect such rents, issues and profits, including those past due and unpaid, and apply the same, less costs and expenses of operation and collection, including reasonable attorney's fees, upon any indebtedness secured hereby, and in such order as Beneficiary may determine. The entering upon and taking possession of said property, the collection of such rents, issues and profits and the application thereof as aforesaid, shall not cure or waive any default or notice of default hereunder or invalidate any act done pursuant to such notice.

11. That upon default by Trustor in payment of any indebtedness secured hereby or in performance of any agreement hereunder, Beneficiary may declare all sums secured hereby immediately due and payable by delivery to Trustee of written declaration of default and demand for sale and of written notice of default and of election to cause to be sold said property, which notice Trustee shall cause to be filed for record. Beneficiary also shall deposit with Trustee this Deed, said note and all documents evidencing expenditures secured hereby.

    After the lapse of such time as may then be required by law following the recordation of said notice of default and notice of sale having been given as then required by law, Trustee, without demand on Trustor, shall sell said property at the time and place fixed by it in said notice of sale, either as a whole or in separate parcels, and in such order as it may determine, at public auction to the highest bidder for cash in lawful money of the United States, payable at time of sale. Trustee may postpone sale of all or any portion of said property by public announcement at such time and place of sale, and from time to time thereafter may postpone such sale by public announcement at the time fixed by the preceding postponement. Trustee shall deliver to such purchaser its deed conveying the property so sold but without any covenant or warranty, express or implied. The recitals in such deed of any matters or facts shall be conclusive proof of the truthfulness thereof. Any person, including Trustor, Trustee, or Beneficiary as hereinafter defined, may purchase at such sale.

    After deducting all costs, fees and expenses of Trustee and of this Trust, including cost of evidence of title in connection with sale, Trustee shall apply the proceeds of sale to payment of: all sums expended under the terms hereof, not then repaid, with accrued interest at the amount allowed by law in effect at the date hereof; all other sums then secured hereby; and the remainder, if any, to the person or persons legally entitled thereto.

12. Beneficiary, or any successor in ownership of any indebtedness secured hereby, may from time to time, by instrument in writing, substitute a successor or successors to any Trustee named herein or acting hereunder, which instrument, executed by the Beneficiary and duly acknowledged and recorded in the office of the recorder of the County or Counties where said property is situated, shall be conclusive proof of proper substitution of such successor Trustee or Trustees, who shall, without conveyance from the Trustee predecessor, succeed to all its title, estate, rights, powers and duties. Said instrument must contain the name of the original Trustor, Trustee and Beneficiary hereunder, the book and page where this Deed is recorded and the name and address of the new Trustee.

13. That this Deed applies to, inures to the benefit of, and binds all parties hereto, their heirs, legatees, devisees, administrators, executors, successors and assigns. The term Beneficiary shall mean the owner and holder, including pledgees, of the note secured hereby, whether or not named as Beneficiary herein. In this Deed, whenever the context so requires, the masculine gender includes the feminine and/or neuter, and the singular number includes the plural.

14. That Trustee accepts this Trust when this Deed, duly executed and acknowledged, is made a public record as provided by law. Trustee is not obligated to notify any party hereto of pending sale under any other Deed of Trust or of any action or proceeding in which Trustor, Beneficiary or Trustee shall be a party unless brought by Trustee.

REQUEST FOR FULL RECONVEYANCE

To be used only when note has been paid.

To OLD REPUBLIC TITLE COMPANY, Trustee: Dated_____

The undersigned is the legal owner and holder of all indebtedness secured by the within Deed of Trust. All sums secured by said Deed of Trust have been fully paid and satisfied; and you are hereby requested and directed, on payment to you of any sums owing to you under the terms of said Deed of Trust, to cancel all evidences of indebtedness, secured by said Deed of Trust, delivered to you herewith together with said Deed of Trust, and to reconvey, without warranty, to the parties designated by the terms of said Deed of Trust, the estate now held by you under the same.

Mail Reconveyance To:

_____
_____
_____   By_____
_____   By_____

Do not lose or destroy this Deed of Trust OR THE NOTE which it secures. Both must be delivered to the Trustee for cancellation before reconveyance will be made.

OLD REPUBLIC TITLE COMPANY

SHORT FORM DEED OF TRUST AND ASSIGNMENT OF RENTS

FIGURE 8-9

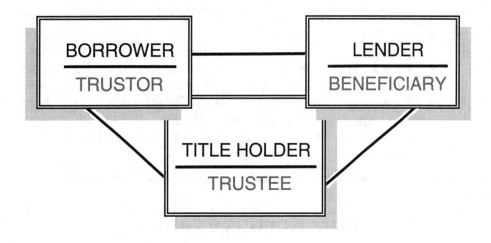

A trustor signs a trust deed that makes the real property security for the promissory note (loan). A trustee has "right to sell," if trustor defaults on loan.

A trust deed must have all three parties: trustor, trustee and beneficiary. The trust deed and note form the lien, which conveys the "bare naked title" of the property to the trustee. The trustee holds title to the real property until the trust deed is paid in full, at which time the title is reconveyed to the trustor through a reconveyance. If the trustor defaults in payments, the beneficiary will instruct the trustee to start the default period, which could ultimately lead to a trustee foreclosure sale.

The lender of the money is called the beneficiary who holds the trust deed and note. A "beneficiary statement" shows the unpaid balance and the condition of the debt.

EQUITABLE TITLE *is held by a trustor while he or she is repaying a trust deed and note.* It is **true** ownership in that the trustor may enjoy all customary rights of title and possession.

LEGAL TITLE, "Bare Naked Legal Title," *is held by a trustee until the terms of a trust deed and note have been fulfilled.* When the trustor has paid the note in full, the trustee will reconvey the bare naked legal title.

The trustee receives the naked legal title along with the power to sell the property if the trustor defaults, or reconveys title back to the trustor when paid in full.

FULL RECONVEYANCE (PROOF OF PAYMENT IN FULL)

A **FULL RECONVEYANCE** *provides proof that a promissory note and the accompanying trust deed have been paid in full.* When the note has been paid in full, the beneficiary requests the trustee to grant a full reconveyance, which makes the trustor's legal title a part of the public record and gives evidence that the debt has been paid off. A full reconveyance **must be recorded** to give public notice, on the county records, that it has been paid. The reconveyance is paid for by the trustor. See Figure 8-10 for more information about a full reconveyance and Figure 8-11 for an example.

FIGURE 8-10

Full Reconveyance

A full reconveyance is a simple written document that offers proof that a loan on real property has been paid off in full. If a trust deed (loan on real property) is to be paid off in full, a request for full reconveyance is to be signed by the beneficiary and sent to the trustee for recording.

The trustor (borrower), who is in the process of paying off a loan secured by a note and deed of trust on a certain piece of real property, wants the following:

1. The return of the original note;

2. The return of the original trust deed; and

3. A "Reconveyance deed" should be recorded in the county recorder's office where the deed of trust is recorded.

When the trustor originally borrowed the money to purchase property or later obtained a loan secured by the property, he or she signed a promissory note and a trust deed. This trust deed, when recorded, became a specific lien. If the trustor tries to sell or refinance the property, this lien will show up on all title searches or title reports until the deed of trust has been "reconveyed."

So it is extremely important for the trustor to have the deed of trust and note returned along with having the beneficiary sign a "Request for Full Reconveyance." Under California Civil Code Section 2941, the beneficiary must forward a deed of reconveyance, within 90 days of receiving the "Request for Full Reconveyance," to the trustee. Violation of this law is a misdemeanor punishable by a $300 fine, plus damages, and/or six months in jail.

FIGURE 8-11

RECORDING REQUESTED BY

AND WHEN RECORDED MAIL TO

SPACE ABOVE THIS LINE FOR RECORDER'S USE

TITLE ORDER NO.   TRUSTEE SALE NO.   COMPUTER NO.

FULL RECONVEYANCE

now duly appointed Trustee under Deed of Trust   EXECUTED BY:

TRUSTOR(S)
TRUSTEE

TO:

Recorded on   as Document no.   Book   Page
of Official Records in the office of the Recorder of   County,
California, having been requested in writing, by the holder of the obligation secured by said deed of trust, to reconvey the estate granted to trustee under said deed of trust, DOES HEREBY RECONVEY to the person or persons legally entitled thereto, without warranty, all the estate, title, and interest acquired by trustee under said deed of trust.
Brief description of property:

DATE:

BY: _____
                        Assistant Secretary

STATE OF CALIFORNIA
                                    } SS.
COUNTY OF _____ }
On this the_____ day of_____ 19____,
before me the, the undersigned, a Notary Public in and for
said County and State, personally appeared _____

personally known to me or proved to me on the basis of
satisfactory evidence to be the person who executed the within
instrument as an Assistant Secretary, on behalf of the corporation therein named, and acknowledged to me that such
corporation executed the within instrument pursuant to its by-
laws or a resolution of its board of directors.

_____
Notary's Signature   Full Reconveyance
SAFECO Stock No. **CA-BNL-0110**

DEFAULT AND FORECLOSURE OF A TRUST DEED

DEFAULT ON A TRUST DEED

In California, the procedure and remedy for nonpayment of a trust deed is well established by law. The trust deed is a lien on the property involved. The lender has the legal right to receive the trust deed payment on time. By law the lender can start default action after the 10- to 15-day grace period. A **GRACE PERIOD** *is a set number of days in which a lender will allow a payment to be late without any penalty.* The lender, at any time after the grace period, may start default action against the trustor. Figure 8-12 shows the sequence of events that will follow if the trustor does not make the trust deed payments.

> *If a note and deed of trust is "silent" on the grace period, the law states it must be more than 10 days.*

When a borrower defaults on his or her payments under the trust deed and note, the beneficiary's remedy is to start default action. The beneficiary notifies the trustee of the trustor's failure to make the payments. The trustee then records a notice of default, which will start the foreclosure action.

FIGURE 8-12

Payment Past-due	3 Months Minimum	20 Days Minimum	1 Day
NOTICE OF DEFAULT RECORDED	REINSTATEMENT PERIOD	PUBLISHING PERIOD	TRUSTEE'S SALE

When the trustee is notified by the lender (beneficiary) of the trustor's nonpayment, the trustee records the "notice of default" (See Figure 8-13). This notice contains all the pertinent information about the default. Within 10 days after the recording, the borrower (trustor) and all people who have filed a "request for notice," such as junior lienholders, will receive (by certified or registered mail) notification from the trustee of the default. In addition, the notice of default must be published in a newspaper of general circulation once a week for three weeks.

FIGURE 8-13

RECORDING REQUESTED BY

WHEN RECORDED MAIL TO

———————— SPACE ABOVE THIS LINE FOR RECORDER'S USE ————————

TRUST ORDER NO.

Notice of Default and Election to Sell Under Deed of Trust

NOTICE IS HEREBY GIVEN: That _____ , a corporation, is Trustee, or successor Trustee, or substituted Trustee under a deed of trust dated_____ , executed by_____

_____ as Trustor,
to secure certain obligations in favor of _____

as Beneficiary, recorded_____ , in Book_____ , Page_____ , of Official
Records in the office of the Recorder of _____ County, California, describing land therein as:

said obligations including_____note____for the_____ sum of $_____ ,

That the beneficial interest under such deed and the obligations secured thereby have been transferred to the undersigned ;
That a breach of, and default in, the obligations for which such deed is security has occurred in that payment has not been made of:

That by reason thereof, the undersigned, present beneficiary under such deed, has executed and delivered to said Trustee, or successor Trustee, or substituted Trustee a written Declaration of Default and Demand for sale, and has deposited with said Trustee, or successor Trustee, or substituted Trustee such deed and all documents evidencing obligations secured thereby, and has declared and does hereby declare all sums secured thereby immediately due and payable and has elected and does hereby elect to cause the trust property to be sold to satisfy the obligations secured thereby.

Dated _____

STATE OF CALIFORNIA
COUNTY OF _____ } SS.
On _____
before me, the undersigned, a Notary Public in and for said County and State, personally appeared

known to me to be the person___ whose name_____
subscribed to the within instrument and acknowledged that_____
executed the same.
WITNESS my hand and official seal.

(Seal) _____
Notary Public in and for said County and State
NOTARY—PLEASE PRINT OR TYPE YOUR NAME BELOW SIGNATURE

THIS NOTICE MUST BE RECORDED BY ←

TRUST ORDER NO._____

TRUSTOR'S RIGHT OF REINSTATEMENT

Reinstatement Period (Three Months)

During the three-month reinstatement period after the notice of default is filed, the trustor may reinstate the loan. The ***REINSTATEMENT PERIOD*** *is the time within which the trustor may pay all past due payments*. To do this, the trustor must pay the beneficiary the following:

      1. All past due payments, penalties, taxes and interest.
      2. Any other costs to the beneficiary.
      3. All costs and fees owed to the trustee.

> *The trustor can reinstate a loan up until five days prior to foreclosure. If reinstated, it is again in good standing.*

If the trustor does not pay the past due payments, taxes, interest and other charges within the three-month reinstatement period, the reinstatement rights are lost. This reinstatement period runs until five days before the date of sale. Sometimes in special circumstances, and always at the discretion of the lender, the trustor may still be allowed to reinstate the loan after this period. If the beneficiary decides to foreclose, however, he or she will start the process by recording a "notice of sale."

Notice Of Sale (21 Days)

The ***NOTICE OF SALE*** *is a recorded notice stating the time, place, property description and type of sale*. See Figure 8-13, which is a notice of default. It also serves as the notice of sale. The notice must be published in a newspaper of general circulation once a week, not more than seven days apart, during the 21-day publishing period. A copy of the notice must also be posted on the property and in a public place, such as the city hall. Most title insurance companies also post a copy if they are acting as trustee.

The Trustee's Sale (Foreclosure Sale)

> *A trustee's sale is only for the real property backing up the trust deed.*

The trustee's sale is held at the time and place stated in the notice of sale. At the public sale, the trustee states the purpose of the sale and describes the property to be sold. All bids must be in the form of cash or cashier's checks.

The first deed holder may bid up to the total amount of the debt without cash. Because it costs the first trust deed holder nothing more than what he or she is already owed, that person will usually make the first bid. The highest bidder obtains the property and will be issued a trustee's deed. Any money more than the amount owed is reimbursed to the trustor. The new owner is entitled to immediate possession.

> *A trustee's sale is an out of court procedure under the "power of sale clause" in the deed of trust and promissory note.*

Judicial Court Foreclosure For A Trust Deed (Rare)

In rare cases, a beneficiary (lender) in California may want to foreclose by court action instead of the simpler trustee's sale. The reason would be to obtain a deficiency judgment if it was not a purchase money trust deed. See the purchase money section below for more information.

Deed In Lieu Of Foreclosure

A **DEED IN LIEU OF FORECLOSURE** *is a deed given by an owner (borrower) to a lender to prevent the lender from bringing foreclosure proceedings.* It is up to the lender to accept or reject such an offer. This could save the borrower's credit in some circumstances.

LIENS NOT ELIMINATED BY FORECLOSURE SALE

Most junior liens are eliminated by a foreclosure sale. The following liens are not necessarily eliminated:

1. Federal tax liens.
2. State, county and city taxes or assessments.
3. Mechanic's liens for work begun before the trust deed was recorded.

PURCHASE MONEY TRUST DEED OR MORTGAGE

A **PURCHASE MONEY INSTRUMENT** *is a trust deed or mortgage obtained during the purchase of a home (1-to-4 units, owner-occupied).* It is called a purchase money instrument **only when** it is obtained at the time of purchase, not on a refinanced loan. It is an automatic protection given to homeowners (nothing is signed and nothing is mentioned). This is important because if the property is forced into foreclosure, a purchase money trust deed holder, or mortgage lender, cannot obtain a deficiency judgment.

A **DEFICIENCY JUDGMENT** *is the deficient difference between the money that a property brings at a court foreclosure sale and the amount owed on the property.* If a home was sold at a court foreclosure sale for $217,000 and $240,000 was owed on the property, a lender would have a $23,000 deficiency judgment against the borrower. If it were a purchase money instrument, however, there would be no deficiency judgment.

The purchase money instrument only protects owners of residential dwellings of 1-to-4 units where the owner lives in one unit. Owners of properties having more than four units or properties that do not have a purchase money instrument are not protected against possible deficiency judgments. Remember: deficiency judgments can only be obtained if the owner doesn't have a purchase money instrument and is foreclosed upon in a court foreclosure sale.

SECOND TRUST DEEDS (Junior TD's)

SECOND TRUST DEEDS

(JUNIOR TRUST DEEDS - 2NDS, 3RDS, 4THS. . .)

> *When the current financial market is tight, a seller may have to take back a second trust deed as part of his or her equity in order to make the sale.*

Even if a buyer qualifies for a loan to cover 80% of the cost of a home, he or she may still have a difficult time scraping together the 20% needed for the down payment. When a buyer does not have enough cash to cover the gap between the sale's price and the loan amount, another loan, or "second" trust deed, is sometimes obtained (often from the seller).

Besides seconds, it is also possible for borrowers who qualify to obtain "third" or "fourth" trust deeds, but they are all commonly referred to as second trust deeds or junior liens. They all may be called second trust deeds but their priority is determined by the order in which they were recorded. *Any loan on real property obtained after the first trust deed and secured by a second, third or subsequent trust deed, is known as a* **JUNIOR LIEN**. The most senior lien, on the other hand, is the first trust deed.

> *Private lenders are the greatest source of junior loans.*

Let's look at an example: Smith is buying a house with a sale's price of $150,000. She assumes the seller's loan on the property of $100,000. She applies to her company credit union and is given a second trust deed of $30,000, so all she needs is a cash down payment of $20,000, plus closing costs, to complete the transaction.

HOMEOWNER EQUITY LOANS

Second trust deeds are not only obtainable as part of the financing package when a property is first being purchased. Seconds and other junior liens may be arranged any time a qualified borrower wants to borrow money, for whatever reason, so long as there is sufficient equity and enough ready income to support the payments. *EQUITY is the fair market value of a property, minus the amount of money owed to lenders and all other lienholders. HOMEOWNER EQUITY LOANS are loans based on the homeowner's increase in equity caused by inflation, rising property values and the reduction, by payments, of the existing loan balance.*

Let's suppose Smith, who purchased that new home for $150,000, finds herself in need of money after a few years. Fortunately, her property has increased in market value and is now worth more than $200,000. Even though Smith is already mortgaged up to her ears, she can borrow on her equity; the difference between what she owes and what her property is worth.

> *Second trust deed notes have a stated interest rate, so they are sold at a discount (reduction in value).*

Homeowner equity loans are generally secured by second (junior) trust deeds. They are available from institutional lenders, small finance companies and individuals who specialize in this area. Lenders will charge a higher interest rate on seconds and other junior trust deeds because they are less secure than primary financing.

HOLDER OF A SECOND TRUST DEED (LENDER)

Sometimes when purchasing a property, additional funds will be required beyond the cash down payment and the first trust deed. As a result the seller may loan the buyer more money through the use of a second trust deed. Usually the second trust deed has a higher rate of interest and a shorter payoff period because of the higher risk involved. The usual monthly payment is one percent of the loan.

Second trust deeds often require a balloon payment at the end of the term because they are not fully amortized. The holder of a second trust deed or any junior trust deed has the same rights as does the holder of the first deed of trust. He or she is entitled to his or her payment each month, as is the first trust deed holder. If the trustor defaults on the second, the second trust deed holder, just like the first trust deed holder, can start default action. In addition, if the trustor defaults on the first trust deed, the second trust deed holder can reinstate the first trust deed and start default action against the trustor. If the property's market value is higher than the total amount owed on the first trust deed, it is a wise move for the second trust deed holder to start his or her own default and sale action.

REQUEST FOR NOTICE

When a ***REQUEST FOR NOTICE*** *is recorded, the trustee is required to notify all persons who request notice if a "notice of default" is recorded on a particular property.* See Figure 8-14. Any person who has an interest in a particular trust deed, usually a second or third trust deed holder, should want to be informed if the buyer is not paying on the first deed of trust. This information not only informs the junior deed holders of nonpayment on the first trust deed, but it also allows them time to prepare to purchase the trust deed at the forthcoming trustee's sale. It will also give them time to start default actions on their own junior trust deeds.

This request for notice is recorded in the county recorder's office where the property is located. If a seller takes back a second or even a third trust deed, thereby becoming a junior trust deed holder on the property that person has just sold, that person would be wise to record a request for notice. Some request for notice forms are incorporated into the trust deed form, so the request for notice is automatically filed.

LAND CONTRACT
(CONDITIONAL INSTALLMENT SALES CONTRACT)

Trust deeds, mortgages and land contracts are all methods of financing: They are financing instruments referred to as "security devices."

FIGURE 8-14

AND WHEN RECORDED MAIL TO

NAME
ADDRESS
CITY &
STATE

——— SPACE ABOVE THIS LINE FOR RECORDER'S USE ———

REQUEST FOR NOTICE

In accordance with section 2924b, Civil Code, request is hereby made that a copy of any notice of default

and a copy of any notice of sale under the deed of trust recorded   19

in Book   page   of official records of   County, (or filed for record

with recorder's serial No.

County) California, executed by

as trustor in which

is named as beneficiary and

as trustee be mailed to   whose

address is

Signature ....

FOR NOTARY SEAL OR STAMP

STATE OF CALIFORNIA

COUNTY OF   SS.

On this the   day of   19   , before me.
the undersigned. a Notary Public in and for said County and State.
personally appeared

, personally known
to me or proved to me on the basis of satisfactory evidence to be the
person   whose name   subscribed to the within
instrument and acknowledged that
executed the same.

NOTARY SIGNATURE

STATE OF CALIFORNIA
COUNTY OF_____
On this the_____ day of _____ 19_____ before
me, the undersigned, a Notary Public in and for said County and State,
personally appeared_____
_____ , personally
known to me or proved to me on the basis of satisfactory evidence to
be the_____ President, and_____
_____ , personally
known to me or proved to me on the basis of satisfactory evidence to
be _____ Secretary of the corporation that executed the
within instrument on behalf of the corporation therein named, and
acknowledged to me that such corporation executed the within instrument pursuant to its by-laws or a resolution of its board of directors.

_____
NOTARY SIGNATURE

Title Order No.   Escrow No.

LAND CONTRACT

The **LAND CONTRACT** *is an instrument of finance in which the seller retains legal ownership of the property until the buyer has made the last payment.* It is usually called a land contract in California, but may also be referred to as a "contract of sale," "agreement of sale," "conditional sales contract" or an "installment sales contract." Since this is a contract between the buyer and seller, the requirements as to the down payment and other conditions of the land contract are negotiable.

When financing is hard to obtain, this can be an alternative to the usual financing methods. Although it is not widely used, it is a valid financing device. See Figure 8-15.

> *An installment sales contract (land contract) can be for both real and personal property. Mortgages and trust deeds are only for real property.*

An *owner selling under a land contract is known as a* **VENDOR.** *A* **VENDEE** *is a buyer using a land contract.* A vendor can sell his or her store (real property) and store fixtures (personal property), by use of a land contract, to a vendee. A land contract is a common way to sell a business.

> *With a conditional sales contract, the seller (vendor) gives the buyer (vendee) equitable title and possession but keeps legal title. The vendor is the lender and the vendee is the borrower.*

With a land contract the buyer holds **equitable title**, like a borrower purchasing under a trust deed. He or she is entitled, though, to the full use and enjoyment of the property. **Legal title** is held by the seller until the land contract terms have been completely fulfilled. A grant deed to the property is only given when the land contract is paid off in full.

> *A land contract is also called a "real property sales contract," an "agreement of sale," an "agreement to purchase" or an "installment sales contract."*

Land contracts can be recorded: If the buyer were to default, his or her interest would show as a cloud on the title. However, the buyer could sign a quitclaim deed that would remove the cloud on the title.

FIGURE 8-15

LAND CONTRACT

RECORDING REQUESTED BY

AND WHEN RECORDED MAIL TO

Name
Street
Address
City &
State

SPACE ABOVE THIS LINE FOR RECORDER'S USE

FORM 1   **LONG FORM SECURITY (INSTALLMENT) LAND CONTRACT WITH POWER OF SALE**   D-120

THIS AGREEMENT, made and entered into .his   day of   , 19   , by and
between   (Vendor's name),
whose address is
(hereinafter sometimes referred to as "Vendor"), and

    (Vendee's name), whose address is
    (hereinafter sometimes referred to as "Vendee"); and
STEWART TITLE, (hereinafter sometimes referred to as "Trustee.")
    W I T N E S S E T H :
WHEREAS, Vendor is now the owner of certain real property situated in the County of
State of California, commonly known as
    (property street address), and described as follows:

WHEREAS, Vendor has agreed to sell, and Vendee has agreed to buy said real property on the terms and conditions hereinafter set
forth;
WHEREAS, Vendor shall retain legal title as a security interest in said real property until the payment of the balance of the purchase
price has been paid by Vendee to Vendor as set forth below.
NOW, THEREFORE, THE PARTIES HERETO DO HEREBY AGREE AS FOLLOWS:
PURCHASE PRICE
1. Vendor agrees to sell, and Vendee agrees to buy all of the aforedescribed real property for the sum of
    (Total purchase price) ($_____),
lawful money of the United States, as hereinafter more fully set forth.

REQUEST FOR NOTICE OF DEFAULT
2. In accordance with Section 2924b, Civil Code, request is hereby made by the undersigned Vendor and
Vendee that a copy of any Notice of Default and a copy of any Notice of Sale under Deed of Trust re-
corded_____in Book_____, Page_____, Official Records of
_____ County, California, as affecting above described property, executed by
_____as Trustor in which_____
is named as beneficiary, and_____as Trustee, be mailed to Vendor
and Vendee at address in paragraph 3 below.
NOTICES AND REQUEST FOR NOTICE
3. Notices required or permitted under this agreement shall be binding if delivered personally to party
sought to be served or if mailed by registered or certified mail, postage prepaid in the United States mail
to the following:
Vendor: _____

    _____   Trustee: Stewart Title
    505 North Brand, 12th Floor
Vendee: _____   Glendale, California 91203

    _____

Vendor and Vendee hereby request that notice of default and notice of sale hereunder be mailed to them at the above address.

PAYMENT OF PURCHASE PRICE
4. Vendee shall pay said purchase price of $_____as follows:
    (a) Vendee shall pay to Vendor the sum of $_____(Down Payment) as and for a down payment.
    (b) Vendee shall take subject to and pay the balance due on that certain note secured by a first trust deed on the above men-
tioned real property, the principal balance of which is $_____, together with interest thereon at the rate of
percent per annum, payable in installments of
$_____, (monthly payments amount; add "or more" if applicable) per month on the   day of each and
every month with the whole of the then outstanding balance thereof due on the   day of
19   . Each such payment includes payment of the following items under the terms of said note and trust deed:
    (1) Principal and interest;
    (2) Impounds for taxes;   (Strike out
    (3) Impounds for fire insurance;   inapplicable
    (4) Impounds for   items.)
Payments shall be made by Vendee directly to beneficiary of said first trust deed at the following address:
    _____
    _____
    (If a second trust deed exists, complete (c) below)
(c) Vendee shall take subject to and pay the balance due on that certain note secured by a second trust deed on the above
mentioned real property, principal balance of which is $_____ together with interest thereon at the rate of
percent per annum, payable in installments of $_____(monthly payment amount; add "or more"

Land contracts are legal documents that should be drawn by, and discussed with, an attorney before use. Legal problems associated with a land contract are: obtaining marketable title, non-recorded status, intervening liens, foreclosure and quiet title action. As you can see, legal advice is necessary.

> *The seller (vendor) keeps legal title (grant deed) under a land contract until all the terms of the contract are met.*

WRAP-AROUND OR ALL INCLUSIVE TRUST DEEDS (A.I.T.D.)

An *ALL INCLUSIVE TRUST DEED (WRAP-AROUND) is a second trust deed with a face value of both the new amount it secures and the balance due under the first trust deed.* A wrap-around can take the form of a land contract or a deed of trust. The wrap-around is seldom used except when a property is difficult to sell or credit is tight (high interest rates). This form of security may be used to increase the lender's yield upon the sale of property and to provide easy financing for the buyer. Rather than having a new buyer assume an existing loan, the seller carries back a wrap-around trust deed at a higher rate of interest. The seller continues to pay off the old trust deed out of the payment received from the buyer. Since these payments are larger, the seller gets a margin of profit. The buyer, in turn, gets easy financing and avoids the new loan fees charged by institutional lenders. As always, an attorney should be consulted because wrap-around contracts may require special handling and will not be available with all loans.

> **Let's look at an example**: Smith has a $100,000 property with an existing 10% interest loan of $50,000. He makes a $500 loan payment every month. Jones wants to buy the property and gives Smith $30,000 in cash down, while Smith carries a wrap-around trust deed for the remaining $70,000 owed. He charges Jones 13% interest payable in monthly installments of $1,100. When Smith receives his $1,100 each month, he uses $500 of it to pay off his 10% loan while pocketing the remaining $600.

TRUTH IN LENDING ACT
Regulation "Z" and Other Acts

> *The purpose of the Federal Truth in Lending Act is for the lender to disclose the cost of credit terms to the borrower. This disclosure must be presented to the borrower within 3 business days of receiving the borrower's loan application.*

"Regulation Z" applies to dwellings with only one-to-four residential units. Agricultural loans are exempt from the truth in lending law as are business and commercial loans.

TRUTH IN LENDING

The Truth in Lending Act, known as Regulation Z, was enacted to protect the consumer by requiring that the lender (creditor) tell the borrower how much he or she is paying for credit. This enables the consumer to make comparisons between various credit sources. Regulation Z also states that the lender (creditor) must express all related financing costs as a percentage, known as the annual percentage rate (APR).

Regulation Z requires a creditor to make the following important financial disclosures:

1) Annual Percentage Rate
2) Finance charges
3) Amount financed
4) Total number of payments
5) Total sales price (credit sales).

Regulation Z is enforced by the Federal Trade Commission (FTC). The Federal Real Estate Loan Disclosure Statement is used to implement Regulation Z. See Figure 8-16. See Figure 8-17 and 8-18 for an example of CAR's Seller Financing Addendum and Disclosure form.

Annual Percentage Rate (APR)

APR is the "relative cost of credit" expressed in percentage terms. It is a percentage rate, not an interest rate. If the APR appears in an advertisement, no other disclosure of terms need be stated because it includes all credit costs.

The **ANNUAL PERCENTAGE RATE (APR)** *represents the relationship between the total of the finance charges (interest rate, points and the loan fee) and the total amount financed, expressed as a percentage.* It must be computed to the nearest one-quarter of one percent and must be printed on the loan form more conspicuously than the rest of the printed material.

Chapter 8

FIGURE 8-16

FEDERAL REAL ESTATE LOAN DISCLOSURE STATEMENT
CALIFORNIA ASSOCIATION OF REALTORS® (CAR) STANDARD FORM

Broker: Creditor:

_____   _____
(name)   (name)

_____   _____
(address)   (address)

YOUR LOAN IN THE AMOUNT OF $ _____ IS TO BE SECURED BY A DEED OF TRUST IN FAVOR OF CREDITOR
ON REAL PROPERTY LOCATED AT _____

ANNUAL PERCENTAGE RATE The cost of your credit as a yearly rate. _____ %	FINANCE CHARGE The dollar amount the credit will cost you. $	AMOUNT FINANCED The amount of credit provided to you or on your behalf. $	TOTAL OF PAYMENTS The amount you will have paid after you have made all payments as scheduled. $

YOUR PAYMENT SCHEDULE WILL BE:

Number of Payments	Amount of Payments	When Payments Are Due

ITEMIZATION OF THE AMOUNT FINANCED OF $ _____

Amount given to you $ _____
Amount paid on your account $ _____
Amount paid to others on your behalf:
         1. Appraisal .... $ _____
         2. Credit report .... $ _____
         3. Notary............................... $ _____
         4. Recording .... $ _____
         5. Title insurance .... $ _____
         6. Document preparation .... $ _____
         7. Property insurance .... $ _____
         8. Other _____ (DESCRIBE) $ _____
         9. Other _____ (DESCRIBE) $ _____

<u>Insurance:</u>
    Property insurance may be obtained by Borrower through any person of his choice. If it is to be purchased through Broker or Creditor, you will pay
$ _____ .
    Credit life and disability insurance are not required to obtain this loan.
<u>Late Charge:</u> If any payment is not made within _____ days after it is due, a late charge must be paid by Borrower as follows:
_____ .

<u>Prepayment:</u> If you pay off early, you ☐ MAY ☐ WILL NOT have to pay a penalty.
<u>Acceleration:</u> If the property securing this loan is sold or otherwise transferred, the Creditor ☐ HAS ☐ DOES NOT have the option to
require immediate payment of the entire loan amount.
SEE YOUR CONTRACT DOCUMENTS FOR ANY ADDITIONAL INFORMATION ABOUT NONPAYMENT, DEFAULT, ANY REQUIRED
REPAYMENT IN FULL BEFORE THE SCHEDULED DATE, AND PREPAYMENT REFUNDS AND PENALTIES.

                                               I HAVE READ AND RECEIVED A COMPLETED COPY OF THIS
                                               STATEMENT.

Date _____ , 19 _____ .   Borrower _____

*IMPORTANT NOTE:
Asterisk denotes an estimate   Borrower _____

Copyright⸱ 1970, 1978, by CALIFORNIA ASSOCIATION OF REALTORS⸱
525 South Virgil Avenue, Los Angeles, California 90020
(Revised 1983)   FORM LD-11   SF-July-89

EQUAL HOUSING
OPPORTUNITY

Interest rates can be calculated by many different methods that can be very confusing to the borrower. The APR standardizes these figures, calculating all rates by the same formula. Borrowers should look for the APR figure (usually in a box) to compare and find the best APR available.

The "APR includes all finance charges," including assumption charges, but it does not include 1) cost of a credit report and 2) appraisal fees, which are exempt.

Advertising Terms May Require Additional Disclosures

Anyone placing an advertisement for consumer credit must comply with the advertising requirements of the Truth in Lending Act. Disclosures must be made "clearly and conspicuously." If only the annual percentage (APR) rate is disclosed, additional disclosures are not required. If, however, an advertisement contains any one of the following terms, then the ad must also disclose other credit terms:

1) The amount or percentage of any downpayment.
2) The number of payments or period of repayment.
3) The amount of any payment.
4) The amount of any finance charge.

When advertising a graduated payment loan, differences in monthly payments must be disclosed.

RIGHT TO CANCEL
(FEDERAL NOTICE OF RIGHT TO CANCEL)

Loans subsequent (future loans) have a 3-day right of rescission by the borrower.

The **RIGHT TO CANCEL** *is the federal law that gives a borrower the right to rescind (cancel) any loan transaction only if it is a business loan, or a second trust deed, secured by the borrower's home.* The borrower has until midnight of the third business day following the signing to cancel.

A first trust deed loan to finance the purchase of the borrower's home carries no right of rescission. However, a first loan secured on the borrower's home for any other purpose, or a second loan on the same home, may be canceled within 3 business days. See Figure 8-19.

FIGURE 8-17

CALIFORNIA ASSOCIATION OF REALTORS®

SELLER FINANCING ADDENDUM AND DISCLOSURE
(California Civil Code §§2956-2967)

This is an addendum to the ☐ Residential Purchase Agreement, ☐ Counter Offer, or ☐ Other _____
_____, ("Agreement"), dated _____,
On property known as _____ ("Property"),
In which _____ is referred to as Buyer,
And _____ is referred to as Seller.

Seller agrees to extend credit to Buyer as follows:

1. **PRINCIPAL; INTEREST; PAYMENT; MATURITY TERMS:** ☐ Principal amount $ _____, interest at _____% per annum, payable at approximately $ _____ per ☐ month, ☐ year, or ☐ other _____, remaining principal balance due in _____ years.

2. **LOAN APPLICATION; CREDIT REPORT:** Within **5 (or ☐ _____) Days** After Acceptance: **(a)** Buyer shall provide Seller a completed loan application on FNMA/FHLMC Uniform Residential Loan Application; and **(b)** Buyer authorizes Seller and/or Agent to obtain, at Buyer's expense, a copy of Buyer's credit report. Buyer shall provide any supporting documentation reasonably requested by Seller. Seller may cancel this Agreement in writing if Buyer fails to provide such documents within that time, or if Seller disapproves any above item within **5 (or ☐ _____) Days** After receipt of each item.

3. **CREDIT DOCUMENTS:** This extension of credit by Seller will be evidenced by: ☐ Note and deed of trust; ☐ All-inclusive note and deed of trust; ☐ Installment land sale contract; ☐ Lease/option (when parties intend transfer of equitable title); OR ☐ Other (specify) _____
_____

THE FOLLOWING TERMS APPLY ONLY IF CHECKED. IF NOT CHECKED, THE TERM IS NOT PART OF THE SELLER FINANCING.

4. ☐ **LATE CHARGE:** If any payment is not made within _____ **Days** After it is due, a late charge of either ☐ $ _____, or ☐ _____% of the installment due, may be charged to Buyer. **NOTE:** On single family residences which Buyer intends to occupy, Civil Code §2954.4(a) limits the late charge to no more than 6% of the total monthly payment due and requires a grace period of no less than ten days.

5. ☐ **BALLOON PAYMENT:** The loan will provide for a balloon payment, in the amount of $ _____, plus any accrued interest, which is due on _____ (date).

6. ☐ **PREPAYMENT:** If all or part of this loan is paid early, Seller may charge a prepayment penalty as follows (if applicable): _____
_____. Caution: Civil Code §2954.9 contains limitations on prepayment penalties.

7. ☐ **DUE ON SALE:** If any interest in the Property is sold or otherwise transferred, Seller has the option to require immediate payment of the entire unpaid principal balance, plus any accrued interest.

8.* ☐ **REQUEST FOR COPY OF NOTICE OF DEFAULT:** A Request for a copy of Notice of Default under Civil Code §2924b will be recorded. **If not**, Seller is advised to consider recording a Request for Notice of Default.

9.* ☐ **REQUEST FOR NOTICE OF DELINQUENCY:** A Request for Notice of Delinquency, as defined in Civil Code §2924e, to be signed and paid for by Buyer, will be made to senior leinholders. **If Not**, Seller is advised to consider making a Request for Notice of Delinquency. Seller is advised to check with senior leinholders to verify whether they will honor this request.

10.* ☐ **TAX SERVICE:**
    A. Tax service will be arranged to report to Seller if property taxes on the Property become delinquent. **If Not**, Seller is advised to consider retaining a tax service, or to otherwise determine that property taxes are paid.
    B. ☐ Buyer, ☐ Seller, will be responsible for the initial and continued retention of, and payment for, such tax service.

11. ☐ **TITLE INSURANCE:** Title insurance coverage will be provided to **both** Seller and Buyer, insuring their respective interests in the Property. **If not**, Buyer and Seller are advised to consider securing such title insurance coverage.

12. ☐ **HAZARD INSURANCE:**
    A. The parties' escrow holder or insurance carrier will be directed to include a loss payee endorsement adding Seller to the property insurance policy. **If Not**, Seller is advised to secure such an endorsement, or acquire a separate insurance policy.
    B. Property insurance **does not** include earthquake or flood insurance coverage, unless checked:
    ☐ Earthquake insurance will be obtained; ☐ Flood insurance will be obtained.

13. ☐ **PROCEEDS TO BUYER:** Buyer will receive cash proceeds at the close of the sale transaction. The amount received will be approximately $ _____, from _____ (indicate source of proceeds). Buyer represents that the purpose of such disbursement is as follows: _____

14. ☐ **NEGATIVE AMORTIZATION; DEFERRED INTEREST:** Negative amortization results when Buyer's periodic payments are less than the amount of interest earned on the obligation. Deferred interest also results when the obligation does not require periodic payments for a period of time. In either case, interest is not payable as it accrues. This accrued interest will have to be paid by Buyer at a later time, and may result in Buyer owing more on the obligation than at its origination. The credit being extended to Buyer by Seller will provide for negative amortization or deferred interest as indicated below. (Check A, B, or C. CHECK ONE ONLY.)
    ☐ **A** All negative amortization or deferred interest shall be added to the principal _____ (e.g., annually, monthly, etc.), and thereafter shall bear interest at the rate specified in the credit documents (compound interest);
    OR ☐ **B.** All deferred interest shall be due and payable, along with principal, at maturity;
    OR ☐ **C.** Other: _____

15. ☐ **ALL-INCLUSIVE DEED OF TRUST; INSTALLMENT LAND SALE CONTRACT:** This transaction involves the use of an all-inclusive (or wraparound) deed of trust or an installment land sale contract. That deed of trust or contract shall provide as follows:
    A. In the event of an acceleration of any senior encumbrance, the responsibility for payment, or for legal defense is : _____
    _____ ; OR ☐ **Is Not** specified in the credit or security documents.
    B. In the event of the prepayment of a senior encumbrance, the responsibilities and rights of Buyer and Seller regarding refinancing, prepayment penalties, and any prepayment discounts are: _____ ;
    OR ☐ **Are Not** specified in the documents evidencing credit.
    C. Buyer will make periodic payments to _____ (Seller, collection agent, or any neutral third party), who will be responsible for disbursing payments to the payee(s) on the senior encumbrance(s) and to Seller. NOTE: The Parties are advised to designate a neutral third party for these purposes.

16. ☐ **TAX IDENTIFICATION NUMBERS:** Buyer and Seller shall each provide to the other their social security numbers or taxpayer identification numbers.

17. ☐ **OTHER CREDIT TERMS:** _____

18. ☐ **RECORDING:** The documents evidencing credit (paragraph 3) will be recorded with the county recorder where the Property is located. **If Not**, Buyer and Seller are advised that their respective interests in the Property may be jeopardized by intervening liens, judgments, encumbrances, or subsequent transfers.

19. ☐ **JUNIOR FINANCING:** There will be additional financing, secured by the Property, junior to this Seller financing. Explain: _____
_____

* (For Paragraphs 8-10) In order to receive timely and continued notification, Seller is advised to record appropriate notices and/or to notify appropriate parties of any change in Seller's address.

Buyer and Seller acknowledge receipt of copy of this page, which constitutes Page 1 of _____ Pages.
Buyer's Initials (_____) (_____)   Seller's Initials (_____) (_____)

Published and Distributed by:
REAL ESTATE BUSINESS SERVICES, INC.
a subsidiary of the CALIFORNIA ASSOCIATION OF REALTORS®
525 South Virgil Avenue, Los Angeles, California 90020

OFFICE USE ONLY
Reviewed by Broker
or Designee _____
Date _____

SELLER FINANCING DISCLOSURE AND ADDENDUM (SFA-14 PAGE 1 OF 2) REVISED 5/97

FIGURE 8-18

Property Address: _____ Date: _____

20. SENIOR LOANS; ENCUMBRANCES: The following information is provided on loans and/or encumbrances that will be senior to Seller financing. NOTE: The following are estimates, unless otherwise marked with an asterisk (*). If checked: ☐ A separate sheet with information on additional senior loans/encumbrances is attached.

	1st	2nd
A. Original Balance	$ _____	$ _____
B. Current Balance	$ _____	$ _____
C. Periodic Payment (e.g. $100/month):	$ _____ / _____	$ _____ / _____
Including Impounds of:	$ _____ / _____	$ _____ / _____
D. Interest Rate (per annum)	_____ %	_____ %
E. Fixed or Variable Rate:	_____	_____
If Variable Rate: Lifetime Cap (Ceiling)	_____	_____
Indicator (Underlying Index)	_____	_____
Margins	_____	_____
F. Maturity Date	_____	_____
G. Amount of Balloon Payment	$ _____	$ _____
H. Date Balloon Payment Due	_____	_____
I. Potential for Negative Amortization? (Yes, No, or Unknown)	_____	_____
J. Due on Sale? (Yes, No, or Unknown)	_____	_____
K. Pre-payment penalty? (Yes, No, or Unknown)	_____	_____
L. Are payments current? (Yes, No, or Unknown)	_____	_____

21. BUYER'S CREDITWORTHINESS: (CHECK EITHER A OR B. Do not check both.) In addition to the loan application, credit report and other information requested under paragraph 2:
A. ☐ No other disclosure concerning Buyer's creditworthiness has been made to Seller;
OR B. ☐ The following representations concerning Buyer's creditworthiness are made by Buyer(s) to Seller:

Borrower: _____ Co-Borrower: _____
1. Occupation _____ 1. Occupation _____
2. Employer: _____ 2. Employer: _____
3. Length of Employment _____ 3. Length of Employment _____
4. Monthly Gross Income: _____ 4. Monthly Gross Income: _____
5. Other: _____ 5. Other: _____

22. ADDITIONAL, DELETION OR SUBSTITUTED BUYERS: The addition, deletion or substitution of any person or entity under this Agreement or to title prior to close of escrow shall require Seller's written consent. Seller may grant or withhold consent in Seller's sole discretion. Any additional or substituted person or entity shall, if requested by Seller, submit to Seller the same documentation as required for the original named Buyer. Seller and/or Brokers may obtain a credit report, at Buyer's expense, on any such person or entity.

23. CAUTION:
A. If the Seller financing requires a balloon payment, Seller shall give Buyer written notice, according to the terms of Civil Code 2966, at least 90 and not more than 150 days before the balloon payment is due.
B. If any obligation secured by the Property calls for a balloon payment Seller and Buyer are aware that refinancing of the balloon payment at maturity may be difficult or impossible, depending on conditions in the conventional mortgage marketplace at that time. There are no assurances that new financing or a loan extension will be available when the balloon prepayment, or any prepayment, is due.
C. If any of the existing or proposed loans would require refinancing as a result of a lack of full amortization, such refinancing might be difficult or impossible in the conventional mortgage marketplace.
D. In the event of default by Buyer: (1) Seller may have to reinstate and/or make monthly payments on any and all senior encumbrances (including real property taxes) in order to protect Seller's secured interest; (2) Seller's rights are generally limited to foreclosure on the Property, pursuant to Code of Civil Procedure 580(b); and, (3) the Property may not have sufficient equity to protect Seller's interests because Property may have decreased in value.

If this two-page Addendum and Disclosure is used in a transaction for the purchase of a dwelling for not more than four families, it shall be prepared by an Arranger of Credit as defined in Civil Code §2957(a). (The Arranger of Credit is usually the agent who obtained the offer.)

Arranger of Credit - Print Firm Name _____ By _____ Date _____
Address _____ City _____ State _____ Zip _____ Telephone _____ Fax _____

BUYER AND SELLER ACKNOWLEDGE AND AGREE THAT BROKERS: (A) WILL NOT PROVIDE LEGAL OR TAX ADVICE; (B) WILL NOT PROVIDE OTHER ADVICE OR INFORMATION THAT EXCEEDS THE KNOWLEDGE, EDUCATION AND EXPERIENCE REQUIRED TO OBTAIN A REAL ESTATE LICENSE; OR (C) HAVE NOT AND WILL NOT VERIFY ANY INFORMATION PROVIDED BY EITHER BUYER OR SELLER. BUYER AND SELLER AGREE THAT THEY WILL SEEK LEGAL, TAX, AND OTHER DESIRED ASSISTANCE FROM APPROPRIATE PROFESSIONALS. BUYER AND SELLER ACKNOWLEDGE THAT THE INFORMATION EACH HAS PROVIDED TO THE ARRANGER OF CREDIT FOR INCLUSION IN THIS DISCLOSURE FORM IS ACCURATE. BUYER AND SELLER FURTHER ACKNOWLEDGE THAT EACH HAS RECEIVED A COMPLETED COPY OF THIS DISCLOSURE FORM.

Buyer (Signature) _____ Date _____ Seller (Signature) _____ Date _____
Address _____ Address _____
City _____ State _____ Zip _____ City _____ State _____ Zip _____
Telephone _____ Fax _____ Telephone _____ Fax _____
Buyer (Signature) _____ Date _____ Seller (Signature) _____ Date _____
Address _____ Address _____
City _____ State _____ Zip _____ City _____ State _____ Zip _____
Telephone _____ Fax _____ Telephone _____ Fax _____

This form is available for use by the entire real estate industry. It is not intended to identify the user as a REALTOR®. REALTOR® is a registered collective membership mark which may be used only by members of the NATIONAL ASSOCIATION OF REALTORS® who subscribe to its Code of Ethics.

OFFICE USE ONLY
Reviewed by Broker or Designee ____
Date _____

Page 2 of _____ Pages.

SELLER FINANCING DISCLOSURE AND ADDENDUM (SFA-14 PAGE 2 OF 2) REVISED 5/97

FIGURE   8-19

NOTICE OF RIGHT TO CANCEL
CALIFORNIA ASSOCIATION OF REALTORS* (CAR) STANDARD FORM

Name(s) of Customer(s)_____

Type of Loan _____

Amount of Loan _____ $_____

You have entered into a transaction which will result in a deed of trust or mortgage on your home. You have a legal right under federal law to cancel this transaction, without cost, within three business days from whichever of the following occurs last:

(1)   the date of the transaction, which is _____ ; or

(2)   the date you received your Truth in Lending disclosures; or

(3)   the date you received this notice of your right to cancel.

If you cancel the transaction, the deed of trust or mortgage is also cancelled. Within 20 calendar days after we receive your notice, we must take the steps necessary to reflect the fact that the deed of trust or mortgage on your home has been cancelled, and we must return to you any money or property you have given to us or to anyone else in connection with this transaction.

You may keep any money or property we have given you until we have done the things mentioned above, but you must then offer to return the money or property. If it is impractical or unfair for you to return the property you must offer its reasonable value. You may offer to return the property at your home or at the location of the property. Money must be returned to the address below. If we do not take possession of the money or property within 20 calendar days of your offer, you may keep it without further obligation.

ACKNOWLEDGEMENT OF RECEIPT

I hereby acknowledge receipt of TWO copies of the foregoing Notice of Right to Cancel.

_____ , 19_____   _____
                (Date)   (Customer's Signature)

                                          _____
                                          (All joint owners must sign)

HOW TO CANCEL

If you decide to cancel this transaction, you may do so by notifying us in writing, at the following address:

_____
          (Creditor's Name)

_____
              (Address)

_____
         (City, State, Zip Code)

You may use any written statement that is signed and dated by you and states your intention to cancel, or you may use this notice by dating and signing below. Keep one copy of this notice because it contains important information about your rights.

If you cancel by mail or telegram, you must send the notice no later than midnight of _____

_____ (or midnight of the third business day following
                (date)
the latest of the three events listed above). If you send your written notice to cancel some other way, it must be delivered to the above address no later than that time.

_____ , 19_____   _____
                (Date)   (Customer's Signature)

┌─── OFFICE USE ONLY ───┐
│ Reviewed by Broker or Designee_____ │
│ Date _____ │
└─────────────────────────┘

EQUAL HOUSING OPPORTUNITY
SF-Apr-90

FORM NRC-14

EQUAL CREDIT OPPORTUNITY ACT

The **EQUAL CREDIT OPPORTUNITY ACT** *is a federal law prohibiting those who lend money from discriminating against borrowers based on their race, sex, color, religion, national origin, age or marital status.* It is specifically designed to come to the aid of low income group members (who receive income from public assistance programs), women and the elderly.

This law limits the lender's access to personal information regarding:

> . marriage and divorce
> . receipt of alimony and child support
> . birth control and child bearing.

It can also require lenders to consider individuals on the merits of their personal credit, as distinct from the bad credit history of a joint account. It also insists that lenders respond quickly to loan applications and be prepared to explain any loan refusal.

SOLDIERS AND SAILORS CIVIL RELIEF ACT

The **SOLDIERS AND SAILORS CIVIL RELIEF ACT** *is a law passed by congress to protect persons serving in the military, and their dependents, from loss of real property through foreclosure.*

In general, the law prohibits the sale or foreclosure of real estate owned by a military person without his or her expressed approval or a court order. It also extends foreclosure proceedings and the mortgage redemption period. Career soldiers are exempt.

In case of payment problems, a letter to a military person's commanding officer will usually get the best results.

Chapter 8

TERMINOLOGY - CHAPTER 8

A. Leverage
B. Hypothecation
C. Promissory Note
D. Straight Note
E. Holder In Due Course
F. Acceleration Clause
G. Alienation Clause
H. Assumption
I. Subordination Clause
J. Prepayment Penalty
K. Interest
L. Amortization
M. Amortization Book
N. Adjustable Rate Mortgage

O. Graduated Payment Mortgage
P. Point
Q. Usury
R. Trust Deed
S. Trustor
T. Beneficiary
U. Trustee
V. Equitable Title
W. Legal Title
X. Reconveyance Deed
Y. Default
Z. Grace Period
AA. Reinstatement Period
BB. Trustee's Sale

CC. Junior Lien or Second Trust Deed
DD. Equal Credit Opportunity Act
EE. Equity
FF. Request for Notice (of Default)
GG. Purchase Money Instrument
HH. Deficiency Judgment
II. Land Contract
JJ. Vendor
KK. Vendee
LL. Wrap-around (trust deed)
MM. Truth in Lending Act
NN. Annual Percentage Rate
OO. Right to Cancel

1. ____ An instrument used to transfer title back from a trustee to the equitable owner of real estate.

2. ____ A second trust deed where the monthly payment includes the amount of monthly payment on the existing first trust deed.

3. ____ Federal law granting women financial independence, and preventing lenders from considering such negative credit aspects as the possibility of a woman having children and dropping out of the labor market.

4. ____ A mortgage or deed of trust where the payments increase over the term of the loan. The payments increase hopefully as the buyer's earnings increase.

5. ____ The amount for which the borrower is personally liable on a note and mortgage if the foreclosure sale does not bring enough to cover the debt.

6. ____ A penalty under a note, mortgage or deed of trust, imposed when the loan is paid before it is due.

7. ____ The total cost of financing expressed as one simple annual percentage rate. This rate must be clearly expressed on any loan agreement.

8. ____ A promise in writing, to pay a specified amount during a limited time, or on demand to a named person.

9. ____ Clause used in a deed of trust that gives the lender the right to demand payment in full upon the happening of a certain event.

10. ____ Ownership by one who does not have legal title, such as a vendee under a land contract or, technically, a trustor under a deed of trust.

11. ____ A sale at auction by a trustee under a deed of trust, pursuant to foreclosure proceedings.

12. ____ A type of lien that is subordinate to a prior lien.

13. ____ An instrument, used in place of a mortgage in most western states, that is based on the Spanish legal tradition. Property is transferred to a trustee by the borrower (trustor), in favor of the lender (beneficiary), and reconveyed upon payment in full.

14. ____ A type of acceleration clause, calling for a debt under a mortgage or deed of trust, to be due in its entirety upon transfer of ownership.

15. ____ The use of financing to allow a small amount of cash to purchase and control a large property investment.

16. ____ A period of time past the due date for a payment (mortgage, insurance, etc.) during which a payment may be made and not considered delinquent.

17. ____ Purchaser or buyer, especially on a land contract.

18. ____ A nonamortized note where the principal is due in a lump sum upon maturity.

19. ____ Charging an illegal rate or amount of interest on a loan.

20. ____ Payment of debt in regular, periodic installments of principal and interest, as opposed to interest only payments.

21. ____ The seller of property under a land contract

22. ____ The kind of title held by the vendor under a land contract and the trustee under a deed of trust. They are still owed money by the buyer.

23.____ An installment contract for the sale of land. The seller (vendor) has legal title until paid in full. The buyer (vendee) has equitable title during the contract term.

24.____ A financing charge equal to one percent of the amount of the loan.

25.____ Money charged for the use of money.

26.____ A failure to perform the financial obligation to pay under a loan.

27.____ A holder of a check or note who takes the note in good faith, on the assumption it is valid.

28.____ The borrower under a deed of trust.

29.____ In a deed of trust, the person who acts as an intermediary between the trustor and the beneficiary.

30.____ A lender for whose benefit a trust is created in those states where trust deeds are commonly used instead of mortgages.

31.____ The ownership interest in real property, it is the market value minus any unpaid loan amount.

32.____ Agreement by the buyer to take over the financial responsibility for real property under the existing note and trust deed.

33.____ An agreement by which a lender substitutes a junior loan position for a senior loan position.

34.____ A schedule of monthly payments that varies according to interest rates and number of monthly payments.

35.____ Mortgage loans on which the interest rate is periodically adjusted to more closely coincide with current rates.

36.____ Regulation Z under the Federal Reserve regulations that requires a credit purchaser be advised, in writing, of all costs connected with the credit portion of their purchase.

37.____ The principle of using real property as security for a debt while the borrower retains possession.

38.____ A recorded form requiring the trustee to notify you in the event of a default on the deed of trust to a property.

39.____ A limited amount of time during which the trustor has the right to pay all past due payments and charges due on a loan and bring it current.

40.____ Part of the Truth In Lending Law that allows a borrower to rescind a loan transaction, until midnight of the third business day, on business loans and second trust deeds secured by a borrower's residence.

41.____ The original loan taken out when purchasing a property, not any refinanced or junior loan.

MULTIPLE CHOICE

1. How long is the trust deed reinstatement period after the notice of default has been filed?

   A. 2 months
   C. 4 months

   B. 3 months
   D. 1 month

2. If the beneficiary must foreclose the property, the trustee will start the process by recording a:

   A. Notice of Sale
   C. Notice of Conveyance

   B. Notice of Default
   D. None of the above

3. A request for a "Notice of Default" on a first trust deed is for the benefit of:

   A. Trustee
   C. Beneficiary of junior lien

   B. Vendee
   D. Trustor

4. Any person who has an interest in a particular trust deed (i.e. second or third trust deed holders) should be sure to file a:

   A. trustee's notice
   C. request for notice

   B. lender's notice
   D. deficiency notice

5. In real estate terms, "alienation" means most nearly the opposite of:

   A. origination
   C. amortization

   B. acquisition
   D. reconveyance

6. A minimum of how many days must elapse between the first notice of sale and the actual date of the trustee's sale?

   A. 90
   C. 21

   B. 111
   D. None of the above.

7. The figure that represents the relationship of the total finance charges to the total amount financed is known as the:

   A. lender's percentage rate
   C. annual percentage rate

   B. borrower's percentage rate
   D. finance percentage rate

8. What kind of instrument are we talking about when real property is sold on credit and the seller retains legal title until the debt is paid off?

   A. VA loan
   C. Mortgage

   B. Pledge agreement
   D. Conditional sales contract

9. One month's interest payment on a straight note amounts to $180. At 9% per annum interest rate, what is the face amount of the note?

   A. $26,000
   B. $24,000
   C. $20,000
   D. $27,000

10. Under the Equal Credit Opportunity Act, what information is the lender allowed to obtain regarding the borrower?

   A. Marital status

   C. Length of time on the job

   B. Receipt of any alimony or child support money
   D. Intentions regarding size of family

247

CHAPTER 9
Financial Institutions

http://www.countrywide.com (Large Home Lender)
http://www.norwest.com (Norwest Corporation)

Inflation (prices appreciate) protects both the lender and trustor. There is more equity protecting the lender if there is a default.

The real estate money market, like any other commodity market, changes constantly. Money for financing real estate may be plentiful in one month or quarter, then scarce and expensive in the next. The money market is no longer national, it has become a global market. A broker must be able to finance real estate transactions every month if he or she expects to remain in business. Because of this, a broker must be able to use all the standard financing methods and any unconventional methods that may fit the time and situation.

> *Before you advertise a property or present it to a prospect, try to visualize all the ways the property may be financed. The more alternatives available, the more likely you are to negotiate a sale. Real estate finance continues to become more variable and more complex as time goes on. This chapter will explain the sources of funds available from financial institutions, the government's role and other creative prospects and information that will assist you when offering financing.*

OUR EVER CHANGING ECONOMY (ECONOMIC CYCLES)

General level of prices: When prices decrease, the value of money increases and when prices increase, the value of money decreases.

Because our government's spending and taxing policies shift with every new election, our economy is in a constant state of transition. From month-to-month, it is difficult to predict what amount of financing money will be available and what rate of interest will be charged. These influences, multiplied over a period of years, make it nearly impossible to accurately project long-term trends in the money supply.

INFLATION is the result of too much money chasing too few goods. When the economy is going very well most people are making more money and spending it too freely, thereby driving up the price of real estate and other goods. The Fed, sensing that inflation is out of control, starts applying the brakes and starts restricting the amount of money available. This and higher interest rates decrease borrowing. If the Fed is forced to apply the brakes hard, deflation will occur. *DEFLATION is when prices of real estate, goods and services go down.*

A "seller's market" is when prices rise and a "buyer's market" is when prices fall.

It is a **BUYER'S MARKET** *when the prices of real estate are down, terms are easy and there is usually a great deal of real estate listed for sale or rent.* Buyers have a choice; there is more to pick and choose from, at lower prices. In a **SELLER'S MARKET** *the prices of real estate are up and there is less real estate listed for sale or rent.* This is due to increased demand and lagging supplies.

THE FEDERAL RESERVE SYSTEM (FED)

The Federal Reserve has nothing directly to do with raising and lowering interest rates on government insured FHA loans or guaranteed VA loans; it works to stimulate or slowdown the nation's entire economy.

The Federal Reserve Banking System is the single greatest influence on the cost and supply of money for real estate loans. It is the link between America's private financial institutions and the taxing and spending policies of the federal government. The **FEDERAL RESERVE BANKING SYSTEM (Fed)** *is the nation's central banking authority.* If the Fed makes money tight, thus restricting the amount of available loan funds, demand for the available funds increases, pushing interest rates higher. Conversely, if the Fed increases the amount of money in circulation, interest rates go down. In this way they keep centralized control over the interest rates for not only banks, but for all lending institutions.

A "tight money policy" from the Fed would involve restricting loan activity and increasing interest rates to mercifully slowdown the economy, thus preventing "overheating" and higher, uncontrolled inflation.

These operations and the other important functions of the Federal Reserve System are supervised by the Federal Reserve Board. The *FEDERAL RESERVE BOARD is a seven-member committee, appointed by the President, but politically independent.* In regulating the amount and flow of loan money available to banks, the board has indirect, but far reaching influence, over all lending institutions and the economy as a whole.

The Federal Reserve's monetary policies influence the supply of money by:

1) Buying and selling government T-bonds and T-securities.
2) Raising and lowering the reserve requirement.
3) Raising and lowering the discount rate to member banks.
4) Margin requirements (percentage loaned on stocks and bonds).

http://www.bog.frb.fed.us (Federal Reserve Board)
http://www.ustreas.gov (U.S. Treasury)
http://www.occ.treas.gov (Office of the Comptroller of the Currency)
http://www.frbsf.org (Federal Reserve Bank of San Francisco - 12th District)

GROSS DOMESTIC PRODUCT (MEASURES ECONOMIC ACTIVITY)

We can monitor growth in our economy and the influence of the Fed by watching closely changes in the gross domestic product. The *GROSS DOMESTIC PRODUCT, or GDP, is the total value of all goods and services produced by an economy during a specific period of time.* It serves as a kind of monetary barometer that shows us the rate and areas of greatest growth.

The term Gross Domestic Product (GDP) is the measure of the total value of production (goods and services) from "our home economy"; specifically, the United States.

CHANGING INTEREST RATES (AFFECTS REAL ESTATE)

The credit crunches of recent years are examples of the drastic changes that can occur in the availability of money. Interest rates soared, and only the best properties and most qualified buyers were able to obtain financing. Salespeople found out firsthand how important it is to be creative in the world of real property finance. At other times interest rates are very low, causing increased selling activity and refinancing. *REFINANCING is the process of obtaining a new loan to pay off the old loan.* If interest rates fall dramatically, it is wise to consider refinancing. Figure 9-1 provides a detailed discussion of the steps in obtaining a loan.

FIGURE 9-1 Steps In Obtaining A Loan

1. Application

After deciding that a real estate loan is necessary, the first step in obtaining the loan is filling out a loan application. It would be a good idea to shop around and check for the best rate and terms at various savings institutions before applying because, despite what many people suspect, every lender is different. Finding the right loan is as important as finding the right piece of real estate. The application will request detailed information regarding both the property and the borrower.

2. Analysis

The application generally receives a preliminary screening to determine if there are any obvious and glaring reasons why either the prospective borrower or the property could not qualify for a loan. This is followed by a professional appraisal of the property and an in-depth investigation into the credit background of the applicant. The lender wants to know how likely the borrower is to meet monthly payments and pay back the loan. This is analyzed with reference to the borrower's "capacity" and "desire" to pay.

CAPACITY is determined based upon a borrower's savings, valuable property and income and evaluated in terms of the reliability of these assets. An excellent evidence of capacity would be good collateral. *COLLATERAL is valuable property pledged as a guarantee for payment of a loan.* **DESIRE (to pay)** *is demonstrated by a good credit history reflecting the discipline to make monthly payments on time.* A background of late payments and loan defaults would make it difficult to get loan approval.

3. Processing

If loan analysis proves favorable and financing terms are acceptable to all parties, it is then time to get the terms of the agreement down on paper. Processing involves typing up the loan documents, preparing necessary disclosure statements and issuing instructions to the escrow holder.

4. Escrow

All the paperwork of the loan transaction ends up in escrow along with all the other contracts involved in the purchase of real property. The trust deed and promissory note are signed and passed along to the escrow company where the deal is closed.

5. Servicing

Loan servicing involves mailing monthly loan statements, collecting payments and seeing to it that all records are kept up to date. Some lenders service their own loans while others hire independent mortgage companies to handle the paperwork for them. Loan servicing also involves all correspondence for late and delinquent payments.

Qualifying for a Loan

All lenders set their own standards for evaluating who qualifies and who does not qualify for loan money. These standards are reflected in the interest rates charged. Some lenders have very strict requirements, while others will take a greater risk but charge a higher rate of interest—especially on second trust deeds. Real estate agents can obtain more specific guidelines simply by contacting local lenders.

Traditionally, lending institutions decided whether or not a borrower was qualified based upon a simple formula: The property should not cost more than two-and-a-half times the borrower's annual income. Today, however, many lenders recognize that this method can be very inadequate. It fails to take into account other debts that the borrower might be paying off and doesn't give the middle income property buyer, or those entering the housing market for the first time, much of a chance with today's high cost real estate.

New rules of thumb consider a borrower's other debts along with the housing payments. Long term debts are added to these payments and the sum is referred to as the borrower's total monthly expenses.

One standard rule is that a borrower's monthly expenses should be no more than 25 percent of all total monthly income. Another rule, which is applied to borrowers who are not heavily in debt elsewhere, requires that their annual income be approximately 30 percent of the cost of the property. This is a variation on the traditional formula reflecting a more realistic attitude on the part of lenders.

Appraisal of the Property

Just as the borrower is evaluated during the loan process, lenders evaluate the property being purchased. They want to be certain that the price being paid reflects a fair market value. If a property is overpriced and the borrower defaults, it might be difficult for the lender to recoup the amount of the loan. This process of determining a property's fair market value is known as appraisal and is discussed in detail in Chapters 10 and 11.

Institutional lenders are not likely to loan the entire amount needed for the purchase of a property. Most often they will determine the fair market value and loan a set percentage of that amount. This "loan to value ratio" (L-T-V) is generally 80 percent to 90 percent at banks and savings banks and 70 percent if the loan comes from an insurance company. Collateral is required but most often the property itself (including any structures) is used as security for the loan.

Chapter 9

SHOPPING FOR A LOAN

All the variables of our changing economy come home in a very personal way when a borrower goes out to look for a loan. For the average person, borrowing the money necessary to buy a house is the largest financial obligation he or she is likely to assume in his or her lifetime. It's an extremely important decision, second only to the selection of the property itself. The salesperson should advise caution and careful consideration before a promissory note is signed. Shopping around for a loan from several different loan sources is an excellent idea. Even if the borrower has found financing that he or she feels is acceptable, talking to other lenders should never be discouraged.

LOAN TO VALUE
(PERCENT OF APPRAISED VALUE LENDER WILL LOAN)

LOAN TO VALUE is the percentage of appraised value the lender will loan the borrower to purchase the property. It is abbreviated as L-T-V or L to V. The lower the L to V, the higher the down payment has to be. The lower the L to V, the more equity is required.

Most lenders commonly request an 80 percent L-T-V ratio but this varies depending on many factors. The lower the L-T-V, the greater the down payment (more equity funds are required).

ESTIMATE OF SETTLEMENT COSTS (RESPA)

The lender must give the applicant the HUD booklet that explains closing costs and has until three business days after receipt of a loan application to provide a good faith estimate of the actual settlement costs to the borrower. Figure 9-2 illustrates an estimated settlement cost form.

This disclosure (RESPA) must include:

1. The rate of interest
2. Points to be charged
3. Any additional loan fees and charges
4. Escrow, title and other allowable costs, which could add up to $1000 or more above lender's estimates.

The idea is to alert the borrower to, at the beginning of the loan process, how much cash, besides the down payment, will be needed to close escrow. Usually the lender will provide the complete estimated settlement cost form along with the loan application.

FIGURE 9-2

CALIFORNIA ASSOCIATION OF MORTGAGE BROKERS
MORTGAGE LOAN DISCLOSURE STATEMENT/GOOD FAITH ESTIMATE

Borrower's Name(s): _____

Real Property Collateral: The intended security for this proposed loan will be a Deed of Trust on (street address or legal description) _____

This joint Mortgage Loan Disclosure Statement/Good Faith Estimate is being provided by <u>TMH Home Mortgage Company</u>, a real estate broker acting as a mortgage broker, pursuant to the Federal Real Estate Settlement Procedures Act (RESPA) and similar California law. In a transaction subject to RESPA, a lender will provide you with an additional Good Faith Estimate within three business days of the receipt of your loan application. You will also be informed of material changes before settlement/close of escrow. The name of the intended lender to whom your loan application will be delivered is:

☐ Unknown   ☐ _____ (Name of lender, if known)

GOOD FAITH ESTIMATE OF CLOSING COSTS

The information provided below reflects estimates of the charges you are likely to incur at the settlement of your loan. The fees, commissions, costs and expenses listed are estimates; the actual charges may be more or less. Your transaction may not involve a charge for every item listed and any additional items charged will be listed. The numbers listed beside the estimate generally correspond to the numbered lines contained in the HUD-1 Settlement Statement which you will receive at settlement if this transaction is subject to RESPA. The HUD-1 Settlement Statement contains the actual costs for the items paid at settlement. When this transaction is subject to RESPA, by signing page two of this form you are also acknowledging receipt of the HUD Guide to Settlement Costs.

HUD-1	Item	Paid to Others	Paid to Broker
800	*Items Payable in Connection with Loan*		
801	Lender's Loan Origination Fee	$ _____	$ _____
802	Lender's Loan Discount Fee	$ _____	$ _____
803	Appraisal Fee	$ _____	$ _____
804	Credit Report	$ 55.00	$ _____
805	Lender's Inspection Fee	$ _____	$ _____
808	Mortgage Broker Commission/Fee	$ _____	$ _____
809	Tax Service Fee	$ 69.00	$ _____
810	Processing Fee	$ _____	$ 375.00
811	Underwriting Fee	$ 350.00	$ _____
812	Wire Transfer Fee	$ 35.00	$ _____
____	Misc.	$ 200.00	$ _____
900	*Items Required by Lender to be Paid in Advance*		
901	Interest for _30_ days at $_____ per day	$ _____	$ _____
902	Mortgage Insurance Premiums	$ _____	$ _____
903	Hazard Insurance Premiums	$ _____	$ _____
904	County Property Taxes	$ _____	$ _____
905	VA Funding Fee	$ _____	$ _____
		$ _____	$ _____
1000	*Reserves Deposited with Lender*		
1001	Hazard Insurance: _2_ months at $_____ /mo.	$ _____	$ _____
1002	Mortgage Insurance: _2_ months at $_____ /mo.	$ _____	$ _____
1004	Co. Property Taxes: _2_ months at $_____ /mo.	$ _____	$ _____
		$ _____	$ _____
1100	*Title Charges*		
1101	Settlement or Closing/Escrow Fee	$ _____	$ _____
1105	Document Preparation Fee	$ 150.00	$ _____
1106	Notary Fee	$ _____	$ _____
1108	Title Insurance	$ _____	$ _____
		$ _____	$ _____
1200	*Government Recording and Transfer Charges*		
1201	Recording Fees	$ 50.00	$ _____
1202	City/County Tax/Stamps	$ _____	$ _____
		$ _____	$ _____
1300	*Additional Settlement Charges*		
1302	Pest Inspection	$ _____	$ _____
		$ _____	$ _____

Subtotals of Initial Fees, Commissions, Costs and Expenses $ _____ $ _____

    Total of Initial Fees, Commissions, Costs and Expenses $ _____

Compensation to Broker (Not Paid Out of Loan Proceeds):

    Mortgage Broker Commission/Fee $ _____

    Any Additional Compensation from Lender   ☒ No   ☐ Yes $ _____ (if known)

255

Chapter 9

THE LOAN APPLICATION

The lender needs a loan application from the borrower so that the borrower's financial condition can be analyzed. Figures 9-3 and 9-4 are a copy of the FHLMC/FNMA application form that is used by most financial institutions. The application provides the lender with the following:

1. Information about property being financed.
2. Information about borrower (and co-borrower, if any).
3. Sources of income and analysis.
4. Monthly housing expenses (present and proposed).
5. Balance sheet.
6. Other information relevant to the borrower's financial status.

EQUITY (MARKET VALUE LESS DEBT)

When shopping for a loan, the lender wants to determine your worth, or equity, so they will require you to fill out an accounting balance sheet as part of the application. *EQUITY is your worth; it is the amount that is left after subtracting all that you owe (debt) from what you own (assets).* Lenders want to see your equity on paper. Equity shows them your ability to make the down payment and meet other expenses. It is common practice to ask buyers what the equity is in their current home in order to determine if they financially qualify for the price of a new home.

The equity (worth) you have in a home is its market value minus what you owe on it.

LIQUIDITY (CONVERT ASSETS INTO CASH)

LIQUIDITY is the ability of a borrower to convert assets into cash so that debt obligation can be paid when due. It is not enough to make money; there also must be the ability to pay bills on time. Real estate has very little liquidity. Depending on market conditions, it could take a very long time to sell a piece of real estate. On the other hand, income property may bring in more cash monthly than goes out for expenditures.

OPPORTUNITY COST (COST OF NON-LIQUIDITY)

OPPORTUNITY COST is lost profit that a person could have made if he or she had the cash available to invest now. It is the cost of non-liquidity. If you own a home, the lost return on that equity is referred to as opportunity cost.

FIGURE 9-3

Uniform Residential Loan Application

This application is designed to be completed by the applicant(s) with the lender's assistance. Applicants should complete this form as "Borrower" or "Co-Borrower", as applicable. Co-Borrower information must also be provided (and the appropriate box checked) when ☐ the income or assets of a person other than the "Borrower" (including the Borrower's spouse) will be used as a basis for loan qualification or ☐ the income or assets of the Borrower's spouse will not be used as a basis for loan qualification, but his or her liabilities must be considered because the Borrower resides in a community property state, the security property is located in a community property state, or the Borrower is relying on other property located in a community property state as a basis for repayment of the loan.

I. TYPE OF MORTGAGE AND TERMS OF LOAN

Mortgage Applied for:	☐ VA ☐ FHA	☐ Conventional ☐ FmHA	☐ Other:	Agency Case Number	Lender Case No.

Amount	Interest Rate	No. of Months	Amortization Type:		
$	%		☐ Fixed Rate ☐ GPM	☐ Other (explain): ☐ ARM (type):	

II. PROPERTY INFORMATION AND PURPOSE OF LOAN

Subject Property Address (street, city, state, & ZIP) No. of Units

Legal Description of Subject Property (attach description if necessary) Year Built

Purpose of Loan: ☐ Purchase ☐ Refinance ☐ Construction ☐ Construction-Permanent ☐ Other (explain):

Property will be: ☐ Primary Residence ☐ Secondary Residence ☐ Investment

Complete this line if construction or construction-permanent loan.

Year Lot Acquired	Original Cost	Amount Existing Liens	(a) Present Value of Lot	(b) Cost of Improvements	Total (a + b)
	$	$	$	$	$

Complete this line if this is a refinance loan.

Year Acquired	Original Cost	Amount Existing Liens	Purpose of Refinance	Describe Improvements ☐ made ☐ to be made
	$	$		Cost: $

Title will be held in what Name(s) Manner in which Title will be held Estate will be held in: ☐ Fee Simple ☐ Leasehold (show expiration date)

Source of Down Payment, Settlement Charges and/or Subordinate Financing (explain)

III. BORROWER INFORMATION

Borrower	Co-Borrower
Borrower's Name (include Jr. or Sr. if applicable)	Co-Borrower's Name (include Jr. or Sr. if applicable)

Social Security Number	Home Phone (incl. area code)	Age	Yrs. School	Social Security Number	Home Phone (incl. area code)	Age	Yrs. School

☐ Married ☐ Separated ☐ Unmarried (include single, divorced, widowed)	Dependents (not listed by Co-Borrower) no. ages	☐ Married ☐ Separated ☐ Unmarried (include single, divorced, widowed)	Dependents (not listed by Borrower) no. ages

Present Address (street, city, state, ZIP) ☐ Own ☐ Rent ____ No. Yrs. | Present Address (street, city, state, ZIP) ☐ Own ☐ Rent ____ No. Yrs.

If residing at present address for less than two years, complete the following:

Former Address (street, city, state, ZIP) ☐ Own ☐ Rent ____ No. Yrs. | Former Address (street, city, state, ZIP) ☐ Own ☐ Rent ____ No. Yrs.

Former Address (street, city, state, ZIP) ☐ Own ☐ Rent ____ No. Yrs. | Former Address (street, city, state, ZIP) ☐ Own ☐ Rent ____ No. Yrs.

IV. EMPLOYMENT INFORMATION

Borrower	Co-Borrower

Name & Address of Employer ☐ Self Employed	Yrs. on this job	Name & Address of Employer ☐ Self Employed	Yrs. on this job
	Yrs. employed in this line of work/profession		Yrs. employed in this line of work/profession

Position/Title/Type of Business	Business Phone (incl. area code)	Position/Title/Type of Business	Business Phone (incl. area code)

If employed in current position for less than two years or if currently employed in more than one position, complete the following:

Name & Address of Employer ☐ Self Employed	Dates (from - to)	Name & Address of Employer ☐ Self Employed	Dates (from - to)
	Monthly Income $		Monthly Income $

Position/Title/Type of Business	Business Phone (incl. area code)	Position/Title/Type of Business	Business Phone (incl. area code)

Name & Address of Employer ☐ Self Employed	Dates (from - to)	Name & Address of Employer ☐ Self Employed	Dates (from - to)
	Monthly Income $		Monthly Income $

Position/Title/Type of Business	Business Phone (incl. area code)	Position/Title/Type of Business	Business Phone (incl. area code)

Freddie Mac Form 65   Page 1 of 4   Fannie Mae Form 1003

FIGURE 9-4

V. MONTHLY INCOME AND COMBINED HOUSING EXPENSE INFORMATION

Gross Monthly Income	Borrower	Co-Borrower	Total	Combined Monthly Housing Expense	Present	Proposed
Base Empl. Income *	$	$	$	Rent	$	
Overtime				First Mortgage (P&I)		$
Bonuses				Other Financing (P&I)		
Commissions				Hazard Insurance		
Dividends/Interest				Real Estate Taxes		
Net Rental Income				Mortgage Insurance		
Other (before completing, see the notice in "describe other income," below)				Homeowner Assn. Dues		
				Other:		
Total	$	$	$	Total	$	$

* Self Employed Borrower(s) may be required to provide additional documentation such as tax returns and financial statements.

Describe Other Income *Notice: Alimony, child support, or separate maintenance income need not be revealed if the Borrower (B) or Co-Borrower (C) does not choose to have it considered for repaying this loan.*

B/C		Monthly Amount
		$

VI. ASSETS AND LIABILITIES

This Statement and any applicable supporting schedules may be completed jointly by both married and unmarried Co-Borrowers if their assets and liabilities are sufficiently joined so that the Statement can be meaningfully and fairly presented on a combined basis; otherwise separate Statements and Schedules are required. If the Co-Borrower section was completed about a spouse, this Statement and supporting schedules must be completed about that spouse also.

Completed ☐ Jointly ☐ Not Jointly

ASSETS Description	Cash or Market Value	Liabilities and Pledged Assets. List the creditor's name, address and account number for all outstanding debts, including automobile loans, revolving charge accounts, real estate loans, alimony, child support, stock pledges, etc. Use continuation sheet, if necessary. Indicate by (*) those liabilities which will be satisfied upon sale of real estate owned or upon refinancing of the subject property.	Monthly Payt. & Mos. Left to Pay	Unpaid Balance
Cash deposit toward purchase held by:	$	LIABILITIES		
		Name and address of Company	$ Payt./Mos.	$
List checking and savings accounts below				
Name and address of Bank, S&L, or Credit Union				
		Acct. no.		
		Name and address of Company	$ Payt./Mos.	$
Acct. no.	$			
Name and address of Bank, S&L, or Credit Union				
		Acct. no.		
		Name and address of Company	$ Payt./Mos.	$
Acct. no.	$			
Name and address of Bank, S&L, or Credit Union				
		Acct. no.		
		Name and address of Company	$ Payt./Mos.	$
Acct. no.	$			
Name and address of Bank, S&L, or Credit Union				
		Acct. no.		
		Name and address of Company	$ Payt./Mos.	$
Acct. no.	$			
Stocks & Bonds (Company name/number & description)	$			
		Acct. no.		
		Name and address of Company	$ Payt./Mos.	$
Life insurance net cash value	$			
Face amount: $				
Subtotal Liquid Assets	$			
Real estate owned (enter market value from schedule of real estate owned)	$	Acct. no.		
Vested interest in retirement fund	$	Name and address of Company	$ Payt./Mos.	$
Net worth of business(es) owned (attach financial statement)	$			
Automobiles owned (make and year)	$			
		Acct. no.		
		Alimony/Child Support/Separate Maintenance Payments Owed to:	$	
Other Assets (itemize)	$	Job Related Expense (child care, union dues, etc.)	$	
		Total Monthly Payments	$	
Total Assets a.	$	Net Worth	$	Total Liabilities b.	$

Freddie Mac Form 65 — Page 2 of 4 — Fannie Mae Form 1003

SOURCES OF REAL ESTATE FUNDS

The remainder of this chapter will deal with the different institutions that loan money to finance the purchase of real property. Details concerning the types of lenders and how they make loans will be explained and different kinds of government loan participation are compared and discussed. In addition, the responsibilities of a broker acting as a loan agent or security dealer are outlined.

The three areas of demand for borrowing money are:

    1) Construction funds to build
    2) To finance a purchase
    3) For refinancing.

TRUTH IN SAVINGS ACT

Financial institutions obtain funds from their depositors and pay a modest return in the form of interest or dividends to keep their depositors money invested with them. In order to make money, the spread that a financial institution must make between the interest rate it charges on loans and the interest rate paid to its depositors must be at least 2%. So if a bank pays 7% to depositors it can only make loans at 9% or higher in order to stay in business. See Figure 9-5.

FIGURE 9-5

Truth in Savings Act
"Annual Percentage Yield" defined as APY

The Truth in Savings Act requires depository institutions to furnish "clear, complete and uniform disclosures" of the terms of their savings and checking deposit accounts. It also requires institutions to pay interest on the consumer's daily balance. Certain practices are no longer permitted, such as advertising "Free Accounts" and then charging maintenance or per-check fees, or requiring minimum balances.

This Act introduces a standard method of expressing interest paid to depositors called "Annual Percentage Yield" or APY. This new method takes into account the rate and also the compounding. So if the APY is 4.46 percent, a hundred dollars will earn $ 4.46 in one year. The higher the APY, the more interest is paid.

INSTITUTIONAL LENDERS

INSTITUTIONAL LENDERS are very large corporations that lend the money of their depositors to finance real estate transactions. Their principal function is to act as financial intermediaries; transfer money from those who have funds to those who wish to borrow. Figure 9-6 illustrates which groups are institutional and which are noninstitutional lenders.

> *Institutional lenders are big lenders who pool funds so they can lend to individual borrowers. They include: insurance companies, savings banks, banks and mutual saving banks.*

FIGURE 9-6

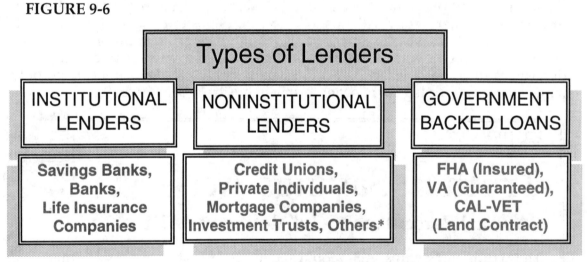

Types of Lenders

INSTITUTIONAL LENDERS	NONINSTITUTIONAL LENDERS	GOVERNMENT BACKED LOANS
Savings Banks, Banks, Life Insurance Companies	Credit Unions, Private Individuals, Mortgage Companies, Investment Trusts, Others*	FHA (Insured), VA (Guaranteed), CAL-VET (Land Contract)

*Pension plans are now a form of noninstitutional lender.

FEDERAL DEPOSIT INSURANCE CORPORATION (FDIC)

The *FEDERAL DEPOSIT INSURANCE CORPORATION (FDIC) is a government corporation that, for a fee, insures each account of a depositor up to $100,000.* All the deposits in savings banks and banks in California are insured by the FDIC because they pay for the premiums. If a depositor has more than the insured $100,000 in any one account, then he or she may lose that amount in excess of $100,000 if there is a savings bank or bank failure.

http://www.fdic.gov
(Federal Deposit Insurance Corp.)

Each depositor insured to $100,000

FDIC

FEDERAL DEPOSIT INSURANCE CORPORATION

SAVINGS BANKS
(GREATEST SOURCE OF MONEY FOR HOME LOANS)

In California, most of the home purchases are financed by savings banks. They make more real estate loans than any other financial institution. This is because, until recently, all the money that savings banks lent out was in the form of real estate loans. Even with current changes in the banking industry, savings banks are still the primary home mortgage lenders. Savings banks are either federally or state licensed.

This is a brief description of how a savings bank works: A person wishing to deposit funds, in exchange for interest, would open an account (savings, money market, checking, etc.) at a savings bank. These funds would then be invested in real estate loans, which yield higher rates of interest for the institution than is being paid out to depositors. This system allows savers to obtain interest from savings bank accounts and at the same time provide a source of loan funds to home buyers. All savings banks can make 80% loans on any amount that is acceptable to them. Savings banks will occasionally make 90 and 95 percent (loan-to-value) loans if the loans are covered by private mortgage insurance.

Savings banks primarily make loans on single family homes or condos that are owner-occupied. They will also make loans on apartment buildings and mobilehomes. Larger savings banks will often make construction loans for a tract and then supply each owner with permanent, long-term financing.

Savings banks, like banks and insurance companies, charge points and loan fees. Points will range from one to five percent (points) of the total loan amount. Loan fees are usually $300 to $500 while appraisal costs start at $200, but vary depending on the property. All institutional lenders tend to charge comparable points and fees according to economic conditions in the market place.

Savings banks are primary sources for residential loans because they invest most of their money in home loans.

Figure 9-7 compares the lending priorities of savings banks with banks and life insurance companies.

FIGURE 9-7

PRIORITIES OF INSTITUTIONAL LENDERS

SAVINGS BANKS	BANKS	INSURANCE COMPANIES
(Residential Lenders)	(General Purpose Lenders)	(Big Money Lenders)
1. Single family homes and condos	1. Business and auto loans	1. Large shopping centers and office buildings
2. Apartment buildings	2. Conventional home loans	2. Hotels and industrial properties
3. Home improvement loans	3. Government backed FHA and VA home loans	3. FHA and VA home loans through mortgage companies
4. Mobilehomes	4. Credit cards	
	5. Construction loans	

BANKS

Banks are **general purpose lenders**, which means they lend money for anything from real estate to sailboats. Even so, they are the second largest lenders for real estate in California. All national banks are required to be members of the Federal Reserve System, while a state bank may be a member by choice. There is no great difference between real estate loans that a state bank makes and loans that the federal banks make. Interest rates and other loan terms are comparable to those offered by savings banks.

Any commercial bank may lend money on real property if it is a first loan on that property. In general, there are three types of real estate financing:

1. **First Trust Deed Loans** — The bank finances long-term loans for existing land and the buildings.

2. **Construction Loans (or Interim loans)** — Money is provided for the construction of a building, to be repaid when the construction is complete.

3. **Take-Out Loans (Replaces Interim "Construction loan")** — Money arranged by the owner, builder or developer for the buyer. The construction loan made for the construction of the improvements is usually paid in full from the proceeds of this more permanent loan.

A construction loan (or interim loan) is a short term loan.

4. **Home Improvement Loans** — This type of loan is for repairing and modernizing existing buildings.

LIFE INSURANCE COMPANIES

A primary source for a very large loan would be a life insurance company. Obtaining a small ($20,000) loan would be least likely from an insurance company.

Life insurance companies have more money to lend than either a bank or a savings bank. They are more conservative lenders and specialize in large loans for commercial projects, but they also make conventional loans on all types of property. These companies supply most of the loan funds for properties where a great deal of capital is required (such as high-rise office buildings, shopping centers, industrial properties and hotels).

Life insurance companies seldom make construction loans.

Life insurance companies also invest large amounts of money in trust deeds that are either insured by the FHA or guaranteed by the VA. Mortgage companies make such loans for insurance companies. Quite often, these mortgage companies, in return for a servicing fee, collect the loan payments for the insurance company.

Life insurance companies are governed by the laws of the state in which they are incorporated, as well as the laws of the states in which they do business. There is no state restriction concerning the number of years for which a loan can be made. However, company policy usually restricts the term to no more than 30 years and requires a loan to be amortized.

Life insurance companies in California, when making loans, are restricted to a 75 percent maximum of market value of any given property. This is not a requirement if the loan is insured by the Federal Housing Administration (FHA) or guaranteed by the Veterans Administration (VA).

Life insurance companies use mortgage companies to obtain and service their trust deeds.

NONINSTITUTIONAL LENDERS

Noninstitutional lenders are smaller lenders. Noninstitutional lenders include: private lenders, mortgage companies, investment trusts, pension plans and credit unions.

NONINSTITUTIONAL LENDERS *are individuals and organizations that lend on a private or individual basis.* Both institutional and noninstitutional lenders make loans that may be or may not be backed by one of the government loan programs.

CONVENTIONAL LOANS *are loans that are not insured or guaranteed by the United States government.*

Conventional loans are NOT insured or guaranteed by the federal government.

PRIVATE INDIVIDUALS

Any real estate loan by an individual is considered a private individual loan. Most individuals who lend money on real estate are sellers who take back a second trust deed as part of the real estate transaction. The seller will be a likely lender when the buyer needs a little more money to purchase a property. Most second trust deed loans are of this type and are the most important type of secondary financing in California.

When the current money market is tight, it often means that a seller will have to take back a second trust deed as part of the equity in his or her home.

Many second loans on real estate, called junior loans (second trust deeds), are obtained from private investors.

Common second trust deed terms are:

1. The loan amount is usually relatively small (under $50,000).
2. There is a relatively high interest rate (10% to 20%).
3. The loan term is usually from 3 to 7 years, with payments on a monthly basis.
4. Loan payments are usually 1% of the original loan and there is usually a balloon payment at the end of the term (if more than six years).
5. There is usually an acceleration clause that makes the entire loan due if any payment is missed or the property is transferred.

CREDIT UNIONS

A **CREDIT UNION** *is a co-operative association organized to promote thrift among its members and provide them with a source of credit.*

Under the Federal Credit Union Act of 1934, a credit union charter may be given to any group having a common bond of association or occupation—a factory, store, office, church, trade group, club or fraternal organization.

Although there are thousands of credit unions across the country, they play a much smaller role than banks, savings banks and insurance companies in financing real estate. The typical credit union is smaller than the average commercial bank or savings bank.

Most credit unions are incorporated and accumulate funds by selling shares to members. From this pool of funds, loans are made at an interest rate equal to or below the current market rate. Low interest rate loans to members are a big plus for credit unions.

The modern credit union offers: savings plans, credit cards, ATM cards, travelers' checks, vehicle loans, signature loans and real estate loans. All deposit accounts have FDIC insurance up to $100,000.

http://www.ncua.gov (National Credit Union Administration [NCUA])

Recent changes in the law have enabled credit unions to make not only second trust deed loans, but also first trust deed loans. This source of real estate funding is expected to grow and expand in coming years.

REAL ESTATE INVESTMENT TRUST (REIT)

A **REAL ESTATE INVESTMENT TRUST (REIT)** *is a type of company that sells securities specializing in real estate ventures.* If the company distributes 90 percent or more of its income to its shareholders, it does not pay federal income taxes on that distribution. Because of these formalities, a real estate investment trust is taxed like any other real estate investment.

A REIT requires a minimum of 100 investors.

Real estate investment trusts are of two types: (1) equity trust and (2) mortgage trust. An **EQUITY TRUST** *is an investment in real estate itself or several real estate projects.* The **MORTGAGE TRUST** *is a company that invests in mortgages and other types of real estate loans or obligations.* Now there are even combination trusts that invest in real estate and lend money in the form of real estate mortgages.

PENSION PLANS

A **PENSION PLAN** *is an investment organization that obtains funds from people before they retire and invests this money for their clients' retirement.* Company pension plans have become a popular source of real estate funds and are expected to grow even larger in the future. Enormous amounts of money, gathered through deductions from each pay period, are held by these plans. Those who administer pension money are becoming more and more inclined to invest it directly in large real estate projects rather than playing the stock market or simply socking it away in investment programs with savings institutions and insurance companies.

MORTGAGE BANKERS (COMPANIES)
SECONDARY MORTGAGE MARKET

The secondary mortgage market is a resale market place where smaller lenders sell their loans to larger lenders.

MORTGAGE BANKERS (COMPANIES) *usually loan their own money or roll it over so they can originate, finance and close first trust deeds or mortgages secured by real estate. They then sell the loans to institutional investors and service the loans through a contractual relationship with the investors. In California, the brokerage function is one of the prime sources for loans on homes and income property, and they are the largest originator of FHA and VA trust deeds or mortgages. Sometimes private mortgage insurance is necessary to make a loan.*

A mortgage banker establishes a good line of credit with a bank to obtain available funds. Mortgage companies like to make loans that can be sold easily on the secondary mortgage market. "Warehousing" is the action of a mortgage banker collecting loans prior to sale.

PRIVATE MORTGAGE INSURANCE (PMI)

PRIVATE MORTGAGE INSURANCE is a guarantee to lenders that the upper portion of a conventional loan will be repaid if a borrower defaults and a deficiency occurs at the foreclosure sale.

> *Let's look at an example: Smith is buying a property for $100,000 but he only has $5,000 for a down payment. He approaches lender Jones for financing. Lender Jones is eager to see this sale go through but he does not feel entirely comfortable putting up $95,000 when normally he would limit the loan to 80%, or $80,000. He is uncomfortable lending Smith the extra $15,000. He agrees to make the loan if Smith will pay for private mortgage insurance to cover the upper portion ($15,000) of the $95,000 loan.*

Private mortgage insurance is obtainable on properties with one-to-four units and generally covers the top 20% of the loan amount. The borrower generally pays an initial premium or an annual fee of one-half of one percent on the remaining principal balance.

GOVERNMENT FINANCING PROGRAMS

The government is very involved in helping people obtain homes. The three programs we will discuss have already helped millions to enjoy "owning a home," the American dream. FHA insurance (part of Housing and Urban Development - HUD) and VA guarantees are federal programs. They **approve** loans made by private lenders, but lend no actual money. The CAL-VET program makes direct loans to qualified borrowers from the state of California. See Figure 9-8 and the chart in Figure 9-9.

FIGURE 9-8

FIGURE 9-9   **Federal Housing Administration**
                                     (FHA) TITLE II (203B)

ELIGIBILITY	Anyone residing in the United States
SOURCE OF FUNDS	Approved Lenders
LOAN INSTRUMENT	Trust Deed or Mortgage
TERM	30 years
INTEREST RATE	current interest rates plus mortgage insurance premiums paid up front, prior to close of escrow
MAXIMUM PURCHASE	No Maximum
MAXIMUM LOAN AMOUNT (For high cost areas)	97% of the maximum for the county average: house-condo $160,950; duplex $205,912; tri-plex $248,887 & 4-unit $309,339
DOWN PAYMENT	3% of first $25,000 5% of appraisal balance 100% over appraisal
SECONDARY FINANCING	Allowed
PREPAYMENT PENALTY	None (30 days notice)
ASSIGNABLE	After 2 year if owner-occupant
POINTS PAID BY	Buyers or Sellers
BORROWER'S MONTHLY PAYMENTS	Monthly principal & Interest 29% to 41% of annual gross income
MONTHLY SALARY (AFTER FEDERAL TAXES)	Approximately 3 times total monthly payment

VA Veterans Administration	CAL-VET State of California
W. W. II, Korean War of Active Duty for 181 Days	California Veteran, W. W. II, Korean War, Vietnam, Persian Gulf *or certain medal winners
Approved Lenders	California Bond Issues
Trust Deed or Mortgage	Conditional Sales Contract
30 Year Maximum	40 Year Maximum (Starts at 25 years)
Set by Veterans Administration	Set by State of California But may increase later
No Maximum	None
1 to 4 Units, Owner-occupied, up to CRV No loan maximum but usually under $203,000 Guarantee maximum is $50,750	Mobile home is Park - $70,000 House - $250,000 Farm - $300,000
None required, lender may require down payment	House -- 3% under $60,000 House -- 5% over $60,000 Farm 5% of Appraisal
Only up to amount of CRV	Allowed up to 90% of appraisal
None	6 months interest (within 5 years)
After 3 years Most qualify for loans	To a Cal-Vet YES
Buyer or Seller	No Points
Monthly principal & Interest 29% to 41% of annual gross income	Monthly principal & Interest 28% to 50% of annual gross income
Approximately 3 times total monthly payment	Approximately 2 times total monthly payment

MINIMUM PROPERTY REQUIREMENTS (MPR)

All of these government-backed finance programs have increased the number of houses and condominiums that people in California can afford to buy. They also have an indirect influence on the quality of homes constructed because they require, as a prerequisite to financing, that the home involved meet minimum property requirements. *MINIMUM PROPERTY REQUIREMENTS (MPR) are set standards of materials and construction required for FHA and VA loans.* These requirements are often more restrictive than the building codes. As a real estate licensee, you should be familiar with the basic financing programs and qualification requirements. In addition, most mortgage companies will help you qualify the buyer and complete the necessary forms for FHA and VA loans.

> *Minimum Property Requirements (or MPR) have been established so that there are minimum quality standards.*

FHA INSURED LOANS
(A DIVISION OF HUD)

http://www.hud.gov/history.html (Housing and Urban Development)
http://www.hud.gov/oig/oigindex.html (Office of The Inspector General - OIG)

The FHA has two main programs that affect California homeowners and buyers: 1) Title I home improvement loans, and 2) Title II (Section 203b) purchase and construction loans. There are other types of FHA financing available. For information, contact a lender who specializes in FHA loans. See Figure 9-9.

FHA TITLE I: HOME IMPROVEMENT LOANS

> *FHA Title I: Home improvement loans*

The FHA can make home improvement loans to a maximum of $25,000. The funds can only be used for home improvement purposes.

FHA TITLE II: HOME PURCHASE OR BUILD LOANS

> *Section 203b program: Insures home loans (1-to-4 units) for anyone who is financially qualified. An FHA loan is based on the selling price when it is lower than the appraisal.*

The maximum FHA loan amount varies from area-to-area in California and could change each year if median home prices change or Federal National Mortgage Association (FNMA) loan amounts change.

The maximum FHA loan amount is the lesser of 1) 95% of an area's median home price or 2) 75% of the Federal National Mortgage Association (FNMA) conforming loan amount.

The maximum loan amount is determined as follows:

1) 97% of the first $25,000 of the loan,
2) then 95% of the loan amount between $25,001 and $125,000,
3) then 90% of the remainder to the maximum loan allowed.

Example of the purchase of a $150,000 home:

Sales price and FHA appraisal	$150,000
Nonrecurring closing cost	= + 3,000
Acquisition cost	**$153,000**

Maximum loan is:

97% of $ 25,000		= $ 24,250
95% of $100,000	(25,001-125,000)	= $ 95,000
90% of $ 28,000	(125,000-153,000)	= $ 25,200
		$144,450

$153,000 Acquisition cost = $144,450 Maximum loan

http://www.comerica.com/mortgage/fha.html (Independent FHA Lender)
http://www.fix.net/~chase/fha.html (Independent FHA lender)

All FHA home buyers must obtain loans at an approved lender's office. The approved local lender (such as banks, insurance companies and mortgage companies) will make the loan if the FHA qualifies the buyer. The FHA has many requirements for its different loan programs. Both the borrower and the property must meet these criteria. If either the borrower or the property does not meet the minimum standards, it would probably be better to look for a lender who deals in conventional rather than FHA loans.

FHA does NOT lend money, do NOT apply at a FHA office, but rather at an approved lender's office.

The FHA does not lend the money, it only insures the approved lender against foreclosure loss. The FHA collects a fee for this insurance called the mortgage insurance premium. The **MORTGAGE INSURANCE PREMIUM (MIP)** *is the protection for the lender that insures the loss if there is a foreclosure.* It is an up-front fee (paid by the borrower) in cash, or through insurance as part of the loan.

MIP is the FHA insurance protection for the "lender" of the loan amount if the owner defaults.

ADVANTAGES & DISADVANTAGES OF "FHA" FINANCING

The advantages and disadvantages of FHA financing include:

ADVANTAGES

1) Low down payment compared to conventional loans.
2) Loans are assumable. Loans before December 15, 1989, without credit or income check. Loans December 15, 1989, and after require approval of the FHA and nonowner-occupied are prohibited after that date.
3) No prepayment penalty is allowed by the FHA.
4) Minimum property requirements (MPR's) give buyer a quality home.
5) A seller receives all cash because of the high loan-to-value ratio.

DISADVANTAGES

1) Lots of processing time and red tape.
2) Existing properties may require repairs necessary to meet minimum property requirements.

VETERANS ADMINISTRATION

http://www.va.gov (VA Loans)

VA LOANS (GUARANTEED LOANS)

The Congress of the United States has passed legislation to assist veterans in obtaining housing. A **VA LOAN** *is not a loan, but rather a guarantee to an approved institutional lender.*

Veteran's Eligibility

Veterans are eligible for a Veterans Administration (VA) loan guarantee if they served on active duty for 181 days or more and were honorably discharged.

Veterans who have served a minimum of 181 days active duty or completed six years in the reserves or national guard qualify. Vets with service-related disabilities are not restricted by time requirements.

American citizens who served in the armed forces of our Allies in World War II may also apply. Widows or widowers of service people or veterans who were eligible at the time of death, but did not use their benefits, may apply to use their husbands' or wives' benefits. Also, the VA Adjudication Board, at its discretion, may give eligibility to any veteran who received other than an honorable discharge.

Veterans May Be Entitled To More Than One Loan

A veteran may restore his or her eligibility and apply for an additional loan if the previous home was sold and its loan paid in full. Other veterans who are eligible for a new VA loan program may apply even if they have a prior VA loan, if the prior loan is not in default and if the veteran no longer owns the property. The previous VA loan need not be paid off. The veteran who purchased a home under a previous program may be eligible again under a new program.

CERTIFICATE OF REASONABLE VALUE (CRV)

A **CERTIFICATE OF REASONABLE VALUE** *is an appraisal of the property to be purchased by the veteran.* The property is appraised by an independent fee appraiser who is appointed by the Veterans Administration. Although the appraisal may be paid for by the veteran, it is usually paid for by the seller. The CRV appraisal expires after six months.

VA LOAN PROVISIONS

VA loans require no down payment, but may require the veteran to pay an origination fee of up to 3% of the loan amount. In addition, the seller may have to pay discount points.

No down payment VA loans can be for any amount, but California lenders will only make a loan up to $203,000. The VA guarantees home loans to veterans up to the lesser of the maximum entitlement established by law (currently $50,750) or 40% of the purchase price (or CRV). Since most lenders will not lend more than four times the guarantee ($50,750 x 4), $203,000 is the maximum loan amount.

A CRV of $100,000 has a guarantee of (40% x $100,000) $40,000. A CRV of $210,000 has a guarantee of $50,750 ($203,000 loan) because of the maximum.

The veteran has the choice of several types of VA loans. They include fixed rate mortgages, graduated payment mortgages, growing equity mortgages and buy-down loans. The time span of a VA loan is generally 30 years. Discount points charged sellers and interest rates vary according to the current economic conditions. The main advantage to the veteran is that no down payment is needed, unless the property's price exceeds the VA's appraisal. This "no money down" feature is unique among government programs. Loans can be above the guaranteed maximum loan amount, but must be in the form of a cash down payment.

ADVANTAGES AND DISADVANTAGES OF "VA" FINANCING

The advantages and disadvantages of VA financing include:

ADVANTAGES

1) No down payment, but a funding fee paid by the veteran
2) Low interest rate because of the VA loan guarantee
3) No prepayment penalty is allowed by the VA.

DISADVANTAGES:

1) Creditworthiness is required for assumption; VA must approve credit and a fee of up to $500; assumption only after one year if owner-occupied or after two years if investor owned
2) Buyer or seller can pay discount points
3) Lengthy processing time and red tape.

CAL-VET (Land Contract)

http://www.ns.net/cadva /calvet.htm (Cal-Vet Loans)

CAL-VET (DIRECT LOANS)

Land contracts (real property purchase contracts) are used and legal title is held by the California Department of Veteran Affairs until the loan is paid in full.

The *CAL-VET loan program is administered by the California Department of Veterans Affairs.* The State of California has developed and operates a program to assist its veterans in purchasing a farm, home or mobilehome. Home property must be a single family dwelling, condominium.

Funds for the Cal-Vet loans come from the sale of Veterans Bonds, voted into law by the people of California. All money loaned to veterans is repaid through installments (including principal, property taxes, insurance and interest) at a rate to cover all operating costs. The bonds are retired at maturity from veterans' loan payments without cost to the State of California.

Funds may not be immediately available for loans to all applicants. The availability of money for this type of loan varies, so a veteran should first check with the Department of Veterans Affairs.

A veteran who intends to obtain a Cal-Vet loan should contact a representative of the Department of Veterans Affairs for complete California Farm and Home Purchase Plan information before committing to purchase a property. To apply for a loan, he or she should obtain the necessary information and forms from one of the Department of Veterans Affairs offices throughout the state.

The Cal-Vet maximum for the purchase of a home is $250,000 and up to $300,000 for a farm. A farm loan, however, may not exceed 95 percent of the Cal-Vet appraisal. The veteran must pay to the seller the difference between the sale's price and the Cal-Vet loan.

The loan term is determined by the amount of the loan, and the age and income of each applicant. Most loans are for 30 years. New loan interest rates are usually lower than current market rates, but may vary according to economic conditions, during the life of the loan.

A loan may be paid in full at any time, but there is a prepayment penalty of six months' interest within the first five years. A Cal-Vet loan can be obtained for a mobilehome if the ownership of the land is included. The maximum mobilehome loan is $70,000 in a park and $90,000 on a single family lot.

Cal-Vet has no points; no one pays for points.

Eligibility

To be eligible for a Cal-Vet loan, a veteran was previously required to be a native Californian or, at the time of entry into active military duty, a bonafide resident of the state. Now there is no residence requirement and all veterans are eligible for the Cal-Vet program.

To qualify, a California veteran must have served at least 90 days active duty in the armed forces of the United States and have been released from service under honorable conditions. A portion of his or her service must have been within one of the following war periods:

WORLD WAR II — December 7, 1941 to December 31, 1946

KOREAN WAR — June 27, 1950 to January 31, 1955

VIETNAM WAR — August 5, 1964 to May 7, 1975

PERSIAN GULF WAR — August 2, 1990 to a date yet to be determined

Also eligible is a California veteran who:

1. Participated in a campaign or expedition for which a medal was awarded by the government of the United States;

2. Was discharged with less than **90 days active duty** because of service-connected disability incurred during his or her qualifying service period.

A qualified veteran must apply for a Cal-Vet loan within 30 years following release from active military duty. However, those who were wounded or disabled during war, or who were prisoners of war, have an indefinite period in which to apply.

All veterans are eligible for the Cal-Vet program. The same person could be eligible for a FHA, a VA and a Cal-Vet loan.

STATE LENDING CORPORATIONS

CALIFORNIA HOUSING FINANCE AGENCY (CHFA) is a state agency that sells bonds so that it can provide funds for low-income family housing on project or individual home basis. It is self-supporting and has political support across party lines. Figure 9-10 explains CHFA in detail.

LENDING CORPORATIONS AND THE SECONDARY MORTGAGE MARKET

PRIVATE AND QUASI-GOVERNMENTAL CORPORATIONS

There were once three federal corporations that used cash to buy and sell trust deeds between financial institutions. These corporations are now either private or quasi-governmental, and provide stability and flexibility for real estate financing in the United States. Each has different programs and areas of focus, but all work together to keep sufficient financing money available at lending institutions so they can make home loans.

FIGURE 9-10

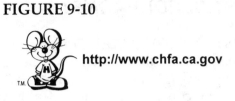

http://www.chfa.ca.gov

CHFA
California Housing Finance Agency

1121 "L" STREET 7TH FLOOR · SACRAMENTO, CA 95814 · (916) 322-3991

The **California Housing Finance Agency** is an exciting program providing real estate funds for low income families, encouraging homeownership over a wider spectrum than has been possible in recent years. This plan is being hailed as a boon from all quarters because it provides a desperately needed funding source and helps stimulate the real estate industry. At the same time, it is entirely self-supporting.

Bonds Issued

Seb Sterpa, past president of CAR, is credited with originating the idea for this program and promoting it to the governor and house speaker. The money for these loans is provided by the issuance of tax free bonds by the state. These bonds sell quickly at a very favorable rate. Because this rate is below the current level, it enables approved lenders to provide loans with affordable rates of interest and still make a reasonable return.

Entirely Self-Supporting

Everyone benefits from this program. Housing in California has become more accessible to buyers with restricted resources. Young couples starting out are now able to enter the housing market. The market is stimulated by the influx of new participants. Investors who purchase the bonds enjoy this profitable form of investment. No tax money is involved and the program is entirely self-supporting.

Support Across Party Lines

Because of the universal benefits, this program claims support across traditional party lines. Democrats favor this program because of the opportunity it offers to the economically disadvantaged. Many Republicans in the state are delighted because of the boost these loans bring to the real estate industry and the state economy in general.

SECONDARY MORTGAGE (TRUST DEED) MARKET

The **SECONDARY MORTGAGE (TRUST DEED) MARKET** *provides an opportunity for financial institutions to buy from, and sell first mortgages (trust deeds) to, other financial institutions.* California has a growing real estate market that will pay higher interest rates than other parts of the country. Therefore, California's financial institutions will make trust deed loans and sell them to other institutions for a profit. The secondary mortgage market enables lenders to keep an adequate supply of money for new loans.

> *The secondary mortgage market is the market where lenders buy and sell mortgages. The secondary mortgage market is the transfer of mortgages among mortgagees.*

http://www.fanniemae.com (Fannie Mae Home Site)
http://www.hud/gov/funcgnma.html (Ginnie Mae Home Site)
http://www.freddiemac.com (Freddie Mac Home Site)

Federal National Mortgage Association (Fannie Mae - Private)

The Federal National Mortgage Association (FNMA), which is commonly referred to as Fannie Mae, dominates the secondary mortgage market. Originally it bought and sold only FHA and VA trust deeds. In 1968 it became a private corporation and now sells securities over the stock exchange to get money so that it can buy and sell conventional loans, besides government backed notes.

> *"Fannie Mae," the Federal National Mortgage Association (FNMA), helps set loan standards and helps to maintain the secondary mortgage market. The FNMA is not a demand source to borrow money.*

Government National Mortgage Association (Ginnie Mae)

The Government National Mortgage Association (GNMA) is a government corporation referred to as Ginnie Mae. It sells secondary mortgages to the public and provides the federal government with cash. These trust deeds are grouped together in pools, and shares are sold on the stock market exchange. All shares are federally guaranteed, making this one of the safest investments available.

Federal Home Loan Mortgage Corporation (Freddie Mac)

The Federal Home Loan Mortgage Corporation (FHLMC), commonly known as Freddie Mac, is a government corporation that issues preferred stock to the public. It is supervised by the Federal Home Loan Bank Board. It helps savings banks maintain a stable and adequate money supply by purchasing their home loan mortgages and repackaging them for sale to investors. The savings banks use the money obtained to make new loans available for home buyers.

The Federal Home Loan Mortgage Corporation, commonly called "Freddie Mac," increases the availability of funds through its involvement in the maintenance of the secondary mortgage market.

FINAL WORD ON CONVENTIONAL LOANS (RISK - LOANS WITHOUT GOVERNMENT BACKING)

Since conventional loans are loans made without government backing or guarantees, they are riskier. Even if conventional loans have lower loan-to-value (LTV) ratios, which makes them safer, government-backed loans are the safest. This is because the government will pay-off if there is a foreclosure, whereas the conventional lender must take the gamble that the foreclosed property will sell for more than what is owed the lender.

Conventional loans have lower "loan-to-value" ratios, which offer greater protection for the lender. Despite the above, conventional loans generally have higher risk. Compared to FHA loans, conventional loans are riskier.

The higher the risk, the higher the interest rates.

More risk = higher interest rates
More risk = higher points

REAL ESTATE BROKER CAN MAKE LOANS

The broker or salesperson, as part of most real estate transactions, may help the buyer fill out a loan application for a financial institution or arrange financing for the buyer. In either case, there are certain restrictions that apply to a real estate licensee acting as a loan broker in buying, selling or exchanging loans. Most of these loans are in the form of a trust deed since it is the usual financing instrument in California.

The "Mortgage Loan Broker Law" (sections 10240-10248 of Article 7) of the Business and Professions Code requires loan brokers to give a Mortgage Loan Disclosure Statement to all borrowers before they become obligated for the loan.

MORTGAGE LOAN BROKER'S STATEMENT (LOAN DISCLOSURE STATEMENT)

A real estate licensee negotiating a loan for a prospective borrower must present to that person completed loan disclosure statements. This statement must be given to the borrower prior to his or her signing the loan documents. It is usually referred to as the Mortgage Loan Disclosure Statement.

A *MORTGAGE LOAN DISCLOSURE STATEMENT is a form that completely and clearly states all the information and charges connected with a particular loan.* It must be kept on file for three years. See Figures 9-11 and 9-12.

> *Loan broker must keep the Mortgage Loan Broker's Disclosure Statement (disclosure given to borrower) on file for three years for the commissioner's inspection.*

Besides providing the borrower with the disclosure statement, the broker is prohibited from doing certain things, and is restricted as to the amount of commission that he or she may charge the borrower.

Anyone negotiating real estate loans must be a real estate licensee. If you make collections on real estate loans and you make more than ten a year or collect more than $40,000, you must also be a licensed real estate broker.

Many brokers establish a regular, ongoing business relationship with individuals or financial institutions that will loan money to prospective buyers.

COMMISSIONS AND OTHER REQUIREMENTS (LOAN BROKER LAWS - ARTICLE 7)

> *On loans of $30,000 and over for first trust deeds, and $20,000 and over for junior deeds of trust, the broker may charge as much as the borrower will agree to pay.*

Brokers negotiating trust deed loans are subject to certain limitations regarding commissions and expenses and must meet other requirements set out by the real estate commissioner. Legislation also requires that brokers provide both the borrower and the lender, on property for first trust deed loans under $30,000 and seconds under $20,000, with copies of the appraisal report. Anyone performing these services, whether soliciting borrowers or lenders, in home loans secured by real property must have a real estate license. This restriction applies even if no advance fee is paid.

FIGURE 9-11

CALIFORNIA ASSOCIATION OF REALTORS®

MORTGAGE LOAN DISCLOSURE STATEMENT (BORROWER)
(As required by the Business and Professions Code §10241
and Title 10, California Administrative Code, §2840)

_____
(Name of Broker/Arranger of Credit)

_____
(Business Address of Broker)

I. SUMMARY OF LOAN TERMS
A. PRINCIPAL AMOUNT . . . . $ _____
B. ESTIMATED DEDUCTIONS FROM PRINCIPAL AMOUNT
   1. Costs and Expenses (See Paragraph III). . . . . $ _____
   *2. Broker Commission/Organization Fee (See Paragraph III) . . . . $ _____
   3. Lender Origination Fee/Discounts (See Paragraph III-B) . . . . $ _____
   4. Additional compensation will/may be received from lender not deducted from loan proceeds.
     _____ YES $ _____ (if known) _____ NO
   5. Amount to be Paid on Authorization of Borrower (See Paragraph III) . . . . $ _____
C. ESTIMATED CASH PAYABLE TO BORROWER (A less B). . . . . $ _____

II. GENERAL INFORMATION ABOUT LOAN
A. If this loan is made, Borrower will be required to pay the principal and interest at _____% per year, payable as
follows: _____ _____ payments of $ _____
       (number of payments)   (monthly/quarterly/annually)
and a **FINAL/BALLOON** payment of $ _____ to pay off the loan in full.

NOTICE TO BORROWER: IF YOU DO NOT HAVE THE FUNDS TO PAY THE BALLOON PAYMENT WHEN IT COMES DUE, YOU MAY HAVE TO OBTAIN A NEW LOAN AGAINST YOUR PROPERTY TO MAKE THE BALLOON PAYMENT. IN THAT CASE, YOU MAY AGAIN HAVE TO PAY COMMISSIONS, FEES AND EXPENSES FOR THE ARRANGING OF THE NEW LOAN. IN ADDITION, IF YOU ARE UNABLE TO MAKE THE MONTHLY PAYMENTS OR THE BALLOON PAYMENT, YOU MAY LOSE THE PROPERTY AND ALL OF YOUR EQUITY THROUGH FORECLOSURE. KEEP THIS IN MIND IN DECIDING UPON THE AMOUNT AND TERMS OF THIS LOAN.

B. This loan will be evidenced by a promissory note and secured by a deed of trust on property identified as (street address or legal description):
_____
_____

C. 1. Liens presently against this property (do not include loan being applied for):

Nature of Lien	Priority	Leinholder's Name	Amount Owing
_____	_____	_____	_____
_____	_____	_____	_____
_____	_____	_____	_____

   2. Liens that will remain against this property after the loan being applied for is made or arranged (including loan being applied for):

Nature of Lien	Priority	Leinholder's Name	Amount Owing
_____	_____	_____	_____
_____	_____	_____	_____
_____	_____	_____	_____

NOTICE TO BORROWER: Be sure that you state the amount of all liens as accurately as possible. If you contract with the broker to arrange this loan, but it cannot be arranged because you did not state these liens correctly, you may be liable to pay commissions, fees and expenses even though you do not obtain the loan.

D. If Borrower pays all or part of the loan principal before it is due, a PREPAYMENT PENALTY computed as follows may be charged:
_____
_____
_____

E. Late Charges: _____ YES, see loan documents _____ NO
F. The purchase of credit life or credit disability insurance by borrower is not required as a condition of making this loan.
G. The real property which will secure the requested loan is an "owner-occupied dwelling." YES _____ NO _____
                (Borrower initial opposite YES or NO)
An "owner-occupied dwelling" means a single dwelling unit in a condominium or cooperative or residential building of four or fewer separate dwelling units, one of which will be owned and occupied by a signatory to the mortgage or deed of trust for this loan within 90 days of the signing of the mortgage or deed of trust.

Borrower hereby acknowledges receipt of copy of this page, which constitutes Page 1 of 2 Pages.
Borrower's Initials (_____) (_____)

THIS FORM HAS BEEN APPROVED BY THE CALIFORNIA ASSOCIATION OF REALTORS® (C.A.R.). NO REPRESENTATION IS MADE AS TO THE LEGAL VALIDITY OR ADEQUACY OF ANY PROVISION IN ANY SPECIFIC TRANSACTION. A REAL ESTATE BROKER IS THE PERSON QUALIFIED TO ADVISE ON REAL ESTATE TRANSACTIONS. IF YOU DESIRE LEGAL OR TAX ADVICE, CONSULT AN APPROPRIATE PROFESSIONAL.

The copyright laws of the United States (17 U.S. Code) forbid the unauthorized reproduction of this form by any means, including facsimile or computerized formats. Copyright © 1991-1997, CALIFORNIA ASSOCIATION OF REALTORS®

Published and Distributed by:
REAL ESTATE BUSINESS SERVICES, INC.
a subsidiary of the CALIFORNIA ASSOCIATION OF REALTORS®
525 South Virgil Avenue, Los Angeles, California 90020

OFFICE USE ONLY
Reviewed by Broker
or Designee _____
Date _____

EQUAL HOUSING OPPORTUNITY

MORTGAGE LOAN DISCLOSURE STATEMENT (BORROWER) (MS-14 PAGE 1 OF 2) REVISED 12/96

FIGURE 9-12

Property Address _____ Date _____

III. DEDUCTIONS FROM LOAN PROCEEDS

A. Estimated Maximum Costs and Expenses of Arranging the Loan to be Paid Out of Loan Principal:

PAYABLE TO

	Broker	Others
1. Appraisal fee	_____	_____
2. Escrow fee	_____	_____
3. Title insurance policy	_____	_____
4. Notary fees	_____	_____
5. Recording fees	_____	_____
6. Credit investigation fees	_____	_____
7. Other costs and expenses:		
_____	_____	_____
_____	_____	_____
_____	_____	_____
Total Costs and Expenses	$ _____	

* B. Compensation. . . . . $ _____
  1. Brokerage Commission/Origination Fee . . . . $ _____
  2. Lender Origination Fee/Discounts. . . . . $ _____

C. Estimated Payment to be Made out of Loan Principal on Authorization of Borrower

PAYABLE TO

	Broker	Others
1. Fire or other hazard insurance premiums	_____	_____
2. Credit life or disability insurance premiums (see Paragraph II-F)	_____	_____
3. Beneficiary statement fees	_____	_____
4. Reconveyance and similar fees.	_____	_____
5. Discharge of existing liens against property:		
_____	_____	_____
_____	_____	_____
6. Other:		
_____	_____	_____
_____	_____	_____
_____	_____	_____
Total to be Paid on Authorization of Borrower	$ _____	

If this loan is secured by a first deed of trust on dwellings in a principal amount of less than $30,000 or secured by a junior lien on dwellings in a principal amount of less than $20,000, the undersigned licensee certifies that the loan will be made in compliance with Article 7 of Chapter 3 of the Real Estate Law.

*This loan **may / will / will not** (delete two) be made wholly or in part from broker-controlled funds as defined in Section 10241(j) of the Business and Professions Code.

*NOTICE TO BORROWER: This disclosure statement may be used if the broker is acting as an agent in arranging the loan by a third person or if the loan will be made with funds owned or controlled by the broker. If the broker indicates in the above statement that the loan "may" be made out of broker-controlled funds, the broker must notify the borrower prior to the close of escrow if the funds to be received by the borrower are in fact broker-controlled funds.

_____		_____
Name of Broker		Broker Representative
_____		_____
License Number		License Number
_____	OR	_____
Signature of Broker		Signature

NOTICE TO BORROWER:

DO NOT SIGN THIS STATEMENT UNTIL YOU HAVE READ AND UNDERSTAND ALL OF THE INFORMATION IN IT. ALL PARTS OF THE FORM MUST BE COMPLETED BEFORE YOU SIGN.

Borrower hereby acknowledges the receipt of a copy of this statement.

DATED: _____ _____
                                                          (Borrower)

                                             _____
                                                          (Borrower)

OFFICE USE ONLY
Reviewed by Broker
or Designee _____
Date _____

Page 2 of 2 Pages.

MORTGAGE LOAN DISCLOSURE STATEMENT (BORROWER) (MS-14 PAGE 2 OF 2) REVISED 12/96

Loans on owner-occupied homes negotiated by brokers for a term of six years or less may not have a balloon payment. If nonowner occupied, loans are exempt from balloon payments when the term is less than three years. Neither of these restrictions apply to transactions where the seller extends credit to the buyer. When such transactions have balloon payments, the seller is obligated to notify the buyer 60 to 150 days before the payment is due. Also, the broker is obligated to inform the buyer regarding the likelihood of obtaining new financing.

THRESHOLD REPORTING (BIG LENDING - $2,000,000)

THRESHOLD REPORTING is the requirement of reporting annual and quarterly loan activity (review of trust fund) to the Department of Real Estate if, within the past 12 months, the broker has negotiated any combination of 20 or more loans to a subdivision or a total of more than $2,000,000 in loans. In addition, advertising must be submitted to the DRE for review. This regulation is intended to protect the public by over-seeing the loan activity of big lenders who are using their real estate broker's licenses.

ARTICLE 5

BROKER RESTRICTIONS

The licensee is prohibited from pooling funds. A broker may not accept funds except for a specifically identified loan transaction. Before accepting a lender's money, the broker must:

1. Own the loan or have an unconditional written contract to purchase a specific note

2. Have the authorization from a prospective borrower to negotiate a secured loan.

ARTICLE 6

REAL PROPERTY SECURITIES DEALER

DRE broker's license and endorsement are required. A $100 fee plus a $10,000 surety bond. DRE permit is required to sell specific security.

No real estate investment type security shall be sold to the public without first obtaining a permit from the commissioner. A ***COMMISSIONER'S PERMIT*** *is the approval of the proposed real property security and plan of distribution.* If, in the commissioner's opinion, the security and proposed plan of distribution is fair, just and equitable, he or she will authorize the sale, subject to any limiting conditions. A permit is not an endorsement or recommendation of the security, it is only a permit to sell. The application for the permit is extensive, and may require supplementary filings. The duration of the permit is one year, and the permit may not be used in advertising unless it is used in its entirety.

A commissioner's permit requires a $10,000 bond.

REAL PROPERTY SECURITIES DEALER ENDORSEMENT

A ***REAL PROPERTY SECURITIES DEALER (RPSD)*** *is any person acting as principal or agent who engages in the business of selling real property securities (such as promissory notes or sales contracts).* RPSD dealers also accept, or offer to accept, funds for reinvestment in real property securities or for placement in a account. Before a licensed real estate broker may act in this capacity, he or she must obtain an RPSD endorsement on his or her broker's license. To obtain an RPSD endorsement on a broker's license, submit the appropriate endorsement fee ($100) along with proof of a properly executed $10,000 surety bond. (For information on Real Property Securities, call the DRE.)

EDITOR'S UPDATE: As of the latest printing of this text, Article 6, Real Property Securities Dealers, Commissioner's permits, and endorsements are no longer under the jurisdiction of the DRE, but the Department of Corporations.

"Equity Sharing"
A different financing and ownership idea

EQUITY SHARING (SHARED EQUITY FINANCING) is a contractual arrangement whereby an investor shares any equity gain with a homeowner. Since California has high housing costs that require a large down payment, many potential homeowners cannot qualify or do not have the cash for a down payment. The concept is that an investor puts up most of the down payment, receives no interest deductions but shares in any equity gain when the property is sold. The homeowner gets his or her home quickly with a minimum down payment, with relaxed credit and with full income tax write-offs. Consult an attorney or CPA before investing.

A. Federal Reserve (Fed) system
B. Federal Reserve Board
C. Gross Domestic Product (GDP)
D. Collateral
E. Institutional Lenders
F. Noninstitutional Lenders
G. Conventional Loan
H. FDIC
I. Soft Money Financing

J. Seller's Market
K. Credit Union
L. Mortgage Companies
M. Mortgage Banker
N. CAL-VET Loans
O. Equity Investment Trust
P. Mortgage Investment Trust
Q. Private Mortgage Insurance (PMI)
R. Minimum Property Requirements (MPRs)

S. VA Loan
T. Certificate of Reasonable Value (CRV)
U. California Housing Finance Agency (CHFA)
V. Fannie Mae
W. Ginnie Mae
X. Freddie Mac
Y. Mortgage Loan Disclosure Statement
Z. Buyer's Market

1.____ A company providing mortgage financing with its own funds rather than simply bringing together lender and borrower, as does a mortgage broker. The mortgages are sold to investors within a short time.

2.____ (FHLMC) Federal Home Loan Mortgage Corporation. A federal Agency purchasing first mortgages, both conventional and federally insured, from members of the Federal Reserve System.

3.____ A company authorized to service real estate loans, charging a fee for this service.

4.____ The federal corporation that insures against loss of deposits in banks, up to a maximum amount (currently $100,000).

5.____ Insurance issued by a private insurance company against a loss by a lender in the event of default by a borrower (mortgagor). The premium is paid by the borrower and is included in the mortgage payment.

6.____ Loans made under a land contract directly from the California Department of Veterans Affairs, which has its own specific qualifications.

7.____ A mortgage or deed of trust not obtained under a government insured or guaranteed program.

8.____ The money value of all goods and services produced by a nation's economy for a given period of time.

9.____ Government National Mortgage Association: A federal corporation, working with the FHA, which offers special assistance in obtaining mortgages, and purchases mortgages in the secondary market.

10.____ Banks, savings banks loan associations, and other businesses which make loans to the public in the ordinary course of business, rather than individuals, or companies which may make loans to employees.

11.____ Housing loans to veterans by banks, savings banks, or other lenders that are guaranteed by the Veteran's Administration, enabling veterans to buy a residence with little or no down payment.

12.____ A private corporation that acts as a secondary market for the purchase of existing first mortgages, at a discount.

13.____ The central banking system that controls the amount of money and the rate of interest in the United States.

14.____ The powerful seven-member banking panel which controls the destiny of the United States' monetary system. Along with the President of the United States, the Chairman is one of the most powerful positions in the country.

15.____ A form that California law requires be given to the borrower, breaking down all the costs and fees of securing out a loan.

16.____ An agency, sponsored by the state of California, which sponsors special housing projects and certain types of loans.

17.____ The real estate pledged to back up a loan. The value of the real estate should be worth substantially more than the loan amount.

18.____ Smaller lenders such as sellers, credit unions and pension plans that lend money on real estate.

19.____ An appraisal document stating the fair market value of real estate under a VA loan.

20.____ The minimal property standards for a property to qualify for an FHA loan.

21.____ A loan made by the seller to the buyer as part of the purchase transaction.

22.____ A market condition favoring the seller, when fewer homes are for sale than there are interested buyers.

23.____ A trust company specializing in making mortgages as an investment.

24.____ A trust company that specializes in taking an ownership position in other projects.

25.____ A market condition favoring the buyer, when more homes are for sale than there are interested buyers.

26.____ An organization whose members have a common bond of occupation. Considered a growing source of real estate funds.

MULTIPLE CHOICE

1. Which of the following would NOT be considered institutional lenders?

    A. Savings Banks
    C. Life insurance companies

    B. Banks
    D. Credit Unions

2. A corporation, or an unincorporated association of 100 or more real estate investors, that serves as a conduit for its investors is called a:

    A. pension plan
    C. real estate investment trust (REIT)

    B. mortgage company
    D. credit union

3. The central banking system for the United States is the:

    A. United Banks
    C. U.S. Banking Reserve

    B. Federal Reserve
    D. California Banking System

4. Which is NOT a government-backed loan?

    A. FHA
    C. APR

    B. VA
    D. CAL-VET

5. To be eligible for a VA loan, a veteran must have served how much time on active duty?

    A. 91 days
    C. 1 year

    B. 181 days
    D. 2 years

6. Which of the following is NOT a government lending corporation?

    A. Fannie Mae
    C. Big Mac

    B. Ginnie Mae
    D. Freddie Mac

7. If a real estate licensee negotiates a loan, he or she must give a Mortgage Loan Disclosure Statement to the:

    A. seller
    C. lender

    B. borrower
    D. none of the above

8. No real estate investment type security (like stock market securities) shall be sold without first obtaining a permit from the DRE commissioner. A commissioner's permit requires a:

    A. broker license endorsement
    C. $10,000 surety bond

    B. $100 fee
    D. all of the above

9. The total value of all goods and services produced by the U.S. during a specific period of time is called the:

    A. GDP
    C. FSLIC

    B. federal reserve
    D. FDIC

10. Why do buyers prefer FHA and VA loans?

    A. Low down payment
    C. No prepayment penalty

    B. Low interest rates
    D. All of the above

CHAPTER 10
Appraisal Basics

In California, appraisers for federally insured (regulated) lending institutions must be licensed by the Office of Real Estate Appraisers. In effect, all appraisers must be licensed.

http://www.appraisalfoundation.org (The Appraisal Foundation)
http://www.orea.cahwnet.gov (California Office of Real Estate Appraisers)

WHAT IS AN APPRAISAL?

An *APPRAISAL is an opinion as to the value of a particular property at a given date.* One of the most important factors for you to consider in deciding whether to sell or buy a home, or any specific piece of real estate, is its selling price. Each parcel of land (and the buildings on it) is unique. No two are exactly alike, so prices vary. The *MARKET PRICE (SELLING PRICE) is the total price, including down payment and financing, that a property actually brought when sold.* Market price is what it sold for, whereas market value is what it should have sold for in a competitive market.

> *An appraisal is an estimate or opinion of value (based on judgment and professional experience) for a specific property as of a certain date.*

The market value is what the property is actually worth. *MARKET VALUE is the price that a willing buyer will pay and a willing seller accept, both being fully informed and with the sale property exposed for a reasonable period.* The courtroom definition is even more technical:

"The highest price, estimated in terms of money, that a property will bring if it is exposed for sale in the open market, allowing a reasonable length of time to find a buyer who buys with full knowledge of all the uses to which it is adapted and for which the property is capable of being used."

Current market value is not affected in any way by the original cost of the property. The market value of a particular property is an **opinion** or **estimate** of worth, by an appraiser, based on analysis of actual and relevant data, as of a given date. Appraisers must have the required experience, education and have passed one of the three California State Appraisal Exams. See end of Chapter 11.

FOUR ESSENTIAL ELEMENTS OF VALUE

VALUE is a relationship between the thing desired and a potential purchaser. Four elements must be present to create and maintain value. The **four essential elements of value** are:

D 1) **Demand** — the desire, need and ability to purchase
U 2) **Utility** — usefulness; ability to instill a desire for possession
S 3) **Scarcity** — in short supply, usually more expensive
T 4) **Transferability** — can change ownership, as with a deed.

Cost is NOT an element of value.

THE APPRAISAL PROCESS
(FOUR LOGICAL STEPS)

An appraisal is the solution to the problem of determining value. To solve this problem an orderly procedure has been developed; it is called the appraisal process. The *APPRAISAL PROCESS is an orderly program by which the problem is defined, the work is planned, the data is gathered, analyzed and correlated to estimate the value.* Although the characteristics of real property differ, this is an orderly procedure for solving any appraisal problem. See Figure 10-1.

The appraisal process consists of four logical steps:

1. Defining and clarifying the problem (Chapter 10)
2. Gathering the data (Chapter 10)
3. Performing the three appraisal methods (Chapter 11)
4. Correlating the three methods and determining the final estimate of value. (Chapter 11)

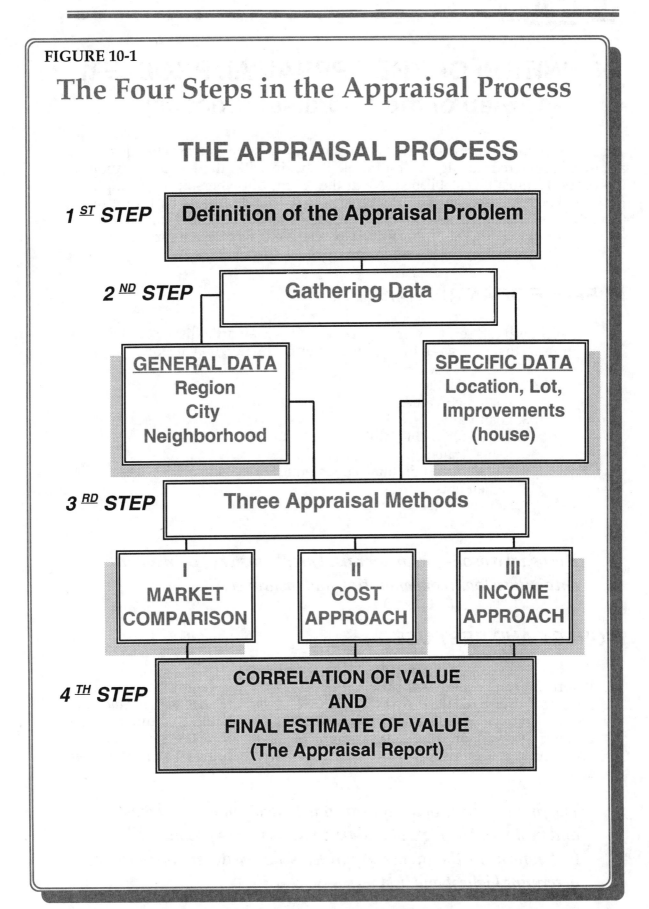

FIGURE 10-1

The Four Steps in the Appraisal Process

THE APPRAISAL PROCESS

1 ST STEP — **Definition of the Appraisal Problem**

2 ND STEP — **Gathering Data**

GENERAL DATA
Region
City
Neighborhood

SPECIFIC DATA
Location, Lot,
Improvements
(house)

3 RD STEP — **Three Appraisal Methods**

I	II	III
MARKET COMPARISON	COST APPROACH	INCOME APPROACH

4 TH STEP — **CORRELATION OF VALUE AND FINAL ESTIMATE OF VALUE (The Appraisal Report)**

Chapter 10

DEFINITION OF THE APPRAISAL PROBLEM
(1ˢᵗ Step of the Appraisal Process)

The first step in the appraisal process must include a definition of what questions are to be answered during the appraisal. To begin with, the precise location of the property must be established. Next, the extent of ownership (fee simple or partial) to be appraised must be identified. The date and purpose of the appraisal (usually to establish market value) is then determined. Any limiting conditions (facts unknown to the appraiser) must be clarified. Finally, the appraiser will determine the fee for his or her services.

PURPOSE OF AN APPRAISAL

An appraisal can serve several purposes. Here is a partial list of the kinds of appraisals that you, as an owner, or a potential owner, may need:

1. Market Value
2. Insurance Value
3. Loan Value
4. Tax Assessment Value
5. Rental Value
6. Value for certain Internal Revenue Service Purposes
7. Settlements
8. Salvage Value
9. Other

The usual reasons for an appraisal are: Transfer of ownership, obtaining a loan, condemnation and insurance.

HIGHEST AND BEST USE

Before we can properly appraise a property, we must determine its highest and best use. *HIGHEST AND BEST USE is the use that will produce the maximum amount of profit or net return.* For example, should we build a house or an apartment on an available piece of land? From the standpoint of economics, it would be best to build that which brings the highest net return.

The first objective of an appraisal is to determine the highest and best use. The highest and best use increases productivity (net return) to the owner. Appraisers do a site analysis to determine highest and best use.

GATHERING DATA
(2<u>nd</u> Step of the Appraisal Process)

There are logical reasons why one home is worth more than another that appears comparable, and why the choice of a neighborhood is as important, or even more important, than the house itself. There are also differences in location within a neighborhood that must be taken into account. Differences in the actual building construction must also be considered. The background information needed for real estate appraisal is very broad, but there is a simple, sensible way to make a wise decision about buying a home or investment property. Start with the largest aspects and work toward the details. Look at:

A. GENERAL DATA

> 1. REGION
> 2. CITY
> 3. NEIGHBORHOOD

B. SPECIFIC DATA (site analysis)

> 4. LOCATION
> 5. LOT
> 6. IMPROVEMENTS (HOUSE)

GENERAL DATA
(Region, City, Neighborhood)

The gathering of general data (regional, city or county and neighborhood information) allows us to understand whether the area is prospering, holding its own or declining and, if so, why.

REGION (A STATE IS DIVIDED INTO REGIONS)

> *A state can be divided into economic regions for analysis purposes. Example: San Diego, Los Angeles, Fresno, San Francisco, Sacramento and Northern California.*

The condition of the nation's economy can be reflected in the California real estate market and can affect the ease with which financing is available. But real estate markets are essentially regional and local. If the regional or local economy is expanding, people are working and can afford to buy homes because lending institutions are eager to grant loans. In a recession, jobs are less secure, confidence is low and financing may not be as easy to obtain. So, the economic mood of the nation as a whole can indirectly affect the economic mood in California, but it is the local and regional economy that directly affects the mood in a particular real estate market.

A regional economy is affected by upturns and also downtrends. Not only do large areas reflect the national picture, but they also respond to more localized forces, such as the rapid growth of large cities and industrial complexes and the down-sizing of defense-related industries or even the weather in agricultural areas. California is divided into north and south regions and many sub-regions and cities.

California, like most large states, is a very geographically diverse state. Geographical considerations can easily affect an entire region. For example, if an area has snow for eight months of the year the value of the property may be reduced when compared to regions that have year-round moderate or sunny climates.

CITY (OR COUNTY)

A desirable city or county is a growing area where people can get good jobs and where people want to live. If the city is undesirable or even unsafe, people want to leave. Features to look for in cities, besides the availability of work and safety, are good public facilities, parks, good school systems and active citizens who care and take part in the city's affairs.

NEIGHBORHOOD

The neighborhood where you want to buy is more important than the house because it is desirability of the area that sets value. An individual can change the appearance of his or her house but he or she alone cannot change the appearance of the neighborhood.

A *RESIDENTIAL NEIGHBORHOOD is normally a limited area where the homes are physically similar and where the occupants have a certain degree of social and economic background in common.* It may cover a few square miles or it may be only one block square. Boundaries may be defined by physical, social or economic differences. The important thing is that your neighborhood is the environment in which you live day-in and day-out. THE NEIGHBORHOOD IN WHICH YOU LIVE IS USUALLY A MORE IMPORTANT FACTOR THAN THE HOUSE ITSELF! This is because the surroundings of a house influence the property value even more than the house itself does.

Neighborhoods influence homeowners' location decisions more than renters'. The reason is that many people rent apartments in neighborhoods in which they would never think of buying, because they plan to stay there for only a short time. Renters may rent in a less desirable area, but when they buy they will select a neighborhood they like.

A neighborhood has similar physical structures based on common social, economic and political characteristics of the people. Owner-occupied homes lend economic stability to a neighborhood and lessen the possibility of turnover.

The selection or acceptance of a neighborhood should come before the actual decision of whether to buy a particular house or not. The four primary forces that affect value of a neighborhood are shown in Figure 10-2.

Neighborhoods are always changing, sometimes at a fast pace, but usually at a slow, steady pace. The four considerations we will discuss can change a prestigious area to a shabby neighborhood or vice versa. Each consideration can change the outlook for any neighborhood.

FIGURE 10-2

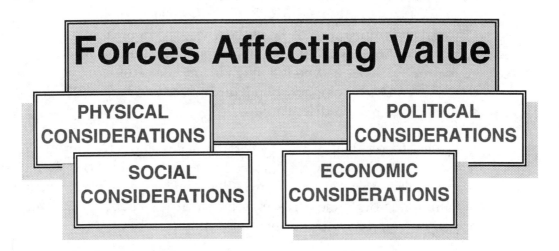

The four forces affecting value are: physical, social, economic and political considerations.

PHYSICAL CONSIDERATIONS

A neighborhood that is close to a commercial area is generally highly desirable. Being close to downtown areas, employment centers and major shopping areas only adds to this desirability, as long as an owner is not located right next to such a facility. If the street patterns are curved and there are wide boulevards, the neighborhood also looks more attractive.

Access to transportation is necessary. The availability of freeways, transit systems and convenient parking is an important consideration in making comparisons between various areas. However, this factor is less important in high value suburban areas where estate living is desirable.

Balanced Land Use

The best efficiency and highest value come when there is a balance between different types of use. A city is a naturally attractive environment when it has a proper balance between residential, commercial, industrial and recreational space.

Families are attracted to a neighborhood with good schools. Certain private or parochial schools may create a demand for homes in that area. Churches are also a definite benefit. Other institutions such as libraries, colleges and universities may also enhance a community.

The first trip into a neighborhood may be impressive, or, on the other hand, it may be depressing. First impressions are important: the landscaping, architectural style and the streets can create either impression. Well-maintained buildings show pride of ownership and suggest a positive character of the residents in that area.

Physical conditions such as lakes, beaches, rivers or hilly areas may be either advantageous or disadvantageous depending on where they are. A feature such as a wooded hillside or lake front property would probably enhance a neighborhood, but a river that frequently floods the surrounding area is a disadvantage.

Invasion of a residential area by commercial or industrial usage around it is usually a disadvantage, especially if the neighborhood is exposed to noise or odors. A bar located across from a home is usually a devaluing factor. Some areas may be hazardous because of landslides or simply from heavy truck and auto traffic.

SOCIAL CONSIDERATIONS

The social characteristics of a neighborhood may influence its value more than any other consideration. If the people there are happy living around each other, then it is a harmonious neighborhood. It is then the proper setting for a person or family with similar characteristics. Race, religion, income, education, cultural background and lifestyle may influence the compatibility of the neighborhood.

Negative social changes usually begin with a few sales to people of different backgrounds. As a result of this, older residents usually flood the market with homes for sale, which depresses selling prices. These depressed prices attract more newcomers until there is a general shift in ownership. At this point prices usually start to firm up and advance again.

"Blight" occurs when a neighborhood is only partially developed. Poor upkeep, gangs and divergent uses of property are difficult to restrict or control.

ECONOMIC CONSIDERATIONS

Population growth is an indication of the economic health of a neighborhood. If more people want to live in an area, then it must be desirable: an economically alive neighborhood has well-maintained lawns and buildings, whereas in a deteriorating neighborhood the lack of maintenance is obvious and so is the lowered value of the homes.

The rents charged and income levels of the people indicate a community's prestige (or lack of it). The larger the percentage of home ownership versus those renting, the more economically stable the area is. If many rentals are vacant, you can surmise that renters are disinterested in the area. New construction, on the other hand, indicates that the area is growing and its value is increasing.

POLITICAL CONSIDERATIONS

Property tax rates vary from area-to-area. Wealthy, more stable economic areas usually have a slightly higher tax rate because the residents are willing and have the ability to pay for more public services. In areas where the taxes are very high, potential buyers are often scared off. Special assessments for lighting, sewers and street improvements may temporarily turn some people away, but they generally add to the property's total value.

Some cities use **zoning and building codes** as devices to insure the continued stability of a neighborhood. If the desirability of the neighborhood warrants such regulation, then the city will continue to be a growing one. In the end, most city leaders politically control changes in their cities by enacting zoning and building codes.

SPECIFIC DATA (Property Itself)

The most important economic characteristic is area preference (location).

There is plenty of land in the world, but the exact location of each parcel makes it unlike any other on earth. Its location is the major factor that determines its value.

LOCATION

A low-income buyer would choose location as the prime factor in selecting a home: it would have an important impact on transportation problems and costs of getting to work.

A **SITE** *is a particular parcel within a neighborhood.* Since each parcel is unique, the individual site that one selects for a home should be chosen with care. There are several site selection factors that affect the value of the home, but the personal needs and objectives of the buyer should be of the utmost concern.

Site: the location of a plot of ground for a building.

LOT (TYPES)

There are six major types (See Figure 10-3) of lots:

1. **Cul-de-sac (Lot A)**

2. **Corner (Lot B)**

3. **Key (Lot C)**

4. **T-Intersection (Lot D)**

5. **Interior (Lot E)**

6. **Flag (Lot F)**

Cul-De-Sac Lot

The **CUL-DE-SAC LOT** *is a lot facing the turnaround portion of a dead-end street.* Figure 10-3 shows that Lot A is a cul-de-sac. The main advantage of a cul-de-sac lot is privacy and lack of traffic one gets by living on a "not a through" street. Due to its pie-shaped design, it has the disadvantage of a small front yard, but this is offset by generally having a large backyard. The design makes it more secluded and limits through traffic from both autos and pedestrians. Limited parking and front yard space does not stop it from rivaling the corner lot as one of the most desirable types of lots. A cul-de-sac lot's desirability may vary due to view, size, area and family characteristics. Figure 10-3, Lot A, Cul-de-sac.

FIGURE 10-3

Corner Lot

The **CORNER LOT** *is a lot that is located at the intersection of two streets.* A corner site frequently has a higher value than a lot fronting only on one street. Figure 10-3, Lot B, Corner. The appraiser must be careful to look at the local market in determining the actual effects of a corner influence on the surrounding lots. **CORNER INFLUENCE** *is the theory that a variety of forces affect corner lots (and also lots located near a corner) to a greater degree than most other lots.* A corner lot is generally more desirable if there is access to the backyard for items such as a trailer or camper. Other people like it because there are fewer homes nearby, which allows for more light, fresh air and also more lot area for gardens and other types of landscaping.

The main disadvantage of a corner lot is the loss of privacy and higher cost, since both sides of the lot require off-site improvements, such as streets, curbs, gutters and sidewalks. Also, zoning setbacks may reduce the buildable lot space. Usually commercial corner lots benefit because of easy access and added traffic exposure.

Chapter 10

Key Lot

Usually the least desirable lot because it has so many adjunct neighbors; it is bordered by more than three lots.

KEY LOT is a lot that is bordered on the side by the back of other lots that front on another street. Key lots are the least desirable lots because of the lack of privacy caused by the close proximity of several neighbors abutting the side of the property. Figure 10-3, Lot C, Key.

T-Intersection Lot

The *T-INTERSECTION LOT is an interior lot that is faced head-on by a street; it is the lot at the end of a dead-end street.* The streets form a "T" shape. It is an interior lot with one advantage and two disadvantages. The advantage is a clear view down the street, which gives a more spacious feeling. Intersection noise and annoying headlights at night are its disadvantages. Figure 10-3, Lot D, T-Intersection.

Interior Lot

An *INTERIOR LOT is a lot generally surrounded by other lots on three sides.* It is usually in the shape of a rectangle, but can be almost any shape. It is the most common type of lot and it is preferred by most people. Interior lots have larger backyards than corner lots, which make them much better for recreational purposes. Since the front yards are smaller than those found on corner lots, they require less yard maintenance and benefit from less intersection noise. Because of typical long block design, interior lots are by far the most numerous. The disadvantages are limited backyard access and three or more adjoining neighbors. Figure 10-3, Lot E, Interior.

Flag Lot

A *FLAG LOT is a rear lot, in back of other lots, with a long, narrow access driveway.* This type of lot takes on the shape a flag. The flag lot's shape allows for a maximum of privacy and can be easily gated. In hilly areas, flag lots have some of the better views, while others can be pushed up against a steep mountain side. The value of a flag lot verses other types of lots depends on the circumstances. The same can be said about all other types of lots: their value depends on the specifics of each lot and the local market conditions. But it is up to the salesperson to gain a working knowledge of lot shapes and the pluses and minuses attributed to each type of lot. Figure 10-3, Lot F, Flag.

PHYSICAL ASPECTS OF A LOT

The major physical aspects of the actual site are:

1. Size and shape
2. Slope, drainage and soil (lot design layouts)
3. View, exposure to sun and weather
4. Improvements (on-site and off-site)

Size And Shape Of Lot

Lots or parcels can be subdivided into almost any shape imaginable, but most lots are rectangular and front onto a street. Any lot is valuable if it offers enough area to build a house that is compatible with the surroundings. In general, the more land or frontage on the street, the higher the value of the land. An example of a depth table will explain this concept. A *DEPTH TABLE is a percentage table that illustrates how the highest value is located in the front part of a lot.* Figure 10-4 is an example of the "4-3-2-1" depth table.

FIGURE 10-4

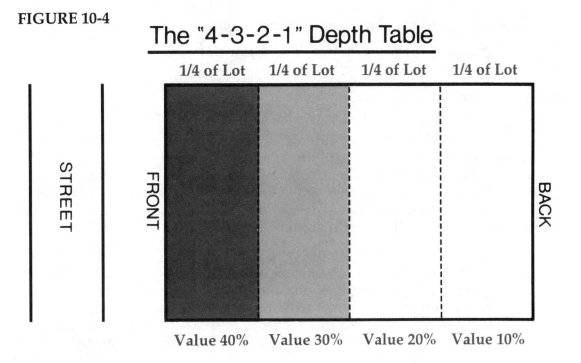

The "4-3-2-1" Depth Table

| 1/4 of Lot | 1/4 of Lot | 1/4 of Lot | 1/4 of Lot |

STREET   FRONT   BACK

| Value 40% | Value 30% | Value 20% | Value 10% |

The "4-3-2-1 rule" is best used by appraisers to determine the value of commercial properties on which the lots vary in depth.

The percentage of value for each 1/4 or 25% section of the lot varies: 40%, 30%, 20% to 10% in value for each quarter back from the front.

In Figure 10-4, the highest value is in the front portion of the lot. For example, a small backyard will not affect the value of the property as much as a small front yard. This is especially true with commercial property such as shopping centers, where there is plenty of parking in the back, but most people prefer to park in the front. Remember, though, that the percentage and values of a depth table vary from property to property.

> *Front footage is a pricing tool mostly used to sell commercial property.*

Since the front portion of the lot has the most value, the more frontage there is, the better. **FRONT FOOTAGE** *is the width of the property in the front, along the street.* Generally speaking we can say that a house with a large front yard is worth more than the same house with a large backyard. But people do have different preferences, such as large backyards for swimming pools, tennis courts or other recreational activities.

> *Plottage brings under single ownership two or more contiguous lots, previously owned separately.*

Lot Design Layouts

There are several ways to lay out lots in a parcel of land being subdivided. Zoning regulations usually state the minimum amount of square feet a lot can have, but a developer can get better prices if he or she divides the land wisely. Figures 10-5 and 10-6 show the same parcel of land twice. Plan 1 is a good design, giving a variety of desirable lots. Plan 2 is a poor design, giving too little variation, too little front area and too much depth.

The layout of lots in a large subdivision is illustrated in Figure 10-7. Often a subdivision tract with fewer, well-planned lots will bring a higher total sales price than a poorly designed tract with more lots. The best tract layout is the one that considers all the costs involved and the marketability of all the lots. This kind of planning is not easy and requires the services of a specialist.

Slope, Drainage And Soil

The slope of a lot will lower its value if it will be costly to improve. A lot that is higher or lower in relation to the street level may be costly to improve because of possible slope and drainage problems. Erosion may also be a part of slope or drainage problems. These problems, however, can be easily offset by an excellent view or location.

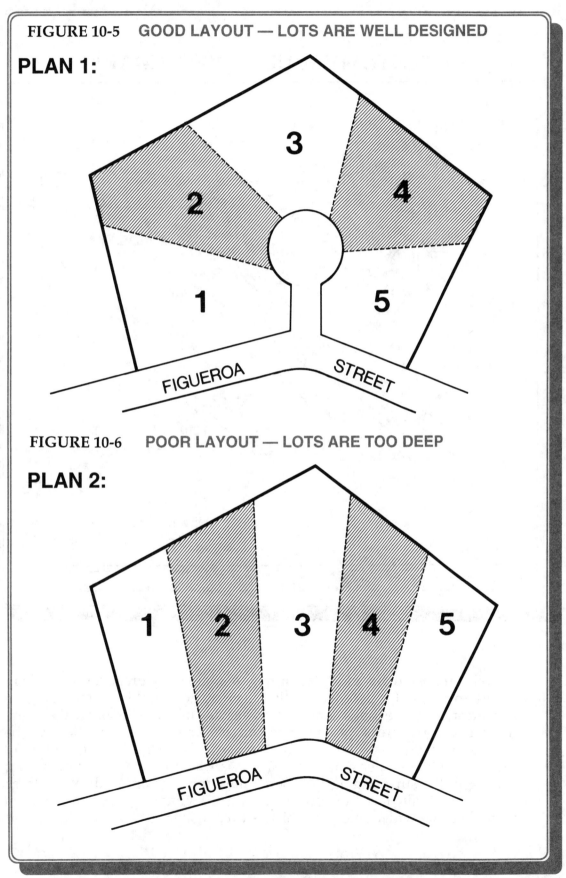

FIGURE 10-5   GOOD LAYOUT — LOTS ARE WELL DESIGNED

PLAN 1:

FIGUEROA   STREET

FIGURE 10-6   POOR LAYOUT — LOTS ARE TOO DEEP

PLAN 2:

FIGUEROA   STREET

FIGURE 10-7

TENTATIVE SUBDIVISION MAP

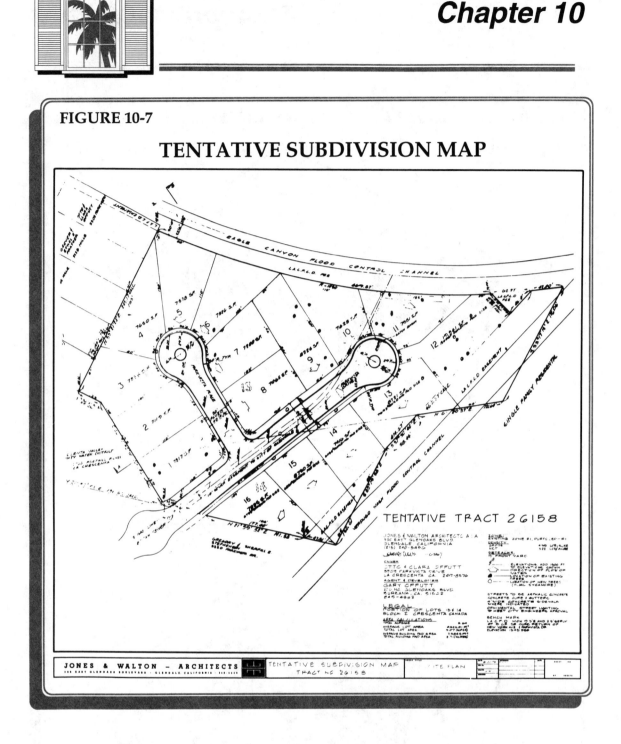

The soil composition of a lot may or may not be of any great concern. There are certain types of soil, however, that may create a problem depending on your lifestyle or possible construction needs. In some regions there are certain peat moss areas that must be corrected before a foundation can be poured. In other areas the soil content can destroy a pipeline within 10 years. If you like gardens and plant life, it is wise to see how the plants are growing in the surrounding lots. Some hillside tracts are built on bedrock covered by a thin layer of topsoil; to dig a swimming pool might even require blasting with dynamite, which is very costly.

View, Exposure To Sun And Weather
(Orientation)

> *The south and west sides of streets are preferred by merchants: pedestrians seek the shady side and displayed merchandise is not damaged by the sun.*

Most people appreciate a good view from their homes: it is pleasant to sit back and enjoy the beautiful surroundings. In a new tract of homes, the lots with the best views usually sell first and apartments with views rent for more. Places like Nob Hill (in San Francisco), Lake Tahoe and La Jolla are examples of areas that are expensive because of their beautiful views.

ORIENTATION is planning the most advantageous place on a parcel of land for an improvement to be located. The exposure of a house to the sun and weather elements may influence a person's decision to buy a house. If the wind usually blows from the northwest, it is best for the house to face the northwest. In this case the house can be a shield for backyard entertaining. The exposure to the sun is a different matter. Most people prefer the sun to shine on their backyard, so the backyard should face the south or the west. In this way the backyard receives the best exposure throughout the day. In windy areas on the coast, sheltered patios, away from cold sea breezes, are desirable.

Amenity properties are usually single-family residences. *AMENITIES are those improvements or views that increase the desirability or enjoyment rather than the necessities of the residents.* For example, a view of the ocean, mountains or city lights at night increase the value of a home. Amenity improvements would include: Jacuzzis, swimming pools and tennis courts.

IMPROVEMENTS

Real estate is logically divided into land (site) and improvements. *IMPROVEMENTS are any buildings, walkways, pools and other structures. CAPITAL IMPROVEMENTS are permanent improvements made to increase the useful life of the property or increase the property's value.* These include off-site improvements (streets and utilities) and on-site improvements (buildings). *OFF-SITE IMPROVEMENTS are the improvements made to areas adjoining the parcel that add to the parcel's usefulness and sometimes its value.* Examples of off-site improvements are: streets, street lights, sewers, sidewalks, curbs and gutters. These items generally add value to urban property but may be of little value in rural areas. Off-site improvements are usually paid for by the homeowners through the levying of special assessments. On the other hand, *ON-SITE IMPROVEMENTS are structures erected permanently for use on a site, such as buildings and fences.* Figure 10-8 is a diagram of a house.

FIGURE 10-8

1. Open Sheathing
2. Building Paper
3. Flashing
4. Rafters
20. Ridge Board
19. Joists
18. Bracing
19. Joists
17. Studs
16. Fire Stop
15. Header
14. Sole Plate
13. Anchor Bolt
12. Footing
11. Foundation
10. Crawl Space
9. Mud Sill
8. Sill
7. Cripple
6. Closed Sheathing
2. Building Paper
5. Eave

EXPLANATION OF DIAGRAM DETAILS

1. Open Sheathing	Boards nailed to rafters as foundation for the roof covering. Open sheathing is used with wood shingles.
2. Building Paper	Heavy waterproof paper used between sheathing and roof covering or siding.
3. Flashing	Sheet metal used to protect against water seepage.
4. Rafters	Sloping members of a roof used to support the roof boards and shingles (Maximum 24″ apart).
5. Eave	Protruding underpart of roof overhanging exterior walls.
6. Closed Sheathing	Boards nailed to studding as foundation for exterior siding. "Closed" means butted together.
7. Cripple	Stud above or below a window opening or above a doorway.
8. Sill	Bottom portion lining doorway or window.
9. Mud Sill	Treated lumber (or redwood) bolted to the foundation.
10. Crawl Space	Unexcavated area under the house (Min. 18″).
11. Foundation	Concrete base of house.
12. Footing	Expanded portion of concrete foundation.
13. Anchor Bolt	Large bolt used for fastening mud sill to foundation. Bolt is anchored into concrete foundation.
14. Sole Plate	Support on which the studs rest.
15. Header	The beam over a doorway or window.
16. Fire Stop	Blocking used to restrict flames from spreading to attic. May be placed horizontally or diagonally.
17. Studs	Vertical 2″ x 4″ framework in the walls spaced 16″ on center.
18. Bracing	Board running diagonally across the wall framing to prevent sway.
19. Joists	Structural parts supporting floor or ceiling loads. A beam which supports them would be called a girder.
20. Ridge Board	Highest point of construction in a frame building.

HOUSE STRUCTURE ILLUSTRATED

This section identifies different parts of a house. Figure 10-8 was a diagram of a house that illustrates the 20 most used construction terms. Figure 10-9 shows roof types. Each part is labeled and defined so that it can be identified. Figure 10-10 lists construction and other terms.

http://www.nahb.com (National association of Home builders)

ROOF TYPES

Before purchasing a house, a potential buyer should carefully evaluate the structure, checking to see that its style of architecture is compatible with that of the surrounding neighborhood. This should also be an element of consideration when building a new house or remodeling.

Examining the type of roof, the way it is framed and finished, is one of the simplest ways to assess the architectural compatibility of a given house.

Pictured below are several of the most common roof types. One is likely to see examples of hip, gambrel, flat, gable, mansard and pyramid roofs throughout California.

FLAT   GABLE   HIP

GAMBREL   MANSARD   PYRAMID

FIGURE 10-10

Construction and other terms

Backfill — The replacement of excavated earth against a structure (wall).

Bearing Wall — A strong wall supporting any vertical load in addition to its own weight, usually a roof or floor above.

Boardfoot — A unit quantity for lumber equal to the volume of a board 12 x 12 x 1 inches.

BTU (British Thermal Unit) — A unit of measurement used to calculate heat - the quantity of heat required to raise one pound of water one degree Fahrenheit.

Capital Assets — Expenditures of a permanent nature that increase property values. Examples: buildings and street improvements.

Cash Flow — In investment property, the actual cash the investor will receive after deduction of operating expenses and debt servicing (loan payment) from his or her gross income.

Conduit — A flexible metal pipe used to protect the electrical wiring inside.

Dry Wall — Plaster walls that are installed in dry sheets.

EER (Energy Efficiency Ratio) — A measure of energy efficiency; the higher the EER, the higher the efficiency.

Elevation Sheet — A rendering which shows the front and side views of a building; it shows the exterior views.

Foundation Plan — Plan that shows footing, piers and sub-flooring.

H_2O Pressure — Testing water pressure by turning on all faucets and flushing all toilets.

Hoskold Tables — Concept of a "sinking fund" as a compound interest-bearing account, into which the portion of the investment returned each year is reinvested immediately.

CONTINUED

Construction and other terms

Inwood Tables — Concept of using present value of income in a perpetuity table to help appraisers.

Kiosk — An information booth.

Local Building Inspector — Person who enforces construction standards.

Over-Improvement — Is an expenditure to a property that doesn't improve its value.

Percolation Test — A test to determine how well water is absorbed by the soil.

Plot Map — The directional orientation of buildings on a lot.

Potable Water — Drinkable water.

Property Residual, Building Residual and Land Residual — All are methods of working backwards, to find the unknown variable, when appraising property.

R-Value — A measure used to calculate the heat resistance of insulation (the higher the better). Insulation is considered adequate if the temperature on the inside of an exterior wall is the same as the temperature on an interior wall.

Rehabilitation — The restoration of a property to a satisfactory condition without changing the interior or exterior design.

Soil Pipe — A pipe used to carry waste and sewage from a property.

Toxic Waste Report — A report evaluating how harmful the dangerous material is on a property.

Turnkey Project — Built, equipped or installed complete and ready to occupy.

Unearned Increment — An increase in value of real estate due to no effort on the part of the owner; often caused by population increase.

Wainscoting — The wood lining of the lower portion of an interior wall with the upper portion wallpapered or covered with another material different from the lower portion.

HOME WARRANTY PLANS

A warranty plan is a good sales tool. It is usually paid for by the seller and assures the buyer that major repairs for defects will be fixed under the terms of the warranty contract.

A *WARRANTY PLAN is an insurance plan that provides financial protection against defects in any major home construction.* There are a growing number of such warranty plans in California. These warranty plans insure the new owner of an existing home against such things as malfunction of built-in appliances and defects in major systems such as structure, roof, heating, plumbing and electrical wiring. For this protection, the previous owner or the buyer pays a fee that varies according to the type of coverage received. Some companies inspect the property (thereby giving notice of any existing defects). The CAR® deposit receipt informs buyers and sellers that there are warranty plans available. But this item, along with who pays for the warranty plan, is negotiable. Note: All new homes automatically carry a one-year warranty, from the contractor, against labor or material defects.

http://www.bhwc.com (Buyers Home Warranty Company)

BASIC APPRAISAL PRINCIPLES

There are several "principles of appraisal." These principles are valid economic concepts that are applied to the appraisal of real estate. A few of the basic principles are explained so that you can understand the logic and reasons why a particular home is worth more than another. Figure 10-11 shows you six of the basic appraisal principles.

PRINCIPLE OF SUPPLY AND DEMAND

Scarcity is an economic characteristic of real estate. If the population of an area increases, the relative scarcity of housing will cause price increases.

The principle of supply and demand shows why "location" is important. The principle of *SUPPLY AND DEMAND states that as the supply of land decreases, the value of land increases, because more people are competing for the desirable land.* Living next to the Pacific Ocean is expensive because the land is scarce. Even small lots bring very high selling prices in these areas. To beach lovers, these are the most desirable neighborhoods because there are only so many ocean view lots. In areas where there are many lots available, like the desert, the supply is large and the price of a lot can be very low. Downtown high-rise commercial locations in cities like San Francisco, Los Angeles and San Diego are scarce and therefore expensive.

Downtown high-rise commercial locations in cities like San Francisco, Los Angeles and San Diego are scarce and therefore expensive.

Purchasing power and dollars follow demand.

FIGURE 10-11

PRINCIPLE OF CHANGE

The principle of **CHANGE** *is that real property is constantly changing.* Value is influenced by changes in such things as: population size, shopping centers, schools and colleges, freeways, economic and social trends. It is hard to see change on a day-to-day basis, but if you go back to the area where you grew up, the change is apparent.

A trend is a series of changes brought about by a chain of events (causes and effects).

The real property life cycle goes through three stages: development, maturity and old age, which are illustrated in Figure 10-12.

FIGURE 10-12

REAL PROPERTY LIFE CYCLE (AGE CYCLE)

Change is evidenced by the fact that neighborhoods tend to pass through the three stages of the real estate life cycle.

Development (Integration)

This is the stage when the land is subdivided into lots, the streets are paved and street lights are installed. Soon, homes are built and the community starts. As new people move in, landscaping and fences improve the homes.

Maturity (Equilibrium)

The maturity stage starts when the homes become older and the children grow up and move away. Most of the residents are long-time homeowners and the community has a solid, well-established look.

Old Age (Disintegration)

In this stage, the buildings show some wear and tear and the oldest buildings are starting to deteriorate. As the useful life of the property declines, lower social or economic groups move into the area. Large homes may be converted into multiple family use.

The life cycle of real property may take a few years, such as that of a mining town going "bust," or may span a century, such as that of a community that constantly revitalizes itself.

PRINCIPLE OF CONFORMITY

The principle of **CONFORMITY** *states that the maximum value is obtained when a reasonable degree of building similarity is maintained in the neighborhood.* So, if all the homes in an area are similar (not identical), the maximum value of real property is created. The word "similar" is the key. If all the tract homes are identical, as if they were all made with the same cookie cutter, the maximum value is not present.

The principle of conformity is one of the primary reasons for zoning regulations (discussed in Chapter 12). They protect the neighborhood from other nonconforming uses, and from infiltration of incompatible structures. An attractive neighborhood would quickly decline in value if zoning did not help protect its conformity.

PRINCIPLE OF CONTRIBUTION

The principle of **CONTRIBUTION** *states that the value of a particular component is measured in terms of its contribution to the value of the whole property.* Consequently, cost does not necessarily equal value. It either adds more or less to the value of real property.

> **For example:** If an apartment building produces a 10% return to investors, a $50,000 investment in a swimming pool, without an equal ($50,000 x 10%) $5,000 or higher increase in rents, would not be a good idea.

Thus, in some cases, a property's market value may not increase even if it has had additions, alterations or has been rehabilitated. If the swimming pool were added, the property would be considered **"over-built."** The principle of contribution is also referred to as increasing and (decreasing) "diminishing returns" in economic textbooks.

PRINCIPLE OF SUBSTITUTION

With the **SUBSTITUTION PRINCIPLE**, *a buyer will not pay more for a particular property if it costs less to buy a similar property of equal utility and desirability.* People prefer the less expensive price if all other things are considered equal. When appraisers use the principle of substitution, they compare properties to adjust for differences. The maximum value of a property tends to be set by the cost of acquiring an equally desirable substitute property.

PRINCIPLE OF REGRESSION

The **REGRESSION PRINCIPLE** *states that between properties in the same neighborhood, the value of the best property will be adversely affected by the value of the other properties.* For example, if a house that would easily be worth $290,000 in a neighborhood of similar homes was to be built in a neighborhood of $135,000 homes, it would not sell for $290,000. Anyone in the market for a $290,000 house would not want to live in a tract where the average price of a house was $135,000. Because of its superior quality or size, the house would undoubtedly sell for more than the average house in the tract, but it would not approach $290,000.

The same principle applies to the over-improved home. When owners invest very large sums in major additions, lavish landscaping and swimming pools, and the other residents do not improve their homes, the house is no longer similar to the others. The owners of the over-built house will not receive the full value for the cost of improvements they have made.

PRINCIPLE OF PROGRESSION

In the **PROGRESSION PRINCIPLE**, *the value of a lesser residence is increased in value by its location in a neighborhood of better homes.* This is the opposite of the principle of regression. A smaller, unattractive and poorly maintained home in an exclusive area will sell for much more than if it were located in a comparable neighborhood. People who wish to live in an exclusive area would think of the smaller home as a bargain.

A. Appraisal	I. Corner Lot	Q. Supply and Demand
B. Market Price	J. Interior Lot	R. Change
C. Market Value	K. T-intersection Lot	S. Conformity
D. Highest and Best Use	L. Key Lot	T. Progression Principle
E. Appraisal Process	M. Depth Table	U. Regression Principle
F. Neighborhood	N. Frontage	V. Flag Lot
G. Site	O. Off-Site Improvements	
H. Cul-de-sac Lot	P. Warranty Plan	

1.____ The appraisal principle that maintains the maximum value of a property is realized when a reasonable degree of similarity is present in the area where the property is located.

2.____ The least desirable type of lot because the back ends of other lots face one of its sides.

3.____ A general term describing people living or working together in an area of similar properties with similar social, economic and political backgrounds.

4.____ The highest price a willing buyer would pay and a willing seller accept, both being fully informed, and the property exposed for a reasonable period of time. This value may be different from the price a property can actually be sold for at a given time.

5.____ Not a corner lot, but an inside lot; the most common type of lot.

6.____ Development of large parcels into smaller lots suitable for construction. This includes sidewalks, curbs, streets, sewers, streetlights, etc.

7.____ A lot at the U-shaped end of a street. Even though they are narrower in the front and wider in the back, these lots are popular because the street itself makes the area exclusive.

8.____ An opinion or estimate of real property value based upon a factual analysis by a qualified (licensed) person with education and experience.

9.____ The use of land that will bring the greatest economic return over a given time.

10.____ The price a property sells for, which may be higher or lower than its actual market value.

11.____ The orderly process of determining the fair market value of real property by: 1) defining the problem, 2) gathering the data, 3) applying the three methods of appraisal (cost approach, market comparison approach, income approach) and 4) correlating the information for a final estimate of value.

12.____ A general term for a lot or plot of land.

13.____ A lot with both the front and side facing different streets. Such a residential lot is generally more desirable because of its increased exposure to light and fresh air. A commercial lot benefits from better street access and exposure to traffic patterns.

14.____ An interior lot facing down a street into traffic. Such a lot benefits from the view down the open street but suffers from additional traffic noise and on-coming headlights at night.

15.____ A lot with a long, narrow entrance, forming the shape of a flag. While it has limited frontage, such a lot can be very desirable if the odd shape is accompanied by a spectacular view in the back.

16.____ A chart illustrating the principle that the greatest value exists in the front portion of the lot, and the value of the land decreases the further back from the street you go.

17.____ The linear measure of the front portion of a parcel facing a major street, walkway, lake or ocean.

18.____ An insurance plan covering the major systems of a home such as electrical, heating, plumbing and major appliances.

19.____ A principle of real estate appraisal suggesting that the value of property increases when there is more demand and a short supply in an area. Conversely, the value decreases when there is an abundant supply and less demand.

20.____ The concept that although changes may be imperceptible, neighborhoods are constantly changing. Population shifts and economic changes, along with many other variables, will constantly work to alter the value of property.

21.____ The real estate principle that a smaller, low quality home will gain value if larger, nicer homes are being built in the neighborhood .

22.____ The real estate principle that a larger, nicer home will not enjoy its full value if it is located in a neighborhood of smaller, low quality homes.

MULTIPLE CHOICE

1. Vertical 2" x 4" framework in walls spaced 16" on center are:

   A. studs
   C. footing

   B. rafters
   D. cripple

2. A bearing wall is defined as:

   A. an interior wall with a doorway
   C. a wall made of studs and cross-bracing

   B. a solid wall of concrete
   D. a wall that supports a floor or ceiling

3. The process of determining whether to build a house or an apartment building on a particular piece of land is known as:

   A. highest and best use
   C. the cost process

   B. the market comparison approach
   D. the appraisal process

4. All new homes in California automatically carry a warranty against labor or material defects for a period of:

   A. 6 months
   C. 8 months

   B. 12 months
   D. 16 months

5. A limited area, where the homes are physically similar and the residents have a certain degree of economic background in common, is known as a:

   A. city
   C. housing tract

   B. township
   D. neighborhood

6. "Backfill" is a term that most closely means:

   A. a special soil made of rock
   C. to refill excavated earth against a wall

   B. to fill holes in concrete blocks
   D. placing grout between ceramic joints

7. The beam over a window or door is called a:

   A. cripple
   C. stud

   B. joist
   D. header

8. What does it mean to buy a "turnkey" house?

   A. This is a technical construction term
   B. The FHA will turn the keys over to the new buyer
   C. A house that has been completed and is ready for occupancy
   D. A federal subsidized housing program turns the key over to a low income family

9. If a customer is deciding between two look-alike clothes dryers, the one with the highest energy efficiency rating (EER) is:

   A. more efficient
   C. produces more BTUs

   B. less efficient
   D. requires more voltage

10. Conduit in the building trade would most likely be used by a (an):

    A. carpenter
    C. plumber

    B. electrician
    D. roofer

CHAPTER 11
Appraisal Methods

http://www.appraisalinstitute.org (Appraisal Institute)
http://www.agri-associations.org (American Society of Farm Managers and
Rural Appraisers)
http://aicanada.org (The Appraisal Institute of Canada)

*To establish a "sales price," a salesperson or broker may
appraise a property without an appraisal license.*

Real estate salespeople need to know enough about appraisal techniques and
practices so that they can determine, in advance, the approximate selling price of
a property. Salespeople have the advantage of determining the probable sales
price of a property quickly because they see what similar properties in their area
sell for each day. They can be on top of the market because of their multiple
listing service and close contact with other knowledgeable agents. They are
constantly being updated as to the current listing and selling prices.

Figure 11-1 is an example of the Competitive Market Analysis. It is presented to
sellers so that they can see at a glance the selling prices of other houses or condos
in their neighborhood. This enables the sellers to "price their listings" close to a
realistic selling price.

FIGURE 11-1

CALIFORNIA ASSOCIATION OF REALTORS® (CAR) STANDARD FORM

COMPETITIVE MARKET ANALYSIS

CALIFORNIA ASSOCIATION OF REALTORS®

PROPERTY ADDRESS _____ DATE _____

PROPERTY DESCRIPTION: BD rms | Ba | FR Den | Reported Sq. Ft. | Other

EXISTING LOANS

FIRST | Reported Balance | Rate | Type

SECOND | Reported Balance | Rate | Type

List Price | Days on Mkt

SELLER MAY CARRY | Amount | Rate | Term

NEW FINANCING | OTHER TERMS & COMMENTS

ON MARKET NOW

REPORTED SOLD PAST 12 MONTHS

Sale Price | Financing | Date Sold | Other Terms & Comments

REPORTED EXPIRED PAST 12 MONTHS

Amount | Rate | Term | Other Terms & Comments

GENERAL COMMENTS: _____

PROBABLE MARKETING RANGE $ _____

Information reported herein is based upon published reports or matters of public record. No representation is made or intended that this information is accurate or complete. Financing information may not reflect specific loan terms.

The undersigned acknowledge receipt of a copy.

_____ Date _____

COMPANY _____
AGENT _____ Date _____
PHONE _____

CMA-11

APPRAISAL METHODS

A licensed (expert) appraiser will use all three of the valuation approaches to determine the value of a property, but will emphasize only one to establish the final value.

These approaches are:

1. COMPARATIVE (MARKET DATA) APPROACH
2. COST (REPLACEMENT) APPROACH
3. CAPITALIZATION (INCOME) APPROACH

The appraisal is also an opinion of a value "range." Let us assume that a range of $222,000 to $245,000 is established from the three appraisal approaches mentioned above. By correlating the economic information from the three approaches, an experienced appraiser can estimate a more precise value. The results of the three approaches can be weighed and it can then be determined which method has provided the best information about the property. In this case, let's say that the appraiser felt he or she should emphasize the market comparison approach that was $243,000. The appraiser would state that, in his or her opinion, the property was worth $243,000; but the value "ranged" from $222,000 to $245,000.

COMPARATIVE APPROACH
(MARKET DATA METHOD)

Of the three approaches previously mentioned, the market comparison method is the one most frequently used. It is easy for an alert student to master this technique within a short time, and it is the most logical way to appraise a house.

The market data method uses the "principle of substitution" to compare similar properties.

The *MARKET COMPARISON APPROACH* simply takes the current selling prices of similar properties and adjusts those prices for any differences. The comparative (market data) approach uses the principle of substitution; a person will not pay more for a property if he or she can buy something similar for less.

Simply adjust the value of the comparable sales price. If a house is comparable, except that it has a pool, sells for $320,000 and the value of the $20,000 pool is subtracted, the house we are appraising is valued at $300,000.

HOW TO ADJUST FOR A COMPARABLE SALE (COMPS)

The market comparison approach is basically common sense. If your neighbor has a similar house to yours that he just sold for $160,000, then yours is worth about $160,000. The only problem is that adjustments must be made for any differences between the houses. For example, if a similar $160,000 house had a fireplace worth $2,500 and yours did not, then your house would be worth $157,500 ($160,000 - $2,500). Adjustments should be made to the selling price of the comparable house for any differences between the properties. **The usual adjustments are made for differences in location, age, lot size, building size, condition of the property and any time difference between the sales.**

Subtract or add from or to the selling price of the comparable property to adjust for differences. The term "Comps" is used to mean comparable properties.

If the comparable property has an item not present in the subject property, the appraiser subtracts the value of the item from the comparable property's selling price. Likewise, if the subject property has an item not present in the comparable property, the appraiser adds the value of the item to the comparable property's selling price. After all these adjustments are made to the comparable selling price, the resulting figure gives the appraiser the subject property's value.

By comparing recent selling prices of properties in the same area, it is easy to see the trends in selling prices and why certain properties sell for more than others. The more comparable sales you gather, the more reliable the results. Real estate salespeople often refer to comparable sales as "comps."

Unsold properties are important when using the market comparison approach. If a property has been listed "for sale" for a long time, it is usually overpriced. Such comparable "unsold properties" suggest an upper limit of value. Unsold listings can therefore help establish the highest comparable price. An experienced appraiser can easily estimate the amount of an adjustment. The adjustment is an estimate or opinion determined solely by the appraiser, and reflects his or her broad experience and education.

Comparable sales information can be obtained from many different sources. Brokers and salespeople are familiar with property sales prices in their area, so naturally they are a good source for appraisal data. In addition, most brokers are members of the local multiple listing service and have access to past sales information. Other people in the real estate field, such as loan officers, title insurance agents and escrow officers can also supply comparable sales information.

It is essential that: 1) the information is from a reliable source; 2) there is an adequate number of comparable sales; and 3) the comparable sales are truly comparable.

The comparison method is the most common approach for houses and condominiums. It is also the best method for appraising lots and vacant land (unimproved property).

Figures 11-2 and 11-3 show the Uniform Residential Appraisal Report that is accepted by Fannie Mae and Freddie Mac.

ADVANTAGES OF THE MARKET APPROACH

The market comparison approach is best for single family residences (houses or condos) and vacant land (lots).

This method is excellent for appraising single family homes. Here are the reasons why:

1. The Market Comparison (Data) Approach is easy to learn, and with a little experience it is easy to apply.

2. Since there are usually many recent comparable sales, the required information is readily available.

3. This method is used mostly for houses or condos, which makes this method the most relevant to us as homeowners, salespeople or investors.

The most difficult part of the market data approach is to adjust similar properties for differences. The market data approach is limited when market conditions are rapidly changing.

Marketability and desirability of a property are the primary concerns when appraising a residential property.

DISADVANTAGES OF THE MARKET APPROACH

The disadvantages of using the market comparison approach are concentrated into several areas which are listed below:

1. This method requires many recent comparable sales of similar properties.

FIGURE 11-2

Property Description   **UNIFORM RESIDENTIAL APPRAISAL REPORT**   File No.   DEMO

SUBJECT

Property Address 1234 EASY STREET	City VACAVILLE State CA Zip Code 95687
Legal Description LOT 2 GREEN ACRES ESTATES UNIT 1 LOT 43	County SOLANO

Assessor's Parcel No. 0136-261-170   Tax Year 96-97 R.E. Taxes $1999.20 Special Assessments $ NONE

Borrower JOHNNY & MARY CASH   Current Owner JOHNNY CASH   Occupant: [X] Owner [ ] Tenant [ ] Vacant

Property rights appraised [X] Fee Simple [ ] Leasehold   Project Type [ ] PUD [ ] Condominium (HUD/VA only) HOA$ /Mo

Neighborhood or Project Name GREEN ACRES   Map Reference PAGE 453 E2   Census Tract 2529.07

Sale Price $ 160,000   Date of Sale 09/08/10   Description and $ amount of loan charges/concessions to be paid by seller NONE

Lender/Client ALLCASH MORTGAGE CO   Address 123 GOLD STREET, LOS ANGELES CA 90200

Appraiser ED STAHL, CA AG 001573   Address 110 ALAMO DRIVE, VACAVILLE, CA 95688

NEIGHBORHOOD

Location	[X] Urban	[ ] Suburban	[ ] Rural	Predominant occupancy	Single family housing	Present land use %	Land use change
Built up	[X] Over 75%	[ ] 25-75%	[ ] Under 25%		PRICE $(000) / AGE (yrs)	One family 100	[X] Not likely [ ] Likely
Growth Rate	[ ] Rapid	[X] Stable	[ ] Slow	[X] Owner	130 Low 5	2-4 family	[ ] In process
Property values	[ ] Increasing	[X] Stable	[ ] Declining	[ ] Tenant	200 High 20	Multi-family	To:
Demand/supply	[ ] Shortage	[X] In balance	[ ] Over supply	[X] Vacant (0-5%)	Predominant	Commercial	
Marketing time	[ ] Under 3 mos.	[X] 3-6 mos.	[ ] Over 6 mos.	[ ] Vacant (Over 5%)	150 10	( )	

Note: Race and the racial composition of the neighborhood are not appraisal factors.

Neighborhood boundaries and characteristics: NORTH: ALAMO DRIVE   SOUTH: VACAVILLE CITY LIMIT
EAST: Vanden Road   WEST: PEABODY ROAD   Residential

Factors that affect the marketability of the properties in the neighborhood (proximity to employment and amenities, employment stability, appeal to market, etc.)
No adverse factors affecting marketability were observed. Amenities closeby
include all schools, shopping and parks. Close to two major employers:
Travis Air Force Base and California Prison, Solano. This home is located
in Travis Unified School District, a district with an excellent reputation

Market conditions in the subject neighborhood (including support for the above conclusions related to the trend of property values, demand/supply, and marketing time
-- such as data on competitive properties for sale in the neighborhood, description of the prevalence of sales and financing concessions, etc.)
Market showing evidence of stability from a long decline with signs of
recovery. Purchase financings and refinancing are readily available. Data
supported by MLS statistics and public records

PUD

Project Information for PUDs (If applicable) - - Is the developer/builder in control of the Home Owners' Association (HOA)? [ ] Yes [ ] No

Approximate total number of units in the subject project   Approximate total number of units for sale in the subject project

Describe common elements and recreational facilities:

SITE

Dimensions 60 X 100 SEE PARCEL MAP		Topography LEVEL AT GRADE
Site area 6,000 SF 0.14 ACRE Corner Lot [ ] Yes [X] No		Size TYPICAL FOR AREA
Specific zoning classification and description Single Family Residential		Shape RECTANGLE
Zoning Compliance [X] Legal [ ] Legal nonconforming (Grandfathered use) [ ] Illegal [ ] No zoning		Drainage APPEARS ADEQUATE
Highest & best use as improved: [X] Present use [ ] Other use (explain)		View RESIDENTIAL

Utilities	Public	Other	Off-site Improvements	Type	Public	Private	
Electricity	[X]		Street	ASPHALT	[X]	[ ]	Landscaping TYPICAL FOR AREA
Gas	[X]		Curb/gutter	CONCRETE	[X]	[ ]	Driveway Surface CONCRETE
Water	[X]		Sidewalk	CONCRETE	[X]	[ ]	Apparent easements SEE TITLE REPORT
Sanitary sewer	[X]		Street lights	YES	[X]	[ ]	FEMA Special Flood Hazard Area [ ] Yes [X] No
Storm sewer	[X]		Alley	NONE			FEMA Zone C Map Date 8/2/82

FEMA Map No. 060373 0011B

Comments (apparent adverse easements, encroachments, special assessments, slide areas, illegal or legal nonconforming zoning use, etc.):
No apparent adverse easements, encroachments or other adverse conditions
Site is fully developed with all underground utilities installed

DESCRIPTION OF IMPROVEMENTS

GENERAL DESCRIPTION	EXTERIOR DESCRIPTION	FOUNDATION	BASEMENT	INSULATION
No. of Units 1	Foundation CONCRET	Slab YES	Area Sq. Ft. NONE	Roof [ ]
No. of Stories 1	Exterior Walls STUCCO	Crawl Space NO	% Finished	Ceiling [X]
Type (Det./Att.) Detach	Roof Surface TILE	Basement NONE	Ceiling	Walls [X]
Design (Style) 1 story	Gutters & Dwnspts. Galvinizd	Sump Pump NONE	Walls	Floor [ ]
Existing/Proposed EXISTIN	Window Type DUAL PANE	Dampness NONE	Floor	None [ ]
Age (Yrs.) 8	Storm/Screens SCREENS	Settlement NONE	Outside Entry	Unknown [ ]
Effective Age (Yrs.) 4	Manufactured House NO	Infestation NONE		

ROOMS	Foyer	Living	Dining	Kitchen	Den	Family Rm.	Rec. Rm.	Bedrooms	# Baths	Laundry	Other	Area Sq. Ft.
Basement												
Level 1	1	1	1	1		1		3	2	1		1600
Level 2												

Finished area **above** grade contains: 8   Rooms: 3   Bedroom(s): 2   Bath(s): 1600   Square Feet of Gross Living Area

INTERIOR	Materials/Condition	HEATING		KITCHEN EQUIP.		ATTIC		AMENITIES		CAR STORAGE:	
Floors	CARPET/AVERG	Type	ForAir	Refrigerator	[ ]	None	[X]	Fireplace(s) #1	[X]	None	[ ]
Walls	DRYWALL/AVER	Fuel	GAS	Range/Oven	[X]	Stairs	[ ]	Patio	[X]	Garage	# of cars
Trim/Finish	WOOD/AVERAGE	Condition	AVERAGE	Disposal	[X]	Drop Stair	[ ]	Deck	[X]	Attached	2 CARS
Bath Floor	VINYL/AVERAG	COOLING		Dishwasher	[X]	Scuttle	[ ]	Porch	[X]	Detached	
Bath Wainscot	TILE/AVERAGE	Central	YES	Fan/Hood	[X]	Floor	[ ]	Fence	[X]	Built-In	
Doors	WOOD/AVERAGE	Other		Microwave	[X]	Heated	[ ]	Pool	[ ]	Carport	
		Condition	AVERAG	Washer/Dryer	[X]	Finished	[ ]			Driveway	CONCRE

COMMENTS

Additional features (special energy efficient items, etc.): THE SUNSHINE floor plan 1,600 sq ft per builder
Attractive landscape plan/Automatic lawn sprinklers

Condition of the improvements, depreciation (physical, functional, and external), repairs needed, quality of construction, remodeling/additions, etc.:
There are no apparent functional or external inadequacies. The construction
is typical for the area. All homes built by same builder.

Adverse environmental conditions (such as, but not limited to, hazardous wastes, toxic substances, etc.) present in the improvements, on the site, or in the
immediate vicinity of the subject property: There are no known or apparent adverse environmental
conditions that would negatively impact value.

Homeputer• Forms Processing System For Laser Printers 1 (802) 773-3018

ED STAHL APPRAISALS, 110 ALAMO DRIVE, VACAVILLE, CA 95688   Ph (707) 448-6140

FIGURE 11-3

UNIFORM RESIDENTIAL APPRAISAL REPORT File No. DEMO

Valuation Section

COST APPROACH

ESTIMATED SITE VALUE	= $	50,000
ESTIMATED REPRODUCTION COST-NEW OF IMPROVEMENTS:		
Dwelling 1,600 Sq Ft @ $ 63.00	= $	100,800
Sq Ft @ $	=	
Garage/Carport 440 Sq Ft @ $ 18.00	=	7,920
Total Estimated Cost New	= $	108,720
Less Physical / Functional / External		
Depreciation 2500	= $	2,500
Depreciated Value of Improvements	= $	106,220
"As-is" Value of Site Improvements	= $	5,000
INDICATED VALUE BY COST APPROACH	= $	161,220

Comments on Cost Approach (such as, source of cost estimate, site value, square foot calculation and, for HUD, VA and FmHA, the estimated remaining economic life of the property):

Remaining economic life = 30 yr Land value from market and recent land sales. See addendum for cost calculations based on Marshall & Swift Residential Cost Handbook (Los Angeles, CA 90026) Physical depreciation based on Age/Life method. Site to total value ratio is typical for area

SALES COMPARISON ANALYSIS

ITEM	SUBJECT	COMPARABLE NO. 1		COMPARABLE NO. 2		COMPARABLE NO. 3	
Address	1234 EASY STREET VACAVILLE	1235 EASY STREET SOUTH VACAVILLE		1234 SUNSHINE ST SOUTH VACAVILLE		2356 EASY STREET SOUTH VACAVILLE	
Proximity to Subject		WITHIN 1 MILE		WITHIN 1 MILE		WITHIN 1 MILE	
Sales Price	$ 160,000	$ 163,000		$ 162,000		$ 160,000	
Price/Gross Liv. Area	$ 100.00 ☑	$ 101.88 ☑		$ 101.25 ☑		$ 100.00 ☑	
Data and/or	INSPECTION	MLS #371294		MLS #371255		MLS #372254	
Verification Sources	INSPECTION	DOC #43284		DOC #33501		DOC #33547	
VALUE ADJUSTMENTS	DESCRIPTION	DESCRIPTION	+ (-) $ Adjustment	DESCRIPTION	+ (-) $ Adjustment	DESCRIPTION	+ (-) $ Adjustment
Sales or Financing		CONVEN LOAN		VA LOAN		CONVEN LOAN	
Concessions		SELLER PAID	-2387	SELLER PAID	-2000	$150,000	
Date of Sale/Time		07/15/10		05/30/10		06/02/10	
Location	AVERAGE	AVERAGE		AVERAGE		AVERAGE	
Leasehold/Fee Simple	FEE	FEE		FEE		FEE	
Site	6,000 SF	6,000 SF		6,000 SF		6,000 SF	
View	RESIDENTIAL	RESIDENTIAL		RESIDENTIAL		RESIDENTIAL	
Design and Appeal	1 story	1 STORY		1 STORY		1 STORY	
Quality of Construction	AVERAGE	AVERAGE		AVERAGE		AVERAGE	
Age	8	8 YEARS		8 YEARS		8 YEARS	
Condition	AVERAGE	AVERAGE		AVERAGE		AVERAGE	
Above Grade	Total Bdrms Baths	Total Bdrms Baths		Total Bdrms Baths		Total Bdrms Baths	
Room Count	8 3 2	8 3 2		8 3 2		8 3 2	
Gross Living Area	1600 Sq. Ft.	1600 Sq. Ft.		1600 Sq. Ft.		1600 Sq. Ft.	
Basement & Finished	NONE	NONE		NONE		NONE	
Rooms Below Grade	NONE	NONE		NONE		NONE	
Functional Utility	AVERAGE	AVERAGE		AVERAGE		AVERAGE	
Heating/Cooling	FAG/CENTRAL	FAG/CENTRAL		FAG/CENTRAL		FAG/CENTRAL	
Energy Efficient Items	DUAL PANE	DUAL PANE		DUAL PANE		DUAL PANE	
Garage/Carport	2 CAR GARAG	2 CAR GARAG		2 CAR GARAG		2 CAR GARAG	
Porch, Patio, Deck,	PATIO	PATIO		PATIO		PATIO	
Fireplace(s), etc.	1 FIREPLACE	1 FIREPLACE		1 FIREPLACE		1 FIREPLACE	
Fence, Pool, etc.	FENCED	FENCED		FENCED		FENCED	
Net Adj. (total)		☐ + ☒ - $	2,387	☐ + ☒ - $	2,000	☐ + ☐ - $	0
Adjusted Sales Price of Comparable		$ 160,613		$ 160,000		$ 160,000	

Comments on Sales Comparison (including the subject property's compatibility to the neighborhood, etc.):
All sales similar location, lot size, home size, construction, age & price
All sales area closed sales from public records and MLS files
SALE NO 1: SELLER PAID $2,387 FOR BUYER'S CLOSING COSTS
SALE NO 3: SELLER PAID $2,000 FOR BUYER'S CLOSING COSTS
SALE NO 3: SIMILAR HOME IN AREA

ITEM	SUBJECT	COMPARABLE NO. 1	COMPARABLE NO. 2	COMPARABLE NO. 3
Date, Price and Data	NONE	NONE	NONE	NONE
Source for prior sales	N/A	N/A	N/A	N/A
within year of appraisal	METROSCAN	METROSCAN	METROSCAN	METROSCAN

Analysis of any current agreement of sale, option, or listing of the subject property and analysis of any prior sales of subject and comparables within one year of the date of appraisal:
Estimated value of subject is consistent with the above sales analysis.
Prior sales of the comparable properties occured more than one year ago

INDICATED VALUE BY SALES COMPARISON APPROACH	$	160,000
INDICATED VALUE BY INCOME APPROACH (If Applicable) Estimated Market Rent $ N/A /Mo. x Gross Rent Multiplier N/A	= $	

RECONCILIATION

This appraisal is made ☒ "as is" ☐ subject to the repairs, alterations, inspections, or conditions listed below ☐ subject to completion per plans and specifications

Conditions of Appraisal: No warranty of the appraisal is given or implied. No liability is assumed for the structural or mechanical elements of the property.

Final Reconciliation: Due to a lack of rental data, the Income Approach is not given. Most weight is given to the Sales Comparison Approach as it best reflects the typical value of a prudent buyer. Cost approach supports this value estimate

The purpose of this appraisal is to estimate the market value of the real property that is the subject of this report, based on the above conditions and the certification, contingent and limiting conditions, and market value definition that are stated in the attached Freddie Mac Form 439/Fannie Mae Form 1004B (Revised 6/93)

I (WE) ESTIMATE THE MARKET VALUE, AS DEFINED, OF THE REAL PROPERTY THAT IS THE SUBJECT OF THIS REPORT, AS OF SEPTEMBER 8, 2010 (WHICH IS THE DATE OF INSPECTION AND THE EFFECTIVE DATE OF THIS REPORT) TO BE $ 160,000

APPRAISER:	SUPERVISORY APPRAISER (ONLY IF REQUIRED):	
Signature	Signature	☐ Did ☐ Did Not
Name Edward S Stahl Phone 707-448-6140	Name	Inspect Property
Date Report Signed SEPTEMBER 8, 2010	Date Report Signed	
State Certification # AG 001873 State CA	State Certification #	State
Or State License # State	Or State License #	State

Freddie Mac Form 70 6-93   10 CH.   PAGE 2 OF 2   Fannie Mae Form 1004 6-93

2. This method is least reliable when there are rapid economic changes. If market prices are increasing rapidly, the comparables, which are based on past sales prices, lag behind. If prices are decreasing rapidly, the comparables, which are based on past sales prices, still remain high.

3. The market comparison approach is less valid with certain income properties because a separate analysis of the income is required.

Listings set ceiling on market value, since they are asking prices.

COST APPROACH
(REPLACEMENT COST METHOD)

The *COST APPROACH is the process of calculating the cost of the land and buildings (as if they were new today) and then subtracting the accrued depreciation to arrive at the current value of the property.* To use the cost approach, the appraiser must be able to determine the new construction cost of replacing the building today, using current construction methods. Depreciation is estimated by the appraiser and is then subtracted from the estimated cost of the new building. The value of the lot and depreciated building is then added to find the market value.

> *The cost approach objective is to determine the land value plus the cost to replace the improvements new (minus depreciation) while maintaining the same utility value.*

Of the three approaches, the cost approach tends to set what the appraisers call an "upper limit of value." Most home buyers or investors prefer a newer building over an older one if the price is about the same. The cost approach therefore tends to set the highest price that a knowledgeable person will pay for a property. Why not build if the construction cost of a newer building is close to the sales price of an older building?

> *In relation to the other appraisal methods, the cost approach tends to set the "upper limit of value" (highest price someone will pay).*

The cost approach is most useful when appraising 1) new buildings and 2) special purpose or unique structures. Estimating depreciation is critical in this approach. As a building gets older, the depreciation becomes more difficult to estimate, eventually making the cost approach impractical. Since newer structures have little depreciation, the cost approach is the most suitable. The cost approach may also be preferred for special purpose or unique structures as they have few, if any, market comparable sales. Special purpose structures, such as an airplane factory, a city hall or a church, are best appraised by the cost approach.

The cost approach is more appropriate for new buildings because there is almost no depreciation.

It is limited in its effectiveness for appraising old buildings because determining depreciation is the most difficult part of the cost approach for the appraiser.

Some properties **require** the use of the cost approach. If, for example, there have been no recent sales in an area, the market comparison approach cannot be used effectively. Furthermore, if there is no income (as for example, from government owned properties) the appraiser must rely solely on the cost approach.

Value of the land plus (+) new cost of buildings today minus (-) depreciation equals (=) current market value of the property.

COSTS ARE BOTH DIRECT AND INDIRECT

Any method used for estimating cost requires the calculation of direct (hard) or indirect (soft) costs. Both types of costs are equally necessary for construction and must be measured accurately.

DIRECT COSTS are expenditures for labor and materials used in the construction of the improvement(s). A contractor's overhead and profit are generally treated as direct costs.

INDIRECT COSTS are expenditures other than material and labor costs. Examples are administrative costs, professional fees, financing costs, insurance and taxes. Indirect costs are usually calculated separately from direct costs.

STEPS IN THE COST APPROACH

The steps used in the cost approach are easy to follow, but studying Figure 11-4 will help to explain each step.

FIGURE 11-4

1. Estimate the value of the land (use the market comparison approach).
2. Estimate the replacement cost of the building as if it were new.
3. Deduct estimated depreciation from the replacement cost of the building.
4. Add the value of the lot (Step 1) and the replacement cost of a new building and subtract estimated depreciation (Steps 2 and 3) to find the total value (Step 4).

STEP 1 - APPRAISE THE LAND (LOT) SEPARATELY

Appraise the land (lot) separately. The value of the vacant land is determined by comparing the lot of the property to be appraised with similar lots that have just been sold. The market comparison approach is used by the appraiser to estimate the lot value of the appraised property.

The cost approach requires the appraiser to identify land values separately by the use of the market data approach.

STEP 2 - ESTIMATE REPLACEMENT COST

Estimate the replacement cost of the improvements to the land. This includes all the buildings and the landscaping improvements.

Replacement Cost

> *REPLACEMENT COST is the cost of building a similar (having utility equivalent) new structure today using modern construction methods.* These methods may differ from the original building techniques, but are becoming an important factor due to the ever increasing costs of new construction. As construction costs increase for new homes, the replacement cost of existing homes also increases. Therefore, well-located older homes will keep rising in value year after year, no matter how old they are, because the newer substitutes are so costly. This is not necessarily because of excellent upkeep, but because it is becoming impossible to find a newer home with the same features at a reasonable price. *REPRODUCTION OR REPLICATION COST is the cost of reproducing a structure (usually destroyed) at current prices using similar (older) style materials and methods as used in the original structure.* This method is rarely used, but it is the type, for example, used by Disneyland to recreate its historical Main Street.

The rarely used reproduction (replication) method is an exact replica ... it is the most expensive. New construction methods (replacement costs) are almost always cheaper.

Appraisal Methods

Three Replacement Methods

The **COMPARATIVE-UNIT METHOD** *is used to derive a cost estimate in terms of dollars per square foot or per cubic foot, based on known costs of similar structures and adjusted for time and physical differences.* The comparative-unit method represents a relatively uncomplicated, practical approach to a cost estimate and is widely used (illustrated below).

The **UNIT-IN-PLACE METHOD** *employs unit costs for the various building components such as foundations, floors, walls, windows and roofs as installed and uses square foot, linear foot or other appropriate units of measurement to estimate each component part.* These estimates include labor and overhead. To use this method, the appraiser must have specialized construction knowledge.

The **QUANTITY SURVEY METHOD** *involves detailed estimates of the quantities of raw materials used, such as brick, lumber, cement, the price of such materials and the labor costs.* It is the most comprehensive and accurate method of cost estimating but too complicated to fully explain here.

Comparative-Unit Method is the most commonly used replacement cost method.

Although there are several ways to determine replacement cost, the simplest way is to *measure the outside of the building to determine SQUARE FOOTAGE.* After you determine the square footage, multiply it by the current cost of construction, per square foot, to get the value (as if it was new) of the building.

To determine square feet, use the formula: **LENGTH X WIDTH**

Square foot cost for a smaller house is higher than the square foot cost for a larger house. If other factors are equal, including square footage, the cost of building a two-story house is up to 50% cheaper than a one-story house.

The cubic foot method is used to appraise warehouses. To determine cubic feet, use the formula: **LENGTH X WIDTH X HEIGHT**

A warehouse building is appraised by the cubic foot but is usually rented by the square foot. Caution: the industrial land the warehouse is on is appraised by the square foot.

As construction costs vary from city-to-city and from builder-to-builder, many appraisers use cost engineers to help them determine the square foot cost of different types of construction. One of the most popular building cost information services is:

 http://www.marshallswift.com (Cost Engineers)

Marshall & Stevens, Inc.
Valuation Engineers
707 Wilshire Blvd., Ste. 5200
Los Angeles, CA 90017
(213) 612-8000

They annually compile a residential cost handbook that details the current cost of most types of residential construction in California.

STEP 3 - ESTIMATE AND DEDUCT DEPRECIATION

DEPRECIATION is a reduction in the value of a property due to any cause. The difference between replacement cost of a property and its market value is depreciation.

Depreciation is a loss in value from any cause. Depreciation is either curable (profitable to repair) or incurable (unprofitable to repair).

Estimate and deduct the depreciation from the replacement cost of the building being appraised. This accumulated depreciation is sometimes called accrued depreciation. *ACCRUED DEPRECIATION (OBSERVED) is the loss in value of improvements from any cause at the date of the appraisal.* Accrued depreciation is what has happened in the past, whereas the accrual for depreciation is the amount of future depreciation. There are five methods of estimating accrued depreciation:

1) Capitalized Income
2) Market
3) Straight-line (Most common and explained below)
4) Engineering
5) Breakdown

The straight-line method is explained here. For information on the other methods, please see an appraisal book. The ***STRAIGHT-LINE METHOD (AGE LIFE)*** *assumes the value declines in equal amounts of depreciation each year, until it reaches zero.* A building with an economic life of 50 years would depreciate 2 percent (100 percent/50 years = 2 percent) in value each year. ***ACTUAL AGE*** *is the current (real) age of the building.* When using the age life method, an appraiser will use an age other than the actual age of the building. This is known as the effective age. ***EFFECTIVE AGE*** *is determined by the condition of the building rather than the age.* If a building has been maintained, its effective age may be less than the actual age; if there has been inadequate maintenance, it may be greater. ***ECONOMIC LIFE*** *is the estimated number of years of anticipated usefulness of the improvements.*

"Effective age" is determined by the condition and usefulness of the property, not the actual age.

ACCRUAL FOR DEPRECIATION *is the concept of estimating the amount of depreciation there will be in the future.* The accrual for depreciation is used in the income approach, discussed next.

To accurately estimate accrued depreciation, the appraiser must have experience, skill and good judgment. He or she must not only estimate the physical wear and tear on the building, but also the losses in value due to outmoded styles, poor design and neighborhood changes that tend to reduce the value of the improvements. A property can lose value through three different types of depreciation.

The three types of depreciation are: 1) physical, 2) functional and 3) economic.

Physical Deterioration (Curable Or Incurable)

PHYSICAL DETERIORATION *is the loss in value due to wear and tear.* As a building gets older, its age will start to show visibly. Since most types of physical deterioration can be repaired, we usually think of it as curable depreciation. On the other hand, severe structural deterioration may not be curable. So physical deterioration can be either curable or incurable. ***CURABLE DEPRECIATION*** *are repairs that add more to a building's value than they cost.* ***INCURABLE DEPRECIATION*** *refers to repairs that would be so expensive they are not economically feasible.*

Examples of physical deterioration (curable or incurable) are:

- a) all forms of wear and tear
- b) damage from dryrot and termites
- c) negligent care (deferred maintenance)
- d) depreciation that has already occurred.

Chapter 11

Functional Obsolescence (Curable Or Incurable)

FUNCTIONAL OBSOLESCENCE is the loss in value due to outmoded style or non-usable space. Examples of functional obsolescence would be a bedroom that can be reached only by walking through another bedroom. By modern standards this is very inconvenient, and reduces the value of the second bedroom. Another devaluing factor is a home with a single car garage. Functional depreciation is hard to cure. If the cost of curing the defect adds at least the same amount to the property's value, then it is worth the investment.

Types of functional obsolescence (curable or incurable) are:

> a) an out-dated kitchen
> b) antique fixtures
> c) a four bedroom, one bath home
> d) a one car garage
> e) massive cornices

Economic Obsolescence (Incurable)

ECONOMIC OBSOLESCENCE (ALSO REFERRED TO AS SOCIAL OBSOLESCENCE) is the loss in value due to changes in the neighborhood and is external to the property itself. It is always incurable. If a freeway is built next to your property, your home will decrease in value because of the noise and nuisance factor. On the other hand, if the freeway is three blocks away, your house will increase in value because of improved freeway access. If social or economic factors cause a neighborhood to become shabby and run-down, the value of your property will decrease accordingly.

Since economic obsolescence results from "off the property" causes, it is always incurable. Economic (profitable) life remaining is the main concern when purchasing an older property.

Types of economic obsolescence (incurable) are:

> a) over supply of similar or competitive units
> b) beyond the confines of the property
> c) aircraft noise

332

d) adverse zoning and legislative acts
e) economic recession
f) departure of major industries from the area
g) rental increases (tenants in area are prospering)

STEP 4 - VALUE OF THE PROPERTY

The last step in the cost approach is to add the depreciated value of any improvements to the value of the land. This figure is the market value of the property using the cost approach.

ADVANTAGES & DISADVANTAGES OF THE COST APPROACH

The cost approach is best for new, unique architecture & public buildings.

The main advantages of the cost approach is that it can be used on: 1) newly constructed buildings, 2) unique structures and 3) public buildings. Since there is little depreciation, if any, to calculate on newer buildings and there is available construction cost data, the value can be easily determined using the cost approach. Unique structures, public buildings and one-of-a-kind structures have no comparables so the cost approach may be the only logical way to appraise them.

The cost approach is limited (least reliable) for an older property. Older properties are harder to appraise because depreciation is difficult to estimate.

The disadvantages of using the cost approach are listed below:

1. There must be an accurate value of the site (land).

2. Since determining depreciation is more difficult as buildings age, the reliability of the depreciation estimate may be questioned.

3. This approach may be difficult to apply to condos or planned unit developments because the land, improvements and marketing costs are not always easy to determine just for appraising one unit.

CAPITALIZATION APPROACH
(INCOME APPROACH)

The income approach is concerned with the "present worth of future benefits."

The **INCOME APPROACH** *is the process of changing the net income projection from a property into its market value.* Another word for this process is **capitalization.** The appraiser, when using the income approach, is determining the present property value based upon the information he or she has on future income and expenses of that given property.

The actual process of capitalization is simple. Divide a capitalization rate into the net income; the answer you obtain is the value of the property.

$$\frac{\text{NET INCOME}}{\text{CAPITALIZATION RATE}} = \text{VALUE OF PROPERTY}$$

$$\frac{\$11,000}{10\%} = \$110,000$$

Rent producing (income) properties such as apartments, offices, warehouses and manufacturing concerns can best be appraised by the income approach. This is because the people who invest in such projects are primarily interested in the income that they will receive. It is only natural that an investor would choose the property producing the highest return. The income approach allows a comparison of different types of income producing real estate and, at the same time, analyzes each as to the return of income to be received from that investment in the future.

The basis for the income approach is to determine the quality, quantity and durability of the property's net income (future income).

STEPS IN THE INCOME APPROACH

There are five basic steps to establish value using the income approach:

1. Determine the annual effective gross income
2. List and Deduct operating expenses to obtain
3. Net Income
4. Divide by the appropriate capitalization rate to determine
5. Total Value

Figure 11-5 illustrates the five steps.

FIGURE 11-5

Step 1 - Calculate The Annual Effective Gross Income

Calculate the annual effective gross income from the investment property. **EFFECTIVE GROSS INCOME** *is the gross income minus any vacancies or rental losses.* In the case of rental properties, the annual gross rental income will be the annual rent that a owner receives if he or she charges the going rental rates with no vacancies. Sometimes managers charge rents that are below the market level, resulting in a very low number of vacancies. On the other hand, rents that are set too high usually yield a higher vacancy rate. The *VACANCY FACTOR is the loss in rents due to any cause.* This is commonly expressed as a percentage. The vacancy factor increases while trying to find a new tenant or because of cleaning, repairs or non-paying renters.

Subtract deductions from the gross rental income for vacancies or any rental losses to arrive at the effective gross income.

Step 2 - Complete An Operating Expense Statement

Complete an operating expense statement. The seven basic operating expense categories for this type of statement are listed below:

1. Property taxes
2. Insurance and licenses
3. Manager fees
4. Utilities
5. Maintenance and repairs
6. Services (i.e., gardener)
7. Replacement reserves

Management fees and replacement reserves must always be included in the basic operating expenses.

The expenses listed in the operating statement should represent the actual cost of each item. Though costs may vary, it is the appraiser's responsibility to determine what actual costs are on an annual basis.

Never deduct mortgage payments of principal or interest from the operating expense statement. They are part of an investor's analysis, not an appraisal.

An item that may need explanation is the replacement reserve. A **REPLACEMENT RESERVE** *consists of funds set aside for the purpose of replacing items in the future.* An example of a replacement reserve cost would be a $2,000 water heater with a life expectancy of five years. The replacement reserve for this item would be $400 per year ($2,000/5.)

"Variable costs" are operating expenses that can vary (utilities and repairs). "Fixed costs" remain constant; such as property taxes and fire insurance.

Step 3 - Deduct The Related Operating Expenses

To determine net income, simply deduct the related operating expenses (Step 2) from the annual effective gross income (Step 1).

To arrive at net income, deduct the above operating expenses from effective gross income.

Step 4 - Divide Net Income By The Appropriate Capitalization Rate

Divide the net income by the appropriate capitalization rate.

Rule: Always convert a monthly or quarterly net income into an annual net income before dividing by the capitalization rate.

Selection of a capitalization rate can be a delicate task. A one percent change in the capitalization rate, for example, can alter the estimated value of a property by up to ten percent or more. The capitalization rate is composed of a return to the investor "on" his or her original investment and "of" the amount to replace the building later.

For example, an investor may want an annual return of eight percent "on" his or her original investment, but two percent a year is needed to replace the building when its economic life is over. Determination of the appropriate capitalization rate takes skill and training.

The greater the risk, the greater the cap-rate.

There are several ways to select the proper capitalization rate. One way of selecting the appropriate capitalization rate is to sample similar recent apartment sales. Simply divide the net income by the sales price to obtain the capitalization rate used in that particular area.

Establishing the capitalization rate is the most difficult step for appraisers using the income approach.

The capitalization rate is composed of two parts: (1) a rate of return "on" the money invested and (2) a return "of" the asset that may be decreasing in value, but is rising in replacement cost. This is commonly referred to as the recapture rate, or depreciation. See Figure 11-6.

FIGURE 11-6

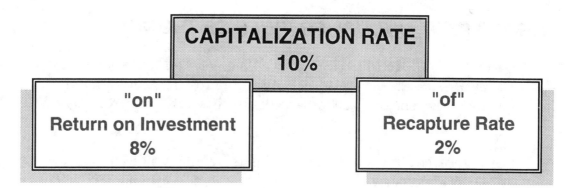

The capitalization rate is composed of two parts: the rate "on" the money invested (expected investor's return) and the annual rate "of" depreciation (recapture) on the improvements.

Capitalization rates can be determined by these advanced methods (not discussed here):

    1. Comparison
    2. Summation
    3. Bands of Investment

Step 5 - Result Of Dividing Net Income By Capitalization Rate

This is the easiest and final step in the income approach. It is simply the result of dividing net income by the capitalization rate.

Net Income divided by Capitalization Rate = Market Value

$$\frac{\text{Net income } \$65,000}{\text{Capitalization Rate } 10\% \ (.10)} = \ \$650,000 \text{ Estimated Market Value}$$

THE MARKET VALUE WHEN USING THE INCOME APPROACH IS $650,000

The appraised value increases when the "capitalization rate" is decreased. The capitalization rate represents the integration of the 1) rate on income, expressed as interest, and the 2) rate of recapture, expressed as depreciation.

GROSS RENT MULTIPLIER (RULE OF THUMB)

GROSS RENT MULTIPLIER is a multiplication rule of thumb used to convert the rental value into market value. If we use a gross rent multiplier of 125 times the monthly rent of $1,000, the property is worth approximately $125,000 (125 x $1,000).

See Figure 11-7 for more details. This is definitely not an accurate way to appraise a property, but it does give a quick estimate of value. Many professional investors use it as a screening device to eliminate undesirable investment opportunities. This monthly gross multiplier is often used for single family homes and apartment buildings.

A quick way to convert gross income into the approximate value is to use the gross rent multiplier.

The *GROSS RENT is the money received from a property before any expenses are deducted.* To use an annual gross rent multiplier, simply determine the total annual rents and multiply this times the annual gross rent multiplier.

FIGURE 11-7

GROSS RENT MULTIPLIER

The *GROSS RENT MULTIPLIER is a rough, quick way of converting gross rent into market value.* To obtain the gross rent multiplier, divide the rent into the "sales" price. It is not a very accurate method, but it is a good estimator because it is so easy.

$$\frac{\text{SALES PRICE}}{\text{RENT}} = \text{GROSS MULTIPLIER}$$

Typical Problems:

If a house that rented for $600 a month sold for $78,000, what is the gross multiplier?

$$\frac{\$78,000 \text{ Sales price}}{\text{Monthly Rent } \$600} = 130 \text{ (Gross Multiplier)}$$

If a similar house down the street is renting for $690, what would the selling price be?

Monthly Rent $690 x 130 (Gross Multiplier) = $89,700.

CAN *ANNUAL* RENTS BE USED?

The gross multiplier is not a percentage, so it can be expressed as either a monthly or an annual figure. If the above problem were expressed as an annual rent figure, the gross multiplier would have to be divided by 12. The gross annual multiplier is 10.83 (130/12.)

If a house that rents for $7,200 a year sold for $78,000, what is the annual gross multiplier?

$$\frac{\$78,000 \text{ Sales Price}}{\text{Annual Rent } \$7,200} = 10.83 \text{ Annual Gross Multiplier}$$

In the real estate investment field, it is common knowledge that the annual gross income multiplier of "x 6.2" is a good "rule of thumb" for an investment. For example, if the annual gross income from an apartment project is $40,000, its value should be approximately $248,000 ($40,000 x 6.2). The annual gross rent multiplier varies from "x 5" to "x 10," depending upon the location of the property and the condition of the individual buildings. Remember: this is an approximation device and should be used only as a quick estimate—not in place of an actual appraisal.

A desert cabin which rents for $150 per month just sold for $24,000. A similar property rents for $165 per month, so the market value is most likely to be near $26,400.

Remember the rule! Confirmed sales price ($24,000) divided by gross monthly rent ($150) equals gross rent multiplier of 160 ... then it follows that the gross rent multiplier of 160 times the rent ($165) of a similar property equals a $26,400 market value.

BEST FOR "INCOME PROPERTIES" (ADVANTAGE & DISADVANTAGE)

The advantage of the income approach method is that no other method focuses solely on determining the present value of the future income stream from the subject property. It is a little different than the other two methods of determining value in that "If the purpose of the property is to generate income; use the income approach." For example a house that is zoned for commercial use may be valued at a much higher amount when used as an insurance office rather than as a house. The location may bring in a great deal of income; as a house the market value is low, but as an income producing property the market value may be very high.

The "present worth of future benefits" is what the income approach is all about.

It is most often used for multi-family residential income property but could be used on any type of property that generates income.

The disadvantage of the income approach is that it may be difficult to determine the proper capitalization rate. For example, it may be impossible to ascertain the cap-rate for a theme park or alligator farm. These other items used in the income approach may also be difficult to estimate: vacancy rate, economic rent, operation expenses and reserve requirements.

CORRELATION OF VALUE (BRACKETING)

The last and most important part of the appraisal process is the correlation (sometimes referred to as reconciliation) of the three approaches to value. *CORRELATION is the process of selecting the most appropriate approach for the particular appraisal job and giving it the most consideration in pinpointing the final value.* Although all three methods are used in appraisal, one is usually most appropriate for a specific appraisal problem.

> *In general, the market comparison approach is best for single-family homes or lots; the cost approach is best for new, unique or unusual structures; and the income approach is best for properties that can be used to generate income.*

FINAL ESTIMATE OF VALUE (APPRAISAL REPORT)

The appraisal report is the documentation of the appraiser's findings. It can be fashioned in a simple letter style, a prepared fill-in form may be used or it may be delivered orally. However, if it is complicated or subject to close interpretation, the report should be written in a narrative form with supporting data contained in supplemental exhibits. In practice most appraisal reports are written.

There are three main types of appraisal reports:

1. **Short form** (a form with checks and explanations)
2. **Letter form** (a short written report)
3. **Narrative report** (most complete and extensive)

Many community colleges and universities offer courses in appraisal or investment properties to acquaint you with the techniques involved in the income approach.

http://www.mtsac.edu/info_tech/learning_res/other.html
(Information on the California Community Colleges)

Whether the report is a simple one page report or an extensive volume, the following information should be presented:

1. An adequate description for the property that is being appraised.
2. A statement as to the purpose and scope of the appraisal.
3. An adequate description of the neighborhood.
4. The date on which the value is estimated.
5. The qualifying conditions and assumptions.
6. The factual data, maps and photos with their analyses and interpretations.
7. The processing of the data by one or more of the three approaches to value (correlation).
8. The estimate of value.
9. The name, address, type of license (and any certifications) and signature of the appraiser.

There is no information about the buyer's or seller's financial condition on an appraisal report.

COST OF AN APPRAISAL

Appraisal costs can vary from relatively small amounts to thousands of dollars. The cost of an appraisal may be affected by its purpose, the qualifications of the appraiser and how detailed the appraisal. An appraisal used to document a court case could cost several thousand dollars.

It would be impractical to spend thousands of dollars for a home appraisal just to determine a selling price. If you are thinking about selling your home, your local real estate broker will probably do this at no cost. Local brokers are familiar with your area and are knowledgeable about current sales prices of similar homes in your neighborhood. On the other hand, appraisal of large parcels, commercial buildings and apartment houses, or appraisals to be used in court, may require the services of a highly skilled appraiser. Although the fees are higher, they reflect the experience and ability of the appraiser. The appraisal fee and an outline of what is to be accomplished in the appraisal should be set in advance. It is unethical to set an appraisal fee as part of the determined value. This may influence the appraiser to increase the value.

Appraisal Report Copies

A lender must provide a notice to a loan applicant stating that the applicant is entitled to a copy of the appraisal report if the applicant requests and pays for the report.

The notice must be provided on any loan secured by residential property and on purchase money financing (or refinancing of purchase money debt) on non-residential property.

LICENSING, FEE APPRAISERS & APPRAISAL ORGANIZATIONS

APPRAISAL LICENSE AND CERTIFICATION

All appraisers are required to be licensed or certified. See figure 11-8. The license/certification categories are:

1. **TRAINEE LICENSE**
2. **RESIDENTIAL LICENSE**
3. **CERTIFIED RESIDENTIAL LICENSE**
4. **CERTIFIED GENERAL LICENSE**

For more information write to the Office of Real Estate Appraisers:

Office of Real Estate Appraisers
P.O. Box 942874
Sacramento, California 94274-0001
http://www.orea.cahwnet.gov (Office of Real Estate Appraisers)

FIGURE 11-8

APPRAISER LICENSE/CERTIFICATION

1. TRAINEE LICENSE

A minimum of 90 hours of appraisal and 15 hours of Uniform Standards of Professional Appraisal Practice (USPAP) education is required. The trainee must also pass the (AQB) approved residential exam.

Education: 90 hours.

2. RESIDENTIAL LICENSE

Appraisals (non-complex) of one-to-four residential units up to a transaction value of $1 million and complex appraisals of one-to-four residential units up to a transaction value of $250,000.

Education: 2,000 hours of acceptable experience. Plus 90 hours of education and at least 15 hours of USPAP education.

3. CERTIFIED RESIDENTIAL LICENSE

Appraisal of residential transactions without regard to transaction value or complexity.

Education: 2,500 hours and 2 and 1/2 years of acceptable experience. Plus 120 hours of education and at least 15 hours of USPAP education.

4. CERTIFIED GENERAL LICENSE

Appraisals of all real estate transactions without regard to transaction value or complexity.

Education: 3,000 hours and 2 and 1/2 years of acceptable experience and at least 1 and 1/2 years of non-residential acceptable experience. Plus 180 hours of education and at least 15 hours of USPAP education.

All licensed and certified appraisers must complete 14 hours of approved continuing education each calendar year.

An appraisal license or certification is required to appraise a property that involves a loan from a financial institution that carries federal (FDIC) insurance or is backed by VA, FHA, FNMA, FHLMC or GNMA. In effect, most of the appraisals that require financing also require a Licensed Appraiser, a Certified Residential Appraiser or a Certified General Appraiser.

Appraisal Methods

FEE APPRAISERS

It is permissible to accept an appraisal fee for servicing on a property in which the appraiser has an interest, provided the fact has been disclosed to his or her client in writing.

A *FEE APPRAISER* *is an independent, self-employed appraiser; he or she appraises for a fee or charge.* In California a license or certification is required to appraise real estate as a profession. Other appraisers are dependent on large corporations or organizations for their employment. Gas, electric, telephone and other utility companies have appraisal departments. Banks, savings banks, mortgage companies and other lenders often have in-house appraisal staffs. Most cities and counties have large appraisal staffs in their assessors' offices. There are also various state agencies, such as Cal-Trans, that maintain appraisal staffs.

A fee appraiser is self-employed; he or she appraises for a fee or charge. Remember: appraisers and real estate agents are concerned with the marketability of residential properties.

http://naifa.com (National Association of Independent Fee Appraisers)
http://www.iami.org/narea.html (National Association of Real Estate Appraisers)

PROFESSIONAL APPRAISAL ORGANIZATIONS

As the leading organization of professional real estate appraisers, the Appraisal Institute has general appraisal members who hold the MAI, SRPA, or SREA designation and residential appraisal members who hold the SRA or RM designation. Currently, the Appraisal Institute confers one general designation, the MAI, and one residential designation, the SRA.

The primary objectives of this organization are to provide education and to have their members adhere to a strictly enforced Code of Professional Ethics and Standards of Professional Appraisal Practice. The minimal candidate includes: 1) a certain number of years of actual appraisal experience; 2) successful completion of a comprehensive written exam; and 3) approval of at least one narrative appraisal report.

Appraisal Institute
875 N. Michigan Avenue
Chicago, Illinois 60611-1980

APPRAISAL INSTITUTE

To keep its members informed, the Appraisal Institute publishes educational material monthly in the *APPRAISAL JOURNAL*. If you are interested in additional educational material or candidacy requirements, you may write directly to this organization:

Appraisal Institute
875 N. Michigan Avenue
Chicago, Illinois 60611-1980

http://www.appraisalinstitute.org (Appraisal Institute)
http://www.frea.com (Foundation of Real Estate Appraisers)

Appraisal Methods

TERMINOLOGY - CHAPTER 11

A. Market Comparison	**I.** Income Approach	**Q.** Effective Gross Income
B. Cost Approach	**J.** Vacancy Factor	**R.** Direct Costs
C. Replacement Cost	**K.** Replacement Reserve	**S.** Indirect Costs
D. Square Footage	**L.** Gross Rent Multiplier	**T.** Reproduction Cost
E. Depreciation	**M.** Correlation	**U.** Accrued Depreciation
F. Physical Deterioration	**N.** Actual Age	**V.** Accrual for Depreciation
G. Functional Obsolescence	**O.** Effective Age	**W.** Curable Depreciation
H. Economic Obsolescence	**P.** Economic Life	**X.** Incurable Depreciation

1.____ The estimated percentage of vacancies in a rental property, such as in an apartment building.

2.____ The use of different appraisal methods to reach an estimate of the value of a property. The methods must be weighed as to which is most appropriate for the type of property being appraised.

3.____ The theoretical cost of replacing a building with one of equivalent usefulness.

4.____ A simple method of using gross monthly or yearly rents to obtain an approximate value of an income property.

5.____ The need to replace part of a structure because new improvements have come along that make the older structure inefficient by comparison. For example, a one bathroom, eight bedroom house.

6.____ An appraisal method, estimating the replacement cost of a structure, less depreciation, plus land value.

7.____ Loss of desirability and useful life of a property through economic forces, such as zoning changes, traffic pattern changes, etc., rather than wear and tear.

8.____ A decrease in the value of real property improvements for any reason.

9.____ An appraisal method to determine the present value today of rental property by estimating the income it will generate over the life of the structure.

10.____ A way of measuring real property in 1 ft. by 1 ft. segments.

11.____ The method of estimating the value of real property by adjusting the sales price of comparable properties for differences.

12.____ Gradual physical wear and tear on a structure that decreases its value.

13.____ Periodically setting money aside to replace systems and appliances in a building. For example, a landlord putting aside a portion of monthly rents toward a new roof or water heater.

14.____ The chronological age of a structure as opposed to its effective or economic life.

15.____ Accumulation of depreciation.

16.____ Construction costs (material and labor).

17.____ The cost of reproducing a property (usually one that has been destroyed) at current prices using the same materials.

18.____ Repairs that would be so expensive they are not economically feasible.

19.____ Age of a structure as estimated by its condition rather than its actual age.

20.____ Repairs that are economically logical to do.

21.____ Costs other than labor and materials.

22.____ Amount of depreciation in the future, not past.

23.____ The "profitable" life of an improvement. Generally shorter than the physical life.

24.____ Gross income of a building if fully rented, less an allowance for estimated vacancies.

MULTIPLE CHOICE

1. An army base moved out of an area, which caused unemployment and housing values to drop. This is referred to as:

    A. economic obsolescence
    C. physical obsolescence
    B. functional obsolescence
    D. none of the above

2. In the appraisal of residential property, the cost approach is most useful in the case of:

    A. single-family dwellings
    C. middle-aged properties
    B. older, greatly depreciated properties
    D. new structures

3. Which is the best method for appraising single-family homes?

    A. Market approach
    C. Cost approach
    B. Income approach
    D. Correlation approach

4. The appraiser must determine the construction expense of replacing a building today, using current construction methods, with the:

    A. market approach
    C. income approach
    B. cost approach
    D. expense approach

5. Wear and tear on the roof of an urban office building would constitute:

    A. physical deterioration
    C. economic depreciation
    B. functional obsolescence
    D. commercial damages

6. If an appraiser lowered the value of a house due to functional obsolescence, he would be referring to:

    A. termites
    C. single-car garage
    B. economic decline in the neighborhood
    D. damage to the foundation

7. Loss of value due to changes in the neighborhood and external to the property is called:

    A. economic obsolescence
    C. functional obsolescence
    B. physical deterioration
    D. income obsolescence

8. A mathematical rule of thumb used to convert the rental value into market value is known as the:

    A. correlation multiplier
    C. gross rent multiplier
    B. net multiplier
    D. evaluation process

9. A water heater costs $1000 and is expected to last five years. The $200 a year that would be put aside for this expense is called the:

    A. maintenance cost
    C. replacement reserve
    B. plumbing reserve
    D. operating expense

10. Which of the following would NOT normally be appraised by the income method?

    A. Apartments
    C. Warehouses
    B. Government land
    D. Offices

CHAPTER 12
Subdivisions & Government Control

http://dre.cahwnet.gov/submenu.htm (DRE—Subdivisions, Public Report)
http://www.ca.gov/s/history/people.html (People of California—History)

There will be about 36 million people in California by the year 2000; we are adding over 1,700 new residents each day.

With a population of more than thirty-two million people, California has more people than any other state. That means we have approximately 12% of the United States population. Since we are such a fast growing and mobile state, the problems encountered can be tremendous. The state and local governments have the responsibility (under the doctrine of police power) to enact and enforce legislative acts to protect the general public. This public protection in the real estate area prevents fraud, misrepresentation and deceit.

POLICE POWER

Police power is the right of public officials to control the use of private property for the health, safety and general welfare of the public.

POLICE POWER *is the power to make rulings to control the "use and taking of private property" for the protection of the public's health, safety and welfare.* Police power allows the state, county or city to protect its citizens by controlling how land is being used.

Police power provides for the regulation of lot design and physical improvements for the orderly and proper development of the community, the construction of streets, highways and parking facilities adequate for our car-oriented society and the certainty of an adequate water supply. It ensures the protection of life and property by police and firemen, the maintenance of the purity of air we breathe, the control of noise, the disposal of sewage and waste and the provision, under public or private regulation, for essential utility services. Figure 12-1 shows seven basic areas of government control at either the state or local level.

FIGURE 12-1

Subdivision & Government Control

THE BASIC SUBDIVISION LAWS

When anyone divides a parcel of land into five or more parcels with the intent to sell, lease or finance them now or in the future, they have created a **SUBDIVISION**. *But if there is some form of common or mutual ownership rights in one parcel, this is also a subdivision.* A condominium is sometimes referred to as a "one lot subdivision."

There are two basic laws under which subdivisions are controlled in California:

(1) Subdivision Map Act (City or County)
(2) Subdivided Lands Law (Department of Real Estate)

These two laws were enacted for different purposes, and were adopted to achieve the objective for which each was designed.

SUBDIVISION MAP ACT
(ENFORCED BY LOCAL CITY OR COUNTY)

The primary objective of the **SUBDIVISION MAP ACT** *is to provide an outline of the methods for the subdivision filing procedure at the city or county level and to make sure subdividers comply with the city's master plan.* This law permits the local government of the city or county to enact subdivision ordinances. Thus, the direct control of the kind and type of subdivision for each community, and the public physical improvements to be installed, is left to the local city (if incorporated) or county (if unincorporated). This act has two major objectives:

1. To coordinate the subdivision plans including lot design, street patterns, drainage and sewers, etc., with the community pattern (master plan) as laid out by the local planning authorities.

2. To ensure, by the filing of the subdivision maps, that parts of the subdivision area will be dedicated to the city or county for public purposes. These dedications include public streets and other public areas, dedicated by the subdivision so that they will not be an unmanageable future burden upon the taxpayers of the community.

State law now requires that each community (city or county government) shall enact local subdivision ordinances. Before the Department of Real Estate will approve the subdivision, a tentative subdivision map must be approved by the local government.

353

SUBDIVIDED LANDS LAW
(STATE LAW ENFORCED BY THE DRE)

This law is statewide in its operation and is directly administered by the California Real Estate Commissioner. The basic objective of the **SUBDIVIDED LANDS LAW** *is to protect the purchasers of property in new subdivisions from fraud, misrepresentation or deceit in the marketing of subdivided lots, parcels, condominiums or other undivided property interests in the state of California.*

No subdivision unit can be offered for sale in California unless the commissioner has issued a subdivision public report. This applies not only to tracts located in California, but also to subdivided lands lying partly outside the state's boundaries. The public report is a factual account of the subdivided property.

The report is not issued until the commissioner is satisfied that the subdivider has met all the statutory requirements, with particular emphasis on the establishment and facilities included in the offering, and demonstrates that the lots or parcels can be used for the purpose for which they are being offered.

PUBLIC REPORT (CONSUMER INFORMATION)

> *The public report (issued by the Department of Real Estate) is required reading by any purchaser.*

As provided by the Subdivided Lands Law, purchasers of a home in a new subdivision must receive a Public Report from the California Real Estate Commissioner's office. A **PUBLIC REPORT** *is a formal disclosure report of the important facts regarding a subdivision.* It is, in a sense, a developer's "permit" to sell. It is not, however, a recommendation pro or con. Figures 12-2 to 12-6 illustrate a five-page public report. The report makes clear the physical characteristics of the land, so that the buyer can know exactly what he or she is buying. The buyer is told the size, arrangement and location of the lot and exactly what off-site improvements and recreation facilities to expect.

> *A subdivider must give a copy of the commissioner's public report to anyone who requests one.*

There may be two public reports. The optional preliminary report may be submitted to the Department of Real Estate for tentative approval. The required final report must be issued and given to the buyer. The **PRELIMINARY PUBLIC REPORT (PINK)** *is a tentative public report that must be given to each prospective purchaser.* The report is printed on pink paper, making it easily recognizable. It is given to a buyer when he or she makes a reservation to purchase or lease a lot, unit or parcel in a subdivision.

Preliminary reports allow subdividers to only obtain reservations: they cannot sell and the deposit is fully refundable. Any preliminary report issued will expire when the final report is published or after one year passes, whichever is first.

A prospective purchaser must be given a copy of the preliminary report and sign a receipt to that effect. A copy of the reservation agreement is signed by the prospective buyer and the money deposited with a neutral escrow company. **The reservation to buy or lease must contain a clause allowing the buyer the option to cancel his or her reservation at any time and immediately have the deposit returned.** Any preliminary report issued will expire when the final report is published or after one year passes, whichever occurs first. The subdivider must keep receipts taken for any public report on file for three years.

In the event that the R. E. Commissioner wishes to stop sales for violations, a "Desist and Refrain Order" would be issued.

The **FINAL PUBLIC REPORT (WHITE)**, *"Real Estate Commissioner's Final Subdivision Public Report,"* is the official report that must be given to the buyer. The buyer must receive a copy of the final public report even if he or she has a preliminary public report. After having enough time to read it, the buyer must sign a receipt stating that the report has been received. There is a five-year time limit on the report and it can be updated and renewed.

Important! Do not buy into any new subdivision unless you have read the report and have checked out all questions that you may have.

FIGURE 12-2

*Department of Real Estate
of the
State of California*

FINAL SUBDIVISION PUBLIC REPORT

In the matter of the application of

ROLLINGWOOD GREEN ASSOCIATES, INC.
a California Corporation

FILE NO.   :   025053SA-F00

ISSUED   :   SEPTEMBER 21, 1988

EXPIRES   :   SEPTEMBER 20, 1993

for a Final Subdivision Public Report on

ROLLINGWOOD GREEN (PHASE TWO)

SACRAMENTO COUNTY, CALIFORNIA

JAMES A. EDMONDS, JR.
Commissioner

by _____ S.S. Turner

Deputy Commissioner

CONSUMER INFORMATION

❖ THIS REPORT IS NOT A RECOMMENDATION OR ENDORSEMENT OF THE SUBDIVISION; IT IS INFORMATIVE ONLY.

❖ BUYER OR LESSEE MUST SIGN THAT (S)HE HAS RECEIVED AND READ THIS REPORT.

❖ A copy of this subdivision public report along with a statement advising that a copy of the public report may be obtained from the owner, subdivider, or agent at any time, upon oral or written request, *must* be posted in a conspicuous place at any office where sales or leases or offers to sell or lease interests in this subdivision are regularly made. *[Reference Business and Professions (B&P) Code Section 11018.1(b)]*

This report expires on the date shown above. All material changes must be reported to the Department of Real Estate. *(Refer to Section 11012 of the B&P Code; and Chapter 6, Title 10 of the California Administrative Code, Regulation 2800.)* Some material changes may require amendment of the Public Report; which Amendment must be obtained and used in lieu of this report.

Section 12920 of the California Government Code provides that the practice of discrimination in housing accommodations on the basis of race, color, religion, sex, martial status, national origin, physical handicap or ancestry, is against public policy.

Under Section 125.6 of the B&P Code, California real estate licensees are subject to disciplinary action by the Real Estate Commissioner if they discriminate or make any distinction or restriction in negotiating the sale or lease of real property because of the race, color, sex, religion, ancestry, national origin, or physical handicap of the client. If any prospective buyer or lessee believes that a licensee is guilty of such conduct, (s)he should contact the Department of Real Estate.

READ THE ENTIRE REPORT ON THE FOLLOWING PAGES BEFORE CONTRACTING TO BUY OR LEASE AN INTEREST IN THIS SUBDIVISION.

RE 618 (Rev. 12/87)

Page 1 of 5   File No. 025053SA-F00

FIGURE 12-3

COMMON INTEREST DEVELOPMENT
GENERAL INFORMATION

The project described in the attached Subdivision Public Report is known as a common-interest development. Read the Public Report carefully for more information about the type of development. The development includes common areas and facilities which will be owned and/or operated by an owners' association. Purchase of a lot or unit automatically entitles and obligates you as a member of the association and, in most cases, includes a beneficial interest in the areas and facilities. Since membership in the association is mandatory, you should be aware of the following information before you purchase:

Your ownership in this development and your rights and remedies as a member of its association will be controlled by governing instruments which generally include a Declaration of Restrictions (also known as CC&R's), Articles of Incorporation (or association) and bylaws. The provisions of these documents are intended to be, and in most cases are, enforceable in a court of law. Study these documents carefully before entering into a contract to purchase a subdivision interest.

In order to provide funds for operation and maintenance of the common facilities, the association will levy assessments against your lot or unit. If you are delinquent in the payment of assessments, the association may enforce payment through court proceedings or your lot or unit may be liened and sold through the exercise of a power of sale. The anticipated income and expenses of the association, including the amount that you may expect to pay through assessments, are outlined in the proposed budget. Ask to see a copy of the budget if the subdivider has not already made it available for your examination.

CALIFORNIA
DEPARTMENT
OF REAL ESTATE

RE 646 (Rev. 2/86)

A homeowner association provides a vehicle for the ownership and use of recreational and other common facilities which were designed to attract you to buy in this development. The association also provides a means to accomplish architectural control and to provide a base for homeowner interaction on a variety of issues. The purchaser of an interest in a common-interest development should contemplate active participation in the affairs of the association. He or she should be willing to serve on the board of directors or on committees created by the board. In short, "they" in a common interest development is "you". Unless you serve as a member of the governing board or on a committee apointed by the board, your control of the operation of the common areas and facilities is limited to your vote as a member of the association. There are actions that can be taken by the governing body without a vote of the members of the association which can have a significant impact upon the quality of life for association members.

Until there is a sufficient number of purchasers of lots or units in a common interest devolopment to elect a majority of the governing body, it is likely that the subdivider will effectively control the affairs of the association. It is frequently necessary and equitable that the subdivider do so during the early stages of development. It is vitally important to the owners of individual subdivision interests that the transition from subdivider to resident-owner control be accomplished in an orderly manner and in a spirit of cooperation.

When contemplating the purchase of a dwelling in a common interest development, you should consider factors beyond the attractiveness of the dwelling units themselves. Study the governing instruments and give careful thought to whether you will be able to exist happily in an atmosphere of cooperative living where the interests of the group must be taken into account as well as the interests of the individual. Remember that managing a common interest development is very much like governing a small community . . . the management can serve you well, but you will have to work for its success. [B & P Code Section 11018.1(c)]

Page 2 of 5   File No. 025053SA-F00

FIGURE 12-4

<u>SPECIAL NOTES</u>

1. IF YOU HAVE RECEIVED A PRELIMINARY PUBLIC REPORT FOR THIS SUBDIVISION, YOU ARE ADVISED TO CAREFULLY READ THIS FINAL PUBLIC REPORT SINCE IT CONTAINS INFORMATION THAT IS MORE CURRENT AND PROBABLY DIFFERENT THAN THAT INCLUDED IN THE PRELIMINARY REPORT.

2. IF YOU ENTER INTO AN AGREEMENT TO PURCHASE OR LEASE AN INTEREST IN THE PROPERTY COVERED BY THIS PUBLIC REPORT, AND YOU SIGNED A RESERVATION AGREEMENT UNDER THE AUTHORITY OF A SHORT FORM PRELIMINARY PUBLIC REPORT, YOU HAVE A RIGHT TO RESCIND (CANCEL) THE AGREEMENT AND TO THE RETURN OF ANY MONEY OR OTHER CONSIDERATION THAT YOU HAVE GIVEN TOWARD THE PURCHASE OR LEASE UNTIL MIDNIGHT OF THE FIFTH CALENDAR DAY FOLLOWING THE DAY YOU EXECUTE THE CONTRACT TO PURCHASE OR LEASE. YOU MAY EXERCISE THIS RIGHT WITHOUT GIVING ANY REASON FOR YOUR ACTION AND WITHOUT INCURRING ANY PENALTY OR OBLIGATION BY NOTIFYING THE DEVELOPER (OR THE DEVELOPER'S AUTHORIZED REPRESENTATIVE) OF SUCH CANCELLATION BY TELEGRAM, MAIL, OR OTHER WRITTEN NOTICE SENT OR DELIVERED NOT LATER THAN MIDNIGHT OF THE FIFTH CALENDAR DAY FOLLOWING THE DATE THE CONTRACT WAS SIGNED. THE NOTIFICATION SHOULD BE SENT TO:

    ROLLINGWOOD GREEN ASSOCIATES, INC.,
    A CALIFORNIA CORPORATION
    ATTN: JAMES D. FLOOD
    9274 MADISON AVENUE
    ORANGEVALE, CA 95662

3. THIS PUBLIC REPORT COVERS ONLY RESIDENTIAL LOTS 19 THROUGH 40, INCLUSIVE, GARAGE LOTS 19G THROUGH 33G, INCLUSIVE, AND COMMON AREA LOT C.

4. THIS PROJECT IS A COMMON-INTEREST SUBDIVISION OF THE TYPE REFERRED TO AS A "PLANNED DEVELOPMENT". IT INCLUDES COMMON AREAS AND COMMON FACILITIES WHICH WILL BE MAINTAINED BY AN INCORPORATED OWNERS ASSOCIATION.

5. THE ASSOCIATION HAS THE RIGHT TO LEVY ASSESSMENTS AGAINST YOU FOR THE MAINTENANCE OF THE COMMON AREAS AND OTHER PURPOSES. YOUR CONTROL OF OPERATIONS AND EXPENSES IS LIMITED TO THE RIGHT OF YOUR ELECTED REPRESENTATIVES TO VOTE ON CERTAIN PROVISIONS AT MEETINGS.

6. WARNING: WHEN YOU SELL YOUR LOT TO SOMEONE ELSE, YOU MUST GIVE THAT PERSON A COPY OF THE DECLARATION OF RESTRICTIONS, ARTICLES OF INCORPORATION, THE BYLAWS AND A TRUE STATEMENT CONCERNING ANY DELINQUENT ASSESSMENTS, PENALTIES, ATTORNEYS' FEES OR OTHER CHARGES, PROVIDED BY THE CC&R'S OR OTHER MANAGEMENT DOCUMENTS ON THE LOT AS OF THE DATE THE STATEMENT WAS ISSUED.

    <u>NOTE:</u>   IF YOU FORGET TO DO THIS, IT MAY COST YOU A PENALTY OF $500.00 -- PLUS ATTORNEY'S FEES AND DAMAGES (SEE CIVIL CODE SECTION 1368).

    THE SUBDIVIDER MUST MAKE AVAILABLE TO YOU, COPIES OF THE ASSOCIATION GOVERNING INSTRUMENTS, A STATEMENT CONCERNING ANY DELINQUENT ASSESSMENTS AND RELATED CHARGES AS PROVIDED BY THE GOVERNING INSTRUMENTS AND, IF AVAILABLE, A CURRENT FINANCIAL AND RELATED STATEMENTS (SEE BUSINESS AND PROFESSIONS CODE SECTION 11018.6).

FIGURE 12-5

<u>INTERESTS TO BE CONVEYED</u>: You will receive fee title to a specified lot, together with a membership in the "Rollingwood Green Homeowners Association" and rights to use the common area.

<u>LOCATION AND SIZE</u>: This subdivision is located in Sacramento County at Madison Avenue near Hazel Avenue.

This is the second increment which consists of approximately 1.306 acres divided into twenty-two residential lots, and including the common area which consists of Lot "C".

Common facilities consisting of lighting, paving and landscaping will be constructed on the common area.

This increment is part of a total project which, if developed as proposed, will consist of a total of three increments containing 58 residential lots within the overall projected development.

There is no assurance that the total project will be completed as proposed.

<u>MANAGEMENT AND OPERATION</u>: The Rollingwood Green Homeowners Association, which you must join, manages and operates the common areas in accordance with the Restrictions, Articles of Incorporation, and the Bylaws.

<u>MAINTENANCE AND OPERATIONAL EXPENSES</u>: The subdivider has submitted budgets for the maintenance and operation of the common areas and for long-term reserves when the subdivision is substantially completed (built-out budget), and an interim budget applicable to this increment. These budgets were reviewed by the Department of Real Estate in October, 1986. You should obtain copies of these budgets from the subdivider.

<u>EASEMENTS</u>: Easements for utilities, planting, rights of way, and other purposes are shown on the Title Report and Subdivision Map recorded in the Office of the Sacramento County Recorder, Book 176 of Maps, Map No. 19 on July 14, 1987.

<u>RESTRICTIONS</u>: This subdivision is subject to Restrictions recorded in the Office of the Sacramento County Recorder, Book 8608-01, Page 522 et. seq., on August 1, 1986 and Declaration of Annexation, Book 8708-11, Page 2018 on August 11, 1987.

> FOR INFORMATION AS TO YOUR OBLIGATIONS AND RIGHTS, YOU SHOULD READ THE RESTRICTIONS. THE SUBDIVIDER SHOULD MAKE THEM AVAILABLE TO YOU.

<u>TAXES</u>: The maximum amount of any tax on real property that can be collected annually by counties is 1% of the full cash value of the property. With the addition of interest and redemption charges on any indebtedness, approved by voters prior to July 1, 1978, the total property tax rate in most counties is approximately 1.25% of the full cash value. In some counties, the total tax rate could be well above 1.25% of the full cash value. For example, an issue of general obligation bonds previously approved by the voters and sold by a county water district, a sanitation district or other such district could increase the total tax.

<u>ASSESSMENTS</u>: This subdivision lies within the boundaries of the Fair Oaks Irrigation District and the Sacramento Municipal Utilities District and is subject to any taxes, assessments and obligations thereof.

<u>CONDITIONS OF SALE - INTEREST TO BE CONVEYED</u>: If your purchase involves financing, a form of deed of trust and note will be used. The provisions of these documents may vary depending upon the lender selected.

> BEFORE SIGNING, YOU SHOULD READ AND <u>THOROUGHLY</u> UNDERSTAND ALL LOAN DOCUMENTS.

FIGURE 12-6

PURCHASE MONEY HANDLING: The subdivider must impound all funds received from you in an escrow depository until legal title is delivered to you. (Refer to Sections 11013, 11013.1 and 11013.2(a) of the Business and Professions Code.)

The subdivider advises that individual escrows will not close until 51 percent of the lots have been sold (applies only to lot purchasers obtaining financing from a lender imposing such a requirement).

If the escrow has not closed on your lot within twelve (12) months of the date of your escrow opening, you may request return of your deposit.

The subdivider has no such interest in the escrow company which is to be used in connection with the sale or lease of lots in this subdivision.

SOILS CONDITIONS: A Soils Report is available at Sacramento County Department of Public Works, 827 7th Street, Room 105, Sacramento, CA 95814.

GEOLOGIC CONDITIONS: THE UNIFORM BUILDING CODE, CHAPTER 70, PROVIDES FOR LOCAL BUILDING OFFICIALS TO EXERCISE PREVENTIVE MEASURES DURING GRADING TO ELIMINATE OR MINIMIZE DAMAGE FROM GEOLOGIC HAZARDS SUCH AS LANDSLIDES, FAULT MOVEMENTS, EARTHQUAKE SHAKING, RAPID EROSION OR SUBSIDENCE. THIS SUBDIVISION IS LOCATED IN AN AREA WHERE SOME OF THESE HAZARDS MAY EXIST. SOME CALIFORNIA COUNTIES AND CITIES HAVE ADOPTED ORDINANCES THAT MAY OR MAY NOT BE AS EFFECTIVE IN THE CONTROL OF GRADING AND SITE PREPARATION.

STREETS AND ROADS: The paved areas within this project will be maintained by the homeowner association. The costs of repair and maintenance of these paved areas are included in the budget and are a part of your regular assessment.

FIRE PROTECTION: The Fair Oaks Fire Protection District advises as follows:

"The above mentioned subdivision is within the Fair Oaks Fire Protection District. The project will be provided with a full range of fire and life safety services. Certain fees for service may be imposed for services provided, pursuant to Ordinance 85-1.

The closest fire station is approximately one and one half miles away.

This project will be served by public water and fire hydrants are required to be installed by the developer.

WATER: Fair Oaks Irrigation District.

GAS: Pacific Gas & Electric.

ELECTRIC: Sacramento Municipal Utilities District.

TELEPHONE: Pacific Bell.

For further information in regard to this subdivision, you may call or examine the documents at the Department of Real Estate, Subdivisions North, 2201 Broadway, Sacramento, California, 95818, (916) 739-3631.

Page 5 of 5   File No. 025053SA-F00

PUBLIC REPORT RECEIPTS

Subdivider must keep receipt of public report for a three-year period.

The receipt stating that the buyer has received a copy of any public report, and had the opportunity to read it, must be kept on file by the owner, his or her agent or the subdivider. Receipts for any public reports are subject to inspection, by the commissioner, for a three-year period. An approved reservation agreement form is furnished by the Department of Real Estate (See Figure 12-7). This form, or a form similar to it, is to be used when taking reservations and deposits under a preliminary public report or deposits under the final public report.

A subdivider must comply with the minimum housing standards that are the most rigid or stringent. If there is a discrepancy between local and state building codes, the highest standard of safety will prevail. A developer is responsible for streets, curbs and utilities in a new subdivision.

MATERIAL CHANGES (NOTIFY COMMISSIONER)

Change in price is not a material fact.

Any material change in the subdivision, or its handling, after the filing is made, or the public report is issued, must be reported to the Commissioner of Real Estate. This not only includes physical changes, such as changes in the lot or street lines, but any new condition or development that may affect the value of the subdivision or the terms of how it is offered to the public.

The owner of a standard type subdivision or planned development must report to the commissioner the sale of five or more parcels. The sale to a single purchaser of two or more units in a community apartment, condominium or stock cooperative project must also be reported. Failure to report material changes not only violates the law, but may furnish a basis for rescission, by court action, of purchases.

If a person purchases, or has an option to purchase, five or more lots in a subdivision, whether contiguous or not, the subdivider must immediately notify the Department of Real Estate with the name and address. The reason for this is that another subdivision has been created within the original subdivision, so a new Final Public Report will be required.

FIGURE 12-7

REGULATION 2795.1

REQUIRED RECEIPT FOR PUBLIC REPORT

The following form shall be duplicated and used by the owner, subdivider or agent as the prospective purchaser's receipt for the copy of the Public Report which was given to said prospective purchaser.

It shall also be used pertinent to all prospective purchasers who sign a reservation agreement under the authority of a Preliminary Public Report or a Short Form Preliminary Public Report.

The receipt is to be kept on file by the subdivider or his/her representative/agent for three years

---

RECEIPT FOR PUBLIC REPORT

The Laws and Regulations of the Real Estate Commissioner require that you as a prospective purchaser or lessee be afforded an opportunity to read the public report for this subdivision before you make any written offer to purchase or lease a subdivision interest or before any money or other consideration toward purchase or lease of a subdivision interest is accepted from you.

In the case of a preliminary subdivision public report, you must be afforded an opportunity to read the report before a written reservation or any deposit in connection therewith is accepted from you.

DO NOT SIGN THIS RECEIPT UNTIL YOU HAVE RECEIVED A COPY OF THE REPORT AND HAVE READ IT.

I have read the Commissioner's Public Report on

"CENTURY PARK PLACE"

054916LA-A04	37164, Phase 4, Lot 1
(File No.)	(Tract No. or Name)

I understand the report is not a recommendation or endorsement of the subdivision, but is for information only.

The date of the public report which is received and read is: _6/7/XX_ .

Vic Lester
Name

1307 Arden Street
Address

_6/7/XX_
Date

Subdivision & Government Control

SUBDIVISION DEFINED BY LAW

Although the definitions of the Subdivided Lands Law and the Subdivision Map Act are in many ways similar, there are some differences. Both define a subdivision as improved or unimproved land divided for the purpose of sale, leasehold or financing into several parcels. This law is not applied only to residential land, but includes lands used for any purpose, including business, industry, recreation or agriculture.

There are several differences between the two Acts. In general, the Subdivided Lands Law applies to five or more units while the Subdivision Map Act applies to two or more units. They both, however, cover two or more units where cooperative ownership apartments or condominiums are concerned.

Full compliance with all the provisions of the Subdivision Map Act and the Subdivided Lands Law is required by law. Subdividers and their professional consultants should be thoroughly familiar with the provisions of the state laws and with the specific city and county provisions that affect the particular community in question. Many variations are found in local subdivision ordinances due to the great diversity of communities and conditions throughout the state.

LAND PROJECTS (STATE LAW)

In recent years, lots in some subdivisions located in sparsely populated areas have been sold by intensive promotional efforts that tend to obscure the gamble involved in such speculations. Such subdivisions are referred to as land projects. A *LAND PROJECT is a remote subdivision of 50 or more vacant lots in a rural area (having less than 1500 registered voters within two miles).*

Certain laws have been established to protect the public from these risky ventures. By law, any contract to buy or lease in a land project may be rescinded, without cause, through written notice before midnight on the fourteenth day after the sales contract is signed.

OUT OF STATE BUYERS (FEDERAL LAW)

Subdividers of large subdivisions to be sold interstate are registered with HUD.

Under the Interstate Land Sales Full Disclosure Act, a federal law, such sales are subjected to special registration and control. A contract for the purchase or lease of a lot of this kind is voidable at the option of the buyer if the contract is made without prior inspection of the site. The buyer has seven days after receiving the property report to rescind the contract.

COMMON INTEREST DEVELOPMENT (CID)

A *COMMON INTEREST DEVELOPMENT (CID) is project where there are common areas used by all; excepting separate interests for the use of individual living units and managed by a nonprofit association.* The four basic types of common interest development ownership, which are defined as subdivisions, include:

> **1.** Planned Development (PD)
> **2.** Community Apartment
> **3.** Condominium (including Timesharing)
> 4. Stock Cooperative

To be defined as subdivisions by the Department of Real Estate as part of the Subdivided Lands Law, a planned unit development must have five or more lots, but all the other types only need two units.

PLANNED DEVELOPMENTS (PD)

> *"Common area" means to own as one.*

A *PLANNED DEVELOPMENT is a subdivision where lots are owned separately, but certain areas are owned, in common, by all owners.* Generally, an owner's association is elected by all the owners to manage and maintain the common areas. The *COMMON AREA is that part of a lot or unit in a subdivision that is shared equally by all owners (undivided interest).* An *UNDIVIDED INTEREST is the right of any owner to use any part of the project.*

> *An example of a PD would be a subdivided tract of homes, each on its own lot, that share a swimming pool on a separate lot, which is owned, in common, by all the tract owners.*

COMMUNITY APARTMENT PROJECT

COMMUNITY APARTMENT PROJECTS *are two or more apartments, defined as a subdivision, where the operation, maintenance and control is usually exercised by a governing board elected by the owners of the fractional interests.* An owner receives an undivided interest in the land together with an exclusive leasehold right to occupy a unit. There is only one property tax bill for the entire project.

> *Purchasers receive only a leasehold interest in an apartment, while a condominium purchaser gets a deed (fee interest) to a unit.*

CONDOMINIUM (MOST COMMON TYPE)

A **CONDOMINIUM** *is the ownership of the land and buildings in common with other owners and the individual ownership of specific air spaces.* Condominiums may be used for residential, industrial or commercial purposes, although the residential type is most commonly seen in California.

> *A condominium is the ownership of your unit (airspace) and shared ownership of the land and all improvements. Each condo unit has its own separate grant deed, trust deed and tax bill. You "own what you see"; the airspace between the paint on one wall to the paint on the other wall.*

In effect, the buyer of a condominium owns, in fee simple, the air space in which his or her particular unit is situated and receives a separate tax bill for private airspace and percentage share of the common area. Each airspace unit is given a grant deed and the owner can acquire a title insurance policy. The common area, which is the land and buildings, is managed by an elected governing board. Condominium projects having two or more condominiums are defined as subdivisions.

> *With the sale of a condominium, the seller must provide the buyer with a copy of the:*
>
> *(1) C, C & R's (covenants, conditions, restrictions)*
> *(2) by-laws (governing rules of the association)*
> *(3) financial statement (the condos most recent).*

STOCK COOPERATIVES (CORP. IS THE OWNER)

A **STOCK COOPERATIVE** *is a corporation that is formed to own the land and improved real property.* A stock cooperative either owns or leases real property. The buyer does not receive a grant deed but owns a share of the corporation and the right to occupy a certain unit. The right to occupy can only be transferred with the share of stock in the corporation.

There is one property tax bill in the name of the corporation. A forerunner of the condominium.

TIMESHARING

http://www.ired.com/dir/timeshar.htm (Ired Timeshare)
http://www.timesharetravelers.com (Travels World Marketplace)
http://www.timeshare-users-group.com (or tug2.net)
http://www.holiday-timeshares.com (Holiday Group)
http://www.timeshare-resorts.com (Timeshare Resorts, International)

TIMESHARING *is a form of ownership where each investor holds a share in a specific unit or home and possesses the right to occupy that home for a specified period each year.* See Figure 12-8.

Fifty-two owners may each own a specific one-week share in one unit at a resort property.

SUBDIVISION ADVERTISING

Guidelines for subdividers in advertising and promotions have been developed by the Department of Real Estate. The pamphlet contains filing procedures, requirements and prohibitions on advertising. Since misleading advertising is watched very carefully, it is now a requirement that the public report must be given to each advertising media selected by the subdivider. In addition, a true copy of any advertising proposed for use in connection with a land project offering must be submitted as part of the documentation required prior to the issuance of the public report.

ENVIRONMENTAL LAWS

In recent years there has been increasing attention focused on the problems of our environment. These problem areas include energy, water pollution, air pollution, population growth, preservation of wild life, waste disposal and the quality of life in general. In response, the federal, state and local governments have passed laws and made regulations to help protect us and our environment.

FIGURE 12-8

TIMESHARING:

Pro or Con? — You Decide! *A chalet at Lake Tahoe...a penthouse on Nob Hill...a gold condo in Palm Springs...beachfront property in La Jolla...*

TIMESHARING *is a form of ownership where each investor holds a share in a specific unit or home and possesses the right to occupy that home for a specified period each year.* For instance, fifty-two owners may each own a one-week share in the property. Each is given a grant deed and each has the right to sell his or her share, rent out the week or stay there for one seven-day period every year. The ownership week is fixed but it is possible to trade with other owners. Similarly, there are timesharing groups across the country and around the world which allow investors to exchange time with owners of comparable properties in other desirable locations.

Advantages

The advantages to this kind of ownership are obvious. The buyer has a vacation home without the expense of purchasing the complete home outright. This kind of plan provides access to some of the most unique and scenic property in the world. Once these very special locations are sold, they are gone, they cannot be replaced in the marketplace.

Disadvantages

On the negative side, these properties tend to be disproportionately high priced. For instance, if you multiplied the cost of one share in a week-based timeshare by 52, it would total much more than the market value of the property purchased. Those selling timeshares are burdened with tremendous marketing expenses. Rather than selling once, each property must be sold many times, complete with financing and paperwork.

Restrictions

A brokerage license is required to sell a timeshare package but, just as with other forms of home sales, owners have the right to transfer their ownership shares without a real estate license.

An **ENVIRONMENTAL IMPACT REPORT (EIR)** *is a study of how a subdivision will affect the ecology of a subdivision's surroundings.* An EIR may be required by either city or county authorities prior to their approval of the subdivision map, but some projects may be exempt. In rare cases, the responsibility for the preparation of the EIR will belong to the Department of Real Estate.

Negative results (nothing found) on an EIR report means it's a good report.

The voters of California passed Proposition 20 that established the state Coastal Commission to preserve the coastline. This commission has set construction standards for private and public projects within 1,000 yards of the Pacific Ocean or any other body of water. Its purpose is to establish land use planning, which has considerable economic, social and political overtones. As part of this law, the commission had to establish a long-range coastal plan. No one seems to agree on the economic effects of Proposition 20, but it did have the result of reducing the number and size of coastal construction projects and required an average of six weeks to pass a project through the commission.

LEAD-BASED PAINT DISCLOSURE (FEDERAL GOVERNMENT)

Lead-Based Paint Disclosure Pamphlet

Residential Lead-Based Paint Hazard Reduction Act

The seller or lessor must provide the buyer or lessee with a lead hazard information pamphlet (including disclosure form) and disclose the known presence of any lead-based paint.

The CAR® Residential Purchase Agreement and Deposit Receipt contains a Lead Warning Statement and a statement, to be signed by the buyer, that the buyer has read the warning statement.

The agent, on behalf of the seller or lessor, must ensure compliance with the requirements of the law. The purchaser has a 10-day opportunity to inspect before becoming obligated under the contract.

GEOLOGICAL HAZARD ZONES

Before any real estate development or large structure is built in California, a geological report must be submitted. This report must be compiled by a registered geologist and given to the city in which the development is planned. In the case of a development in an unincorporated area, the report is submitted to the county in which the planned development is located.

If given the approval of the state geologist, the city or county department may waive such a report as long as there is no earthquake fault activity.

The California Division of Mines and Geology has mapped every earthquake fault that has hazardous potential or recent activity. These special study zones are found throughout California and new ones are added to the map (Figure 12-9).

Any person buying within such a zone should be informed either by the seller or the real estate licensee of this fact. A buyer who is thinking of building should be cautioned as to the regulations and requirements that may have to be met to develop the land. See Figure 12-10 for specifics on the Alquist-Priolo Special Studies Zones Act. There are approximately 205 different Geological Survey areas in California. If you want more information about these hazardous zones or copies of the maps, they can be obtained for a small fee from:

CALIFORNIA DIVISION OF MINES AND GEOLOGY
1416 "9" Street
Sacramento, CA 95814   (916) 445-1825
http:www.consrv.ca.gov (California Division of Mines & Geology)

PLANNING COMMISSION

In recent years the belief has been that the best way of curing problems is to prevent them from first appearing. The *CITY or COUNTY PLANNING COMMISSIONS are usually appointed to draft proposals for construction and orderly development before these actions are initiated.* These city or county organizations gather information, cite other examples and come up with their own innovations in an attempt to make some order out of the chaos into which a city may have fallen. The primary responsibility of a planning commission is to prepare and adopt comprehensive, long-term general plans for the physical development of its area of jurisdiction. Commissions have discovered that preplanning exactly which types of buildings can go where, before they are constructed, saves more time and money than all the zoning laws made after the building is done. Such planning commissions make predictions to guarantee that today's residential, commercial and industrial areas will not collide in the future due to expansion of both areas.

Chapter 12

FIGURE 12-9

Preliminary Fault Activity Map of California

Division of Mines and Geology

1975, 1980 and 1992
Scale 1: 750,000
1 inch equals 12 miles

Caution this fault map and any accompanying text are for use as a guide only and should not be used to replace site specific evaluations.

Compiled and interpreted by Charles Jennings

DMG open file report 92-03

http://www.consrv.ca.gov/dmg/index.html
(California Division of Mines & Geology)

FIGURE 12-10

Earthquake Zones

Alquist - Priolo Special Studies Zones Act

It is a zoning act designed to control the development in the vicinity (1/4 mile on each side) of hazardous earthquake faults for the benefit of public safety.

The purpose of the Alquist-Priolo Special Studies Zones Act is to assist governmental jurisdictions in the exercise of their responsibility to prohibit the development of structures for human occupancy across active earthquakes faults as defined by the state geological survey maps. Developments or structures in existence prior to May 4, 1975, are not affected.

A zone normally extends one-quarter of a mile or more in width, centered on the trace of a fault, and includes an area that may be hazardous for development or construction of a structure for human occupancy due to surface faulting or fault creep.

Maps for special studies zone

These maps can be consulted at any district office of the California Division of Mines and Geology. Individuals can obtain copies of these maps at many different local jurisdictions. As a practical matter, the local Multiple Listing Office is one of the most convenient locations to see a map.

"Any person who is acting as a agent for a seller of real estate that is located within a delineated special studies zone, or the seller if acting without an agent, shall disclose the fact that the property is located within a delineated special studies zone."

MASTER PLAN

Every city and county must have a planning commission. The primary purpose of a city's Master Plan is to set forth existing and future matters concerning seismic safety, districts, streets and highways.

Entire new cities can be pre-planned so that zoning laws exist only to enforce and execute the city's master plan. The *MASTER PLAN is a comprehensive guide through which zoning establishes an ideal plan for the city's development in the future. DIRECTIONAL GROWTH is the actual growth path of urban development. Properties in the direction of growth tend to increase in value especially if the growth is steady and rapid.* It is used, by smart investors, to determine where future development will be most profitable. A good example of preplanning is the Irvine Ranch in Orange County, where there is a balance between residential, recreational, commercial and manufacturing areas.

The essential elements of a general, or master plan, are:

1. The designation of proposed general distribution, location and extent of land uses within certain areas.
2. The determination of general traffic patterns, including the extensions of existing and proposed transportation routes, terminals and other public utility facilities.
3. The setting of standards of population density and building units per acre of various districts and the estimation of future population growth trends. A number of other elements may also be included.

ZONING (USE)

Zoning is the city or county exercise of "police power"; rulings are made to control the use of private property for the protection of the public's health, safety and welfare.

ZONING LAWS regulate the use of property by prescribing what uses that land can be put to, and by establishing uniformity throughout the community. For example, zoning laws may indicate that a specific property can be used only as a single family home, multiple family housing or for commercial or industrial use. It is possible for the planning commission to change zoning. It can change an area from commercial to residential or change a residential area from R-4 to R-1. This is called down zoning. *DOWN ZONING means the land will have less use density.*

Changing the zoning from R-4 to R-1 is a example of down zoning.

Zoning laws use the "police power" granted to every county and city to regulate the use, planning and setbacks of land. Such regulations protect the health, safety, comfort and general welfare of the community. These ordinances are public restrictions to the uses of private property. Counties and cities can set their own standards, which can be much higher than the minimums set by the state. For example zoning, which regulates the use of lands and buildings, may specify the following:

1. Location and type of building
2. Height of the structure
3. Size of the building
4. Percentage of a lot the building may occupy
5. Setback requirements from front, back and sides of the property boundaries.

Who can petition for zone changes? Owners, subdividers and government agencies.

Figures 12-11 and 12-12 are examples of a Los Angeles zoning plan. You will notice that there are many symbols that indicate the regulated uses for all the different parts of Los Angeles.

Each symbol represents a different type of zone, but it is possible to make the following generalization about some of the common zoning symbols:

A — This symbol usually indicates an *agricultural* area such as farm or ranch land. In a few isolated areas a symbol beginning with "A" stands for an airport.

C — The "C" symbol represents *commercial* areas. In these areas anything from an office building to a community shopping center may exist. There are other, more specific, "C" symbols regulating the construction of such commercial properties.

M — Stands for *manufacturing*. Industrial complexes must be built only in zones classified "M."

P — Although there are many different interpretations of the "P" symbol, the most important categories it covers are *parking lots and parks*.

R — The "R" symbol is probably the most important symbol to the real estate person. This symbol (and its derivations) designates those areas in which *homes, condominiums or apartments* may be built or maintained.

FIGURE 12-11

SUMMARY OF ZONING REGULATIONS
CITY OF LOS ANGELES

CLASSIFICATION	ZONE	USE	MAXIMUM HEIGHT STORIES	MAXIMUM HEIGHT FEET	REQUIRED YARDS FRONT	REQUIRED YARDS SIDE	REQUIRED YARDS REAR	MINIMUM PER LOT	AREA PER DWELLING UNIT	MINIMUM LOT WIDTH	PARKING SPACE	EAGLE PRISMACOLOR PENCIL CHART
AGRICULTURAL	A1	AGRICULTURAL ONE-FAMILY DWELLINGS - PARKS - PLAYGROUNDS - COMMUNITY CENTERS - GOLF COURSES - TRUCK GARDENING - EXTENSIVE AGRICULTURAL USES	3	45 FT.	25 FT.	25 FT. MAXIMUM 10% LOT WIDTH 3 FT. MINIMUM	25 FT.	5 ACRES	2½ ACRES	300 FT.	TWO SPACES PER DWELLING UNIT	909 GRASS GREEN
AGRICULTURAL	A2	AGRICULTURAL A1 USES	3	45 FT.	25 FT.	25 FT. MAXIMUM 10% LOT WIDTH 3 FT. MINIMUM	25 FT.	2 ACRES	1 ACRE	150 FT.	TWO SPACES PER DWELLING UNIT	912 APPLE GREEN
AGRICULTURAL	RA	SUBURBAN LIMITED AGRICULTURAL USES	3	45 FT.	25 FT.	10'-1&2 STORIES 11'-3 STORIES	25 FT.	17,500 SQ. FT. ✳	17,500 SQ. FT. ✳	70 FT. ✳	TWO GARAGE SPACES PER DWELLING UNIT	910 TRUE GREEN
RESIDENTIAL / ONE FAMILY	RE40	RESIDENTIAL ESTATE ONE-FAMILY DWELLINGS PARKS PLAYGROUNDS COMMUNITY CENTERS TRUCK GARDENING	3	45 FT.	25 FT.	10 FT.	25 FT.	40,000 SQ. FT. ✳	40,000 SQ. FT. ✳	80 FT. ✳	TWO GARAGE SPACES PER DWELLING UNIT	950 GOLD
	RE20				25 FT.	10 FT.	25 FT.	20,000 SQ. FT. ✳	20,000 SQ. FT. ✳	80 FT. ✳		
	RE15				25 FT.	10 FT. MAXIMUM 10% LOT WIDTH 5 FT. MINIMUM	25 FT.	15,000 SQ. FT. ✳	15,000 SQ. FT. ✳	80 FT. ✳		
	RE11				25 FT.	5'-1&2 STORIES 6'-3 STORIES	25 FT.	11,000 SQ. FT. ✳	11,000 SQ. FT. ✳	70 FT. ✳		
	RE9				25 FT.	5 FT. MAXIMUM 10% LOT WIDTH 3 FT. MINIMUM	25 FT.	9,000 SQ. FT. ✳	9,000 SQ. FT. ✳	65 FT. ✳		
	RS	SUBURBAN ONE-FAMILY DWELLINGS - PARKS PLAYGROUNDS - TRUCK GARDENING	3	45 FT	25 FT.	5'-1&2 STORIES 6'-3 STORIES	20 FT.	7,500 SQ. FT.	7,500 SQ. FT.	60 FT.	TWO GARAGE SPACES PER DWELLING UNIT	911 OLIVE GREEN
	R1	ONE-FAMILY DWELLING RS USES	3	45 FT	20 FT.	5'-1 & 2 STORIES 6'-3 STORIES	15 FT.	5,000 SQ. FT.	5,000 SQ. FT.	50 FT.	TWO GARAGE SPACES PER DWELLING UNIT	916 CANARY YELLOW
	RW1	ONE-FAMILY RESIDENTIAL WATERWAYS ZONE	3	45 FT.	10 FT.	4' PLUS 1' EACH STORY ABOVE 2ND 10% LOT WIDTH ●	15 FT.	2,300 SQ. FT.	2,300 SQ. FT.	28 FT.	TWO GARAGE SPACES PER DWELLING UNIT	914 CREAM
	RW2	TWO-FAMILY RESIDENTIAL WATERWAYS ZONE							1,150 SQ. FT.			
	R2	TWO-FAMILY DWELLING R1 USES TWO-FAMILY DWELLINGS	3	45 FT.	20 FT.	5'-1&2 STORIES 6'-3 STORIES	15 FT.	5,000 SQ. FT.	2,500 SQ. FT.	50 FT.	TWO SPACES ONE IN A GARAGE	917 YELLOW ORANGE
MULTIPLE RESIDENTIAL	RD1.5	RESTRICTED DENSITY MULTIPLE DWELLING ZONE TWO-FAMILY DWELLING APARTMENT HOUSES MULTIPLE DWELLINGS			20 FT.	6 FT.	20 FT.	6,000 SQ. FT.	1,500 SQ. FT.	60 FT.	ONE SPACE EACH DWELLING UNIT OF LESS THAN THREE ROOMS ONE AND ONE HALF SPACES EACH DWELLING UNIT OF THREE ROOMS TWO SPACES EACH DWELLING UNIT OF MORE THEN THREE ROOMS ONE SPACE EACH GUEST ROOM (FIRST THIRTY)	940 SAND
	RD2		HEIGHT DISTRICT NO. 1 3 STORIES 45 FT.		20 FT.	10 FT.	25 FT.	12,000 SQ. FT.	2,000 SQ. FT.	70 FT.		
	RD3								3,000 SQ. FT.			
	RD4								4,000 SQ. FT.			
	RD5		HEIGHT DISTRICT NOS. 2,3 OR 4 6 STORIES 75 FT.						5,000 SQ. FT.			
	RD6								6,000 SQ. FT.			
	R3	MULTIPLE DWELLING R2 USES APARTMENT HOUSES MULTIPLE DWELLINGS			15 FT.	5'-1 & 2 STORIE 6'-3 STORIES	15 FT.	5,000 SQ. FT.	800 TO 1,200 SQ FT	50 FT.		918 ORANGE
	R4	MULTIPLE DWELLING R3 USES CHURCHES HOTELS-SCHOOLS	UNLIMITED ✳		15 FT.	5' PLUS 1' EACH STORY ABOVE 2ND 16 FT. MAX.	15' PLUS 1' EACH STORY ABOVE 3RD 20 FT. MAX	5,000 SQ. FT.	400 TO 800 SQ FT	50 FT		943 BURNT OCHRE
	R5	MULTIPLE DWELLING R4 USES CLUBS-HOSPITALS LODGES-SANITARIUMS	UNLIMITED ✳		15 FT.	5' PLUS 1' EACH STORY ABOVE 2ND 16 FT. MAX.	15' PLUS 1' EACH STORY ABOVE 3RD 20 FT. MAX.	5,000 SQ. FT.	200 TO 400 SQ FT	50 FT		946 DARK BROWN

✳ SEE HEIGHT DISTRICTS AT THE BOTTOM OF PAGE 2

● FOR TWO OR MORE LOTS THE INTERIOR SIDE YARDS MAY BE ELIMINATED, BUT 4 FT IS REQUIRED ON EACH SIDE OF THE GROUPED LOTS.

✳ "H" HILLSIDE OR MOUNTAINOUS AREA DESIGNATION MAY ALTER THESE REQUIREMENTS IN THE RA-H OR RE-H ZONES, SUBDIVISIONS MAY BE APPROVED WITH SMALLER LOTS, PROVIDING LARGER LOTS ARE ALSO INCLUDED EACH LOT MAY BE USED FOR ONLY ONE SINGLE-FAMILY DWELLING SEE MINIMUM WIDTH & AREA REQUIREMENTS BELOW.

ZONE COMBINATION	MINIMUM TO WHICH NET AREA MAY BE REDUCED	MINIMUM TO WHICH LOT WIDTH MAY BE REDUCED
RA-H	14,000 SQ FT	63 FT
RE9-H	7,200 SQ FT	60 FT
RE11-H,	8,800 SQ FT	63 FT
RE15-H	12,000 SQ FT	72 FT
RE20-H	16,000 SQ FT	72 FT
RE40-H	32,000 SQ FT	NO REDUCTION

SHEET 1 OF 2   CP FORM 10

PREPARED BY CITY PLANNING DEPARTMENT

FIGURE 12-12

SUMMARY OF ZONING REGULATIONS
CITY OF LOS ANGELES

CLASSIFICATION	ZONE	USE	MAXIMUM HEIGHT		REQUIRED YARDS			MINIMUM AREA PER LOT AND UNIT	MINIMUM LOT WIDTH	LOADING SPACE	PARKING SPACE	EAGLE PRISMACOLOR PENCIL CHART
			STORIES	FEET	FRONT	SIDE	REAR					
COMMERCIAL — RESIDENTIAL USES (EXCEPT HOTELS) PROHIBITED UNLESS CONDITIONAL USE IS APPROVED BY ZONING ADMINISTRATOR	CR	LIMITED COMMERCIAL — BANKS, CLUBS, HOTELS, CHURCHES, SCHOOLS, BUSINESS & PROFESSIONAL OFFICES, PARKING AREAS	6	75 FT	10 FEET	5'-10' CORNER LOT, RESIDENTIAL USE "A" OR "R" ZONE SAME AS R4 ZONE	15' PLUS 1' EACH STORY ABOVE 3rd	SAME AS R4 FOR DWELLINGS OTHERWISE NONE	50 FEET FOR RESIDENCE USE OTHERWISE NONE	HOSPITALS, HOTELS INSTITUTIONS, AND WITH EVERY BUILDING WHERE LOT ABUTS ALLEY	ONE SPACE FOR EACH 500 SQ. FT. OF FLOOR AREA	939 FLESH
	CI	LIMITED COMMERCIAL — LOCAL RETAIL STORES, OFFICES OR BUSINESSES, HOTELS, LIMITED HOSPITALS AND/OR CLINICS, PARKING AREAS	UNLIMITED *			3'-5' CORNER LOT OR ADJOINING AN "A" OR "R" ZONE	5' PLUS 1' EACH STORY ABOVE 3rd RESIDENTIAL USE OR ABUTTING AN "A" OR "R" ZONE	SAME AS R3 FOR DWELLINGS EXCEPT 5000 SQ FT. PER UNIT IN CI-H ZONES — OTHERWISE NONE		MINIMUM LOADING SPACE 400 SQUARE FEET	ONE SPACE FOR EACH 500 SQUARE FEET OF FLOOR AREA IN ALL BUILDINGS ON ANY LOT	929 PINK
	CI.5	LIMITED COMMERCIAL — CI USES — DEPARTMENT STORES, THEATRES, BROADCASTING STUDIOS, PARKING BUILDINGS, PARKS & PLAYGROUNDS				RESIDENTIAL USE SAME AS R4 ZONE OTHERWISE NONE				ADDITIONAL SPACE REQUIRED FOR BUILDINGS CONTAINING MORE THAN 50,000 SQUARE FEET OF FLOOR AREA	MUST BE LOCATED WITHIN 750 FEET OF BUILDING	928 BLUSH
	C2	COMMERCIAL — CI.5 USES — RETAIL BUSINESSES WITH LIMITED MANUFACTURING, AUTO SERVICE STATION & GARAGE, RETAIL CONTRACTORS BUSINESSES, CHURCHES, SCHOOLS			NONE			SAME AS R4 FOR DWELLINGS OTHERWISE NONE				922 SCARLET RED
	C4	COMMERCIAL — C2 USES — (WITH EXCEPTIONS, SUCH AS AUTO SERVICE STATIONS, AMUSEMENT ENTERPRISES, CONTRACTORS BUSINESSES, SECOND-HAND BUSINESSES)				NONE FOR COMMERCIAL BUILDINGS RESIDENTIAL USES — SAME AS IN R4 ZONE	NONE FOR COMMERCIAL BUILDINGS RESIDENTIAL USES — SAME AS IN R4 ZONE			NONE REQUIRED FOR APARTMENT BUILDINGS 20 UNITS OR LESS	SEE CODE FOR ASSEMBLY AREAS, HOSPITALS AND CLINICS	924 CRIMSON RED
	C5	COMMERCIAL — C2 USES — LIMITED FLOOR AREAS FOR LIGHT MANUFACTURING OF THE CM - ZONE TYPE										925 CRIMSON LAKE
	CM	COMM'L MANUFACTURING — WHOLESALE BUSINESSES, STORAGE BUILDINGS, CLINICS, LIMITED MANUFACTURING, C2 USES - EXCEPT HOSPITALS, SCHOOLS, CHURCHES						SAME AS R3 FOR DWELLINGS OTHERWISE NONE				905 AQUA-MARINE
INDUSTRIAL — RESIDENTIAL USES PROHIBITED IN ALL INDUSTRIAL ZONES	MR I	RESTRICTED INDUSTRIAL — CM USES — LIMITED COMMERCIAL & MANUFACTURING USES, HOSPITALS, CLINICS, SANITARIUMS, LIMITED MACHINE SHOPS			15 FT.	NONE FOR INDUSTRIAL OR COMMERCIAL BUILDINGS RESIDENTIAL USES - SAME AS IN R4 ZONE	NONE FOR INDUSTRIAL OR COMMERCIAL BUILDINGS RESIDENTIAL USES - SAME AS IN R4 ZONE		50 FEET FOR RESIDENCE USE OTHERWISE NONE	HOSPITALS, HOTELS INSTITUTIONS, AND WITH EVERY BUILDING WHERE LOT ABUTS ALLEY MINIMUM LOADING SPACE 400 SQUARE FEET	ONE SPACE FOR EACH 500 SQUARE FEET OF FLOOR AREA IN ALL BUILDINGS ON ANY LOT	901 INDIGO BLUE
	MR 2	RESTRICTED LIGHT INDUSTRIAL — MR I USES — ADDITION INDUSTRIAL USES, MORTUARIES, AGRICULTURE	UNLIMITED *					SAME AS R4 FOR DWELLINGS OTHERWISE NONE			MUST BE LOCATED WITHIN 750 FEET OF BUILDING	906 COPENHAGEN BLUE
	M1	LIMITED INDUSTRIAL — CM USES — LIMITED INDUSTRIAL & MANUFACTURING USES — NO "R" ZONE USES, NO HOSPITALS, SCHOOLS OR CHURCHES								ADDITIONAL SPACE REQUIRED FOR BUILDINGS CONTAINING MORE THAN 50,000 SQUARE FEET OF FLOOR AREA		904 LIGHT BLUE
	M2	LIGHT INDUSTRIAL — M1 USES — ADDITIONAL INDUSTRIAL USES, STORAGE YARDS OF ALL KINDS, ANIMAL KEEPING — NO "R" ZONE USES			NONE						SEE CODE FOR ASSEMBLY AREAS, HOSPITALS AND CLINICS	902 ULTRA-MARINE
	M3	HEAVY INDUSTRIAL — M2 USES — ANY INDUSTRIAL USES — NUISANCE TYPE - 500 FT. FROM ANY OTHER ZONE — NO "R" ZONE USES				NONE	NONE	NONE —NOTE— "R" ZONE USES PROHIBITED	NONE	NONE REQUIRED FOR APARTMENT BUILDINGS 20 UNITS OR LESS		931 PURPLE
PARKING	P	AUTOMOBILE PARKING - SURFACE & UNDERGROUND — PROPERTY IN A "P" ZONE MAY ALSO BE IN AN "A" OR "R" ZONE — PARKING PERMITTED IN LIEU OF AGRICULTURAL OR RESIDENTIAL USES						NONE UNLESS ALSO IN AN "A" OR "R" ZONE	NONE UNLESS ALSO IN AN "A" OR "R" ZONE	—	—	967 COLD GREY LIGHT
	PB	PARKING BUILDING — AUTOMOBILE PARKING WITHIN OR WITHOUT A BUILDING	* *	—	0', 5', OR 10' DEPENDING ON ZONING IN BLOCK AND ACROSS STREET	5' PLUS 1' EACH STORY ABOVE 2nd IF ABUTTING OR ACROSS STREET FROM "A" OR "R" ZONE	5' PLUS 1' EACH STORY ABOVE 2nd IF ABUTTING AN "A" OR "R" ZONE, TO A 16' MAXIMUM	NONE	NONE	—	—	936 SLATE GREY
SPECIAL	SL	SUBMERGED LAND ZONE — COMMERCIAL SHIPPING, NAVIGATION, FISHING, RECREATION										919 SKY BLUE
	(T)	TENTATIVE CLASSIFICATION — USED IN COMBINATION WITH ZONE CHANGE ONLY - DELAYS ISSUANCE OF BUILDING PERMIT UNTIL SUBDIVISION OR PARCEL MAP RECORDED										
	(F)	FUNDED IMPROVEMENT CLASSIFICATION — AN ALTERNATE MEANS OF EFFECTING ZONE CHANGES AND SECURING IMPROVEMENTS (WHEN NO SUBDIVISION OR DEDICATIONS ARE INVOLVED)										
	(Q)	QUALIFIED CLASSIFICATION — USED IN COMBINATION WITH ZONE CHANGES ONLY EXCEPT WITH RA, RE, RS OR RI ZONES - RESTRICTS USES OF PROPERTY AND ASSURES DEVELOPMENT COMPATIBLE WITH THE SURROUNDING PROPERTY										

SUPPLEMENTAL USE DISTRICTS: G ROCK AND GRAVEL • O OIL DRILLING • S ANIMAL SLAUGHTERING • RPD RESIDENTIAL PLANNED DEVELOPMENT — K HORSE - KEEPING
(ESTABLISHED IN CONJUNCTION WITH ZONES)

HEIGHT DISTRICT				MAXIMUM PB ZONE HEIGHTS		
*	Nº 1	FLOOR AREA OF MAIN BUILDING MAY NOT EXCEED THREE TIMES THE BUILDING AREA OF THE LOT		* *	Nº 1	2 STORIES AND ROOF
	Nº 1L	SAME AS Nº 1 AND MAXIMUM HEIGHT - 6 STORIES OR 75 FT.			Nº 2	6 STORIES
	Nº 1-VL	SAME AS Nº 1 AND MAXIMUM HEIGHT - 3 STORIES OR 45 FT.			Nº 3	10 STORIES
	Nº 2	FLOOR AREA OF MAIN BUILDING MAY NOT EXCEED SIX TIMES THE BUILDABLE AREA OF THE LOT			Nº 4	13 STORIES
	Nº 3	FLOOR AREA OF MAIN BUILDING MAY NOT EXCEED TEN TIMES THE BUILDABLE AREA OF THE LOT				
	Nº 4	FLOOR AREA OF MAIN BUILDING MAY NOT EXCEED THIRTEEN TIMES THE BUILDABLE AREA OF THE LOT				

NOTE: ALL INFORMATION GENERAL - FOR SPECIFIC DETAILS CHECK WITH DEPARTMENT OF BUILDING AND SAFETY

SHEET 2 OF 2

PREPARED BY CITY PLANNING DEPARTMENT

Each of these symbols is usually followed by a number, for example "R" may be followed by 1, 2, 3 or 4. The number indicates a higher density or use for that particular zone. The following will help explain each use:

R1 - is for a *single family* dwelling

R2 - is for *two dwelling* units

R3 - is for *multiple dwellings* depending on square footage and height of apartment buildings, condominiums, etc.

R4 - is for *higher density multiple dwellings with certain square footage*

R5 - *requirements and maximum height allowable* . . . motels, hotels and high-rise apartments or condominiums.

Zoning restrictions reduce the buildable area by requiring setbacks from the front, back and sides of the lot lines.

Figure 12-13 is a math problem using setbacks to determine the buildable area of a lot. Remember that all the above explanations are general and may vary. You should investigate any individual symbol for its exact meaning in your city or county before interpreting it.

Title insurance does not give protection for zoning changes.

ZONING REGULATION (CONTROLS USE)

Zoning is police power that controls only the "use" of the property, not ownership.

Most planning commissions, boards or city councils have an established procedure for a change of zoning. As part of a logical procedure, four steps are usually followed. They are:

1. Giving public notice of any proposed zoning changes.

2. Calling a public hearing where interested people can voice their opinions before any changes are made.

3. Adoption or rejection of a zoning regulation.

4. If rejected, an appeal can be made to the city council, which can overrule the planning commission.

Once zoning regulations are enacted, the objecting parties have the right to appeal to the courts on the basis that the ordinance may be arbitrary or unreasonable. The usual grounds for appeal is equal protection under the ordinance. Zoning ordinances have been held invalid when it was shown that a monopoly would be created, the new ordinance rendered an adjoining lot worthless or when it prohibited an existing business that did not create a nuisance.

Although the intent of zoning is to create reasonable uniformity, total uniformity is not required. Spot zoning might benefit the public in some cases. *SPOT ZONING is a small area that is zoned differently from the surrounding area. For example, controlled use of commercial stores and service stations can enhance the value and utility of the residential area.*

NONCONFORMING USE

As conditions in the area change, the zoning of existing parcels may also change. The change may cause some of the existing structures to become nonconforming. *NONCONFORMING USE is a property that is not used according to the current zoning.* An example of nonconforming use would be an apartment with one parking space per unit where zoning changes require two parking spaces per unit. It is a general policy to let nonconforming uses continue for a time if conformity creates unnecessary hardships. However, the growing trend is for cities to charge large fees for nonconforming properties as a source of income.

VARIANCE (FOR PRIVATE HARDSHIP)

One way to provide reasonable conformity is to allow zoning variances. A *VARIANCE is an exception to the existing zoning regulations in cases of special need for circumstances that might create serious hardship for property owners.* Zoning restrictions such as setbacks may be removed by petitioning for a variance.

Variance is for one lot; re-zoning is for many lots.

For example, if an individual wants to construct a building that does not comply with the local zoning rule, he or she may petition for a variance. When filing this petition, the individual must prove that the construction of the building will not be detrimental to the public. Variances are often granted with special conditions such that both plans and construction be approved and initiated within a specified time.

A "grandfather" clause allows an owner to continue using his or her property in a way prohibited by the new zoning.

Chapter 12

FIGURE 12-13

SETBACK PROBLEM
(ZONING REGULATIONS)

BUILDABLE AREA is the maximum allowable area of a lot that a city or county allows for a building after deducting setbacks from the front, back and sides.

DETERMINING USABLE AREA

Question: What is the buildable space of a lot 150 feet by 50 feet if the city requires deducting a 20-foot setback from the front and deducting 4 feet from each side and the back?

150 Feet X 50 Feet

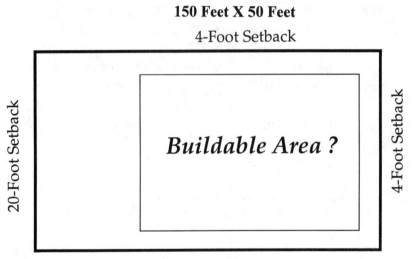

Answer:

Width: 50 feet minus (4 feet on both the left and right side) = ?
50 feet - 8 Feet = <u>42 feet</u> buildable width

Length: 150 feet minus (20-foot front setback and a 4-foot rear setback) = ?
150 feet - 24 feet = <u>126 feet</u> buildable length

TOTAL:
Width X Length = Area
42 feet X 126 feet = Area
42 feet X 126 feet = <u>5,292 square feet</u>

CONDITIONAL USE PERMIT (FOR PUBLIC BENEFIT)

A *CONDITIONAL USE PERMIT is an exception to the current zoning for the public welfare or benefit.* Variances, on the other hand, are based on hardship.

Since zoning ordinances may be altered, most title insurance policies do not insure against zoning changes. For a small fee, an endorsement may be added to the title insurance policy that covers any losses due to zoning changes. Zoning is an environmental control that attempts to ensure uniform land use while also meeting the occasional special needs of the community.

HOUSING, BUILDING AND HEALTH LAWS

The basic control of housing, building and health standards is held at the state level. Although building codes and health standards are usually enforced by the local county and city agencies, contractors, factory home builders and house builders are always regulated at the state level.

Regulatory authority of the housing and construction industry is accomplished by the state contractor's license laws, the local building codes and the State Housing Law.

STATE HOUSING LAW

California has adopted a State Housing Law that sets the minimum construction and occupancy requirements for all apartments, hotels and other dwellings. It should be noted that any city or county may impose more stringent requirements if it so wishes. Construction regulations under this law are handled by local building inspectors. Occupancy and sanitation regulations are enforced by local health officers.

LOCAL BUILDING CODES

When there are two conflicting laws, you must comply with the most stringent.

Most cities and counties have additional, more stringent construction standards than the state. The *BUILDING CODE is the basic minimum construction standard for a structure.* This code includes regulation of all the basic methods, materials and components of a structure from the foundation to the plumbing and electrical system. Local building inspectors enforce both the state and local building codes.

The local building inspector enforces construction standards (codes).

New construction or building alterations require a building permit. A **BUILDING PERMIT** *is an approved building application that includes plans, specifications and a plot plan.* After an examination of the application, plans and any revisions of the plans, the building permit is issued. No construction or alteration can be started until the building permit has been issued.

GOVERNMENT FINANCING REQUIREMENTS

To obtain certain forms of government financing toward the purchase of a home, various construction requirements must be met. These **Minimum Property Requirements** (**MPRs**) are usually more restrictive than state housing or local building codes. This indirect type of regulation must be considered if any FHA, VA or Cal-Vet financing is needed.

FACTORY-BUILT HOUSING LAW

The state has preempted local building codes concerning factory-built housing (prefabricated homes). These are homes that are built in sections in a factory and assembled on site. Each section is checked at the factory by state inspectors. Local inspectors oversee only the site hookup of water lines and other on-site facilities.

MOBILE HOMES (MANUFACTURED HOUSING)

Real estate licensees can sell a mobile home that is over one year old, whereas licensed mobile home dealers can sell new or used mobile homes.

A **MOBILE HOME**, *commonly referred to as* **MANUFACTURED HOUSING**, *is a transportable structure in one or more eight-foot (or more) wide by 40-foot (or more) long sections that will cover 320 or more square feet when erected on a site.* Built on a permanent chassis, it is designed to be used with or without permanent foundation when connected to the necessary utilities. If sold in California, it must meet the California Department of Housing standards.

Real estate salespeople can also sell, lease or finance mobile homes as soon as they have been transformed into real property (wheels removed, placed on a foundation and having a building permit).

Real Estate brokers can sell mobile homes once they are considered real property. A real estate broker must report all sales of mobile homes, within ten calendar days, to the Department of Housing and Community Development (HCD). Registration cards, title and fees are also sent there.

A new mobile home dealer must be licensed by the Department of Housing and Community Development (HCD).

New mobile homes can only be sold by licensed mobile home dealers. This industry is growing and CAR® (Figure 12-14) has developed a Deposit Receipt especially designed for mobile home sales.

A licensee must withdraw any advertisement of a mobile home within 48 hours after notice that it is no longer available for sale.

CONTRACTOR'S STATE LICENSE LAW

Contractors are licensed at the state level by the Contractor's State License Board, whose main purpose is to protect the public against incompetent building contractors and subcontractors. This protection is achieved by requiring construction to be done only by licensed persons. This includes subcontract work as well as general and engineering contract work.

The construction field is divided into general engineering, general building and specialty contracting. A license is required to perform work in any of these categories. Examinations are prepared on legal matters affecting construction and cost estimation. Each applicant is further required to have a certain amount of actual experience in his or her particular field. Only construction work done on one's own home without intent to sell or lease may be undertaken without a license, but still requires a building permit.

The state housing law, administered by the codes and standards division, is designed to provide that minimum construction and occupancy standards are met.

HEALTH AND SANITATION (COUNTY FUNCTION)

The California State Department of Health regulates a statewide health program. Even though the state regulates it, local health officials are required, by law, to be appointed in every city or county. These officials

FIGURES 12-14

CALIFORNIA ASSOCIATION OF REALTORS®

MANUFACTURED HOME PURCHASE CONTRACT AND RECEIPT FOR DEPOSIT
(For Sale of Manufactured Homes on Leased or Rented Real Property)

DATE: _____ at _____, California,
RECEIVED FROM _____ ("Buyer")
A DEPOSIT OF _____ Dollars $ _____ TOWARD
THE PURCHASE PRICE OF _____ Dollars $ _____
FOR PURCHASE OF THE MANUFACTURED HOME ("Property") located in: _____,
County of _____, California, at (Address) _____, Space No. _____
Park Name _____,
Manufacturer's Name _____ Model _____ DOM _____ (year) DFS _____
Property is: ☐ On Local Property Tax Roll, ☐ Department of Housing and Community Development ("HCD") registered.
Approximate Width _____ Approximate Length _____ Expando Size _____ HCD/HUD License/Decal Number _____

SERIAL NUMBERS: 1. _____ 2. _____ 3. _____ 4. _____
                  (Single Wide)   (Multiple Units)

HCD/HUD Label/Insignia: 1. _____ 2. _____ 3. _____ 4. _____
                     (Single Wide)   (Multiple Units)

1. **FINANCING: THE OBTAINING OF THE LOANS BELOW IS A CONTINGENCY OF THIS PURCHASE CONTRACT AND RECEIPT FOR DEPOSIT ("AGREEMENT"). Buyer shall act diligently and in good faith to obtain the designated loans.**

    A. **LOAN CONTINGENCY** shall remain in effect until: (Check only ONE of the following:)
    - ☐ **(1)** The designated loans are funded and/or the assumption of existing financing is approved by lender and completed.
    - OR ☐ **(2)** _____ **days** from acceptance of the offer, by which time Buyer shall give to Seller written notice of Buyer's election to cancel this Agreement because of Buyer's inability to obtain the designated loans or obtain approval of assumption of existing financing. If Buyer does not give Seller such notice, the contingency of obtaining the designated loans shall be removed by the method specified in paragraph 23.

    B. ☐ **APPRAISAL CONTINGENCY:** (If checked) This Agreement is contingent upon lender appraising Property at no less than the specified total purchase price. The Appraisal contingency shall remain in effect for the period specified for Loan Contingency in paragraph 1A, until such loan contingency is removed.

    C. **BUYER'S DEPOSIT,** to be deposited ☐ with Escrow Holder, ☐ into Broker's trust account, ☐ or _____ $ _____
    by Personal Check, ☐ Cashier's Check, ☐ Cash, or ☐ _____.
    to be held uncashed until the next business day after acceptance, or ☐ _____.

    D. **INCREASED DEPOSIT** within _____ **days** from acceptance shall be deposited with _____. $ _____

    E. **BALANCE OF DOWN PAYMENT** to be deposited with Escrow Holder within sufficient time to close escrow .... $ _____

    F. **FIRST LOAN IN THE AMOUNT OF** : . . . . $ _____
    ☐ NEW Security Agreement and Certificate of Title designating ☐ LENDER, ☐ SELLER, as legal owner; OR
    ☐ ASSUMPTION of Existing Security Agreement and Certificate of Title encumbering the Property, securing a note
    payable at approximately $ _____ per month at maximum interest of _____% fixed rate
    or _____% initial adjustable rate with a maximum lifetime interest rate cap of _____%, balance due in _____ years.
    Buyer shall pay loan fees/points not to exceed _____.

    G. **SECOND LOAN IN THE AMOUNT OF** . . . . $ _____
    ☐ NEW Security Agreement and Certificate of Title designating ☐ LENDER, ☐ SELLER, as legal owner; OR
    ☐ ASSUMPTION of Existing Security Agreement and Certificate of Title encumbering the Property, securing a note
    payable at approximately $ _____ per month at maximum interest of _____% fixed rate
    or _____% initial adjustable rate with a maximum lifetime interest rate cap of _____%, balance due in _____ years.
    Buyer shall pay loan fees/points not to exceed _____.

    H. **ADDITIONAL FINANCING TERMS:** _____
    _____

    I. **TOTAL PURCHASE PRICE,** not including sales tax, if applicable, costs of obtaining loans and other closing costs . . . . $ _____

    J. **OBTAINING DEPOSIT, DOWN PAYMENT, and CLOSING COSTS** by Buyer is NOT a contingency unless agreed in writing.

    K. **CAL VET/VA FINANCING:** ☐ (If checked) The following terms apply ONLY to CAL VET/VA financing.
    - **(1)** Seller shall pay _____% of the loan as discount points.
    - **(2)** Seller shall pay other fees which Buyer is not permitted to pay, not to exceed $ _____.
    - **(3)** Seller shall pay the cost of repairs required by lender not otherwise provided for in this Agreement, not to exceed $ _____.
    - **(4)** All other charges to obtain financing shall be paid by Buyer unless otherwise agreed in writing.
    - **(5)** OTHER: _____

    L. **IF THIS IS AN ALL CASH OFFER,** Buyer shall, within 5 (or ☐ _____) days from acceptance, provide to Seller written verification of sufficient funds to close this transaction. Seller may cancel this Agreement in writing within 5 (or ☐ _____) days (1) after receipt of the verification, if Seller disapproves it, or (2) after the time to provide the verification expires, if Buyer fails to provide it.

    M. **LOAN APPLICATIONS; PREQUALIFICATION:**
    - **(1) For NEW and ASSUMED lender financing:** Within 10 (or ☐ _____) days from acceptance, Buyer shall provide to Seller a letter from lender stating that, based on a review of Buyer's written application and credit report, Buyer is prequalified for the NEW and/or ASSUMED loans indicated above. If Buyer fails to provide such letter within that time, Seller may cancel this Agreement in writing.
    - **(2) For SELLER financing:** Within 5 (or ☐ _____) days after acceptance: (a) Buyer shall submit to Seller a completed loan application on FNMA/FHLMC Uniform Residential Loan Application; (b) Buyer authorizes Seller and/or Brokers to obtain, at Buyer's expense, a copy of Buyer's credit report; (c) Buyer shall provide any supporting documentation reasonably requested by Seller. Seller may cancel this Agreement in writing if Buyer fails to provide such documents within that time, or if Seller disapproves the application, credit report, or supporting documentation within 5 (or ☐ _____) days from receipt of those documents.

Buyer and Seller acknowledge receipt of copy of this page, which constitutes Page 1 of _____ Pages.
Buyer's Initials (_____) (_____)   Seller's Initials (_____) (_____)

THIS FORM HAS BEEN APPROVED BY THE CALIFORNIA ASSOCIATION OF REALTORS® (C.A.R.). NO REPRESENTATION IS MADE AS TO THE LEGAL VALIDITY OR ADEQUACY OF ANY PROVISION IN ANY SPECIFIC TRANSACTION. A REAL ESTATE BROKER IS THE PERSON QUALIFIED TO ADVISE ON REAL ESTATE TRANSACTIONS. IF YOU DESIRE LEGAL OR TAX ADVICE, CONSULT AN APPROPRIATE PROFESSIONAL.

The copyright laws of the United States (17 U.S. Code) forbid the unauthorized reproduction of this form by any means, including facsimile or computerized formats.
Copyright © 1989-1997, CALIFORNIA ASSOCIATION OF REALTORS®

Published and Distributed by:
REAL ESTATE BUSINESS SERVICES, INC.
a subsidiary of the CALIFORNIA ASSOCIATION OF REALTORS®
525 South Virgil Avenue, Los Angeles, California 90020

OFFICE USE ONLY
Reviewed by Broker
or Designee _____
Date _____

EQUAL HOUSING OPPORTUNITY

MANUFACTURED HOME PURCHASE CONTRACT (MHD-14 PAGE 1 OF 6) REVISED 12/96

382

enforce either state or local health laws, whichever is stricter. Health inspectors also act as health advisors. They can close down any proposed development that may cause contamination of the water supply or drainage systems, as well as any development that would cause improper sewage disposal. Furthermore, the sanitary condition of all housing is subject to control by the health authorities.

EMINENT DOMAIN

EMINENT DOMAIN
(INVOLUNTARY TAKING - CONDEMNATION)

With eminent domain, the government "takes for compensation." It is not police power. Eminent domain is an involuntary conversion process, which means that the owner receives money and is allowed to buy another property, within three years, without incurring taxes.

INVOLUNTARY CONVERSION *is the legal conversion of real property to personal property (money) without the voluntary act of the owner.* This occurs when property is taken by eminent domain (condemnation).

The owner is allowed to convert back to real property (buy another property) without paying tax on the gain from the condemnation. This must be done within a three-year period and the prices of the old and new property are considered to form a new tax base.

EMINENT DOMAIN *is the right of the government to take private property from a landowner (with the fair market value paid as compensation to that owner) for the "public good."* The use of the right of eminent domain is often referred to as "condemnation." In most condemnation cases, the main issue is the amount of just compensation required to be paid to the property owner. If a portion of a parcel is condemned, then there may be severance damages. ***SEVERANCE DAMAGE*** *is the compensation paid an owner for "devalued remaining property" as the result of an eminent domain action.* In some instances, the property owner will feel that the property is so devalued that he or she will file an inverse condemnation action. ***INVERSE CONDEMNATION*** *is an action where the property owner files suit to force the government to take all of the property, not just a part.*

Condemnation is the process of taking for compensation.

Some examples of private property being taken through eminent domain to benefit the general public are: improvement committees (urban renewal), K-12 schools, colleges and public utilities.

Eminent domain is the supreme power of a government agency to take private property for public use, by paying the fair market value for it.

REDEVELOPMENT (CITY AND COUNTY AGENCIES)

REDEVELOPMENT is the process of purchasing land in a run-down area (blighted) and constructing new buildings, parks, etc.. Early efforts at redevelopment were made by organizations such as syndication groups, realty boards and large insurance companies. However, the difficulty of assembling the necessary parcels by negotiation alone proved to be an impossible task. There was need for a government agency that could exercise its right of eminent domain to bring, by process of law, the court condemnation orders. Redevelopment organizations have been replaced by redevelopment agencies. *REDEVELOPMENT AGENCIES are city or county run redevelopment organizations that direct the spending of federal and state money.* The cities or counties have found a new way to rebuild their areas with government money.

MUTUAL WATER COMPANY

A *MUTUAL WATER COMPANY is organized by water users in a given district to supply ample water at a reasonable rate.* It is usually a corporation wherein the owner of each parcel of land is given a share of stock. The stock is appurtenant to the land, that is, each share of stock is attached to the land and cannot be sold separately. This enables the water company to develop uniformity and prevents speculation in the shares of stock.

Stock in a mutual water company is appurtenant to the land; it is real property.

No cash dividends are declared by these companies, but credits are given to water users if surpluses occur. On the other hand, assessments may be levied if operating revenues are not sufficient. Directors are elected by the stockholders, who usually employ one officer to operate the company, supervise the clerical help and advise stockholders regarding any water problems.

FAIR HOUSING LAWS

California first passed the Unruh Civil Rights Act (no discrimination in business, including real estate agents' services), then the Rumford Act (no discrimination in housing). These were later reinforced by the Federal Civil Rights Act of 1968.

California was among the first states with fair housing laws. Our first law was the **Unruh Civil Rights Act (no discrimination in business)**, then the **Rumford Act (no discrimination in housing)** and later these were reinforced with the Federal Civil Rights Act of 1968 (expanded in 1988). Figure 12-15 describes the different types of civil rights violations.

STATE LAW - UNRUH CIVIL RIGHTS ACT
(NO DISCRIMINATION IN BUSINESS)

The Unruh Civil Rights Act was the first civil rights act in California; it prohibits "steering" and "block busting" as a real estate business practice.

California first passed the Unruh Civil Rights Act that declares:

"All persons within the jurisdiction of this state are free and equal, and no matter what their race, color, religion, ancestry or national origin, they are entitled to the full and equal accommodations, advantages, facilities, privileges or services in all business establishments of every kind whatsoever. . ."

STATE LAW - RUMFORD ACT
(CALIFORNIA FAIR EMPLOYMENT AND HOUSING ACT)

The Rumford Act (California Fair Employment and Housing Act) established the Commission of Fair Employment and Housing to hear complaints of discrimination (and levy fines) with regards to the selling, renting, leasing or financing of housing.

FIGURE 12-15

FAIR HOUSING VIOLATIONS & POSSIBLE REMEDIES

REDLINING ——————— The refusal of a loan or insurance based upon a property's location (zip code).

STEERING ——————— Showing a client property in only one type of neighborhood, such as a Caucasian buyer in a Caucasian neighborhood, and the refusal to communicate the availability of housing in other neighborhoods.

OWNER TELLS AGENT NOT TO SHOW PROPERTY TO MINORITY — The agent is relieved of the duty to show the property to anyone, including a minority who has requested to see the property.

CONTRACT REFUSED TO BUYER BECAUSE OF RACE — ADVISE BUYER of the right to complain to the Fair Employment and Housing (FEH) and WARN SELLER that he or she has violated fair housing laws.

RACE RESTRICTIONS ——— Any race restriction is UNENFORCEABLE. It has NO LEGAL effect upon a transaction.

PANIC SELLING OR BLOCK BUSTING AND PANIC PEDDLING — An agent intentionally incites existing homeowners to sell their properties by saying that property values will fall because persons of a different race or religion have targeted a move into their neighborhood.

SALE OF PROPERTY - AGENT ASKED TO DISCRIMINATE — Agent must REFUSE the listing.

The **California Fair Employment and Housing Act, known as the Rumford Act (no discrimination in housing)**, established the Department of Fair Employment and Housing to investigate and take action against property owners, financial institutions and real estate licensees who engage in discriminatory practices. It clearly defines discrimination as the refusal to sell, rent or lease housing accommodations, including misrepresentation as to availability, inferior terms and cancellations on the basis of race, color, religion, sex, family status, national origin, ancestry and age. It also outlaws sale or rental advertisements containing discriminatory information.

STATE LAW - HOLDEN ACT
(HOUSING FINANCIAL DISCRIMINATION ACT)

The Housing Financial Discrimination Act of 1977 (Holden Act) prohibits financial institutions from engaging in discriminatory loan practices called "redlining."

In remedying such violations, the state may force a landowner to proceed with the rental or sale in question, provide comparable housing accommodations if the original is no longer available or pay punitive damages up to $1,000. Under the **Housing Financial Discrimination Act of 1977 (Holden Act)**, the practice of redlining is specifically outlawed. *REDLINING is the practice, by financial institutions, of denying loans or varying finance terms based on the location of a given property, regardless of the credit worthiness of the borrower.* This law explicitly forbids discrimination because of the race of the borrower or the racial composition of the neighborhood in which the borrower's home is located.

The Holden Act (no redlining) covers 1-to-4 units (at least one owner-occupied) used for residential purposes, but an owner seeking a home improvement loan need not occupy the property. A grievance under the Holden Act is directed to the U. S. Department of Business, Transportation and Housing. Lending institutions in violation of the Holden Act may be required to pay for damages, limited to $1,000 for each offense.

FEDERAL LAWS (FEDERAL CIVIL RIGHTS ACT OF 1968)

Federal law prohibits discrimination on the part of owners of property and their agents based on the **U.S. Supreme Court Case** *Jones vs. Mayer* (after the Civil War) and Title VIII of the Civil Rights Act of 1968.

For all practical purposes, discrimination laws evolved from the U.S. Supreme Court Case Jones vs. Mayer, Title VIII of the Civil Rights Act of 1968 and the 13th Amendment to the U.S. Constitution. To sum up: Real estate licensees must not discriminate, and to that end should not accept restrictive listings or make, print or publish any notice, statement or advertisement, with respect to a sale or rental of a dwelling, that suggests discrimination because of race, color, religion or national origin.

At the federal level, the Federal Civil Rights Act of 1968 reinforced the Unruh and Rumford Acts: 1) Any discrimination that the two acts did not prohibit was explicitly outlawed. **THERE ARE NO EXCEPTIONS;** 2) It makes it illegal for real estate licensees to engage in discriminatory practices regardless of any instructions the agent may have received from the seller or landlord. If asked to discriminate in the sale of a property, the salesperson must refuse to accept the listing; 3) It bars real estate boards or multiple listing services from discriminating by denying participation or restricting terms and conditions of membership; 4) It requires a fair housing poster to be displayed at all real estate offices and subdivision model homes. The poster (Figure 12-16) must also be displayed at all financial institutions or by mortgage lenders who make loans to the general public.

The U.S. Fair Housing Act became effective in 1968. Fair Housing Posters must be displayed at real estate offices and lending institutions.

FEDERAL CIVIL RIGHTS ACT EXPANDED IN 1988
(HUD CAN INITIATE HOUSING DISCRIMINATION CASES)

A 1988 federal law allows the U.S. Government to take court action if it believes discrimination exists in home sales or apartment rentals. Landlords are explicitly forbidden to discriminate against families with children under 18 years of age. The only exemptions from this would be in retirement communities where most of the residents are more than 55 years of age.

FIGURE 12-16

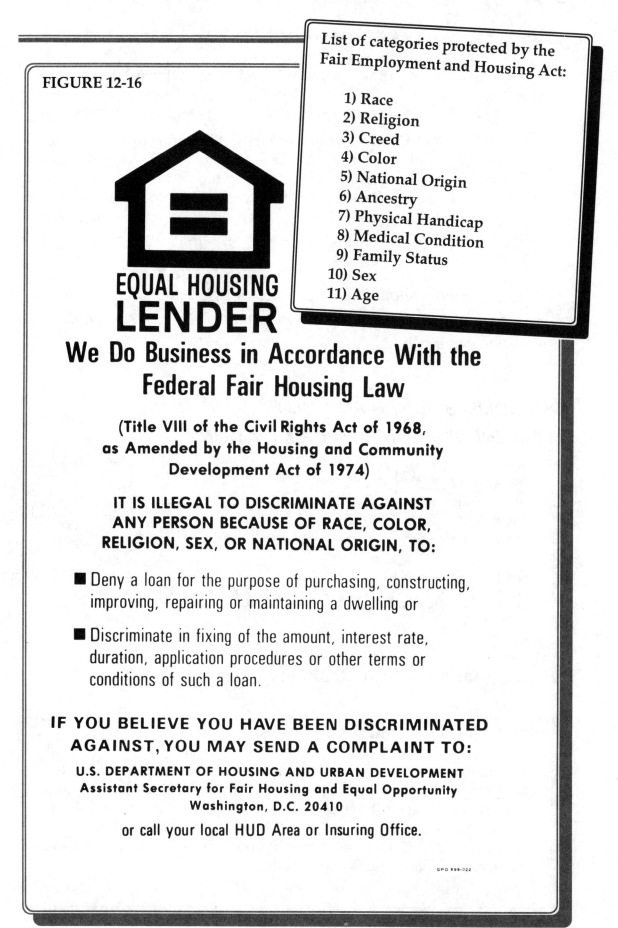

List of categories protected by the Fair Employment and Housing Act:

1) Race
2) Religion
3) Creed
4) Color
5) National Origin
6) Ancestry
7) Physical Handicap
8) Medical Condition
9) Family Status
10) Sex
11) Age

EQUAL HOUSING LENDER

We Do Business in Accordance With the Federal Fair Housing Law

(Title VIII of the Civil Rights Act of 1968, as Amended by the Housing and Community Development Act of 1974)

IT IS ILLEGAL TO DISCRIMINATE AGAINST ANY PERSON BECAUSE OF RACE, COLOR, RELIGION, SEX, OR NATIONAL ORIGIN, TO:

■ Deny a loan for the purpose of purchasing, constructing, improving, repairing or maintaining a dwelling or

■ Discriminate in fixing of the amount, interest rate, duration, application procedures or other terms or conditions of such a loan.

IF YOU BELIEVE YOU HAVE BEEN DISCRIMINATED AGAINST, YOU MAY SEND A COMPLAINT TO:

U.S. DEPARTMENT OF HOUSING AND URBAN DEVELOPMENT
Assistant Secretary for Fair Housing and Equal Opportunity
Washington, D.C. 20410

or call your local HUD Area or Insuring Office.

GPO 899-022

This federal law also extends protections to handicapped home buyers or tenants. As of 1991, builders of all new apartment buildings were required to include ground floor rooms suitable for use by residents in wheelchairs.

The Housing and Urban Development (HUD) Department is authorized to bring enforcement action against sellers and landlords who defy this law. Fines of up to $10,000 have been authorized for first time violators, up to $25,000 for a second offense within five years and up to $50,000 for a third offense within seven years. Those accused of violating this tough statute would face an administrative judge unless they specifically requested a jury trial.

Complaints should be filed with Housing & Urban Development (HUD). Fair Employment & Housing will enforce any action.

THE COMMISSIONER AND "NAR"
ALSO ENFORCE ANTI-DISCRIMINATION

The Commissioner

Regulations of the Real Estate Commissioner

(10177 of the Business and Professions Code)

Regulations have been issued by the real estate commissioner that cover any discrimination with regards to housing. Disciplinary action will be taken against any real estate licensee who violates these regulations. This could include a suspension, fine, revocation of license or prosecution by the local district attorney. See Chapter 14 for more about the Commissioner's Regulations.

The National Association of Realtors®

Code of Ethics

The National Association of Realtors (NAR)® Code of Ethics and Fair Practices forbids discrimination against any minority group. Any violation by a real estate licensee could subject that licensee to disciplinary action from the local board of Realtors®.

Article 10 states that the Realtor® shall not deny equal service (or be a party to any plan or agreement to deny service) to any person for reasons of race, color, religion, handicap, family status or national origin.

http://www.realtor.com (National Association of Realtors)

A. Subdivision Map Act	J. Condominium	T. Conditional Use Permit
B. Subdivided Lands Law	K. Redevelopment Agency	U. Building Code
C. Public Report	L. Eminent Domain	V. Building Permit
D. Redlining	M. Environmental Impact Report	W. Mobilehomes
E. Mutual Water Company	N. Planning Commission	X. Severance Damages
F. Land Project	O. Master Plan	Y. Unruh Act
G. Planned Unit Development	P. Zoning Laws	Z. Rumford Act
H. Common Area	Q. Spot Zoning	AA. Holden Act
I. Community Apartment Project	R. Nonconforming Use	BB. Jones vs. Mayer
	S. Variance	CC. Civil Rights Act of 1968

1.____ A comprehensive zoning plan to help a city grow in an orderly and sound manner, both economically and ecologically.

2.____ A water company in which the owners are the customers.

3.____ A permit given by a local government to construct a building or make improvements.

4.____ A report given to a prospective purchaser (s) in a new subdivision.

5.____ Zoning on a parcel-by-parcel basis, rather than a comprehensive general or master plan. Considered poor planning.

6.____ The outlining in red on a map of certain "high risk" areas where lenders will not extend credit, regardless of the qualifications of the applicants (illegal practice).

7.____ The local government board which must approve proposed building projects according to zones; it must answer to the county board or city council.

8.____ A subdivision where there is private ownership of individual lots as well as common ownership of another lot, usually a swimming pool or a recreation room.

9.____ A report of the probable effect of a development on the ecology of the surrounding area. The report is prepared by an independent company and follows federal, state or local guidelines.

10.____ An isolated rural subdivision, operating under federal guidelines, with certain rights of rescission.

11.____ Permission to change a portion of zoning requirements without changing the entire zoning.

12.____ Loss in value to the remaining property when part of a parcel is condemned and seized by the government for public use.

13.____ A corporation formed for the purpose of holding title to a building. Each shareholder receives the right to occupy a dwelling unit but must pay property taxes and insurance in common with the other owners.

14.____ The area owned in common by all the owners of condominiums or planned unit developments.

15.____ A property that does not conform to the current zoning of the area. Usually, the property was built in conformity and then the zoning was changed.

16.____ A structure of two or more units, the interior spaces of which are individually owned; the balance of the property is owned in common by the owners of the individual units.

17.____ A comprehensive set of laws that control the construction of buildings, including design, materials used, repair, remodeling and other similar factors.

18.____ Generally, the improvement of land in accordance with a city renewal project.

19.____ A governmental right to acquire private property for public use by condemnation, and the payment of just compensation.

20.____ Homes that are not truly mobile but are constructed in the same manner as trailers, as opposed to conventional, on-site construction.

21.____ Laws that require cities and counties to specify the uses allowable for real property in different areas or zones.

22.____ An Act requiring developers to obtain local government (city or county) approval for the detailed construction plan of their subdivision.

23.____ A specific exception to zoning laws, granted for the general good of the community.

24.____ A law requiring an acknowledgment from the Department of Real Estate that a subdivision has met the minimum requirements for filing the necessary reports.

25.____ Established far-reaching federal anti-discrimination laws. Requires that fair housing posters be displayed at real estate offices and lending institutions.
26.____ Civil War-era court case that was the basis for current civil rights laws.
27.____ State fair housing law established to eliminate redlining.
28.____ Established the California Fair Employment and Housing Act.
29.____ The state fair housing law that disallowed discrimination in business, including real estate agent's services.

MULTIPLE CHOICE

1. The law that permits the local government at the city or county level to enact subdivision ordinances is called the:

   A. State Redevelopment Act
   C. Subdivided Lands Act
   B. Subdivision Map Act
   D. Fair Housing Act

2. The receipt stating that the buyer has received a copy of any public report must be kept on file by an owner for:

   A. 1 year
   C. 3 years
   B. 120 days
   D. 5 years

3. Any material change in a subdivision, after the filing of the public report is issued, must be reported to the:

   A. Real Estate Commissioner
   C. Fair Housing Administration
   B. Department of Corporations
   D. State Department of Subdivisions

4. A study of how a subdivision will effect the ecology of a subdivision's surroundings is called a (an):

   A. Coastal Commission Report
   C. Pollution Control Report
   B. Environmental Impact Report
   D. Subdivision Impact Report

5. Unless provided for in the policy, title insurance will NOT protect against:

   A. recorded liens
   C. forgeries
   B. zoning changes
   D. acts of minors

6. Real estate brokers cannot sell mobilehome that:

   A. are new
   C. are permanently stationed in a mobile park
   B. have been registered for more than one year
   D. have their axles removed

7. What is eminent domain often referred to as?

   A. Police power
   C. Spot zoning
   B. Condemnation
   D. Easement appurtenant

8. The Rumford Act established:

   A. The Unruh Civil Rights Act
   C. The Housing Financial Discrimination Act
   B. The Department of Fair Employment and Housing
   D. HUD

9. Display of the fair housing poster became mandatory under the:

   A. Housing Financial Discrimination Act
   C. Civil Rights Act of 1968
   B. Rumford Act
   D. Garn Act

10. Which of the following may NOT generally exercise the power of eminent domain?

   A. Improvement committees
   C. Public education institutions
   B. Private individuals
   D. Utility companies

CHAPTER 13
Taxation of Real Estate

Taxes are an important aspect of all real estate transactions. Property owners are taxed annually on the property they own. In addition, there are other state and federal taxes that must be paid in order to buy, sell or give away real property. Figure 13-1 illustrates the five taxes with which every taxpayer, investor and salesperson should be familiar. The amount of tax and who must pay the tax are often major factors to consider in the transfer of real estate.

PROPERTY TAXES

A city or county receives most of its operating revenue from the assessment and collection of real property taxes. *REAL PROPERTY TAXES are taxes determined according to the value of the real property, and are paid annually or semi-annually.* These taxes are called ad valorem taxes. An *AD VALOREM TAX is a tax that is charged in proportion to the value of the property.* Property taxes are based on the concept that taxes should be assessed in accordance with a person's ability to pay. In the case of real estate, the higher the value of the property, the higher the property taxes.

Ad valorem means taxed according to value. Real property is reassessed each time it is transferred (sold) at of its selling price. Annual property taxes are 1% of selling price.

 http://www.co.la.ca.us/assessor (L. A. County Assessor)

FIGURE 13-1

The **COUNTY ASSESSOR** *is the county officer who has the responsibility of determining the assessed valuation of land, improvements and personal property used in business.* The county assessor determines the value of both county and city properties, except in a few cities that use their own assessors. In Los Angeles County, the City of Pasadena has its own assessor who assess the property in that city. San Francisco is unique because the city and county are combined, so the city and county assessor functions are combined.

In general all real property, except that which is owned by the government, and all tangible personal property, except inventory used in a business, is subject to property tax assessment in California. Intangible personal property, such as shares of stock, promissory notes, as well as household furnishings and personal effects of individuals, are not assessed or taxed.

> *County Assessor assesses; County Tax Collector collects;*
> *County Board of Supervisors sets tax rate.*

The **COUNTY TAX COLLECTOR** *is the county officer who collects the real property taxes.* He or she only collects taxes; the county tax collector has nothing to do with determining how much tax is levied. If the real property taxes are not paid, the county tax collector will eventually require that the property be sold at a tax sale.

http://www.cacttc.org/start.html (List of Assessors)

PROPOSITION 13

PROPOSITION 13 limits the amount of taxes to a maximum of 1%* of the March 1, 1975, market value of the property plus the cumulative increase of 2% in market value each year thereafter. Improvements made after March 1, 1975, are added to the value in the year they are made. If ownership has changed after March 1, 1975, the tax is limited to 1%* of the market value plus the 2% cumulative increase each succeeding year. Any state-allowed exemptions are deducted after figuring the basic tax. See Figure 13-2.

*Voted indebtedness may increase this rate beyond 1%, from area-to-area, with voter approval.

REAL PROPERTY TAX BASE IS TRANSFERABLE

Under the following conditions, homeowners may be permitted to transfer their current Proposition 13 tax base with them when they move:

1. Homeowners over the age of 55
2. Replacement home of equal or lesser value
3. Purchased within two years of original sale
4. New home must be in the same county; or another participating county (check first).

This allows "empty-nesters" to purchase a new home while holding on to their low tax base, thus freeing up larger multiple bedroom homes for younger families.

ASSESSED VALUATION is set at 100% of the property's selling price or fair market value, whichever is higher, plus a 2% increase for every year the property has been owned, but only as far back as March 1, 1975. The tax rate is set at 1% of selling price (or fair market value, whichever is higher) plus any voter-approved indebtedness. Properties that are transferred and new construction are subject to a new appraisal based upon the current market value or selling price, whichever is higher. Existing structures are given a new assessment each year as of January 1st. New construction and transfers are assessed immediately upon the first day of the next month. See Figures 13-3 and 13-4 for an example of a property tax bill.

PROPERTY TAXES BECOME A SPECIFIC LIEN

Property taxes due upon real property are, in effect, liens against that specific property. Business personal property taxes (trade fixtures) also become liens against that specific real property on the same tax bill. For example, the furniture in furnished apartments is taxed as business personal property and is usually included on the property tax bill.

FIGURE 13-2

PROPOSITION 13

That Article XII A is added to the Constitution to read:

Section 1.

(a) The maximum amount of any ad valorem tax on real property shall not exceed one percent (1%)*of the full cash value of such property. The one percent (1%)*tax to be collected by the counties and apportioned according to law to the districts within the counties.

(b) The limitation provided for in subdivision (a) shall not apply to ad valorem taxes or special assessments to pay the interest and redemption charges on any indebtedness approved by the voters prior to the time this section becomes effective.

Section 2.

(a) The full cash value means the county assessors valuation of real property as shown on the 1975-76 tax bill under "full cash value," or thereafter, the appraised value of real property when purchased, newly constructed, or a change in ownership has occurred after the 1975 assessment. All real property not already assessed up to the 1975-76 tax levels may be reassessed to reflect that valuation.

(b) The fair market value base may reflect from year to year the inflationary rate not to exceed two percent (2%) for any given year or reduction as shown in the consumer price index or comparable data for the area under taxing jurisdiction.

Section 3.

From and after the effective date of this article, any changes in state taxes enacted for the purpose of increasing revenues collected pursuant thereto whether by increased rates or changes in methods of computation must be imposed by an Act passed by not less than two-thirds of all members elected to each of the two houses of the Legislature, except that no new ad valorem taxes on real property, or sales or transaction taxes on the sales of real property may be imposed.

Section 4.

Cities, counties and special districts, by a two-thirds vote of the qualified electors of such district, may impose special taxes on such district, except ad valorem taxes on real property or a transaction tax or sales tax on the sale of real property within such city, county, or special district.

Section 5.

This article shall take effect for the tax year beginning on July 1 following the passage of this Amendment, except Section 3 which shall become effective upon the passage of this article.

Section 6.

If any section, part, clause, or phrase hereof is for any reason held to be invalid or unconstitutional, the remaining sections shall not be affected but will remain in full force and effect.

Voted indebtedness may increase this rate beyond 1% from local area to area with voter approval.

FIGURE 13-3 ## JOINT CONSOLIDATED ANNUAL TAX BILL

CITIES, COUNTY, SCHOOLS AND ALL OTHER TAXING AGENCIES IN LOS ANGELES COUNTY
SECURED PROPERTY TAX FOR FISCAL YEAR JULY 1, 1997 TO JUNE 30, 1998
LARRY J. MONTEILH, TREASURER AND TAX COLLECTOR

OWNER OF RECORD AS OF JANUARY 1, 1997
SAME AS BELOW

```
4225 011 081
HUBER, WALTER R AND DEBBIE R
27 KETCH ST NO 1
MARINA DL REY CA 90292-5946
```

PROPERTY LOCATION AND / OR PROPERTY DESCRIPTION
```
27 KETCH ST NO 1                    LOS ANGELE
*TR=P M 72-26-27  CONDOMINIUM*UNITS
1 AND A
```

DETAIL OF TAXES DUE	RATE	AMOUNT
GENERAL TAX LEVY		
ALL AGENCIES	1 000000	1930 01
VOTED INDEBTEDNESS		
COUNTY	001584	3 06
CITY-LOS ANGELES	031098	60 02
METRO WATER DIST	008900	17 17
FLOOD CONTROL	002197	4 39
UNIFIED SCHOOLS	012017	23 19
DIRECT ASSESSMENTS		
FLOOD CONTROL		10 09
CTY LAND/LT 96-1		15 07
CITY 911 FUND		12 07
LA WEST MOSQ AB		3 27
COUNTY PARK DIST		15 38
CTY FIRE/PRAMDCS		13 07
LA STORMWATER		8 05
FIRST INSTALLMENT TAXES DUE		1057 42
SECOND INSTALLMENT TAXES DUE		1057 42
TOTAL TAXES DUE		2114 84

**BEFORE CALLING A COUNTY OFFICE
SEE REVERSE SIDE FOR
IMPORTANT TAXPAYER INFORMATION**

ELECTRONIC FUND TRANSFER NUMBER
ID#: 19 4225 011 081 9 YR:97 SEQ:0004

COUNTY OF LOS ANGELES

ACCOUNT NO.	PRINT NO.	DIVISION INDEX BATCH NO.	REG.	ASSESSOR'S ID. NO.					TRA
				Year	Seq. No.	Map Book	Page	Parcel	
	531189		07	97	000	4225	011	081	00067

ROLL YEAR 97-98	CURRENT ASSESSED VALUE	TAXABLE VALUE
LAND	114470	114470
IMPROVEMENTS	85531	85531
FIXTURES		

	TOTAL	200001
	LESS EXEMPTION HOME	7000
	NET TAXABLE VALUE	193001

THERE WILL BE A $49.85 SERVICE CHARGE FOR ANY CHECK RETURNED BY THE BANK.

KEEP THIS UPPER PORTION FOR YOUR RECORDS   YOUR CANCELLED CHECK IS YOUR RECEIPT

Property taxes for the following fiscal year become a lien against the real property on January 1st of the current year. Officially, the first installment for half of the taxes becomes due on November 1st and is delinquent after 5pm on December 10th. The second installment is due on February 1st and is delinquent if not paid by 5pm on April 10th. If either December 10th or April 10th falls on a Saturday, Sunday or legal holiday, the delinquency date is extended to the close of the next business day.

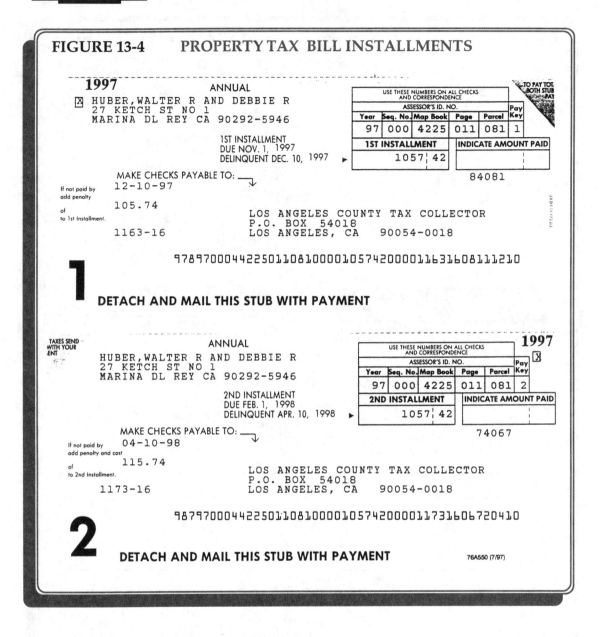

FIGURE 13-4   PROPERTY TAX BILL INSTALLMENTS

PROPERTY TAX TIME TABLE

The city or county fiscal year starts on July 1st and ends on June 30th. All revenues and expenditures are planned for this period of time. Figure 13-5 illustrates all the important dates that are associated with property taxes. Assessable property is evaluated by the assessor on January 1st for the upcoming year in the name of the property's legal owner on that date. Most cities allow the county assessor to evaluate the property in both the county and the incorporated parts of the county, which are the cities. In a few rare cases as stated earlier, cities may use their own assessors. County assessors complete their assessment rolls by July 1st, the beginning of the fiscal year.

FIGURE 13-5

PROPERTY TAX TIME TABLE

January 1	July 1	November 1	February 1
Property tax becomes a lien on real property	Fiscal year starts	1st installment is due and delinquent after December 10 at 5:00 P.M.	2nd installment is due and delinquent after April 10 at 5:00 P.M.

Important tax dates can be remembered "**N**o **D**arn **F**ooling **A**round" as follows:

    N   November 1 (first installment)
    D   December 10 (first installment is delinquent)
    F   February 1 (second installment)
    A   April 10 (second installment is delinquent)

The governmental fiscal tax year is July 1 through June 30.

PROPERTY TAX PRORATION PROBLEM

Proration question: Who owes whom how much?

If the seller of the subject property has paid both the 1st and 2nd installments of the property taxes for a total annual bill of $2,760, what is the proration of property taxes for both the seller and buyer if the buyer takes possession on May 1st?

Remember: Escrow prorates property taxes using old (seller's) assessed value (tax bill).

The first step is to determine the amount of taxes per month. The annual tax bill of $2,760 is divided by 12 months to determine that the monthly tax is $230. Since the seller paid the property taxes through the month of June (the end of the fiscal tax year, which is July 1st through June 30th), and the buyer took possession on May 1st, two months of paid property taxes are owed the seller. The buyer would owe the seller for two months (May and June) that were already paid by the seller. This amount would be $460 (2 X $230).

When a property is sold, the buyer will receive one new property tax bill, but it may be followed by other updated property tax bills, referred to as supplemental property tax bills. See Figure 13-6.

FIGURE 13-6

SUPPLEMENTAL PROPERTY TAX BILLS

The law (SB 813) requires reassessment of property **immediately** when it changes ownership or when new construction is completed. While the amount of the supplemental assessment is still determined in accordance with Proposition 13, the actual effect is to "speed up" reassessment of property. In fact, prior to the change in the law, property was generally not reappraised until January 1st.

The Office of Assessor enters the new property value onto the assessment roll as of the first of the month following the month in which the property changes ownership or new construction is completed.

Depending upon the date you purchase property, or the date construction is completed, you will receive **one or more** supplemental tax bills in addition to your regular tax bill. Taxes on the supplemental tax roll become a lien against the real property on the date of change in ownership or the date new construction is completed.

HOMEOWNER'S PROPERTY TAX EXEMPTION

Homeowner's property tax exemption is $7,000 of assessed valuation. Not the same as a homestead exemption.

The *HOMEOWNER'S PROPERTY TAX EXEMPTION is a deduction, on the property tax bill, of the first $7,000 of assessed value of an owner-occupied property.*

A homeowner's exemption on your home does the following:

1. All personal property of the homeowner is exempt from property taxes.

2. A resident owner receives a $7,000 homeowner's exemption in assessed value if the property is the principal residence on the 1st of March.

The time to file for the homeowner's exemption is from January 1st to April 15th in order to receive the full exemption. Once the exemption is filed, it remains on the property until the homeowner terminates it. If the exemption is terminated, a new claim form must be obtained from, and filed with, the assessor to regain eligibility.

Qualifying residential property that is owner-occupied receives a $7,000 homeowner's exemption. For example, an assessed value of $200,000 minus the homeowner's exemption of $7,000 is $193,000.

RENTERS' CREDIT

EDITOR'S UPDATE: As of the latest printing of this text, a single renter who's income is under $25,000 may qualify for a renter's credit of $60; if married and earn under $50,000, the renters' credit is $120.

HOMEOWNERS AND RENTERS PROPERTY TAX REBATE (SENIOR CITIZENS AND DISABLED PERSONS)

This is a property tax relief law for any resident who is 62 years of age or older as of January 1st, and has a household income of not more than $12,000 for the calendar year. The applicant must have owned and occupied his or her home within the fiscal year. Persons under the age of 62 who are totally disabled also qualify for this rebate. A similar program provides a rebate to elderly and disabled persons who rent their homes or apartments.

All relief is in the form of a property tax rebate granted to the applicant. The amount of the property tax rebate is a percentage of household income on the first $8,500 of assessed valuation. The exact amount of rebate is determined by the Senior Citizen's Property Tax Assistance branch of the State Franchise Tax Board.

Rebate applicants pay property taxes as usual during the year and their application must be filed between May 16th and August 31st. The claim form is processed and the rebate checks are sent directly to the applicant. The form may be obtained from the local Franchise Tax Board office.

SENIOR CITIZEN'S PROPERTY TAX ASSISTANCE
P. O. BOX 1588
SACRAMENTO, CALIFORNIA 95807

DISABLED AND SENIOR CITIZENS (PROPERTY TAX POSTPONEMENT)

Seniors who are 62 years of age or older, and have a household income of $24,000 or less, may qualify for this tax postponement assistance program. This program offers them the option of having the state pay all or part of the taxes on their homes. In return, a lien is placed on the property for the amount that the state has to pay. This lien becomes payable when the taxpayer moves or dies. In effect, the homeowner is relieved of his or her tax burden in exchange for title to his or her home upon death. California has extended this program to include persons under the age of 62 who are legally disabled. Further information is available from the State Franchise Tax Board.

VETERAN'S EXEMPTION

Any California resident who served in the military during a time of war is entitled to an annual $4,000 property tax exemption against the assessed value of one property. This exemption also applies to the widow, widowed mother, or pensioned father of a deceased veteran. However, the exempted property is limited to an assessed value of less than $5,000 for a single veteran or $10,000 if he or she is married. For disabled California veterans who qualify, however, the assessment limit can be raised up to $100,000.

Note: A veteran cannot have a veteran's exemption and a homeowner's property tax exemption on the same property.

TAX EXEMPT PROPERTY

In California there are some properties that are partially or totally tax exempt. All real property that is owned by the federal, state, county or city government is automatically tax exempt.

Since California has many national and state parks, the majority of land in this state is tax exempt. Any property that is used exclusively by non-profit organizations for religious, charitable, medical or educational purposes is also tax exempt. In addition, 50 percent of all growing crops, young orchard trees, immature timber and young grapevines are tax exempt.

Property of non-profit organizations used for religious, charitable, medical or educational purposes is tax exempt.

PROPERTY TAX APPEALS

Over-assessments can be taken to the appeals board.

People who feel that the assessment of their property is not correct may appeal the assessment. Appeals would be directed to the Board of Equalization (the property tax assessment appeals board), in the county in which the property is located, between July 2nd and August 26th (in most counties). After it considers the case, the Board may reduce an assessment, or it may increase it, or it may issue a new assessment if the property has not been assessed before.

In most small and many medium sized counties, the County Board of Supervisors serves as the Board of Equalization. In larger counties, with a larger number or properties to assess, a special Tax Appeals Board is usually established. This board has no control over tax rates in general, but is the government body that makes individual assessment decisions on individual properties.

If a property owner wishes to protest the real property tax assessment, he or she can do so by contacting the appeals board office for detailed information. This Board of Equalization agency may reduce an assessed value that has been appealed.

DELINQUENT TAX SALE (FIRST SALE)

Each year, on or before June 8th, the county tax collector publishes a list of tax delinquent properties. This is his or her "notice of intent to sell" all such properties on which the property taxes have not been paid for one year. Strictly speaking, this is not a true sale, but is a formality that starts a five year redemption period. If the property is not redeemed within five years, it will be deeded over to the state.

Properties may be redeemed by anyone upon the payment of taxes, interest, costs and redemption penalties. The tax collector gives a receipt called a "certificate of redemption" as evidence of payment. If the owner cannot pay for all past due taxes and costs at once, he or she may pay them in five annual installment payments, providing all current taxes are paid.

If taxes are not paid on or before June 30th, the property is sold to the state. This sale starts the running of the redemption period which is five years.

SECOND SALE (AFTER FIVE YEARS)

After five years, if the property has not been redeemed, the delinquent property is deeded to the state. This is the official sale, and the former owner may now only redeem the property if the state has not sold the property at public auction.

Although property taxes are not paid, a owner can remain in possession and could redeem for 5 years.

SALE TO THE PUBLIC

The county tax collector will sell the state-owned properties to other taxing agencies or to the highest bidder at a public tax auction. The minimum bid is established by the tax collector and approved by the county board of supervisors. All such sales are for cash at the time of the sale. The purchaser then receives a tax deed. Most title insurance companies will insure the tax deed sale after one year has elapsed. But, if any difficulties are encountered, the buyer may clear title through a "quiet title" court action.

SPECIAL ASSESSMENT TAX

A *SPECIAL ASSESSMENT TAX is levied by a city council or a county board of supervisors, with the voters' approval, for the cost of specific local improvements such as streets, sewers, irrigation or drainage.* It differs from property taxes in that property taxes finance the general functions of government, whereas a special assessment is levied once (usually) by the city, county or "improvement district" for a particular work or improvement.

The official body that levies a special assessment is called a SPECIAL ASSESSMENT DISTRICT BOARD. According to state law, any self-governing area, such as a city or county, may establish a special assessment district for the purpose of levying a special assessment.

As a rule, a district issues its own bonds to finance particular improvements such as water distribution systems, parking facilities, street lighting and many other types of developments. To repay the funds borrowed through the bonds issued, these districts have the power to assess all lands included in the district on an ad valorem basis. Such loans constitute liens on the land until paid. These liens can be foreclosed by sale similar to a tax sale and have priority over private property interests.

Special assessments are for improvements only. If you purchase a lot for $40,000 and assume a $1,200 assessment bond, your cost basis for income tax purposes would be $41,200.

STREET IMPROVEMENT ACT OF 1911

The **STREET IMPROVEMENT ACT OF 1911** *finances street and highway improvements through an assessment to property owners based upon the frontage they enjoy facing the improved street.* Also called the Bond Act of 1911, it allows property owners, through the issuance of municipal bonds, up to 30 years to pay off their portion of the improvement assessment.

THE MELLO-ROOS COMMUNITY FACILITIES ACT

The Mello-Roos Community Facilities Act is another type of improvement bond. Figure 13-7 explains Mello-Roos in detail.

DOCUMENTARY TRANSFER TAX

Paid only on the new amount of money (cash down and new financing), not on any assumed financing.

The **DOCUMENTARY TRANSFER TAX** *is a tax that is applied to the consideration paid or money borrowed when transferring property, except for any remaining loans or liens on the property.* This tax is computed at the rate of 55 cents for each $500 of consideration or any fraction thereof that exceeds $100. The consideration is any amount of cash payment plus any new loans. However, this tax does not apply to any liens or encumbrances that remain on the property as part of the transfer. If a house were sold for $230,000 and a buyer assumed the old loan of $30,000, the documentary transfer tax would be $220.

$$\frac{\$200,000}{\$500} \times \$.55 = \$220$$

The documentary transfer tax is charged to the seller and is handled as part of the escrow. According to state law the county is allowed to charge this tax. However, a city within a county can charge that county for 1/2 of this tax. Therefore, in most cities, the county collects the documentary transfer tax and

FIGURE 13-7

Mello-Roos Liens
DISCLOSURE REQUIRED

Failure to disclose allows buyer a 3-day right of rescission, and results in agent disciplinary action

MELLO-ROOS LIENS are municipal bonds issued to fund streets, sewers and other infrastructure needs before a housing development is built. This financial device allows developers to raise money to complete off-site improvements in a house or condo subdivision. The developer is usually responsible for making payments on the bond until the home is sold. The homeowner then becomes responsible for payment via a special tax.

The Mello-Roos Community Facilities Act is a way that a city or governmental district can skirt the property tax limitations of Proposition 13. The city can include the cost and maintenance of infrastructure items in the property tax bill as a special tax, which is allowed to go above the limits of Proposition 13.

This has been a boon for developers who need help financing their projects and for municipalities anxious to upgrade new developments under the restrictions of Proposition 13. The downside is that if something goes wrong with the economy or the project, the municipality may have to foreclose on the developer.

A broker must disclose to property buyers that a project is subject to a Mello-Roos special tax levy. If the agent fails to provide this disclosure, he or she is subject to discipline by the Real Estate Commissioner. A notice of special tax is required on the sale or lease (for more than five years) of property subject to this lien. Failure to give notice before signing the sales contract permits the buyer or tenant a three-day right of rescission after receipt of the notice.

Warning: Whereas property taxes are totally deductible from state and federal income taxes, Mello-Roos taxes may only be partially deductible depending upon whether they are for maintenance or improvements. Consult with your C.P.A. before claiming such a deduction.

gives half of it to the city. Based on the information found at the county recorder's office, the documentary transfer tax can be used to determine a previous sale price of a property. Simply divide 55 cents into the amount of the documentary transfer tax and multiply by $500. If any loans have been assumed by the new owner, also add that amount to arrive at the total prior sale price of the property.

If any old loans or liens are to remain on the property, this fact must be stated on the deed or on a separate paper filed with the deed. Then add the value of the cash down payment and any new loans together with any remaining loan on the property to find the total selling price.

— CITY TRANSFER TAXES —

The city of Los Angeles initiated a transfer tax to be paid by sellers when a property is sold. The current charge is $4.50 per $1,000 of selling price.

— WATCH FOR A VERSION OF THIS TAX IN YOUR CITY —

GIFT AND ESTATE TAXES

For federal purposes, the transfer of property by a gift or inheritance is taxed. Exemptions may reduce the taxes and sometimes eliminate them. Figure 13-8 illustrates the federal taxes encountered by transferring property as a gift or by inheritance.

A gift of real estate may avoid federal estate taxes. So if a person wants to give a property away, it will most likely escape (the future) federal estate taxes. But, if you are to avoid federal gift taxes, usually only a fractional interest in the property should be given away each year. For example, you could give a son and daughter each a 1/30 interest in your home every year for 15 years to give the house to your children.

FIGURE 13-8

FEDERAL GIFT TAXES

Estate taxes and income taxes on appreciated property can be avoided by giving it away or by donating it to a non-profit organization; see a CPA or tax expert for advice.

Frequently, as an individual family matures, the value of the real property owned by the family increases and the owning family may consider bestowing it as a gift. When a family gives property, whether real or personal, to another individual there may be federal gift taxes that must be paid. If the value of the property is higher than an exempt amount, the donor must pay a gift tax. A **DONOR** *is the person or persons giving the property as a gift.* Generally, people give their property away to relatives on a systematic basis so that taxes are avoided. The **DONEE** *is the person or persons who receive the property as a gift.* The federal gift tax law also provides for a $10,000 annual exemption per donee.

FEDERAL ESTATE TAX

A **FEDERAL ESTATE TAX** *return must be filed for the estate of every resident of the United States whose gross estate exceeds $600,000 in value at the date of death.* Estate tax exemptions will gradually increase the size of estates that are exempt from taxation from $600,000 to $1,000,000 by 2014.

NO STATE GIFT AND INHERITANCE TAXES

> State Inheritance Tax
> None (Repealed June 8, 1982)
> State Gift Tax
> None (Repealed June 8, 1982)

FEDERAL, STATE & LOCAL INCOME TAXES

The annual Federal Income Tax Form 1040 (See Figure 13-9) and the State Income Tax Form 540 are bookkeeping or accounting summaries of the prior year's financial facts. These facts are a history and cannot be altered at the time of filing the income tax return.

 http://www. irs.ustreas.gov (Internal Revenue Service)

FIGURE 13-9

Form 1040
Department of the Treasury—Internal Revenue Service
U.S. Individual Income Tax Return **19XX** (0)
IRS Use Only—Do not write or staple in this space.

For the year Jan. 1–Dec. 31, 1992, or other tax year beginning   , 1992, ending   , 19 | OMB No. 1545-0074

Label

(See instructions on page 10.)

Use the IRS label. Otherwise, please print or type.

Your first name and initial   Last name

Your social security number

If a joint return, spouse's first name and initial   Last name

Spouse's social security number

Home address (number and street). If you have a P.O. box, see page 10.   Apt. no.

City, town or post office, state, and ZIP code. If you have a foreign address, see page 10.

For Privacy Act and Paperwork Reduction Act Notice, see page 4.

Presidential Election Campaign
(See page 10.)

Do you want $1 to go to this fund? . . . .   Yes [ ]   No [ ]

If a joint return, does your spouse want $1 to go to this fund? .   Yes [ ]   No [ ]

Note: Checking "Yes" will not change your tax or reduce your refund.

Filing Status
(See page 10.)

Check only one box.

1 Single
2 Married filing joint return (even if only one had income)
3 Married filing separate return. Enter spouse's social security no. above and full name here. ▶ _____
4 Head of household (with qualifying person). (See page 11.) If the qualifying person is a child but not your dependent, enter this child's name here. ▶ _____
5 Qualifying widow(er) with dependent child (year spouse died ▶ 19   ). (See page 11.)

Exemptions
(See page 11.)

6a [ ] **Yourself.** If your parent (or someone else) can claim you as a dependent on his or her tax return, **do not** check box 6a. But be sure to check the box on line 33b on page 2

b [ ] **Spouse** . . . .

c Dependents:

(1) Name (first, initial, and last name)	(2) Check if under age 1	(3) If age 1 or older, dependent's social security number	(4) Dependent's relationship to you	(5) No. of months lived in your home in 1992

If more than six dependents, see page 12.

d If your child didn't live with you but is claimed as your dependent under a pre-1985 agreement, check here ▶ [ ]
e Total number of exemptions claimed . . . .

No. of boxes checked on 6a and 6b ___

No. of your children on 6c who:
• lived with you
• didn't live with you due to divorce or separation (see page 13)

No. of other dependents on 6c ___

Add numbers entered on lines above ▶ [ ]

Income

Attach Copy B of your Forms W-2, W-2G, and 1099-R here.

If you did not get a W-2, see page 9.

Attach check or money order on top of any Forms W-2, W-2G, or 1099-R.

7 Wages, salaries, tips, etc. Attach Form(s) W-2 . . . . | 7 |
8a **Taxable** interest income. Attach Schedule B if over $400 . . . | 8a |
b **Tax-exempt** interest income (see page 15). DON'T include on line 8a | 8b | |
9 Dividend income. Attach Schedule B if over $400 . . . . . . | 9 |
10 Taxable refunds, credits, or offsets of state and local income taxes from worksheet on page 16 | 10 |
11 Alimony received . . . . | 11 |
12 Business income or (loss). Attach Schedule C or C-EZ . . . . | 12 |
13 Capital gain or (loss). Attach Schedule D . . . . | 13 |
14 Capital gain distributions not reported on line 13 (see page 15) . . | 14 |
15 Other gains or (losses). Attach Form 4797 . . . . | 15 |
16a Total IRA distributions . | 16a | | b Taxable amount (see page 16) | 16b |
17a Total pensions and annuities | 17a | | b Taxable amount (see page 16) | 17b |
18 Rents, royalties, partnerships, estates, trusts, etc. Attach Schedule E . . | 18 |
19 Farm income or (loss). Attach Schedule F . . . . | 19 |
20 Unemployment compensation (see page 17) . . . . | 20 |
21a Social security benefits | 21a | | b Taxable amount (see page 17) | 21b |
22 Other income. List type and amount—see page 18 . . . . | 22 |
23 Add the amounts in the far right column for lines 7 through 22. This is your **total income** ▶ | 23 |

Adjustments to Income
(See page 18.)

24a Your IRA deduction from applicable worksheet on page 19 or 20 | 24a |
b Spouse's IRA deduction from applicable worksheet on page 19 or 20 | 24b |
25 One-half of self-employment tax (see page 20) . . . | 25 |
26 Self-employed health insurance deduction (see page 20) | 26 |
27 Keogh retirement plan and self-employed SEP deduction | 27 |
28 Penalty on early withdrawal of savings . . . . . | 28 |
29 Alimony paid. Recipient's SSN ▶ | 29 |
30 Add lines 24a through 29. These are your **total adjustments** . . . . ▶ | 30 |

Adjusted Gross Income

31 Subtract line 30 from line 23. This is your **adjusted gross income.** If this amount is less than $22,370 and a child lived with you, see page EIC-1 to find out if you can claim the "Earned Income Credit" on line 56 . . . . . ▶ | 31 |

Cat. No. 11320B   Form **1040**

California has both state and federal income taxes. See Figure 13-10. That's right! California residents pay both income taxes, which ranks us among the most taxed people in the United States. It is no wonder that Californians are very interested in understanding the effects of income taxes on both their personal residence and income producing property.

Tax matters should be considered prior to buying and continued during ownership until the estate's ultimate disposition.

We will discuss only the most basic concepts of reducing the income tax bite for the average citizen. A basic knowledge of the requirements necessary to take advantage of federal and state income tax incentives is helpful. Arranging the purchase of real estate in a manner that reduces your personal income taxes is the purpose of tax planning. This may allow you to reduce the income taxes you pay, or at least postpone such taxes.

> *Tax shelters are the reduction in income taxes. Now is the time to start tax planning for your future income tax returns.*

FIGURE 13-10

CALIFORNIA vs. FEDERAL INCOME TAX:
Emphasis is on the Federal

California state income tax laws tend to conform with federal laws in most respects. There are, however, several important income tax exceptions listed below:

1. State does not tax Social Security benefits
2. State does not allow tax breaks for IRA plans (simple)
3. State does not tax lottery winnings

The state taxes at a lower rate (a maximum of 9.3 percent) but tends to be more restrictive on deductions. State taxes paid are themselves deductible from the federal return.

Most state and local tax laws are considered by many insiders to be antiquated. Tax reform on these levels has become a much slower process than that by the federal government. Focus is on the federal government which taxes at higher rates and sets the tone for state and local taxes. For more detailed information on preparing personal income taxes, a tax attorney or CPA should certainly be consulted.

Figure 13-11 shows the five main areas of the federal and state income tax laws that are incentives to owning real estate. Each area will be explained only to give the general concepts or ideas behind the laws. To obtain the exact meaning and clauses of the law, an owner or investor should seek the help of a Certified Public Accountant for advice on the accounting, or an attorney who is familiar with tax problems. Remember, these are only generalizations and our income tax laws are more complex than the basic concepts presented here.

FIGURE 13-11

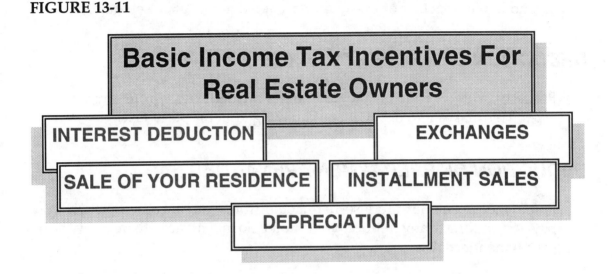

TAXES ON PERSONAL RESIDENCE

Homeowners can annually deduct these three items from their income taxes based on their personal residence:

1) Mortgage Interest on Loan (Trust Deeds)
2) Property Taxes
3) Prepayment Penalties

By the way, you cannot deduct the cost of personal residence repairs from your federal taxes, except for uninsured casual losses. For example, if your roof blows off and you have no insurance to cover it, the replacement cost can be deducted from your federal income taxes.

DEDUCTION OF INTEREST

Deduction of interest on your home loan from your income taxes is one of the major tax advantages of owning real estate. Buying a first and second home provides the average family with the biggest buffer against income taxes that it is likely to enjoy.

Despite recent income tax reforms, the federal tax laws still provide incentives to those who purchase a first and even a second home. When buying these homes you may finance up to $1 million ($1,000,000) with all the interest paid out during the year fully tax deductible. An additional deduction is available on the interest from home equity loans, taken for any purpose, even buying a second home, of up to $100,000 in principal. The $1,000,000 and $100,000 debit limit is a total applied against both first and second homes together or one owner-occupied home taken separately.

DEDUCTION OF PROPERTY TAXES

Property taxes on your 1st and 2nd homes are deductible from your income taxes. This makes us feel better about paying local property taxes.

DEDUCTION OF PREPAYMENT PENALTIES

Prepayment penalties are also deductible from your income taxes. If you pay off or drastically reduce your home loan balance, there may be a prepayment penalty.

Interest, property taxes and prepayment penalties paid on your personal residence can be deducted from your income taxes.

SALE OF YOUR RESIDENCE

When selling a personal residence, the seller can deduct up to $250,000 ($500,000 if married) of any financial gain (profit) for each spouse. This could be used only once every two years.

Federal income tax laws allow a taxpayer to exclude up to $250,000 of gain for each individual ($500,000 if married and on the title). This benefit may only be used once every two years for a residence.

If a married couple's home increases in value (approximately $500,000); all they have to do is simply sell and buy another residence to avoid any income tax liability.

This is a good way for you, as a homeowner, to eliminate income taxes, as long as you keep buying and selling a new residence, making sure not to make more than $250,000 each time if you are single ($500,000 if married and owned together).

You can deduct a loss on sale of a personal residence if you have turned it into income producing property by renting it.

The only way to deduct a loss on a personal residence is to turn that property into income producing property first by renting it. Then any loss based on its sale is deductible because it is income producing property, not a personal residence.

TAXES FOR INCOME PRODUCING PROPERTIES

Investors of income producing properties can annually deduct these items from their income taxes:

1) Mortgage Interest on Loans (no maximum)
2) Property Taxes
3) Prepayment Penalties

In addition they can deduct:

4) Operating Expenses
5) Depreciation of Improvements

In addition to deducting mortgage interest (no maximum), property taxes and prepayment penalties, income property owners can deduct operating expenses and depreciation. Owners cannot deduct losses due to vacancies.

DEPRECIATION OF (BUSINESS) PROPERTY (FEDERAL & STATE)

DEPRECIATION FOR TAX PURPOSES is a yearly tax deduction for wear, tear and obsolescence on investment property that is deducted from the taxpayer's income on his or her income tax form. This deduction applies only to investment property or property used in a business, **not on a taxpayer's personal residence.** Apartment buildings, commercial buildings and any building improvements to investment property can be depreciated. The land itself cannot be depreciated.

> *Only the buildings and other improvements can be depreciated, not the land.*

One can only depreciate property that is improved. Since land cannot be depreciated, only the improvements can be depreciated. Currently, the straight-line method is the accepted way to depreciate buildings and other improvements.

> *Residential (homes & apartments) property depreciation schedule:*
>
> *Minimum 27 $^{1/2}$ years (Straight-line).*
>
> *Commercial improvements depreciation schedule:*
>
> *Minimum 39 years (Straight-line).*

The amount of depreciation must be spread uniformly over the useful life of the property, with the same amount deducted each year (straight-line depreciation). Since most buildings in these inflationary times actually increase in value, depreciation is usually just a technique for postponing income taxes until the property is sold.

> Example: If you own a cabin in the desert that you rent to vacationers and the cabin cost $100,000 and the land value is $17,500, this leaves improvements of $82,500. Divide this $82,500 by 27 1/2 years giving you a depreciation of $3,000 for each year of the 27 1/2 years. If we had used a 27 1/2 year formula, the yearly depreciation amount would be slightly higher.

Remember: A property owner can deduct depreciation on income, trade or business real property, not on a residence.

ADVANTAGES OF "SALE - LEASEBACK"
(BUYER GETS TO DEPRECIATE NEW BUILDING COST)

If the owner of a business sells her building for cash, and then leases it back, the seller has become a lessee and the buyer the lessor.

The advantage to the seller: all lease payments can be deducted from income taxes and she has received cash for her building.

The advantage to the buyer: he can use the purchase price as the new basis for depreciation and establishes a new depreciation schedule.

Seller, now renter, deducts 100% of future rents paid. Buyer can depreciate new cost of buildings (even if they have been depreciated previously).

SALE OF REAL PROPERTY

CAPITAL ASSETS (GAINS AND LOSSES)

In real estate a capital asset includes your personal residence (including your second home) and any other real estate because they are long-term investments. When you sell your home or other real estate there is either a capital gain or loss. A *CAPITAL GAIN is taxed at a lower rate than is ordinary income.* It is in the public interest to foster investment in land and buildings and other long-term assets so that businesses are encourage to expand. This in turn creates more job opportunities for everyone.

Congress and the president, the same group that promised tax simplification, has established four capital gains tax rates as follows:

20% maximum capital gains tax rate if held for more than 18 months
15% maximum capital gains tax rate if held for more than 7 years
10% capital gains tax rate if net income is less than $50,000
5% capital gains tax rate (over 7 years) if net income is less than $50,000

Gains are taxed at the lower capital gains tax rates (lower than ordinary income tax rates).

There should be a tax benefit to encourage entrepreneurs to risk investing long-term in things such as equipment, stocks, bonds and real estate in order to obtain capital gains or losses. Other countries, like Japan and Germany, have very low capital gain tax rates which encourage investment in companies so that more career opportunities are generated for their employees. The size of the nation's "economic pie," which everyone enjoys, increases.

FEDERAL INCOME TAX RATES

As the old saying goes, "There is nothing surer than death and taxes." One other certainty is the constant change in federal tax rates. Income tax rates are progressive. *PROGRESSIVE TAXES are taxes where the rates (percentage paid) increase as the amount to be taxed increases.* So as you make more money, not only does the amount increase, but the rate at which income is taxed also increases. The end effect is that higher income families (the exact ones who usually own businesses and can expand job opportunities) pay most of the income taxes.

MARGINAL TAX RATE is the rate that the next dollar earned puts you into.

REGRESSIVE TAXES use the same rate no matter how much is spent or earned. Sale tax is an example of a regressive tax. The rate is the same, so in effect the poor pay a higher percent of their income.

Income tax rates are progressive. Sale taxes are regressive.

ACCOUNTING FOR THE SALE OF REAL ESTATE

The method of determining a profit or loss on the sale of real property is spelled out by the Internal Revenue Service. Steps 1 and 2 must be completed before determining the profit or loss on a sale (Step 3).

(1) Cost Basis (Purchase price)	$500,000
+ Improvements	200,000
	$700,000
- Depreciation (tax records)	30,200
= Adjusted Cost Basis	$669,800
(2) Sale price	$1,000,000
- Sale Expenses	32,500
= Adjusted Sale Price	$967,500
(3) Adjusted Sale Price	$967,500
- Adjusted Cost Basis	669,800
= Gain	$297,700

"Adjusted cost basis" is the base cost, plus capital improvements, minus depreciation and sale expenses. A broker's commission is an expense of the sale.

INSTALLMENT SALES & EXCHANGES

INSTALLMENT SALES OF REAL ESTATE

An **INSTALLMENT SALE** *is the sale of real estate where the payments for the property extend over more than one calendar year.* Installment sales are used to spread a gain over two or more calendar years so that the entire gain is not taxed all in the first year. Our income tax system has progressive rates, which means that the higher the income the higher the income tax rate for that year. If a person can spread a gain over more than one calendar year, the same income may be taxed at a lower rate.

By doing this the seller avoids the disadvantages of paying for his or her entire gain in one year, and thereby has a substantial savings on his or her income taxes. This method is usually used when selling large tracts of land held for a period of time, or large buildings owned by one individual.

Installment sales are used because a gain is only taxed in the year that it is received. Spreading the gain over several years may drop you into a lower tax bracket (marginal tax rate).

A sale of a large lot for $100,000 all at once might force you into a higher tax rate. So by having an installment sale of $25,000 for each of the next four years, you may substantially reduce the total income taxes paid. An installment sale may be a good way to defer income taxes if your income varies from year-to-year: Just arrange to get larger installment payments in years when your ordinary income is low.

EXCHANGES TAX-DEFERRED (FEDERAL & STATE) (SECTION 1031 OF I.R.S. CODE)

In an exchange, the adjusted cost basis of the old property becomes the basis of the new property.

Chapter 13

An **EXCHANGE** *is a transfer of real estate where one party trades property for another's property.* The property must be of "like kind" in nature or character, not in use, quality or grade. The exchange may be a straight trade (tax-free) or one party may receive cash in addition to the property (partially tax-free). An exchange can be income tax free, partially taxed, or fully taxed, depending on the cost factors in each particular exchange. Exchanges are too detailed to explain here, but it is a way of deferring or possibly eliminating income taxes on the transfer of real estate.

Any net cash or net mortgage relief that a participant in an exchange might receive in addition to the actual property is known as **BOOT.** All boot is taxable to the extent of the gain in this partially tax-free exchange. See Figure 13-12.

Boot is cash or debt relief. Receiver has recognized gain. If there is no boot in an exchange, the old basis is the new basis.

FIGURE 13-12

Tax Deferred Exchanges

Boot is defined as cash or mortgage relief.

In a tax-free exchange, boot is defined as cash or mortgage relief given in addition to the property. Boot is the amount received to balance the equities in the exchange. Brokers often encounter the term "boot" when talking with a client about income taxes.

The person receiving boot has a net gain and has to pay taxes on it. When no boot is given or received, then the basis remains the same.

In a tax free exchange, properties must be of a "like kind" in nature or character, not in use, quality or grade. "Tax free" merely means to DEFER the payment of taxes until a later time. Since you can move your equity to another property, it is almost like buying and selling without paying income taxes.

The actual techniques used to understand exchanging are too complex to be explained here, but many six-hour seminars and exchange clubs are available to interested people.

Exchanges are popular among apartment owners and commercial property investors. This is because these owners are usually in high income tax brackets and exchanging enables them to move up to a more valuable property, without paying taxes on the gain. People in higher income tax brackets usually keep their money invested in real estate, and they find exchanges to be a way of selling and buying simultaneously.

WE ARE NOW TAX COLLECTORS
(Federal & State Income Tax Laws—Escrow Usually Takes Care of This)

FEDERAL TAX COLLECTION REQUIREMENTS AND EXEMPTIONS (IF A FOREIGNER)

Persons buying property from foreign investors (sellers) are required to set aside 10% of the purchase price for the Internal Revenue Service. This 10% withholding is kept by the IRS to insure that property capital gains taxes are paid on the transaction. Both the buyer and broker share liability. If this amount is not withheld, the broker may be liable for the full amount of the tax not paid.

In effect, this law holds brokers responsible to check the citizenship of all sellers and see to it that the buyer retains either a 10% deposit, an affidavit from the seller stating that he or she is not a foreigner or a waiver from the IRS. Residential property purchased for under $300,000 to be used as the buyer's residence is exempted from this withholding.

The key points for licensees to remember are these:

1. **Inquire** into the citizenship of all sellers of residential or commercial properties priced at $300,000 or more, even if a foreigner holds only partial or syndicate interest.

2. **Require** a statement of citizenship as part of the listing agreement and then follow up in escrow by having the seller or sellers sign a sworn affidavit.

3. **Do not discriminate.** Require this information of all sellers in transactions of $300,000 or more. Even if someone does not appear to be an alien, they might hold foreign citizenship.

FIGURE 13-13

CALIFORNIA
ASSOCIATION
OF REALTORS®

SELLER'S AFFIDAVIT OF NONFOREIGN STATUS
AND/OR CALIFORNIA RESIDENCY

FOREIGN INVESTMENT IN REAL PROPERTY TAX ACT (FIRPTA)
AND CALIFORNIA NONRESIDENT WITHHOLDING LAW

Section 1445 of the Internal Revenue Code provides that a transferee of a U.S. real property interest must withhold tax if the transferor is a "foreign person." Section 18662 of the California Revenue and Taxation Code provides that a transferee of a California real property interest must withhold tax if the transferor's proceeds will be disbursed to a financial intermediary of the transferor or to the transferor with a last known street address outside of California. Section 18662 of the California Revenue and Taxation Code includes additional provisions for corporation.

I understand that this affidavit may be disclosed to the Internal Revenue Service and to the California Franchise Tax Board by the transferee and that any false statement I have made herein (if an entity Transferor, on behalf of the Transferor) could be punished by fine, imprisonment, or both.

1. **PROPERTY ADDRESS** (the address of property being transferred): _____

_____

2. **TRANSFEROR'S INFORMATION:**
   A. **NAME/ADDRESS:** The full name and address of all owners (transferors) whose interests are being transferred are required. Use HOME address for individual transferors. Use OFFICE address for corporations, partnerships, limited liability companies, trusts, and estates (entities).
   B. **TRANSFER No. 1:** Full Name: _____ Telephone No.: _____
      Address: _____
      Social Security No., federal Employer Identification No., or California Corporation No.: _____
      TRANSFER No. 2: Full Name: _____ Telephone No.: _____
      Address: _____
      Social Security No., federal Employer Identification No., or California Corporation No.: _____
3. **AUTHORITY TO SIGN:** If this is signed on behalf of an entity Transferor, THE UNDERSIGNED INDIVIDUAL DECLARES THAT HE/SHE HAS AUTHORITY TO SIGN THIS DOCUMENT ON BEHALF OF THE TRANSFEROR.
4. **FEDERAL LAW:** I, the undersigned individual, declare under penalty of perjury that I am exempt (or if signed on behalf of an entity transferor, the entity is exempt) from the federal (FIRPTA) withholding law, and that:

   ○ □ (For individual Transferors) I am not a nonresident alien for purposes of U.S. income taxation.

   ○ □ (For corporation, partnership, limited liability company, trust, and estate Transferors) The Transferor is not a foreign corporation, foreign partnership, foreign limited liability company, foreign trust, or foreign estate, as those term are defined in the Internal Revenue Code and Income Tax Regulations.

Transferor No. 1 mark applicable circles (○) and sign here: _____ Date _____
_____ (Transferor's Signature)

Title _____ Typed or printed name: _____
_____ (If signed on behalf of entity Transferor)

Transferor No. 2 mark applicable boxes (□) and sign here: _____ Date _____
_____ (Transferor's Signature)

Title _____ Typed or printed name: _____
_____ (If signed on behalf of entity Transferor)

5. **CALIFORNIA LAW:** I, the undersigned individual, declare under penalty of perjury that I am exempt (or if signed on behalf of an entity transferor, the entity is exempt) from the California nonresident withholding law, and that:

   ○ □ (For individual Transferors) I am a resident of California. My home address is: _____
   _____ .

   ○ □ (For individual Transferors) The **PROPERTY ADDRESS** (property being transferred) was my principal residence within the meaning of Internal Revenue Code Section 1034.

   ○ □ (For corporation Transferors) The Transferor is a corporation qualified to do business in California, or has a permanent place of business in California at the address shown in "Transferor's Information," paragraph 2.

   ○ □ (For limited liability company (LLC)Transferors) The Transferor is an LLC and recorded title to the property being transferred is in the name of the LLC.

   ○ □ (For trust Transferors) The Transferor is an irrevocable trust in which at least one trustee is a California resident, or is a revocable/grantor trust in which all grantors are California residents.

   ○ □ (For estate Transferors) The Transferor is an estate of a decedent who was a California resident at the time of his/her death.

   ○ □ (For tax exempt entity and nonprofit organization Transferors) The Transferor is exempt from tax under California or federal law.

TRANSFER No. 1 mark applicable circles (○) and sign here: _____ Date _____
_____ (Transferor's Signature)

Title _____ Typed or printed name: _____
_____ (If signed on behalf of entity Transferor)

TRANSFER No. 2 mark applicable boxes (□) and sign here: _____ Date _____
_____ (Transferor's Signature)

Title _____ Typed or printed name: _____
_____ (If signed on behalf of entity Transferor)

OFFICE USE ONLY
Reviewed by Broker
or Designee _____
Date _____

EQUAL HOUSING
OPPORTUNITY

FORM AS-14 REVISED 7/95

The CAR® Seller's Affidavit of Nonforeign Status and/or California Residency form is a form for the seller to sign (Figure 13-13) swearing that he or she is not a nonresident alien. If the seller completes the lower portion of this sworn statement, the buyer and broker may no longer be liable for any portions of unpaid taxes.

Figure 13-14 shows a Buyer's Affidavit form available from CAR. This form states that the sales price is less than $300,000 and that the property will be used as a residence. It is signed by the buyer under penalty of perjury. If these two considerations can be met, the buyer is immediately exempted from the withholding requirement. If neither of these forms can truthfully be completed, then the broker should see to it that 10% of the sales price is withheld in escrow or that the proper waiver is obtained from the IRS. The escrow officer will help you with this matter.

STATE TAX COLLECTION REQUIREMENTS & EXEMPTIONS (IF A FOREIGNER OR RESIDENT OF ANOTHER STATE)

Persons buying property from foreign or out-of-state investors may be required to set aside 3 1/2% of the sales price for the Franchise Tax Board. If this amount is not withheld, the broker and buyer may be liable for the full amount of income taxes not paid. Escrow usually handles this, but the buyer and broker are responsible.

The exemptions from the buyer withholding 3 1/2% of the sales price for the Franchise Tax Board are:

1. Sales price is $100,000 or less.
2. Property is seller's principle residence, under certain conditions.
3. Seller signs California Residency Declaration.
4. Seller receives a waiver - Franchise Tax Board Form 567A.

Both of these laws put the burden on the buyer, not the seller. Escrow officers will help with these requirements. Buyer and broker must retain the documentation for 5 years.

FIGURE 13-14

CALIFORNIA
ASSOCIATION
OF REALTORS®

BUYER'S AFFIDAVIT
That Buyer is acquiring property for use as a residence
and that sales price does not exceed $300,000.
(FOREIGN INVESTMENT IN REAL PROPERTY TAX ACT)

1. I am the transferee (buyer) of real property located at _____
_____.

2. The sales price (total of all consideration in the sale) does not exceed $300,000.

3. I am acquiring the real property for use as a residence. I have definite plans that I or a member of my family will reside in it for at least 50 percent of the number of days it will be in use during each of the first two 12 month periods following the transfer of the property to me. I understand that the members of my family that are included in the last sentence are my brothers, sisters, ancestors, descendents, or spouse.

4. I am making this affidavit in order to establish an exemption from withholding a portion of the sales price of the property under Internal Revenue Code §1445.

5. I understand that if the information in this affidavit is not correct, I may be liable to the Internal Revenue Service for up to 10 percent of the sales price of the property, plus interest and penalties.

   Under penalties of perjury, I declare that the statements above are true, correct and complete.

Date _____   Signature _____

                                    Typed or Printed Name _____

Date _____   Signature _____

                                    Typed or Printed Name _____

IMPORTANT NOTICE: An affidavit should be signed by each individual transferee to whom it applies. Before you sign, any questions relating to the legal sufficiency of this form, or to whether it applies to a particular transaction, or to the definition of any of the terms used, should be referred to an attorney, certified public accountant, other professional tax advisor, or the Internal Revenue Service.

Published and Distributed by:
REAL ESTATE BUSINESS SERVICES, INC.
a subsidiary of the CALIFORNIA ASSOCIATION OF REALTORS®
525 South Virgil Avenue, Los Angeles, California 90020

Page _____ of _____ Pages.

OFFICE USE ONLY
Reviewed by Broker
or Designee _____
Date _____

EQUAL HOUSING OPPORTUNITY

BUYER'S AFFIDAVIT (AB-11 PAGE 1 OF 1) REVISED 2/91

OTHER TAXES PAID BY BROKERS

BUSINESS LICENSE TAXES (CITY INCOME TAX)

A city may levy a tax against real estate brokerage firms, which is based upon the gross receipts, through a BUSINESS LICENSE TAX. In most areas of California, this annual city business license tax is a nominal amount, which usually starts at about $100. Other city taxes may also include employee payroll taxes.

A city tax on a real estate brokerage firm's gross receipts is called a business license tax.

A. Real Property Taxes
B. Ad Valorem
C. County Assessor
D. County Tax Collector
E. Proposition 13
F. Assessed Valuation
G. Homeowners Property Tax Exemption
H. Renters Credit
I. Special Assessment Tax
J. Donor
K. Donee

L. Documentary Transfer Tax
M. Federal Estate Tax
N. Federal Gift Tax
O. Federal and State Income Taxes
P. Depreciation for Tax Purposes
Q. Installment Sale
R. Exchange
S. Boot
T. Two Years
U. $125,000

1.____ Value placed upon property, for property tax purposes, by the tax assessor.

2.____ The sale of property in installments that spreads tax on profit from a sale of property over a number of years.

3.____ A tax charged according to the value of the property.

4.____ One who gives a gift.

5.____ Federal taxes paid on the giving of gifts.

6.____ One who receives a gift.

7.____ In a tax-deferred exchange, any cash or other property included in the transaction to make the exchange an even proposition.

8.____ The trading of parcels of real property to obtain tax benefits that might not be available in a normal sale. Generally considered tax-deferred, not tax-exempt.

9.____ An annual tax that applies to real estate; based on the assessed valuation of the property.

10.____ The person, in a given political division within a state, who is responsible for collecting property taxes.

11.____ One who estimates the value of property for property tax purposes.

12.____ A renter's deduction allowed from state income taxes payable, under certain circumstances.

13.____ A loss in value of improvements as an accounting procedure; used as a deduction on income taxes.

14.____ A lien assessed against real property, in a given district, by a public authority to pay costs of special public improvements.

15.____ A tax on the sale of real property, usually based on the sales price and paid on or before the recordation of the deed.

16.____ A tax against the property of a deceased, based on the value of the estate.

17.____ Limits the amount of taxes to a maximum of 1% of the March 1, 1975, market value of the property plus the cumulative increase of 2% in market value each year thereafter.

18.____ Personal taxes paid annually on your taxable income.

19.____ A deduction of up to $7,000 from an owner-resident's assessed valuation on his or her property tax bill. Must be filed between March 1st and April 15th, each year, to receive the full deduction.

20.____ The length of time (before or after) that a person is allowed to purchase an equally or more expensive property without having to pay income taxes.

21.____ The amount, if 55 or older, that is exempt from taxation (once in a lifetime).

MULTIPLE CHOICE

1. The second installment on property taxes would be considered delinquent on:

   A. July 11th
   C. December 11th

   B. April 11th
   D. March 11th

2. The first installment on property taxes becomes due on:

   A. June 30th
   C. March 1st

   B. April 15th
   D. November 1st

3. Of the following, which one would best describe income taxes?

   A. Regressive
   C. Marginal

   B. Progressive
   D. Repressive

4. A tax that is charged in proportion to the value of the property is referred to as a (an):

   A. ad valorem tax
   C. progressive tax

   B. progression tax
   D. excise tax

5. Proposition 13 set property taxes at what percent of the selling price or fair market value (whichever is higher)?

   A. 1%
   C. 5%

   B. 2%
   D. 10%

6. A person can buy a new house of equal or greater value and NOT pay income taxes on the sale of the old house provided they purchased the new house within:

   A. one year before or after the sale
   C. five years before or after the sale

   B. two years before or after the sale
   D. ten years before or after the sale

7. On what date does the county or city fiscal year begin?

   A. January 1st
   C. July 1st

   B. December 10th
   D. April 10th

8. The documentary transfer tax is how much per $500 of new loans and considerations?

   A. 6%
   C. $.55

   B. $1.10
   D. none of the above

9. Which of the following taxes is for specific improvements?

   A. Special assessments
   C. Inheritance taxes

   B. Property taxes
   D. Estate taxes

10. The person who gives a gift is called a:

    A. trustor
    C. donor

    B. donee
    D. none of the above

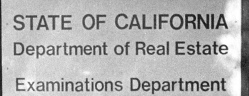

STATE OF CALIFORNIA
Department of Real Estate

Examinations Department

→

Information

CHAPTER 14
Licensing, Education and Associations

 http://www.dre.cahwnet.gov (Department of Real Estate)

A person working for compensation (agent) must have a real estate license from the DRE.

DEPARTMENT OF REAL ESTATE (DRE)

In California all real estate agreements are under the jurisdiction of the **CALIFORNIA DEPARTMENT OF REAL ESTATE,** *which is the regulatory agency for real estate in California.* The main purpose of this department is to protect the public by enactment and enforcement of laws relating to real estate and by establishing requirements for real estate salespersons' or brokers' licenses.

The California Department of Real Estate is responsible for the enforcement of real estate laws. These laws help protect both the individual citizen and the real estate profession. There are obvious benefits derived by shielding citizens from dishonest or incompetent real estate licensees. The reputation of the real estate profession is upheld by making sure that all practicing salespeople and brokers are both honest and capable of performing their jobs properly.

The Real Estate Commissioner, deputies and clerks (as employees of the Department of Real Estate) are not allowed to have an interest in any real estate company or brokerage firm.

The California Department of Real Estate is governed by the Real Estate Commissioner. The Commissioner, who sets all the rules and regulations for the Department of Real Estate, receives his or her power from the state legislature. The legislature, in turn, used police power to create the position of Commissioner. *POLICE POWER is the right to enact and enforce laws beneficial to the health, safety, morals and general welfare of the public.*

REAL ESTATE COMMISSIONER (APPOINTED BY THE GOVERNOR)

The governor appoints the Real Estate Commissioner, who is defended by the state Attorney General. The Real Estate Commissioner issues rules and regulations that have the force and effect of law.

http://www.ca.gov (Governor of California)

In addition to his or her position as chairperson of the State Real Estate Advisory Commission, the *REAL ESTATE COMMISSIONER is the chief executive of the Department of Real Estate.* It is the Commissioner's duty, therefore, to mold the department's policy and to enforce Real Estate Law (found in the Business and Professions Code) so that both real estate purchasers and real estate licensed agents benefit from his or her rulings. The Commissioner's other duties include:

1. Decide the business policy of the State Department of Real Estate.

2. Inform the Governor and other state officials as to what services the department can render to the state and provide them with descriptions of the department's licenses.

3. Recommend changes in policy that may have been deemed necessary for the good of the public and the business of real estate in California.

4. Regulation of the sales of subdivisions.

5. Decide if applicants for real estate licenses have met all the experience and education requirements.

6. The investigation of complaints against allegedly incompetent license holders.

7. The investigation of complaints against those performing acts without the required license.

The Commissioner cannot settle commission disputes. It must be remembered that the Commissioner does not take the place of a court of law and does not give legal advice.

The Real Estate Commissioner has the power to call formal hearings to discuss any issue concerning an applicant for a license, a current license holder or a subdivider. The commissioner may subsequently suspend, revoke or deny a license. He or she could also halt sales (desist and refrain order) in a subdivision. Remember: The Commissioner cannot take the place of a court of law.

A licensee can be disciplined by the Real Estate Commissioner, but the local District Attorney prosecutes for the Real Estate Commissioner.

REAL ESTATE ADVISORY COMMISSION

The *REAL ESTATE ADVISORY COMMISSION recommends and makes suggestions to the Commissioner.* The Advisory Commission has ten members, all appointed by the Commissioner and serving at his or her pleasure. Six members must be licensed California real estate brokers and four must be chosen from the general public; they are not paid a salary, but their actual and necessary expenses are reimbursed. They meet with and advise the Commissioner on matters relating to the Department of Real Estate's function and to the real estate profession in the state.

The Commissioner is required to call Advisory Committee meetings at least four times a year, and the proceedings of all meetings must be made public. At such meetings, the views and suggestions of the public and of the licensees of the Department are heard.

REAL ESTATE LICENSE REQUIREMENTS

As mentioned in the preceding section, the Real Estate Commissioner's main purpose is the regulation of the real estate business in the state of California. This regulation is accomplished by imposing mandatory licenses on those individuals who choose to work in the field of real estate. Who is required to have these licenses? In short, any person who is actively involved in a real estate transaction at the service of another, in the expectation of receiving a commission, must be licensed.

WHO MUST HAVE A LICENSE

A person is required to have a license if he or she:

1. Sells or offers to sell, buys or offers to buy and solicits buyers or sellers.

2. Solicits or obtains listings.

3. Negotiates the purchase, sale or exchange of real property or business opportunities.

4. Leases or rents, collects rents or negotiates the sale, purchase or exchange of leases.

5. Assists in the purchase of leases on lands owned by the state or federal government.

6. Negotiates loans, collects payments or performs services for borrowers or lenders.

Any person found to be involved in such actions without a license may be guilty of breaking the Real Estate Law, under which stiff penalties can be imposed.

WHEN A LICENSE IS NOT REQUIRED

It should be noted that there are a few exceptions to these regulations. The following people, because of the nature of their work, are exempt from the licensing regulations (NO LICENSE REQUIRED):

1. Employees of lending institutions

2. Lenders making federally insured or guaranteed loans

3. Certain agricultural associations

4. Licensed personal property brokers

5. Cemetery authorities

6. Collectors of loans made on real property

7. Certain clerical help

A person who is not a real estate salesperson or broker may solicit for the sale of real property (according to Section 10133 of the Real Estate Law) as long as he or she is:

1. the owner.

2. holding power of attorney for the owner.

3. an attorney at law acting on behalf of the owner.

4. a receiver or court appointee.

5. a trustee, selling under a deed of trust.

OBTAINING THE SALESPERSON'S LICENSE

The candidate for a real estate salesperson's license examination must:

1. be 18 years of age to apply for a license, although there is no age restriction for taking the exam,
2. be honest and truthful,
3. complete a college-level Real Estate Principles course and
4. pass the required examination.

For further information call or write any district office of the Department of Real Estate. Ask for the pamphlet, *Instructions to License Applicants* (Figure 14-1). At the same time, ask for the examination application and a license application.

The salesperson exam takes "three hours, fifteen minutes," has 150 questions and requires a 70% correct score to pass.

FIGURE 14-1

PRINCIPAL OFFICE

SACRAMENTO—2201 Broadway, Sacramento, CA 95818 (916) 227-0931

 http://www.dre.ca.gov (DRE)

DISTRICT OFFICES

SAN DIEGO—1350 Front Street, Suite 3064 San Diego, CA 92101-3687 (619) 525-4192

OAKLAND—1515 Clay St., Suite 702 Oakland, CA 94612-1402 (510) 622-2552

LOS ANGELES—320 W. 4th. St. Suite 350 Los Angeles, CA 90013-1105 (213) 620-2072

FRESNO—2550 Mariposa Mall, Room 3070 Fresno, CA 93721-2273 (559) 445-5009

CONDITIONAL SALESPERSON'S LICENSE
(THE 18-MONTH LICENSE)

To obtain a conditional salesperson's license (18-month), the applicant must 1) complete a college level Real Estate Principles course; 2) pass the DRE salesperson's exam; and 3) pay the necessary fees. A *CONDITIONAL SALESPERSON'S LICENSE is the license of a person who has only taken the Real Estate Principles course. This license expires 18 months after issuance unless the salesperson has submitted evidence to the DRE of the completion of two other college level (broker required) real estate courses.*

FOUR-YEAR SALESPERSON'S LICENSE
(REGULAR, RENEWABLE LICENSE)

To obtain a regular four-year salesperson's license, the applicant must:

1) complete a college level Real Estate Principles course and two other approved college level (broker required) courses;
2) pass the DRE salesperson's exam; and
3) pay the necessary fees.

With a conditional salesperson's license, the licensee must furnish, within 18 months, transcript evidence to the DRE that he or she has successfully completed two additional (broker required) three semester-unit (or equivalent quarter-unit) courses. See Figure 14-3 for details of DRE educational (broker required) course requirements.

If an applicant has already completed a college level Real Estate Principles course and at least two other (broker required) approved courses, he or she can apply for the regular four-year salesperson's license.

SALESPERSON'S EXAMINATION

To pass, an applicant must achieve a score of at least 70% in the three hour fifteen minute salesperson's exam, which has 150 multiple choice questions. Exams are usually scheduled during the morning or afternoon. A non-refundable fee of $60.00 is required to take the test. If you fail, you may take the exam as often as you wish, but you must pay $60.00 for each exam application. See Figures 14-2 and 14-3 for the salesperson's and broker's requirements.

The use of silent, battery-operated, pocket-sized **electronic calculators** that are non-programmable and do not have a printout capability is permitted.

FIGURE 14-2
EXAMINATION —SUBJECT AREAS

	SALESPERSON EXAM	BROKER EXAM
Property Ownership/Land Use Controls Class of Property, Land Characteristics, Encumbrances, Types of Ownership, Descriptions of Property, Government Rights in Land, Public and Private Control	15%	10%
Transfer of Property Title Insurance, Deeds, Escrow, Reports, Tax Aspects, Probate	10%	10%
Valuation/Market Analysis Value, Methods of Estimating Value/Appraisal Process, Competitive Market Analysis	10%	15%
Financing General Concepts, Types of Loans, Sources, Government Programs, Mortgages/Deeds of Trust, Finaincing/Credit	15%	15%
Laws of Agency/Mandated Disclosures Law, Definition & Nature of Agency, Relationships, Types of Agencies & Agents, Creation of Agency & Agency Agreements Responsibilities of Agent to Principal, Responsibilities to Buyer & Third Parties, Disclosure of Agency, Disclosure of Acting as Principal or Other Interest, Termination of Agency, Commissions and Fees	20%	20%
Contracts General, Listing Agreements, Advance Fee Agreements, Buyer/Broker Agreements, Officers/Purchase Agreements, Counteroffers/Multiple Counteroffers, Leases as Contracts, Options Rescission of Agreements, Broker/Salesperson Agreements	15%	15%
Real Estate Practice Trust Accounts, Fair Housing Laws, Advertising, Record Keeping Requirements, Agent Supervision Continuing Education Requirements, Disciplinary Actions, Unauthorized Law Practice, Specialty Areas	15%	15%

**Dept. of Real Estate
% of Exam Questions
Testing Emphasis**

FIGURE 14-3 SALESPERSON AND BROKER COURSES
(The statutory required college level courses)

The statutory required college level courses for people wishing to qualify for either the real estate salesperson or broker license examination.

APPLICANTS FOR THE SALESPERSON'S EXAM

1. To qualify to take an examination for a real estate **salesperson's** license, an applicant must have completed the **REAL ESTATE PRINCIPLES** college level course.

2. In order for the applicant to obtain the original four-year salesperson's license, he or she must also, either prior to the salesperson's exam, or within 18 months after issuance of the conditional salesperson's license, complete two additional basic real estate courses selected from among the following:

Real Estate Practice	Real Estate Economics
Real Estate Appraisal	Escrows
Accounting Business Law	Property Management
Legal Aspects of Real Estate	Real Estate
Real Estate Financing	Office Administration

3. **Salespersons** who qualify to take the examination by completing only the **Real Estate Principles** course shall have their licenses automatically suspended, effective 18 months after issuance of the conditional license, unless the two additional courses have been completed within that time.

APPLICANTS FOR THE BROKER'S EXAM

1. An applicant for the broker license examination must have completed eight courses in addition to the experience requirements. These eight courses must include the following five:

Real Estate Practice	Real Estate Economics
Real Estate Appraisal	(or Accounting)
Legal Aspects of Real Estate	Real Estate Finance

2. The remaining three courses are to be selected from the following:

R E Office Administration	Business Law
Advanced Legal Aspects of R E	Property Management
Advanced Real Estate Appraisal	Escrows
Advanced Real Estate Finance	Mortgage Loan Brokering and
Real Estate Principles	Lending

Thanks to Thomas L. Mabry, Real Estate Manager Il, Education, Research and Publications, California Department of Real Estate.

NOTIFICATION OF EXAMINATION RESULTS

You will be notified of your examination results by mail only, normally within five working days after the examination.

To pass the examination, you must correctly answer at least 70% of the questions. The examination is qualifying in nature; applicants who pass are not informed of their score. You will be notified of the actual score, and the percentage of questions answered correctly in each of the seven subject areas, only when unsuccessful. Those who pass will receive an application for a license. Those who do not receive a passing grade will automatically receive a reexamination form.

You may not apply for a reexamination until after notification of failure of a prior test. Another $60 application fee payment will be required.

There is no limitation to the number of reexaminations you may take during the two-year period following the date of the filing of the original application. If you wish to take additional examinations after the two-year period, you must complete a new application.

ELECTRONIC FINGERPRINT SCANS REQUIREMENTS (SALESPERSON AND BROKER)

> *Applicants for the salesperson's license must apply for a license within one year from the exam date.*

If you have taken Principles plus the two other courses and have passed the examination, you are qualified to apply for a four-year renewable license by submitting $65 for an active license and $32.00 for processing the live scan fingerprints. ($90 for the conditional 18-month license, if you have completed only the Principles but not the two other courses.)

> *Upon completion of the real estate license exam a copy of the Live Scan Service Request Form will be mailed to all applicants. A list of providers is listed on the DRE web site.*

BROKER'S LICENSE (RENEWABLE FOUR-YEAR LICENSE)

A BROKER'S LICENSE is required of any individual who wants to operate a real estate office. The candidate for a real estate broker's license examination must:

Chapter 14

1. Be 18 years of age to apply for a license, although there is no age restriction for taking the exam.

2. Have had previous experience (two years or college education).

3. Complete the required eight broker courses.

4. Be honest and truthful.

5. Pass the required examination.

BROKER'S QUALIFYING EXPERIENCE

A candidate must also be able to prove that he or she has experience in real estate before applying for a broker's license. Generally, two years of full-time work (104 forty-hour weeks) as a salesperson is required. This two-year requirement may be replaced by an equivalent amount of part-time salesperson work. Such experience must have been completed within the five years immediately preceding the date of application.

Sometimes the State Real Estate Commissioner will accept experience in fields other than real estate sales. These fields include contract work, lease, escrow, title insurance, bonds, mortgage company or experience in another area directly involved in real estate.

Besides direct experience in these fields, education may qualify as full or partial experience. For example, the commissioner has ruled that any individual with a four-year college degree is exempt from the two-year experience requirement. But, all candidates **must** complete the eight required real estate courses, regardless of their educational degree. A community college graduate with the required real estate courses needs only one year of experience.

All students are encouraged to submit an equivalency request with the Department of Real Estate. All decisions made by the commissioner are final.

> *B.S. or B.A. (four year degree) = 2 years of experience*
> *A.A. (two year degree) = 1 year of experience*

Most California colleges and universities offer courses and majors in real estate. See Figure 14-4.

 http://www.mtsac.edu/info_tech/learning_res/other.html (California Community Colleges)

The broker's 200-question exam takes five hours to complete. The applicant must answer 75% of the questions correctly to pass.

FIGURE 14-4

ADVANCED EDUCATION IN REAL ESTATE

As the study of real estate becomes more complex and more intertwined with other business disciplines, students of real estate find it rewarding to continue their studies beyond those levels required to enter the field as a salesperson or broker. Many real estate professionals, after obtaining their A.A. degrees from community colleges, have gone on to pursue bachelor's and master's degrees.

CALIFORNIA STATE UNIVERSITY SYSTEM

Bakersfield
Chico
Dominguez Hills
Fresno
Fullerton
Hayward
Humboldt
Long Beach
Los Angeles
Northridge

Pomona*
Sacramento*
San Bernardino
San Diego*
San Francisco
San Jose
San Luis Obispo
San Marcos
Sonoma
Stanislaus

regional centers for RELUI
Real Estate and Land Use Institute
Cal State University, Sacramento
Sacramento, CA 95819

UNIVERSITY OF CALIFORNIA SYSTEM

Berkeley**
Davis
Irvine
Los Angeles***
Monterey

Riverside
San Diego
San Francisco
Santa Barbara
Santa Cruz

The U.C. Berkeley Center for Real Estate and Urban Economics publishes a newsletter, **Quarterly Report, which may be obtained by instructors and school libraries by writing (on college stationery) to Kenneth T. Rosen, Center for Real Estate and Urban Economics, 156 Barrows Hall, University of California, Berkeley, CA 94720.*

***The U.C.L.A. Housing, Real Estate and Urban Land Studies Program publishes its quarterly newsletter, **Real Estate Indicators**, which is available to instructors and college libraries. Apply on school stationary to Frank Mittelbach, Housing, Real Estate and Urban Land Studies Program, Graduate School of Management, University of California, Los Angeles, CA 90024.*

EXTENSION COURSES

The UC and Cal State University campuses also offer extension programs for persons interested in a more in-depth study of certain areas of real estate without the constraints of a degree program. Classes are generally offered in the evening or on weekends.

BROKER'S REQUIRED EDUCATION (EIGHT COURSES)

Applicants for the real estate broker's license examination must have successfully completed the eight statutory-required college-level courses. The required salesperson's courses can be found on the list of required broker's courses, only the number of required courses is different; three for the regular salesperson's license and eight for the broker's license. An applicant's choice of eight (broker required) courses must be taken by all broker candidates. Refer back to Figure 14-3.

Once all of these requirements have been completed, a candidate may apply to take the broker's examination. By filing the $95.00 examination fee, plus proof of 2 year's experience or the equivalent thereof, and transcripts showing that the eight statutory classes have been completed, the applicant will receive his or her admission card for the test. The cost of a broker's license is $110.

RENEWAL OF LICENSE - EVERY 4 YEARS (SALESPERSON AND BROKER)

Broker's and salesperson's licenses can be renewed; a conditional (18-month) salesperson's license cannot.

Once the license has expired, no licensed activity can be performed by the salesperson until the license has been renewed. The late renewal period (often referred to as the "grace" period) simply allows the licensee to renew on a late basis without retaking the examination; it does not allow the licensee to conduct licensed activity during the late renewal period. The license renewal fee for a salesperson is $65 if filed on time, and $97 if filed late. A broker's renewal costs $110 if on time and $165 if late. Fees may be changed annually.

Whenever a real estate salesperson enters the employ of a real estate broker, or whenever the salesperson is terminated, the broker shall immediately notify the Department of Real Estate in writing.

CONTINUING EDUCATION REQUIREMENT (45 HOURS EVERY 4 YEARS TO RENEW YOUR LICENSE)

The continuing education requirement (45 hours every 4 years for license renewal) is NOT the same as the required broker courses.

All real estate licensees are required to attend **45 clock hours** of Commissioner approved courses, seminars or conferences during the four-year period preceding license renewal. Three of these hours must be in an Ethics course and three hours must be in Agency. On a salesperson's license first renewal, only the Ethics and Agency courses are required. Thereafter, however, the 45-clock-hour requirement continues indefinitely with every renewal. Figure 14-5 shows distribution of continuing education courses.

FIGURE 14-5

45 HOURS OF REQUIRED CONTINUING EDUCATION

A three-hour continuing education course in Agency and a three-hour continuing education course in Ethics and Professional Conduct is a necessary part of the 45 hours. The required 45 hours of continuing education include:

3 hours of Ethics and Professional Conduct
3 hours of Agency
3 hours of Trust Fund Accounting & Handling
3 hours of Fair Housing
33 hours of Consumer Protection (18 minimum; up to 33 hours)

45 TOTAL HOURS (Required)

After 2000, A "Six-Hour C E Survey" Course Is Available

The *Six-Hour CE Survey* course can replace the 12-hour combination of four separate 3-hour courses in (Ethics, Agency, Trust Fund Handling and Fair Housing), starting with your second license renewal. So if a licensee takes the *Six-Hour CE Survey* course, he or she still needs an additional 39 hours of CE to complete the 45 total hours required every four years at license renewal time.

Mineral, Oil, And Gas Broker License (MOG) (Has Been Phased Out)

EDITOR'S UPDATE: The DRE no longer issues MOG licenses.

Prepaid Rental Listing Service License

A *PREPAID RENTAL LISTING SERVICE (PRLS) license is required when running a business that supplies prospective tenants with listings of residential real property for rent or lease while collecting a fee for such service.* Negotiation of the rental of property is not a part of this activity. An individual may obtain, without examination, a two-year license to conduct PRLS activities.

Prior to issuance of the PRLS license, the applicant must submit, and have approved by the DRE, a contract to be entered into between the licensee and client (prospective tenant). Fingerprints and a $2,500 surety bond are required for each business location.

Real Property Securities Dealer Endorsement

A *REAL PROPERTY SECURITIES DEALER (RPSD) is any person acting as a principal or agent who engages in the business of selling real property securities (such as promissory notes or sales contracts).* RPSD's also accept, or offer to accept, funds for reinvestment in real property securities or for placement in an account. Before a licensed real estate broker may act in the capacity of a RPSD, he or she must obtain a permit from the Department of Corporations. (For information on Real Property Securities, contact the Department of Corporations.)

http://www.corp.ca.gov (Department of Corporations)

BUSINESS OPPORTUNITY BROKERAGE

http://www.census.gov (U.S. Census Bureau)
http://www.sbaonline.sba.gov (Small Business Administration)

In a sale of a business (Business Opportunity), the real property is transferred by "deed" and the personal property is transferred by a "bill of sale." If money is owed on the business, the proper forms are filed with the Secretary of State's office.

Your real estate license also authorizes you to practice in the specialized field of "Business Opportunities." This is a different area of real estate, and requires knowledge and experience beyond that which is needed for real property transactions. The business opportunity broker's transactions usually include the three items shown in figure 14-6.

FIGURE 14-6

Sale of a Business

REAL PROPERTY	PERSONAL PROPERTY	GOODWILL
Sale or Lease	Equipment and Fixtures	Reputation and Established Sales

BUSINESS OPPORTUNITY SALE

A *BUSINESS OPPORTUNITY is the sale or lease of a business, including the goodwill of an existing business.* It involves the sale of personal property and must also conform to the rules and laws that govern the transfer of chattels (personal property). A more common definition of a *BUSINESS is an establishment whose main purpose is the buying and reselling of goods, or the performance of services, with the intention of making a profit.* The most common types of business opportunities are small, locally owned neighborhood businesses like grocery stores, liquor stores, Laundromats, service stations and restaurants.

The three documents in a personal property security transaction are: 1) a promissory note; 2) a security agreement; and 3) compliance with the UCC-1 financing statement.

BUSINESS OPPORTUNITY LISTING

A business opportunity salesperson should have a working knowledge of business practices and a thorough understanding of accounting or bookkeeping principles. The seller of the business must give you all the pertinent information as part of the listing agreement. The accuracy of the information, however, should be validated by the listing broker.

Business opportunities can involve the transfer of both real and personal property and usually use one escrow.

The business opportunity listing should include all the information necessary for a real property sale. But, in addition, it should include:

1. Name of business and owner.
2. Nature and location of business.
3. Price and terms of sale.
4. Encumbrances and items that are to be assumed by the buyer.

In addition, if there is a lease, the terms should be stated. The important income information should detail the gross income, expenses and net income. If there is competition in the area, it should be so stated. The usual business hours each day and the square footage of the building should also be stated. If the current employees are expected to stay, salary and any existing fringe benefits should be explained in detail.

Buyers of businesses differ. They are usually motivated by the thought of becoming their own boss or the need for a steady income, and they usually fall into one of these two categories:

1. The experienced individual with a background in the field or business he or she is buying.

2. The new buyer who is usually young and inexperienced.

The experienced individual will usually only need the basic facts in order to decide whether to purchase or not. The inexperienced buyer needs more help but is sometimes hesitant to ask questions, so all pertinent facts should be explained, in detail, to that person. He or she should also be informed of applicable laws that govern that particular business. See Figure 14-7 for information about buying a bar or liquor store.

BULK SALES (TRANSFER OF BUSINESS INVENTORY) (NOTICE TO CREDITORS REQUIRED)

A *BULK TRANSFER is any sale of a substantial part of the 1) inventory, items purchased for resale; 2) other supplies and equipment associated with a business.* Division 6 of the Uniform Commercial Code (UCC) requires the purchaser (transferee) in a bulk transfer to give the seller's (transferor's) creditors fair warning that a sale of all or a major part of the inventory is about to take place.

FIGURE 14-7

(ABC)
ALCOHOLIC BEVERAGE CONTROL

Any California real estate licensee who is interested in negotiating business opportunity transactions should be familiar with the legal controls on the transfer of licenses for the sale of alcoholic beverages.

The Department of Alcoholic Beverage Control (ABC) administers the Alcoholic Beverage Control Act and issues all licenses thereunder.

Alcoholic beverage licenses are issued to qualified adults, partnerships, fiduciaries and corporations for use at a particular premises, which also has to be approved by the ABC. The ABC may refuse to issue a license to any person who has a criminal record or has violated the ABC Act. The premises may be disapproved for various reasons, including over concentration of alcoholic beverage licenses in the area, the creation of a police problem or the proximity to a school, playground or church.

With the sale of a business opportunity involving a liquor license, you cannot automatically assume that the ABC will permit the transfer. An escrow is legally required and no consideration may be paid out before the license and the sale of the business is approved. Each application and transfer is subject to protest by local officials and private parties within 30 days of the posted notice of intention to sell alcoholic beverages.

New licenses for bars (on-sale) and liquor stores (off-sale) are usually obtained through a lottery type system in each county. The maximum sales price for a new license is $6,000.00, but after a period of five years from the date of the original issuance, this restriction is lifted and the purchase price is usually considerably more.

DEPARTMENT OF ALCOHOLIC BEVERAGE CONTROL
1901 BROADWAY
SACRAMENTO, CALIFORNIA

http://www.abc.ca.gov (Alcoholic Beverage Control)

Buyer (Transferee) Must Comply With The UCC

If a retail or wholesale merchant transfers a substantial part of his or her materials, supplies, merchandise or inventory, the transferee involved in the transfer must give notice by:

1. **Twelve business days** prior to transfer, recorded notice with the County Recorder's Office.

2. **Twelve business days** prior to transfer, published notice in a newspaper of general circulation in the county or judicial district.

3. **Twelve business days** prior to transfer, delivered notice (by hand or registered mail) to the County Tax Collector.

Protection For Creditors

This notice must include:

1. notification that the transfer is going to take place;
2. the name and any business addresses used by the seller;
3. the location and a description of the property;
4. the place and date of the transfer.

If all of the conditions listed are not met, any transfer of bulk that takes place is considered fraudulent and void against creditors, but valid between buyer and seller.

CALIFORNIA SALES TAXES (SELLING RETAIL)

SALES TAXES are taxes imposed on the sale of tangible personal property by retailers. This is important to brokers and salespeople who are in transactions involving the sale of businesses where sales of tangible personal property is involved. A *SELLER'S PERMIT from the State Board of Equalization is the permit that allows sellers to buy at wholesale without paying sales tax as long as they collect sales taxes from their customers and forward these taxes to the State Board of Equalization.* Before selling a business, escrow should check to see if there are any past due sales taxes.

Licensing, Education and Associations

REAL ESTATE LAW AND REGULATIONS

California laws affecting real estate are included in several different acts and codes. The *CALIFORNIA REAL ESTATE LAW is the portion of the Business and Professions Code that refers to licensing and subdivisions.* On the other hand, the *COMMISSIONER'S REGULATIONS are rules that form part of the California Administrative Code established and enforced by the Commissioner of Real Estate.* All licensees should be familiar with the Real Estate Law, the Commissioner's Regulations and (as mentioned before) the Subdivided Lands Act administered by the Commissioner.

ENFORCEMENT OF REAL ESTATE LAW

Licensing and regulatory law is effective only to the extent that it is enforced. The Commissioner, as the chief officer of the Department of Real Estate, is duty bound to enforce the provisions of the Real Estate Law. The Commissioner may, by his or her own choice, and must upon a verified complaint in writing, investigate the actions of any person engaged in the real estate business or acting in the capacity of a licensee within this state. He or she has the power to suspend any real estate license or to revoke it permanently. The Commissioner also has the authority to deny a license to an applicant if the applicant does not meet the full requirements of the law. If, through the screening process (including the fingerprint record) of an applicant for license, it is found that he or she has a criminal record or some other record that may adversely reflect on his or her character, an investigation is made by the commissioner's staff. A formal hearing may be ordered to determine whether or not the applicant meets the requirements of honesty, truthfulness and good reputation.

HEARINGS FOR LICENSE VIOLATIONS

One function of Real Estate Law is to hold a hearing when there is a question as to the rights of persons to obtain or keep their real estate licenses. All hearings must be conducted in accordance with certain legal regulations. These regulations are set forth in the Administrative Procedure Act. The Department of Real Estate and other licensing agencies must conduct hearings with strict regard for the rules, since the rights of the individual are protected by the act. Before denying, suspending or revoking any license, the licensee is served a statement, and the commissioner acts as the complainant. The licensee, or respondent as he or she is known in the hearing procedures, may appear with or without counsel. The hearing is conducted according to rules of evidence in civil matters.

A decision is made by the hearing officer based upon his or her findings. The commissioner may reject or accept the proposed decision or reduce the proposed penalty, and then make his or her official decision. The respondent has the right of appeal to the courts.

If the charges are not sustained at the hearing, they are dismissed. On the other hand, if the testimony substantiates the charges and they appear to be sufficiently serious, the license of the respondent is suspended or revoked. After a license is revoked, the person affected may not apply for reinstatement until one year has passed. Deputies in the department also investigate persons or firms who appear to be operating improperly or without benefit of a license, or who subdivide land without complying with the subdivision laws enforced by the commissioner.

LICENSES: REVOKE, RESTRICT, SUSPEND

The real estate commissioner can revoke, restrict or suspend the license of any real estate agent for misconduct.

> *REVOKE ... is to take away the license.*
>
> *RESTRICT ... is to limit the use of the license.*
>
> *SUSPEND ... is to take away the license for a period of time.*

COMMON REAL ESTATE LAW VIOLATIONS

Figures 14-8 and 14-9 illustrate most of the common real estate law violations. **Section 10176** of the Business and Professions Code is the legal guideline for the licensee engaged in the practice and performance of any of the acts within the scope of the Real Estate Law. **Section 10177** of the Business and Professions Code applies to situations where the licensee involved was not necessarily acting as an agent or as a licensee.

SECTION 10176
LICENSEE ACTING IN A LICENSEE CAPACITY

This section of the Real Estate Law is for violations by those licensees who are acting within the scope of their licenses. (See Figures 14-8 and 14-9.)

FIGURE 14-8

Section 10176
(Real Estate Licensee
<u>Acting</u> As Licensee)

Grounds for Revocation or Suspension

Misrepresentation - Section 10176(a)

The licensee must disclose to his or her principal all material facts that the principal should know. Failure to do so is cause for disciplinary action. A great majority of the complaints received by the commissioner allege misrepresentation on the part of the broker or his or her salespeople.

False Promise - Section 10176(b)

A false promise is a false statement about what the promisor is going to do in the future. Many times a false promise is proved by showing that the promise was impossible to perform, and that the person making the promise knew it was impossible.

Misrepresentation by Agents - Section 10176(c)

This section gives the commissioner the right to discipline a licensee for a continued and flagrant course of misrepresentation or making of false promises through real estate agents or salespeople.

Divided Agency - Section 10176(d)

This section requires a licensee to inform all his or her principals if he or she is acting as agent for more than one party in a transaction.

Commingling - Section 10176(e)

Commingling takes place when a broker has mixed the funds of his or her principals with his or her own money. A broker should keep all funds separate.

FIGURE 14-9 Continued

Section 10176
(Real Estate Licensee
<u>Acting</u> As Licensee)

Grounds for Revocation or Suspension

Definite Termination Date - Section 10176(f)

A specified termination date, in writing, is required for all exclusive listings transactions.

Secret Profit - Section 10176(g)

Secret profit cases usually arise when the broker makes a low offer, usually through a "dummy" purchaser, when he or she already has a higher offer from another buyer. The difference is the secret profit.

Listing Option - Section 10176(h)

This section requires a licensee, when he or she has used a form which is both an option and a listing, to obtain the written consent of his or her principal approving the amount of such profit before the licensee may exercise the option. This does not apply where a licensee is using an option only.

Dishonest Dealing - Section 10176(i)

Dishonest dealing is a catchall section used when the acts of the person required a license but he or she did not have a license.

Signatures of Prospective Purchasers - Section 10176(j)

Brokers must obtain a written (business opportunities) authorization to sell from an owner before securing the signature of a prospective purchaser to the agreement. This section strikes at what was once a common practice in some areas, in the sale of business opportunities, where the prospective purchaser was forced to deal with the broker who furnished him or her with the listing.

SECTION 10177
LICENSEE NOT NECESSARILY ACTING AS A LICENSEE

Section 10177 applies to situations where the affected party was not necessarily acting in the capacity of an agent or as a real estate licensee. (See Figures 14-10 and 14-11.) The vast majority of brokers and salespeople are honest and perform their services in a straightforward manner. Occasionally, a section of the Real Estate Law may be violated inadvertently and without intent. In such cases the Commissioner would most likely consider restriction of the real estate license. On the other hand, a flagrant violation would most likely cause a revocation of the license.

Examples: It is "blind advertising" if an agent gives the impression that he or she is the owner of the property for sale; The Real Estate Commissioner does not approve of pocket listings (kept within real estate office)—they are not part of the professional code and guidelines.

Importance of Section 10176 and Section 10177
REGULATIONS OF THE COMMISSIONER

The Real Estate Commissioner is empowered to adopt Regulations for the administration and enforcement of the Real Estate Law and the Subdivided Lands Law. Duly adopted regulations become part of the California Code of Regulations and, in effect, have the force and authority of the law itself. Therefore, all licensees, prospective licensees and subdividers should be thoroughly familiar with the Real Estate Commissioner's Regulations.

10176. The commissioner may, upon his own motion, and shall, upon the verified complaint in writing of any person, investigate the actions of any person engaged in the business or acting in the capacity of a real estate licensee within this state, and he may temporarily suspend or permanently revoke a real estate license at any time where the licensee, while a real estate licensee, in performing or attempting to perform any of the acts within the scope of this chapter, has been guilty of any act listed in this Section

10177. The commissioner may suspend or revoke the license of any real estate licensee, or may deny the issuance of a license to an applicant, who has done, or may suspend or revoke the license of, or deny the issuance of a license to, a corporate applicant if an officer, director, or person owning or controlling 10 percent or more of the corporation's stock has done, any of the acts listed in this section.

 http://www.dre.ca.gov (California Department of Real Estate)

FIGURE 14-10

Section 10177
(R.E.Licensee <u>Not Necessarily Acting</u> as a Licensee)

Grounds for Revocation or Suspension

Obtaining License by Fraud - Section 10177(a)

This section gives the Commissioner the power to take action against a licensee for misstatements of fact in an application for a license and in those instances where licenses have been procured by fraud, misrepresentation or deceit.

Convictions - Section 10177(b)

This section permits proceedings against a licensee after a criminal conviction for either a felony or a misdemeanor which involves moral turpitude (anything contrary to justice, honesty, modesty or good morals).

False Advertising - Section 10177(c)

This section makes licensees who are parties to false advertising subject to disciplinary action. The ban extends to subdivision sales as well as general property sales.

Violations of Other Sections - Section 10177(d)

This section gives the Department authority to proceed against the licensee for violation of any of the other sections of the Real Estate Law, the regulations of the commissioner and the subdivision laws.

Misuse of Trade Name - Section 10177(e)

Only active members of the national association or local associations of real estate boards are permitted to use the term "Realtor®." This is a term belonging exclusively to such members, and no licensee may advertise or hold himself or herself out as a "Realtor®" without proper entitlement.

Conduct Warranting Denial - Section 10177(f)

This is a general section of the Real Estate Law and almost any act involving crime or dishonesty will fall within it. An essential requirement for the issuance of a license is that the applicant be honest, truthful and of good reputation.

Negligence or Incompetence - Section 10177(g)

Demonstrated negligence or incompetence, while acting as a licensee, is just cause for disciplinary action. The department proceeds in those cases where the licensee is so careless or unqualified that to allow him or her to handle a transaction would endanger the interests of his or her clients or customers.

FIGURE 14-11

Section 10177
(R.E. Licensee <u>Not Necessarily Acting</u> as a Licensee)
Grounds for Revocation or Suspension

Supervision of Salespersons - Section 10177(h)

A broker is subject to disciplinary action if he or she fails to exercise reasonable supervision over the activities of his or her salespersons.

Violating Government Trust - Section 10177(i)

Prescribes disciplinary liability for using government employment to violate the confidential nature of records thereby made available.

Other Dishonest Conduct - Section 10177(j)

Specifies that any other conduct which constitutes fraud or dishonest dealings may subject the ones involved to license suspension or revocation.

Restricted License Violation - Section 10177(k)

Makes violation of the terms, conditions, restrictions and limitations contained in any order granting a restricted license grounds for disciplinary action.

Inducement of Panic Selling - Section 10177(l)

It is a cause for disciplinary action to solicit or induce the sale, lease, or the listing for sale or lease, of residential property on the grounds of loss of value because of entry into the neighborhood of a person or persons of another race, color, religion, ancestry or national origin.

Violation of Franchise Investment Law - Section 10177(m)

Violates any of the provisions of the Franchise Investment Law or any regulations of the Corporations Commissioner pertaining thereto.

Violation of Securities Law - Section 10177(n)

Violates any of the provisions of the Corporations Code or any regulations of the Commissioner of Corporations relating to securities as specified.

REGULATIONS OF THE COMMISSIONER (FOUND IN THE ADMINISTRATIVE CODE)

The Real Estate Commissioner's regulations are, in effect, laws.

Real Estate Law empowers the Commissioner to issue regulations to aid in the administration and enforcement of the law. These regulations, which are known formally as the Regulations of the Real Estate Commissioner, have the force and effect of the law itself. Licensees and prospective licensees should be familiar with these regulations. The California Department of Real Estate produces a factual law book entitled *Real Estate Law* (Real Estate Law and Regulations of the Real Estate Commissioner), which can be obtained from their office.

REAL ESTATE GENERAL FUND

All the money collected from license and exam fees goes into the Real Estate General fund. Eight percent of this money is used for the operating expenses of the Department of Real Estate. Twenty percent of the Real Estate General Fund is set aside as follows:

> 1) eight percent to the Real Estate Education and Research Fund;
> 2) twelve percent to the Recovery Fund.

The *RECOVERY FUND was established for the payment of damages and arbitration awards to people who have suffered financial loss due to the wrongful act of a licensee in a real estate transaction.* To qualify for these funds, plaintiffs must first obtain a judgment in civil court (or through arbitration) against a licensee on the grounds of fraud, misrepresentation, deceit or conversion of trust funds. If, after reasonable effort, the judgment remains uncollected, a claim may be filed with the Commissioner's office.

> *A license is suspended until the fund is reimbursed (plus interest).*

The total liability of the recovery fund in any one transaction is $20,000 and the total series of judgments against any individual licensee is limited to $100,000. California is one of the few states that actively helps protect the public against fraudulent acts by real estate licensees.

Licensing, Education and Associations

TRADE AND PROFESSIONAL ASSOCIATIONS

A *TRADE OR PROFESSIONAL ASSOCIATION is a voluntary, non-profit organization made up of independent firms in the same industry.* It is formed to promote progress, aid in solving the industry's problems and enhance its service to the community. We will discuss the role of local boards of Realtors®, the California Association of Realtors® (CAR), the National Association of Realtors® (NAR) and its Code of Ethics and the term Realtist.

A "Realtor®" is a member of a real estate trade association.

Local Real Estate Boards

The *LOCAL BOARD OF REALTORS is a voluntary organization of real estate licensees in a particular community.* A broker is entitled to full membership, a salesperson may be an associate member and a non-realtor (who is in a real estate related field) may be an affiliate member. For example, an affiliate member might work for a title insurance company, an escrow company, a lender or any other business having an interest in local real estate activities.

Local boards usually provide a multiple listing service for their members so that all members can be equally informed. Most local boards provide services such as distribution of educational material, seminars, library services and other worthwhile services for the local Realtors®.

http://www.bhbr.com (Example; Beverly Hills, California, Board of Realtors)
http://www.abr.org (Altlanta, Georgia, Board of Realtors)
http://hilo.mlshawaii.com (Hilo, Hawaii, Board of Realtors)
http://vail.net/real_estate// (Vail, Colorado, Board of Realtors)

California Association Of Realtors® (CAR)

The *CALIFORNIA ASSOCIATION OF REALTORS® is the state division of the National Association of Realtors®.* It is a voluntary organization whose membership includes local realty boards throughout the state and individual members who are not affiliated with any particular local board. With the exception of NAR, CAR is the largest Realtor® organization in the United States, with over 100,000 members in California.

The objectives of the California Association of Realtors® are:
1. To promote high standards and unite its members.
2. To safeguard the property buying public.
3. To foster legislation for the benefit and protection of the real estate field.
4. To cooperate in the economic growth and development of the state.

CAR has many standing committees that meet at director's meetings, seminars and annual conventions. These committees specialize in specific areas such as education, ethics, legislation, political affairs, real property taxation, professional standards and many other areas. There are also many divisions of CAR.

 http://www.car.org (California Association of Realtors - CAR)
http://www.ca.realtor.com (California Association of Realtors - CAR)

> **California Association of Realtors®**
> **525 South Virgil Avenue**
> **P. O. Box 76917**
> **Los Angeles, California 90076**

Most of the people who are successful salespeople are also member of the California Association of Realtors®. We suggest you become a member of this or some other trade association when you are serious about selling real estate.

National Association Of Realtors® (NAR)

The *NATIONAL ASSOCIATION OF REALTORS® is the national trade association for all the state associations and local boards of Realtors® in the United States*. NAR unifies the real estate industry at the national level. It encourages legislation favorable to the real estate industry and enforces professional conduct standards in behalf of its members across the nation.

 http://www.realtor.com (National Association of Realtors - NAR)

TRADE NAME

Only active members of the National Association of Realtors® (NAR) or the California Association of Realtors® (CAR), through their local real estate boards, are permitted to use the term Realtor®. This is a term belonging exclusively to such members and no licensee may advertise or present himself or herself to be a Realtor® if not associated with such a group.

Use of the term "Realtor®" without proper group affiliation
is grounds for revocation of your license.

FIGURE 14-12

Real Estate Associations

Counselors of Real Estate (CRE)

CRE is a recognized problem-solver that provides counseling services.

Commercial Investment Real Estate Institute (CIREI)

CIREI enhances the professional development of those engaged in commercial-investment real estate.

Institute of Real Estate Management (IREM)

IREM is committed to enhancing the knowledge and professionalism of the real estate management industry.

 http://www.ccim.com

Real Estate Brokerage Managers Council (CRB)

CRB is recognized throughout the industry as the professional peer organization for brokerage owners and managers.

 http://www.crb.com (Real Estate Brokerage Managers Council)

Realtors® National Marketing Institute (RNMI)

RNMI promotes professional competence in real estate sales and brokerage, and real estate brokerage management.

 http://www.realtor.com (NAR)
(These association can be accessed here)

FIGURE 14-13

Real Estate Associations

http://rebc.com/links
(CAR-Real Estate Business Services/links)

Realtors® Land Institute (RLI)

RLI brings together real estate professionals interested in the improvement of their professional competence in activities related to land.

Real Estate Buyer's Agent Council (REBAC)

REBAC (Real Estate Buyer's Agent Council) serves Realtors® members who wish to devote all or part of their business to the practice of buyer's agency.

Residential Sales Council

The Residential Sales Council serves the real estate industry's top producing residential specialists.

http://www.cre.org

Society of Industrial and Office Realtors® (SIOR)

An international organization whose 1,700 members specialize in a variety of commercial real estate activities.

http://www.sior.com (Society of Industrial and Office Realtors)

Women's Council of Realtors® (WCR)

WCR provides an extensive referral network and education programs for personal and career growth.

Figures 14-12 and 14-13 show the affiliated Institutes, Societies and Councils of the National Association of REALTORS®.

The National Association of REALTORS® has ten affiliated Institutes, Societies and Councils that provide a wide-ranging menu of programs and services that assist members in increasing skills, productivity and knowledge. They include:

1. Counselors of Real Estate (CRE)
2. Commercial Investment Real Estate Institute (CIREI)
3. Institute of Real Estate Management (IREM)
4. Real Estate Brokerage Managers Council (CRB)
5. Realtors® Land Institute (RLI)
6. Realtors® National Marketing Institute (RNMI)
7. Real Estate Buyer's Agent Council (REBAC)
8. Residential Sales Council
9. Society of Industrial and Office Realtors (SIOR)
10. Women's Council of Realtors® (WCR)

CODE OF ETHICS

See Figures 14-14 through 14-20 for the National Association of Realtors® Code of Ethics. These guidelines show not only how one **should** act but also how one **must** act.

The National Association of Realtors® and its state and local divisions form a composite organization of brokers whose objective is to forward the interests of brokers, encourage education of practitioners and the public, raise the standard of real estate practice and increase the esteem in which brokers are held by their fellow citizens. To this end, a code of ethics has been formulated and adopted. It is the generally accepted code of ethics for real estate people and every Realtor® swears to abide by it.

"Under all is the land" are the beginning words of the NAR Code of Ethics.

FIGURE 14-14

Code of Ethics and Standards of Practice of the National Association of Realtors®

Effective January 1, 1997

Where the word REALTORS® is used in this Code and Preamble, it shall be deemed to include REALTOR-ASSOCIATE®S.

While the Code of Ethics establishes obligations that may be higher than those mandated by law, in any instance where the Code of Ethics and the law conflict, the obligations of the law must take precedence.

Preamble...

Under all is the land. Upon its wise utilization and widely allocated ownership depend the survival and growth of free institutions and of our civilization. REALTORS® should recognize that the interests of the nation and its citizens require the highest and best use of the land and the widest distribution of land ownership. They require the creation of adequate housing, the building of functioning cities, the development of productive industries and farms, and the preservation of a healthful environment.

Such interests impose obligations beyond those of ordinary commerce. They impose grave social responsibility and a patriotic duty to which REALTORS® should dedicate themselves, and for which they should be diligent in preparing themselves. REALTORS®, therefore, are zealous to maintain and improve the standards of their calling and share with their fellow REALTORS® a common responsibility for its integrity and honor.

In recognition and appreciation of their obligations to clients, customers, the public, and each other, REALTORS® continuously strive to become and remain informed on issues affecting real estate and, as knowledgeable professionals, they willingly share the fruit of their experience and study with others. They identify and take steps, through enforcement of this Code of Ethics and by assisting appropriate regulatory bodies, to eliminate practices which may damage the public or which might discredit or bring dishonor to the real estate profession.

Realizing that cooperation with other real estate professionals promotes the best interests of those who utilize their services, REALTORS® urge exclusive representation of clients; do not attempt to gain any unfair advantage over their competitors; and they refrain from making unsolicited comments about other practitioners. In instances where their opinion is sought, or where REALTORS® believe that comment is necessary, their opinion is offered in an objective, professional manner, uninfluenced by any personal motivation or potential advantage or gain.

The term REALTORS® has come to connote competency, fairness, and high integrity resulting from adherence to a lofty ideal of moral conduct in business relations. No inducement of profit and no instruction from clients ever can justify departure from this ideal.

In the interpretation of this obligation, REALTORS® can take no safer guide than that which has been handed down through the centuries, embodied in the Golden Rule, "Whatsoever ye would that others should do to you, do ye even so to them."

Accepting this standard as their own, REALTORS® pledge to observe its spirit in all of their activities and to conduct their business in accordance with the tenets set forth below.

Duties to Clients and Customers

Article 1

When representing a buyer, seller, landlord, tenant, or other client as an agent, REALTORS® pledge themselves to protect and promote the interests of their client. This obligation of absolute fidelity to the client's interests is primary, but it does not relieve REALTORS® of their obligation to treat all parties honestly. When serving a buyer, seller, landlord, tenant or other party in a non-agency capacity, REALTORS® remain obligated to treat all parties honestly. (Amended 1/93)

Standard of Practice 1-1

REALTORS®, when acting as principals in a real estate transaction, remain obligated by the duties imposed by the Code of Ethics. (Amended 1/93)

Standard of Practice 1-2

The duties the Code of Ethics imposes on agents/representatives are applicable to REALTORS® acting as agents, transaction brokers, facilitators, or in any other recognized capacity except for any duty specifically exempted by law or regulation. (Adopted 1/95)

Standard of Practice 1-3

REALTORS®, in attempting to secure a listing, shall not deliberately mislead the owner as to market value.

Standard of Practice 1-4

REALTORS®, when seeking to become a buyer/tenant representative, shall not mislead buyers or tenants as to savings or other benefits that might be realized through use of the Realtor's services. (Amended 1/93)

Standard of Practice 1-5

REALTORS® may represent the seller/landlord and buyer/tenant in the same transaction only after full disclosure to and with informed consent of both parties. (Adopted 1/93)

Standard of Practice 1-6

REALTORS® shall submit offers and counter-offers objectively and as quickly as possible. (Adopted 1/93, Amended 1/95)

http://lakeland.net/~lar/code.html
(DRE Code of Ethics)

FIGURE 14-15

Standard of Practice 1-7

When acting as listing brokers, REALTORS® shall continue to submit to the seller/landlord all offers and counter-offers until closing or execution of a lease unless the seller/landlord has waived this obligation in writing. REALTORS® shall not be obligated to continue to market the property after an offer has been accepted by the seller/landlord. REALTORS® shall recommend that sellers/landlords obtain the advice of legal counsel prior to acceptance of a subsequent offer except where the acceptance is contingent on the termination of the pre-existing purchase contract or lease. (Amended 1/93)

Standard of Practice 1-8

REALTORS® acting as agents of buyers/tenants shall submit to buyers/tenants all offers and counter-offers until acceptance but have no obligation to continue to show properties to their clients after an offer has been accepted unless otherwise agreed in writing. REALTORS® acting as agents of buyers/tenants shall recommend that buyers/tenants obtain the advice of legal counsel if there is a question as to whether a pre-existing contract has been terminated. (Adopted 1/93)

Standard of Practice 1-9

The obligation of REALTORS® to preserve confidential information provided by their clients continues after the termination of the agency relationship. REALTORS® shall not knowingly, during or following the termination of a professional relationship with their client: 1) reveal confidential information of the client; or 2) use confidential information of the client to the disadvantage of the client; or 3) use confidential information of the client for the Realtor's advantage or the advantage of a third party unless: a) the client consents after full disclosure; or b) the REALTORS® is required by court order; or c) it is the intention of the client to commit a crime and the information is necessary to prevent the crime; or d) it is necessary to defend the REALTORS® or the Realtor's employees or associates against an accusation of wrongful conduct. (Adopted 1/93, Amended 1/97)

Standard of Practice 1-10

REALTORS® shall, consistent with the terms and conditions of their property management agreement, competently manage the property of clients with due regard for the rights, responsibilities, benefits, safety and health of tenants and others lawfully on the premises. (Adopted 1/95)

Standard of Practice 1-11

REALTORS® who are employed to maintain or manage a client's property shall exercise due diligence and make reasonable efforts to protect it against reasonably foreseeable contingencies and losses. (Adopted 1/95)

Article 2

REALTORS® shall avoid exaggeration, misrepresentation, or concealment of pertinent facts relating to the property or the transaction. REALTORS® shall not, however, be obligated to discover latent defects in the property, to advise on matters outside the scope of their real estate license, or to disclose facts which are confidential under the scope of agency duties owed to their clients. (Amended 1/93)

Standard of Practice 2-1

REALTORS® shall only be obligated to discover and disclose adverse factors reasonably apparent to someone with expertise in those areas required by their real estate licensing authority. Article 2 does not impose upon the REALTORS® the obligation of expertise in other professional or technical disciplines. (Amended 1/96)

Standard of Practice 2-2

When entering into listing contracts, REALTORS® must advise sellers/landlords of: 1) the Realtor's general company policies regarding cooperation with subagents, buyer/tenant agents, or both; 2) the fact that buyer/tenant agents, even if compensated by the listing broker, or by the seller/landlord will represent the interests of buyers/tenants; and 3) any potential for the listing broker to act as a disclosed dual agent, e.g. buyer/tenant agent. (Adopted 1/93)

Standard of Practice 2-3

When entering into contracts to represent buyers/tenants, REALTORS® must advise potential clients of: 1) the Realtor's general company policies regarding cooperation with other firms; and 2) any potential for the buyer/tenant representative to act as a disclosed dual agent, e.g. listing broker, subagent, landlord's agent, etc. (Adopted 1/93)

Standard of Practice 2-4

REALTORS® shall not be parties to the naming of a false consideration in any document, unless it be the naming of an obviously nominal consideration.

Standard of Practice 2-5

Factors defined as "non-material" by law or regulation or which are expressly referenced in law or regulation as not being subject to disclosure are considered not "pertinent" for purposes of Article 2. (Adopted 1/93)

Article 3

REALTORS® shall cooperate with other brokers except when cooperation is not in the client's best interest. The obligation to cooperate does not include the obligation to share commissions, fees, or to otherwise compensate another broker. (Amended 1/95)

Standard of Practice 3-1

REALTORS®, acting as exclusive agents of sellers/landlords, establish the terms and conditions of offers to cooperate. Unless expressly indicated in offers to cooperate, cooperating brokers may not assume that the offer of cooperation includes an offer of compensation. Terms of compensation, if any, shall be ascertained by cooperating brokers before beginning efforts to accept the offer of cooperation. (Amended 1/94)

Standard of Practice 3-2

REALTORS® shall, with respect to offers of compensation to another REALTORS®, timely communicate any change of compensation for cooperative services to the other REALTORS®

FIGURE 14-16

prior to the time such REALTORS® produces an offer to purchase/lease the property. (Amended 1/94)

Standard of Practice 3-3

Standard of Practice 3-2 does not preclude the listing broker and cooperating broker from entering into an agreement to change cooperative compensation. (Adopted 1/94)

Standard of Practice 3-4

REALTORS®, acting as listing brokers, have an affirmative obligation to disclose the existence of dual or variable rate commission arrangements (i.e., listings where one amount of commission is payable if the listing broker's firm is the procuring cause of sale/lease and a different amount of commission is payable if the sale/lease results through the efforts of the seller/landlord or a cooperating broker). The listing broker shall, as soon as practical, disclose the existence of such arrangements to potential cooperating brokers and shall, in response to inquiries from cooperating brokers, disclose the differential that would result in a cooperative transaction or in a sale/lease that results through the efforts of the seller/landlord. If the cooperating broker is a buyer/tenant representative, the buyer/tenant representative must disclose such information to their client. (Amended 1/94)

Standard of Practice 3-5

It is the obligation of subagents to promptly disclose all pertinent facts to the principal's agent prior to as well as after a purchase or lease agreement is executed. (Amended 1/93)

Standard of Practice 3-6

REALTORS® shall disclose the existence of an accepted offer to any broker seeking cooperation. (Adopted 5/86)

Standard of Practice 3-7

When seeking information from another REALTORS® concerning property under a management or listing agreement, REALTORS® shall disclose their REALTORS® status and whether their interest is personal or on behalf of a client and, if on behalf of a client, their representational status. (Amended 1/95)

Standard of Practice 3-8

REALTORS® shall not misrepresent the availability of access to show or inspect a listed property. (Amended 11/87)

Article 4

REALTORS® shall not acquire an interest in or buy or present offers from themselves, any member of their immediate families, their firms or any member thereof, or any entities in which they have any ownership interest, any real property without making their true position known to the owner or the owner's agent. In selling property they own, or in which they have any interest, REALTORS® shall reveal their ownership or interest in writing to the purchaser or the purchaser's representative. (Amended 1/91)

Standard of Practice 4-1

For the protection of all parties, the disclosures required by Article 4 shall be in writing and provided by REALTORS® prior to the signing of any contract. (Adopted 2/86)

Article 5

REALTORS® shall not undertake to provide professional services concerning a property or its value where they have a present or contemplated interest unless such interest is specifically disclosed to all affected parties.

Article 6

When acting as agents, REALTORS® shall not accept any commission, rebate, or profit on expenditures made for their principal, without the principal's knowledge and consent. (Amended 1/92)

Standard of Practice 6-1

REALTORS® shall not recommend or suggest to a client or a customer the use of services of another organization or business entity in which they have a direct interest without disclosing such interest at the time of the recommendation or suggestion. (Amended 5/88)

Standard of Practice 6-2

When acting as agents or subagents, REALTORS® shall disclose to a client or customer if there is any financial benefit or fee the REALTORS® or the Realtor's firm may receive as a direct result of having recommended real estate products or services (e.g., homeowner's insurance, warranty programs, mortgage financing, title insurance, etc.) other than real estate referral fees. (Adopted 5/88)

Article 7

In a transaction, REALTORS® shall not accept compensation from more than one party, even if permitted by law, without disclosure to all parties and the informed consent of the Realtor's client or clients. (Amended 1/93)

Article 8

REALTORS® shall keep in a special account in an appropriate financial institution, separated from their own funds, monies coming into their possession in trust for other persons, such as escrows, trust funds, clients' monies, and other like items.

Article 9

REALTORS®, for the protection of all parties, shall assure whenever possible that agreements shall be in writing, and shall be in clear and understandable language expressing the specific terms, conditions, obligations and commitments of the parties. A copy of each agreement shall be furnished to each party upon their signing or initialing. (Amended 1/95)

Standard of Practice 9-1

For the protection of all parties, REALTORS® shall use reasonable care to ensure that documents pertaining to the purchase, sale, or lease of real estate are kept current through the use of written extensions or amendments. (Amended 1/93)

Duties to the Public

Article 10

REALTORS® shall not deny equal professional services to any person for reasons of race, color, religion, sex, handicap, familial

FIGURE 14-17

status, or national origin.

REALTORS® shall not be parties to any plan or agreement to discriminate against a person or persons on the basis of race, color, religion, sex, handicap, familial status, or national origin. (Amended 1/90)

Standard of Practice 10-1

REALTORS® shall not volunteer information regarding the racial, religious or ethnic composition of any neighborhood and shall not engage in any activity which may result in panic selling. REALTORS® shall not print, display or circulate any statement or advertisement with respect to the selling or renting of a property that indicates any preference, limitations or discrimination based on race, color, religion, sex, handicap, familial status or national origin. (Adopted 1/94)

Article 11

The services which REALTORS® provide to their clients and customers shall conform to the standards of practice and competence which are reasonably expected in the specific real estate disciplines in which they engage; specifically, residential real estate brokerage, real property management, commercial and industrial real estate brokerage, real estate appraisal, real estate counseling, real estate syndication, real estate auction, and international real estate.

REALTORS® shall not undertake to provide specialized professional services concerning a type of property or service that is outside their field of competence unless they engage the assistance of one who is competent on such types of property or service, or unless the facts are fully disclosed to the client. Any persons engaged to provide such assistance shall be so identified to the client and their contribution to the assignment should be set forth. (Amended 1/95)

Standard of Practice 11-1

The obligations of the Code of Ethics shall be supplemented by and construed in a manner consistent with the Uniform Standards of Professional Appraisal Practice (USPAP) promulgated by the Appraisal Standards Board of the Appraisal Foundation.

The obligations of the Code of Ethics shall not be supplemented by the USPAP where an opinion or recommendation of price or pricing is provided in pursuit of a listing, to assist a potential purchaser in formulating a purchase offer, or to provide a broker's price opinion, whether for a fee or not. (Amended 1/96)

Standard of Practice 11-2

The obligations of the Code of Ethics in respect of real estate disciplines other than appraisal shall be interpreted and applied in accordance with the standards of competence and practice which clients and the public reasonably require to protect their rights and interests considering the complexity of the transaction, the availability of expert assistance, and, where the REALTORS® is an agent or subagent, the obligations of a fiduciary. (Adopted 1/95)

Standard of Practice 11-3

When REALTORS® provide consultive services to clients which involve advice or counsel for a fee (not a commision), such advice shall be rendered in an objective manner and the fee shall not be contingent on the substance of the advice or counsel given. If brokerage or transaction services are to be provided in addition to consultive services, a separate compensation may be paid with prior agreement between the client and REALTORS®. (Adopted 1/96)

Article 12

REALTORS® shall be careful at all times to present a true picture in their advertising and representations to the public. REALTORS® shall also ensure that their professional status (e.g., broker, appraiser, property manager, etc.) or status as REALTORS® is clearly identifiable in any such advertising. (Amended 1/93)

Standard of Practice 12-1

REALTORS® may use the term "free" and similar terms in their advertising and in other representations provided that all terms governing availability of the offered product or service are clearly disclosed at the same time. (Amended 1/97)

Standard of Practice 12-2

REALTORS® may represent their services as "free" or without cost even if they expect to receive compensation from a source other than their client provided that the potential for the REALTORS® to obtain a benefit from a third party is clearly disclosed at the same time. (Amended 1/97)

Standard of Practice 12-3

The offering of premiums, prizes, merchandise discounts or other inducements to list, sell, purchase, or lease is not, in itself, unethical even if receipt of the benefit is contingent on listing, selling, purchasing, or leasing through the REALTORS® making the offer.

However, REALTORS® must exercise care and candor in any such advertising or other public or private representations so that any party interested in receiving or otherwise benefiting from the Realtor's offer will have clear, thorough, advance understanding of all the terms and conditions of the offer. The offering of any inducements to do business is subject to the limitations and restrictions of state law and the ethical obligations established by any applicable Standard of Practice. (Amended 1/95)

Standard of Practice 12-4

REALTORS® shall not offer for sale/lease or advertise property without authority. When acting as listing brokers or as subagents, REALTORS® shall not quote a price different from that agreed upon with the seller/landlord. (Amended 1/93)

Standard of Practice 12-5

REALTORS® shall not advertise nor permit any person employed by or affiliated with them to advertise listed property without disclosing the name of the firm. (Adopted 11/86)

Standard of Practice 12-6

REALTORS®, when advertising unlisted real property for sale/lease in which they have an ownership interest, shall disclose their status as both owners/landlords and as REALTORS® or real estate licensees. (Amended 1/93)

FIGURE 14-18

Standard of Practice 12-7

Only REALTORS® who participated in the transaction as the listing broker or cooperating broker (selling broker) may claim to have "sold" the property. Prior to closing, a cooperating broker may post a "sold" sign only with the consent of the listing broker. (Amended 1/96)

Article 13

REALTORS® shall not engage in activities that constitute the unauthorized practice of law and shall recommend that legal counsel be obtained when the interest of any party to the transaction requires it.

Article 14

If charged with unethical practice or asked to present evidence or to cooperate in any other way, in any disciplinary proceeding or investigation, REALTORS® shall place all pertinent facts before the proper tribunals of the Member Board or affiliated institute, society, or council in which membership is held and shall take no action to disrupt or obstruct such processes. (Amended 1/90)

Standard of Practice 14-1

REALTORS® shall not be subject to disciplinary proceedings in more than one Board of REALTORS® or affiliated institute, society or council in which they hold membership with respect to alleged violations of the Code of Ethics relating to the same transaction or event. (Amended 1/95)

Standard of Practice 14-2

REALTORS® shall not make any unauthorized disclosure or dissemination of the allegations, findings, or decision developed in connection with an ethics hearing or appeal or in connection with an arbitration hearing or procedural review. (Amended 1/92)

Standard of Practice 14-3

REALTORS® shall not obstruct the Board's investigative or disciplinary proceedings by instituting or threatening to institute actions for libel, slander or defamation against any party to a professional standards proceeding or their witnesses. (Adopted 11/87)

Standard of Practice 14-4

REALTORS® shall not intentionally impede the Board's investigative or disciplinary proceedings by filing multiple ethics complaints based on the same event or transaction. (Adopted 11/88)

Duties to REALTORS®

Article 15

REALTORS® shall not knowingly or recklessly make false or misleading statements about competitors, their businesses, or their business practices. (Amended 1/92)

Article 16

REALTORS® shall not engage in any practice or take any action inconsistent with the agency of other REALTORS®.

Standard of Practice 16-1

Article 16 is not intended to prohibit aggressive or innovative business practices which are otherwise ethical and does not prohibit disagreements with other REALTORS® involving commission, fees, compensation or other forms of payment or expenses. (Adopted 1/93, Amended 1/95)

Standard of Practice 16-2

Article 16 does not preclude REALTORS® from making general announcements to prospective clients describing their services and the terms of their availability even though some recipients may have entered into agency agreements with another REALTORS®. A general telephone canvass, general mailing or distribution addressed to all prospective clients in a given geographical area or in a given profession, business, club, or organization, or other classification or group is deemed "general" for purposes of this standard.

Article 16 is intended to recognize as unethical two basic types of solicitations:

First, telephone or personal solicitations of property owners who have been identified by a real estate sign, multiple listing compilation, or other information service as having exclusively listed their property with another REALTORS®; and Second, mail or other forms of written solicitations of prospective clients whose properties are exclusively listed with another REALTORS® when such solicitations are not part of a general mailing but are directed specifically to property owners identified through compilations of current listings, "for sale" or "for rent" signs, or other sources of information required by Article 3 and Multiple Listing Service rules to be made available to other REALTORS® under offers of subagency or cooperation. (Amended 1/93)

Standard of Practice 16-3

Article 16 does not preclude REALTORS® from contacting the client of another broker for the purpose of offering to provide, or entering into a contract to provide, a different type of real estate service unrelated to the type of service currently being provided (e.g., property management as opposed to brokerage). However, information received through a Multiple Listing Service or any other offer of cooperation may not be used to target clients of other REALTORS® to whom such offers to provide services may be made. (Amended 1/93)

Standard of Practice 16-4

REALTORS® shall not solicit a listing which is currently listed exclusively with another broker. However, if the listing broker, when asked by the REALTORS®, refuses to disclose the expiration date and nature of such listing; i.e., an exclusive right to sell, an exclusive agency, open listing, or other form of contractual agreement between the listing broker and the client, the REALTORS® may contact the owner to secure such information and may discuss the terms upon which the REALTORS® might take a future listing or, alternatively, may take a listing to become effective upon expiration of any existing exclusive listing. (Amended 1/94)

FIGURE 14-19

Standard of Practice 16-5

REALTORS® shall not solicit buyer/tenant agency agreements from buyers/tenants who are subject to exclusive buyer/tenant agency agreements. However, if a buyer/tenant agent, when asked by a REALTORS®, refuses to disclose the expiration date of the exclusive buyer/tenant agency agreement, the REALTORS® may contact the buyer/tenant to secure such information and may discuss the terms upon which the REALTORS® might enter into a future buyer/tenant agency agreement or, alternatively, may enter into a buyer/tenant agency agreement to become effective upon the expiration of any existing exclusive buyer/tenant agency agreement. (Adopted 1/94)

Standard of Practice 16-6

When REALTORS® are contacted by the client of another REALTORS® regarding the creation of an agency relationship to provide the same type of service, and REALTORS® have not directly or indirectly initiated such discussions, they may discuss the terms upon which they might enter into a future agency agreement or, alternatively, may enter into an agency agreement which becomes effective upon expiration of any existing exclusive agreement. (Amended 1/93)

Standard of Practice 16-7

The fact that a client has retained a REALTORS® as an agent in one or more past transactions does not preclude other REALTORS® from seeking such former client's future business. (Amended 1/93)

Standard of Practice 16-8

The fact that an agency agreement has been entered into with a REALTORS® shall not preclude or inhibit any other REALTORS® from entering into a similar agreement after the expiration of the prior agreement. (Amended 1/93)

Standard of Practice 16-9

REALTORS®, prior to entering into an agency agreement, have an affirmative obligation to make reasonable efforts to determine whether the client is subject to a current, valid exclusive agreement to provide the same type of real estate service. (Amended 1/93)

Standard of Practice 16-10

REALTORS®, acting as agents of buyers or tenants, shall disclose that relationship to the seller/landlord's agent at first contact and shall provide written confirmation of that disclosure to the seller/landlord's agent not later than execution of a purchase agreement or lease. (Amended 1/93)

Standard of Practice 16-11

On unlisted property, REALTORS® acting as buyer/tenant agents shall disclose that relationship to the seller/landlord at first contact for that client and shall provide written confirmation of such disclosure to the seller/landlord not later than execution of any purchase or lease agreement.

REALTORS® shall make any request for anticipated compensation from the seller/landlord at first contact. (Amended 1/93)

Standard of Practice 16-12

REALTORS®, acting as agents of sellers/landlords or as subagents of listing brokers, shall disclose that relationship to buyers/tenants as soon as practicable and shall provide written confirmation of such disclosure to buyers/tenants not later than execution of any purchase or lease agreement. (Amended 1/93)

Standard of Practice 16-13

All dealings concerning property exclusively listed, or with buyer/tenants who are exclusively represented shall be carried on with the client's agent, and not with the client, except with the consent of the client's agent or except where such dealings are initiated by the client. (Adopted 1/93, Amended 1/97)

Standard of Practice 16-14

REALTORS® are free to enter into contractual relationships or to negotiate with sellers/landlords, buyers/tenants or others who are not represented by an exclusive agent but shall not knowingly obligate them to pay more than one commission except with their informed consent. (Amended 1/94)

Standard of Practice 16-15

In cooperative transactions REALTORS® shall compensate cooperating REALTORS® (principal brokers) and shall not compensate nor offer to compensate, directly or indirectly, any of the sales licensees employed by or affiliated with other REALTORS® without the prior express knowledge and consent of the cooperating broker.

Standard of Practice 16-16

REALTORS®, acting as subagents or buyer/tenant agents, shall not use the terms of an offer to purchase/lease to attempt to modify the listing broker's offer of compensation to subagents or buyer's agents nor make the submission of an executed offer to purchase/lease contingent on the listing broker's agreement to modify the offer of compensation. (Amended 1/93)

Standard of Practice 16-18

REALTORS® shall not use information obtained by them from the listing broker, through offers to cooperate received through Multiple Listing Services or other sources authorized by the listing broker, for the purpose of creating a referral prospect to a third broker, or for creating a buyer/tenant prospect unless such use is authorized by the listing broker. (Amended 1/93)

Standard of Practice 16-19

Signs giving notice of property for sale, rent, lease, or exchange shall not be placed on property without consent of the seller/landlord. (Amended 1/93)

Article 17

In the event of contractual disputes or specific non-contractual disputes as defined in Standard of Practice 17-4 between REALTORS® associated with different firms, arising out of their relationship as REALTORS®, the REALTORS® shall submit the dispute to arbitration in accordance with the regulations of their Board or Boards rather than litigate the matter.

FIGURE 14-20

In the event clients of REALTORS® wish to arbitrate contractual disputes arising out of real estate transactions, REALTORS® shall arbitrate those disputes in accordance with the regulations of their Board, provided the clients agree to be bound by the decision. (Amended 1/97)

Standard of Practice 17-1

The filing of litigation and refusal to withdraw from it by REALTORS® in an arbitrable matter constitutes a refusal to arbitrate. (Adopted 2/86)

Standard of Practice 17-2

Article 17 does not require REALTORS® to arbitrate in those circumstances when all parties to the dispute advise the Board in writing that they choose not to arbitrate before the Board. (Amended 1/93)

Standard of Practice 17-3

REALTORS®, when acting solely as principals in a real estate transaction, are not obligated to arbitrate disputes with other REALTORS® absent a specific written agreement to the contrary. (Adopted 1/96)

Standard of Practice 17-4

Specific non-contractual disputes that are subject to arbitration pursuant to Article 17 are:

Where a listing broker has compensated a cooperating broker and another cooperating broker subsequently claims to be the procuring cause of the sale or lease. In such cases the complainant may name the first cooperating broker as respondent and arbitration may proceed without the listing broker being named as a respondent. Alternatively, if the complaint is brought against the listing broker, the listing broker may name the first cooperating broker as a third-party respondent. In either instance the decision of the hearing panel as to procuring cause shall be conclusive with respect to all current or subsequent claims of the parties for compensation arising out of the underlying cooperative transaction. (Adopted 1/97)

Where a buyer or tenant representative is compensated by the seller or landlord, and not by the listing broker, and the listing broker, as a result, reduces the commission owed by the seller or landlord and, subsequent to such actions, another cooperating broker claims to be the procuring cause of sale or lease. In such cases the complainant may name the first cooperating broker as respondent and arbitration may proceed without the listing broker being named as a respondent. Alternatively, if the complaint is brought against the listing broker, the listing broker may name the first cooperating broker as a third-party respondent. In either instance the decision of the hearing panel as to procuring cause

shall be conclusive with respect to all current or subsequent claims of the parties for compensation arising out of the underlying cooperative transaction. (Adopted 1/97)

Where a buyer or tenant representative is compensated by the buyer or tenant and, as a result, the listing broker reduces the commission owed by the seller or landlord and, subsequent to such actions, another cooperating broker claims to be the procuring cause of sale or lease. In such cases the complainant may name the first cooperating broker as respondent and arbitration may proceed without the listing broker being named as a respondent. Alternatively, if the complaint is brought against the listing broker, the listing broker may name the first cooperating broker as a third-party respondent. In either instance the decision of the hearing panel as to procuring cause shall be conclusive with respect to all current or subsequent claims of the parties for compensation arising out of the underlying cooperative transaction. (Adopted 1/97)

Where two or more listing brokers claim entitlement to compensation pursuant to open listings with a seller or landlord who agrees to participate in arbitration (or who requests arbitration) and who agrees to be bound by the decision. In cases where one of the listing brokers has been compensated by the seller or landlord, the other listing broker, as complainant, may name the first listing broker as respondent and arbitration may proceed between the brokers. (Adopted 1/97)

The Code of Ethics was adopted in 1913. Amended at the Annual Convention in 1924, 1928, 1950, 1951, 1952, 1955, 1956, 1961, 1962, 1974, 1982, 1986, 1987, 1989, 1990, 1991, 1992, 1993, 1994, 1995 and 1996.

Explanatory Notes

The reader should be aware of the following policies which have been approved by the Board of Directors of the National Association:

In filing a charge of an alleged violation of the Code of Ethics by a REALTORS®, the charge must read as an alleged violation of one or more Articles of the Code. Standards of Practice may be cited in support of the charge.

The Standards of Practice serve to clarify the ethical obligations imposed by the various Articles and supplement, and do not substitute for, the Case Interpretations in Interpretations of the Code of Ethics.

Modifications to existing Standards of Practice and additional new Standards of Practice are approved from time to time. Readers are cautioned to ensure that the most recent publications are utilized.

REALTIST DEFINED

"Realtist" is the name for a member of a predominantly black real estate broker trade association.

The National Association of Real Estate Brokers, or "Realtist," is a national organization of brokers with a predominance of black members, but whose membership is by no means limited to black membership. The organization has local boards in the largest cities in most states. The organization in this state, called the California Association of Real Estate Brokers, has four board affiliations:

1. Associated Real Property Brokers, Oakland
2. Consolidated Real Estate Brokers, Sacramento
3. Consolidated Realty Board, Los Angeles
4. Logan Heights Realty Board, San Diego

A Realtist must be a member of a local board as well as a member of the national organization. Both on the local and national levels, Realtists work for better housing in the communities they serve. In many instances, individuals are both Realtors® and Realtists by virtue of dual membership. For more information contact:

National Association of Real Estate Brokers
1629 K Street NW
Washington, DC 20006
202-785-4477
202-785-1244 (Fax)

 http://www.nareb.org/index.htm (National Association of Real Estate Brokers)

INDEPENDENT BOARDS

There are also several "independent" boards in California, some of which are large in membership and influential in their communities. Most of these boards are organized for some particular purpose, such as a multiple listing service. Many members of independent boards are also members of boards affiliated with CAR.

OTHER ASSOCIATIONS

In addition to the above mentioned organizations, there are many trade associations and professional bodies that are related to the real estate business, such as:

1. American Bankers Association
2. American Savings and Loan Institute
3. Building Owners and Managers Association
4. Mortgage Bankers Association
5. National Association of Home Builders
6. National Association of Mutual Savings Banks
7. Prefabricated Home Manufacturers Institute

REAL ESTATE INSTRUCTOR & LICENSING ASSOCIATIONS

In addition to the above mentioned organizations, there are real estate instructor organizations and other professional bodies that are related to real estate education and licensing. See Figure 14-21.

NO AFFILIATION NECESSARY

A real estate licensee need not be a member of any trade or professional association. In this case, he or she is simply referred to as a salesperson or broker. There is no compulsion for any licensee of the Department of Real Estate to join or affiliate with any local or state organization. That decision is strictly individual and personal.

FIGURE 14-21

REAL ESTATE TEACHERS' GROUPS

California Real Estate Educators Association (CREEA)

Real estate instructors from throughout the state have come together with the formation of CREEA, the California Real Estate Educators Association. This organization constitutes a chapter of REEA, the Real Estate Educators Association, a private trade association, which is international in scope. REEA has a reputation throughout the world for its comprehensive representation.

California Real Estate Education Association
P.O. Box 1230 Costa Mesa, CA 92628
Tel. (714) 751-2787 Ext. 211

Real Estate Educators Association
10565 Lee Highway, Suite 104, Fairfax, VA 22030 Phone: (703) 352-6688

http://www.creea.org (CREEA)

http://www.reea.org (REEA)

http://www.yosemite.cc.ca.us/realestate/ (CCCREEC)

http://www.arello.org (Association of Real Estate Law Officials)

CALIFORNIA COMMUNITY COLLEGES
REAL ESTATE EDUCATION CENTER

California Community Colleges Real Estate Education Center is a real estate instructors group sponsored by the California Department of Real Estate. This fund publishes a quarterly newsletter and sponsors educators' conferences throughout the year in cooperation with the California Community College chancellor's office. The newsletter, called *The Informer*, is a useful reference source to keep educators up to date on new laws and real estate practices. The conferences, held at convenient locations throughout the state, are well attended by educators from all segments. For information about The *Informer* and Endowment Fund contact:

George Bairey, Director
California Community Colleges
Real Estate Education Center
Yosemite Community College District
P.O. Box 4065, Modesto, CA 95352
(209) 575-6465

Association of Real Estate License
Law Officials (ARELLO)
P. O. BOX 129
Centerville, Utah 84014-0129

    A. Department of Real Estate (DRE)   **K.** Local Board of Realtors
    B. Police Power   **L.** California Association of Realtors (CAR)
    C. Real Estate Advisory Commission   **M.** National Association of Realtors (NAR)
    D. Broker's License   **N.** Continuing Education Requirements
    E. Business Opportunity and Bulk Sales   **O.** NARELLO
    F. Business   **P.** Commissioner's Code of Ethics (2785)
    G. Real Estate Law   **Q.** Realtor
    H. Commissioner's Regulations   **R.** Realtist
    I. Recovery Fund   **S.** NAR Code of Ethics
    J. Trade Association

1.____ A national trade association of real estate professionals who call themselves Realtors®.

2.____ The sale of a business.

3.____ The right of the government to enact laws for the protection of the general public. Laws such as zoning ordinances, building codes and health and safety requirements are common in real estate.

4.____ Any legitimate activity by which people expect to earn money.

5.____ The division of the state government responsible for the licensing and regulation of persons engaged in the real estate business. Heading the department is the Real Estate Commissioner.

6.____ Composed of ten members, it recommends and makes suggestions to the Commissioner.

7.____ A voluntary, nonprofit organization made up of independent firms in the same industry. CAR and NAR are examples.

8.____ A license that allows a person to represent, for compensation, one or more parties in a real estate transaction.

9.____ Established to compensate people who have suffered financial loss due to the wrongful act of a real estate licensee.

10.____ Rules that form part of the California Administrative Code. Established regulations are enforced by the Commissioner of Real Estate.

11.____ The portion of the Business and Professions Code that refers to licensing and subdivisions.

12.____ A local voluntary organization, in a given community, made up of real estate licensees.

13.____ The state division of the National Association of Realtors.

14.____ The 45 clock hours of Commissioner-approved courses that must be taken by all real estate licensees during the four-year period preceding license renewal.

15.____ The association made up of real estate license law officials.

16.____ Standards of professional conduct and business practices established by the commissioner to enhance the professionalism of the California real estate industry.

17.____ A term reserved for active members of the National Association of Realtors or the California Association of Realtors.

18.____ Members of the National Association of Real Estate Brokers.

19.____ In order to be a realtor, a person must swear to uphold this code

MULTIPLE CHOICE

1. The Real Estate Commissioner is:

   A. appointed by the Governor
   C. appointed by the Board of Governors

   B. appointed by the Legislature
   D. elected by members of CAR

2. Which of the following would be required to have a real estate license?

   A. A person who solicits or obtains listings
   C. A person who is an employee of a lending institution

   B. A person who is a cemetary owner
   D. A person who collects loans made on real property

3. How many clock hours of continuing education are required for renewal of a real estate license?

   A. 10
   C. 45

   B. 20
   D. 60

4. The salesperson's examination process consists of:

   A. 150 multiple choice question test
   C. 3 1/4 hour exam period

   B. photo identification required for entry
   D. all of the above

5. Bulk sales of inventory supplies and associated equipment requires, by law, notice to the:

   A. creditors
   C. Deparment of Motor Vehicles

   B. Department of Real Estate
   D. buyers

6. The name for a member of a real estate trade association that consists of predominantely Black members is:

   A. Realtor
   C. salesperson

   B. Realist
   D. Realtist

7. With regard to the recovery fund, what is the total maximum payable for one salesperson's offense?

   A. $20,000
   C. $50,000

   B. $40,000
   D. $100,000

8. To secure a salesperson's license, a person is NOT required to:

   A. be 18 years old
   C. be a U.S. citizen

   B. pass the exam
   D. file a set of fingerprints

9. A real estate licensee may sell a business in addition to real estate. This is called:

   A. business opportunities
   C. resale license

   B. business sales
   D. none of the above

10. Any person who is a salesperson or broker must also be a:

    A. Realtor
    C. independent board member

    B. Realtist
    D. none of the above

CHAPTER 15
Real Estate Math

Real estate, as you have learned, can be an extremely profitable profession. The licensee who is able to compute quickly and accurately the mathematics underlying most transactions will be in a better position to capitalize on opportunities as they arise.

This chapter will illustrate and explain some basic mathematical skills useful to a career in real estate. Familiarity with fundamental arithmetic and a few simple formulas along with plain common sense will provide the necessary background. Such knowledge will not only assist in the practice of real estate, but should also prove advantageous in passing the licensing exam. Figure 15-1 is a table of common measurements.

It might also prove to your advantage to bring a calculator with you when taking the salesperson's examination. The state permits applicants to use electronic calculators as long as they are battery operated, non-programmable, silent and without printout capability. Such a device will free you from tedious and time consuming arithmetic work in order to concentrate on the reasoning behind the problems you will encounter.

FIGURE 15-1

MEASUREMENTS

(A SALESPERSON SHOULD BE FAMILIAR WITH THESE)

LINEAR

1 foot (ft) = 12 inches (in.)
1 yard (yd) = 3 feet (ft.)
1 rod = 16.5 ft = 5.5 yd
1 mile = 5,280 ft = 1,760 yd = 320 rods

SQUARE

1 sq. ft. = 144 sq. in.
1 sq. yd. = 9 sq. ft.
1 acre = 43,560 sq. ft. = 4,840 sq. yd. = 160 sq. rods

CUBIC

1 cu. ft. = 1,728 cu. in.
1 cu. yd. = 27 cu. ft.

LAND DESCRIPTION

1 link = 7.92 inches
1 rod = 25 links
1 chain = 100 links = 66 ft. = 4 rods
1 mile = 80 chains
1 Acre = 43,560 sq. ft.
1 Township = 36 sections = 36 square miles = 23,040 acres
1 section = 1 mile square = 640 acres
= 1/36 of a township
1 circle = 360 degrees (°)
1 quadrant = 90 degrees (°)
1 degree (°) = 60 minutes (')
1 minute (') = 60 seconds (")

AREA MEASUREMENT

LAND AREA is the surface space between lot lines measured in square feet.

AREA OF A RECTANGULAR LOT

A RECTANGULAR LOT is a four-sided parcel whose opposite sides are equal in length and right angles are formed by the intersection of the sides. The dimensions of a rectangle are equal on two sides. Most lots encountered will be rectangular in shape.

How Do We Get "Square" Measurement?

The area of a rectangular or square lot is determined by multiplying the length by the width. The result is expressed in square feet, square yards or some similar expression. The formula is:

$$A = L \times W$$

$$AREA = LENGTH \times WIDTH$$

EXAMPLE: How many square feet would there be in a rectangular parcel 100 feet long and 50 feet wide?

$$A = L \times W$$

$$AREA = LENGTH \times WIDTH$$

$$AREA = 100 \text{ FEET} \times 50 \text{ FEET}$$

$$A = 100 \times 50$$

$$A = 5,000 \text{ SQUARE FEET}$$

ANSWER: The area of this lot is calculated to be 5,000 square feet.

AREA OF A TRIANGULAR LOT

A TRIANGULAR LOT is a three-sided parcel.

In order to determine the area of a triangular parcel, we must know the measurements of its base and height.

The *BASE OF A TRIANGULAR LOT* is the side that is horizontal. The *HEIGHT OF A TRIANGULAR LOT* is the perpendicular distance from the base to the highest point.

The area of a triangular parcel is determined by multiplying the base by the height, and then dividing by two. This is normally expressed by the formula:

$$A = \frac{B \times H}{2}$$

$$AREA = \frac{BASE \times HEIGHT}{2}$$

Here is a sample exercise for you to try:

EXAMPLE: How many square feet would there be in a triangular lot with a 150 foot base and a height of 100 feet?

$$A = \frac{B \times H}{2}$$

$$AREA = \frac{BASE \times HEIGHT}{2}$$

$$AREA = \frac{150 \text{ FEET} \times 100 \text{ FEET}}{2}$$

$$A = \frac{150 \times 100}{2}$$

$$A = \frac{15,000}{2}$$

$$A = 7,500 \text{ SQUARE FEET}$$

ANSWER: The area of this lot is 7,500 square feet.

AREA OF AN IRREGULAR LOT

An *IRREGULAR LOT is a parcel that does not consist of a single known shape.* Often the area of an irregular or circular parcel cannot be measured accurately without the help of a land measurement expert, such as a surveyor. Many times, though, an irregular lot is simply made up of a series of rectangles and triangles, the combined measures of which make up the measure of the whole. In these cases the square footage of the parcel can be determined through the use of techniques already described in this chapter.

The area of an irregular parcel is determined by breaking the lot up into the various rectangles and triangles which comprise it, and totaling their areas.

An Irregular Lot Problem

EXAMPLE: What would be the total area of the irregular lot shown below? Use the dimensions given to calculate your answer.

ANSWER: The irregular lot is broken up into a square, a rectangle and a triangle. The area of the parcel is the total of the areas of each of these.

TOTAL AREA = AREA (S) + AREA (R) + AREA (T)

TOTAL AREA = AREA SQUARE + AREA RECTANGLE + AREA TRIANGLE

AREA (S) = L X W

AREA (S) = LENGTH X WIDTH

AREA (S) = 40 FEET X 40 FEET

AREA (S) = 40 X 40

AREA (S) = 1,600 SQUARE FEET

The area of the square is 1,600 square feet.

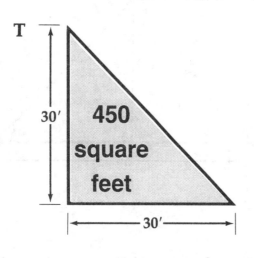

AREA (R) = L x W

AREA (R) = LENGTH x WIDTH

AREA (R) = 30 FEET x 25 FEET

AREA (R) = 30 x 25

AREA (R) = 750 SQUARE FEET

The area of the rectangular section is 750 square feet.

$$\text{AREA (T)} = \frac{B \times H}{2}$$

$$\text{AREA (T)} = \frac{BASE \times HEIGHT}{2}$$

$$\text{AREA (T)} = \frac{30 \text{ FEET} \times 30 \text{ FEET}}{2}$$

$$\text{AREA (T)} = \frac{30 \times 30}{2}$$

$$\text{AREA (T)} = \frac{900}{2}$$

AREA (T) = 450 SQUARE FEET

The area of the triangle is 450 square feet.

Irregular Problem Solution

AREA (S) = 1,600 SQUARE FEET

AREA (R) = 750 SQUARE FEET

AREA (T) = 450 SQUARE FEET

TOTAL AREA = AREA (S) + AREA (R) + AREA (T)

TOTAL AREA = 1,600 + 750 + 450

TOTAL AREA = 2,800 SQUARE FEET

The total area of this irregular lot is 2,800 square feet.

CONVERSION: SQUARE FEET TO SQUARE YARDS

Many questions on area will ask that you present the answer in square yards, rather than square feet. Conversion of square feet to square yards is a simple matter of dividing the answer by nine, because there are nine square feet in a square yard.

(3 feet x 3 feet = 9 square feet or 1 square yard)

Square yards, likewise, may be converted into square feet through multiplication by nine.

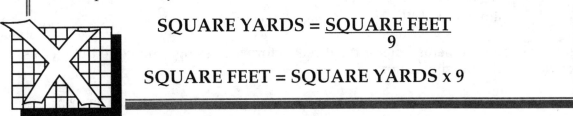

SQUARE YARDS = $\dfrac{\text{SQUARE FEET}}{9}$

SQUARE FEET = SQUARE YARDS x 9

VOLUME OF A STRUCTURE

STRUCTURAL VOLUME is the square or cubic measure of the space within a structure. Structural volume measurement is generally used when renting space in a warehouse type structure. Square measure is the area of the floor space, and it is determined through the use of the same techniques that apply to finding the square footage of a lot. Cubic measure is the area volume or total air space. **The cubic volume of a structure is determined by multiplying the interior length by the width and the height.** This can be expressed by the formula:

$$V = L \times W \times H$$

VOLUME = LENGTH x WIDTH x HEIGHT

EXAMPLE: How many cubic feet would there be in a room that is 15 feet long, 10 feet wide and 10 feet high?

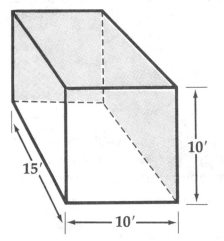

$$V = L \times W \times H$$
VOLUME = LENGTH x WIDTH x HEIGHT
VOLUME = 15 FEET x 10 FEET x 10 FEET
VOLUME = 15 x 10 x 10
VOLUME = 150 x 10
VOLUME = 1,500 CUBIC FEET

ANSWER: The cubic volume of this room would be 1,500 cubic feet.

PERCENTAGE PROBLEMS

The majority of math problems that you will encounter in real estate involve the use of percent. It is important, therefore, for you to understand certain general rules about percent problems before dealing with any of the particular types.

There are three factors in any percentage problem:

1. The amount *PAID (P)* *is the amount invested.*
2. The *RATE (%)* *is the percentage.*
3. The amount *MADE (M)* *is the amount earned.*

In percentage problems, **one** of the three factors is missing. There are three rules for finding the missing factor:

1) To find the amount **PAID (P)**, divide **MADE (M)** by the **RATE (%)**

2) To find the amount **MADE (M)**, multiply **PAID (P)** by **RATE (%)**

3) To find the **RATE (%)**, divide **MADE (M)** by **(PAID (P)**.

OTHER FACTOR TERMS

MADE	PAID	% RATE
Return	Investment	Rate of return
Profit	Cost	Rate of profit
Commission	Price	Rate of commission
Net income	Value	Rate of capitalization
Interest	Principal	Rate of interest

Whenever you are working a percent problem, you will be dealing with one of these equations, or a modification of one of them. The typical percent problem will supply you with two of the variables. You may easily determine the third through the use of the proper equation.

HUBER'S PYRAMID

If you feel that you might have trouble committing the percent equations to memory, you might want to make use of Huber's percent problem pyramid instead. Shown in Figure 15-2, this diagram points out what operation is required to find each of the variables.

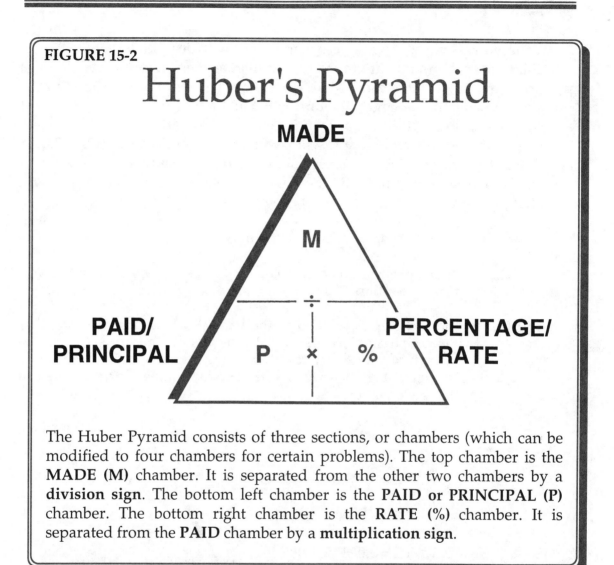

FIGURE 15-2

Huber's Pyramid

MADE

M

÷

PAID/
PRINCIPAL

P × %

PERCENTAGE/
RATE

The Huber Pyramid consists of three sections, or chambers (which can be modified to four chambers for certain problems). The top chamber is the **MADE (M)** chamber. It is separated from the other two chambers by a **division sign**. The bottom left chamber is the **PAID or PRINCIPAL (P)** chamber. The bottom right chamber is the **RATE (%)** chamber. It is separated from the **PAID** chamber by a **multiplication sign**.

To use the Huber Pyramid, simply cover the chamber you are trying to find and then perform the required math:

1) **To find M, cover M and multiply P x %**

2) **To find P, cover P and divide M by %**

3) **To find %, cover % and divide M by P**

When doing a math problem involving three or more variables, first draw the Huber Pyramid and plug in the available figures, then perform the required action.

Your success in solving percent problems will depend largely on your ability to spot and identify the three variables as they are presented. In most problems the **PAID** and the **MADE** will both be labeled as money. But the **PAID** (generally the larger amount) will usually be given as a base amount such as a price, investment or loan balance. The **MADE**, on the other hand, (generally the smaller amount) will be a sum made or lost from the **PAID**. Returns, profits, net income, taxes, interest and commissions are all common labels identifying the **MADE**. The **RATE** is easy to identify because it will always be given as some form of a percentage (%).

Here is a sample percent exercise for you to try:

EXAMPLE: Your agency purchases a lot for $9,000. In selling it later, you made a profit of $3,000. What was your percentage of profit?

ANSWER: The first step is to identify the variables. The principal (paid) is the purchase price of $9,000. The result (made) is the $3,000 margin of profit that resulted from the transaction. The rate is the percentage that we are asked to determine. To find it we use the rate equation.

$$\% = \frac{M}{P}$$

RATE = MADE ÷ PAID

RATE = $3,000 ÷ $9,000

RATE = 3,000 ÷ 9,000

RATE = .3333 = 33.33%

So, your agency made a 33.33% profit on the transaction.

The above problem was looking for the rate (a percentage). The decimal number .3333 is not a percentage and so it had to be converted into a percentage in the final step of the sample exercise.

To convert a decimal number into a percentage, you simply move the decimal point two spaces to the right, adding zeros if needed. Figure 15-3 gives some examples of this type of conversion.

FIGURE 15-3
DECIMAL TO PERCENT

.095 = 9.5%

1.2 = 120%

.009 = .9%

In problems where you are asked to compute the results (paid) and the principal (made) it will be necessary for you to multiply or divide by the rate. In these cases you will have to convert the percentage into a decimal before completing the operation. This is done by reversing the process above: Move the decimal point two spaces to the left, and drop the percent sign. This changes a percent into its equivalent decimal form. Figure 15-4 demonstrates this process.

FIGURE 15-4
PERCENT TO DECIMAL

8.5% = .085

50.% = .5

110% = 1.1

Another simple way to remember percents is to relate them to dollars and cents.

10 cents = .10	10% = .10
50 cents = .50	50% = .50
$1.50 = 1.50	150% = 1.50

DETERMINING COMMISSIONS AND SELLING PRICE

A *COMMISSION RATE is a percentage of the selling price that is used to calculate the commission.* The *COMMISSION is the dollar amount received by a real estate agent for completing the sale.* A real estate agent wants to know how much he or she will be paid for doing his or her job. Most real estate salespeople are paid on a commission basis. As a licensed real estate agent, one of your most pleasant duties will be determining your commission.

When dealing with math problems in real estate, it is important to translate "words" into "math words" and "math symbols."

WORD	MATH WORD	MATH SYMBOL
OF	MULTIPLY	X
IS	EQUALS	=

In commission problems you are supplied with the principal **(PAID)**, which is the property selling price, and the rate **(%)**, which is the rate of commission and asked to find the result **(MADE)**, the agent's commission. Such problems use the result equation: **M = P x %.**

EXAMPLE: You have completed the sale of a $100,000 home. The rate of commission is 6%. How much money have you made?

$$M = P \times \%$$

MADE = PAID x RATE

MADE = $100,000 x 6% (.06)

MADE = $6,000

ANSWER: Your commission is $6,000.

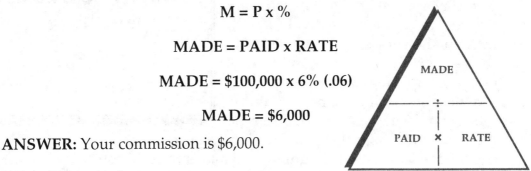

Splitting Commissions

Most often when you have completed a sale, your brokerage will not be entitled to the entire commission. If you were representing the seller, for example, you might very likely split your commission with a broker and salesperson for the buyer. You will have earned a percentage of the amount earned by your broker, depending on the percentage both of you have agreed to in advance. The rates here are negotiable and usually vary with your experience and success.

When determining the splits of a commission, you use the result **(MADE)** equation. The total commission represents the principal **(PAID)** and the percentage **(RATE)** is whatever rate of commission was agreed to between the parties. Figure 15-5 illustrates how a commission might be split.

FIGURE 15-5

$2,100 + $900 + $1,800 + $1,200 = $6,000

PROFIT AND LOSS

When dealing with profit and loss problems, you must establish the value, or cost, before profit (+) or loss (-).

The terms "value" and "cost" are interchangeable in real estate math problems; **it is what you paid for the property.**

Key terms when working profit and loss problems:

1) **SELLING PRICE** - the value **after** the profit or loss has been added or subtracted from the original cost.

2) **COST -** the value **before** the profit or loss has been added or subtracted. Cost is often stated as **purchase price** or **original price**.

3) **1 + % PROFIT** - in a profit problem, the percent used in the formula will **always** be greater than 100%; in other words, the original cost (100%) plus the percent of profit. If you sold your property for 40% more than you paid for it, your selling price (100% + 40% = 140%) would be the cost x 140 % (1.40). To find the amount of profit (+40%), you would subtract the **cost** from the **selling price**.

4) **1 - % LOSS** - for a loss problem, the percent used will **always** be less than 100%; in other words, the original cost (100%) minus the percent of loss. If you sold your property for 25% less than what you paid for it, your selling price (100% - 25% = 75%) would be the cost x 75% (.75). To find the amount of loss (-25%), you would subtract the **selling price** from the **cost**.

The key to working these types of problems is to determine what percent to use.

Chapter 15

EXAMPLE: Ms. Smith sold her home for $250,000, which was 8% more than she paid for the property. How much did Ms. Smith pay for the property?

SOLUTION: Remember that profit is **always a % of cost**. If we use the Huber Pyramid, we know the Selling price (MADE) is $250,000 and the rate (%) is 108% (100% + 8%). To find the cost (PAID), we would divide **MADE by %**.

ANSWER: (rounded)
$250,000 divided by 108% (1.08) = **$231,481**
Ms. Smith paid $231,481 for her property.

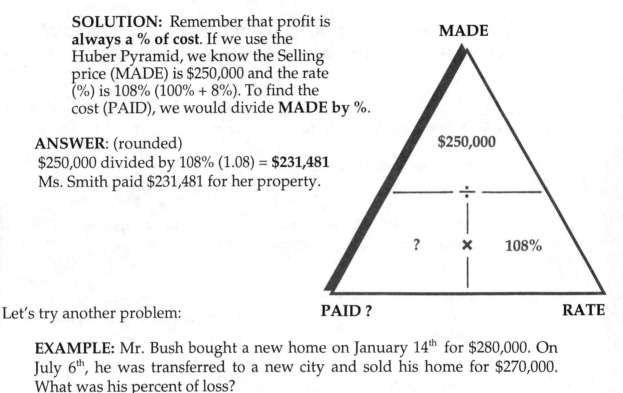

Let's try another problem:

EXAMPLE: Mr. Bush bought a new home on January 14th for $280,000. On July 6th, he was transferred to a new city and sold his home for $270,000. What was his percent of loss?

REMEMBER: the percent of loss is based on what the home **cost**, not what it sold for.

SOLUTION: First we determine the **amount of loss**: $280,000 - $270,000 = $10,000. Now we plug in the figures: MADE ($10,000) divided by PAID ($280,000) = percent (%) of loss.

ANSWER: Mr. Bush's percent of loss was 4% (.03572, or .04).

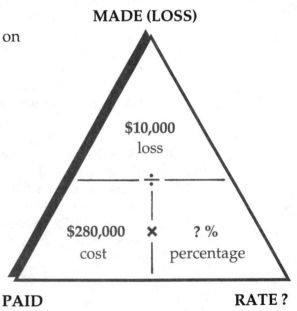

Remember: In profit problems, percent will always be greater than 100%. In loss problems, percent will always be less than 100%.

PRINCIPAL AND INTEREST CALCULATIONS

Use a 30-day month (banker's month) in calculating interest payments; thus 1 year = 360 days (statutory year).

Great amounts of capital are necessary to complete most real estate transactions. As a licensed real estate agent, financing will often be one of the major concerns of your clients. It will be advantageous, therefore, for you to be able to provide loan counseling as a part of your services. Essential to this service will be your ability to readily calculate principal and interest payments.

INTEREST *is a fee paid for the use of other people's money, stated in dollars and cents.* When one leases an apartment, he or she pays rent to the landlord for the use of the property. Similarly, when one borrows money he or she pays "rent" to the lender for the use of the money. This "rent" is called interest. **SIMPLE INTEREST** *is the term used to describe interest on the unpaid balance.*

Most interest problems will supply you with the principal **(PAID)**, which is the amount borrowed, and the rate **(%)**, which is the percentage being charged. You are asked to determine the interest **(MADE)**. We learned this formula earlier:

$$M = P \times R \, (\%)$$

There is an extra variable that is a factor in all interest problems: time. The duration of the loan determines how much interest is owed at the annual rate. One year equals one, one month equals 1/12 and one day equals 1/360. In order to take this factor into consideration, we modify the MADE equation slightly, with **MADE (M)** becoming **INTEREST (I)**:

$$I = P \times R \times T$$

INTEREST (MADE) = PRINCIPAL (PAID) x RATE (%) x TIME

When doing principal and interest problems, you are trying to find one of four unknowns: **INTEREST (I), PRINCIPAL (P), INTEREST RATE (R) OR TIME (T).**

We will use this modified Huber
Pyramid to work these types of problems:

> **Remember:** To use the Huber Pyramid, simply cover the chamber you are trying to find and then perform the required math.

$$I = P \times R \times T$$

Interest Problem

INTEREST is the payment made for using other people's money. The formula for finding interest is:

$$I = P \times R \times T$$

Here is a sample exercise for you to try:

EXAMPLE: What would be the interest due on a loan of $10,000, borrowed at 9%, for a period of 2 years?

$I = P \times R \times T$

INTEREST = PRINCIPAL x RATE x TIME

INTEREST = $10,000 x 9% x 2 YEARS

INTEREST = $10,000 x .09 x 2

INTEREST = $900 x 2

INTEREST = $1,800

ANSWER: The interest would be $1,800.

Principle Problem

As used in real estate finance problems, **PRINCIPAL** *is the amount borrowed in dollars.* To find the principal (amount borrowed), we would use the following formula:

$$P = \frac{I}{R \times T}$$

EXAMPLE: Mr. Johnson has a trust deed loan with annual interest payments of $5,200. If the rate of interest is 10%, how much did he borrow?

SOLUTION: We know that the **INTEREST (I)** is $5,200, the **RATE (%)** is 10% (.10) and the **TIME (T)** is 1 year. Using the above formula:

$$P = \frac{\$5,200}{.10 \times 1} = \frac{\$5,200}{.10} = \$52,000$$

ANSWER: Mr. Johnson borrowed $52,000.

Interest Rate Problem

Figure 15-6 explains some useful terms in calculating interest rate problems.

FIGURE 15-6 *In calculating interest rate problems:*

Annual = once a year
Semiannual = twice a year at 6 month intervals
Biannual = twice a year
Bimonthly = 6 times a year (every 2 months)
Monthly = 12 times a year
Semimonthly = twice a month
Biennial = once every 2 years
1 Year = 12 months = 52 weeks = 360 days
1 Month = 30 days

The **INTEREST RATE** *is the percent of interest charged.* The purpose of principal and interest problems is to determine what we are paying (**INTEREST**) for the use of the amount borrowed (**PRINCIPAL**) and expressing that amount as a percentage (**INTEREST RATE**). We use the following formula to find the interest rate:

$$R = \frac{I}{P \times T}$$

EXAMPLE: Ms. Bishop borrows $150,000 from 1ST Bank to purchase a condominium. If, after the first year, she owes the lender $15,500 interest, what is the rate of interest?

SOLUTION: We know that the **INTEREST (I)** is $15,000, the **PRINCIPAL (P)** is $150,000 and the **TIME (T)** is one year.

Using the above formula:

$$R = \frac{\$15,000}{\$150,000 \times 1} = \frac{\$15,000}{\$150,000} = (.10) \text{ or } 10\%$$

ANSWER: Ms. Bishop's rate of interest is 10%.

Unless stated otherwise, the interest rate is assumed to be in annual terms.

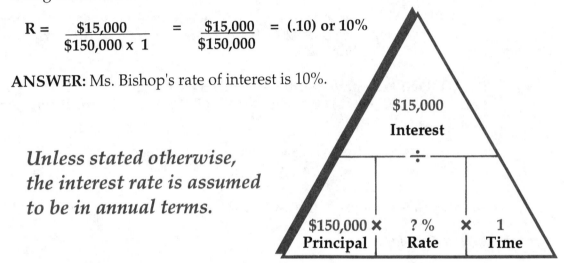

Time Problem

TIME is used for periods less than or greater than one year. Time is expressed as a fraction or percent of a year (1/12th or .0833) if a payment is to be made monthly. As stated earlier, **interest rates** are assumed to be annual unless otherwise stated. However the payment of **principal and interest** is usually done on a monthly basis. The previous problems used a one year time period. If the time period is more or less than a year, then **TIME (T)** takes on a different value:

Monthly payment: T = 1/12   or   .0833

Semiannual payment: T = 1/2   or   .5

EXAMPLE: Mr. Philips borrows $200,000 at 9.5 % interest. What is the monthly interest payment?

SOLUTION: PRINCIPAL (P) is $200,000, **RATE (R)** is 9.5% and **TIME (T)** is 1/12 or .0833.

$$I = P \times R \times T$$

I = $200,000 x .095 x .0833 = $1,583

ANSWER: Mr. Philips makes a monthly interest payment of $1,583.

DISCOUNT POINTS (POINTS)

1 discount point = 1% of the loan amount

1 discount point raises yield 1/8 of 1%

DISCOUNT POINTS *are charges made by a lender to increase the yield on a loan: one point equals 1% of the loan and one point raises the loan yield by 1/8 of 1% for 8 years.*

EXAMPLE: Mr. and Mrs. Majors are purchasing a house for $155,000. They will put $30,000 down and borrow the rest, which will include a 4 point charge by the savings bank. How much will the points cost them?

SOLUTION: First we must determine the amount being borrowed:

$$\$155,000 - \$30,000 = \$125,000$$

Next we compute the discount rate:

1 point = 1% of the loan amount = .01 x $125,000 = $1,250

Finally, we calculate the amount of discount:

4 x $1,250 = $5,000

ANSWER: The Majors will pay $5,000 for the discount points

DETERMINING PRORATIONS

Buyer's ownership starts on the day of closing.

PRORATION *is the process of proportionately dividing (prorating) expenses or income to the precise date that escrow closes, or any other date previously agreed upon. Its purpose is to apportion income and expense items correctly between the parties of a sale. These are divided (or **prorated**) in proportion to the time that each owned or will own the property. In analyzing proration problems, you will need to determine **who** will be credited with a dollar amount at closing. The next thing that you need to consider is **how much** will be credited.*

Items that are normally prorated include mortgage interest, taxes, fire insurance premiums, rent and assessments. In some areas, prorations are also known as **adjustments** or **apportionments**.

Proration involves dividing the dollar amount associated with the time an expense or income occurred between two parties (the buyer and seller). Rent and interest are usually paid in one month intervals, property taxes are paid every six months or once a year and fire insurance premiums can be for one, two or even as many as five years. A important question that must be answered is who gets credit for an item. The rules are simple.

BUYER'S AND SELLER'S SETTLEMENT STATEMENTS (ALSO SEE CHAPTER 7)

DOUBLE-ENTRY BOOKKEEPING is the procedure used to complete a settlement statement. (Accountants will find this the opposite of true accounting.) The statement consists of two parts: a **buyer's statement** and a **seller's statement**. Each of these is divided into a **debit column** and a **credit column**.

A *DEBIT is something that is owed.* A debit entry for a buyer is anything charged against or subtracted from his or her account. The purchase price of the property is an example of something debited to the buyer. A debit entry for a seller means the same thing. Unpaid property taxes are a good example.

A *CREDIT is something that is received.* A credit entry for a buyer is anything received or added to his or her account. The deposit made on the property is a good example of something credited to the buyer. A good example of a credit entry for the seller would be prepaid property taxes.

If an item was **paid** before closing, the buyer's closing statement will be debited and the seller's statement will be credited. If **income** was received before closing, the buyer's statement will be credited and the seller's statement will be debited. Though items on closing statements follow no set order of entry, the **purchase price is usually the first entry and the amount due from/to buyer to close and the amount due to/from seller to close are the last entries.**

On an escrow statement a CREDIT is something that is received and a DEBIT is something that is owed.

RENTS (INCOME)

In determining the proration of rents, it is important to remember that all escrow companies use a **30-day base month** (banker's month) and a **360-day statutory year**. The portion of income that is granted to each party can be represented as a fraction. The denominator will be 30, while the numerator will vary depending upon what day in the month escrow closes. It is important to remember that the buyer's ownership starts on the day of closing.

> **EXAMPLE:** If the escrow closes on the 21st day of the month, how would you divide a prepaid rent of $1,500 between the seller and the buyer?

> **ANSWER:** The seller's share would be 20/30 of the whole, because he holds ownership **through** the 20th day. The share of the other 10 days (10/30) would go to the buyer.

> | SELLER'S SHARE | BUYER'S SHARE |
> |---|---|
> | $\dfrac{20}{30}$ X 1,500 = $1,000 | $\dfrac{10}{30}$ X 1,500 = $500 |

So, the seller would receive $1,000 of the rent money, while the buyer would be prorated $500.

PROPERTY TAXES (EXPENSES) BUYER'S AND SELLER'S

Property taxes are prorated either from July 1st, the beginning of the fiscal year, or January 1st, the middle of the fiscal year. Since each of these two installments covers a six-month period, the portion of the expense prorated to each party is represented as a fraction with a denominator of 6. The numerator varies depending upon what month in the six-month period escrow closes.

> **EXAMPLE:** The second installment of property tax on a home is $500. The seller has paid this tax, which covers a six-month period ending July 1st. If he sells this property and escrow closes on April 1st, how much of the $500 is his share in the expense? How much would the buyer have to reimburse?

> **ANSWER:** The seller's share would be 3/6 of the tax bill, while the buyer would also be responsible for 3/6. This is because both the seller and the buyer owned the property for 3 months during the six-month period.

SELLER'S SHARE	BUYER'S SHARE
$\dfrac{3}{6} \times 500 = \$250$	$\dfrac{3}{6} \times 500 = \$250$

Each would be responsible for $250 of the property tax; the buyer having to reimburse the seller, who already paid the entire property tax bill.

DEPRECIATION (For Tax Purposes)

DEPRECIATION (for income taxes) is a loss in the value of buildings and other improvements. All new depreciation schedules for normal income tax purposes involving real property must be straight-line.

STRAIGHT-LINE DEPRECIATION

STRAIGHT-LINE DEPRECIATION is a method of computing depreciation for income tax purposes in which the difference between the original cost and no salvage value is deducted in installments evenly over the life of the asset. It is based upon the assumption that depreciation is dependent solely on the passage of time. Depreciation is spread uniformly over the useful life of a property (building).

> *When doing depreciation problems, it is important to remember that land does not depreciate.*

To find depreciation using the straight-line method use:

ANNUAL DEPRECIATION (A) = $\dfrac{\text{COST OF IMPROVEMENTS (V)}}{\text{ECONOMIC LIFE (E)}}$

 or simplified:

$$A = \frac{V}{E}$$

Let's try a problem using straight-line depreciation:

EXAMPLE: Mr. and Mrs. Roberts purchased some real property for $475,000. The land was valued at $200,000. The improvements had an estimated economic life of 27.5 years. What would be the depreciated value of the property after 17 years?

ANSWER: We must first determine the value of the depreciable asset (improvements) because land is not depreciated.

$475,000 (land and improvements)
- 200,000 (land)
$275,000 (value of improvements)

$$A = \frac{V}{E} \;=\; A = \frac{\$275,000}{27.5} = \$10,000 \text{ depre. per year}$$

$10,000 x 17 years = $170,000 accumulated depreciation

$275,000 - $170,000 = $105,000 depreciated value of the improvements only

$105,000 + $200,000 (value of land) = $305,000

$305,000 is the depreciated book value of the property.

The IRS allows straight line depreciation of 27.5 years on residential properties and 39 years on commercial properties.

TM

I wish you the best of luck in your real estate career, whether it be as a homeowner, investor or salesperson. The future is yours!

http://etc.com (Educational Textbook Company)

Walter Roy Huber

Chapter 15

A. Area
B. Rectangular Lot
C. Triangular Lot
D. Debit
E. Credit
F. Irregular Lot
G. Cubic Area
H. Principal (amount paid)

I. Interest Rate
J. Result (amount made)
K. Commission
L. Interest
M. Proration
N. Depreciation
O. Straight-line Depreciation
P. Discount Points (points)

1.____ The amount of money borrowed.

2.____ Money owed; it is shown as what on the settlement statement.

3.____ The up-front charge by a lender to obtain and to increase the yield on a loan.

4.____ The amount paid to a real estate broker usually expressed as a percentage of the sale price.

5.____ To divide property taxes, insurance premiums, rental income, etc. between buyer and seller proportionately to time of use, or the date of closing.

6.____ Decrease in value to real property improvements by any cause.

7.____ The rent, or charge, for the use of money.

8.____ The surface of land or building. Length (in feet) times width (in feet).

9.____ The area of this shaped lot is obtained by multiplying base times height and dividing by 2.

10.____ Money received; it is shown as what on the settlement statement.

11.____ Principal (paid) times rate (%) equals?

12.____ The percentage paid for the use of borrowed money. Usually expressed as an annual percentage.

13.____ Equal amount of depreciation each year. A loss in the value of improvements, used as an accounting (income tax) procedure.

14.____ A lot with an unusual shape.

15.____ The result of multiplying length times width times height.

16.____ Four-sided figure with opposite sides equal in length and intersecting corners forming right angles.

MULTIPLE CHOICE

1. Ms. Donaldson exchanged her fourplex (fair market value $100,000 with a loan of $52,000) for a larger building (fair market value $150,000 with a loan of $42,000). Using only the above figures, how much money did Donaldson have to pay to complete the exchange?

   A. $48,000
   C. $60,000
   B. $52,000
   D. $108,000

2. Carol borrowed $5,200 and signed a straight note with an interest rate of 7% per annum. If she paid $1,125 in interest during the term of the note, what was the term of the note?

   A. 22 months
   C. 32 months
   B. 27 months
   D. 37 months

3. A woman owns a rental unit that nets her $450 per month. She realizes a 10% return on her investment each year. What is her investment in the property?

   A. $45,000
   C. $54,000
   B. $48,500
   D. None of the above

4. The assessed value of a piece of property is $48,700. The tax rate is $1.02 per $100 of assessed valuation. The tax is:

   A. $496.74
   C. $584.40
   B. $489.60
   D. $594.14

5. How much would have to be invested at 7% in order to provide an investor with $640 monthly income?

   A. $9,143
   C. $109,714
   B. $91,429
   D. $53,760

6. The second quarter interest on a $7,600 term loan at 8% interest is:

   A. $76
   C. $608
   B. $152
   D. none of the above

7. An apartment complex cost $450,000. It brings in a net income of $3,000 per month. The owner is making what percentage of return on her investment?

   A. 7%
   C. 11%
   B. 8%
   D. 12%

8. Broker Jones negotiates a lease for 3,000 square feet of warehouse storage space at a monthly rental of $0.50 per square foot. Jones' commission is 8% of the first year's gross. Jones will receive:

   A. $1180
   C. $1440
   B. $1340
   D. none of the above

9. Frank holds a five-year trust deed and note that was paid off at 7.2% interest per annum. If the total interest he received from the borrower was $4,140, what, approximately, was the original amount of the loan?

   A. $11,500
   C. $33,650
   B. $29,700
   D. $57,500

10. A builder constructed a home for $350,000 and sold it for a 20% profit. What is the amount of the profit?

    A. $17,500
    C. $35,000
    B. $20,000
    D. $70,000

Appendix A
Glossary

ALTA Title Policy (American Land Title Association): A type of title insurance policy issued by title insurance companies which expands the risks normally insured against under the standard type policy to include unrecorded mechanic's liens; unrecorded physical easements; facts a physical survey would show; water and mineral rights; and rights of parties in possession, such as tenants and buyers under unrecorded instruments.

ALTA Owner's Policy (Standard Form B1962, as amended 1969): An owner's extended coverage policy that provides buyers or owners the same protection the ALTA policy gives to lenders.

Abatement of Nuisance: Extinction or termination of a nuisance.

Absolute Fee Simple Title: Absolute or fee simple title is one that is absolute and unqualified. It is the best title one can have.

Abstract of Judgment: A condensation of the essential provisions of a court judgment.

Abstract of Title: A summary or digest of the conveyances, transfers, and any other facts relied on as evidence of title, together with any other elements of record which may impair the title.

Abstraction: A method of valuing land. The indicated value of the improvement is deducted from the sale price.

Acceleration Clause: Clause in trust deed or mortgage giving lender right to call all sums owing him to be immediately due and payable upon the happening of a certain event.

Acceptance: When the seller's or agent's principal agrees to the terms of the agreement of sale and approves the negotiation on the part of the agent and acknowledges receipt of the deposit in subscribing to the agreement of sale, that act is termed an acceptance.

Access Right: The right of an owner to have ingress and egress to and from his property.

Accretion: An addition to land from natural causes as, for example, from gradual action of the ocean or river waters.

Accrued Depreciation: The difference between the cost of replacement new as of the date of the appraisal and the present appraised value.

Accrued Items of Expense: Those incurred expenses which are not yet payable. The seller's accrued expenses are credited to the purchaser in a closing statement.

Acknowledgment: A formal declaration before a duly authorized officer by a person who has executed an instrument that such execution is his act and deed.

Acoustical tile: Blocks of fiber, mineral or metal, with small holes or rough textured surface to absorb sound, used as covering for interior walls and ceilings.

Acquisition: The act or process by which a person procures property.

Acre: A measure of land equaling 160 square rods, or 4,840 square yards, or 43,560 square feet, or a tract about 208.71 feet square.

Adjustments: A means by which characteristics of a residential property are regulated by dollar amount or percentage to conform to similar characteristics of another residential property.

Administrator: A person appointed by the probate court to administer the estate of a person deceased.

Ad Valorem: A Latin phrase meaning, "according to value." Usually used in connection with real estate taxation.

Advance: Transfer of funds from a lender to a borrower in advance on a loan.

Advance Commitment: The institutional investor's prior agreement to provide long-term financing upon completion of construction.

Advance Fee: A fee paid in advance of any services rendered. Specifically that unethical practice of obtaining a fee in advance for the advertising of property or businesses for sale, with no obligation to obtain a buyer, by persons representing themselves as real estate licensees, or representatives of licensed real estate firms.

Adverse Possession: The open and notorious possession and occupancy under an evident claim or right, in denial or opposition to the title of another claimant.

Affiant: A person who has made an affidavit.

Affidavit: A statement or declaration reduced to writing sworn to or affirmed before some officer who has authority to administer an oath or affirmation.

Affidavit of Title: A statement in writing, made under oath by seller or grantor, acknowledged before a Notary Public in which the affiant identifies himself and his marital status certifying that since the examination of title on the contract date there are no judgments, bankruptcies or divorces, or unrecorded deeds, contracts, unpaid repairs or improvements or defects of title known to him and that he is in possession of the property.

Affirm: To confirm, to aver, to ratify, to verify.

AFLB: Accredited Farm and Land Broker.

Agency: The relationship between principal and agent which arises out of a contract, either expressed or implied, written or oral, wherein the agent is employed by the principal to do certain acts dealing with a third party.

Agent: One who represents another from whom he has derived authority.

Agreement of Sale: A written agreement or contract between seller and purchaser in which they reach a meeting of minds on the terms and conditions of the sale.

Air Rights: The rights in real property to use the air space above the surface of the land.

Alienation: The transferring of property to another; the transfer of property and possession of lands, or other things, from one person to another.

Allodial Tenure: A real property ownership system where ownership may be complete except for those rights held by government. Allodial is in contrast to feudal tenure.

Alluvion: (Alluvium) Soil deposited by accretion. Increase of earth on a shore or bank of a river.

Amenities: Satisfaction of enjoyable living to be derived from a home; conditions of agreeable living or a beneficial influence arising from the location or improvements.

American Institute of Real Estate Appraisers: A trade association of real estate appraisers.

AMO: Accredited Management Organization.

Amortization: The liquidation of a financial obligation on an installment basis; also, recovery: over a period, of cost or value.

Amortized Loan: A loan that is completely paid off, interest and principal, by a series of regular payments that are equal or nearly equal. Also called a Level Payments Loan.

Annuity: A series of assured equal or nearly equal payments to be made over a period of time or it may be a lump sum payment to be made in the future. The installment payments due to the landlord under a lease is an Annuity. So are the installment payments due to a lender. In real estate finance we are most concerned with the first definition.

Anticipation, Principle of: Affirms that value is created by anticipated benefits to be derived in the future.

Appraisal: An estimate and opinion of value; a conclusion resulting from the analysis of facts.

Appraiser: One qualified by education, training and experience who is hired to estimate the value of real and personal property based on experience, judgment, facts, and use of formal appraisal processes.

Appropriation of: A legal term including the act or acts involved in the taking and reducing to personal possession of water occurring in a stream or other body of water, and if applying such water to beneficial uses or purposes.

Appurtenance: Something annexed to another thing which may be transferred incident to it. That which belongs to another thing, as a barn, dwelling, garage, or orchard is incident to the land to which it is attached.

Architectural Style: Generally the appearance and character of a building's design and construction.

ASA: American Society of Appraisers.

Assessed Valuation: A valuation placed upon property by a public officer or board, as a basis for taxation.

Assessed Value: Value placed on property as a basis for taxation.

Assessment: The valuation of property for the purpose of levying a tax or the amount of the tax levied.

Assessor: The official who has the responsibility of determining assessed values.

Assignment: A transfer or making over to another of the whole of any property, real or personal, in possession or in action, or of any estate or right therein.

Assignor: One who assigns or transfers property.

Assigns; Assignees: Those to whom property shall have been transferred.

Assumption Agreement: An undertaking or adoption of a debt or obligation primarily resting upon another person.

Assumption Fee: A lender's charge for changing over and processing new records for a new owner who is assuming an existing loan.

Assumption of Mortgage: The taking of title to property by a grantee, wherein he assumes liability for payment of an existing note secured by a mortgage or deed of trust against the property; becoming a co-guarantor for the payment of a mortgage or deed of trust note.

Attachment: Seizure of property by court order, usually done to have it available in event a judgment is obtained in a pending suit.

Attest: To affirm to be true or genuine; an official act establishing authenticity.

Attorney in Fact: One who is authorized to perform certain acts for another under a power of attorney; power of attorney may be limited to a specific act or acts, or be general.

Avulsion: The sudden tearing away or removal of land by action of water flowing over or through it.

Axial Growth: City growth which occurs along main transportation routes. Usually takes the form of star-shaped extensions outward from the center.

Backfill: The replacement of excavated earth into a hole or against a structure.

Balloon Payment: Where the final installment payment on a note is greater than the preceding installment payments and it pays the note in full, such final installment is termed a balloon payment.

Bargain and Sale Deed: Any deed that recites a consideration and purports to convey the real estate; a bargain and sale deed with a covenant against the grantor's acts is one in which the grantor warrants that he himself has done nothing to harm or cloud the title.

Baseboard: A board placed against the wall around a room next to the floor.

Base and Meridian: Imaginary lines used by surveyors to find and describe the location of private or public lands.

Base Molding: Molding used at top of baseboard.

Base Shoe: Molding used at junction of baseboard and floor. Commonly called a carpet strip.

Batten: Narrow strips of wood or metal used to cover joints, interiorly or exteriorly; also used for decorative effect.

Beam: A structural member transversely supporting a load.

Bearing Wall or Partition: A wall or partition supporting any vertical load in addition to its own weight.

Bench Marks: A location indicated on a durable marker by surveyors.

Beneficiary: (1) One entitled to the benefit of a trust; (2) One who receives profit from an estate, the title of which is vested in a trustee; (3) The lender on the security of a note and deed of trust.

Bequeath: To give or hand down by will; to leave by will.

Bequest: That which is given by the terms of a will.

Betterment: An improvement upon property which increases the property value and is considered as a capital asset or distinguished from repairs or replacements where the original character or cost is unchanged.

Bill of Sale: A written instrument given to pass title of personal property from vendor to the vendee.

Binder: An agreement to consider a down payment for the purchase of real estate as evidence of good faith on the part of the purchaser. Also, a notation of coverage on an insurance policy, issued by an agent, and given to the insured prior to issuing of the policy.

Blacktop: Asphalt paving used in streets and driveways.

Blanket Mortgage: A single mortgage which covers more than one piece of real estate.

Blighted Area: A declining area in which real property values are seriously affected by destructive economic forces, such as encroaching inharmonious property usages, infiltration of lower social and economic classes of inhabitants, and/or rapidly depreciating buildings.

Board foot: A unit of measurement of lumber; one foot wide, one foot long, one inch thick; 144 cubic inches.

Bona Fide: In good faith, without fraud.

Bond: An obligation under seal. A real estate bond is a written obligation issued on security of a mortgage or trust deed.

Bracing: Framing lumber nailed at an angle in order to provide rigidity.

Breach: The breaking of a law, or failure of duty, either by omission or commission.

Breezeway: A covered porch or passage, open on two sides, connecting house and garage or two parts of the house.

Bridging: Small wood or metal pieces used to brace floor joists.

Broker: A person employed by another, to carry on any of the activities listed in the license law definition of a broker, for a fee.

B.T.U.: British thermal unit. The quantity of heat required to raise the temperature of one pound of water one degree Fahrenheit.

Building Code: A systematic regulation of construction of buildings within a municipality established by ordinance or law.

Building Line: A line set by law a certain distance from a street line in front of which an owner cannot build on his lot. (A setback line.)

Building, Market Value of: The sum of money which the presence of that structure adds to or subtracts from the value of the land it occupies. Land valued on the basis of highest and best use.

Building Paper: A heavy waterproofed paper used as sheathing in wall or roof construction as a protection against air passage and moisture.

Built-in: Cabinets or similar features built as part of the house.

Bundle of Rights: Beneficial interests or rights.

CBD: Central Business District.

CCIM: Certified Commercial Investment Member.

CC and R's: Abbreviation for covenants, conditions and restrictions.

CPM: Certified Property Manager, a designation of the Institute of Real Estate Management.

Capital Assets: Assets of a permanent nature used in the production of an income, such as: land, buildings, machinery, and equipment, etc. Under income tax law, it is usually distinguishable from "inventory" which comprises assets held for sale to customers in ordinary course of the taxpayers' trade or business.

Capital Gain: Income from a sale of an asset rather than from the general business activity. Capital gains are generally taxed at a lower rate than ordinary income.

Capitalization: In appraising, determining value of property by considering net income and percentage of reasonable return on the investment. Thus, the value of an income property is determined by dividing *annual net income* by the *Capitalization Rate.*

Capitalization Rate: The rate of interest which is considered a reasonable return on the investment, and used in the process of determining value based upon net income. It may also be described as the yield rate that is necessary to attract the money of the average investor to a particular kind of investment. In the case of land improvements which depreciate to this yield rate is added a factor to take into consideration the annual amortization factor necessary to recapture the initial investment in improvements. This amortization factor can be determined in various ways: (1) straight-line depreciation method, (2) Inwood Tables, and (3) Hoskold Tables. (To explore this subject in greater depth, the student should refer to current real estate appraisal texts.)

Casement Window: Frames of wood or metal, which swing outward.

Cash Flow: The net income generated by a property before depreciation and other noncash expenses.

Caveat Emptor: "Let the buyer beware." The buyer must examine the goods or property and buy at his own risk.

Center of Influence: One, who, by nature of his relationships is in a position to sway others.

Certificate of Reasonable Value (CRV): The federal Veterans Administration appraisal commitment of property value.

Certificate of Taxes Due: A written statement or guaranty of the condition of the taxes on a certain property, made by the County Treasurer of the county wherein the property is located. Any loss resulting to any person from an error in a tax certificate shall be paid by the county which such treasurer represents.

Chain: A unit of measurement used by surveyors. A chain consists of 100 links equal to 66 feet.

Chain of Title: A history of conveyances and encumbrances affecting the title from the time the original patent was granted, or as far back as records are. available.

Change, Principle of: Holds that it is the future, not the past, which is of prime importance in estimating value.

Characteristics: Distinguishing features of a (residential) property.

Chattel Mortgage: A claim on personal property (instead of real property) used to secure or guarantee a promissory note. (See definition of *A Security Agreement* and *Security Interest.*)

Chattel Real: An estate related to real estate, such as a lease on real property.

Chattels: Goods or every species of property movable or immovable which are not real property.

Circuit Breaker: An electrical device which automatically interrupts an electric circuit when an overload occurs; may be used instead of a fuse to protect each circuit and can be reset.

Clapboard: Boards usually thicker at one edge used for siding.

Closing Statement: An accounting of funds made to the buyer and seller separately. Required by law to be made at the completion of every real estate transaction.

Cloud on the Title: Any conditions revealed by a title search which affect the title to property; usually relatively unimportant items but which cannot be removed without a quitclaim deed or court action.

Collar Beam: A beam that connects the pairs of opposite roof rafters above the attic floor.

Collateral: This is the property subject to the security interest. (See definition of *Security Interest.*)

Collateral Security: A separate obligation attached to contract to guarantee its performance; the transfer of property or of other contracts, or valuables, to insure the performance of a principal agreement.

Collusion: An agreement between two or more persons to defraud another of his rights by the forms of law, or to obtain an object forbidden by law.

Color of Title: That which appears to be good title but which is not title in fact.

Combed Plywood: A grooved building material used primarily for interior finish.

Commercial Acre: A term applied to the remainder of an acre of newly subdivided land after the area devoted to streets, sidewalks and curbs, etc., has been deducted from the acre.

Commercial Paper: Bills of exchange used in commercial trade.

Commission: An agent's compensation for performing the duties of his agency; in real estate practice, a percentage of the selling price of property, percentage of rentals, etc.

Commitment: A pledge or a promise or firm agreement.

Common Law: The body of law that grew from customs and practices developed and used in England "Since the memory of man runneth not to the contrary."

Community: A part of a metropolitan area that has a number of neighborhoods that have a tendency toward common interests and problems.

Community Property: Property accumulated through joint efforts of husband and wife living together.

Compaction: Whenever extra soil is added to a lot to fill in low places or to raise the level of the lot, the added soil is often too loose and soft to sustain the weight of the buildings. Therefore, it is necessary to compact the added soil so that it will carry the weight of buildings without the danger of their tilting, settling or cracking.

Comparable Sales: Sales which have similar characteristics as the subject property and are used for analysis in the appraisal process.

Competent: Legally qualified.

Competition, Principle of: Holds that profits tend to breed competition and excess profits tend to breed ruinous competition.

Component: One of the features making up the whole property.

Compound Interest: Interest paid on original principal and also on the accrued and unpaid interest which has accumulated.

Conclusion: The final estimate of value, realized from facts, data, experience and judgment.

Condemnation: The act of taking private property for public use by a political subdivision; declaration that a structure is unfit for use.

Condition: A qualification of an estate granted which can be imposed only in conveyances. They are classified as *conditions precedent* and *conditions subsequent.*

Condition Precedent: A condition that requires certain action or the happening of a specified event before the estate granted can take effect. Example: most installment real estate sale contracts take all payments shall be made at the time specified before the buyer may demand transfer of title.

Condition Subsequent: When there is a condition subsequent in a deed, the title vests immediately in the grantee, but upon breach of the condition the grantor has the power to terminate the estate if he wishes to do so. Example: A condition in the deed prohibiting the grantee from using the premises as a liquor store.

Conditional Commitment: A commitment of a definite loan amount for some future unknown purchaser of satisfactory credit standing.

Conditional Sales Contract: A contract for the sale of property stating that delivery is to be made to the buyer, title to remain vested in the seller until the conditions of the contract have been fulfilled. (See definition of *Security Interest.*)

Condominium: A system of individual fee ownership of units in a multifamily structure, combined with joint ownership of common areas of the structure and the land. (Sometimes referred to as a vertical subdivision.)

Conduit: Usually a metal pipe in which electrical wiring is installed.

Confession of Judgment: An entry of judgment upon the debtor's voluntary admission or confession.

Confirmation of Sale: A court approval of the sale of property by an executor, administrator, guardian or conservator.

Confiscation: The seizing of property without compensation.

Conformity, Principle of: Holds that the maximum of value is realized when a reasonable degree of homogeneity of improvements is present.

Conservation: The process of utilizing resources in such a manner which minimizes their depletion.

Consideration: Anything of value given to induce entering into a contract; it may be money, personal services, or even love and affection.

Constant: The percentage which, when applied directly to the face value of a debt, develops the annual amount of money necessary to pay a specified net rate of interest on the reducing balance and to liquidate the debt in a specified time period. For example, a 6% loan with a 20 year amortization has a constant of approximately 8 1/2%. Thus, a $10,000 loan amortized over 20 years requires an annual payment of approximately $850.00.

Construction Loans: Loans made for the construction of homes or commercial buildings. Usually funds are disbursed to the contractor builder during construction and after periodic inspections. Disbursements are based on an agreement between borrower and lender.

Constructive Eviction: Breach of a covenant of warranty or quiet enjoyment, e.g., the inability of a lessee to obtain possession because of a paramount defect in title, or a condition making occupancy hazardous.

Constructive Notice: Notice given by the public records.

Consummate Dower: A widow's dower interest which, after the death of her husband, is complete or may be completed and become an interest in real estate.

Contour: The surface configuration of land.

Contract: An agreement, either written or oral, to do or not to do certain things.

Contribution, Principle of: Holds that maximum real property values are achieved when the improvements on the site produce the highest (net) return commensurate with the investment.

Consumer Goods: These are goods used or bought for use primarily for personal, family or household purposes.

Conventional Mortgage: A mortgage securing a loan made by investors without governmental underwriting, i.e., which is not F.H.A. insured or G.I. guaranteed.

Conversion: Change from one character or use to another.

Conveyance: This has two meanings. One meaning refers to the process of transferring title to property from one person to another. In this sense it is used as a verb. The other meaning refers to the document used to effect the transfer of title (usually some kind of deed). In this last sense, it is used a noun.

Cooperative Ownership: A form of apartment ownership. Ownership of shares in a cooperative venture which entitles the owner to use, rent, or sell a specific apartment unit. The corporation usually reserves the right to approve certain actions such as a sale or improvement.

Comer Influence Table: A statistical table that may be used to estimate the added value of a corner lot.

Corporation: A group or body of persons established and treated by law as an individual or unit with rights and liabilities or both, distinct and apart from those of the persons composing it. A corporation is a creature of law having certain powers and duties of a natural person. Being created by law it may continue for any length of time the law prescribes.

Corporeal Rights: Possessory rights in real property.

Correction Lines: A system for compensating inaccuracies in the Government rectangular Survey System due to the curvature of the earth. Every fourth township line, 24 mile intervals, is used as a correction line on which the intervals between the north and south range lines are remeasured and corrected to a full 6 miles.

Correlate the Findings: Interpret the data and value estimates to bring them together to a final conclusion of value.

Correlation: To bring the indicated values developed by the three approaches into mutual relationship with each other.

Cost: A historical record of past expenditures, or an amount which would be given in exchange for other things.

Cost Approach: One of three methods in the appraisal process. An analysis in which a value estimate of a property is derived by estimating the replacement cost of the improvements, deducting therefrom the estimated accrued depreciation, then adding the market value of the land.

Counterflashing: Flashing used on chimneys at roofline to cover shingle flashing and to prevent moisture entry.

Covenant: Agreements written into deeds and other instruments promising performance or nonperformance of certain acts or stipulating certain uses or nonuses of the property.

Crawl Hole: Exterior or interior opening permitting access underneath building, as required by building codes.

CRB: Certified Residential Broker.

CRE: Counselor of Real Estate. Members of American Society of Real Estate Counselors.

Cubage: The number or product resulting by multiplying the width of a thing by its height and by its depth or length.

Curable Depreciation: Items of physical deterioration and functional obsolescence which are customarily repaired or replaced by a prudent property owner.

Curtail Schedule: A listing of the amounts by which the principal sum of an obligation is to be reduced by partial payments and of the dates when each payment will become payable.

Curtesy: The right which a husband has in a wife's estate at her death.

Damages: The indemnity recoverable by a person who has sustained an injury, either in his person, property, or relative rights, through the act or default of another.

Data Plant: An appraiser's file of information on real estate.

Debenture: Bonds issued without security.

Debtor: This is the party who "owns" the property which is subject to the Security Interest. Previously he was known as the *mortgagor* or the *pledgor*, etc.

Deciduous Trees: Lose their leaves in the autumn and winter.

Deck: Usually an open porch on the roof of a ground or lower floor, porch or wing.

Decree of Foreclosure: Decree by a court in the completion of foreclosure of a mortgage, contract, or lien.

Dedication: An appropriation of land by its owner for some public use accepted for such use by authorized public officials on behalf of the public.

Deed: Written instrument which, when properly executed and delivered, conveys title.

Deed Restrictions: This is a limitation in the deed to a property that dictates certain uses that may or may not be made of the property.

Default: Failure to fulfill a duty or promise or to discharge an obligation; omission or failure to perform any act.

Defeasance Clause: The clause in a mortgage that gives the mortgagor the right to redeem his property upon the payment of his obligations to the mortgagee.

Defeasible Fee: Sometimes called a base fee or qualified fee; a fee simple absolute interest in land that is capable of being defeated or terminated upon the happening of a specified event.

Deferred Maintenance: Existing but unfulfilled requirements for repairs and rehabilitation.

Deferred Payment Options: The privilege of deferring income payments to take advantage of the tax statutes.

Deficiency Judgment: A judgment given when the security pledge for a loan does not satisfy the debt upon its default.

Depreciation: Loss of value in real property brought about by age, physical deterioration or functional or economic obsolescence. Broadly, a loss in value from any cause.

Depth Table: A statistical table that may be used to estimate the value of the added depth of a lot.

Desist and Refrain Order: An order directing a person to desist and refrain from committing an act in violation of the real estate law.

Deterioration: Impairment of condition. One of the causes of depreciation and reflecting the loss in value brought about by wear and tear, disintegration, use in service, and the action of the elements.

Devisee: One who receives a bequest made by will.

Devisor: One who bequeaths by will.

Directional Growth: The location or direction toward which the residential sections of a city are destined or determined to grow.

Discount: An amount deducted in advance from the principal before the borrower is given the use of the principal (see point(s)).

Disintermediation: The relatively sudden withdrawal of substantial sums of money savers have deposited with savings and loan associations, commercial banks, and mutual savings banks. This term can also be considered to include life insurance policy purchasers borrowing against the value of their policies. The essence of this phenomenon is financial intermediaries losing within a short period of time billions of dollars as owners of funds held by those institutional lenders exercise their prerogative of taking them out of the hands of these financial institutions.

Disposable Income: The after-tax income a household receives to spend on personal consumption.

Dispossess: To deprive one of the use of real estate.

Documentary Transfer Tax: A state enabling act allowing a county to adopt a documentary transfer tax to apply on all transfer of real property located in the county. Notice of payment is entered on face of the deed or on a separate paper filed with the deed.

Donee: A person to whom a gift is made.

Donor: A person who makes a gift.

Dower: The right which a wife has in her husband's estate at his death.

Duress: Unlawful constraint exercised upon a person whereby he is forced to do some act against his will.

Earnest Money: Down payment made by a purchaser of real estate as evidence of good faith.

Easement: Created by grant or agreement for a specific purpose, an easement is the right, privilege or interest which one party has in land of another. (Example: right of way.)

Eaves: The lower part of a roof projecting over the wall.

Ecology: The relationship between organisms and their environment.

Economic Life: The period over which a property will yield a return on the investment, over and above the economic or ground rent due to land.

Economic Obsolescence: A loss in value due to factors away from the subject property but adversely affecting the value of the subject property.

Economic Rent: The reasonable rental expectancy if the property were available for renting at the time of its valuation.

Effective Age of Improvement: The number of years of age that is indicated by the condition of the structure.

Effective Date of Value: The specific day the conclusion of value applies.

Effective Interest Rate: The percentage of interest that is actually being paid by the borrower for the use of the money.

Eminent Domain: The right of the government to acquire property for necessary public or quasi-public use by condemnation; the owner must be fairly compensated. The right of the government to do this and the right of the private citizen to get paid is spelled out in the 5th Amendment to the United States Constitution.

Encroachment: Trespass, the building of a structure or construction of any improvements, partly or wholly on the property of another.

Encumbrance: Anything which affects or limits the fee simple title to property, such as mortgages, easements or restrictions of any kind. Liens are special encumbrances which make the property security for the payment of a debt or obligation, such as mortgages and taxes.

Equity: The interest or value which an owner has in real estate over and above the liens against it; branch of remedial justice by and through which relief is afforded to suitors in courts of equity.

Equity of Redemption: The right to redeem property during the foreclosure period, such as a mortgagor's right to redeem within a year after foreclosure sale.

Erosion: The wearing away of land by the action of water, wind or glacial ice.

Escalation: The right reserved by the lender to increase the amount of the payments and/or interest upon the happening of a certain event.

Escalator Clause: A clause in a contract providing for the upward or downward adjustment of certain items to cover specified contingencies.

Escheat: The reverting of property to the State when heirs capable of inheriting are lacking.

Escrow: The deposit of instruments and funds with instructions to a third neutral party to carry out the provisions of an agreement or contract; when everything is deposited to enable carrying out the instructions, it is called a complete or perfect escrow.

Estate: As applied to the real estate practice, the term signifies the quantity of interest, share, right, equity, of which riches or fortune may consist, in real property. The degree, quantity, nature, and extent of interest which a person has in real property.

Estate of Inheritance: An estate which may descend to heirs. All freehold estates are estates of inheritance, except estates for life.

Estate for Life: A freehold estate, not of inheritance, but which is held by the tenant for his own life or the life or lives of one or more other persons, or for an indefinite period which may endure for the life or lives of persons in being and beyond the period of life.

Estate from Period to Period: An interest in land where there is no definite termination date but the rental period is fixed at a certain sum per week, month, or year. Also called a periodic tenancy.

Estate at Sufferance: An estate arising when the tenant wrongfully holds over after the expiration of his term. The landlord has the choice of evicting the tenant as a trespasser or accepting such tenant for a similar term and under the conditions of the tenant's previous holding. Also called a tenancy at sufferance.

Estate of Will: The occupation of lands and tenements by a tenant for an indefinite period, terminable by one or both parties.

Estate for Years: An interest in lands by virtue of a contract for the possession of them for a definite and limited period of time. A lease may be said to be an estate for years.

Estimate: To form a preliminary opinion of value.

Estimated Remaining Life: The period of time (years) it takes for the improvements to become valueless.

Estoppel: A doctrine which bars one from asserting rights which are inconsistent with a previous position or representation.

Ethics: That branch of moral science, idealism, justness, and fairness, which treats of the duties which a member of a profession or craft owes to the public, to his clients or patron, and to his professional brethren or members.

Eviction: Dispossession by process of law. The act of depriving a person of the possession of lands, in pursuance of the judgment of a court.

Exclusive Agency Listing: A written instrument giving one agent the right to sell property for a specified time but reserving the right of the owner to sell the property himself without the payment of a commission.

Exclusive Right to Sell Listing: A written agreement between owner and agent giving agent the right to collect a commission if the property is sold by anyone during the term of his agreement.

Execute: To complete, to make, to perform, to do, to follow out; to execute a deed, to make a deed, including especially signing, sealing, and delivery; to execute a contract is to perform the contract, to follow out to the end, to complete.

Executor: A person named in a will to carry out its provisions as to the disposition of the estate of a person deceased.

Expansible House: Home designed for further expansion and additions in the future.

Expansion Joint: A bituminous fiber strip used to separate units of concrete to prevent cracking due to expansion as a result of temperature changes.

Expenses: Certain items which may appear on a closing statement in connection with a real estate sale.

Facade: Front of a building.

Farmers Home Administration: An agency of the Department of agriculture. Primary responsibility is to provide financial assistance for farmers and others living in rural areas where financing is not available on reasonable terms from private sources.

Fair Market Value: This is the amount of money that would be paid for a property offered on the open market for a reasonable period of time with both buyer and seller knowing all the uses to which the property could be put and with neither party being under pressure to buy or sell.

Federal Deposit Insurance Corporation: (FDIC) Agency of the federal government which insures deposits at commercial banks and savings banks.

Federal Home Loan Bank: (FHLB) A district bank of the Federal Home Loan Bank system that lends only to member savings and loan associations.

Federal Home Loan Bank Board: (FHLBB) The administrative agency that charters federal savings and loan associations and exercises regulatory authority over the FHLB system.

Federal Housing Administration: (FHA) An agency of the federal government that insures mortgage loans.

Federal National Mortgage Association: (FNMA) "Fanny Mae" a quasi-public agency being converted into a private corporation whose primary function is to buy and sell FHA and VA mortgages in the secondary market.

Federal Savings and Loan Association: An association chartered by the FHLBB in contrast to a state-chartered savings and loan association.

Federal Savings and Loan Insurance Corporation: (FSLIC) An agency of the federal government that insures savers' accounts at savings and loan associations.

Fee: An estate of inheritance in real property.

Fee Simple: In modern estates, the terms "Fee" and "Fee Simple" are substantially synonymous. The term "Fee" is of Old English derivation. "Fee Simple Absolute" is an estate in real property, by which the owner has the greatest power over the title which it is possible to have, being an absolute estate. In modern use, it expressly establishes the title of real property in the owner, without limitation or end. He may dispose of it by sale, or trade or will, as he chooses.

Feudal Tenure: A real property ownership system where ownership rests with a sovereign who, in turn, may grant lesser interests in return for service or loyalty. In contrast to allodial tenure.

Feuds: Grants of land.

Fidelity Bond: A security posted for the discharge of an obligation of personal services.

Fiduciary: A person in a position of trust and confidence, as between principal and broker; broker as fiduciary owes certain loyalty which cannot be breached under the rules of agency.

Filtering Down: The process of making housing available to successively lower income groups.

Financial Intermediary: Financial institutions such as commercial banks, savings and loan associations, mutual savings banks and life insurance companies which receive relatively small sums of money from the public and invest them in the form of large sums. A considerable portion of these funds are loaned on real estate.

Financing Statement: This is the instrument which is filed in order to give public notice of the security interest and thereby protect the interest of the secured parties in the collateral. See definitions of *Security Interest and Secured Party*.

Finish Floor: Finish floor strips are applied over wood joists, deadening felt and diagonal subflooring before finish floor is installed; finish floor is the final covering on the floor: wood, linoleum, cork, tile or carpet .

Fire Stop: A solid, tight closure of a concealed space, placed to prevent the spread of fire and smoke through such a space.

First Mortgage: A legal document pledging collateral for a loan (see "mortgage") that has first priority over all other claims against the property except taxes and bonded indebtedness.

Fiscal Controls: Federal tax revenue and expenditure policies used to control the level of economic activity.

Fixity of Location: The physical characteristic of real estate that subjects it to the influence of its surroundings.

Fixtures: Appurtenances attached to the land or improvements, which usually cannot be removed without agreement as they become real property; examples: plumbing fixtures, store fixtures built into the property, etc.

Flashing: Sheet metal or other material used to protect a building from seepage of water.

Footing: The base or bottom of a foundation wall, pier, or column.

Foreclosure: Procedure whereby property pledged as security for a debt is sold to pay the debt in event of default in payments or terms.

Forfeiture: Loss of money or anything of value, due to failure to perform .

Foundation: The supporting portion of a structure below the first floor construction, or below grade, including the footings.

Franchise: A specified privilege awarded by a government or business firm which awards an exclusive dealership.

Fraud: The intentional and successful employment of any cunning, deception, collusion, or artifice, used to circumvent, cheat or deceive another person, whereby that person acts upon it to the loss of his property and to his legal injury.

Freehold: An estate of indeterminable duration, e.g., fee simple or life estate.

Frontage: Land bordering a street.

Front Foot: Property measurement for sale or valuation purposes; the property measures by the front foot on its street line--each front foot extending the depth of the lot.

Front Money: The minimum amount of money necessary to initiate a real estate venture.

Frostline: The depth of frost penetration in the soil. Varies in different parts of the country. Footings should be placed below this depth to prevent movement.

Functional Obsolescence: A loss of value due to adverse factors from within the structure which affect the utility of the structure.

Furring: Strips of wood or metal applied to a wall or other surface to even it, to form an air space, or to give the wall an appearance of greater thickness.

Future Benefits: The anticipated benefits the present owner will receive from his property in the future.

Gable Roof: A pitched roof with sloping sides.

Gambrel Roof: A curb roof, having a steep lower slope with a flatter upper slope above.

General Lien: A lien on all the property of a debtor.

Gift Deed: A deed for which the consideration is love and affection and where there is no material consideration.

Girder: A large beam used to support beams, joists and partitions.

Grade: Ground level at the foundation.

Graduated Lease: Lease which provides for a varying rental rate, often based upon future determination; sometimes rent is based upon result of periodical appraisals; used largely in long-term leases.

Grant: A technical term made use of in deeds of conveyance of lands to import a transfer.

Grant Deed: A deed in which "grant" is used as the word of conveyance. The grantor impliedly warrants that he has not already conveyed to any other person, and that the estate conveyed is free from encumbrances done, made or suffered by the grantor or any person claiming under him, including taxes, assessments, and other liens.

Grantee: The purchaser; a person to whom a grant is made.

Grantor: Seller of property; one who signs a deed.

GRI: Graduate, Realtors Institute.

Grid: A chart used in rating the borrower risk, property, and the neighborhood.

Gross Income: Total income from property before any expenses are deducted.

Gross National Product: (GNP) The total value of all goods and services produced in a economy during a given period of time.

Gross Rate: A method of collecting interest by adding total interest to the principal of the loan at the outset of the term.

Gross Rent Multiplier: A figure which, times the gross income of a property, produces an estimate of value of the property.

Ground Lease: An agreement for the use of the land only, sometimes secured by improvements placed on the land by the user.

Ground Rent: Earnings of improved property credited to earnings of the ground itself after allowance is made for earnings of improvements; often termed economic rent.

Habendum Clause: The "to have and to hold" clause in a deed.

Header: A beam placed perpendicular to joists and to which joists are nailed in framing for chimney, stairway, or other opening.

Highest and Best Use: An appraisal phrase meaning that use which at the time of an appraisal is most likely to produce the greatest net return to the land and/or buildings over a given period of time; that use which will produce the greatest amount of amenities or profit. This is the starting point for appraisal.

Hip Roof: A pitched roof with sloping sides and ends.

Holder in Due Course: One who has taken a note, check or bill of exchange in due course:

> I. Before it was overdue;

> 2. In good faith and for value;

> 3. Without knowledge that it has been previously dishonored without notice of any defect at the time it was negotiated to him.

Holdover Tenant: Tenant who remains in possession of leased property after the expiration of the lease term.

Homestead: A home upon which the owner or owners have recorded a Declaration of Homestead, as provided by Statutes in some states; protects home against judgments up to specified amounts.

Hundred Percent Location: A city retail business location which is considered the best available for attracting business.

Hypothecate: To give a thing as security without the necessity of giving up possession of it.

Impounds: A trust-type account established by lenders for the accumulation of funds to meet taxes, FHA mortgage insurance premiums, and/or future insurance policy premiums required to protect their security. Impounds are usually collected with the note payment.

Inchoate Right of Dower: A wife's interest in the real estate of her husband during his life which upon his death may become a dower interest.

Income Approach: One of the three methods in the appraisal process; an analysis in which the estimated gross income from the subject residence is used as a basis for estimating value along with gross rent multipliers derived.

Incompetent: One who is mentally incompetent, incapable; any person who, though not insane, is by reason of old age, disease, weakness of mind, or any other cause, unable, unassisted, to properly manage and take care of himself or his property and by reason thereof would be likely to be deceived or imposed upon by artful or designing persons.

Incorporeal Rights: Nonpossessory rights in real estate.

Increment: An increase. Most frequently used to refer to the increase of value of land that accompanies population growth and increasing wealth in the community. The term unearned increment is used in this connection since values are supposed to have increased without effort on the part of the owner.

Indenture: A formal written instrument made between two or more persons in different interests.

Indirect Lighting: The light is reflected from the ceiling or other object external to the fixture.

Indorsement: The act of signing one's name on the back of a check or note, with or without further qualification.

Injunction: A writ or order issued under the seal of a court to restrain one or more parties to a suit or proceeding from doing an act which is deemed to be inequitable or unjust in regard to the rights of some other party or parties in the suit or proceeding.

Input: Data, information, etc., that is fed into a computer or other system.

Installment Contract: Purchase of real estate wherein the purchase price is paid in installments over a long period of time, title is retained by seller, upon default the payments are forfeited. Also known as a land contract.

Installment Note: A note which provides that payments of a certain sum or amount be paid on the dates specified in the instrument.

Installment Reporting: A method of reporting capital gains by installments for successive tax years to minimize the impact of the totality of the capital gains tax in the year of the sale.

Instrument: A written legal document; created to effect the rights of the parties.

Interest: The charge in dollars for the use of money for a period of time. In a sense, the "rent" paid for the use of money.

Interest Rate: The percentage of a sum of money charged for its use.

Interim Loan: A short-term loan until long-term financing is available.

Intestate: A person who dies having made no will, or one which is defective in form in which case his estate descends to his heirs at law or next of kin.

Involuntary Lien: A lien imposed against property without consent of an owner; example: taxes, special assessments, federal income tax liens, etc.

Inwood Tables — Concept of using present value of income in a perpetuity table to help appraisers.

Irrevocable: Incapable of being recalled or revoked; unchangeable.

Irrigation Districts: Quasi-political districts created under special laws to provide for water services to property owners in the district; an operation governed to a great extent by law.

Jalousie: A slatted blind or shutter, like a venetian blind but used on the exterior to protect against rain as well as to control sunlight.

Jamb: The side post or lining of a doorway, window or other opening.

Joint: The space between the adjacent surfaces of two components joined and held together by nails, glue, cement, mortar, etc.

Joint Note: A note signed by two or more persons who have equal liability for payment.

Joint Tenancy: Joint ownership by two or more persons with right of survivorship; all joint tenants own equal interest and have equal rights in the property.

Joint Venture: Two or more individuals or firms joining together on a single project as partners.

Joist: One of a series of parallel beams to which the boards of a floor and ceiling laths are nailed, and supported in turn by larger beams, girders, or bearing walls.

Judgment: The final determination of a court of competent jurisdiction of a matter presented to it; money judgments provide for the payment of claims presented to the court, or are awarded as damages, etc.

Judgment Lien: A legal claim on all of the property of a judgment debtor which enables the judgment creditor to have the property sold for payment of the amount of the judgment.

Junior Mortgage: A mortgage second in lien to a previous mortgage.

Jurisdiction: The authority by which judicial officers take cognizance of and decide causes; the power to hear and determine a cause; the right and power which a judicial officer has to enter upon the inquiry.

Laches: Delay or negligence in asserting one's legal rights.

Land Contract: A contract ordinarily used in connection with the sale of property in cases where the seller does not wish to convey title until all or a certain part of the purchase price is paid by the buyer; often used when property is sold on small down payment.

Land and Improvement Loan: A loan obtained by the builder developer for the purchase of land and to cover expenses for subdividing.

Landlord: One who rents his property to another.

Later Date Order: The commitment for an owner's title insurance policy issued by a title insurance company which covers the seller's title as of the date of the contract. When the sale closes the purchaser orders the title company to record the deed to purchaser and bring down their examination to cover this later date so as to show purchaser as owner of the property.

Lateral Support: The support which the soil of an adjoining owner gives to his neighbors' land.

Lath: A building material of wood, metal, gypsum, or insulating board fastened to the frame of a building to act as a plaster base.

Lease: A contract between owner and tenant, setting forth conditions upon which tenant may occupy and use the property, and the term of the occupancy.

Leasehold Estate: A tenant's right to occupy real estate during the term of the lease. This is a personal property interest.

Legal Description: A description recognized by law; a description by which property can be definitely located by reference to government surveys or approved recorded maps.

Lessee: One who contracts to rent property under a lease contract.

Lessor: An owner who enters into a lease with a tenant.

Level Payment Mortgage: A loan on real estate that is paid off by making a series of equal (or nearly equal) regular payments. Part of the payment is usually interest on the loan and part of it reduces the amount of the unpaid balance of the loan. Also sometimes called an "amortized mortgage."

Lien: A form of encumbrance which usually makes property security for the payment of a debt or discharge of an obligation. Example: judgments, taxes, mortgages, deeds of trust, etc.

Life Estate: An estate or interest in real property which is held for the duration of the life of some certain person.

Limited Partnership: A partnership composed of some partners whose contribution and liability are limited.

Lintel: A horizontal board that supports the load over an opening such as a door or window.

Lis Pendens: Suit pending, usually recorded so as to give constructive notice of pending litigation.

Liquidated Damages: A sum agreed upon by the parties to be full damages if a certain event occurs.

Listing: An employment contract between principal and agent authorizing the agent to perform services for the principal involving the latter's property; listing contracts are entered into for the purpose of securing persons to buy, lease or rent property. Employment of an agent by a prospective purchaser or lessee to locate property for purchase or lease may be considered a listing.

Loan Administration: Also called loan servicing. Mortgage bankers not only originate loans, but also "service" them from origination to maturity of the loan.

Loan Application: The loan application is a source of information on which the lender bases his decision to make the loan, defines the terms of the loan contract; gives the name of the borrower, place of employment, salary, bank accounts, and credit references; and, describes the real estate that is to be mortgaged. It also stipulates the amount of loan being applied for, and repayment terms.

Loan Closing: When all conditions have been met, the loan officer authorizes the recording of the trust deed or mortgage. The disbursal procedure of funds is similar to the closing of a real estate sales escrow. The borrower can expect to receive less than the amount of the loan, as title, recording, service, and other fees may be withheld, or he can expect to deposit the cost of these items into the loan escrow. This process is sometimes called "funding" the loan.

Loan Commitment: Lender's contractual commitment to a loan based on the appraisal and underwriting.

Loan Value Ratio: The percentage of a property's value that a lender can or may loan to a borrower. For example, if the ratio is 80% this means that a lender may loan 80% of the property's appraised value to a borrower.

Louver: An opening with a series of horizontal slats set at an agle to permit ventilation without admitting rain, sunlight, or vision.

MAI: Member o f the Appraisal Institute. Designates a person who is a member of the' American Institute of Real Estate Appraisers of the National Association of Realtors.

Margin of Security: The difference between the amount of the mortgage loan(s) and the appraised value of the property.

Marginal Land: Land which barely pays the cost of working or using.

Market Data Approach: One of the three methods in the appraisal process. A means of comparing similar type residential properties, which have recently sold, to the subject property.

Market Price: The price paid regardless of pressures, motives or intelligence.

Market Value: (1) The price at which a willing seller would sell and a willing buyer would buy, neither being under abnormal pressure; (2) as defined by the courts, is the highest price estimated in terms of money which a property will bring if exposed for sale in the open market allowing a reasonable time to find a purchaser with knowledge of property's use and capabilities for use.

Marketable Title: Merchantable title; title free and clear of objectionable liens or encumbrances.

Material Fact: A fact is material if it is one which the agent should realize would be likely to affect the judgment of the principal in giving his consent to the agent to enter into the particular transaction on the specified terms.

Mechanics' Lien: A lien created by statute which exists against real property in favor of persons who have performed work or furnished materials for the improvement of the real estate.

Memory Bank: Data and information held in storage in the computer.

Meridians: Imaginary north-south lines which intersect base lines to form a starting point for the measurement of land.

Metes and Bounds: A term used in describing the boundary lines of land, setting forth all the boundary lines together with their terminal points and angles.

Mile: 5,280 feet.

Minor: All persons under 18 years of age.

Misplaced Improvement: Improvements on land which do not conform to the most profitable use of the site.

Modular: A building composed of modules constructed on an assembly line in a factory. Usually, the modules are self-contained.

Moldings: Usually patterned strips used to provide ornamental variation of outline or contour, such as cornices, bases, window and door jambs.

Monetary Controls: Federal Reserve tools for regulating the availability of money and credit to influence the level of economic activity.

Monument: A fixed object and point established by surveyors to establish land locations.

Moratorium: The temporary suspension, usually by statute, of the enforcement of liability for debt.

Mortgage: An instrument recognized by law by which property is hypothecated to secure the payment of a debt or obligation; procedure for foreclosure in event of default is established by statute.

Mortgage Contracts with Warrants: Warrants make the mortgage more attractive to the lender by providing both the greater security that goes with a mortgage, and the opportunity of a greater return through the right to buy either stock in the borrower's company or a portion of the income property itself.

Mortgage Guaranty Insurance: Insurance against financial loss available to mortgage lenders from Mortgage Guaranty Insurance Corporation, a private company organized in 1956.

Mortgagee: One to whom a mortgagor gives a mortgage to secure a loan or performance of an obligation, a lender. (See definition of *Secured Party*.)

Mortgagor: One who gives a mortgage on his property to secure a loan or assure performance of an obligation; a borrower. (See definition of *Debtor*.)

Multiple Listing: A listing, usually an exclusive right to sell, taken by a member of an organization composed of real estate brokers, with the provisions that all members will have the opportunity to find an interested client; a cooperative listing.

Mutual Water Company: A water company organized by or for water users in a given district with the object of securing an ample water supply at a reasonable rate; stock is issued to users.

NAREB: National Association of Real Estate Brokers.

NAR: National Association of Realtors.

Narrative Appraisal: A summary of all factual materials, techniques and appraisal methods used by the appraiser in setting forth his value conclusion.

Negotiable: Capable of being negotiated; assignable or transferable in the ordinary course of business.

Net Listing: A listing which provides that the agent may retain as compensation for his services all sums received over and above a net price to the owner.

Nominal Interest Rates: The percentage of interest that is stated in loan documents.

Notary Public: An appointed officer with authority to take the acknowledgment of persons executing documents, to sign the certificate and affix his seal.

Note: A signed written instrument acknowledging a debt and promising payment.

Notice: Actual knowledge acquired by being present at the occurrence.

Notice of Nonresponsibility: A notice provided by law designed to relieve a property owner from responsibility for the cost of work done on the property or materials furnished therefor; notice must be verified, recorded and posted.

Notice to Quit: A notice to a tenant to vacate rented property.

Obsolescence: Loss in value due to reduced desirability and usefulness of a structure because its design and construction become obsolete; loss because of becoming old-fashioned and not in keeping with modern needs, with consequent loss in income.

Offset Statement: Statement by owner of property or owner of lien against property, setting forth the present status of liens against said property.

Open-end Mortgage: A mortgage containing a clause which permits the mortgagor to borrow additional money after the loan has been reduced, without rewriting the mortgage.

Open Housing Law: Congress passed a law in April 1968 which prohibits discrimination in the sale of real estate because of race, color, or religion of buyers.

Open Listing: An authorization given by a property owner to a real estate agent wherein said agent is given the non-exclusive rights to secure a purchaser; open listings may be given to any number of agents without liability to compensate any except the one who first secures a buyer ready, willing and able to meet the terms of the listing, or secures the acceptance by the seller of a satisfactory offer.

Opinion of title: An attorney's evaluation of the condition of the title to a parcel of land after his examination of the abstract of title to the land.

Option: A right given for a consideration to purchase or lease a property upon specified terms within a specified time.

Oral Contract: A verbal agreement; one which is not reduced to writing.

Orientation: Placing a house on its lot with regard to its exposure to the rays of the sun, prevailing winds, privacy from the street and protection from outside noises.

Overhang: The part of the roof extending beyond the walls, to shade buildings and cover walks.

Over Improvement: An improvement which is not the highest and best use for the site on which it is placed by reason of excess size or cost.

Parquet Floor: Hardwood flooring laid in squares or patterns.

Participation: In addition to base interest on mortgage loans on income properties, a small percentage of gross income is required, sometimes predicated on certain conditions being fulfilled, such as minimum occupancy or a percentage of net income after expenses, debt service and taxes.

Partition Action: Court proceedings by which co-owners seek to sever their joint ownership.

Partnership: A decision of the California Supreme Court has defined a partnership in the following terms: "A partnership as between partners themselves may be defined to be a contract of two or more persons to unite their property, labor or skill, or some of them, in prosecution of some joint or lawful business, and to share the profits in certain proportions."

Party Wall: A wall erected on the line between two adjoining properties, which are under different ownership, for the use of both properties.

Par Value: Market value, nominal value.

Patent: Conveyance of title to government land.

Penalty: An extra payment or charge required of the borrower for deviating from the terms of the original loan agreement. Usually levied for being late in making regular payment or for paying off the loan before it is due.

Penny: The term, as applied to nails, serves as a measure of nail length and is abbreviated by the letter "d"

Percentage Lease: Lease on the property, the rental for which is determined by amount of business done by the lessee; usually a percentage of gross receipts from the business with provision for a minimum rental.

Perimeter Heating: Baseboard heating, or any system in which the heat registers are located along the outside walls of a room, especially under the windows.

Personal Property: Any property which is not real property.

Physical Deterioration: Impairment of condition. Loss in value brought about by wear and tear, disintegration, use and actions of the elements.

Pier: A column of masonry, usually rectangular in horizontal cross section, used to support other structural members.

Pitch: The incline or rise of a roof.

Planned Unit Development: (PUD) A land use design which provides intensive utilization of the land through a combination of private and common areas with prearranged sharing of responsibilities for the common areas.

Plate: A horizontal board placed on a wall or supported on posts or studs to carry the trusses of a roof or rafters directly; a shoe, or base member as of a partition or other frame; a small flat board placed on or in a wall to support girders, rafters, etc.

Pledge: The depositing of personal property by a debtor with a creditor as security for a debt or engagement.

Pledgee: One who is given a pledge or a security. (See definition of *Secured Party.*)

Pledgor: One who offers a pledge or gives security. (See definition of *debtor.*)

Plottage Increment: The appreciation in unit value created by joining smaller ownerships into one large single ownership.

Plywood: Laminated wood made up in panels; several thickness of wood glued together with grain at different angles for strength.

Points: Under FHA-insured or VA-guaranteed loans, discounts or points paid to lenders are, in effect, prepaid interest, and are used by lenders to adjust the effective interest rate so that it is equal to or nearly equal to the prevailing market rate (the rate charged on conventional loans). The discounts are absorbed by the sellers and a point is one percent of the loan amount. On FHA-insured and VA-guaranteed loans, buyers may be charged only one percent "service charge". This restriction does not apply to conventional loans. Under conventional loans the charge for making a loan at most institutions is usually called a "loan fee," "service charge," "commitment fee," or may be referred to as "points to the buyer."

Police Power: The right of the State to enact laws and enforce them for the order, safety, health, morals and general welfare of the public.

Power of Attorney: An instrument authorizing a person to act as the agent of the person granting it, and a general power authorizing the agent to act generally in behalf of the principal. A special power limits the agent to a particular or specific act as: a landowner may grant an agent special power of attorney to convey a single and specific parcel of property. Under the provisions of a general power of attorney, the agent having the power may convey any or all property of the principal granting the general power of attorney.

Prefabricated House: A house manufactured and sometimes partly assembled, before delivery to building site.

Prepaid Items of Expense: Prorations of prepaid items of expense which are credited to the seller in the closing statement.

Prepayment: Provision made for loan payments to be larger than those specified in the note.

Prepayment Penalty: Penalty for the payment of a mortgage or trust deed note before it actually becomes due if the note does not provide for prepayment.

Present Value: The lump sum value today of an annuity. A $100 bill to be paid to someone in *one year is* worth *less* than if it were a $100 bill to be paid to someone *today*. This is due to several things, one of which is that the money has *time value*. How much the $100 bill to be paid in one year is worth today will depend on the interest rate that seems proper for the particular circumstances. For example, if 6% is the appropriate rate, the $100 to be paid one year from now would be worth $94.34 today.

Presumption: A rule of law that courts and judges shall draw a particular inference from a particular fact, or from particular evidence, unless and until the truth of such inference is disproved.

Prima Facie: Presumptive on its face.

Principal: This term is used to mean either the employer of an agent or the amount of money borrowed or the amount of the loan.

Principal Note: The promissory note which is secured by the mortgage or trust deed.

Privity: Mutual relationship to the same rights of property, contractual relationship.

Procuring Cause: That cause originating from series of events that, without break in continuity, results in the prime object of an agent's employment producing a final buyer.

Progression, Principle of: The worth of a lesser valued residence tends to be enhanced by association with many higher valued residences in the same area.

Promissory Note: Following a loan commitment from the lender, the borrower signs a note, promising to repay the loan under stipulated terms. The promissory note establishes personal liability for its repayment.

Property: The rights of ownership. The right to use, possess, enjoy, and dispose of a thing in every legal way and to exclude everyone else from interfering with these rights. Property is generally classified into two groups, personal property and real property.

Proration: Adjustments of interest, taxes, and insurance, etc., on a prorate basis as of the closing date. Fire insurance is normally paid for three years in advance. If a property is sold during this time, the seller wants a refund on that portion of the advance payment that has not been used at the time the title to the property is transferred. For example, if the property is sold two years later, he will want to receive 1/3 of the advance premium that was paid.

Proration of Taxes: To divide or prorate the taxes equally or proportionately to time of use.

Proximate Cause: That cause of an event is that which, in a natural and continuous sequence unbroken by any new cause, produced that event, and without which the event would not have happened. Also, the procuring cause.

Public Trustee: The county public official whose office has been created by statute, to whom title to real property, in certain states, e.g., Colorado, is conveyed by Trust Deed for the use and benefit of the beneficiary, who usually is the lender.

Purchase and Installment Sale-back: Involves purchase of the property upon completion of construction and immediate sale-back on a long-term installment contract.

Purchase of Land, Leaseback and Leasehold Mortgages: An arrangement whereby land is purchased by the lender and leased back to the developer with a mortgage negotiated on the resulting leasehold of the income property constructed. The lender receives an annual ground rent, plus a percentage of income from the property.

Purchase and Leaseback: Involves the purchase of property subject to an existing mortgage and immediate leaseback.

Purchase Money Mortgage or Trust Deed: A trust deed or mortgage given as part or all of the purchase consideration for property. In some states the purchase money mortgage or trust deed loan can be made by a seller who extends credit to the buyer of property or by a third party lender (typically a financial institution) that makes a loan to the buyer of real property for a portion of the purchase price to be paid for the property. (In many states there are legal limitations upon mortgagees and trust deed beneficiaries collecting deficiency judgments against the purchase money borrower after the collateral hypothecated under such security instruments has been sold through the foreclosure process. Generally no deficiency judgment is allowed if the collateral property under the mortgage or trust deed is residential property of four units or less with the debtor occupying the property as a place of residence.)

Quantity Survey: A highly technical process in arriving at cost estimate of new construction, and sometimes referred to in the building trade as the *price takeoff* method. It involves a detailed estimate of the quantities of raw material lumber, plaster, brick, cement, etc. used, as well as the current price of the material and installation costs. These factors are all added together to arrive at the cost of a structure. It is usually used by contractors and experienced estimators.

Quarter round: A molding that presents a profile of a quarter circle.

Quiet Enjoyment: Right of an owner to the use of the property without interference of possession.

Quiet Title: A court action brought to establish title; to remove a cloud on the title.

Quitclaim Deed: A deed to relinquish any interest in property which the grantor may have.

Radiant Heating: A method of heating, usually consisting of coils or pipes placed in the floor, wall, or ceiling.

Rafter: One of a series of boards of a roof designed to support roof loads. The rafters of a flat roof are sometimes called *roof* joists.

Range: A strip of land six miles wide determined by a government survey, running in a north-south direction.

Ratification: The adoption or approval of an act performed on behalf of a person without previous authorization.

Real Estate Board: An organization whose members consist primarily of real estate brokers and salesmen.

Real Estate Settlement Procedures Act: A federal disclosure law effective June 20, 1975 requiring new procedures and forms for settlements (closing costs) involving federally related loans.

Real Estate Trust: A special arrangement under Federal and State law whereby investors may pool funds for investments in real estate and mortgages and yet escape corporation taxes.

Realtist: A real estate broker holding active membership in a real estate board affiliated with the National Association of Real Estate Brokers.

Realtor: A real estate broker holding active membership in a real estate board affiliated with the National Association of Realtors.

Recapture: The rate of interest necessary to provide for the return of an investment. Not to be confused with interest rate, which is a rate of interest on an investment.

Reconveyance: The transfer of the title of land from one person to the immediate preceding owner. This particular instrument of transfer is commonly used when the performance or debt is satisfied under the terms of a deed of trust, when the trustee conveys the title he has held on condition back to the owner.

Recording: The process of placing a document on file with a designated public official for everyone to see. This public official is usually a county officer known as the *County Recorder*. He designates the fact that a document has been given to him by placing his stamp upon it indicating the time of day and the date when it was officially placed on file. Documents filed with the Recorder are considered to be placed on open notice to the general public of that county. Claims against property usually are given a priority on the basis of the time and the date they are recorded with the most preferred claim status going to the earliest one recorded and the next claim going to the next earliest one recorded, and so on. This type of notice is called "constructive notice" or "legal notice."

Redemption: Buying back one's property after a judicial sale.

Refinancing: The paying-off of an existing obligation and assuming a new obligation in its place.

Reformation: An action to correct a mistake in a deed or other document.

Rehabilitation: The restoration of a property to satisfactory condition without drastically changing the plan, form or style of architecture.

Release Clause: This is a stipulation that upon the payment of a specific sum of money to the holder of a trust deed or mortgage, the lien of the instrument as to a specific described lot or area shall be removed from the blanket lien on the whole area involved.

Release Deed: An instrument executed by the mortgagee or the trustee reconveying to the mortgagor the real estate which secured the mortgage loan after the debt has been paid in full. Upon recording it cancels the mortgage lien created when the mortgage or trust deed was recorded.

Remainder: An estate which takes effect after the termination of the prior estate, such as a life estate.

Remainder Depreciation: The possible loss in value of an improvement which will occur in the future.

Replacement Cost: The cost to replace the structure with one having utility equivalent to that being appraised, but constructed with modern materials, and according to current standards, design and layout.

Reproduction Costs: The cost of replacing the subject improvement with one that is the exact replica, having the same quality of workmanship, design and layout.

Rescission of Contract: The abrogation or annulling of contract; the revocation or repealing of contract by mutual consent by parties to the contract, or for cause by either party to the contract.

Reservation: A right retained by a grantor in conveying property.

RESPA: Real Estate Settlement Procedures Act.

Restriction: The term as used relating to real property means the owner of real property is restricted or prohibited from doing certain things relating to the property, or using the property for certain purposes. Property restrictions fall into two general classifications--public and private. Zoning ordinances are examples of the former type. Restrictions may be created by private owners, typically by appropriate clauses in deeds, or in agreements, or in general plans of entire subdivisions. Usually they assume the form of a covenant, or promise to do or not to do a certain thing. They cover a multitude of matters including use for residential or business purposes, e.g. houses in tract must cost more than $25,000 etc.

Retrospective Value: The value of the property as of a previous date.

Reversion: The right to future possession or enjoyment by the person, or his heirs, creating the preceding estate.

Reversionary Interest: The interest which a person has in lands or other property, upon the termination of the preceding estate.

Ridge: The horizontal line at the junction of the top edges of two sloping roof surfaces. The rafters at both slopes are nailed at the ridge.

Ridge Board: The board placed on edge at the ridge of the roof to support the upper ends of the rafters; also called roof tree, ridge piece, ridge plate or ridgepole.

Right of Survivorship: Right to acquire the interests of a deceased joint owner; distinguishing feature of a joint tenancy.

Right of Way: A privilege operating as an easement upon land, whereby the owner does by grant, or by agreement, give to another the right to pass over his land, to construct a roadway, or use as a roadway, a specific part of his land, or the right to construct through and over his land, telephone, telegraph, or electric power lines, or the right to place underground water mains, gas mains, or sewer mains.

Riparian Rights: The right of a landowner to water on, under, or adjacent to his land.

Riser: The upright board at the back of each step of a stairway. In heating, a riser is a duct slanted upward to carry hot air from the furnace to the room above.

Risk Analysis: A study made, usually by a lender, of the various factors that might affect the repayment of a loan.

Risk Rating: A process used by the lender to decide on the soundness (syn) of making a loan and to reduce all the various factors affecting the repayment of the loan to a qualified rating of some kind.

Roman Brick: Thin brick of slimmer proportions than standard building brick.

Sales Contract: A contract by which buyer and seller agree to terms of a sale.

Sale-leaseback: A situation where the owner of a piece of property wishes to sell the property and retain occupancy by leasing it from the buyer.

Sandwich Lease: A leasehold interest which lies between the primary lease and the operating lease.

Sash: Wood or metal frames containing one or more window panes.

Satisfaction: Discharge of mortgage or trust deed lien from the records upon payment of the evidenced debt.

Satisfaction Piece: An instrument for recording and acknowledging payment of an indebtedness secured by a mortgage.

Scribing: Fitting woodwork to an irregular surface.

Seal: An impression made to attest the execution of an instrument.

Secondary Financing: A loan secured by a second mortgage or trust deed on real property. These can be third, fourth, fifth, sixth--on and on ad infinitum.

Secured Party: This is the party having the security interest. Thus the *mortgagee*, the *conditional seller*, the *pledgee*, etc., are all now referred to as the secured party.

Security Agreement: An agreement between the secured party and the debtor which creates the security interest.

Security Interest: A term designating the interest of the creditor in the property of the debtor in all types of credit transactions. It thus replaces such terms as the following: *chattel mortgage; pledge; trust receipt; chattel trust; equipment trust; conditional sale; inventory lien;* etc.

Section: Section of land is established by government survey and contains 640 acres.

Seizin: Possession of real estate by one entitled thereto.

Separate Property: Property owned by a husband or wife which is not community property; property acquired by either spouse prior to marriage or by gift or devise after marriage.

Septic Tank: An underground tank in which sewage from the house is reduced to liquid by bacterial action and drained off.

Servicing: Supervising and administering a loan after it has been made. This involves such things as: collecting the payments, keeping accounting records, computing the interest and principal, foreclosure of defaulted loans, and so on.

Setback Ordinance: An ordinance prohibiting the erection of a building or structure between the curb and the setback line.

Severalty Ownership: Owned by one person only. Sole ownership.

Shopping Center, Regional: A large shopping center with 250,000 to 1,000,000 square feet of store area, serving 200,000 or more people.

Shake: A handsplit shingle, usually edge grained.

Sheathing: Structural covering usually boards, plywood, or wallboards, placed over exterior studding or rafters of a house.

Sheriff's Deed: Deed given by court order in connection with sale of property to satisfy a judgment.

Sill: The lowest part of the frame of a house, resting on the foundation and supporting the uprights of the frame. The board or metal forming the lower side of an opening, as a door sill, window sill, etc.

Sinking Fund: Fund set aside from the income from property which, with accrued interest, will eventually pay for replacement of the improvements.

SIR: Society of Industrial Realtors.

Soil Pipe: Pipe carrying waste out from the house to the main sewer line.

Sole or Sole Plate: A member, usually a 2 by 4, on which wall and partition studs rest.

Span: The distance between structural supports such as walls, columns, piers, beams, girders, and trusses.

Special Assessment: Legal charge against real estate by a public authority to pay cost of public improvements such as: street lights, sidewalks, street improvements, etc.

Special Warranty Deed: A deed in which the grantor warrants or guarantees the title only against defects arising during his ownership of the property and not against defects existing before the time of his ownership.

Specific Liens: Liens which attach to only a certain specific parcel of land or piece of property.

Specific Performance: An action to compel performance of an agreement, e.g., sale of land.

S.R.A.: Designates a person who is a member of the Society of Real Estate Appraisers.

SREA: Society of Real Estate Appraisers.

Standard-Depth: Generally the most typical lot depth in the neighborhood.

Standby Commitment: The mortgage banker frequently protects a builder by a "standby" agreement, under which he agrees to make mortgage loans at an agreed price for many months in the future. The builder deposits a "standby fee" with the mortgage banker for this service. Frequently, the mortgage banker protects himself by securing a "standby" from a long-term investor for the same period of time, paying a fee for this privilege.

Statute of Frauds: State law which provides that certain contracts must be in writing in order to be enforceable at law. Examples: real property lease for more than one year; agent's authorization to sell real estate.

Statutory Warranty Deed: A short form warranty deed which warrants by inference that the seller is the undisputed owner and has the right to convey the property and that he will defend the title if necessary. This type of deed protects the purchaser in that the conveyor covenants to defend all claims against the property. If he fails to do so, the new owner can defend said claims and sue the former owner.

Straight Line Depreciation: Definite sum set aside annually from income to pay cost of replacing improvements, without reference to interest it earns.

String, Stringer: A timber or other support for cross members. In stairs, the support on which the stair treads rest.

Studs or Studding: Vertical supporting timbers in the walls and partitions.

Subject to Mortgage: When a grantee takes a title to real property subject to mortgage, he is not responsible to the holder of the promissory note for the payment of any portion of the amount due. The most that he can lose in the event of a foreclosure is his equity in the property. See also "assumption of mortgage" in this section. In neither case is the original maker of the note released from his responsibility.

Sublease: A lease given by a lessee.

Subordinate: To make subject to, or junior to.

Subordination Clause: Clause in a junior or a second lien permitting retention of priority for prior liens. A subordination clause may also be used in a first deed of trust permitting it to be subordinated to subsequent liens as, for example, the liens of construction loans.

Subpoena: A process to cause a witness to appear and give testimony.

Subrogation: The substitution of another person in place of the creditor, to whose rights he succeeds in relation to the debt. The doctrine is used very often where one person agrees to stand surety for the performance of a contract by another person.

Substitution, Principle of: Affirms that the maximum value of a property tends to be set by the cost of acquiring an equally desirable and valuable substitute property, assuming no costly delay is encountered in making the substitution.

Sum of the Years Digits: An accelerated depreciation method.

Supply and Demand, Principle of: Affirms that price or value varies directly, but not necessarily proportionally with demand, and inversely, but not necessarily proportionately with supply.

Surety: One who guarantees the performance of another: Guarantor.

Surplus Productivity, Principle of: Affirms that the net income that remains after the proper costs of labor, organization and capital have been paid, which surplus is imputable to the land and tends to fix the value thereof.

Survey: The process by which a parcel of land is measured and its area is ascertained.

Syndicate: A partnership organized for participation in a real estate venture. Partners may be limited or unlimited in their liability.

Takeout Loan: The loan arranged by the owner or builder developer for a buyer. The construction loan made for construction of the improvements is usually paid from the proceeds of this loan.

Tax-Free Exchange: Income property exchanged on an even basis for other income property which does not have to pay a capital gain tax at the time.

Tax Sale: Sale of property after a period of nonpayment of taxes.

Tenancy in Common: Ownership by two or more persons who hold undivided interest, without right of survivorship; interests need not be equal.

Tenants by the Entireties: Under certain state laws, ownership of property acquired by a husband and wife during marriage which is jointly owned. Upon death of one spouse, it becomes the property of the survivor.

Tentative Map: The Subdivision Map Act requires subdividers to submit initially a tentative map of their tract to the local planning commission for study. The approval or disapproval of the planning commission is noted on the map. Thereafter a final map of the tract embodying any changes requested by the planning commission is required to be filed with the planning commission.

Tenure in Land: The mode or manner by which an estate in lands is held.

Termites: Ant-like insects which feed on wood.

Termite Shield: A shield, usually of noncorrodible metal, placed on top of the foundation wall or around pipes to prevent passage of termites.

Testator: One who leaves a will in force at his death.

Threshold: A strip of wood or metal beveled on each edge and used above the finished floor under outside doors.

Time Is the Essence: One of the essential requirements to forming of a binding contract; contemplates a punctual performance.

Title: Evidence that owner of land is in lawful possession thereof, an instrument evidencing such ownership.

Title Insurance: Insurance written by a title company to protect property owner against loss if title is imperfect.

Title Report: A report which discloses condition of the title, made by a title company preliminary to issuance of title insurance.

Title Theory: Mortgage arrangement whereby title to mortgaged real property vests in the lender.

Topography: Nature of the surface of land; topography may be level, rolling, mountainous.

Torrens Title: System of title records provided by state law (no longer used in California).

Tort: A wrongful act; wrong, injury; violation of a legal right.

Township: A territorial subdivision six miles long, six miles wide and containing 36 sections, each one mile square.

Trade Fixtures: Articles of personal property annexed to real property, but which are necessary to the carrying on of a trade and are removable by the owner.

Trade-in: An increasingly popular method of guaranteeing an owner a minimum amount of cash on sale of his present property to permit him to purchase another. If the property is not sold within a specified time at the listed price, the broker agrees to arrange financing to purchase the property at an agreed upon discount.

Treads: Horizontal boards of a stairway.

Trim: The finish materials in a building, such as moldings, applied around openings (window trim, door trim) or at the floor and ceiling (baseboard, cornice, picture molding).

Trust Account: An account separate and apart and physically segregated from broker's own funds, in which broker is required by law to deposit all funds collected for clients.

Trust Deed: Just as with a mortgage, this is a legal document by which a borrower pledges certain real property or collateral as guarantee for the repayment of a loan. However, it differs from the mortgage in a number of important respects. For example, instead of there being two parties to the transaction, there are three. There is the borrower who gives the trust deed and who is called the trustor. There is the third, neutral party (just as there is with an escrow) who receives the trust deed and who is called the trustee. And, finally, there is the lender who **is called the beneficiary since** he is the one who benefits from the pledge arrangement in that in the event of a default the trustee can sell the property and transfer the money obtained at the sale to him as payment of the debt.

Trustee: One who holds property in trust for another to secure the performance of an obligation.

Trustor: One who deeds his property to a trustee to be held as security until he has performed his obligation to a lender under terms of a deed of trust.

Under Improvement: An improvement which, because of its deficiency in size or cost, is not the highest and best use of the site.

Underwriting: The technical analysis by a lender to determine the borrower's ability to repay a contemplated loan.

Undue Influence: Taking any fraudulent or unfair advantage of another's weakness of mind, or distress or necessity.

Unearned Increment: An increase in value of real estate due to no effort on the part of the owner; often due to increase in population.

Uniform Commercial Code: Establishes a unified and comprehensive scheme for regulation of security transactions in personal property, superseding the existing statutes on chattel mortgages, conditional sales, trust receipts, assignment of accounts receivable and others in this field.

Unit-in-place Method: The cost of erecting a building by estimating the cost of each component part, i.e. foundations, floors, walls, windows, ceilings, roofs, etc. (including labor and overhead).

Urban Property: City property; closely settled property.

Usury: On a loan, claiming a rate of interest greater than that permitted by law.

Utilities: Refers to services rendered by public utility companies, such as: water, gas, electricity, telephone.

Utility: The ability to give satisfaction and/or excite desire for possession.

Valid: Having force, or binding force; legally sufficient and authorized by law.

Valley: The internal angle formed by the junction of two sloping sides of a roof.

Valuation: Estimated worth or price. Estimation. The act of valuing by appraisal .

Vendee: A purchaser; buyer.

Vendor: A seller; one who disposes of a thing in consideration of money.

Veneer: Thin sheets of wood.

Vent: A pipe installed to provide a flow of air to or from a drainage system or to provide a circulation of air within such system to protect trap seals from siphonage and back pressure.

Verification: Sworn statement before a duly qualified officer to correctness of contents of an instrument.

Vested: Bestowed upon someone; secured by someone, such as a title to property.

Void: To have no force or effect; that which is unenforceable.

Voidable: That which is capable of being adjudged void, but is not void unless action is taken to make it so.

Voluntary Lien: Any lien placed on property with consent of, or as a result of, the voluntary act of the owner.

Wainscoting: The covering of an interior wall with wood (usually panels), tiles, etc., from the floor to a point about half way to the ceiling. The remaining portion is painted, wallpapered or covered with another material different from the lower portion.

Waive: To relinquish, or abandon; to forego a right to enforce or require anything.

Warranty Deed: A deed used to convey real property which contains warranties of title and quiet possession, and the grantor thus agrees to defend the premises against the lawful claims of third persons. It is commonly used in many states but in others the grant deed has supplanted it due to the modern practice of securing title insurance policies which have reduced the importance of express and implied warranty in deeds.

Waste: The destruction, or material alteration of, or injury to premises by a tenant for life or years.

Water Table: Distance from surface of ground to a depth at which natural groundwater is found.

Wrap Around Mortgage: A second trust deed with a face value of both the new amount it secures and the balance due under the first trust deed. A wrap-around can take the form of a land contract or a deed of trust.

Yield: The interest earned by an investor on his investment (or bank on the money it has lent). Also called *Return.*

Yield Rate: The yield expressed as a percentage of the total investment. Also called *Rate of Return.*

Zone: The area set off by the proper authorities for specific use; subject to certain restrictions or restraints.

Zoning: Act of city or county authorities specifying type of use to which property may be put in specific areas.

http://www.homequest.com/glossary.html (San Diego's Exclusive Buyer's Agent)
gopher://gopher.gsa.gov/00/staff/pa/cic/housing/hmvocab.txt (HUD)
http://www.countrywide.com/cw_g/customers/Info/glossary.html (Country Wide)

Appendix B
INDEX

Appendix C - Answers to Multiple Choice Questions

Chapter 1
1) d
2) d
3) c
4) c
5) c
6) c
7) a
8) a
9) d
10) b

Chapter 2
1) a
2) b
3) a
4) c
5) d
6) d
7) a
8) b
9) d
10) b

Chapter 3
1) d
2) c
3) a
4) a
5) b
6) d
7) d
8) a
9) d
10) a

Chapter 4
1) c
2) c
3) b
4) d
5) c
6) b
7) d
8) a
9) c
10) b

Chapter 5
1) d
2) b
3) c
4) d
5) b
6) d
7) b
8) a
9) b
10) d

Chapter 6
1) b
2) a
3) b
4) d
5) b
6) a
7) d
8) a
9) b
10) d

Chapter 7
1) c
2) a
3) a
4) b
5) b
6) b
7) b
8) a
9) d
10) a

Chapter 8
1) b
2) b
3) c
4) c
5) b
6) c
7) c
8) d
9) b
10) c

Chapter 9
1) d
2) c
3) b
4) c
5) b
6) c
7) b
8) d
9) a
10) d

Chapter 10
1) a
2) d
3) a
4) b
5) d
6) c
7) d
8) c
9) a
10) b

Chapter 11
1) a
2) d
3) a
4) b
5) a
6) c
7) a
8) c
9) c
10) b

Chapter 12
1) b
2) c
3) a
4) b
5) b
6) a
7) b
8) b
9) c
10) b

Chapter 13
1) b
2) d
3) b
4) a
5) a
6) b
7) c
8) c
9) a
10) c

Chapter 14
1) a
2) a
3) c
4) d
5) a
6) d
7) d
8) c
9) a
10) d

Chapter 15
1) c
2) d
3) c
4) a
5) c
6) b
7) b
8) c
9) a
10) d

Appendix D
Answers to Matching Terminology

Chapter 1

1. R
2. M
3. N
4. H
5. Q
6. E
7. L
8. A
9. O
10. G
11. S
12. C
13. J
14. V
15. I
16. U
17. T
18. F
19. P
20. D
21. K
22. B

Chapter 2

1. V
2. R
3. CC
4. I
5. A
6. AA
7. F
8. BB
9. E
10. D
11. Z
12. T
13. Y
14. U
15. W
16. B
17. Q
18. H
19. K
20. P
21. C
22. J
23. L
24. N
25. DD
26. X
27. G
28. O
29. EE
30. M
31. S

Chapter 3

1. P
2. Y
3. A
4. H
5. X
6. K
7. B
8. J
9. W
10. V
11. M
12. E
13. L
14. I
15. F
16. D
17. Z
18. C
19. G
20. AA

21. N
22. U
23. Q
24. R
25. O
26. S
27. T
28. BB
29. CC
30. DD

Chapter 4

1. W
2. Q
3. X
4. M
5. A
6. P
7. Y
8. D
9. H
10. E
11. I
12. U
13. F
14. N
15. R
16. S
17. T
18. L
19. K
20. BB
21. Z
22. AA
23. V
24. C
25. B
26. G
27. J
28. O

Chapter 5

1. DD
2. U
3. F
4. II
5. EE
6. I
7. M
8. W
9. X
10. J
11. FF
12. Y
13. V
14. A
15. R
16. C
17. D
18. E
19. Q
20. O
21. P
22. N
23. S
24. T
25. Z
26. AA
27. CC
28. HH
29. KK
30. JJ
31. B
32. GG
33. BB
34. L
35. G
36. H
37. K
38. LL

Chapter 6

1. U
2. F
3. Y
4. M
5. A
6. E
7. X
8. B
9. W
10. I
11. Q
12. O
13. P
14. C
15. N
16. G
17. D
18. J
19. H
20. K
21. L
22. R
23. T
24. Z
25. S
26. V

Chapter 7

1. I
2. A
3. G
4. D
5. B
6. C
7. K
8. J
9. F
10. E
11. M
12. O
13. N
14. L
15. H

Chapter 8

1. X
2. LL
3. DD
4. O
5. HH
6. J
7. NN
8. C
9. F
10. V
11. BB
12. CC
13. R
14. G
15. A
16. Z
17. KK
18. D
19. Q
20. L
21. JJ
22. W
23. II
24. P
25. K
26. Y
27. E
28. S
29. U
30. T
31. EE
32. H
33. I
34. M
35. N
36. MM
37. B
38. FF
39. AA
40. OO
41. GG

Chapter 9

1. M
2. X
3. L

4. H
5. Q
6. N
7. G
8. C
9. W
10. E
11. S
12. V
13. A
14. B
15. Y
16. U
17. D
18. F
19. T
20. R
21. I
22. J
23. P
24. O
25. Z
26. K

Chapter 10

1. S
2. L
3. F
4. C
5. J
6. O
7. H
8. A
9. D
10. B
11. E
12. G
13. I
14. K
15. V
16. M
17. N
18. P
19. Q
20. R
21. T
22. U

Chapter 11

1. J
2. M
3. C
4. L
5. G
6. B
7. H
8. E
9. I
10. D
11. A
12. F
13. K
14. N
15. U
16. R
17. T
18. X
19. O
20. W
21. S
22. V
23. P
24. Q

Chapter 12

1. O
2. E
3. V
4. C
5. Q
6. D
7. N
8. G
9. M
10. F
11. S
12. X
13. I
14. H
15. R
16. J
17. U
18. K
19. L
20. W
21. P
22. A
23. T
24. B
25. CC
26. BB
27. AA
28. Z
29. Y

Chapter 13

1. F
2. Q
3. B
4. J
5. N
6. K
7. S
8. R
9. A
10. D
11. C
12. H
13. P
14. I
15. L

16. M
17. E
18. O
19. G
20. T
21. U

Chapter 14

1. M
2. E
3. B
4. F
5. A
6. C
7. J
8. D
9. I
10. H
11. G
12. K
13. L
14. N
15. O
16. P
17. Q
18. R
19. S

Chapter 15

1. H
2. D
3. P
4. K
5. M
6. N
7. L
8. A
9. C
10. E
11. J
12. I
13. O
14. F
15. G
16. B

Student's Notes

TO THE OWNER OF THIS BOOK:

We hope that you found *California Real Estate Principles, Eighth Edition,* by Professor Walt Huber useful. So that this book can be improved in a future edition, would you take the time to complete this sheet and return it? Thank you.

Instructor's name:_____

Department:_____

School and address:_____

_____

1. My general reaction to this book is:_____

_____

2. What I like most about this book is:_____

_____

3. What I like least about this book is:_____

4. Were all of the chapters of the book assigned for you to read? Yes   No

    If not, which ones weren't?_____

5. Do you plan to keep this book after you finish the course? Yes   No

    Why or why not_____

_____

6. On a separate sheet of paper, please write specific suggestions for improving this book and anything else you'd care to share about your experience in using the book.

Optional:

Your name:_____ Date:_____

Please return to:

Educational Textbook Company
P.O. Box 3597
Covina, CA 91722
(626) 339-7733 Fax (626) 332-4744